Windows Server® 2008 Networking and Network Access Protection (NAP)

by Joseph Davies and Tony Northrup
with the Microsoft Networking Team

PUBLISHED BY
Microsoft Press
A Division of Microsoft Corporation
One Microsoft Way
Redmond, Washington 98052-6399

Library of Congress Control Number: 2007940507

Printed and bound in the United States of America.

1 2 3 4 5 6 7 8 9   QWT   2 1 0 9 8 7

Distributed in Canada by H.B. Fenn and Company Ltd.

A CIP catalogue record for this book is available from the British Library.

Microsoft Press books are available through booksellers and distributors worldwide. For further information about international editions, contact your local Microsoft Corporation office or contact Microsoft Press International directly at fax (425) 936-7329. Visit our Web site at www.microsoft.com/mspress. Send comments to mspinput@microsoft.com.

Acquisitions Editor: Martin DelRe
Developmental Editor: Karen Szall
Project Editor: Maria Gargiulo
Editorial Production: Interactive Composition Corporation
Technical Reviewer: Bob Hogan; Technical Review services provided by Content Master, a member of CM Group, Ltd.
Cover: Tom Draper Design

Body Part No. X14-31173

For David Wright
—Joseph Davies

For Jenny Lozier
—Tony Northrup

Contents at a Glance

Table of Contents

What do you think of this book? We want to hear from you!

Microsoft is interested in hearing your feedback so we can continually improve our books and learning resources for you. To participate in a brief online survey, please visit:

www.microsoft.com/learning/booksurvey/

Part III ## Network Access Infrastructure

9 ## Authentication Infrastructure **231**

Part IV   Network Access Protection Infrastructure

What do you think of this book? We want to hear from you!

Microsoft is interested in hearing your feedback so we can continually improve our books and learning resources for you. To participate in a brief online survey, please visit:

www.microsoft.com/learning/booksurvey/

Acknowledgments

Joseph Davies and Tony Northrup would like to thank the numerous Windows Server 2008 product team members and other experts at Microsoft who have contributed hundreds of hours of their valuable time toward this project by carefully reviewing chapter content for technical accuracy, by contributing content, and by tirelessly giving us their advice, encouragement, and support as we worked on this project.

We would in particular like to express our thanks to the following contributors at Microsoft for writing the Direct from the Source sidebars that provide in-depth information that only these experts could know (in order by chapter):

- Dmitry Anipko, a developer in the Windows Core Networking Group
- Sean Siler, an IPv6 program manager in the Windows Core Networking Group
- Santosh Chandwani, the lead program manager in the Enterprise Networking Group
- Ian Hameroff, the senior product manager in Security and Access Product Marketing
- Gabe Frost, the product manager of Windows Core Networking
- Rade Trimceski, the program manager of the Windows Networking and Devices Group
- Jeff Westhead, a senior software development engineer in the Enterprise Networking Group
- Anthony Witecki, a senior consultant in Microsoft Services, Public Sector
- Chris Irwin, a premier field engineer in the Premier Field Engineering Group
- Clay Seymour, a support escalation engineer in Enterprise Platform Support
- Tim Quinn, a support escalation engineer in Enterprise Platform Support
- James McIllece, a technical writer in the Windows Server User Assistance Group
- Samir Jain, a lead program manager in the India Development Center
- Greg Lindsay, a technical writer in the Windows Server User Assistance Group
- John Morello, a senior program manager in the Windows Server Customer Connection Group

We wrote this book while Windows Server 2008 was in development, and many of the most brilliant people at Microsoft reviewed our chapters in rough form to make corrections, alert us to changes in the operating system, and suggest additions. Many thanks to our reviewers (in order by chapter):

Mike Barrett, Dmitri Anipko, Ben Shultz, Thiago Hirai, Mahesh Narayanan, Santosh Chandwani, Jason Popp, Hermant Banavar, Osama Mazahir, Ian Hameroff, Rade Trimceski,

Alireza Dabagh, Chandra Nukala, Arren Conner, Jeff Westhead, Sudhakar Pasupuleti, Yi Zhao, Subhasish Bhattacharya, Tim Quinn, Clay Seymour, Chris Irwin, Greg Lindsay, James MacIllece, Anthony Leibovitz, Sreenivas Addagatla, Arvind Jayakar, Brit Weston, Lee Gibson, Drew Baron, Brit Weston, Dhiraj Gupta, Samir Jain, Puja Pandey, Tushar Gupta, Manu Jeewani, Jim Holtzman, Kevin Rhodes, Steve Espinosa, Tom Kelnar, Kedar Mohare, Pat Fetty, Gavin Carius, Wai-O Hui, Harini Muralidharan, Richard Costleigh, Ryan Hurst, Chris Edson, Chandra Nukala, Abhishek Tiwari, Aanand Ramachandran, John Morrello, and Barry Mendonca.

Additional thanks go to the Microsoft Security Review Board for their careful review of all the content in this book.

If we've forgotten to include anyone in the above list, please forgive us!

Joseph would like to personally thank and honorably mention Greg Lindsay for devoting his time and effort of many hours for meetings, discussions, technical review, and multiple sidebars for the Network Access Protection (NAP) chapters of this book.

Tony would also like to personally thank Bob Hogan for going above and beyond what was required of him as a technical editor, and Hayley Bellamy for assistance troubleshooting a critical hardware problem.

Finally, we would also like to collectively thank our outstanding editorial team at Microsoft Press for this project, including Martin DelRe, Jenny Moss Benson, Maureen Zimmerman, and Maria Gargiulo, and Susan McClung, Joel Rosenthal, Bob Hogan, Mary Rosewood, and Seth Maislin of Interactive Composition Corporation, for their unflagging energy and tireless commitment to making this book a success.

–Joseph and Tony

Introduction

Welcome to *Windows Server 2008 Networking and Network Access Protection (NAP)*.

You can use the deployment guidelines in Part I of this book to build an addressing and packet flow infrastructure that uses Internet Protocol version 4 (IPv4) and Internet Protocol version 6 (IPv6), Dynamic Host Configuration Protocol (DHCP), host-based firewalling and Internet Protocol security (IPsec), policy-based Quality of Service (QoS), and scalable networking technologies.

You can use the deployment guidelines in Part II of this book to build a name resolution infrastructure with the Domain Name System (DNS) and Windows Internet Name Service (WINS).

You can also use the guidelines in Part III of this book to deploy a network access infrastructure consisting of Active Directory domain services, a public key infrastructure, Group Policy, and centralized authentication, authorization, and accounting with Remote Authentication Dial-In User Service (RADIUS). This network access infrastructure supports a variety of authenticated and authorized network access methods, including Institute of Electrical and Electronics Engineers (IEEE) 802.11 wireless, authenticating switch, and virtual private network (VPN) connections.

Once your addressing and packet flow, name resolution, and network access infrastructures are in place, you can use the guidelines in Part IV of this book to deploy Network Access Protection (NAP) to enforce system health requirements for IPsec-protected communication, IEEE 802.1X–authenticated wireless and wired access, remote access VPN connections, and DHCP address configuration.

Document Conventions

The following conventions are used in this book to highlight special features or usage:

Reader Aids

The following reader aids are used throughout this book to point out useful details:

Reader Aid	Meaning
Note	Underscores the importance of a specific concept or highlights a special case that might not apply to every situation.
More Info	Refers you to another resource for further information.
On the Disc	Calls attention to a related link on the Companion CD that helps you perform a task described in the text.

Sidebars

The following sidebars are used throughout this book to provide added insight, tips, and advice concerning networking and network access protection (NAP):

Sidebar	Meaning
Direct from the Source	Contributed by experts at Microsoft to provide "from-the-source" insight into how technologies work, best practices, and trouble-shooting tips.
How It Works	Provides unique glimpses of features and how they work.

Command-Line Examples

The following style conventions are used in documenting command-line examples throughout this book:

Style	Meaning
Bold font	Used to indicate user input (characters that you type exactly as shown).
Italic font	Used to indicate variables for which you need to supply a specific value (for example *file_name* can refer to any valid file name).
`Monospace font`	Used for code samples and command-line output.
%SystemRoot%	Used for environment variables.

About the Companion CD-ROM

The companion CD-ROM included with this book contains the following:

- **eBook form of this book**   Adobe Portable Document Format (PDF) version of this book, which allows you to view it online and perform text searches.

- **eBook of *TCP/IP Fundamentals for Microsoft Windows***   The most current version of TCP/IP Fundamentals for Microsoft Windows is available at *http://technet.microsoft.com/en-us/library/bb726983.aspx*. Adobe PDF version of *TCP/IP Fundamentals for Microsoft Windows* by Joseph Davies.

- **eBook of *Understanding IPv6*, Second Edition**   Adobe PDF version of *Understanding IPv6*, Second Edition by Joseph Davies.

- **Link to Network Monitor 3.1**   Link to Network Monitor 3.1, available as a free download from the Microsoft.com Download Center. You can also install Network Monitor 3.1 from *http://go.microsoft.com/fwlink/?LinkID=92844*. For the latest information about Network Monitor, see the Network Monitor blog at *http://blogs.technet.com/netmon*.

> **Find Additional Content Online**   As new or updated material becomes available that complements your book, it will be posted online on the Microsoft Press Online Windows Server and Client Web site. Based on the final build of Windows Server 2008, the type of material you might find includes updates to book content, articles, links to companion content, errata, sample chapters, and more. This Web site will be available soon at *http://www.microsoft.com/learning/books/online/serverclient* and will be updated periodically.

System Requirements

To view the eBooks, you need any system that is capable of running Adobe Reader, available from *http://www.adobe.com*. For more detailed information about system requirements, refer to the System Requirements page in the back of the book.

Technical Support

Every effort has been made to ensure the accuracy of this book and the contents of the companion CD-ROM. Microsoft Press provides corrections for books in the Microsoft Knowledge Base. If you have comments, questions, or ideas regarding this book or the companion CD, please send them to Microsoft Press by using either of the following methods:

E-mail: mspinput@microsoft.com

Postal Mail:

Microsoft Press
Attn: *Windows Server 2008 Networking and Network Access Protection (NAP)* Editor
One Microsoft Way
Redmond, WA 98052-6399

For additional support information regarding this book and the CD-ROM (including answers to commonly asked questions about installation and use), visit the Microsoft Press Book and CD Support Web site at *http://www.microsoft.com/learning/support/books*. To connect directly to the Microsoft Knowledge Base search page and enter a query, visit *http://support.microsoft.com/search*. For support information regarding Microsoft software, please visit *http://support.microsoft.com*.

Part I
Addressing and Packet Flow Infrastructure

Chapter 1

IPv4

Today, the vast majority of networked computers communicate using Internet Protocol version 4 (IPv4) and the suite of protocols collectively called Transmission Control Protocol/Internet Protocol (TCP/IP). To plan, deploy, maintain, and troubleshoot Microsoft Windows networking, you must first understand the fundamentals of TCP/IP.

This chapter provides information about how to design, deploy, maintain, and troubleshoot IPv4 networks. Most of the information in this chapter applies equally to the Windows Server 2008, Windows Vista, and Windows Server 2003 operating systems and other recent versions of Windows. For information about IPv6, refer to Chapter 2, "IPv6." This chapter assumes that you have a general understanding of TCP/IP and some networking experience.

Concepts

This section provides a brief overview of important TCP/IP concepts, including IPv4 addressing, multicasting, User Datagram Protocol (UDP), and TCP.

Network Layers

Network protocols are organized into layers, with each layer interacting only with the layers directly above and below it. The most commonly used model is the seven-layer Open Systems Interconnection (OSI) model. Table 1-1 lists the seven OSI layers and examples of protocols at each layer.

Table 1-1 OSI Layers

Layer Number	Layer Name	Examples
Layer 1	Physical Layer	Wired cabling and wireless frequency standards
Layer 2	Data-Link Layer	Ethernet, Wi-Fi
Layer 3	Network Layer	IPv4, IPv6, Internet Control Message Protocol (ICMP)
Layer 4	Transport Layer	TCP, UDP
Layer 5	Session Layer	NetBIOS
Layer 6	Presentation Layer	Rarely used
Layer 7	Application Layer	Hypertext Transfer Protocol (HTTP), Simple Mail Transfer Protocol (SMTP), Post Office Protocol (POP), Domain Name System (DNS)

This chapter focuses on IPv4, a Layer 3 protocol, but also discusses how IPv4 interacts with Layer 2 and Layer 4 protocols.

IPv4 Addressing

IPv4 addresses are four bytes, for a total length of 32 bits. (One byte equals eight bits.) Each byte (known as an *octet*) is written as a decimal number from 0–255 and separated by a period (called a *dot* when speaking). For example, the following are valid IP addresses:

- 192.168.1.32

- 10.1.1.1

- 127.0.0.1

The beginning portion of an IP address is the *network address,* and the remainder is the *host address,* which identifies an individual computer on the subnet. Routers use the network address to forward packets to the correct destination network, and computers use the host address to determine which packets are destined for them. Figure 1-1 illustrates how routers move a packet across a network to the destination computer.

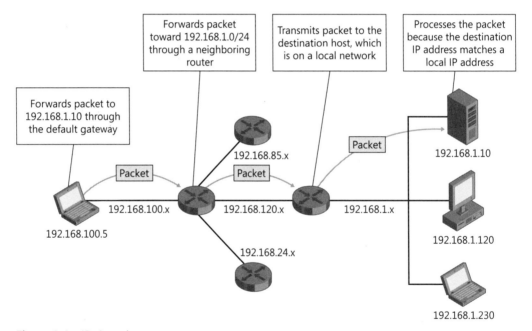

Figure 1-1   IPv4 routing

In Figure 1-1, the first three octets of the IP address are the network address (such as 192.168.1 or 192.168.10), and the last octet is the host address (such as .5 or .10). Although this is the most common way to divide an IP address between the host and network, you can:

- Use a shorter network address (such as 192.168) to dedicate more bits to the host address. This gives you fewer networks but allows more hosts on each network.

- Use a longer network address and dedicate fewer bits to the host address. This gives you more subnets but a smaller number of unique hosts on each network.

Hosts use subnet masks to indicate how many bits of the IP address are dedicated to the network address. The subnet mask 255.255.255.0 indicates that the first three octets of the IP address are dedicated to the network address, and is commonly referred to as a *Class C* network. The subnet mask 255.255.0.0 indicates that the first two octets of the IP address are dedicated to the network address and is commonly referred to as a *Class B* network. Though rarely used, a *Class A* network has a subnet mask of 255.0.0.0 and indicates that only the first octet of the IP address is used as the network address.

Direct from the Source: Network Classifications

The "A,B,C" classful networking is obsolete. Classless Inter-Domain Routing (CIDR), introduced by RFC 1519, is not only about notation, but about how address space is actually split. One of the differences is that in classful networking, a router in the middle can determine the subnet mask given just the address, and thus can determine whether a particular address is a subnet broadcast. In CIDR, in general, only routers directly connected to a subnet can determine the actual subnet mask.

Dmitry Anipko, Developer

Windows Core Networking

The subnet mask 255.255.255.0 indicates that the first 24 of the 32 bits in an IP address are dedicated to the network address. Rather than writing the entire subnet mask, you can use Classless Inter-Domain Routing (CIDR, pronounced *cider*) notation to indicate the number of bits dedicated to the network address by adding a forward slash (/) symbol followed by the number of bits in the network address after the IP address. For example, a 24-bit subnet mask could be written as 192.168.10.0/24. If you wanted to subdivide that network into four smaller networks, you could use a 26-bit network address (leaving only 6 bits for the host address). The four networks would be written as shown in Table 1-2.

Table 1-2   Subdividing the 192.168.10.0/24 Network

Network ID	IP Address Range
192.168.10.0/26	192.168.10.0–192.168.10.63
192.168.10.64/26	192.168.10.64–192.168.10.127
192.168.10.128/26	192.168.10.128–192.168.10.191
192.168.10.192/26	192.168.10.192–192.168.1.255

How It Works: Binary Math

Although IP addresses are expressed in decimal octets, you must use binary math (also known as *Boolean* math) if you want to use anything other than an 8-bit, 16-bit, or 24-bit subnet mask. For example, consider the IP address 192.168.14.222 with a 24-bit subnet mask, as shown in Figure 1-2. In this example, the network ID and host ID are divided along 8-bit boundaries, making it simple to separate the two in decimal numbering.

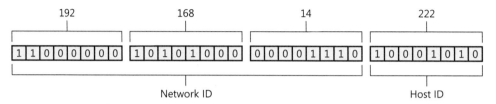

Figure 1-2   24-bit subnet mask

Now, consider the same IP address with a 26-bit subnet mask, as shown in Figure 1-3. In this example, the network ID uses the highest two bits from the last octet. Although this is more difficult to visualize in decimal form because the last octet is partially dedicated to the network ID and partially dedicated to the host ID, in binary, the network ID is simply a 26-bit number, whereas the host ID is a 6-bit number.

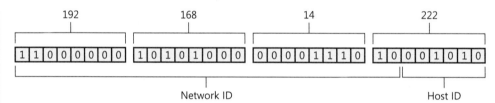

Figure 1-3   26-bit subnet mask

In Figure 1-3, the network ID would be written as 192.168.14.128/26, and host IP addresses would be in the range 192.168.14.129 to 192.168.14.190. Assigning a host IP address below 128 or above 192 would require changing one of the two highest two bits in the last octet, which would also change the network ID.

If you find this confusing, you're not alone. IPv4 was designed to support only 8-bit, 16-bit, or 24-bit subnet masks (also known as *classful* subnet masks). Variable-length subnet masks were added decades later when CIDR was introduced in 1993. IPv6, discussed in Chapter 2, takes a more straightforward approach.

Table 1-3 shows commonly used subnet mask bit lengths, the number of host IP addresses available in each, and the number of subnets you could create if you had been allocated a 24-bit network address space such as 192.168.10.0/24.

Table 1-3   Subnet Mask Bit Lengths and Available Host IP Addresses

Subnet Mask Bit Length	Available Network Addresses	Available IP Addresses
24	1	256
25	2	128
26	4	64
27	8	32

Note that the available number of host IP addresses is actually a bit lower than indicated in Table 1-3. The highest and lowest IP addresses on a subnet (in binary, all 0s and all 1s) are reserved for broadcast messages. Additionally, the router will require at least one IP address on the subnet. Therefore, the number of IP addresses available for computers on the network is actually three lower than the theoretical number of IP addresses shown in Table 1-3.

Private IPv4 Addresses

Several IP address ranges are reserved for private use on internal networks, as listed in Table 1-4. Addresses in these ranges cannot be accessed from the public Internet because Internet routers won't have the addresses in their routing tables. However, private IP addresses can be routed on your internal network, and you can use network address translation (NAT) to allow clients with a private IP address to communicate on the Internet. NAT is discussed later in this chapter.

Table 1-4   Private IPv4 Address Ranges

Network	Available 24-bit Networks	Available IP Addresses
192.168.0.0–192.168.255.255	256	65,536
172.16.0.0–173.1.255.255	4,096	1,048,576
10.0.0.0–10.255.255.255	65,536	16,777,216

Private IP addresses are defined in RFC 1918, available at *http://tools.ietf.org/html/rfc1918*.

Automatic Private IP Addressing (APIPA)

If a computer running Microsoft Windows 98 or a later version of Windows does not have a static IP address configured and cannot obtain an IP address from a Dynamic Host Configuration Protocol (DHCP) server, it will use Automatic Private IP Addressing (APIPA) to assign a random IP address from the link-local address range 169.254.1.0 to 169.254.254.255. APIPA, also known as *IPv4 Link-Local* (IPv4LL), *Zero Configuration Networking,* or *Zeroconf,* is described in RFC 3330 (available at *http://tools.ietf.org/html/rfc3330*) and RFC 3927 (available at *http://tools.ietf.org/html/rfc3927*).

APIPA allows computers to communicate on a local area network (LAN), such as an ad-hoc wireless network, without a DHCP server or static IP address configuration. If a computer has an APIPA IP address on a network that has a DHCP server, it means that the computer could not contact the DHCP server. Either the computer is not properly connected to the network, or the DHCP server was offline.

> **Note**   APIPA addresses should never have a default gateway because APIPA is designed to function only on a single subnet.

Computers with APIPA IP addresses will regularly attempt to contact a DHCP server in case a DHCP server is brought online after the client computer starts.

Multicast Addresses

Addresses in the range 224.0.0.0 through 239.255.255.255 are reserved for multicast communications. Whereas most IP communications are one-to-one (such as a Web browser connecting to a Web server), and some IP communications are broadcast to the local network, such as an Address Resolution Protocol (ARP) request, a relatively small number of communications are multicast to multiple specific listeners.

Often, multicast communications are sent only to other hosts on the local network. For example, Enhanced Interior Gateway Routing Protocol (EIGRP) uses the multicast IP address 224.0.0.10 to allow a router to communicate with a single packet a change in the routing table to all neighboring routers.

However, multicast communications can also be routed between networks. Routed multicasting does not typically work on the Internet; however, private networks can be configured to support multicasting. Private routed multicasting is useful for internal streaming video, for example, to transmit live video of a speech by a company's president to all employee computers.

Figure 1-4 shows the bandwidth used when twelve computers use unicasting to view a 128k streaming video feed. Whereas the relatively low bandwidth used in this example would allow most LANs to support unicasting, a network with hundreds or thousands of computers would be able to support only multicasting live video. Figure 1-5 shows that multicasting the streaming video feed uses significantly less bandwidth, especially on the server's network.

Network Address Translation

There are not enough public IPv4 addresses for every Internet-connected computer. In fact, most ISPs assign only one to four public IP addresses for every business Internet connection, which is obviously not sufficient for the hundreds or thousands of computer an organization might have at a location.

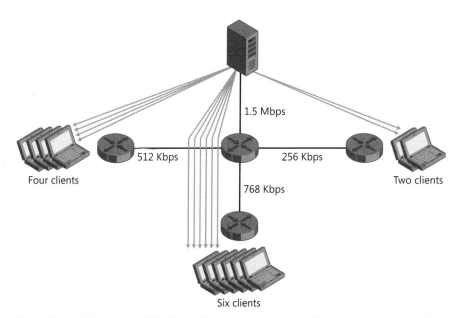

Figure 1-4   Unicasting a 128-Kbps video stream to twelve clients on three networks

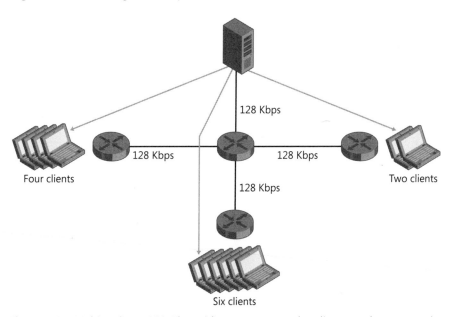

Figure 1-5   Multicasting a 128-Kbps video stream to twelve clients on three networks

IPv4 Address Shortage

In theory, 32-bit IP addresses allow for over four billion addresses, and recent estimates place the total number of Internet-connected computers at a little over one billion. The number of IP addresses actually available for client computers is well below four billion because of the large number of private IP addresses, the range of addresses reserved for multicast communications, and the fact that most subnets have well below 100 percent utilization.

NAT works around the limited number of public IP addresses by allowing computers with private IP addresses to access the Internet. With NAT, you assign private IP addresses (such as 192.168.0.0/16) to computers on your internal network. Your NAT gateway receives a public IP address, intercepts all outgoing connections, and forwards the traffic to the final destination on the Internet. To allow the return traffic to be routed back to your network, the NAT gateway changes the source IP address from the private IP address to its own public IP address. When the NAT gateway receives return traffic, it rewrites the destination IP address to the client computer's private IP address.

Figure 1-6 illustrates how NAT works. Because NAT changes private IP addresses to its own public IP address before sending packets on the Internet, NAT is completely transparent to most network applications. Configuring clients on a NAT network is exactly the same as configuring clients on any other IPv4 network.

You can configure port forwarding on the NAT gateway to allow clients on the Internet to connect to a server on your private network. With port forwarding, the NAT gateway forwards all incoming packets with a specific destination port number to an IP address on your internal network. For example, you could configure incoming requests with a destination TCP port number of 80 to be sent to your Web server and all incoming requests with a destination TCP port number of 25 to be sent to your e-mail server.

Layer 2 and Layer 3 Addressing

Computers that are on the same LAN identify each other using media access control (MAC) addresses. MAC addresses are Layer 2 addresses and are not routable, whereas IP addresses are Layer 3 and can be routed.

The first step in sending an IP packet is to determine whether the remote host is on the same LAN or a remote network:

- If the destination is on the same LAN, the destination MAC address must be the destination host's MAC address.

■ If the destination is on a remote LAN, the destination MAC address must be the default gateway's MAC address. The default gateway will then forward the packet to the next network in the route towards the destination.

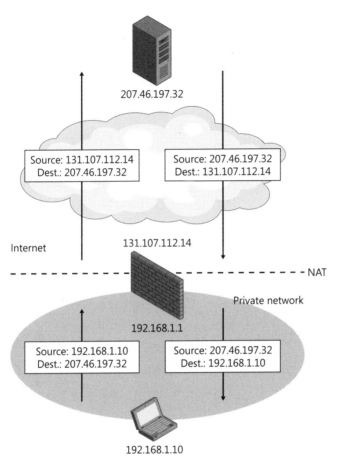

Figure 1-6   How NAT works

Regardless of whether the destination MAC address is that of the default gateway or the final destination host, the destination IP address will always be the IP address of the final destination host. Figure 1-7 illustrates how addressing of packets for the same LAN or a remote LAN differ. Naturally, the source IP address and the source MAC address are those of the source host.

Note   Figure 1-7 uses Ethernet as the model for Layer 2 communications. Other Layer 2 protocols might use a different structure for the MAC address.

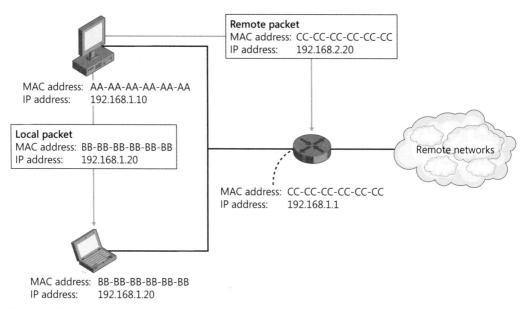

Figure 1-7   Addressing at Layers 2 and 3

Hosts use ARP to determine the MAC address of a computer on the local network. ARP uses this process:

1. The client computer broadcasts an ARP message to the LAN asking for the MAC address of the computer with the specified IP address.

2. All computers on the LAN receive and process the ARP request.

3. The server that owns the IP address specified in the ARP request sends a response back with its MAC address.

4. The client receives the ARP response, adds the address to the ARP cache, and uses the server's MAC address for all future communications.

Layer 4 Protocols: UDP and TCP

Most network applications use one of two Layer 4 protocols:

-   **User Datagram Protocol (UDP)**   Applications that want to minimize network overhead and do not require detecting lost or out-of-order packets use UDP. UDP also supports multicasting, which is not possible with TCP. Most DNS queries and streaming media use UDP. Applications that use UDP can still handle retransmitting lost packets or reordering out-of-order packets; however, it must be handled within the application itself and requires more effort from the application developer.

-   **Transmission Control Protocol (TCP)**   Applications that require detecting and resending lost or corrupted packets use TCP. Using TCP requires a connection to be established before application data can be transmitted. Specifically, the client sends a

SYN packet to request a connection, the server responds with an SYN/ACK packet, and the client confirms the connection with a ACK packet. Requiring these packets to be exchanged before application data can be sent causes TCP to be slower than UDP for short-lived connections. Most applications, including e-mail and Web browsing, use TCP.

A single server typically has several different services listening for incoming connections. To allow Windows to direct incoming traffic to the correct application, incoming network requests include a port number. For example, DNS requests use port 53 by default. Therefore, when Windows receives a packet with a port number of 53, it delivers it to the DNS Server service.

Planning and Design Considerations

It is critical to carefully plan a new IPv4 network, because changing IP addresses after deployment is time consuming. This section guides you through the fundamentals of planning an IPv4 network.

Designing Your Internet Connection

Small organizations, or regional offices that can support only a single subnet, can use the architecture shown in Figure 1-8. This architecture assigns a single public IP address to the NAT gateway and assigns private IP addresses to all computers on the internal network. If a server must be accessible from the Internet, the NAT gateway can be configured with port forwarding.

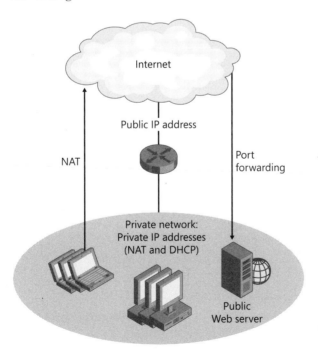

Figure 1-8 Small network architecture without a perimeter network

Most medium-size and large organizations will use a network architecture resembling that shown in Figure 1-9. This architecture provides a separate network for public servers, with public IP addresses, called a *perimeter network* (also known as a *screened subnet*). Internal clients use private DHCP-assigned IP addresses and access the Internet by using a NAT gateway. In the example shown in Figure 1-9, the private network might consist of many different subnets connected with routers.

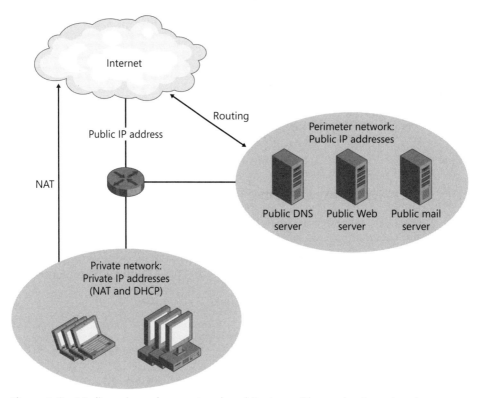

Figure 1-9 Medium-size or large network architecture with a perimeter network

Note The network device shown in the center of Figures 1-8 and 1-9 represents routing, firewall, and NAT gateway services. For small organizations, these services are often performed by a single device. Large organizations often have separate redundant devices for each role.

Creating an IPv4 Addressing Scheme

Plan your IPv4 addressing scheme to simplify routing and IP address configuration on your internal network by following these steps. In the long run, this will simplify router configuration and reduce the complexity of troubleshooting network problems.

1. Choose one of the private address ranges for your internal networks. The 10.0.0.0/8 address space provides the largest number of networks.

2. Choose a random starting point within the private address space. For example, if you are using the 10.0.0.0/8 address space, you could choose 10.187.0.0/16 for your internal networks. Even though your private address space does not need to be unique on the Internet, using a random portion of the address space will minimize the chance for conflict with other internal networks that you might connect to in the future as a result of mergers, acquisitions, or business partnerships. Many organizations start numbering at the bottom of the address space (such as using networks numbered 10.0.0.0/24 or 192.168.0.0/24), which are likely to conflict with other private networks.

3. Allocate portions of your address space to different regional offices. Provide at least ten times the number of addresses each location is likely to require in the near future to allow for future growth and enable network administrators to use logical network numbering without needing to subnet networks for efficiency.

4. Allow each regional office to subnet that address space for their internal networks. To simplify configuration, use 24-bit subnets for each physical network segment. Figure 1-10 illustrates how a private address can be divided between regional offices and then subdivided for individual network segments. These networks must provide address space for both wired and wireless networks.

5. Allocate network space for remote-access clients such as employees who work from home and dial in or connect using a virtual private network (VPN).

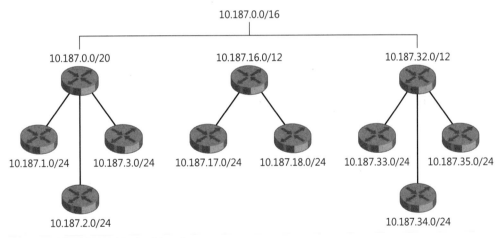

Figure 1-10 Hierarchical addressing

Planning Host Addresses

To improve consistency on your networks and allow administrators to more quickly assess network problems, create a host address plan that you will use on all networks. Whereas the specific servers will vary, Table 1-5 shows a typical host address plan.

Table 1-5   Example Host Address Plan

Role	Host Address
Default gateway	.1
Secondary gateway	.2
DHCP server	.3
Primary DNS server	.4
Secondary DNS server	.5
Primary Windows Internet Name Service (WINS) server	.6
Secondary WINS server	.7
Clients that temporarily require a static IP address	.20–.29
Static clients	.30–.99
DHCP clients	.100–.250

Using VPNs

Today, many organizations choose to use site-to-site VPNs to connect remote offices across the public Internet. Site-to-site VPNs use the Internet to establish an authenticated, encrypted connection between two remote offices. Traffic originating from one office can travel to the remote office just as if the two offices were connected by standard routers.

Figure 1-11 illustrates a traditional approach to connecting remote offices, which relies on private network links such as frame relay networks, asynchronous transfer mode (ATM) networks, or private telco links (such as a T-1). This approach provides guaranteed, consistent bandwidth between offices. However, the cost can be high compared to a VPN-based solution because separate network connections are required for the private wide area network (WAN) and the Internet.

Figure 1-12 illustrates a similar network connected using VPNs. Typically, each location requires an Internet connection anyway, meaning that no additional network links are required to implement the VPN. However, VPNs must share bandwidth with other Internet traffic. Additionally, the performance of communications across the Internet can vary more than in private network links.

Note   Although encryption provides a high level of privacy for VPN data, using a public network to transport private data might not meet some security regulations.

Many firewalls and routers have VPN capabilities built in. Additionally, you can implement a VPN with dedicated network hardware or any recent version of Windows Server, including Microsoft Windows 2000 Server, Windows Server 2003, and Windows Server 2008. Therefore, you can often implement VPNs with little or no additional cost.

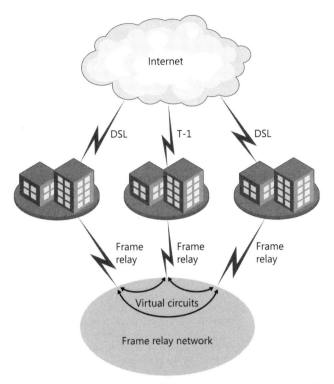

Figure 1-11   A WAN built with dedicated, private network links

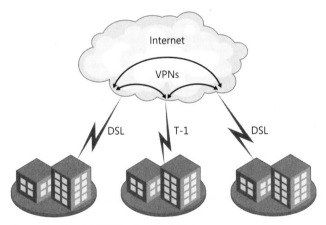

Figure 1-12   A WAN built with VPNs

Planning Redundancy

Your routing infrastructure is the most critical part of your network because without it, all network services are unavailable. Because of this, many environments deploy redundant router configurations. Fortunately, IPv4 was designed for redundancy.

Routers use routing protocols to create a map of the network. They then use this map to build their own routing tables, which allows them to properly forward traffic that is destined for a network not directly connected to the router. If there is more than one path to a destination network, routers can automatically detect the failure of one path and redirect traffic through a functioning path.

Consider the network shown in Figure 1-13. If router B fails, the client can still communicate with the server because router A will detect the failure of router B and forward traffic destined for the server's network through router C.

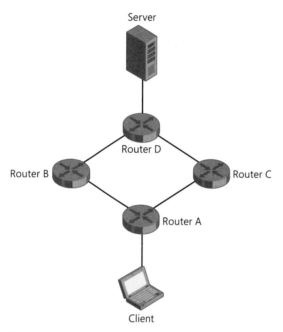

Figure 1-13   Redundant network

However, the network shown in Figure 1-13 still has single points of failure: routers A and D. If one of these routers fails, computers that have the failed router configured as their default gateway will be unable to communicate with hosts on other networks.

Figure 1-14 demonstrates that you can provide redundant default gateways for computers by connecting two routers to a single subnet. When configured with multiple default gateways, computers running Windows will automatically detect when one router has failed and forward traffic through the alternate gateway. This allows continued network access with minimal interruption.

For a more complete discussion of using Windows with multiple routers, read "The Cable Guy–September 2003: Default Gateway Behavior for Windows TCP/IP" at *http://www.microsoft.com/technet/community/columns/cableguy/cg0903.mspx.*

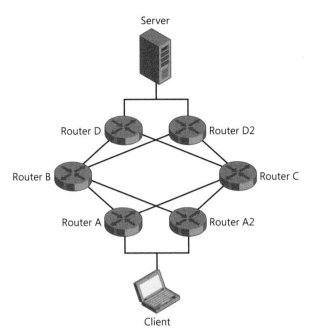

Figure 1-14 Redundant default gateways

Using Multihomed Computers

Computers can be multihomed for several reasons:

- **Scalability** If a server might require more throughput than is possible with a single interface, you can use two network adapters to double the maximum throughput (assuming that the server hardware supports network adapter teaming). For example, if your streaming media is connected to a Gigabit network and needs to transmit 1.2 gigabits per second (Gbps), you could connect two network adapters and achieve a maximum theoretical outgoing throughput of close to 2 Gbps. For more information, refer to Chapter 6, "Scalable Networking."

- **Redundancy** To avoid server downtime if a network adapter fails, configure redundant network adapters. If one network adapter fails, the other will maintain connectivity. Then you can schedule downtime for the server to replace the failed network adapter when users will be minimally impacted.

- **Connecting to disjoint networks** Some servers need to connect to multiple, disjoint networks (networks that are not connected to each other). For example, an update server might connect to your internal network to allow clients to download updates but also need to connect to a disjoint lab network to allow lab computers to download updates. When connecting to disjoint networks, configure a default gateway only on one adapter. If you need to connect to multiple networks through the disjoint network, use the **route add** command to manually configure the computer's routing table.

Note   You can assign multiple IP addresses to a single network adapter. This is a common practice with Web servers that host multiple Web sites.

Deployment Steps

This section provides guidance for deploying IPv4 networks.

Manually Configuring IPv4 Clients

Typically, you should rely on DHCP to provide IP configuration to IPv4 clients. However, DNS, DHCP, and WINS servers require manually configured IP addresses.

To Manually Configure the IP Address of a Computer Running Windows Vista or Windows Server 2008

1.   Click Start, right-click Network, and then click Properties.

2.   Under Tasks, click Manage Network Connections.

3.   Right-click the network adapter you want to configure, and then click Properties.

4.   Select Internet Protocol Version 4 (TCP/IPv4), and then click Properties.

     The Internet Protocol Version 4 (TCP/IPv4) Properties dialog box appears.

5.   On the General tab, click Use The Following IP Address, and then in the appropriate fields, type the IP address, subnet mask, and default gateway. Click Use The Following DNS Server Addresses, and then type the primary and secondary DNS server addresses.

6.   If you need to configure more than one IP address or more than two DNS servers, or you must add a WINS server, click Advanced, and then make the appropriate configuration. Click OK.

Configuring Client Behavior When a DHCP Server Is Not Available

By default, computers running Windows that are configured to receive a DHCP address will assign a random APIPA address if they are unable to connect to a DHCP server. However, you can change this behavior to allow a computer to have a specific static IP address when connected to your internal network (assuming your network lacks a DHCP server) but still acquire a DHCP-assigned IP address when connected to other networks. This is ideal for mobile computers that need static IP addresses.

To Assign the Computer a Static IP Address When a DHCP Server Is Not Available

1.   Click Start, right-click Network, and then click Properties.

2.   Under Tasks, click Manage Network Connections.

3.   Right-click the network adapter you want to configure, and then click Properties.

4. Select Internet Protocol Version 4 (TCP/IPv4), and then click Properties.

   The Internet Protocol Version 4 (TCP/IPv4) Properties dialog box appears.

5. On the Alternate Configuration tab, select User Configured. Type the IP address, subnet mask, default gateway, DNS server addresses, and WINS server addresses.

6. If you need to configure more than two DNS servers or a WINS server, click the General tab, click Advanced, and then make the necessary configuration. Click OK.

Adding Routes to the Routing Table

Most computers access remote networks by using one or more default gateways. If a computer has multiple routers on the local network and must send traffic destined for different networks to different routers, you will need to use the **route** command to configure routes for any networks that should not be sent to the default gateway.

To Add a Route to the Routing Table

1. Open a command prompt with administrative privileges.

2. Run the **route add** *network/bits gateway* command. For example, the following command configures the computer to forward traffic destined for the 192.168.2.0/24 network to the gateway at 192.168.1.1:

   route add 192.168.2.0/24 192.168.1.1 -p

To view the computer's current routing table, run the **route print** command at a command prompt. For complete usage information, run **route /?**.

Ongoing Maintenance

Typically, IPv4 configuration requires no ongoing maintenance other than configuration changes already described in "Deployment Steps" earlier in this chapter.

Troubleshooting

This section provides a brief overview of the troubleshooting tools built into Windows Server 2008.

ARP

Computers use the protocol ARP (discussed earlier in this chapter) to determine the MAC address associated with an IP address on the local subnet. Administrators use Arp (Arp.exe), the command-line tool, to view or clear a computer's ARP cache.

Problems with ARP are rare. The most common problem occurs when an administrator changes the network adapter in a server, or a backup server in a cluster comes online and clients have the old network adapter's MAC address cached. In that scenario, clients will not be able to connect to the server until the cached ARP entry expires or the client computer receives the updated MAC address in a broadcast message from the server. For Windows Vista and Windows Server 2008, cached ARP entries expire 30 seconds after the last valid communication.

Because it typically takes more than two minutes to change a network adapter, you might never need to manually clear the ARP cache. However, you can manually clear the ARP cache by running this command from an administrative command prompt:

arp -d *

To view the ARP cache, run the following command:

arp -a

```
Interface: 192.168.1.161 --- 0x7
  Internet Address       Physical Address      Type
  192.168.1.1            00-19-5b-0d-ed-fc     dynamic
  192.168.1.124          00-90-4b-6d-6c-7e     dynamic
  192.168.1.126          00-17-08-cf-36-1b     dynamic
  192.168.1.205          00-14-6c-83-38-2f     dynamic
  192.168.1.207          00-13-d3-3b-50-8f     dynamic
  192.168.1.255          ff-ff-ff-ff-ff-ff     static
  224.0.0.22             01-00-5e-00-00-16     static
```

If a physical address is 00-00-00-00-00-00, this indicates that the physical link between the two computers is not working correctly.

Ipconfig

You can use Ipconfig (Ipconfig.exe) to quickly view a computer's IP configuration and to retrieve an updated configuration from a DHCP server. To view detailed IP configuration information, open a command prompt and run the following command:

ipconfig /all

```
Windows IP Configuration

   Host Name . . . . . . . . . . . . : Vista1
   Primary Dns Suffix  . . . . . . . : hq.contoso.com
   Node Type . . . . . . . . . . . . : Hybrid
   IP Routing Enabled. . . . . . . . : No
   WINS Proxy Enabled. . . . . . . . : No
   DNS Suffix Search List. . . . . . : hq.contoso.com
                                       contoso.com

Ethernet adapter Local Area Connection:

   Connection-specific DNS Suffix  . : contoso.com
   Description . . . . . . . . . . . : NVIDIA nForce Networking Controller
```

```
Physical Address. . . . . . . . . : 00-13-D3-3B-50-8F
DHCP Enabled. . . . . . . . . . . : Yes
Autoconfiguration Enabled . . . . : Yes
Link-local IPv6 Address . . . . . : fe80::a54b:d9d7:1a10:c1eb%10(Preferred)
IPv4 Address. . . . . . . . . . . : 192.168.1.132(Preferred)
Subnet Mask . . . . . . . . . . . : 255.255.255.0
Lease Obtained. . . . . . . . . . : Wednesday, September 27, 2006 2:08:58 PM
Lease Expires . . . . . . . . . . : Friday, September 29, 2006 2:08:56 PM
Default Gateway . . . . . . . . . : 192.168.1.1
DHCP Server . . . . . . . . . . . : 192.168.1.1
DHCPv6 IAID . . . . . . . . . . . : 234886099
DNS Servers . . . . . . . . . . . : 192.168.1.210
NetBIOS over Tcpip. . . . . . . . : Enabled
```

If the IP address shown is in the range from 169.254.0.0 through 169.254.255.255, Windows used APIPA because the operating system was unable to retrieve an IP configuration from a DHCP server upon startup and there was no alternate configuration. To confirm this, examine the **ipconfig** output for the DHCP Enabled setting without a DHCP server address.

To release and renew a DHCP-assigned IP address, open a command prompt with administrative credentials, and then run the following commands:

ipconfig /release

ipconfig /renew

Windows will stop using the current IPv4 address and will attempt to contact a DHCP server for a new IPv4 address. If a DHCP server is not available, it will either use the alternate configuration or automatically assign an APIPA address in the range of 169.254.0.0 to 169.254.255.255.

Netstat

You can use Netstat (Netstat.exe) to determine the UDP or TCP ports a server is listening for connections on and to list the clients that have active connections. To view open ports and active incoming connections, run the following command at a command prompt:

netstat -a

```
Active Connections

  Proto  Local Address          Foreign Address        State
  TCP    0.0.0.0:135            0.0.0.0:0              LISTENING
  TCP    0.0.0.0:3389           0.0.0.0:0              LISTENING
  TCP    0.0.0.0:49152          0.0.0.0:0              LISTENING
  TCP    192.168.1.132:139      0.0.0.0:0              LISTENING
  TCP    192.168.1.132:3389     192.168.1.196:1732    ESTABLISHED
  TCP    [::]:135               [::]:0                LISTENING
  TCP    [::]:445               [::]:0                LISTENING
  TCP    [::]:2869              [::]:0                LISTENING
  TCP    [::]:3389              [::]:0                LISTENING
```

If you notice that a computer is listening for incoming connections on unexpected ports, you can use the **-b** parameter to resolve applications associated with active connections:

netstat -a -b

```
Active Connections

  Proto  Local Address          Foreign Address        State
  TCP    0.0.0.0:135            0.0.0.0:0              LISTENING
  RpcSs
 [svchost.exe]
  TCP    0.0.0.0:3389           0.0.0.0:0              LISTENING
  Dnscache
 [svchost.exe]
  TCP    0.0.0.0:49152          0.0.0.0:0              LISTENING
 [wininit.exe]
  TCP    0.0.0.0:49153          0.0.0.0:0              LISTENING
  Eventlog
 [svchost.exe]
  TCP    0.0.0.0:49154          0.0.0.0:0              LISTENING
  nsi
 [svchost.exe]
  TCP    0.0.0.0:49155          0.0.0.0:0              LISTENING
  Schedule
 [svchost.exe]
  TCP    0.0.0.0:49156          0.0.0.0:0              LISTENING
 [lsass.exe]
  TCP    0.0.0.0:49157          0.0.0.0:0              LISTENING
 [services.exe]
  TCP    169.254.166.248:139    0.0.0.0:0              LISTENING
Network Monitor
```

Microsoft Network Monitor is a protocol analyzer, also known as a *sniffer*. Network Monitor allows you to examine every detail of raw network communications. To download Network Monitor, visit *http://www.microsoft.com/downloads/* and search for Network Monitor. For detailed instructions on how to use Network Monitor to capture and analyze network communications, refer to the Help.

PathPing

You can use the PathPing tool to identify routers between a client and server, as the following example demonstrates (code in bold indicates user input):

pathping www.contoso.com

```
Tracing route to contoso.com [10.46.196.103]
over a maximum of 30 hops:
  0  contoso-test [192.168.1.207]
  1  10.211.240.1
  2  10.128.191.245
  3  10.128.191.73
  4  10.125.39.213
  5  gbr1-p70.cb1ma.ip.contoso.com [10.123.40.98]
```

```
 6  tbr2-p013501.cb1ma.ip.contoso.com [10.122.11.201]
 7  tbr2-p012101.cgcil.ip.contoso.com [10.122.10.106]
 8  gbr4-p50.st6wa.ip.contoso.com [10.122.2.54]
 9  gar1-p370.stwwa.ip.contoso.com [10.123.203.177]
10  10.127.70.6
```

PathPing can identify routing errors, such as a routing loop where routers send packets continuously between three or more routers. Like Ping, PathPing uses ICMP to identify routers. Therefore, routers that drop ICMP communications will not appear in PathPing output.

Performance Monitor

Performance Monitor enables you to view thousands of real-time counters about your computer or a remote computer. When troubleshooting network performance problems, you can use Performance Monitor to view current bandwidth utilization in a more detailed way than provided by Task Manager or Resource Monitor. Additionally, Performance Monitor provides access to counters measuring retries, errors, and much more.

To Monitor Windows Server 2008 IP Activity in Real Time

1. Click Start, and then click Server Manager.

2. In Server Manager, expand Diagnostics\Reliability And Performance\Monitoring Tools\Performance Monitor.

3. In the Performance Monitor snap-in, click the Add button (green plus sign) on the toolbar.

   The Add Counter dialog box appears.

4. There are several counters useful for monitoring IPv4 utilization:

   ❑ **IPv4\Datagrams Received/Sec and IPv4\Datagrams Sent/Sec**   Counters that display the current rate of incoming and outgoing IPv4 packets.

   ❑ **Network Interface\Bytes Received/Sec and Network Interface\Bytes Sent/Sec**   Counters that display the current rate of incoming and outgoing network communications, including IPv4, IPv6, and any other protocols. Multiply this value by 8 to determine the bits per second.

   ❑ **TCPv4\Connections Active**   The current number of outgoing TCP connections (for connections where the computer is acting as a client).

   ❑ **TCPv4\Connections Passive**   The current number of incoming TCP connections (for connections where the computer is acting as a server).

   ❑ **UDPv4\Datagrams Received/Sec and UDPv4\Datagrams Sent/Sec**   The current number of incoming and outgoing UDP packets.

   ❑ **ICMP\Messages Sent/Sec and ICMP\Messages Received/Sec**   The current number of incoming and outgoing ICMP packets. ICMP is used for Ping and other low-level network communications.

5. Click the counters you want to monitor, and then click Add.

6. Click OK to return to the Performance Monitor snap-in.

Ping

Ping is still the best tool to easily monitor network connectivity on an ongoing basis, despite the fact that many routers and servers drop ICMP communications. After using PathPing to identify network hosts that respond to ICMP requests, you can use Ping to constantly submit Ping requests, allowing you to easily determine whether you currently have connectivity to the host. If you are experiencing intermittent connectivity problems, a Ping loop will indicate whether your connection is active or not at any given time.

To start a Ping loop, run the following command:

ping -t *hostname*

Replies indicate that the packet was sent successfully, whereas Request Timed Out messages indicate that the computer did not receive a response from the remote host, or the remote host could not return a response. The following example indicates how to monitor the connection to a host at the IP address 192.168.1.1:

ping -t 192.168.1.1

```
Pinging 192.168.1.1 with 32 bytes of data:

Reply from 192.168.1.1: bytes=32 time=1ms TTL=64
Reply from 192.168.1.1: bytes=32 time<1ms TTL=64
Reply from 192.168.1.1: bytes=32 time<1ms TTL=64
Reply from 192.168.1.1: bytes=32 time<1ms TTL=64
Request timed out.
Request timed out.
Request timed out.
Request timed out.
Request timed out.
Reply from 192.168.1.1: bytes=32 time<1ms TTL=64
Request timed out.
Request timed out.
Reply from 192.168.1.1: bytes=32 time<1ms TTL=64
```

Note that Ping loops provide only an approximate estimation of connectivity. Ping packets can occasionally be dropped even if connectivity is constant, because routers drop ICMP requests before other types of packets. Additionally, because Ping sends requests sooner if a reply is received than if the reply times out, you cannot use the ratio of replies to time-out errors as a useful indication of network uptime.

Task Manager

You can use the Networking tab of Task Manager (Taskmgr.exe) to quickly view the bandwidth utilization of each of a computer's network adapters. To start Task Manager, click Start, type **Taskmgr**, and then press Enter. Alternatively, you can right-click the taskbar and then click Task Manager, or you can press Ctrl+Shift+Esc.

The Task Manager Networking tab, as shown in Figure 1-15, shows the utilization of each network adapter. The percentage utilization is measured in relation to the reported Link Speed of the adapter. In most cases, network adapters are not capable of 100 percent utilization, and peak utilization is approximately 60 percent to 70 percent.

Windows Network Diagnostics

Windows Network Diagnostics performs automated detection and diagnosis of networking problems and can quickly identify many common connectivity issues. If you are unable to connect to a network, Windows Network Diagnostics should always be the first troubleshooting step because it can often diagnose the problem quicker than even an experienced systems administrator.

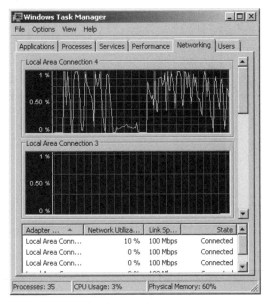

Figure 1-15 The Networking tab of Task Manager

To launch Windows Network diagnostics, follow these steps:

1. Click Start, right-click Network, and then click Properties.

2. Under Tasks, click Manage Network Connections.

3. Right-click the network adapter you want to configure, and then click Diagnose.

Windows Network Diagnostics attempts to identify any problems. It will display any information it finds that might be useful for troubleshooting and can even prompt you to automatically fix the problem if it is software related.

Chapter Summary

IPv4 is by far the most popular networking protocol in use today, and it will almost certainly remain popular for many years to come. Whereas connecting computers to an IPv4 network is straightforward (and often entirely automatic), designing IPv4 networks requires understanding IP addressing concepts and planning for future growth. Although IPv4 requires little ongoing maintenance, as an administrator, you must be familiar with many different troubleshooting tools to solve common connectivity problems.

Additional Information

For additional information about private IP addresses, see RFC 1918 at *http://tools.ietf.org/html/rfc1918*.

For additional information about APIPA, see the following:

- RFC 3330 at *http://tools.ietf.org/html/rfc3330*
- RFC 3927 at *http://tools.ietf.org/html/rfc3927*

For additional information about using multiple routers, see "The Cable Guy—September 2003: Default Gateway Behavior for Windows TCP/IP" at *http://www.microsoft.com/technet/community/columns/cableguy/cg0903.mspx*.

Chapter 2
IPv6

Internet Protocol version 4 (IPv4) was standardized in 1981 (with the publication of RFC 791)—many years before the modern Internet materialized. Although the Internet community has found ways to work around many of IPv4's shortcomings, a new version of the Layer 3 and 4 protocols, known as Internet Protocol version 6 (IPv6), will need to be adopted to allow the Internet to continue to grow in the decades to come.

IPv6 was included with the Windows XP SP1 and Windows Server 2003 operating systems as a core networking technology, but it was disabled by default. IPv6 is enabled by default on the Windows Vista and Windows Server 2008 operating systems. Microsoft has no plans to provide IPv6 support for Microsoft Windows 2000, Windows 98, and older versions of Windows.

This chapter provides information about how to design, deploy, maintain, and troubleshoot IPv6 networks in Windows Server 2008. A complete discussion of IPv6 would warrant an entire book, such as *Understanding IPv6,* Second Edition by Joseph Davies (Microsoft Press, 2008). This chapter focuses on knowledge that Windows Server 2008 systems administrators require to manage computers on IPv6 networks. This chapter assumes that you have a solid understanding of IPv4, which is described in Chapter 1, "IPv4."

Concepts

The single most important feature of IPv6, when compared to IPv4, is the larger address space. The IPv4 address space can never be expanded, and thus upgrading to IPv6 is inevitable if the Internet continues to grow. Additionally, IPv6 supports packets as large as 4 gigabytes (GB), allowing for better performance on very high-speed networks.

IPv6 incorporates many features that required extensions to IPv4. However, because these capabilities are already available for IPv4, they do not drive the adoption of IPv6:

- **Simpler configuration** Most IPv6 clients will automatically configure their own IP addresses—often without the need for a Dynamic Host Configuration Protocol (DHCP) server.

- **Security** Whereas Internet Protocol security (IPsec) extensions provide authentication and encryption for IPv4 communications, IPv6 has those capabilities built in.

- **Quality of Service (QoS)**   IPv6 has QoS built in. QoS extensions allow IPv4 data to be prioritized.

- **More efficient routing**   IPv6 routing is hierarchical and better organized, allowing routers to operate more efficiently and dedicate less memory to routing tables. Routing technology has scaled with the higher demands of IPv4, however, so this improvement will probably not result in a performance increase.

- **Improved extensibility**   IPv6 headers can be extended to support new features. IPv4 supports only 40 bytes of options, most of which have already been filled by extensions such as QoS. IPv6 headers are always exactly 40 bytes, but extension headers can be used to provide almost unlimited extensibility as networking needs change.

Changes from IPv4 to IPv6

Besides the larger address space, most IPv6 changes involve integrating optional extensions created after IPv4 was originally designed. Table 2-1 highlights the most significant changes from IPv4 to IPv6.

Table 2-1   IPv6 Changes

IPv4	IPv6
IP addresses are 32 bits.	IP addresses are 128 bits.
QoS headers are optional.	QoS support is built in.
IPsec support is optional.	IPsec support is required for all hosts.
Header includes a checksum.	Header does not include a checksum.
Header includes options that always consume space in the header.	Optional fields are stored in header extensions (although IPv6 header size is still twice the IPv4 header size).
Hosts use Address Resolution Protocol (ARP) to identify each other on local networks.	Hosts use Neighbor Solicitation messages to identify each other on local networks, which is easier to manage.
Hosts use Internet Group Management Protocol (IGMP) to manage local subnet group memberships for multicasting.	Hosts use Multicast Listener Discovery (MLD) to manage multicast group memberships.
Most hosts receive IP addresses from a DHCP server (although some hosts can use Internet Control Message Protocol, or ICMP, router discovery, it's uncommon).	Most hosts use ICMP Router Solicitation and Router Advertisements to determine their IP address, with an optional DHCPv6 server query for additional configuration settings.
Hosts use broadcast messages to communicate with all hosts on the local network.	Hosts use link-local scope all-nodes multicast instead of broadcast messages.
IPv4 uses interface ID (A) resource records in DNS queries.	IPv6 uses IPv6 interface ID (AAAA) resource records in DNS queries.
IPv4 has a maximum packet size of 65,535 bytes.	An IPv6 Jumbogram can be 4,294,967,295 bytes.

IPv6 has a handful of drawbacks when compared to IPv4:

- **Requires a new routing infrastructure**   IPv6 has a new header format, and IPv4 routers that haven't been designed to support IPv6 can't parse the fields in the IPv6 header. Therefore, organizations must upgrade their routers before adopting IPv6. Layer 2 protocols aren't affected, so Layer 2 switches and hubs don't need to be upgraded, and computers on a LAN can communicate using existing network hardware. Transition technologies, including 6to4, ISATAP, and Teredo (discussed later in this chapter) allow IPv6 to be used across a routing infrastructure that supports only IPv4.

- **Increased overhead**   The IPv6 header is twice as large as the IPv4 header. This difference is insignificant on most LANs and WANs, but on some lower-bandwidth links, performance could be impacted.

- **Difficult-to-memorize IP addresses**   Today, some systems administrators use IP addresses to identify computers and network infrastructure. That is no longer practical with IPv6. Instead, administrators will need to reference host names.

IPv6 Addressing

Perhaps the most significant drawback of IPv4 is the limited address range. IPv4 uses a 32-bit address space, providing a theoretical maximum of a little over four billion addresses (but the practical limit, as discussed in Chapter 1, is much smaller). IPv6 uses a 128-bit address space, providing about 3.4E38 (340 undecillion, if that clarifies the number) addresses. Whereas the practical number of IPv6 hosts is actually much smaller, there are still enough IPv6 addresses to give every man, woman, and child trillions of routable addresses without resorting to work-arounds such as network address translator (NAT).

IPv6 Address Structure

Typically, IPv6 addresses are divided into two parts: a 64-bit network component and a 64-bit host component. The network component identifies a unique subnet, and numbers are assigned to ISPs or large organizations by the Internet Assigned Numbers Authority (IANA). The host component is typically dandomlyderived or based on the network adapter's unique 48-bit media access control (MAC) address, though this can vary. For example, ISATAP (discussed later in this chapter) uses a different address structure.

> **Note**   Generating part of the IP address using the MAC address allows Web sites to track a single computer as long as it uses the same network adapter. To improve privacy for users, RFC 4941 (available at *http://www.ietf.org/rfc/rfc4941.txt*) describes techniques to change the IPv6 address over time so that a single computer cannot be tracked as easily.

IPv6 addresses are written using eight groups of four hexadecimal digits, as the following example shows:

2001:0000:0000:0000:085b:3c51:f5ff:ffdb

You can abbreviate IPv6 addresses by leaving out any leading zeros from any of the groups. This IP address is exactly equivalent to the previous IP address:

2001:0:0:0:85b:3c51:f5ff:ffdb

To shorten an IPv6 address even further, replace groups of zeros with two colons. You can do this only once in a single IPv6 address. Because IPv6 addresses always have eight groups of four hexadecimal digits, you can determine how many groups of 0s have been omitted. For example, the following IP address (which is equivalent to the previous examples) has three groups omitted, because five groups of hexadecimal digits are still shown:

2001::85b:3c51:f5ff:ffdb

Using IPv6 Addresses in Universal Naming Convention (UNC) Paths and URLs

Though you should typically rely on DNS names, you can embed an IPv6 address in a UNC path or a URL with a few minor conversions. To use an IPv6 address as part of a UNC path (such as \\server\share), change the colons to hyphens, and append .ipv6-literal.net. For example, to specify the C$ share of the computer with the IPv6 address of 2001:db8::85b:3c51:f5ff:ffdb, use the UNC path **\\2001-db8--85b-3c51-f5ff-ffdb.ipv6-literal.net\C$**. To specify the zone ID, replace the **%** symbol with an **s**. In this case, the IP address 2001:db8::85b:3c51:f5ff:ffdb%4 would become \\2001-db8--85b-3c51-f5ff-ffdbs4.ipv6-literal.net\C$ in a UNC path. To use this technique with computers running Windows 2000 or Windows Server 2003, add the name to the server by following the steps in Microsoft Knowledge Base article 281308 at *http://support.microsoft.com/kb/281308*.

You can embed an IPv6 address in a URL by enclosing it in brackets, for example, *http://[2001:db8::85b:3c51:f5ff:ffdb]/*. The brackets are required so that you can specify a port number as part of the URL. For example, this URL would connect to the same IPv6 IP address on port 81: *http://[2001:db8::85b:3c51:f5ff:ffdb]:81/*.

Just as IPv4 networks can be written using Classless Inter-Domain Routing (CIDR) notation (such as 192.168.1.0/24), IPv6 addresses use CIDR notation. For example, the following shows a 48-bit network address (note the double colon used to indicate zeros in the interface ID):

2001:db8:4136::/48

IPv6 Address Types

There are several different types of IPv6 addresses:

- **Link-local addresses**   IPv6 addresses that are automatically added for all physical and virtual interfaces and are accessible only on the local network segment

- **Unique local IPv6 unicast addresses**   IPv6 addresses that are routable on your intranet but not accessible from the Internet

- **Global unicast addresses**   IPv6 addresses that can be routed on the *IPv6 Internet,* which is a portion of the Internet that uses IPv6

- **Multicast addresses**   Addresses that allow a single host to communicate with multiple recipients

- **Anycast addresses**   Addresses that can be assigned to multiple interfaces, such as a single address for all the interfaces of a multi-homed server

- **Special addresses**   A variety of different addresses including loopback addresses

Whereas most IPv4 computers have only a single IP address per interface, IPv6 computers typically have both a link-local address and a global or unique local address.

The sections that follow describe each of these in more detail.

Link-Local Addresses   Hosts use link-local addresses when they need to communicate with other hosts on the same network. All IPv6 interfaces have a link-local address even if they also have a global unicast address. Because the network prefix is always the same, link-local addresses cannot be routed.

As shown in Figure 2-1, the first ten bits are always 1111111010, and the remaining 54 bits of the network address are always zero. This creates an address prefix of fe80::/64. As with most IPv6 addresses, the last 64 bits are the interface ID.

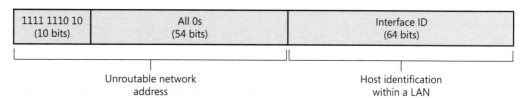

Figure 2-1   Link-local addresses

To view an example of link-local addresses, start any computer running Windows Vista or Windows Server 2008, and run the **ipconfig** command at a command prompt. For each network adapter, **ipconfig** will list a link-local IPv6 address that starts with fe80::.

Direct from the Source: Zone IDs

Link-local addresses should always be used only with zone IDs. As we've learned from experience, people often use them without zone IDs in scripts and applications, and the software will fail once there is a second interface (physical or virtual) on the system.

Dmitry Anipko, Developer

Windows Core Networking

Unique Local Addresses   Unique local addresses (ULAs) are routable between subnets on a private network but are not routable on the public Internet. ULAs are similar in function to the private IPv4 networks (10.0.0.0/8, 172.16.0.0/12, and 192.168.0.0/16) because they allow you to create complex internal networks without having public address space assigned.

As shown in Figure 2-2, the first ten bits are always 11111101, which creates an address prefix of fd00::/8. The next 40 bits of the network address are the global ID, which identifies a site or campus within an organization. Although it's up to the individual organization to assign global IDs, they should be randomly assigned to reduce the risk of address conflicts in future mergers (which would require one of the sites to be renumbered). The remaining 16 bits of the network address are the subnet ID, which allows you to create 65,536 subnets within each site. As with most IPv6 addresses, the last 64 bits are the interface ID.

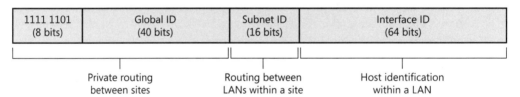

Figure 2-2   Unique local unicast addresses

    Note   Site-local addresses in the feco::10 address prefix originally provided private routing on IPv6 networks, but they were deprecated by RFC 3879.

Global Addresses   Like public IPv4 addresses, global unicast addresses can be reached from the public Internet. This requires Internet routers to have a path in their routing tables for the network portion of all valid global unicast addresses.

As shown in Figure 2-3, the first three bits of global unicast addresses are 001, which creates an address prefix of 2000::/3. The next 45 bits are the global routing prefix, which is used to identify the network on the public Internet. The following 16 bits are the subnet ID, which organizations can use to create up to 65,536 different internal subnets on their private network. As with most IPv6 addresses, the last 64 bits are the interface ID.

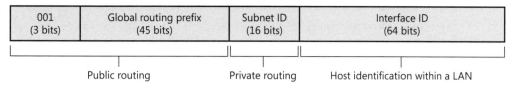

Figure 2-3   Global unicast address structure

Multicast Addresses   Like IPv4, IPv6 reserves a set of addresses for multicast use. Multicast communications allow a single host to send a single packet to multiple recipients. Multicasting is commonly used for streaming live media, for example, to send video of a meeting to several different computers simultaneously. Multicasting is also used to keep multiple computers synchronized (for example, keeping three database servers synchronized) or to deploy an operating system to multiple computers simultaneously. For multicast communications to work between networks, the routing infrastructure must be configured to support multicasting. Typically, multicasting does not work across the public Internet.

As shown in Figure 2-4, the first eight bits of multicast addresses are all ones, which creates an address prefix of FF00::/8. The next four bits are four binary flags (which indicate whether the multicast address is permanent or temporary), followed by four more bits that describe the scope (such as link-local or site-local). The remaining 112 bits are the group ID, which identifies the group of computers subscribed to the multicast. Multicast packets do not have a typical 64-bit interface ID.

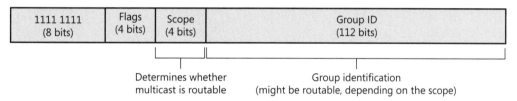

Figure 2-4   Multicast address structure

Anycast Addresses   An *anycast* address is a special address that can be assigned to multiple interfaces. The most commonly used example of an anycast address is the Subnet-Router anycast address, which is the network ID with an interface ID of zero. IPv6 hosts can use the Subnet-Router anycast address to contact any router on the local network.

Special IPv6 Addresses   The following addresses and networks are reserved for special uses:

- **::1/128 (or just ::1)**   The loopback address, which always refers to the local computer.
- **ff01::1/128 (or just ff01::1)**   The interface-local scope all-nodes multicast address.
- **ff02::1/128 (or just ff02::1)**   The link-local scope all-nodes multicast address, which is similar to a broadcast address in IPv4.
- **ff02::2/128 (or just ff02::2)**   The link-local scope all-routers multicast address.

- **ff05::2/128 (or just ff05::2)**   The site-local scope all-routers multicast address.

- **::ffff:0:0/96**   The prefix used for IPv4 mapped addresses.

- **2002::/16**   The prefix used for 6to4 addressing.

- **ff00::/8**   Used for multicast addresses.

- **fe80::/64**   A link-local address, which is an automatically assigned IP address that resembles Automatic Private Internet Protocol Addressing (APIPA) in IPv4. Seeing this address assigned to an interface indicates that a DHCPv6 server was not available. For more information, read "Link-Local Addresses" earlier in this chapter.

- **fc00::/8 or fd00::/8**   ULAs routable on intranets but not routable on the Internet. For more information, read "Unique Local Addresses" earlier in this chapter.

- **2001:db8::/32**   A network reserved for use in documentation.

Additionally, the Teredo and 6to4 transition technologies (discussed later in this chapter) use their own special addressing.

Distinguishing Multiple Interfaces

IPv6 clients always use the fe80::/64 link-local network address for network adapters connected to networks without IPv6 routers or a DHCPv6 server. If a computer running Windows has multiple network adapters connected to different network segments, it distinguishes the networks by using a numeric zone ID following a percent sign after the IP address, as the following examples demonstrate:

- fe80::d84b:8939:7684:a5a4%7

- fe80::462:7ed4:795b:1c9f%8

- fe80::2882:29d5:e7a4:b481%9

The last two characters indicate that the preceding networks are connected to the zone IDs 7, 8, and 9. You should always specify the zone ID when connecting to link-local addresses. Zone IDs are the same as the interface index, which you often use when configuring IPv6 settings on a per-interface basis.

> **Note**   Zone IDs are relative to the sending host. Therefore, different hosts connected to the same network might use different zone IDs to identify that network.

IPv6 Autoconfiguration

Although manual configuration is still an option (and is required for routers), computers will almost always have their IPv6 configuration automatically assigned. When an IPv6 host connects to a network, it sends a local-link multicast request to retrieve configuration parameters. IPv6 hosts can also use DHCPv6 to retrieve IP configuration information from a DHCPv6 server.

> **Note**   All hosts automatically assign themselves a link-local address without communicating with any infrastructure component. Additional configuration is required for unique local addresses, global addresses, or other address types.

Depending on how your IPv6 routers are configured, autoconfiguration can occur in three ways:

- **Stateless**   In stateless mode, IPv6 clients automatically configure their own IPv6 addresses by using IPv6 router advertisements, as discussed in "IPv6 Autoconfiguration" earlier in this chapter. If a DHCPv6 server is available, stateless clients can obtain configuration settings other than their IPv6 address, such as the DNS server address. Technically, stateless configuration occurs if your IPv6 routers transmit Router Advertisement messages with the Managed Address Configuration and Other Stateful Configuration flags set to 0 and one or more Prefix Information options with the A flag set. For more information, refer to RFC 4861.

- **Stateful**   Occurs if a DHCPv6 server provides IPv6 configuration information. A host uses stateful address configuration when it receives Router Advertisement messages with no prefix options when either the Managed Address Configuration flag or the Other Stateful Configuration flag is set to 1. Stateful address configuration also occurs when there are no IPv6 routers available.

- **Both**   Stateless and stateful mode can be used together. For example, IPv6 clients will use stateless autoconfiguration to assign an IPv6 address and then use stateful autoconfiguration to contact a DHCPv6 server and acquire other IPv6 settings, such as DNS server addresses. Technically, this occurs if your IPv6 routers transmit Router Advertisement messages with Prefix Information options set and the Managed Address Configuration or Other Stateful Configuration flags set to 1.

> **Note**   The Microsoft IPv6 implementations for Windows XP and Windows Server 2003 do not support DHCPv6. Windows Vista and Windows Server 2008 do support stateful address configuration with DHCPv6.

If IPv6 Duplicate Address Detection (DAD)—a feature not required for ISATAP, 6to4, or some other special interface types—is enabled, autoconfigured addresses can be in one or more of the following states:

- **Tentative**   Addresses are tentative for the brief period of time between first assigning the address and verifying that the address is unique. Computers use duplicate address detection to identify other computers that have the same IPv6 address by sending out a

Neighbor Solicitation message with the tentative address. If a computer responds, the address is considered invalid. If no other computer responds, the address is considered unique and valid.

- **Valid** Assigned addresses that have been verified as unique. A valid address can be either:

    - Preferred, which means the address can be used for communications. An address remains preferred for a length of time specified in the Preferred Lifetime field of the Router Advertisement message.

    - Deprecated, which means that the address has expired but can still be used for communications. An address remains valid for a length of time specified in the Valid Lifetime field of the Router Advertisement message. The Valid Lifetime should always be at least as long as the Preferred Lifetime, allowing addresses to be considered deprecated during the time span after the Preferred Lifetime has expired but before the Valid Lifetime expires.

- **Invalid** An address that was previously valid but can no longer be used because it has expired.

Figure 2-5 illustrates the relationships between the different Autoconfiguration states:

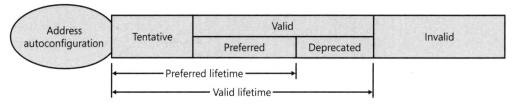

Figure 2-5   Autoconfiguration lifetimes

When a computer with IPv6 enabled starts up, it follows this process to perform autoconfiguration:

1. The computer configures a link-local address using the FE80::/64 address prefix.

2. The computer attempts to perform stateless address autoconfiguration by sending up to three Router Solicitation messages. If a router responds, the computer uses the response to configure the IP address in addition to other IPv6 configuration settings that might be present in the response.

3. If a router did not respond, or the router responded with either or both the Managed Address Configuration flag and the Other Stateful Configuration flag enabled in the Router Advertisement, DHCPv6 (or another stateful configuration method) is used to complete autoconfiguration.

The computer performs duplicate address detection for every IP address configured on it, including the link-local address. If no other host responds to the duplicate address detection, the address is considered valid. If a host responds to the duplicate address detection, the address is considered invalid.

DHCPv6

IPv4 clients automatically query for DHCP servers at startup. IPv6 clients query for address configuration from a router instead and perform a DHCPv6 query only if instructed by the router to perform stateful configuration.

You can configure IPv6 clients by using only your routers. However, using a DHCPv6 server can provide easier manageability because you can manage client configuration settings by using Windows Server 2008 rather than configuring your routers. For more information about DHCP, refer to Chapter 3, "Dynamic Host Configuration Protocol."

Neighbor Discovery

Computers use Neighbor Discovery (ND) to perform the following tasks:

- Identify routers on the local network.

- Identify their own IP addresses, address prefixes, and other network configuration settings.

- Resolve layer 2 addresses (such as a Media Access Control, or MAC, address) given an IPv6 address on the local network, similar to what ARP does in IPv4.

 More Info   For detailed information about Neighbor Discovery, read RFC 4861 at *http://www.ietf.org/rfc/rfc4861.txt*.

IPv6 Security

IPv6 includes built-in (and mandatory) support for IPsec headers. In IPv4, IPsec provides similar capabilities. However, because IPsec is not mandatory for IPv4 hosts, many hosts do not support it. For more information about IP security, read Chapter 4, "Windows Firewall with Advanced Security."

IPv6 Transition Technologies

The Internet is a massive infrastructure, managed by millions of people and run on billions of dollars in hardware and software. Changing something as fundamental as the Layer 3 protocol takes an incredible effort, requiring almost all routing infrastructure to be upgraded or, more likely, completely replaced.

The cost and time required to migrate the Internet to IPv6 is unimaginable, and that transition will not happen soon. However, many organizations have already begun supporting IPv6 on internal networks. Fortunately, there are several technologies you can use to allow IPv4 and IPv6 to coexist and to allow IPv6 to communicate across IPv4 networks.

Table 2-2 compares the different IPv6 transition technologies.

Table 2-2 IPv6 Transition Technologies

Technology	Purpose
Dual IP layer architecture	Allows computers to communicate using both IPv4 and IPv6 simultaneously. This is required for ISATAP and Teredo hosts and for 6to4 routers. (These three terms are defined later in this table and in greater detail later in the chapter.)
IPv6 over IPv4 tunneling	Embeds IPv6 traffic within an IPv4 header with an IP Protocol value of 41. Typically, this tunneling technique is used with ISATAP or 6to4.
Intra-Site Automatic Tunnel Addressing Protocol (ISATAP)	Allows IPv6 hosts to use IPv6 over IPv4 tunneling to communicate on intranets. Hosts identify each other by embedding the IPv4 address in the host portion of the IPv6 address.
6to4	Allows IPv6 hosts to communicate with the IPv6 Internet. A 6to4 router with a public IPv4 address is required.
Teredo	Allows IPv4/IPv6 hosts to communicate with the IPv6 Internet even if they are behind a network address translator (NAT).

The sections that follow provide an overview of each of these IPv6 transition technologies.

More Info   For detailed information, read "IPv6 Transition Technologies" at *http://www.microsoft.com/downloads/details.aspx?FamilyID=afe56282-2903-40f3-a5ba-a87bf92c096d*.

Dual IP Layer Architecture

The most fundamental transition technology is the dual IP layer architecture, shown in Figure 2-6, which is built into Windows Vista and Windows Server 2008. With this technology, computers can use IPv6 to communicate if the client, server, and network infrastructure support it. However, they can also communicate with computers or network services that support only IPv4.

Note   IPv6 on Windows XP and Windows Server 2003 uses a dual-stack architecture, with separate Layer 4 implementations for IPv4 and IPv6. Although the design of Windows XP and Windows Server 2003 is different than that of Windows Vista and Windows Server 2008, the functionality is similar.

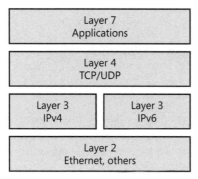

Figure 2-6   The dual IP layer architecture

IPv6 over IPv4 Tunneling

A host that is connected to an IPv4 network, such as the IPv4 Internet, can use tunneling to connect to an IPv6 portion of that network. With tunneling, IPv6 packets are encapsulated within IPv4 packets (as shown in Figure 2-7). Once the tunneled packets reach the IPv6 destination host, the IPv4 header is removed, exposing the native IPv6 packet.

IPv4 header	IPv6 header	Data

Figure 2-7   Tunneling IPv6 packets

Although IPv6 over IPv4 tunneling seems to resemble a traditional VPN, IPv6 over IPv4 tunneling does not typically require any communications to set up the tunnel. Also, the tunneling provides no additional authentication or encryption, unlike most VPNs.

Note   Adding the IPv4 header to the IPv6 packet reduces the maximum transmission unit (MTU) by at least 20 bytes. Additionally, the IPv4 packets should not be fragmented. Windows automatically handles this.

Architecturally, there are three different types of IPv6 over IPv4 tunnels:

■ **Router-to-router**   Allows two IPv6 networks to communicate even though they are connected by IPv4-only networks. This type of tunnel, illustrated in Figure 2-8, is completely transparent to the hosts on the network. You can manually implement a router-to-router tunnel (as described in "How to Configure a Router-to-Router Tunnel" later in this chapter), and 6to4 uses router-to-router tunnels.

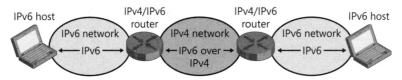

Figure 2-8   Router-to-router tunnel

- **Host-to-router and router-to-host**   Allows IPv6 hosts to communicate with a remote IPv6 network even though the local area network does not support IPv6. This type of connection is illustrated in Figure 2-9. ISATAP and Teredo can use this type of tunnel, though they each use different encapsulation techniques.

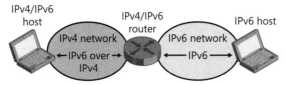

Figure 2-9   Host-to-router tunnel

- **Host-to-host**   Allows two IPv6 hosts to communicate even if none of the network infrastructure supports IPv6. This type of connection is illustrated in Figure 2-10. ISATAP and Teredo can use this type of tunnel, though they each use different encapsulation techniques.

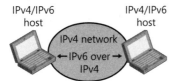

Figure 2-10   Host-to-host tunnel

> **Note**   IPv6 over IPv4 tunneling is a different technology from the similarly-named 6over4, also known as IPv4 multicast tunneling, available for Windows XP and Windows Server 2003.

ISATAP

ISATAP allows IPv6 hosts and routers to communicate across IPv4 networks by combining IPv4 and IPv6 addresses. As shown in Figure 2-11, an *ISATAP address* is an IPv6 address in which the 64-bit interface ID is 0:5EFE:*w.x.y.z*, where *w.x.y.z* is a private IPv4 address, or 200:5EFE:*w.x.y.z*, where *w.x.y.z* is a public IPv4 address.

Network address (64 bits)	0:5EFE or 200:5EFE (32 bits)	IPv4 address (32 bits)

Figure 2-11   ISATAP address structure

The host potion of an ISATAP address contains an embedded IPv4 address that is used to determine the destination IPv4 address for the IPv4 header when ISATAP-addressed IPv6 traffic is tunneled across an IPv4 network.

ISATAP is enabled by default on all versions of Windows that support IPv6. Because IPv6 hosts always receive a link-local address on the fe80::/64 network, computers running Windows will also receive an ISATAP address of fe80::5efe:*w.x.y.z* or fe80:200:5efe:*w.x.y.z* for every IPv4 address assigned. Additionally, they will have an ISATAP address for any other IPv6 address. For example, if an ISATAP host has an IPv4 address of 192.168.1.185, it will have an ISATAP link-local address of fe80::5efe:192.168.1.185.

ISATAP addresses can directly communicate only with other ISATAP addresses. You cannot use an ISATAP address to communicate directly to an IPv4 address or a non-ISATAP IPv6 address.

The value of ISATAP is in its ability to traverse IPv4 intranets. When two ISATAP hosts are on the same IPv4 network segment, ISATAP tunnels the IPv6 packets inside IPv4 packets and sets the IPv4 destination address to the last 32 bits of the destination ISATAP address on the link-local network.

When an ISATAP host must communicate with a remote IPv6 network, as illustrated in Figure 2-12, the IPv4 destination is the local interface of the ISATAP router. The ISATAP router removes the IPv4 header and transmits the IPv6 packets to the next router or to the destination host. Naturally, communicating across a router requires the host to have a unique local or global IPv6 address in addition to the standard link-local address.

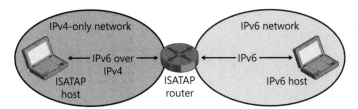

Figure 2-12   ISATAP routing

ISATAP routers advertise their presence, and IPv6 hosts configured to support ISATAP automatically configure the router as the default gateway.

6to4

Like ISATAP, 6to4 tunnels IPv6 packets over an IPv4 network. Whereas ISATAP stores the IPv4 address in the last 32 bits of the IPv6 address, 6to4 stores the IPv4 address of the 6to4 router in bits 17–48, as shown in Figure 2-13. 6to4 addresses are written entirely in hexadecimal, so the IPv4 portion of the address is not as easily readable as it is in an ISATAP address. All 6to4 addresses use the 2002::/16 prefix.

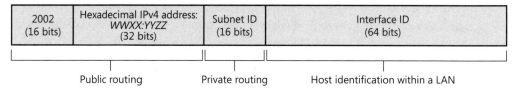

Figure 2-13   6to4 address structure

Every ISATAP host receives an ISATAP address with the encoded IPv4 address as the last 32 bits. With 6to4, only 6to4 routers have their IPv4 address encoded in the IPv6 address. 6to4 hosts receive an IPv6 address on the 6to4 router's network, with a unique interface ID. In other words, 6to4 hosts have their router's IPv4 address embedded in their IPv6 address and do not necessarily require an IPv4 address at all. A sample 6to4 network is shown in Figure 2-14.

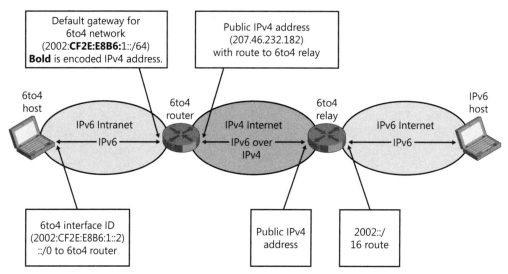

Figure 2-14   Sample 6to4 network

Whereas ISATAP is intended primarily for intranets, 6to4 is intended to be used on the Internet. You can use 6to4 to connect to IPv6 portions of the Internet through a 6to4 relay even if your intranet or your ISP supports only IPv4.

IPv6 routers can advertise 2002:*WWXX:YYZZ*:SubnetID::/64 prefixes so that hosts can create an autoconfigured 6to4 address.

Teredo

Teredo, also known as IPv4 network address translator (NAT) traversal (NAT-T) for IPv6, allows IPv6 hosts to communicate across IPv4 NATs. Although Teredo is similar in function to 6to4, 6to4 requires a 6to4 router with a public IP address, preventing IPv6 hosts from connecting to the IPv6 Internet until the network's edge router can be upgraded. Because networks rely on the edge router for all Internet access, organizations are often reluctant to upgrade them while still testing IPv6. Teredo can provide IPv6 Internet connectivity using your existing edge routers; however, it should be used only if native IPv6, ISATAP, or 6to4 cannot be used.

How It Works: IPv6 Tunneling

ISATAP and 6to4 tunnel IPv6 packets directly in the IPv4 packet and set the Protocol header value to 41 without relying on a Layer 4 protocol such as Transmission Control Protocol (TCP) or User Datagram Protocol (UDP). Many NAT devices do not handle Protocol 41 tunneling correctly and will drop the traffic. Teredo uses IPv4 with UDP, providing better compatibility with existing NAT devices.

For a NAT to be compatible with Teredo, the NAT must support UDP port translation. Teredo is fully compatible with cone and restricted NATs for all versions of Windows that support IPv6. Teredo in Windows XP and Windows Server 2003 are not compatible symmetric NATs. Teredo in Windows Vista and Windows Server 2008 can work between Teredo clients if at most one Teredo client is behind a symmetric NAT. For example, Teredo in Windows Vista and Windows Server 2008 will work if one of the peers is behind a symmetric NAT and the other is behind a cone or restricted NAT.

To allow Teredo to traverse NATs, IPv6 packets are tunneled within IPv4 packets between two IPv6 hosts or between an IPv6 host and a Teredo relay (rather than tunneled between routers, as is the case with 6to4). As with 6to4, a relay (as shown in Figure 2-15) is used to terminate the IPv6 over IPv4 tunnel and forward traffic between the IPv4 Internet and the IPv6 Internet. A Teredo server assists the configuration of Teredo clients and facilitates the initial communication between two Teredo clients or one Teredo client and one IPv6 host. Microsoft provides publicly available Teredo servers identified by the DNS entry teredo.ipv6.microsoft.com, and other organizations can also provide public Teredo servers.

Teredo host-specific relays, also shown in Figure 2-15, are computers running both IPv4 and IPv6 that can forward traffic between the IPv4 Internet and the IPv6 Internet. Computers running Windows can act as Teredo host-specific relays when they have proper connectivity. IPv6 connectivity can be provided by either a native IPv6 connection to the IPv6 Internet or a 6to4 connection.

Figure 2-16 shows the format of Teredo addresses. All Teredo clients use the 2001::/32 prefix. The remaining 32 bits of the network ID are the 32-bit IPv4 address of the IPv4 server (which is always written in hexadecimal). The host ID starts with 16 bits reserved for Teredo flags. The next 16 bits are the external UDP port number used by the NAT, and the final 32 bits are the NAT's IPv4 address (also written in hexadecimal). The NAT port number and IPv4 address are detected by the Teredo server, which provides the information back to the client. The Teredo client obscures the NAT port number and IPv4 address to prevent the NAT from translating them.

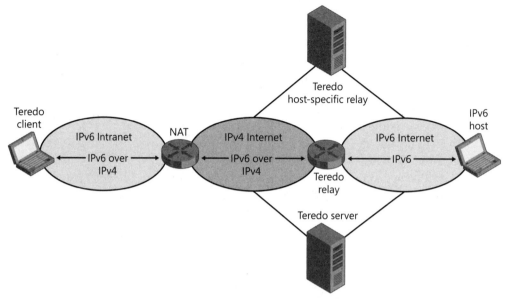

Figure 2-15   Sample Teredo network

3FFE:831F (32 bits)	Teredo server IPv4 address: *WWXX:YYZZ* (32 bits)	Flags (16 bits)	Obscured external port (16 bits)	Obscured external address (32 bits)

Figure 2-16   Teredo address structure

Note   Windows XP and Windows Server 2003 Teredo clients initially used the 3FFE:831F::/32 prefix. Microsoft Security Bulletin MS06-064, available at *http://www.microsoft.com/technet/ security/Bulletin/MS06-064.mspx*, configures these operating systems to use the 2001::/32 prefix.

More Info   For more information about Teredo, read "Teredo Overview" at *http:// www.microsoft.com/technet/network/ipv6/teredo.mspx* and RFC 4380 at *http://www.ietf.org/ rfc/rfc4380.txt*.

Planning and Design Considerations

Because the infrastructure, servers, and clients that comprise the modern Internet are managed by millions of different people and organizations, it will take many years before networks have entirely transitioned to IPv6. In the meantime, IPv4-to-IPv6 transitioning technologies allow hosts to communicate with different parts of the network.

> **Note** The most important transitioning technology is the ability for hosts to use both IPv4 and IPv6 simultaneously. Windows Vista and Windows Server 2008 have both IPv4 and IPv6 enabled by default for all network adapters.

This section provides information to evaluate IPv6 and plan your IPv6 migration.

Migrating to IPv6

Upgrading to an exclusively IPv6 environment should be a long-term goal. You will need to follow these general steps (with proper testing prior to any implementation) to migrate to IPv6:

1. As you deploy new computers or operating systems, configure them to support both IPv6 and IPv4. If you plan to continue using computers running Windows XP and Windows Server 2003, gradually enable IPv6 across your infrastructure for those hosts.

2. Upgrade your routing infrastructure to support native IPv6 routing.

3. Upgrade your DNS infrastructure to support IPv6 AAAA records and PTR records in the IP6.ARPA reverse domain.

4. Connect your routing and DNS infrastructures to the IPv6 Internet by using technologies such as 6to4 or Teredo, if necessary.

5. Work with internal and external developers to upgrade your applications to be independent of IPv6 or IPv4.

6. After thorough testing, convert IPv4/IPv6 nodes to use only IPv6.

Of those steps, the single greatest challenge will be upgrading applications to support IPv6. Enterprises often have thousands of applications that must be tested. Many existing applications will not work properly in an IPv6 environment and will need to be either upgraded or replaced before IPv4 can be entirely disabled.

> **Direct from the Source: Managing the Upgrade to IPv6**
>
> It's worth remembering that deploying IPv6 is not trivial. Just having IPv6 enabled isn't a big deal because most of the other devices on your network aren't going to be using IPv6 (except for other computers running Windows Vista and Windows Server 2008), so if your machine is talking to a printer or other device, it will use just IPv4 by default. Once you start trying to roll out IPv6, though, there is a lot to consider. There are a lot of variables, and not all of the skills you used in IPv4 transfer to IPv6.
>
> You need to plan it out and be ready to troubleshoot during rollout. Maybe some of your applications are just not IPv6 capable, or your older hardware doesn't understand what an IPv6 address is. Maybe it is a configuration error on a host or router. There could be

any number of issues that might cause problems, which is why I strongly recommend setting up an IPv6 test lab now—TODAY!—and testing your devices and applications to determine how they will work in an IPv6 network while building your IPv6 skills.

A lot of people are running IPv6 with Windows and a wide array of stuff and are making it work. To help you get there, we provide tools such as checkv4.exe (available at *http:// msdn2.microsoft.com/en-us/library/ms740624.aspx*) to help you figure out whether your code has any IPv4 calls hardcoded into it, in addition to white papers such as "Manageable Transition to IPv6 using ISATAP" (available at *http://www.microsoft.com/downloads/ details.aspx?FamilyId=B8F50E07-17BF-4B5C-A1F9-5A09E2AF698B*), a joint white paper with Cisco describing how to ease the deployment of IPv6, and "Enabling the Next Generation of Networking with End-to-End IPv6" (available at *http:// www.microsoft.com/downloads/details.aspx?FamilyID=b3611543-58b5-4ccc-b6ce- 677ebb2a520d*), a joint white paper with Juniper discussing IPv6 deployment and benefits. All of these and more are available from *http://www.microsoft.com/ipv6*. In short, we are working with lots of industry partners to simplify IPv6 deployment and make sure that all of our customers can gain the maximum value from IPv6.

Moral to the story? Get cracking on your IPv6 testing today!

Sean Siler, IPv6 Program Manager

Acquiring IPv6 Addresses

As with IPv4 addresses, most organizations will be assigned IPv6 addresses by their Internet service provider (ISP). Contact your ISP for more information.

If you work for an ISP, you can request an IPv6 address block from your Regional Internet Registry (RIR). For example, the American Registry for Internet Numbers (ARIN) is responsible for assigning IPv6 addresses to organizations in most North American countries. To identify your RIR, visit the Number Resource Organization (NRO) at *http://www.nro.org/about/ get_resources.html*.

Note   RIRs are assigned large blocks of IPv6 networks by the Internet Assigned Numbers Authority.

Planning Network Infrastructure Upgrades

For performance reasons, many network components operating at Layer 3 and above (including routers, firewalls, and NATs), are hard-wired to read the IPv4 header structure. Because IPv6 uses a different header structure, these network components often cannot be upgraded to support IPv6. Contact the hardware manufacturer for more information. Layer 2 network components, including hubs and switches, typically do not need to be upgraded to support IPv6.

Because much of your network infrastructure cannot have the software or firmware upgraded to support IPv6, you will probably need to replace network equipment to support native IPv6 networking. To minimize upgrade costs in the future, look for IPv6 support when purchasing new network equipment, even if you do not have immediate plans to migrate to IPv6.

Most organizations can begin testing and implementing IPv6 by using an IPv4-only infrastructure without purchasing upgrades. As discussed in the previous section, ISATAP, 6to4, and Teredo enable IPv6 communications to cross IPv4 networks. Additionally, you can use Windows Server 2008 (in addition to Windows Server 2003, Windows Vista, and Windows XP) as an IPv6 router. For more information about configuring Windows Server 2008 as an IPv6 router, read "How to Configure a Computer as an IPv6 Router" later in this chapter.

If your organization has IPv6 networks that are not directly connected to each other, plan to manually configure IPv6 over IPv4 router-to-router tunnels to connect the IPv6 networks. If you have IPv6 hosts that are connected to IPv4-only networks, plan to use ISATAP to allow the IPv6 hosts to access IPv6-only network resources.

Planning for IPv6 Transition Technologies

You will need to use one or more IPv6 transition technologies during the IPv6 migration process. The sections that follow provide planning information for ISATAP, 6to4, and Teredo.

ISATAP

By default, ISATAP hosts will obtain the IPv4 address of the ISATAP router by using DNS and other IP name resolution techniques to resolve the name ISATAP to an IPv4 address. Once the host has identified the ISATAP router's IP address, it uses IPv4 unicast messages to acquire autoconfiguration information from the router. To ensure that clients can find the ISATAP router, plan to use one of the following techniques:

- If the ISATAP router is a computer, configure the computer name as **ISATAP**.
- Create a DNS entry for every DNS domain.
- Add an entry to the Hosts file.
- Create a static WINS record.
- Run a **netsh** command on all ISATAP hosts.

For detailed instructions, read "How to Configure a Computer as an ISATAP Router" later in this chapter.

6to4

6to4 allows you to access the IPv6 Internet by using your existing IPv4 Internet connection. 6to4 requires you to have a 6to4 router and a public IPv4 address (such as an address assigned by your ISP). IPv4-only routers cannot act as 6to4 routers. Therefore, if you are currently using an IPv4-only router for your Internet access, you will need to upgrade or replace your router.

Before investing in upgrades to support 6to4 or Teredo, evaluate whether the benefits of connecting to the IPv6 Internet outweigh the costs. Unless you need to access a specific resource on the IPv6 Internet that is not accessible on the IPv4 Internet, there might be no practical benefit to connecting to the IPv6 Internet. Generally, public IPv6 Internet resources (such as Web sites) are also available on the IPv4 Internet.

Teredo

You can use Teredo to provide hosts with IPv6 Internet connectivity when you do not have a 6to4 router with a public IPv4 address. For best results with Teredo, choose cone or restricted NATs that support UDP port translation, and avoid symmetric NATs. While implementing Teredo, you might discover that you need to change the NAT or firewall configuration. Therefore, you should be prepared to work with network administrators to provide the connectivity you require.

You can use Microsoft's Internet Connectivity Evaluation Tool to determine whether your current NAT supports Teredo. To use the online tool, open *http://www.microsoft.com/windows/ using/tools/igd/* in Microsoft Windows Internet Explorer, and follow the prompts.

Deployment Steps

Because IPv6 is enabled by default in Windows Vista and Windows Server 2008, and IPv6 automatically configures itself by communicating with IPv6 routers, you typically do not need to perform any host configuration to support IPv6.

This section provides instructions for disabling or manually configuring IPv6. Additionally, this section shows you how to enable ISATAP, 6to4, and Teredo and to configure Windows Server 2008 as an IPv6 router.

How to Disable IPv6

Unlike Windows XP and Windows Server 2003, IPv6 in Windows Vista and Windows Server 2008 cannot be uninstalled. However, you can disable IPv6 from individual network adapters or entire computers in Windows Vista and Windows Server 2008.

Disable IPv6 on a Network Adapter

Even though having IPv6 enabled should not cause any problems on an IPv4-only network, you could choose to disable IPv6 to simplify network troubleshooting. To disable IPv6 on a network adapter, follow these steps:

1. Click Start, right-click Network, and then click Properties.

2. Under Tasks, click Manage Network Connections.

3. Right-click the network adapter, and then click Properties.

4. Clear the Internet Protocol Version 6 check box, and then click OK.

Disabling IPv6 might prevent some applications and services from functioning. For example, some features of Windows Meeting Space (a Windows Vista feature) use IPv6 for peer-to-peer networking on a single network segment.

Disable IPv6 on a Computer

To disable IPv6 on all network adapters, connections, and tunnel interfaces on a computer, add the following registry value (DWORD type) set to **0xFF**:

HKEY_LOCAL_MACHINE\SYSTEM\CurrentControlSet\Services\Tcpip6\Parameters \DisabledComponents

You must restart the computer for this registry value to take effect. This method does not disable the IPv6 loopback interface.

How to Manually Configure IPv6

To manually configure an IPv6 address by using the graphical interface, follow these steps:

1. Click Start, right-click Network, and then click Properties.

    The Network And Sharing Center appears.

2. Under Tasks, click Manage Network Connections.

3. Right-click the network interface, and then click Properties.

4. Select Internet Protocol Version 6 (TCP/IPv6), and then click Properties.

    The Internet Protocol Version 6 (TCP/IPv6) Properties dialog box appears.

5. Click Use The Following IPv6 Address. Type the address, subnet prefix length, and default gateway.

6. Click Use The Following DNS Server Addresses, and then type the preferred and alternate DNS servers.

7. To configure multiple IP addresses, default gateways, or DNS servers, click Advanced, and make the appropriate settings in the presented dialog box.

8. Click OK twice.

The new IP settings take effect immediately.

How to Configure IPv6 from a Script

You can use the Netsh tool to configure a computer's IPv6 settings by using the following syntax:

netsh interface ipv6 add address "*Interface*" *Address*

The following demonstrates how to add the address 2001:db8:: 1c32:29d5:e7a4:b481 to the "Local Area Connection" interface:

netsh interface ipv6 add address "Local Area Connection" 2001:db8::1a49:2aa:ff:fe34:ca8f

Though rarely necessary, you can manually specify the preferred and valid lifetimes by using the same command. For complete usage information, run **netsh interface ipv6 add address ?** at a command prompt.

To configure a router, use the following syntax:

netsh interface ipv6 add potentialrouter "*Interface*" *Address*

To configure a DNS server, use the following syntax:

netsh interface ipv6 add dnsserver "*Interface*" *Address*

How to Enable ISATAP

ISATAP is enabled by default in Windows Vista. It is also enabled by default in Windows XP and Windows Server 2003 if they have IPv6 installed. However, it is disabled by default in Windows Server 2008 and Windows Vista with Service Pack 1 (unless the name ISATAP is resolved). You can view the current state by running the following command:

netsh interface isatap show state

To enable ISATAP on a computer, run the following command:

netsh interface isatap set state enabled

By default, ISATAP hosts will obtain the IPv4 address of the ISATAP router by using DNS and other IP name resolution techniques to resolve the name ISATAP to an IPv4 address. Once the host has identified the ISATAP router's IP address, it uses IPv4 unicast messages to acquire autoconfiguration information from the router. To manually configure an address for the ISATAP router, run the following command:

netsh interface isatap set router *IPv4Address*

Note that the router must respond to unicast IPv4-encapsulated Router Solicitation messages before the ISATAP host will use it as a default gateway.

You can use the Ping tool to test connectivity between two ISATAP hosts. However, you must specify the zone ID of the virtual interface with the ISATAP IPv6 address. To determine the zone ID, run the command **ipconfig /all** at a command prompt. Then, examine the Microsoft ISATAP adapter output, and identify the zone ID at the end of the ISATAP address. The zone ID is shown in bold in this example output:

```
Tunnel adapter Local Area Connection* 8:

    Connection-specific DNS Suffix  . :
    Description . . . . . . . . . . . : Microsoft ISATAP Adapter
    Physical Address. . . . . . . . . : 00-00-00-00-00-00-00-E0
    DHCP Enabled. . . . . . . . . . . : No
    Autoconfiguration Enabled . . . . : Yes
    Link-local IPv6 Address . . . . . : fe80::5efe:192.168.1.185%12(Preferred)
    Default Gateway . . . . . . . . . :
    DNS Servers . . . . . . . . . . . : ::1
                                        127.0.0.1
    NetBIOS over Tcpip. . . . . . . . : Disabled
```

Now, identify the ISATAP address of another host on the same network, and run the **ping** command using the zone ID, as the following example shows:

```
ping fe80::5efe:192.168.1.186%12

Pinging fe80::5efe:192.168.1.186%12 from fe80::5efe:192.168.1.185%12:

Reply from fe80::5efe:192.168.1.186%12: time=3ms
Reply from fe80::5efe:192.168.1.186%12: time=2ms
Reply from fe80::5efe:192.168.1.186%12: time=3ms
Reply from fe80::5efe:192.168.1.186%12: time=3ms

Ping statistics for fe80::5efe:192.168.1.186%12:
    Packets: Sent = 4, Received = 4, Lost = 0 (0% loss),
Approximate round trip times in milli-seconds:
    Minimum = 2ms, Maximum = 3ms, Average = 2ms
```

Note   To ensure that Windows Server 2008–based DNS servers can resolve the ISATAP name for ISATAP hosts, remove the ISATAP entry from the HKEY_LOCAL_MACHINE\System\ CurrentControlSet\Services\DNS\Parameters\Global QueryBlockList registry value.

How to Enable 6to4

Whereas two hosts can use ISATAP to communicate without any IPv6 network infrastructure, 6to4 relies primarily on router configuration. When configuring 6to4, begin by configuring a 6to4 router with a routable IPv4 address on the public Internet. Then configure the 6to4 relay by using the anycast address 2002:c058:6301::, defined in RFC 3068, available at *http://www.ietf.org/rfc/rfc3068.txt*. The anycast prefix for 6to4 relay routers identifies the nearest 6to4 relay by using the Internet routing protocol Border Gateway Protocol (BGP). Depending on your router, the relay might be automatically configured.

Next, configure the IPv6 router to advertise itself as a 6to4 router on your local IPv6 network. It should begin advertising the 2002:*WWXX:YYZZ:SubnetID*::/64 prefix. When IPv6 hosts autoconfigure, they will assign a host ID on that subnet (in addition to the link-local address and any other IPv6 addresses) and configure the 6to4 router as the default gateway.

You can configure a single computer to act as a 6to4 host/router, enabling the computer to communicate with the IPv6 Internet using its own public IPv4 address.

If a computer running Windows and IPv6 has a public IPv4 address assigned to it, it will attempt to automatically configure itself as a 6to4 host/router by performing these tasks:

- Configuring a 6to4 address in the form 2002:*WWXX:YYZZ::WWXX:YYZZ*. On Windows XP and Windows Server 2003, this is assigned to the 6to4 Tunneling Pseudo-Interface. On Windows Vista and Windows Server 2008, this is assigned to the tunnel adapter with the description *Microsoft 6to4 Adapter*.

- Creating a 2002::/16 route to forward all 6to4 traffic to the tunnel interface.

- Attempts to identify a 6to4 relay by querying the DNS address 6to4.ipv6.microsoft.com. If the query is successful, the 6to4 component adds a default route on the 6to4 tunnel interface to send all 6to4 traffic to the 6to4 relay.

If this automatic configuration is successful, the host/router will be able to reach the IPv6 Internet without manual configuration.

To determine whether 6to4 is enabled, run the following command:

netsh interface 6to4 show state

In addition to being enabled, 6to4 must have an interface configured. By default, on computers running Windows Server 2008, no interface is configured. To determine whether an interface is configured and view the configuration of the 6to4 relay, run the following commands:

netsh interface 6to4 show interface

netsh interface 6to4 show relay

To enable 6to4 as a host, run the following commands (where **Interface** is the name of the IPv6 interface):

netsh interface 6to4 set state enabled

netsh interface 6to4 set interface "*Interface*" default

Specify the 6to4 relay by running the following command (where **Relay** is the host name or IP address of the 6to4 relay):

netsh interface 6to4 set relay *Relay*

Now, when you run **ipconfig /all**, you will see a tunnel adapter with the description Microsoft 6to4 Adapter.

> **Note**   To verify connectivity to the IPv6 Internet, you will need an IPv6 address that you can access. For a list of IPv6 accessible Web sites, visit *http://www.ipv6.org/v6-www.html*. You can use Nslookup to determine the IPv6 address associated with a AAAA record. For more information about Nslookup, read "Nslookup" in "Troubleshooting" later in this chapter.

How to Enable Teredo

Teredo is disabled by default for Windows XP, Windows Server 2003, and Windows Server 2008. Although it is enabled by default for Windows Vista, Teredo is typically inactive based on the configuration of the client computer.

When a Windows Teredo client starts, it sends a series of Router Solicitation messages to the Microsoft Teredo servers at teredo.ipv6.microsoft.com. These responses determine the type of NAT the client is behind. To view the type of NAT, run the following command:

netsh interface ipv6 show teredo

To enable Teredo on a computer in an Active Directory environment, run the following command:

netsh interface ipv6 set teredo enterpriseclient

To enable Teredo on a computer in a workgroup environment, run the following command:

netsh interface ipv6 set teredo client

You can view the current state by running the following command:

netsh interface teredo show state

How to Configure a Computer as an IPv6 Router

Traditionally, routers are used to forward packets between network segments. IPv6 routers can also be used to forward packets through a tunnel. For example, a 6to4 router can send packets from an IPv4 network across the IPv4 Internet to a 6to4 relay connected to the IPv6 Internet.

Dedicated network equipment typically offers lower cost, better performance, and easier manageability, but configuring computers as IPv6 routers can allow you to use existing computer hardware to create an IPv6 lab environment. It also allows you to create routed IPv6 networks consisting entirely of virtual machines running in an environment such as Microsoft Virtual Server or Microsoft Virtual PC.

Computers running Windows XP, Windows Vista, Windows Server 2003, and Windows Server 2008 can be configured as native IPv6 routers, 6to4 routers, or ISATAP routers. The sections that follow describe how to configure Windows Server 2008 computers to act as these types of IPv6 routers.

How to Configure a Computer as a Native IPv6 Router

To enable a computer running Windows Vista or Windows Server 2008 to act as an IPv6 router, use the Netsh tool to enable IPv6 forwarding on each interface. To enable advertising, add the **advertise=enabled** parameter. You need to enable advertising only for interfaces that connect to networks that do not yet have an advertising router.

The following two commands demonstrate how to enable routing and advertising between the interfaces named Local Area Connection and Local Area Connection 2:

netsh interface ipv6 set interface "Local Area Connection" forwarding=enabled advertise=enabled

netsh interface ipv6 set interface "Local Area Connection 2" forwarding=enabled advertise=enabled

Before clients can autoconfigure based on the router advertisements, you must publish routes by running the **netsh interface ipv6 add route** command. First, configure routes for all directly attached networks, using the following syntax:

netsh interface ipv6 add route <*network*>::/64 "*Interface*" publish=yes

If Netsh displays The Object Already Exists, the route you are trying to publish was added automatically but might not be published. Run the following command to display all routes:

netsh interface ipv6 show route

If the route you want to publish already exists and is not yet published, use the following syntax to publish the existing route:

netsh interface ipv6 set route <*network*>::/64 "*Interface*" publish=yes

If you want an interface to be the default router for autoconfigured hosts attached to the same network, use the following syntax:

netsh interface ipv6 add route ::/0 "*Interface*" nexthop=*Address* publish=yes

After adding routes, run **netsh interface ipv6 show route** to display all routes, and use the **netsh interface ipv6 delete route** to selectively delete routes.

How to Configure a Router-to-Router Tunnel

You can use a router-to-router tunnel to connect two IPv6 networks that are connected only by an IPv4 network. To create a router-to-router tunnel, run the following command on both computers running Windows Server 2008 that will be acting as a router. In this command, *InterfaceName* is the friendly name for the new interface that will be created to route traffic between the two routers, *LocalIPv4Address* is the IPv4 address of the local router, and *RemoteIPv4Address* is the IPv4 address of the remote router.

netsh interface ipv6 add v6v4tunnel "*InterfaceName*" *LocalIPv4Address* *RemoteIPv4Address*

Next, follow the steps in "How to Configure a Computer as a Native IPv6 Router" earlier in this chapter to complete the router configuration.

How to Configure a Computer as an ISATAP Router

To configure a computer running Windows Server 2008 as an ISATAP router, follow these steps:

1. Connect the computer to both an IPv4 intranet and an IPv6 intranet. Make note of the interface indexes of each interface in addition to the interface index of the ISATAP tunneling interface (with the description *Microsoft ISATAP Adapter*). If *Microsoft ISATAP Adapter* does not appear in the **Ipconfig /all** output, follow the steps in "How to Enable ISATAP" earlier in this chapter.

2. Run the following command to enable forwarding and advertising on the IPv6 interface, where **Index** is the index assigned to your IPv6 interface:

   netsh interface ipv6 set interface *Index* forwarding=enabled

3. Run the following command to enable forwarding and advertising on the ISATAP interface, where **Index** is the index assigned to your ISATAP interface:

   netsh interface ipv6 set interface *Index* forwarding=enabled advertise=enabled

4. Run the following command to add routes to your IPv6 network, where **Network/Prefix** is the network and prefix (such as 2001:db8:0:1::/64), and **Index** is the index assigned to your ISATAP interface:

   netsh interface ipv6 add route *Network/Prefix Index* publish=yes

5. Run the following command to add a default route to your IPv6 network, where **Index** is the index assigned to your intranet interface, and **IPv6Address** is the default gateway:

    netsh interface ipv6 add route ::/0 *Index* **nexthop=***IPv6Address* **publish=yes**

6. Configure clients with the address of the ISATAP router by using one of the following techniques:

    ❑ Name the computer ISATAP, and allow it to automatically register itself in DNS and optionally in WINS.

    ❑ Manually create an A record for the name ISATAP in every DNS domain that contains ISATAP hosts. For example, if the default domain for an ISATAP host is north.contoso.com, you would need to create an A record for isatap.north.contoso.com to identify the ISATAP router. For more information about DNS, read Chapter 7, "Domain Name System."

    ❑ Add an entry to the *%SystemRoot%*\system32\drivers\etc\hosts file with the value *IPv4Address* **ISATAP**.

    ❑ Create a static WINS record with the NetBIOS name **ISATAP <00>** (where **<00>** is the hexadecimal value of the sixteenth character). For more information about WINS, read Chapter 8, Windows Internet Name Service."

    ❑ Run the following command on the ISATAP router and all ISATAP hosts, where *IPv4Address* is the IPv4 address of the ISATAP router:

    netsh interface ipv6 isatap set router *IPv4Address*

> **Note**   ISATAP clients running Windows XP with no service pack attempt to resolve the name _ISATAP (note the leading underscore character) instead of ISATAP.

How to Configure a Computer as a 6to4 Router

The simplest way to configure a computer running Windows Server 2003 or Windows Server 2008 as a 6to4 router is to enable the Internet Connection Sharing (ICS) feature. Enabling ICS on an interface that is assigned a public IPv4 address:

■ Enables IPv6 forwarding on both the 6to4 tunneling and private interfaces.

■ Advertises a 6to4 route on the private intranet using the network 2002:*WWXX:YYZZ:Index*::/64, in which *Index* is the interface index of the private interface.

To enable Internet Connection Sharing, follow these steps:

1. Click Start, right-click Network, and then click Properties.

2. In the Tasks pane, click Manage Network Connections.

3. In the Network Connections window, right-click the interface with the public IPv4 address, and then click Properties.

4. In the network adapter's properties dialog box, on the Sharing tab, select the Allow Other Network Users To Connect Through This Computer's Internet Connection check box. Click the Home Networking Connection list, and select the network adapter associated with the private network.

5. Click OK., and when prompted, click Yes.

ICS will act as an advertising 6to4 router, and IPv6 hosts on the private network will automatically configure themselves with 6to4 interface IDs and be able to access the IPv6 Internet. ICS will perform Network Address Translation (NAT) on IPv4 traffic and act as a 6to4 router for IPv6 traffic.

You can also manually configure a computer as a 6to4 router by following these steps:

1. Configure the computer with a public IPv4 address, and verify that the computer is not receiving Router Advertisement messages from IPv6 or ISATAP routers. Windows Server 2008 will automatically create a 6to4 interface and add a default route to a 6to4 relay router on the IPv4 Internet.

2. Run the following command to enable forwarding and advertising on the interface attached to your intranet, where **Index** is the index assigned to your intranet interface:

    netsh interface ipv6 set interface *Index* forwarding=enabled advertise=enabled

3. Run the following command to enable the 6to4 service:

    netsh interface ipv6 6to4 set state enabled

4. Run the following command to enable forwarding on the 6to4 interface, where **Index** is the index assigned to your Internet interface:

    netsh interface ipv6 set interface *Index* forwarding=enabled

5. Run the following command to add routes for the 6to4 networks, where **WWXX:YYZZ** is the public IPv4 address (*W.X.Y.Z*) in hexadecimal format, and **Index** is the index assigned to your intranet interface:

    netsh interface ipv6 add route 2002:*WWXX:YYZZ:SubnetID*::/64 *Index* publish=yes

If your router has network interfaces connected to multiple intranet networks, repeat steps 2 and 5 for each intranet interface.

Ongoing Maintenance

IPv6 requires no maintenance to maintain the same configuration. However, over time, you should expand the portion of your network that supports IPv6 and change the way you use IPv6 transition technologies. For hosts that currently use Teredo, work to migrate them to ISATAP and 6to4. Then, migrate networks from ISATAP and 6to4 to native IPv6.

Troubleshooting

IPv6 troubleshooting is similar to IPv4 troubleshooting, and you can use the same tools described in the "Troubleshooting" section in Chapter 1. The sections that follow provide some IPv6-specific troubleshooting information.

Netsh

The **netsh interface ipv6** command context contains many commands that are useful for analyzing the current IPv6 configuration and troubleshooting problems. The most useful commands are:

- **netsh interface ipv6 show global**   Displays general IPv6 settings, including the default hop limit. Though you rarely need to modify these settings, you can use the **netsh interface ipv6 set global** command to change them.

- **netsh interface ipv6 show addresses**   Displays all IPv6 addresses in a much more compact format than **ipconfig /all**.

- **netsh interface ipv6 show dnsservers**   Displays all DNS servers that have been configured for IPv6. This does not display any DNS servers that might be configured with IPv4 addresses.

- **netsh interface ipv6 show potentialrouters**   Displays all advertising IPv6 routers that have been detected on the local network.

- **netsh interface ipv6 show route**   Lists the automatically and manually configured routes, including tunneling routes.

- **netsh interface ipv6 show tcpstats**   Lists various IPv6 TCP statistics, including the current number of connections, the total number of both incoming and outgoing connections, and the number of communication errors.

- **netsh interface ipv6 show udpstats**   Lists various IPv6 UDP statistics, including the number of UDP datagrams that have been sent or received and the number of datagrams that resulted in an error.

- **netsh interface ipv6 show neighbors**   Displays all cached IPv6 neighbors. To flush the neighbor cache, run the command **netsh interface ipv6 delete neighbors**.

- **netsh interface ipv6 show destinationcache**   Displays all cached IPv6 hosts that the computer has communicated with. To flush the destination cache, run the command **netsh interface ipv6 delete destinationcache**.

When troubleshooting IPv6 transition technologies, you can use the following commands:

- **netsh interface ipv6 show teredo**   Displays the Teredo configuration, including the Teredo server name and the client port number. You can use the **netsh interface ipv6 set teredo** command to change these configuration settings.

■ **netsh interface ipv6 6to4 show** *command*   By using one of the four commands in this context (**interface**, **relay**, **routing**, and **state**), you can examine the current 6to4 configuration.

■ **netsh interface isatap show** *command*   By using one of the two commands in this context (**router** and **state**), you can examine the current ISATAP configuration.

Ipconfig

You can use the Ipconfig tool (the **ipconfig** command) to quickly view a computer's IPv4 and IPv6 configuration. IPv6 can add several virtual network adapters that appear in the **ipconfig /all** output, as described in Table 2-3.

Table 2-3   IPv6 Network Adapter Descriptions

Adapter Description	Purpose
Microsoft ISATAP Adapter or isatap.{*identifier*}	A virtual interface used for ISATAP tunneling
Teredo Tunneling Pseudo-Interface	A virtual interface used for Teredo tunneling
6TO4 Adapter	A virtual interface used for 6to4 tunneling.

If the *IPv6 Address* line does not appear in the **ipconfig /all** output, but the interface has a Link-local IPv6 Address specified, IPv6 is enabled for the interface, but no advertising router was available when the interface was configured.

To manually initiate IPv6 autoconfiguration (for example, after making a change to the IPv6 router configuration), open a command prompt and run the following commands:

ipconfig /release6

ipconfig /renew6

Nslookup

As described more thoroughly in Chapter 7, you can use the Nslookup tool to test DNS servers. When testing IPv6 communications, run the command **nslookup** at a command prompt without any parameters to open Nslookup in interactive mode. Then, run the **nslookup** command **set type=aaaa** to configure Nslookup to query IPv6 AAAA DNS records. You can then query IPv6 AAAA records by typing the name of the record as a command. The following example shows user input in bold:

nslookup

```
Default Server:  dns.contoso.com Address:  10.100.100.201:53
```

set type=aaaa

ipv6.research.microsoft.com

```
Server:  dns.contoso.com
Address:  10.100.100.201:53

Non-authoritative answer:
Name:    ipv6.research.microsoft.com
Addresses:  2002:836b:4179::836b:4179, ::131.107.65.121
```

As long as you keep Nslookup open, any DNS queries you perform will query only AAAA records.

Troubleshooting Teredo

First, determine the current Teredo configuration by running the following command:

netsh interface teredo show state

If the output includes the message, "Error: client is in a managed network," Teredo is configured as a standard client, which does not function when connected to a domain controller. To resolve this, run the following command:

netsh interface ipv6 set teredo enterpriseclient

If Teredo still does not work, it's likely that your network infrastructure blocks the IPv4 UDP traffic that Teredo uses for communications. Work with your network administrators to ensure that routers and firewalls allow incoming UDP traffic.

You can enable tracing to troubleshoot more complex problems by following these steps:

1. Set the HKEY_LOCAL_MACHINE\SOFTWARE\Microsoft\Tracing\IpHlpSvc\Enable-FileTracing registry key to **1**.

2. Stop the IP Helper service by running the command **net stop iphlpsvc**.

3. Delete the contents of the *%SystemRoot%*\Tracing folder.

4. Start the IP Helper service by running the command **net start iphlpsvc**.

5. Reproduce the problem. For example, you can force Teredo to attempt a connection by running the command **netsh interface teredo show state**.

   Now you can examine the trace logs in the *%SystemRoot%*\Tracing folder or submit the logs to technical support.

6. Set the HKEY_LOCAL_MACHINE\SOFTWARE\Microsoft\Tracing\IpHlpSvc\Enable-FileTracing registry key to **0**.

7. Stop the IP Helper service by running the command **net stop iphlpsvc**, and then restart it by running the command **net start iphlpsvc**.

Chapter Summary

IPv6 is the future of networking, primarily because it offers a vastly greater address space than IPv4. For some organizations, IPv6 is the immediate future, and those organizations must begin adopting IPv6 immediately. For most organizations, an IPv6 infrastructure will not be required for several years. An understanding of IPv6 requirements will allow the latter organizations to make hardware and software purchases today that will still be usable in the future IPv6 network environment.

Even within an organization that is adopting IPv6 today, the transition will not be immediate. To allow IPv6 to function on networks that still support only IPv4, IPv6 supports several important transition technologies: ISATAP, 6to4, and Teredo. With these technologies, you can connect IPv6 hosts on IPv4 networks to remote IPv6 networks (including the IPv6 Internet), connect remote IPv6 networks that are connected only by an IPv4 network, and connect IPv6 hosts behind NATs to the IPv6 Internet.

The vast majority of IPv6 hosts are automatically configured. Because IPv6 is enabled by default on Windows Vista and Windows Server 2008, you do not need to perform any configuration tasks for most computers. The routing infrastructure does require configuration, however. Because many organizations must work with IPv6 in lab environments without purchasing IPv6 network hardware, you might want to configure Windows Server 2008 as an IPv6 router.

While IPv6 requires minimal ongoing maintenance, administrators often need to troubleshoot IPv6 because it is a relatively new networking technology. Fortunately, IPv6 supports the same troubleshooting tools you are already familiar with from troubleshooting IPv4 networks.

Additional Information

For additional information about IPv6, see the following:

- *Understanding, IPv6*, Second Edition by Joseph Davies (Microsoft Press, 2008)
- The Microsoft TechNet IPv6 page (*http://www.microsoft.com/Ipv6*)
- "Introduction to IP Version 6" (*http://technet.microsoft.com/en-us/library/bb726944.aspx*)
- "IPv6 Transition Technologies" (*http://www.microsoft.com/downloads/details.aspx?FamilyID=afe56282-2903-40f3-a5ba-a87bf92c096d*)
- "Teredo Overview" (*http://www.microsoft.com/technet/network/ipv6/teredo.mspx*)
- The Microsoft TechNet IPv6 blog (*http://blogs.technet.com/ipv6/*)

Chapter 3
Dynamic Host Configuration Protocol

Most IPv4 network devices, excluding some servers and network infrastructure equipment, receive IP address configuration from a Dynamic Host Configuration Protocol (DHCP) server. Hosts that are automatically configured with DHCP are much easier to manage than hosts with manually configured IP addresses—especially if you ever need to move hosts to a different subnet, change Domain Name System (DNS) or Windows Internet Name Service (WINS) servers, or update the default gateway.

Some IPv6 network devices can also use DHCP for autoconfiguration, although many IPv6 networks rely entirely on routers to provide hosts with the information they need to connect to the network. Whether you are using IPv4, IPv6, or both, using the DHCP server component of Windows Server 2008 gives you straightforward, enterprise-wide control over the configuration of the majority of your network hosts.

This chapter provides information about how to design, deploy, maintain, and troubleshoot the DCHP server component in Windows Server 2008. This chapter assumes that you have a solid understanding of Transmission Control Protocol/Internet Protocol (TCP/IP).

Concepts

DHCP automatically configures client IP address settings by exchanging a few messages with DHCP clients when they start up or connect to a network. DHCP leases ensure that assigned IP addresses are freed up if they aren't currently in use by a client. The sections that follow provide a brief overview of the DHCP address assignment process and the DHCP life cycle.

The DHCP Address Assignment Process

When a DHCP client starts, it follows the process shown in Figure 3-1 to acquire IP address configuration information from a DHCP server on the same subnet.

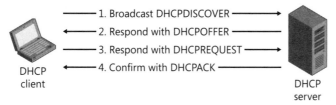

DHCP client

1. Broadcast DHCPDISCOVER →
← 2. Respond with DHCPOFFER
3. Respond with DHCPREQUEST →
← 4. Confirm with DHCPACK

DHCP server

Figure 3-1 The DHCP address assignment process

These four steps represent a successful DHCP address assignment:

1. **Broadcast DHCPDiscover**   The client broadcasts a DHCPDiscover message to the local network to identify any available DHCP servers.

2. **Respond with DHCPOffer**   If a DHCP server is connected to the local network and can provide the DHCP client with an IP address assignment, it sends a unicast DHCPOffer message to the DHCP client. The DHCPOffer message contains a list of DHCP configuration parameters and an available IP address from the DHCP scope. If the DHCP server has an IP address reservation that matches the DHCP client's MAC address, it offers the reserved IP address to the DHCP client. It's possible for more than one DHCP server to respond to the DHCP client.

> **Note**   Most DHCP clients, including Microsoft Windows 2000 and all later versions of Windows, perform IP address detection to verify that an IP address offered in the DHCPOffer message isn't already in use. If it is in use, the DHCP client will send a DHCP-Decline message.

3. **Respond with DHCPRequest**   The DHCP client responds to one of the DHCPOffer messages, requesting the IP address contained in the DHCPOffer message. Alternatively, the DHCP client might request the IP address that was previously assigned.

4. **Confirm with DHCPAck**   If the IP address requested by the DHCP client is still available, the DHCP server responds with a DHCPAck acknowledgement message. The client can now use the IP address.

How It Works: The DHCP Protocol

All DHCP traffic uses the User Datagram Protocol (UDP) Layer 4 protocol. Messages from the DHCP client to the DHCP server use UDP source port 68 and UDP destination port 67. Messages from the DHCP server to the DHCP client use UDP source port 67 and UDP destination port 68.

DHCP IP address assignments typically contain the following basic IP address configuration information (though many different options are available):

- Length of the DHCP lease
- IP address
- Subnet mask
- Default gateway
- Primary and secondary DNS servers
- Primary and secondary WINS servers

DHCP Life Cycle

To prevent an IP address from being indefinitely assigned to a client that has disconnected from the network, DHCP servers reclaim addresses at the end of the DHCP lease period. Halfway through a DHCP lease, the DHCP client submits a lease renewal request to the DHCP server. If the DHCP server is online, the DHCP server typically accepts the renewal, and the lease period restarts. If the DHCP server is not available, the DHCP client will try to renew the DHCP lease again after half the remaining lease period has passed. If the DHCP server is not available when 87.5% of the lease time has elapsed, the DHCP client will attempt to locate a new DHCP server and possibly acquire a different IP address.

If the DHCP client shuts down normally, or an administrator runs the command **ipconfig /release**, the client sends a DHCPRelease message to the DHCP server that assigned the IP address. The DHCP server then marks the IP address as available and can reassign it to a different DHCP client. If the DHCP client disconnects suddenly from the network and does not have the opportunity to send a DHCPRelease message, the DHCP server will not assign the IP address to a different client until the DHCP lease expires. For this reason, it's important to use a shorter DHCP lease period (for example, 6 hours instead of 6 days) on networks where clients frequently connect and disconnect—such as wireless networks.

Planning and Design Considerations

You must carefully plan DHCP on your network to avoid future problems that could result in users who are unable to access network resources. Specifically, consider the following elements:

- **DHCP servers**   DHCP servers should be highly available, so you should consider deploying multiple DHCP servers to provide redundancy. Although you can locate a DHCP server across a WAN link, you must determine whether to accept the risk that a WAN outage will cause the DHCP server to be unavailable.

- **DHCP relay agents**   To contact a DHCP server, DHCP clients broadcast a message to the local network segment. To enable DHCP clients to contact DHCP servers on other network segments, configure DHCP relay agents on every network segment that does not have a DHCP server. Typically, routers will act as DHCP relay agents.

- **DHCP lease durations**   Longer DHCP lease durations minimize network traffic caused by DHCP renewals. However, shorter DHCP lease durations minimize the time that IP addresses remain unused when a DHCP client disconnects from the network. You must identify the ideal DHCP lease duration for every network in your organization.

Before you configure your first DHCP server, you should plan your subnets, scopes, and exclusions. This section will give you the information you need to perform that planning.

> **Note**   Network Access Protection (NAP) prevents clients from connecting to the network until they have been authenticated and authorized. For more information about NAP, see Part IV of this book, "Network Access Protection Infrastructure." For detailed information about how to plan, deploy, maintain, and configure DHCP enforcement, see Chapter 19, "DHCP Enforcement."

DHCP Servers

Hardware requirements for DHCP servers are minimal, and servers that meet the minimum Windows Server 2008 hardware requirements can act as DHCP servers for thousands of client computers. Additionally, you can combine DHCP with DNS, WINS, or other infrastructure services. Although your DHCP servers might never experience a performance bottleneck, at extreme periods of activity (such as when thousands of computers restart after a power failure), disk I/O can be the limiting factor in performance. To optimize disk I/O, use Redundant Array of Independent Disks (RAID) configurations or another high-performance storage technology.

DHCP server storage requirements are minimal. Although the DHCP database is capable of growing to several gigabytes, typical database sizes are less than 100 MB.

For redundancy, you should plan to provide at least two DHCP servers. If a DHCP server is not available when a DHCP client starts, the client typically assigns itself an Automatic Private IP Addressing (APIPA) address that can access only other hosts with APIPA addresses. The result is that, when a DHCP server is not available, DHCP clients will not be able to access any network resources. For more information about APIPA, see Chapter 1, "IPv4."

DHCP Relay Agents

DHCP requests are broadcast messages, which reach only computers on the local network segment. Therefore, you must either have a DHCP server on every network segment that will support DHCP clients, or configure each network segment with a DHCP relay agent.

DHCP relay agents listen for DHCP request broadcast messages and forward the request within a unicast message to a DHCP server on a different subnet, as shown in Figure 3-2. The DHCP server examines the source IP address from the DHCP relay agent and identifies an available IP address from a scope that matches the DHCP client's subnet. Then the DHCP IP address assignment proceeds normally, with all messages being forwarded by the DHCP relay agent.

Most routers support acting as a DHCP relay agent. The capability is often referred to as a *BOOTP relay agent,* referring to the now-outdated BOOTP standard, which DHCP has replaced. Typically, you should configure the router on every subnet as a DHCP relay agent (assuming that the subnet does not have a DHCP server). As described later in this chapter, you can also configure computers as DHCP relay agents.

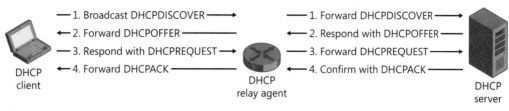

Figure 3-2 A DHCP relay agent forwarding a DHCPDiscover message

Typically, you should configure one DHCP server per location, but you can configure two for redundancy. Although you can use a DHCP relay agent to forward requests across a wide area network (WAN), a failed WAN link would prevent DHCP clients from obtaining an IP address.

DHCP Lease Durations

By default, Windows Server 2008 creates a lease period of 8 days for wired networks and 6 hours for wireless networks. You can accept the default settings on networks that meet the following requirements:

- Less than one-third of the available DHCP scope is in use at any one time.

- Client computers are primarily desktops and remain connected to the network for more than a week at a time.

- IP addresses of DNS servers, WINS servers, and routers are not changed regularly.

If a network does not meet any of these requirements, you might need to use a shorter lease period. For example, wireless networks have a default lease period of 6 hours because wireless computers tend to stay connected for a short period of time. Similarly, wired networks with a large number of mobile computers and remote access connections (such as a virtual private network) should have a shorter lease period because computers are likely to use an IP address for less than a day. If more than half your DHCP scope is in use during peak hours, a shorter lease period reduces the likelihood that the DHCP server will run out of available addresses.

Shorter lease periods allow you to change IP address settings in a shorter time frame. For example, if you are replacing your DNS server with a server that uses a new IP address, you can immediately update the options on the DHCP server. However, you will need to run both the old and the new DNS server during the period of time that DHCP clients retain their original IP settings. With a shorter DHCP lease of 6 hours, you can be assured that DHCP clients will have updated DNS server configuration information by the end of the lease period, allowing you to disconnect the old DNS server the following day. With an 8-day lease period, you would need to leave the old DNS server online for more than a week.

The disadvantage to shorter DHCP lease durations is increased network traffic for DHCP renewals. However, the bandwidth required by DHCP lease renewals in relation to the bandwidth of modern local area networks (LANs) is insignificant. For example, with a relatively short lease period of 6 hours, only two small packets will be transmitted for each DHCP client every three hours. The amount of additional bandwidth required is hardly measurable and will have no impact on network performance. Therefore, you can use shorter DHCP lease durations with no significant penalty.

Designing Scopes

A *DHCP scope* is the range of IP addresses that will be assigned to clients on a subnet. To prevent two different DHCP servers from assigning the same IP address, only a single DHCP server should have any given IP address in its DHCP scope.

The *80/20 rule* suggests using two DHCP servers for any network subnet, a technique called *DHCP split-scope*. Configure the same scope on both DHCP servers, but create an *exclusion range* so that the primary DHCP server assigns 80 percent of the total scope while the secondary DHCP server assigns the remaining 20 percent of IP addresses within the scope. An exclusion range prevents a DHCP server from assigning a range of addresses within a scope.

If the primary DHCP server fails, the secondary server will have enough IP addresses to assign addresses to new clients, assuming that the primary DHCP server is brought back online reasonably quickly (for example, within 24 hours). If the primary DHCP server is going to be offline for an extended amount of time, you can remove the exclusion from the secondary server and allow it to assign IP addresses from the full scope.

Direct from the Source: Determining the Ratio for DHCP Split-Scope Deployment

An 80-20 split of the available address range between the primary and the secondary DHCP servers is most commonly used, but of course you can use any ratio appropriate to your deployment.

A good rule of thumb for determining the ratio is (0.5*Lease Time for the Subnet):(Amount of time it will take you to restore a server). For instance, if the address lease time on your DHCP server is 8 days, then the clients will renew their lease every (0.5 * 8 = 4) days. Say it will take you a maximum of one day to restore a server in case it is down. Then the appropriate ratio would be 4:1 or 80:20. You can vary this based on your requirements/deployment.

Ideally, of course, if you have a lot of free address space available (especially if you are using one of the private address ranges specified by RFC 1918), you can forget about the above rule and use a 50-50 split. Note that in this case the maximum number of clients on the network should correspond to around 50 percent of the available address range. So if you are expecting around 250 clients, you should use a /23 address range for the subnet.

This should help you fine-tune your DHCP deployment.

Santosh Chandwani, Lead Program Manager

Enterprise Networking Group

Server Clustering for DHCP

Although using split-scope might be sufficient to meet your redundancy requirements, you can also use server clustering to provide a highly available DHCP service. Implementing server clustering for the DHCP Server service requires that the server cluster have disk, IP address (which must be static), and name resource types.

After configuring the DHCP Server service on the server cluster nodes, authorize the clustered virtual IP address in Active Directory. Then, configure the database path, audit log file path, and the database backup path on the shared disk by using the Cluster Administrator tool. When configuring the DHCP scopes, remember to exclude the clustered virtual IP address.

For more information about DHCP clusters, see "Centralize management of two or more DHCP servers as a single system by clustering DHCP servers" in Windows Server 2008 Help and Support.

Dynamic DNS

Because DHCP clients can receive different IP addresses, any DNS entries for the DHCP client must also be updated when the client's IP address changes. Dynamic DNS allows for this by enabling clients to send a message to their DNS server to update their DNS resource records. For more information about DNS, read Chapter 7, "Domain Name System."

Some clients, including Microsoft Windows NT 4.0 and earlier versions of Windows, cannot update their own DNS records. For these clients, or for clients that have been configured not to update their own DNS records, the DHCP server can update their DNS records (including both A and PTR records) after assigning an IP address to the DHCP client. DHCP servers can also discard DNS records when a lease is deleted.

Windows Server 2008 is configured by default to perform DNS updates for clients that request it. Therefore, you probably do not need to make any changes to the DHCP server configuration to support dynamic DNS. If you use clients that do not support dynamic DNS (including Windows NT 4.0 and earlier versions of Windows), or your DNS and DHCP servers are not members of the same Active Directory domain, you will need to modify the DHCP server configuration to support dynamic DNS. For more information, see "Configuring Dynamic DNS" in the next section in this chapter, "Deployment Steps."

Deployment Steps

When deploying DHCP, first add the role to the DHCP server, configure the scopes, options, and exclusions, and then authorize the DHCP server. Next, configure your routers as DHCP relay agents to forward requests from subnets that do not have a DHCP server directly attached. Typically, computers other than the DHCP server do not require any configuration, because they are configured to act as DHCP clients by default.

The sections that follow provide step-by-step instructions for deploying DHCP on your network.

DHCP Servers

When configuring a DHCP server, first install the DHCP server role. You can add a single scope when adding the role, and you should add any additional scopes, reservations, exclusions, and options after you have configured the role. Once you have completed the configuration of the DHCP server, if you are in an Active Directory domain environment, authorize the server to make the DHCP server active.

Installing the DHCP Server Roles

You can use computers running Windows Server 2008 as DHCP servers by adding the DHCP server role.

To Add the DHCP Server Role

1. Configure the server with a static IP address. DHCP servers should always have a static IP address, because using a dynamic IP address would require another DHCP server to be present on the network.

2. Click Start, and then click Server Manager.

3. In the left pane, click Roles, and then in the right pane, click Add Roles.

4. If the Before You Begin page appears, click Next.

5. On the Select Server Roles page, select DHCP Server, and then click Next.

6. On the DHCP Server page, click Next.

7. If the Select Network Connection Bindings page appears, as shown in Figure 3-3, select the network interfaces that you want the DHCP server to use to assign IP addresses. This page appears only if the DHCP server has multiple network connections. Click Next.

8. On the Specify IPv4 DNS Settings page, in the Parent Domain field, specify the parent domain that clients will use for name resolution. For example, if you specify a parent domain of **contoso.com,** and a client user types the name **intranet** into the client's Web browser, the client computer will attempt to resolve the name *intranet.contoso.com.* The parent domain does not need to be the same as the Active Directory domain. Then, specify the IP addresses of the primary and secondary DNS servers. Click Next.

9. On the Specify IPv4 WINS Settings page, you can choose whether to provide clients with the IP address of a WINS server. If you do not have a WINS server on your network, leave the default setting of WINS Is Not Required For Applications On This Network. If you do have one or more WINS servers, select WINS Is Required For Applications On This Network, and then type the IP addresses of the primary and secondary WINS servers. Click Next.

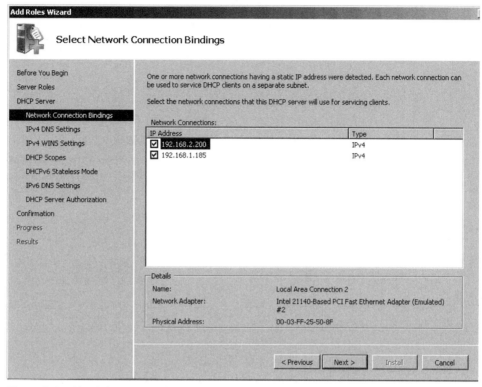

Figure 3-3   The Select Network Connection Bindings page of the Add Roles Wizard

10. On the Add Or Edit DHCP Scopes page, you will configure the range of IP addresses that will be assigned to clients. Follow these steps to add as many DHCP scopes as you require, and then click Next:

   a. Click Add to open the Add Scope dialog box.

   b. In the Scope Name box, type a name for the scope such as **Wired-192.168.1.0/24**.

   c. In the Starting IP Address and Ending IP Address boxes, type the lowest and highest IP addresses you want to assign, such as **192.168.1.100** and **192.168.1.199**.

   d. In the Subnet Mask box, type the subnet mask, such as **255.255.255.0**.

   e. In the Default Gateway box, type the IP address of the network's router.

   f. In the Subnet Type drop-down list, select Wired or Wireless depending on the type of network.

   g. If you want the scope to be immediately active, select the Activate This Scope check box.

   h. Click OK.

11. If the Configure DHCPv6 Stateless Mode page appears, select Disable DHCPv6 Stateless Mode For This Server if you want to use DHCP to configure IPv6 clients. The default setting, Enable DHCPv6 Stateless Mode For This Server, causes DHCP to be disabled for IPv6 clients, which will autoconfigure themselves based solely on information provided by your IPv6 routers. Click Next.

12. If the Specify IPv6 DNS Settings page appears, specify the parent domain and the IPv6 addresses of the primary and secondary DNS servers, and then click Next.

13. If the Authorize DHCP Server page appears, choose whether to use your current credentials to authorize the DHCP server, use different credentials, or skip authorization. If you choose to skip authorization, you can authorize the DHCP server later using the DHCP console. Click Next.

14. On the Confirm Installation Selections page, review your settings, and then click Install.

15. On the Results page, verify that the installation was successful, and then click Close.

Authorizing a DHCP Server

In Active Directory domain environments, a DHCP server will not start unless it is authorized. In other words, an unauthorized DHCP server does not issue DHCP addresses to clients. Requiring servers to be authorized reduces the risk that a user will accidentally create a DHCP server that hands out invalid IP address configuration information to DHCP clients, which might prevent the clients from accessing network resources.

For a DHCP server that is not a member of the Active Directory domain, the DHCP Server service sends a broadcast DHCPInform message to request information about the root Active Directory domain in which other DHCP servers are installed and configured. Other DHCP servers on the network respond with a DHCPAck message, which contains information that the querying DHCP server uses to locate the Active Directory root domain. The starting DHCP server then queries Active Directory for a list of authorized DHCP servers and starts the DHCP Server service only if its own address is in the list.

If a server requires authorization, you will see a red arrow over the IPv4 and IPv6 icons in the DHCP console.

Note Only Windows-based DHCP servers require authorization. Third-party DHCP servers can start up without authorization and might accidentally or maliciously assign invalid IP addresses to clients, preventing those clients from connecting to the network.

To Authorize a DHCP Server

1. Log on as a member of the Domain Admins group.

2. Click Start, click Administrative Tools, and then click DHCP.

3.   Under DHCP, right-click the server name, and then click Authorize.

4.   Right-click the server name again, and click Refresh.

The red arrows should disappear from the IPv4 and IPv6 icons in the DHCP console, indicating that the server is authorized. The server will now begin issuing DHCP addresses. To deauthorize a server, right-click it, and then click Unauthorize.

To Authorize a DHCP Server by Using a Script

To authorize a DHCP server by using a script, run the following command with Domain Admin privileges:

netsh dhcp add server *ServerName [ServerIPv4Address]*

You can list all authorized DHCP servers by running the following command:

netsh dhcp show server

Adding a Scope

A scope is the range of IP addresses that a DHCP server will assign to DHCP clients. Every subnet that a DHCP server assigns IP addresses for, including remote subnets that use a DHCP relay agent, must have a DHCP scope configured. You can add scopes when you add the DHCP server role. If you need to add a scope later, you can use the DHCP console.

To Add an IPv4 Scope

1.   Click Start, click Administrative Tools, and then click DHCP.

2.   Right-click IPv4, and then click New Scope.

The New Scope Wizard appears.

3.   On the Welcome To The New Scope Wizard page, click Next.

4.   On the Scope Name page, type a name and description for the scope, and then click Next.

5.   On the IP Address Range page, type the lowest and highest IP addresses you want to assign, such as **192.168.1.100** and **192.168.1.199**. Then specify the Subnet Mask by either specifying the bits in the Length box or typing the subnet mask (such as 255.255.255.0). If you use Classless Inter-Domain Routing (CIDR) notation to identify networks, such as 192.168.1.0/24, type the number after the "/" in the Length box. Click Next.

6.   On the Add Exclusions page, add any address ranges (within the scope you specified on the previous page) that you do not want to assign addresses for. For example, if you created a scope for the range 192.168.1.100 to 192.168.1.199, but 192.168.1.150 through 192.168.1.155 were already assigned to servers, you would configure that range as an exclusion. To configure an exclusion, follow these steps, and then click Next.

    a. In the Start IP Address box, type the first IP address that you want to be excluded from the DHCP scope.

    b. In the End IP Address box, type the last IP address that you want to be excluded from the DHCP scope. If you want to exclude just a single IP address, type the same address in the Start IP Address box and the End IP Address box.

    c. Click Add.

    d. Repeat these steps to exclude additional ranges.

7. On the Lease Duration page, type the amount of time that you want addresses assigned by DHCP to be valid. For wired networks, this is typically **8** days. For wireless networks, this is **6** hours. Click Next.

8. On the Configure DHCP Options page, select whether you want to configure DHCP Options (such as the default gateway and DNS server addresses) now. Clients cannot connect to network resources without these options enabled, so you should always enable them. Click Next. If you chose not to configure options, skip to the last step of this process.

9. On the Router (Default Gateway) page, type the IP address of the network's default gateway, and then click Add. If the network has multiple default gateways, add each of them. Then, click Next.

10. On the Domain Name And DNS Servers page, in the Parent Domain field, specify the parent domain that clients will use for name resolution. For example, if you specify a parent domain of **contoso.com**, and a client user types the name **intranet** into that client's Web browser, the client computer will attempt to resolve the name *intranet .contoso.com*. The parent domain does not need to be the same as the Active Directory domain. Then, type the host name or IP address of each DNS server, click Add, and then click Next.

11. On the WINS Servers page, you can choose whether to provide clients with the IP address of a WINS server. If you do not have a WINS server on your network, do nothing on this page. If you do have one or more WINS servers, type their host name or IP address, and then click Add. Click Next.

12. On the Activate Scope page, click Yes if you want the scope to be immediately active. Otherwise, click No. Then, click Next.

13. On the Completing The New Scope Wizard page, click Finish.

The new scope will be visible under the IPv4 node in the DHCP console.

To Add an IPv6 Scope

1. Click Start, click Administrative Tools, and then click DHCP.

2. Right-click IPv6, and then click New Scope.

    The New Scope Wizard appears.

3. On the Welcome To The New Scope Wizard page, click Next.

4. On the Scope Name page, type a name and description for the scope, and then click Next.

5. On the Scope Prefix page, type the 64-bit network prefix, such as **2001:db8::1**. Click Next.

6. On the Add Exclusions page, add any address ranges (within the scope you specified on the previous page) that you do not want to assign addresses for. To configure an exclusion, follow these steps, and then click Next.

    a. In the Start IPv6 Address box, type the first IP address that you want to be excluded from the DHCP scope. You must type every byte of the host address, including any zeroes. For example, you could type **0:0:20:20**, but you cannot type **20:20**.

    b. In the End IPv6 Address box, type the last IP address that you want to be excluded from the DHCP scope. If you want to exclude just a single IP address, leave the End IPv6 Address box blank.

    c. Click Add.

    d. Repeat these steps to exclude additional ranges.

7. On the Scope Lease page, type the amount of time that you want addresses assigned by DHCP to be preferred and valid. Typically, the default settings are sufficient. For more information about IPv6 address lifetimes, read Chapter 2, "IPv6." Click Next.

8. On the Completing The New Scope Wizard page, select whether to activate the current scope immediately, and then click Finish.

Before clients can retrieve IPv6 address information from the DHCPv6 server, you must configure your IPv6 routers for stateful autoconfiguration. For more information, refer to Chapter 2.

Adding an Address Reservation

Routers, DNS servers, and WINS servers each require static IP addresses that are the same every time the computer starts. You can manually configure the IP addresses on these hosts to provide a static IP address, or you can add a reservation to the DHCP server. When you configure a reservation, the DHCP server always assigns the same IP address to the host. The DHCP server recognizes the host based on the network adapter's MAC address.

To Add a Reservation

1. Identify the MAC address of the computer's network adapter that you are creating the reservation for. You can identify the MAC address by running the command **ipconfig/ all** at a command prompt on the computer that requires the reservation.

2. Click Start, click Administrative Tools, and then click DHCP.

3. Expand IPv4 or IPv6, and then expand the scope you want to add the reservation to. Click Reservations.

4. Right-click Reservations, and then click New Reservation.

5. In the New Reservation dialog box, type a name for the reservation (such as the computer name you are creating the reservation for), the IP address, and the MAC address. Click Add.

6. Repeat the previous step for every reservation required. Then, click Close.

Adding an Exclusion

If you manually configure a computer with an IP address that is within a DHCP scope, you should add an exclusion to the DHCP server to prevent the server from assigning that IP address to a DHCP client. You should also create exclusions when two DHCP servers have overlapping scopes, as described in "Designing Scopes" earlier in this chapter.

To Add an Exclusion to an IPv4 Scope

1. Click Start, click Administrative Tools, and then click DHCP.

2. Expand IPv4, expand the scope you want to add an exclusion to, and then click Address Pool.

3. Right-click Address Pool, and then click New Exclusion Range.

4. In the Add Exclusion dialog box, type the start and end IP addresses of the range that you would like excluded from the address pool, and then click Add.

5. Repeat the previous step as required, and then click Close.

To Add an Exclusion to an IPv6 Scope

1. Click Start, click Administrative Tools, and then click DHCP.

2. Expand IPv6, expand the scope you want to add an exclusion to, and then click Exclusions.

3. Right-click Exclusions, and then click New Exclusion Range.

4. In the Add Exclusion dialog box, type the start and end IP addresses of the range that you would like excluded from the address pool, and then click Add.

5. Repeat the previous step as required, and then click Close.

Adding or Changing DHCP Options

DHCP options, such as the default gateway, DNS server, or WINS server assigned to DHCP clients, must be changed if an IP address changes.

To Add or Change a DHCP Option

1. Click Start, click Administrative Tools, and then click DHCP.

2. Expand IPv4 or IPv6, and then expand the scope you want to edit.

3. Right-click Scope Options, and then click Configure Options.

   The Scope Options dialog box appears.

4. On the General tab, select the option you want to add or edit. Figure 3-4 shows the Router option selected, which specifies the default gateway for clients. Use the controls in the Data Entry box to configure the value of that option.

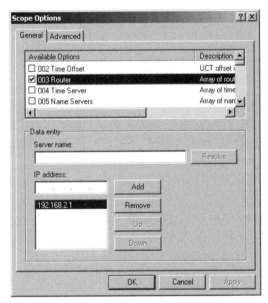

Figure 3-4   The Scope Options dialog box

5. Click OK.

Configuring Dynamic DNS

The default settings for dynamic DNS are sufficient for most organizations. However, you must modify the dynamic DNS settings to provide dynamic DNS support for Windows NT 4.0 and earlier versions of Windows or to manually specify credentials to update the DNS server.

To Update DNS for Windows NT 4.0 and Earlier Versions of Windows

1. Click Start, click Administrative Tools, and then click DHCP.

2. Under DHCP, expand the server name, and then click IPv4.

Note   All IPv6 clients can dynamically update their own DNS records, so this option is not required for DHCPv6.

3. Right-click IPv4, and then click Properties.

4. On the DNS tab, select the Dynamically Update DNS A And PTR Records For DHCP Clients That Do Not Request Updates check box, and then click OK.

To Specify Credentials for Dynamic DNS Updates

1. Click Start, click Administrative Tools, and then click DHCP.

2. Under DHCP, expand the server name, and then click IPv4 or IPv6.

> **Note**   All IPv6 clients can dynamically update their own DNS records, so this option is not required for DHCPv6.

3. Right-click IPv4 or IPv6, and then click Properties.

4. On the Advanced tab, click Credentials.

5. In the DNS Dynamic Update Credentials dialog box, type the user name, domain, and password for the user who has privileges to update the DNS server, and then click OK twice.

DHCP Relay Agents

DCHP relay agents forward DHCP requests to a DHCP server on a remote network. Because DHCP request messages are broadcast messages that reach only other computers on the network segment, DHCP relay agents are required for subnets that do not have a DHCP server.

Typically, you should configure routers as DHCP relay agents. However, you can also configure a computer running Windows Server 2008 as a DHCP relay agent as long as it is not already configured as a DHCP or Internet Connection Sharing (ICS) server and it does not have the network address translation (NAT) routing protocol component with automatic addressing enabled.

To Configure a DHCP Relay Agent

1. Click Start, and then click Server Manager.

2. In the left pane, click Roles, and then in the right pane, click Add Roles.

3. If the Before You Begin page appears, click Next.

4. On the Select Server Roles page, select Network Policy And Access Services, and then click Next.

5. On the Network Policy And Access Services page, click Next.

6. On the Role Services page, select the Routing And Remote Access Services check box. The wizard will automatically select the Remote Access Service and Routing check boxes. Click Next.

7. On the Confirmation page, click Install.

8. After the Add Roles Wizard completes the installation, click Close.

9. In Server Manager, expand Roles, expand Network Policy And Access Services, and then click Routing And Remote Access. Right-click Routing And Remote Access, and then click Configure And Enable Routing And Remote Access.

   The Routing And Remote Access Server Setup Wizard appears.

10. On the Welcome To The Routing And Remote Access Server Setup Wizard page, click Next.

11. On the Configuration page, click Custom Configuration, and then click Next.

12. On the Custom Configuration page, select LAN Routing, and then click Next.

13. On the Completing The Routing And Remote Access Server Wizard page, click Finish.

14. When prompted, click Start Service.

15. In Server Manager, expand Routing And Remote Access. Then, expand either IPv4 (to add a IPv4 DHCP relay agent) or IPv6 (to add a DHCPv6 relay agent). Right-click General, and then click New Routing Protocol.

16. In the New Routing Protocol dialog box, click DHCP Relay Agent or DHCPv6 Relay Agent, and then click OK.

17. Right-click DHCP Relay Agent or DHCPv6 Relay Agent, and then click New Interface.

18. Click the interface you want to add the DHCP relay agent to, and then click OK.

19. In the DHCP Relay Properties dialog box, on the General tab, verify that the Relay DHCP Packets check box is selected. If needed, click the arrows to modify the thresholds. Then, click OK.

You can select the DHCP Relay Agent or DHCPv6 Relay Agent node to view the number of DHCP requests and replies that the DHCP relay agent has processed.

DHCP Client Configuration

Computers running Windows and most other IP hosts use DHCP by default. Therefore, configuring computers as DHCP clients requires absolutely no configuration. Simply connect the computer to a network and power it on.

If you have previously configured a computer running Windows Vista or Windows Server 2008 to use a manually configured IP address, you can return it to its default setting of retrieving an IP address assignment from a DHCP server.

To Configure an IPv4 Computer as a DHCP Client

1. Click Start, right-click Network, and then click Properties.

2. Under Tasks, click Manage Network Connections.

3. Right-click the network adapter you want to configure, and then click Properties.

4. Click Internet Protocol Version 4 (TCP/IPv4), and then click Properties.

   The Internet Protocol Version 4 (TCP/IPv4) Properties dialog box appears.

5. On the General tab, click Obtain An IP Address Automatically and Obtain DNS Server Address Automatically, and then click OK.

You can also configure computers to assign a manually configured IP address if a DHCP server is not available. For more information, refer to Chapter 1.

To Configure an IPv6 Computer as a DHCP Client

1. Click Start, right-click Network, and then click Properties.

2. Under Tasks, click Manage Network Connections.

3. Right-click the network adapter you want to configure, and then click Properties.

4. Click Internet Protocol Version 6 (TCP/IPv6), and then click Properties.

   The Internet Protocol Version 6 (TCP/IPv6) Properties dialog box appears.

5. On the General tab, click Obtain An IPv6 Address Automatically and Obtain DNS Server Address Automatically, and then click OK.

Ongoing Maintenance

DHCP servers should be monitored to ensure that the DHCP service remains available and that the DHCP scopes do not run out of addresses. The maintenance requirements for DHCP servers is minimal, and maintenance is required only when a problem occurs or you need to migrate the DHCP server service to a different computer.

Monitoring DHCP Servers

You can monitor the activity on your DHCP server by using the Performance Monitor console. To monitor the DHCP server activity in real time, follow these steps:

1. Click Start, and then click Server Manager.

2. In Server Manager, expand Diagnostics\Reliability And Performance\Monitoring Tools\Performance Monitor.

3. In the Performance Monitor snap-in, click the green plus button on the toolbar.

   The Add Counter dialog box appears.

4. In the Available Counters list, expand DHCP Server or DHCPv6 Server. Click the counters you want to monitor, and then click Add.

5. Click OK to return to the Performance Monitor snap-in.

You can monitor the following DHCP-related counters:

■ **Packets Received/Sec**   The number of incoming messages received per second. A large number indicates heavy DHCP server traffic.

■ **Discovers/Sec**   The number of DHCP discover messages (DHCPDiscovers) received per second.

■ **Offers/Sec**   The number of DHCP offer messages (DHCPOffers) sent per second by the DHCP server to clients.

■ **Requests/Sec**   The number of DHCP request messages (DHCPRequests) received per second by the DHCP server from clients.

■ **Informs/Sec**   The number of DHCP information messages (DHCPInforms) received per second. DHCP information messages are used when the DHCP server queries for the directory service for the enterprise root and when dynamic updates are being done on behalf of clients by the server.

■ **Acks/Sec**   The number of DHCP acknowledgment messages (DHCPAcks) sent per second by the DHCP server to clients.

■ **Nacks/Sec**   The number of DHCP negative acknowledgment messages (DHCPNaks) sent per second by the DHCP server to clients. A very high value might indicate potential network trouble in the form of misconfiguration of either the server or clients. When servers are misconfigured, one possible cause is a deactivated scope. For clients, a very high value could be caused by computers moving between subnets such as laptop portables or other mobile devices.

■ **Declines/Sec**   The number of DHCP decline messages (DHCPDeclines) received per second by the DHCP server from clients. A high value indicates that several clients have found their addresses to be in conflict, possibly indicating network trouble.

■ **Releases/Sec**   The number of DHCP release messages (DHCPReleases) received per second by the DHCP server from clients, which indicates that a DHCP client is disconnecting from the network (or no longer requires the IP address for a different reason).

■ **Duplicates Dropped/Sec**   The number of duplicated packets per second dropped by the DHCP server. If this value is regularly larger than zero, you might have multiple DHCP relay agents or network interfaces forwarding the same packet to the server. A large number might indicate that the server is responding too slowly.

■ **Milliseconds Per Packet (Avg.)**   The average response time in milliseconds of the DHCP server.

■ **Active Queue Length**   The current length of the DHCP server queue, which stores unprocessed messages.

■ **Packets Expired/Sec**   The number of packets per second that expire and are dropped by the DHCP server after being queued for 30 seconds or more. Any number over zero indicates that the server is overloaded or the network is too busy.

■ **Conflict Check Queue Length**   The current length of the conflict check queue for the DHCP server. This queue holds messages without responses while the DHCP server performs address conflict detection.

Additionally, you can monitor DHCP servers by using Microsoft System Center Operations Manager 2007.

> **More Info**   For more information on Microsoft System Center Operations Manager 2007, visit *http://www.microsoft.com/systemcenter/opsmgr/*.

Manually Backing Up and Restoring a DHCP Server

Server backup software should automatically back up the DHCP configuration. However, you might want to manually back up a DHCP server so that you can immediately restore the configuration on a new server.

To Back Up a DHCP Server

1. Click Start, click Administrative Tools, and then click DHCP.

2. Right-click the server name, and then click Backup.

3. In the Browse For Folder dialog box, select the folder to store the backup file in, and then click OK.

   If you are planning to immediately replace the DHCP server, continue following these steps. Otherwise, the backup process is complete.

4. Right-click the server name, click All Tasks, and then click Stop. Stopping the DHCP server prevents it from issuing new addresses that aren't backed up.

5. Finally, use the Services console to disable the DHCP Server service. Otherwise, the service might start automatically the next time the computer is restarted.

To Restore a DHCP Server

1. Click Start, click Administrative Tools, and then click DHCP.

2. Right-click the server name, and then click Restore.

3. In the Browse For Folder dialog box, select the folder to store the backup file in, and then click OK.

> **Note**   If you need to restore a DHCP server and you have not manually created a backup, check the *%SystemRoot%*\System32\dhcp\backup\ folder and subfolders for an automatically generated backup.

Troubleshooting

DHCP problems occur infrequently. However, when they do occur, they typically prevent a user from accessing the network. Therefore, DHCP problems tend to be very urgent, and all support staff should know how to quickly identify and resolve DHCP problems.

The sections that follow describe how to troubleshoot DHCP clients and servers.

Troubleshooting DHCP Clients

After verifying that a computer is configured to act as a DHCP client (as described in "DHCP Client Configuration" earlier in this chapter), you can force a DHCP client to give up its current IP address, attempt to locate a new DHCP server, and request a new IP address.

To View the DHCP Configuration

1. To view the current IP configuration, run the following command:

    ipconfig /all

For each network adapter, examine the DHCP Enabled line to determine whether DHCP is enabled. Additionally, you can determine the DHCP server that assigned the IP address by examining the DHCP Server line in the Ipconfig output.

If the DHCP client has an IP address in the range 169.254.0.0 to 169.254.255.255, the client has an APIPA address. APIPA addresses are automatically assigned when a DHCP client cannot contact a DHCP server. To solve the problem, verify that the client is connected to the network and that the DHCP server is online. If the DHCP server is connected to a different network than the DHCP client, verify that a DHCP relay agent is connected to the same network as the DHCP client and that the DHCP relay agent is configured with the DHCP server's IP address. Then, with administrative privileges, run **ipconfig /renew** on the DHCP client.

To Request a New DHCP Address

1. Open a command prompt, and run the following commands:

    ipconfig /release

    ipconfig /renew

Troubleshooting DHCP Servers

The most common problems with DHCP servers is that the DHCP Server service is not authorized. In Active Directory domain environments, all DHCP servers must be authorized. For more information, read "Authorizing a DHCP Server" earlier in this chapter.

If the DHCP server still fails to start, review the System event log and the DHCP server audit log files, as described in the next section, for more information.

Using Audit Logging to Analyze DHCP Server Behavior

The DHCP Server service stores an audit log in *%SystemRoot%*\System32\DHCP. The DHCP Server service bases the name of the audit log file on the current day of the week, as determined by checking the current date and time at the server. For example, when the DHCP server starts, if the current date is Monday, October 8, 2007, the IPv4 audit log file is named DhcpSrvLog-Mon, and the IPv6 audit log file is named DhcpV6SrvLog-Mon. The DHCP Server starts a new log file at midnight and overwrites log files from the previous week.

> **Note** Because the previous week's files are automatically overwritten, storage requirements for the audit logs are minimal. On extremely busy DHCP servers, you can enable NTFS compression on the *%SystemRoot%*\System32\DHCP folder to reduce storage requirements significantly.

By default, the DHCP Server service stops audit logging if disk space is less than 20MB or the current log file is larger than one-seventh the maximum allotted space or size for the combined total of all audit logs currently stored on the server. By default, each log file can be a maximum of 10MB. You can change the maximum size by multiplying the desired value by seven (for each day of the week) and storing the value in the HKEY_LOCAL_MACHINE\System\CurrentControlSet\Services\DHCPServer\Parameters\DhcpLogFilesMaxSize registry value.

Each audit log file begins with a description of the different event codes and the fields in the log file. Therefore, audit log files are self-explanatory. Audit logging is enabled by default.

To Enable or Disable Audit Logging

1. Click Start, click Administrative Tools, and then click DHCP.
2. Expand your server name, right-click either IPv4 or IPv6, and then click Properties.
3. On the General tab, select the Enable DHCP Audit Logging check box, and then click OK.

To Change the Audit Log File Path

1. Click Start, click Administrative Tools, and then click DHCP.
2. Expand your server name, right-click either IPv4 or IPv6, and then click Properties.
3. On the Advanced tab, click Browse to select the audit log file path, and then click OK.

Chapter Summary

Practically all IPv4 networks, and many IPv6 networks, require one or more DHCP servers to automatically assign IP addresses to DHCP clients. Ideally, you would have two DHCP servers per location with DHCP relay servers forwarding requests from subnets that do not have a DHCP server.

DHCP clients attempting to obtain an IP address will be unable to connect to network resources if a DHCP server is not available. Therefore, you should plan to have redundant DHCP servers. The most straightforward way to configure redundant DHCP servers is to configure two different DHCP servers using split-scope, where each is configured to assign addresses for a different portion of the scope.

To allow DHCP servers to reuse IP addresses after clients disconnect from the network, DHCP IP address assignments have a limited lease time. For wireless networks, the lease time is typically 6 hours to minimize the unavailable IP addresses when a client disconnects from the network. For wired networks, the lease time is 8 days by default; however, you can use a shorter lease time if you begin to run out of available IP addresses in a scope.

Computers running Windows are configured to act as DHCP clients by default. Therefore, no client configuration is necessary. Windows Server 2008 allows you to add the DHCP Server role by using a wizard interface, and you can perform additional configuration by using the DHCP console. Typically, routers should be configured to act as DHCP relay agents.

Ongoing maintenance and troubleshooting are minimal. For clients, you should use the Ipconfig tool to manually refresh the DHCP configuration. For servers, verify that the server is authorized, and then examine the System event log and DHCP audit logs for additional troubleshooting information.

Additional Information

For additional information about scalable networking in Windows, see the following:

- The Microsoft Windows DHCP Team Blog (*http://blogs.technet.com/teamdhcp/*)
- "The DHCPv6 Protocol" (*http://www.microsoft.com/technet/technetmag/issues/2007/03/CableGuy/default.aspx*)
- RFC 2131, "Dynamic Host Configuration Protocol" (*www.ietf.org/rfc/rfc2131.txt*)

Chapter 4

Windows Firewall with Advanced Security

Windows Firewall in the Windows Server 2008 and Windows Vista operating systems provides both packet filtering and IP Security (IPsec) capabilities. Combined, these features can greatly reduce network security risks including the risk that malicious attackers connecting from the Internet or internal networks will gain access to internal resources.

The default security settings allow most network applications to have full connectivity. Through careful planning, you can tighten this security so that only computers on specific networks, domain member users and computers, or computers you have issued a certificate to can connect to network resources.

This chapter provides information about how to design, deploy, maintain, and troubleshoot the Windows Firewall component in Windows Server 2008. This chapter assumes that you have a solid understanding of Transmission Control Protocol/Internet Protocol (TCP/IP).

Concepts

During the late 1990s, the Internet (and networking in general) grew at an extremely fast pace. At the time, worms—a form of malware that propagate primarily by exploiting vulnerabilities in network services—posed the greatest security threat. Put simply, malware technology advanced faster than operating system countermeasures. As a result, millions of computers connected to the Internet were infected by malware.

Beginning with the Windows XP SP2 and Windows Server 2003 operating systems, Windows includes Windows Firewall. Windows Firewall filters incoming and outgoing traffic and drops incoming traffic that hasn't been specifically approved. Windows Firewall dramatically decreased the number of compromises caused by malicious network communications.

Other, more complex network attacks require the attacker to monitor communications as they cross the network or impersonate a legitimate server to intercept communications. IPsec can reduce the risk of these types of attacks by requiring both authentication and encryption. With Windows Vista and Windows Server 2008, IPsec management is now built into Windows Firewall.

This chapter provides important background information about network security concepts, details about planning Windows Firewall and IPsec implementations, step-by-step instructions for deploying Windows Firewall and IPsec, and guidance for maintaining and troubleshooting network security.

Filtering Traffic by Using Windows Firewall

Windows Firewall gives administrators control over which services can accept incoming network connections and which networks are allowed to connect to a given service. Windows Firewall allows all outbound traffic by default, but administrators can also restrict which applications can send traffic. Examples of the types of rules you can create include:

- On a Domain Name System (DNS) server, allow DNS queries only from internal networks.

- On an e-mail server, allow any host (including hosts on the Internet) to connect to the Simple Mail Transfer Protocol (SMTP) server on TCP port 25, but allow only hosts on internal networks to connect to the Post Office Protocol (POP) server on TCP port 110.

- Block all applications and services from initiating an outgoing connection except for Windows Update.

- Allow hosts on the internal network to ping servers, but block ping requests from external networks.

Direct from the Source: Using IPsec to Tunnel Through a Firewall

On a recent internal discussion alias, a question came up about using IPsec to securely connect Active Directories that are separated by firewalls. This happens to be a very common scenario for IPsec: securely replicating domain controllers on opposite sides of a firewall (or multiple firewalls).

This is a great use for IPsec, leveraging its ability to not only authenticate connections between hosts but also the network tunneling and encryption capabilities. This helps reduce the number of ports you need to open in your firewalls between sites to enable Active Directory replication and helps protect that critical traffic along the way.

Ian Hameroff, Senior Product Manager

Security and Access Product Marketing

Protecting Traffic by Using IPsec

IPsec is a security standard that provides authentication and encryption at the network layer, as part of Internet Protocol version 4 (IPv4) and Internet Protocol version 6 (IPv6). Because IPsec provides protection at the network layer, it can authenticate and encrypt data for any network application.

IPsec encryption is important for preventing sniffing attacks. For example, sharing files across a network does not provide any encryption, and an attacker with access to the physical network could read the contents of a file that was transferred across a network. With IPsec, the network communications could be encrypted, making it almost impossible for an attacker to view the contents of a file as it is transferred.

 Note   IPsec was not part of the original IPv4 standards. However, most recent operating systems, including Microsoft Windows 2000 and later versions of Windows, support IPsec.

Besides encryption, IPsec can also provide authentication. With authentication, IPsec on a server can verify that a client computer is a member of a domain or has a valid computer certificate before allowing the client to connect. Similarly, the client computer can verify that the server is the correct computer. IPsec authentication can prevent complex but powerful man-in-the-middle attacks, as illustrated in Figure 4-1.

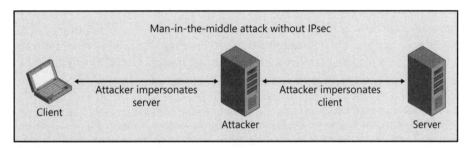
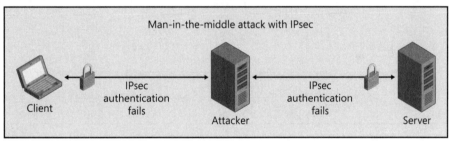

Figure 4-1   IPsec preventing a man-in-the-middle attack

In summary, IPsec provides a high level of protection against:

- Man-in-the-middle attacks
- Sniffing attacks
- *Replay attacks*, which transmit previously captured traffic to bypass authentication
- Unauthorized access to network applications that do not require authentication
- Unauthorized access to network applications that authenticate using only the client's source IP address

Because IPsec operates at the network layer, it's transparent to most applications. IPsec is not compatible with some network infrastructure, however. Because IPsec encrypts traffic, any firewall or other device that inspects traffic will be unable to function. You can often configure these devices to forward IPsec communications; however, they will be unable to monitor the traffic.

> **More Info** This chapter will provide a basic overview of IPsec's functionality. For detailed information, read the following Requests For Comments (RFCs): 3457, 3456, 3281, 3193, 2857, 2709, 2451, and approximately 22 more by searching for *IPsec*. You can obtain copies at *http://www.ietf.org*.

IPsec Transport Mode and Tunnel Mode

IPsec can operate in two different modes: transport mode and tunnel mode. *Transport mode* protects host-to-host communications. In transport mode, IPsec tunnels traffic starting at the transport layer, also known as Layer 4. Therefore, IPsec in transport mode can encrypt the User Datagram Protocol/Transmission Control Protocol (UDP/TCP) protocol header and the original data, but the IP header itself cannot be protected. *Tunnel mode* protects host-to-network and network-to-network communications, such as virtual private network (VPN) uses of IPsec. For more information about VPNs, refer to Chapter 12, "Remote Access VPN Connections."

IPsec encapsulates data within a header and trailer. Depending on the IPsec protocol used, the original contents of the outgoing packets will be encrypted. IPsec's IPv4 transport mode packet structure is shown in Figure 4-2. The diagram shows IPsec using the Encapsulating Security Payload (ESP) protocol, which provides both authentication and encryption. IPsec is an integral part of IPv6.

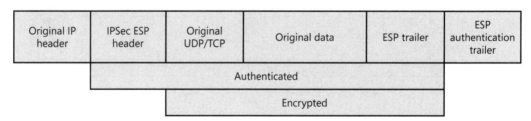

Figure 4-2 IPsec packet structure

IPsec NAT Traversal

Early implementations of IPsec in IPv4 could not pass through a Network Address Translation (NAT) device because NAT devices change the source and destination IP address. IPsec interpreted the changing IP addresses as a packet that had been modified and would drop the packets. IPsec NAT Traversal (NAT-T) allows IPsec traffic to pass through compatible NAT servers. However, both the IPsec hosts and the NAT server must support NAT-T, and the NAT server must be configured to allow traffic on UDP port 4500. All versions of Windows that support IPsec support NAT-T. For more information about NAT-T, refer to RFC 3947.

Not all computers support IPsec. Additionally, IPsec supports many different authentication and encryption standards, and two IPsec-capable hosts might not support the same sets of standards. Therefore, before establishing an IPsec connection, *IPsec negotiation* must take place to allow the hosts to determine whether they both support IPsec and a common set of acceptable authentication and encryption standards.

Internet Key Exchange (IKE) is the algorithm by which the first secure Security Association, or SA (secure channel), is negotiated. IKE is a combination of the Internet Security Association Key Management Protocol (ISAKMP) and the Oakley Key Determination protocol, and it performs a two- or three-phase negotiation: Main Mode and Quick Mode. Additionally, Windows Vista and Windows Server 2008 support User Mode. Generally, the process is:

- **Main Mode**   IKE negotiates the authentication and encryption protocols and authenticates the computer.

- **User Mode (optional)**   If user authentication is configured for IPsec, IKE authenticates the user.

- **Quick Mode**   IKE protects individual traffic flows and changes security keys on a regular basis, but it does not perform authentication in this mode.

> **More Info**   You can read more about IKE negotiation and this process in RFC 2409, at *http://www.ietf.org/rfc/rfc2409.txt.*

The sections that follow describes these modes in more detail.

Main Mode

Main Mode, also known as Phase 1, performs the initial long form of the IKE negotiation to authenticate the hosts and generate the master key to establish an ISAKMP SA between machines. After the ISAKMP SA is established, it remains in place for a period of eight hours, by default, for computers running Windows. If data is actively being transferred at the end of the eight hours, the Main Mode security association will be renegotiated automatically.

Main Mode negotiation occurs in three parts:

- **Negotiation of protection suites**   Part 1 of the Main Mode negotiation uses unencrypted communications to identify the protection suites (including the encryption and hash algorithms, authentication methods, and Diffie-Hellan Oakley groups) that are available and determines which algorithms will be used during the session. The IPsec client will send the IPsec server a list of protection suites that the client supports. The IPsec server then responds to the client with the preferred protection suite.

> ### How It Works: Determining the Preferred Protection Suite
>
> A Windows IPsec client proposes protection suites in the order they are listed in a filter action. A Windows IPsec server uses the first suitable protection suite listed by the client. Therefore, the Windows client determines the priorities of the protection suites, not the server. You should place this sequence in order from most to least secure.

- **Diffie-Hellman exchange** After IPsec negotiates a protection suite, part 2 of the Main Mode negotiation generates a Diffie-Hellman public and private key pair based on the negotiated Diffie-Hellman Oakley group. The IPsec hosts exchange public keys and then separately generate the Main Mode master key. This key will be used to efficiently encrypt the traffic sent between the two hosts.

- **Authentication** Part 3 of the Main Mode negotiation performs authentication. The authentication that occurs for Main Mode negotiation is a computer-based authentication rather than the user-based authentication most applications rely on. Therefore, the authentication process verifies only the identity of the computers, not the individuals using the computers when the authentication process occurs.

User Mode

User Mode is an optional second authentication phase that occurs immediately after Main Mode only if user authentication is required. User Mode authenticates the user to an Active Directory domain controller using Kerberos V5. User Mode authentication was newly introduced with Windows Vista and Windows Server 2008, so it is not available in earlier versions of Windows.

Quick Mode

Quick Mode, also known as *Phase 2*, negotiation establishes a secure channel between the IPsec hosts. The SAs created during Quick Mode are called the *IPsec SAs*. Two SAs are established, each with its own Security Parameter Index (SPI) label. One IPsec SA is used for inbound traffic, and the other is used for outbound traffic. During Quick Mode, keying material is refreshed, or if necessary, new keys are generated. A protection suite is also selected.

By default, computers running Windows perform Quick Mode negotiation every hour or after 100 MB of data has been transferred. Using Quick Mode to renegotiate the keys on a regular basis reduces the risk of an attacker using brute force methods to determine the keys used in the communications, because brute force attacks can be more effective if the attacker is allowed to capture more data.

> **More Info** Establishing the IPsec connection is processor intensive because it uses asymmetric public key cryptography. The data transmitted after the connection is established is encrypted using symmetric shared key cryptography and does not use a significant amount of processing capacity. However, servers with many active IPsec connections might have high processor utilization as a result. To minimize this, choose a network interface with IPsec Offload capabilities. For more information, refer to Chapter 6, "Scalable Networking."

Authentication Header and ESP

IPsec uses two protocols:

- **Authentication Header (AH)** Provides authentication, data integrity, and anti-replay protection for the entire packet including the IP header (except that the hop count and other fields might change during transit). AH does not encrypt data, however, so it is not used as frequently as ESP. AH cannot traverse NAT devices.

- **ESP** Provides authentication, data integrity, anti-replay protection, and optional encryption. ESP supports NAT-T, and it can traverse NAT devices. Because it supports encryption, ESP is almost always the better choice.

By default, Windows will attempt to use ESP and fall back to AH if both hosts cannot support ESP. Falling back to AH should be a rare occurrence, however, because ESP is widely supported.

Planning and Design Considerations

Because Windows Firewall rules have the potential to prevent legitimate users from connecting to critical network resources or allow attackers to connect to resources they might abuse, you must carefully plan Windows Firewall rules. Specifically, you should create packet filtering policies for every server application that allows traffic only from networks used by legitimate users. When creating IPsec policies, you must identify hosts that can and cannot support IPsec and design an isolation strategy that maximizes security but takes advantage of exemptions to allow connectivity for all clients.

> **Note** For information about IPsec enforcement and Network Access Protection (NAP), read Chapter 16, "IPsec Enforcement."

Planning Windows Firewall Policies

The sections that follow provide information for planning Windows Firewall policies. To optimize security, you should understand the default firewall policies configured automatically by Windows Server 2008 and situations that might require custom Windows Firewall rules.

You should also consider whether to narrow the scope of firewall rules and if you need to apply different rules to different Windows Firewall profiles.

Default Firewall Policies

By default, Windows Firewall (in both Windows Vista and Windows Server 2008) blocks all inbound traffic and allows all outbound traffic. In effect, this allows client applications to function without any configuration. Server applications must have an exception created.

To allow system services to function, Windows Firewall includes a default set of inbound and outbound rules. These rules are enabled only when a feature or role is enabled. For example, Windows Firewall includes the World Wide Web Services (Hypertext Transfer Protocol or HTTP Traffic-In) inbound rule, but it is disabled by default. If you add the Application or Web Server role, Windows Server 2008 automatically enables this rule to allow incoming connections to the Web service.

The default firewall policies meet the security needs of most organizations. You can, however, edit the default firewall policies to:

- Allow connections only from specific subnets.
- Allow connections only from specific users or computers.
- Allow only IPsec-protected connections.
- Apply the exception only to specific profiles (which is useful primarily for mobile computers).

Custom Windows Firewall Rules

Some non-Microsoft applications might also automatically create Windows Firewall rules. For those applications that do not, you can create one of the following types of rules:

- **Program** A rule that allows or blocks connections for a specific executable file, regardless of the port numbers it might use.
- **Port** A rule that allows or blocks communications for a specific TCP or UDP port number, regardless of the program generating the traffic.
- **Predefined** A rule that controls connections for a Windows component, such as Active Directory Domain Services, File And Printer Sharing, or Remote Desktop. Typically, Windows enables these rules automatically.
- **Custom** A rule that can combine program and port information.

Typically, you should create program rules because they are the simplest to configure. If a service listens on multiple ports and you want to restrict each port differently, create port rules.

By default, Windows Firewall does not block any outbound traffic. Therefore, you will need to create outbound rules only if you decide to block outbound traffic by default. If you choose to block all outbound traffic that hasn't been explicitly allowed, you can greatly reduce the risk of malware (such as spyware) transmitting confidential data. However, you will need to dedicate significant testing efforts to verify that outbound exceptions have been created for every legitimate application used within your organization.

Controlling the Scope of Firewall Policies

You can edit the properties of a default or custom rule to change the *scope*. The *scope* is the range of IP addresses that are allowed to communicate with the service specified by the Windows Firewall rule. For example, you could edit the DNS inbound rules to allow connections only from your internal subnets, reducing the risk that an attacker on the Internet would query your DNS server to identify the IP addresses of internal resources.

Controlling the scope of inbound rules is one of the best ways to reduce the security risk of network attacks. Ideally, all rules would be configured with a scope that allows connections only from the limited set of IP addresses used by legitimate clients. Controlling scope can increase ongoing management costs, however, because you will need to update the scope each time a new subnet is added or IP addresses change. Additionally, it can complicate troubleshooting, because an administrator must view the properties of a rule to determine whether a specific rule applies to a client that is experiencing problems.

Windows Firewall Profiles

When you create rules, you can apply them to any or all of the following profiles:

- **Domain**   Applies when a computer is connected to its Active Directory domain. Specifically, any time a member computer's domain controller is accessible, this profile will be applied.
- **Private**   Applies when a computer is connected to a private network location. By default, no networks are considered private—users must specifically mark a network location, such as their home office network, as private.
- **Public**   The default profile applied to all networks when a domain controller is not available. For example, the public profile is applied when users connect to Wi-Fi hotspots at airports or coffee shops. By default, the Public profile allows outgoing connections but blocks all incoming traffic that is not part of an existing connection.

Profiles are primarily intended for use with mobile computers. When configuring rules on servers, you will typically apply rules to all three profiles.

Protecting Communications with IPsec

Probably the most significant risk of requiring IPsec for communications is that legitimate users will be prevented from connecting. For this reason, it's important to carefully plan the users and computers that are authorized to connect to a server and test the implementation before requiring IPsec to connect.

IPsec Rule Types

You can create the following types of security rules:

- **Isolation** Allows computers to connect only when they meet criteria you specify such as being a member of your Active Directory domain or meeting health criteria such as having recent Windows updates installed. For more information about using health criteria, refer to Part III of this book, "Network Access Infrastructure."

- **Authentication exemption** Allows specific computers to bypass an authentication requirement specified by another rule.

- **Server-to-server** Requires authentication between specific computers.

- **Tunnel** Some organizations implement IPsec tunnels to allow IPsec traffic to traverse networks that do not support IPsec. This rule type specifies the hosts and destinations that will use the tunnel and the local and remote gateways. For more information about using tunnels, refer to Chapter 13, "Site-to-Site Connections."

- **Custom** Allows you to combine criteria from the different rule types.

Typically, you will create isolation rules for policies that should apply to all network connections, server-to-server rules for policies that apply only to specific networks, and authentication exemption rules for computers that cannot support IPsec.

IPsec Authentication Methods

You can choose the following types of authentication methods for IPsec:

- **Default** Uses the default authentication method for the profile. Table 4-1 lists the default settings.

Table 4-1 Default IPsec Settings in Windows Server 2008

Setting	Value
Authentication method	Computer (Kerberos V5)
Key exchange algorithm	Diffie-Hellman Group 2
Data integrity verification method	SHA1
IPsec authentication protocol	ESP
Encryption key lifetime	60 minutes or 100,000 KB
Encryption method	AES-128 (primary) and 3-DES (secondary)

- **Computer (Kerberos V5)**   Allows connections only from computers that are members of your domain. For IPsec to use Kerberos authentication across a cross-forest trust, you must use fully qualified domain names (FQDNs) to configure the trusts. In addition, you must configure the IPsec client policy to allow communication to any domain controller in the forest domain hierarchy so that IPsec can obtain a Kerberos ticket from a domain controller in the IPsec peer's domain.

- **Computer and user (Kerberos V5)**   Allows connections only from computers with authorized users that are members of your domain. Computer authentication occurs first, and then the user is authenticated using Kerberos V5 to provide an additional layer of protection.

- **Computer certificate**   Allows connections only from computers that have a computer certificate from a specific certification authority (CA). This allows you to use authentication for computers that aren't members of the same Active Directory domain, but it requires you to issue certificates to all computers (for example, by using Active Directory Certificate Services). Before you apply an IPsec policy that can use certificates for authentication, make sure that all target computers have the correct root CA certificates and relevant cross-certificates in addition to valid computer certificates. Additionally, to ensure that certificate authentication works as intended, test your PKI infrastructure with various IPsec policy configurations before deployment.

- **Advanced**   Allows you to configure multiple user or computer authentication methods and to specify the relative priorities. You can also configure Advanced security to use preshared keys for computer authentication, in which you must configure every computer with a key (which acts as a password). You should use preshared key authentication only in lab environments because it's too difficult to change the preshared key in production environments, and you would need to change it if any computer configured with the preshared key were compromised.

You can mix and match authentication methods as needed. For example, you can configure your public Web server to authenticate internal clients by using Kerberos and external clients by using public key certificates. After you configure IPsec, it will compare the source IP address of the remote host against an IPsec policy rule to determine which authentication method to use.

After IPsec authentication occurs, the client can establish a network connection to the server. The application might still require authentication, however. For example, if an authorized user connects to a file server that requires IPsec authentication, IPsec authentication will occur before the client can attempt to connect to the shared folder. If the client successfully authenticates with IPsec and is authorized to connect to the file server at the network level, the user will still need to provide credentials for the specific shared resources on the file server.

Figure 4-3 shows examples of how security can be provided at several different levels, with examples of how security is often used at each level. Using multiple levels of security is a strategy known as *defense-in-depth*, and it provides protection even if a single layer of security fails. In addition to the layers shown in Figure 4-3, many organizations use firewalls as part of their network infrastructure.

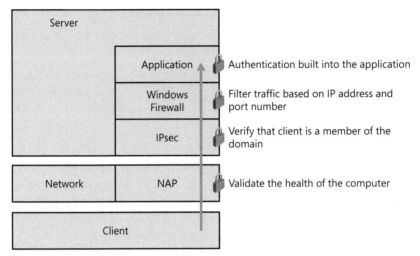

Figure 4-3   IPsec is one part of multi-layer network security.

Server and Domain Isolation

The term *isolation* originally referred to a network architecture technique that placed computers on physically separate networks that were unreachable from outside networks to make it very difficult for an unauthorized user to access the computer across the network. Physical isolation can make it difficult to manage computers and typically prevents mobile clients from connecting.

IPsec can use authentication to provide a high level of logical isolation while still allowing clients to connect from a variety of networks. With server and domain isolation, only authorized computers are allowed to establish network connections. Authentication occurs at the network layer, below the application layer, protecting all network communications. Therefore, even if an attacker gains physical access to your network, protected servers will reject network connection attempts because the attacker's computer will lack the appropriate credentials.

Direct from the Source: Adopting Server and Domain Isolation

Server and domain isolation is a fairly new usage scenario for IPsec. A few years back, our own Microsoft IT (MSIT) department was looking for a way to better protect our corporate network from malicious code attacks (like viruses and worms). As you can imagine, we've got a huge network, with all the challenges related with remote access, contractors and partners "on LAN," et cetera, that many organizations face each and every day.

To add to our existing defense-in-depth approach, MSIT needed a technology that would not require them to completely "rewire" the corporate network but instead could be layered on top of it, to segment (and isolate) the hosts we managed from rogue or unmanaged devices. This was important to further reduce the attack surface area of our network, ensure that machines that are not subject to our host health policies (for example, latest updates, antivirus signatures, host firewall, and so on), are not able to introduce network security threats that could impact our operations, and help us comply with such regulations as Sarbanes-Oxley (SOX).

After looking through a number of options, MSIT built a solution with IPsec, Active Directory Group Policy, and our existing Kerberos and Public Key Infrastructure (PKI) credentialing. This was the first implementation of the Server and Domain Isolation approach, although we learned that a few other customers had also developed a similar solution in the same organic fashion.

So I encourage you to take a look at what Server and Domain Isolation can do for you on your existing Windows infrastructure, all without the need to "rip and replace" your existing security technologies, change your existing network gear, or reengineer your applications.

Ian Hameroff, Senior Product Manager

Security and Access Product Marketing

IPsec also encrypts protected traffic by default, making it almost impossible for an attacker with access to your physical network to intercept your traffic and access the unencrypted network data.

Although IPsec provides very flexible authorization strategies, it is most commonly used in the following ways:

- **Domain isolation**   Only domain members can establish network connections to each other (with some exceptions).
- **Server isolation**   A specific server is configured to accept network connections from trusted domain members or a specific group of domain members. For example, you could configure an Accounting server to accept connections only from computers and users in the Accounting group. Server isolation can also allow connections to computers that are not domain members but have been issued a computer certificate by a trusted CA.

Server and domain isolation can help mitigate these risks:

- Attackers who connect to an unprotected (or rogue) wireless network and access servers that do not require application-layer authentication

- Servers that allow access from any user who can physically connect to the network

- Authorized users who connect using unauthorized computers

Server and domain isolation is only one layer of security, however, and cannot protect against these risks:

- Authorized users with authorized computers who misuse their access

- Attackers who gain access to an authorized computer, and, depending on how IPsec is configured, authorized user credentials

- Worms or other malware that infects an authorized computer and attack other computers across the network

- Attackers accessing servers that are not protected with IPsec

- Unauthorized connections that meet an IPsec exemption

IPSec Exemptions

Exemptions are sets of criteria for bypassing IPsec security requirements. Because Windows Server 2008 does not require IPsec by default, you need exemptions only if you require IPsec for communications. If you do require IPsec, you will need to create exemptions for authorized connections that cannot connect with IPsec. For example, you might create exemptions for:

- Newly deployed computers that haven't been configured for IPsec

- Operating systems that do not support IPsec

- Computers belonging to guests or contractors

Strive to minimize the scope of the exemptions. Grant exemptions only for those resources that must be accessible by computers that do not support IPsec. For example, you might need to create an exemption to allow hosts with an IP address on your guest wireless access point to connect to your proxy server and access the Internet (and only the public Internet). That exemption should not allow those guests to connect to the intranet Web server that lists employee names and phone numbers, however. Further limit the scope of the exemption by allowing access using only specific TCP or UDP ports.

> **Note**   Consider creating an exemption to allow Internet Control Message Protocol (ICMP) traffic. This will allow administrators to ping a computer and verify that it's online, even if an IPsec misconfiguration prevents them from connecting with other protocols.

Many infrastructure servers will require IPsec exemptions:

- **DHCP servers**   DHCP servers must be able to receive DHCP negotiation traffic across UDP port 68 without requiring IPsec.

■ **DNS servers**   To allow clients to locate domain controllers and other network resources, DNS servers should allow DNS queries across UDP port 53 without requiring IPsec.

■ **Windows Internet Name Service (WINS) servers**   If client computers require WINS servers, you should create an exemption for WINS queries using UDP port 137.

■ **Domain controllers**   Domain controllers must be able to accept non-IPsec protected connections for several different communications protocols.

Every exemption you create is a security risk, and you must evaluate every exemption and take steps to minimize the security risk. Think about the possibility for an attacker to abuse access allowed by an exemption to access protected resources or elevate privileges. For example, if you allow unauthenticated guests access to your proxy server, you should verify that guests cannot use the proxy server to access other, protected resources. Similarly, if an exemption allows a computer to connect to an IPsec-enabled computer through Remote Desktop, an attacker could use the Remote Desktop session to access protected resources.

Additionally, you should use physical access and Network Access Protection (NAP) to protect networks with exemptions that allow access to internal resources. For example, if you need to create an exemption for newly deployed computers, use physical locks to limit access to the deployment network. Whenever possible, prevent IPsec-protected computers from accessing resources available to non-IPsec computers; this will reduce the risk of confidential information accidentally leaking to unauthorized computers and reduce the risk of malware from unauthorized computers infecting internal computers.

Finally, apply the defense-in-depth security principle and never rely solely on IPsec for security. If an intranet Web server requires IPsec, you should also require authentication within the Web application. Similarly, if you use IPsec to encrypt communications to your e-mail server, you should still enable application-layer encryption (such as SSL) to minimize the risk if IPsec is circumvented or accidentally disabled.

Figure 4-4 shows how server isolation IPsec policies might be planned on a simple network. In this example, domain isolation should be used to limit IPsec connections to domain members.

Testing IPsec

Begin testing IPsec in a lab environment. Configure computers with the client side and server side of your critical applications, and verify that the lab is functional and accurately simulating the production environment. Your lab environment should have computers with each of the potential IPsec client operating systems because different operating systems support different IPsec functionality. Test application performance both with and without IPsec to verify that IPsec does not significantly slow performance.

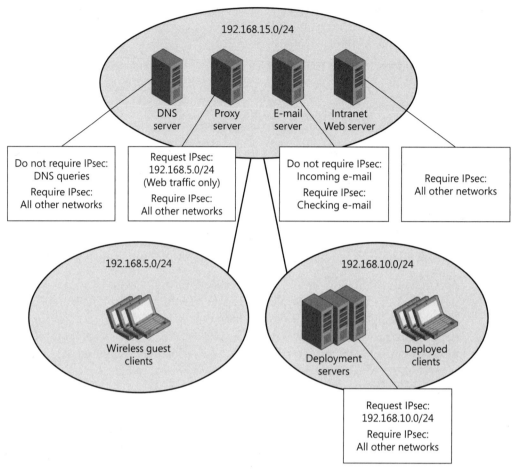

Figure 4-4 Sample isolation architecture with exemptions

Add firewalls, proxy servers, and routers used in your production environment to the lab environment to simulate the potential for those devices to interfere with IPsec communications in the production environment. Test non-IPsec-enabled clients with IPsec-enabled servers, and verify that the connection is either successful or unsuccessful, depending on how you have configured IPsec.

Begin the IPsec rollout with a pilot deployment. During the pilot phase, you should not require IPsec communications on any computer. All computers should allow non-IPsec communications to support computers that are not part of the pilot. You can require IPsec communications only after you have configured all computers to use IPsec.

Note Even if you plan to deploy IPsec to every computer, there will be a transition period during which some computers will not yet have received the IPsec configuration. Therefore, you will need to allow unprotected connections during the IPsec deployment.

Deployment Steps

You can configure Windows Firewall either locally, using the Windows Firewall With Advanced Security console in the Administrative Tools folder, or using the Computer Configuration\Windows Settings\Security Settings\Windows Firewall With Advanced Security\ Windows Firewall With Advanced Security node of a Group Policy Object (GPO). Typically, you will configure policies that apply to groups of computers (including IPsec connection security policies) by using GPOs and edit server-specific policies (such as configuring the range of IP addresses a DNS server accepts queries from) by using local tools.

The sections that follow describe common Windows Firewall configuration tasks.

Firewall Settings with Group Policy

Firewall policies are most effective when implemented throughout an Active Directory domain by using Group Policy Objects. Before creating a firewall policy, determine the executable file used by the application, the TCP or UDP port numbers, or other protocol types that you will use to specify the criteria used to apply the rule. Also think about whether you can limit the scope of the communications to specific computers or networks.

You can use Group Policy to manage Windows Firewall settings for computers running Windows Vista and Windows Server 2008 by using two different nodes:

- **Computer Configuration\Windows Settings\Security Settings\Windows Firewall With Advanced Security\Windows Firewall With Advanced Security**   This node applies settings only to computers running Windows Vista and Windows Server 2008. You should always use this node when possible because it provides a more detailed configuration of firewall rules and allows you to configure new authentication types and the new cryptographic option and because many firewall rules are pre-configured.

- **Computer Configuration\Administrative Templates\Network\Network Connections\ Windows Firewall**   This node applies settings to computers running Windows XP, Windows Server 2003, Windows Vista, and Windows Server 2008. This tool is less flexible than the previously described node; however, settings apply to all versions of Windows that support Windows Firewall. If you are not using the new IPsec features in Windows Vista, you can use this node to configure all your clients.

For best results, create separate GPOs for Windows Vista/Windows Server 2008 and Windows XP/Windows Server 2003. Then, use WMI queries to target the GPOs only to computers running the appropriate version of Windows.

More Info   For more information, read Microsoft Knowledge Base article 555253, "HOWTO: Leverage Group Policies with WMI Filters" at *http://support.microsoft.com/kb/555253*.

Because this chapter is focused on configuring firewall settings for Windows Vista and Windows Server 2008, it provides instructions for using only the Windows Firewall With Advanced Security console.

To Configure General Firewall Settings

1. Open the Group Policy Object in the Group Policy Management Editor.

> **Note**   You can also configure these settings for individual computers by using the Windows Firewall With Advanced Security console, available within the Administrative Tools folder on the Start menu.

2. Select Computer Configuration\Windows Settings\Security Settings\Windows Firewall With Advanced Security\Windows Firewall With Advanced Security.

3. Right-click Windows Firewall With Advanced Security, and then click Properties.

4. On the Domain Profile, Private Profile, and Public Profile tabs, configure settings in three different groups:

   - **State**   Configure whether the firewall is enabled by default and whether inbound and outbound connections are allowed or blocked by default.

   - **Settings**   Click the Customize button in the Settings group to configure whether Windows Firewall displays a notification when a program is blocked from receiving inbound connections, whether unicast responses to multicast or broadcast network traffic are allowed, and whether local firewall and IPsec connection security rules are merged or overridden by Group Policy settings.

   - **Logging**   Click the Customize button in the Logging group to configure whether firewall actions such as dropped packets or successful connections are logged. Logging is disabled by default and should remain disabled unless you are actively troubleshooting a firewall problem.

5. On the IPsec Settings tab, configure settings in two groups:

   - **IPsec defaults**   Click the Customize button to open the Customize IPsec Settings dialog box. From this dialog box, you can configure the encryption technologies and key lifetimes used for both Main Mode and Quick Mode. Typically, however, the default settings are ideal. You can also change the default authentication method, although the chosen authentication method can be overridden by IPsec rules. Click OK.

   - **IPsec exemptions**   Select whether ICMP traffic (such as traffic generated by Ping and Tracert) is exempt from IPsec. This can be useful for systems administrators who want to ping a server that otherwise requires IPsec authentication.

6. Click OK.

To configure general firewall settings from a script, first enter the **netsh advfirewall** context by running the following commands:

netsh

advfirewall

Then, use the **set store** command to choose whether to work with the local store (the default) or an Active Directory GPO. The following commands demonstrate how to select two different stores from within the **netsh advfirewall** context:

set store local

set store gpo="contoso.com\IT"

With the store set, you can run the many different commands to configure general firewall settings. In the following commands, *profile* is **allprofiles**, **domainprofile**, **privateprofile**, or **publicprofile**.

Within the **netsh advfirewall** context, you can use the following command to configure default firewall behavior, which is useful for troubleshooting or temporarily hardening network security configuration:

set *profile* firewallpolicy *inbound,outbound*

Notice that there is no space after the comma. In this command, *profile* must be one of the following values:

- **allprofiles**
- **domainprofile**
- **privateprofile**
- **publicprofile**

The *inbound* parameter must be one of the following values:

- **blockinbound**   Blocks all inbound connections that do not match an inbound rule (the default setting).
- **blockinboundalways**   Blocks all inbound connections even if they match an inbound rule. This can be useful for temporarily increasing the network security of a computer, for example, when connecting a computer to an untrusted network when exceptions have been added to the Public profile.
- **allowinbound**   Allows inbound connections even if you haven't created an exception. This can be useful for temporarily allowing any application to receive incoming connections and for determining whether a problem is being caused by the Windows Firewall configuration.

- **notconfigured** Returns Windows Firewall policy to its default state after being modified by one of the previous commands.

The outbound parameter must be one of the following values:

- **allowoutbound** Allows all outbound connections that do not match an outbound rule.
- **blockoutbound** Blocks all outbound connections that do not match an outbound rule. This can be useful for temporarily stopping applications from communicating on the network.
- **notconfigured** Returns Windows Firewall policy to its default state after being modified by one of the previous commands.

For example, the following command causes both inbound and outbound traffic to be allowed, regardless of whether it matches a rule:

set allprofiles firewallpolicy allowinbound,allowoutbound

And the following command reverts the firewall to its default behavior (which is applicable only when configuring an Active Directory GPO store):

set allprofiles firewallpolicy notconfigured,notconfigured

To restore all default settings from within the Windows Firewall With Advanced Security console, right-click Windows Firewall With Advanced Security, and then click Restore Defaults. To restore default settings from a script, run the following command:

netsh advfirewall reset

For complete usage information, run **netsh advfirewall ?** at a command prompt.

Configuring Default Rules

Windows Firewall includes default inbound and outbound rules for Windows services and applications that require network connectivity. For example, after adding the Active Directory Domain Controller role, Windows Server 2008 adds 13 rules. Combined, these rules consist of a *rule group*, as shown in Figure 4-5.

To Enable or Disable Rules

1. From within the Windows Firewall With Advanced Security console, select the Inbound Rules or Outbound Rules node.

2. Right-click the rule, and then click Enable Rule or Disable Rule.

To use Netsh to enable or disable a single rule, use the following syntax:

netsh advfirewall firewall set rule name="*Rule*" new enable=yes

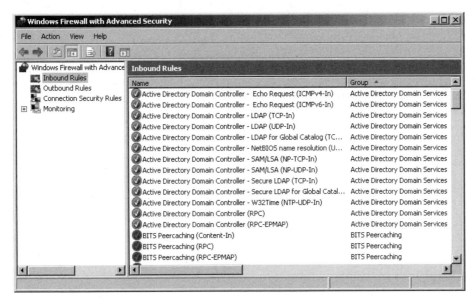

Figure 4-5   The Active Directory Domain Services rule group

Or disable a rule by running the following command:

netsh advfirewall firewall set rule name="*Rule*" new enable=no

For example, the following command enables the BITS Peercaching (RPC) rule (which is disabled by default):

netsh advfirewall firewall set rule name="BITS Peercaching (RPC)" new enable=yes

You can use Netsh to enable an entire rule group by running a single command, using the following syntax:

netsh advfirewall firewall set rule group="*RuleGroup*" new enable=yes

Or disable a rule group by running the following command:

netsh advfirewall firewall set rule group="*RuleGroup*" new enable=no

For example, the following command enables all rules in the BITS Peercaching group (which is disabled by default):

netsh advfirewall firewall set rule group="BITS Peercaching" new enable=yes

To Change the Configuration of a Rule

1.   From within the Windows Firewall With Advanced Security console, select the Inbound Rules or Outbound Rules node.

2.   Right-click the rule, and then click Properties.

3. Edit the configuration of the rule:

    ❏ **To change the scope**   Click the Scope tab, click These IP Addresses, and then
    click Add to specify the local or remote IP addresses.

    ❏ **To require IPsec**   Click the General tab, and then click Allow Only Secure
    Connections.

    ❏ **To allow only specific users or computers to connect**   Click the Users And
    Computers tab, and then select Only Allow Connections From These Computers
    or click Only Allow Connections From These Users. Click the Add button to add
    the users or computers.

    ❏ **To apply the rule to a specific profile**   Click the Advanced tab, click These
    Profiles, and then select the profiles the rule should apply to.

4. Click OK.

Adding New Rules

Many applications and services will automatically configure firewall rules as required. For
other applications, including applications created for earlier versions of Windows, you will
need to manually configure an exception to allow an inbound connection.

To Add a Firewall Exception by Using Group Policy

1. Open the Group Policy Object in the Group Policy Management Editor.

> **Note**   You can also configure these settings for individual computers by using the
> Windows Firewall With Advanced Security console, available within the Administrative
> Tools folder on the Start menu. This tool replaces the IPsec Security Policy Management
> console that was included with Windows XP and Windows Server 2003.

2. Select Computer Configuration\Windows Settings\Security Settings\Windows Fire-
    wall With Advanced Security\Windows Firewall With Advanced Security.

3. Right-click either Inbound Rules (to filter incoming traffic from other computers)
    or Outbound Rules (to filter outgoing traffic sent by applications on the computer
    applying the GPO), and then click New Rule.

    The New Inbound Rule Wizard or New Outbound Rule Wizard appears.

4. On the Rule Type page, click the type of rule you want to create, and then click Next. For
    more information about the types of rules, refer to "Custom Windows Firewall Rules"
    earlier in this chapter.

5. If the Program page appears, click This Program Path, and then type the path of the
    executable file you want the rule to apply to. This file doesn't necessarily need to exist

on the computer you are configuring Group Policy on, and it will apply only if the computer applying the GPO has the file. Click Next.

6. If the Protocols And Ports page appears, complete the following fields, and then click Next.

   ❑ **Protocol Type**   For most applications, you should select either TCP or UDP. You can also select less frequently used protocols if required by the application. Select Custom to type your own Protocol Number.

   ❑ **Protocol Number**   Populated automatically when you select a Protocol Type.

   ❑ **Local Port and Remote Port**   Applies only to TCP and UDP Protocol Types. For firewall exceptions that apply to a server, choose Specific Ports for the Local Port, and leave Remote Port set to All Ports. For firewall exceptions that apply to a client, choose Specific Ports for the Remote Port, and leave Local Port set to All Ports. After selecting Specific Ports, type the port numbers separated by commas. If required by the application, select Dynamic RPC or RPC Endpoint Mapper (used only with the RPCSS service).

   ❑ **Internet Control Message Protocol Settings**   The Customize button is enabled only if you select the ICMPv4 and ICMPv6 Protocol Types. Click Customize to choose specific ICMP types, or accept the default setting of All ICMP Types, and then click Next.

7. If the Scope page appears, leave the default settings to allow traffic to or from any IP address. If you can limit communications to specific IP addresses or networks, click These IP Addresses for either local (to limit the computers that apply the rule) or remote (to limit the servers to which clients are communicating). Then, click Add, specify the IP address, network, or predefined set of computers, and then click OK. Click Customize to choose whether to apply the rule to LAN interfaces, remote access interfaces, or wireless interfaces, click OK, and then click Next.

8. On the Action page, click Allow The Connection to allow all communications that match the criteria you selected on the previous pages. If you want to allow only IPsec communications, click Allow The Connection If It Is Secure, and choose whether to require encryption. If you want to block traffic that matches your criteria, click Block The Connection. Click Next.

9. On the Profile page, select the profiles that you want to apply the rule to, and then click Next. For more information, read "Windows Firewall Profiles" earlier in this chapter.

10. On the Name page, type a name and description for the rule, and then click Finish.

After configuring a rule, you can double-click it in the Group Policy Management Editor to edit the properties. Clients will apply the firewall rule the next time they refresh Group Policy settings.

IPsec Connection Security Rules

IPsec connection security rules allow you to either request or require IPsec for connections that match the criteria you specify. The criteria resemble those used to define Windows Firewall filters. For example, you can set an IPsec security rule for:

- All traffic to or from IP address 10.4.22.17
- All Internet Control Message Protocol (ICMP) traffic to or from the default gateway
- All traffic sent to TCP port 80 except traffic sent from the internal network
- All outbound connections except those to specific servers

Each computer can have only one IPsec policy. If multiple GPOs apply to a computer, each with different IPsec policies, only the IPsec policy defined in the highest priority GPO will be applied.

Adding an IPsec Connection Security Rule

By default, Windows Server 2008 computers have a single local IPsec policy called Request Security. This policy attempts to use IPsec authentication and encryption for all communications but falls back to unprotected communications when IPsec negotiations fail. You must create additional rules to configure computers for server or domain isolation.

To Add an IPsec Security Rule

1. Open the Group Policy Object in the Group Policy Management Editor.

> **Note** You can also configure these settings for individual computers by using the Windows Firewall With Advanced Security console, available within the Administrative Tools folder on the Start menu.

2. Select Computer Configuration\Windows Settings\Security Settings\Windows Firewall With Advanced Security\Windows Firewall With Advanced Security. This node is used to configure computers running Windows Vista and Windows Server 2008. The Computer Configuration\Windows Settings\Security Settings\IP Security Policies On Active Directory node is used to configure Windows XP and earlier versions of Windows.

> **Note** To edit IPsec on an individual computer, open the Windows Firewall With Advanced Security console from within the Administrative Tools folder on the Start menu.

3. Right-click Connection Security Rules, and then click New Rule.

   The New Connection Security Rule Wizard appears.

4. On the Rule Type page, select the rule type, as described in "IPsec Rule Types" earlier in this chapter. Click Next.

5. If the Exempt Computers page appears, click the Add button. Type the IP address, subnet, and IP address range, or select one of the predefined set of computers. Then, click OK. You can add as many sets of exemptions as required. Click Next.

6. If the Endpoints page appears, select the computers that you want to configure the server-to-server connection for. For a connection to match this criteria, the client must appear in one list (either Endpoint 1 or Endpoint 2), and the server must appear in the other list. If both the server and client appear on the Endpoint 1 list, the rule will not apply to the connection. Click Next.

7. If the Tunnel Endpoints page appears, click both Add buttons to specify the computers at either end of the tunnel. Then, type the IP addresses of the local and remote tunnel computers. An IPsec tunnel must be defined at both ends of the connection, and at each end, the entries for the local tunnel computer and remote tunnel computer must be swapped, and the entries for Endpoint 1 and Endpoint 2 must be swapped. Therefore, you will need to create one tunnel endpoint rule for each of the endpoints. Click Next. For more information, refer to "IPsec Rule Types" earlier in this chapter.

8. If the Requirements page appears, choose whether to require or request authentication for inbound and outbound connections. Requesting authentication doesn't offer a significant security benefit, because a malicious client could simply choose not to authenticate. However, requesting authentication provides backward compatibility for clients that do not support IPsec or do not have proper credentials. You should require security for inbound connections only when all legitimate clients support IPsec. You should require security for outbound connections only when all servers the client might connect to (within the profile you select later in the wizard) support IPsec. Click Next.

9. On the Authentication Method page, choose whether to authenticate the computers with a computer certificate or a preshared key (for lab environments only). Alternatively, you can select Advanced and then click Customize to select multiple authentication methods. Click Next.

10. On the Profile page, select the profiles that you want to apply the rule to, and then click Next. For more information, read "Windows Firewall Profiles" earlier in this chapter.

11. On the Name page, type a name and description for the rule, and then click Finish.

After configuring a rule, you can double-click it in the Group Policy Management Editor to edit the properties. This allows you to specify subnets that the rule applies to if the wizard didn't prompt you for that information.

If you want to require IPsec for a specific protocol (for example, to require IPsec to connect to File And Printer Sharing), edit the properties of the appropriate Inbound Rule, and specify an action on the General tab, as described in "To Change the Configuration of a Rule" earlier in this section.

Configuring Domain Isolation

To configure domain isolation, follow these steps in a lab environment and then in a production environment using non-critical servers. Because requiring IPsec can prevent computers from connecting, it has the potential to interrupt critical network applications.

1. Follow the steps in "To Configure General Firewall Settings" to configure the default IPsec authentication and encryption requirements using the IPsec Settings tab of the Windows Firewall With Advanced Security Properties dialog box. By default, only computer authentication is performed using Kerberos V5, which works automatically in domain environments. For additional security, you can choose to use both Computer And User authentication.

2. Follow the steps in "Adding an IPsec Connection Security Rule" earlier in this chapter to add a connection security rule to your Default Domain GPO that requests, but does not require, IPsec.

3. Monitor computers to verify that they are successfully connecting with IPsec and that both authentication and encryption is occurring correctly. For more information, read "Ongoing Maintenance" later in this chapter. Make note of computers that require access to resources but are unable to connect with IPsec.

4. Follow the steps in "Adding an IPsec Connection Security Rule" earlier in this chapter to add connection security rules that exempt computers not capable of supporting IPsec. Be as specific as possible with these rules, granting exemptions to a limited number of computers and allowing them to access the most narrow set of resources possible. In the New Connection Security Rule Wizard, on the Rule Type page, select Authentication Exemption. On the Exempt Computers page, specify the IP addresses of the computers that should be exempt. After completing the wizard, edit the properties for the rule, and then select the Computers tab. If you can grant exempt computers access to only a limited set of network resources, specify the IP addresses of those network resources in the Endpoint 1 group. (The list of exempt computers will be in the Endpoint 2 group.)

5. Create a new GPO that applies only to computers in a pilot group, and then follow the steps in "Adding an IPsec Connection Security Rule" earlier in this chapter to add a connection security rule that requires IPsec. On the Rule Type page, select Isolation. On the Requirements page, select Require Authentication For Inbound And Outbound Connections. For servers, the default settings for the other wizard pages will typically work for most environments. To allow mobile computers to connect to resources on other networks, you might want to apply the rule only to the Domain profile.

6. Monitor the computers in the pilot group to verify that they are able to successfully connect to network resources and that the connections are using IPsec.

7. Gradually expand the scope of the IPsec pilot GPO so that more computers require IPsec. Ultimately, all computers in your domain should require IPsec for connection security.

Work closely with IT operations and support groups so they are aware of the changes and know how to test and modify connection security rules to troubleshoot connectivity problems. If a support person must make a change to allow connectivity, review the change to assess the potential security impact.

Configuring Server Isolation

Server isolation follows a similar process to domain isolation. However, although all client computers should be configured to support security, only the servers you need to protect should be configured to require security for incoming connections. As with domain isolation, create exemptions prior to requiring security.

Whereas domain isolation necessarily uses Kerberos V5 authentication, server isolation can use either Kerberos V5 authentication (if all computers or users are members of the same forest) or computer certificates (if computers are not all domain members). If you are using computer certificates, you must either:

- **Purchase certificates from a public CA**   Certificates from a public CA that Windows trusts by default to connect with IPsec, which is ideal for communicating with partners from outside organizations. Client computers also need certificates.

- **Generate certificates by using an internal CA**   You can generate your own computer certificates by using an internal CA such as that provided by Windows Server 2008 Active Directory Certificate Services. You must configure both servers and clients with computer certificates. All computers must trust your CA.

Configuring an Exemption for ICMP

Administrators often use ICMP to ping servers and determine whether or not they are online. If a problem with IPsec prevents an administrator from connecting to a server, pings will also fail, which might lead the administrator to mistakenly believe the server is offline.

Just as with any other exception, creating an exemption for ICMP incurs a slight security risk. Attackers can use ICMP to create a map of your network or to launch a denial-of-service attack against computers.

To Configure an IPsec Exemption for ICMP

1. In the Windows Firewall With Advanced Security console, right-click Windows Firewall with Advanced Security, and then click Properties.

2. Click the IPsec Settings tab.

3. Click the Exempt ICMP From ICMP drop-down list, click Yes, and then click OK.

Ongoing Maintenance

Ongoing maintenance for Windows Firewall includes:

- Adjusting inbound filtering rules when new server applications are installed. For more information, read "Adding New Rules" earlier in this chapter.

- Adding connection security rules to provide exemptions for new computers and networks that require access to network resources but cannot support IPsec. For more information, read "IPsec Connection Security Rules" earlier in this chapter.

- Updating rules when IP addresses change, which can be done by editing the rule's properties in the Windows Firewall With Advanced Security console.

- Removing exemptions (or expanding coverage of existing rules) when computers are upgraded to an operating system that supports IPsec.

Because Windows Firewall changes can have serious security implications, all changes should follow the standard Microsoft Operations Framework (MOF) management process, as follows:

- **Change request**   Formally initiating a change by submitting a request for change document.

- **Change classification**   Assigning a priority and a category to the change that uses its urgency and its impact on the infrastructure or users as criteria. This assignment affects the implementation speed and route.

- **Change authorization**   Determining whether the change should be allowed by assessing possible negative impacts, including application functionality, network performance, and security risks.

- **Change development**   Planning the change, including testing it in a lab environment and determining whether the new rules will be deployed to all computers at once or to a pilot group.

- **Change release**   The release and deployment of the change into the production environment.

- **Change review**   A post-implementation process that reviews whether the change has achieved the goals that were established for it and determines whether to keep the change in effect or revert to the original state. Specifically, you should verify that IPsec rules are still being enforced and that new exemptions don't accidentally exempt IPsec-capable computers.

For more information about MOF, read "Microsoft Operations Framework Process Model for Operations" at *http://www.microsoft.com/downloads/details.aspx?FamilyID=e0807633-2689-45fa-8d48-1b5b383afc00*.

Troubleshooting

Windows Firewall problems typically take the form of a connectivity failure. In other words, a user will be unable to connect to a server. Unfortunately, connectivity failures can be caused by many different factors. When troubleshooting connectivity problems, begin by determining whether Windows Firewall is the root cause of the problem.

Especially when IPsec is newly deployed, administrators assume that general connectivity problems are actually caused by IPsec. If you have created an ICMP exemption (as described in "Configuring an Exemption for ICMP" earlier in this chapter), you can ping the client and server to verify connectivity. Next, use the Windows Firewall With Advanced Security monitoring features to determine whether a security association is active between the client and server, as described in "Monitoring IPsec Security Associations" later in this section. To determine whether the problem is application-specific, have the client attempt to connect to the server using different protocols—for example, connecting to a shared folder or connecting to a Web server.

Windows Firewall inbound rules can also cause apparent connectivity problems. First, determine whether other clients can connect to the server. If other clients can connect, the problem is frequently one of the following:

- **The client has a general connectivity failure.**   Verify that the client can connect to other network resources and can resolve the server's host name correctly. For more information about troubleshooting name resolution problems, read Chapter 7, "Domain Name System."
- **The client has an outbound rule that is blocking traffic.**   Although Windows Firewall allows all outbound traffic by default, outbound rules are capable of blocking an application's traffic. Verify that no outbound rules apply to the application you are troubleshooting.
- **The application has been misconfigured.**   The client might have the wrong host name or IP address configured for the server. Occasionally, the client application might have a nonstandard port number configured. Verify that the application is configured correctly.

If no clients can connect to the server, begin troubleshooting at the server. The problem is frequently one of the following:

- **The server has a general connectivity failure.**   Verify that the server can connect to other network resources.
- **DNS is misconfigured.**   If the server does not have a resource record in DNS, or the IP address is incorrect, clients will be unable to connect to the server. For more information about resolving DNS problems, read Chapter 7.
- **IPsec rules require connection security.**   Verify that clients support IPsec or that exemptions have been created for the clients.

- **The service has been misconfigured.** The service might be configured to respond on a nonstandard IP address or port number.

- **Authentication is failing.** Many server applications require client authentication. Check the application's event logs to determine whether authentication attempts are failing.

- **No Windows Firewall exception exists.** If the problem is not caused by any of the previous conditions, verify that a Windows Firewall exception exists to allow inbound traffic on the server.

The sections that follow provide detailed information about logging Windows Firewall activity (useful for determining whether incoming connection attempts are being dropped) and using Network Monitor to determine whether IPsec is functioning correctly.

Windows Firewall Logging

If you think Windows Firewall might be blocking important communications, or Windows Firewall does not seem to be blocking communications that you have configured it to filter, you can view detailed information about the traffic Windows Firewall filters in one of two ways:

- **Enable logging to the Pfirewall.log file.** Logs Windows Firewall activity to a text file.
- **Enable auditing to the Security event log.** Logs Windows Firewall activity to the Security event log, where it can be viewed in Event Viewer.

To Enable Windows Firewall Logging

1. Open the Windows Firewall With Advanced Security console, available within the Administrative Tools folder on the Start menu. Alternatively, you can enable logging within a Group Policy Object in the Group Policy Management Editor.

2. Right-click the Windows Firewall With Advanced Security node, and then click Properties.

3. Click the Domain Profile, Private Profile, or Public Profile tab depending on the profile you want to enable logging for.

4. In the Logging group, click the Customize button.

   The Customize Logging Settings dialog box appears.

5. Type a name for the log file, or accept the default location of *%SystemRoot%*\System32\ LogFiles\Firewall\Pfirewall.log.

6. Type a size limit for the log file, which is 4 megabytes (MB) (4096 KB) by default.

7. To log packets that Windows Firewall drops, click the Log Dropped Packets drop-down list, and then click Yes.

8. To log connections that Windows Firewall allows because an exception exists, click the Log Successful Connections drop-down list, and then click Yes.

9. Click OK twice.

You can also enable logging using the following commands:

REM enter the netsh firewall context

netsh

advfirewall

REM the following commands are executed within the netsh firewall context

set allprofiles logging allowedconnections enable

set allprofiles logging droppedconnections enable

set allprofiles logging filename "*filename*"

With logging enabled, re-create the problem that you are troubleshooting. Then, repeat the previous steps to disable logging. Avoid leaving logging enabled, because a large amount of logging can occur and impact system performance. To disable logging from a script, run the following commands:

REM enter the netsh firewall context

netsh

advfirewall

REM the following commands are executed within the netsh firewall context

set allprofiles logging allowedconnections disable

set allprofiles logging droppedconnections disable

View the log file by opening the *%SystemRoot%*\System32\LogFiles\Firewall\Pfirewall.log file (or the file you specified) in Notepad or another text editor. As shown in Figure 4-6, the log file starts with a list of fields that are logged. Each line with an Action of ALLOW indicates one successful connection, and each line with an Action of DROP indicates a dropped packet.

To Enable Windows Firewall Security Auditing

1. To log packets that Windows Firewall drops, run the following command at a command prompt:

    auditpol /set /subcategory:"Filtering Platform Packet Drop" /failure:enable

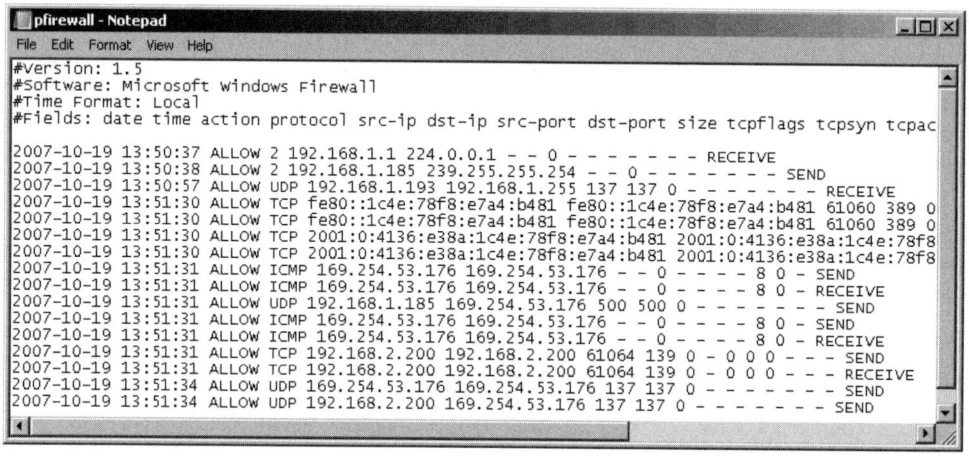

Figure 4-6   The Pfirewall.log file

2. To log connections that Windows Firewall allows because an exception exists, run the following command at a command prompt:

   auditpol /set /subcategory:"Filtering Platform Connection"

3. With logging enabled, re create the problem that you are troubleshooting.

4. If you enabled logging of dropped packets or successful connections, disable it now by running the following command at a command prompt:

   auditpol /clear

Avoid leaving logging enabled, because a large amount of logging can occur and affect system performance.

View the log file by opening the Diagnostics\Event Viewer\Windows Logs\Security log in Server Manager. Firewall events will have a Task Category of Filtering Platform Packet Drop or Filtering Platform Connection. As shown in Figure 4-7, the event details will show the source and destination IP addresses and port numbers.

Monitoring IPsec Security Associations

You can monitor active IPsec sessions by using the Windows Firewall With Advanced Security console. In the console, select the Monitor\Security Associations\Main Mode node or the Monitor\Security Associations\Quick Mode node. Each displays active security associations, including the IP addresses, authentication method, and encryption method.

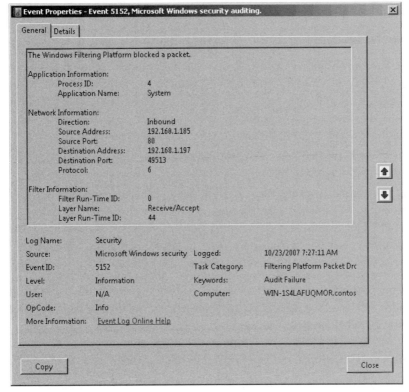

Figure 4-7   A dropped packet logged in the Security event log

Using Network Monitor

Microsoft Network Monitor is a protocol analyzer, also known as a *sniffer*. Network Monitor captures raw network data, including IPsec communications, and allows you to examine it. You cannot use Network Monitor to examine the contents of encrypted IPsec traffic, but you can use it to verify that IPsec is being used and traffic is being encrypted.

To download Network Monitor, visit *http://www.microsoft.com/downloads/search.aspx* and search for Network Monitor. For detailed instructions on how to use Network Monitor to capture and analyze network communications, refer to online Help.

 On the Disc   You can link to the download site for Network Monitor from the companion CD-ROM.

Chapter Summary

Windows Firewall provides two closely related capabilities:

- **Packet filtering**   Windows Firewall can selectively block or allow either incoming or outgoing network communications. This capability gives administrators control over which networks can connect to which services on a server and which applications are allowed to send outgoing traffic. For many organizations, the default settings are sufficient. However, organizations with strict security requirements can use Windows Firewall to carefully control which networks are allowed to access which services.

- **IPsec connection security**   IPsec can request or require authentication and encryption for different applications and networks. You can use this to implement domain isolation, which configures domain member computers to accept connections only from computers or users that are members of the domain. Server isolation provides similar capabilities on a server-by-server basis. Naturally, you can create exemptions for computers that require connectivity but cannot support IPsec.

When implementing any security feature, weigh the benefits against the costs. Modifying the default Windows Firewall settings can dramatically reduce the risks of many types of network attacks. However, this tightened security can cause unexpected connectivity problems and complicate troubleshooting. Thorough testing in a lab environment before deployment, meticulous maintenance procedures, and proper troubleshooting techniques can greatly reduce the costs.

Additional Information

For additional information about planning, deploying, and maintaining Windows Firewall, see the following:

- "Server and Domain Isolation" (*http://www.microsoft.com/sdisolation*)

- "Server and Domain Isolation Using IPsec and Group Policy" (*http://www.microsoft .com/technet/security/guidance/architectureanddesign/ipsec/*)

- "HOWTO: Leverage Group Policies with WMI Filters" (*http://support.microsoft.com/ kb/555253*)

- "Microsoft Operations Framework Process Model for Operations" (*http:// www.microsoft.com/downloads/details.aspx?FamilyID=e0807633-2689-45fa-8d48- 1b5b383afc00*)

Chapter 5
Policy-Based Quality of Service

This chapter provides information about how to design, deploy, maintain, and troubleshoot Quality of Service (QoS) in Windows Server 2008.

This chapter assumes the following:

- That you understand the role of Active Directory and Group Policy for managing Microsoft Windows computers.
- That you have a solid understanding of managing routers in your network infrastructure.

Concepts

As more people and organizations begin to use real-time networking services, such as Voice over Internet Protocol (VoIP), multimedia streaming, and video conferencing, the impact of network performance problems becomes more significant. Ten years ago, a network performance problem would just cause a Web page to open slowly. Today, it can make your phone service unusable, interrupt critical video conference meetings, and prevent financial transactions from being completed.

Simply adding bandwidth won't solve most network performance problems. On many networks, a single large file transfer can monopolize the entire network connection, negatively impacting any real-time communications while the transfer occurs. Quality of Service (QoS) works with your servers, clients, and network infrastructure to prioritize network traffic. With QoS, phone calls and other real-time communications can be given priority over file transfers, e-mail, Web browsing, and other lower-priority communications.

The Causes of Network Performance Problems

Some of the network conditions that can cause performance problems include latency, jitter, out-of-order delivery, and dropped packets. The sections that follow describe these conditions in more detail.

Latency

Latency is the delay it takes for a packet to reach its destination, typically measured in milliseconds (ms). When planning for QoS, round-trip latency (the time it takes for a packet to be sent to a remote host and for a response to be returned) is the most important metric because it has the most significant impact on real-time two-way communications such as VoIP.

Latency comes from several sources:

- **Forwarding delay**   When a router processes a packet and moves it from one network to the next, there is normally an insignificant delay of one or two milliseconds. However, if the router receives traffic faster than it can forward it to the destination network—for example, if it receives communications at 5 megabits per second (Mbps) and must forward it to an interface that supports only 1.54 Mbps—the router must store the packet a queue, causing additional latency.

- **Propagation delay**   Communications take time to travel a distance. For most copper or fiber networks, the speed is about 2/3 the speed of light—around 125,000 miles per second. On local area networks, the propagation delay is negligible. However, for a transmission to travel halfway around the world would take close to 100 ms (because networks are never a straight line). Communications that pass through a satellite link incur a latency of about 500 ms, making them unusable for VoIP. Virtual private networks (VPNs) often cause network communications to take an extremely inefficient path between the source and destination, multiplying the propagation delay.

- **Host processing delay**   If an incoming packet is VoIP or streaming media, the operating system or application will hold the packet in a jitter buffer to minimize the impact of jitter (discussed in the next section) and out-of-order delivery. Jitter buffers vary, but packets are typically held about 20 to 200 ms, adding latency. Once the packets have been held in a jitter buffer for a sufficient time, the application must process the data contained within the packets, which can incur an additional processing delay depending on the speed of the computer and the percentage of processing time currently dedicated to the network application.

Jitter

Jitter is change in latency. For example, a one-way video stream that begins with 10 ms of latency might suddenly have 100 ms of latency if network conditions change. Software uses jitter buffers, as discussed in the previous section, to reduce the impact of jitter. However, the more jitter you have, the longer data must be held in the jitter buffer—increasing latency for all communications.

Out-of-Order Delivery

In IP networks, two consecutive packets can take different routes between the source and the destination. This can cause packets to arrive out of order. Transmission Control Protocol (TCP) handles this automatically by waiting for out-of-order packets and reassembling them. For file transfers and most other communications, out-of-order packets do not cause a problem. However, with real-time communications, such as VoIP or streaming media (which typically use user datagram protocol or UDP), a packet that is received out of order and arrives after the jitter buffer has expired is useless and will be discarded by the client computer.

Dropped Packets

Routers drop packets only when the router's queue is full and no more packets can be stored. When TCP communications are dropped, this can worsen the network congestion problems, because dropped packets must be retransmitted.

How QoS Can Help

QoS can reduce the impact of network problems on high-priority traffic in several ways:

- **Reducing latency** By default, most routers forward traffic on a first-in, first-out (FIFO) basis. With QoS, routers can use a Differentiated Services Code Point (DSCP) value to forward high-priority traffic before low-priority traffic, even if the high-priority traffic arrived last. This increases the latency for the low-priority traffic but decreases it for the high-priority traffic. Adding bandwidth allows the router to empty the queue faster, but it cannot eliminate queuing. Computers that are transmitting traffic also queue packets sent by different applications and can use QoS priorities to transmit high-priority packets first.

> **Note** Even with QoS, bulk communications can still cause a slight forwarding delay at the router. For example, consider a user carrying on a VoIP conversation while trying to use HTTP to upload a large file across a 128 kilobits per second (Kbps) DSL link. After the router forwards all VoIP traffic, it will begin to transfer an HTTP packet, which will often be 1,500 bytes. If a VoIP packet arrives after the router begins forwarding the HTTP packet, it must finish sending the packet before it can forward the new VoIP packet, which would take about 100 ms in this example. That 100 ms forwarding delay could put the total latency above the acceptable latency for VoIP of about 150 ms. To minimize the impact of the latency incurred when transmitting a single large packet, some routers can be configured to fragment low-priority packets into smaller packets.

- **Reducing jitter** By using the same techniques used to reduce latency, QoS can also reduce jitter. Lower amounts of jitter allow you to decrease the time data is held in the jitter buffer, further decreasing total latency. Software often automatically adjusts the jitter buffer as network conditions change. Depending on the layout of your network, you might be able to reduce jitter by routing critical traffic across dedicated, low-latency links.

- **Reducing out-of-order delivery** If you mark communications with DSCP values, you can configure routers to use the same route for all communications of that type, minimizing both jitter and out-of-order delivery.

- **Reducing high-priority dropped packets** If you mark communications with DSCP values, you can configure many routers to drop lower-priority traffic before higher-priority traffic.

QoS for Outbound Traffic

On computers running the Windows Vista and Windows Server 2008 operating systems, you can implement QoS by using two techniques: DSCP and traffic throttling. Ideally, you would combine both to provide the highest level of service.

Figure 5-1 demonstrates how DSCP and traffic throttling can work together. In this example, a high-speed 100-Mbps LAN is connected to a relatively low-speed 1.54-Mbps Internet connection. Server administrators have used traffic throttling to limit to 512 Kbps each the traffic that is bound for the Internet from the Web server and the e-mail server. Therefore, even if the Web site is busy and many users are downloading their e-mail simultaneously, there will still be 512 Kbps of bandwidth remaining for the VoIP server to use. To reduce latency that might occur when the router queues traffic, traffic from each server is labeled with a DSCP number. The router uses these DSCP numbers to prioritize the traffic so that latency-sensitive VoIP traffic always leaves the queue first.

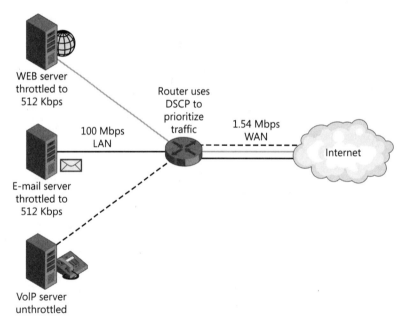

Figure 5-1   DSCP and traffic throttling working together

The sections that follow describe DSCP and traffic throttling in more detail.

DSCP

RFC 2474 defines the Differentiated Services Code Point (DSCP), which adds a value to the IP header of outgoing datagrams that routers can use to prioritize traffic. For example, you could configure Windows Server 2008 to add the DSCP value 10 to FTP traffic and the DSCP value 46 to streaming media traffic. When a router forwards this traffic, it can place traffic with a DSCP value of 10 in the low-priority queue and traffic with a DSCP value of 46 in the high-priority queue.

DSCP is specified by a number from 0 to 63 in the IP header, where 0 indicates that no DSCP value has been provided. In IPv4, DSCP uses the type of service (TOS, defined in RFC 791) octet in the header, as shown in Figure 5-2. In IPv6, DSCP uses the traffic class octet in the header. Though DSCP uses a full eight-bit octet in both IPv4 and IPv6, DSCP uses only the first six bits. The remaining two bits are Explicit Congestion Notification (ECN) bits.

More Info   For more information about ECN, visit *http://www.microsoft.com/technet/community/columns/cableguy/cg1006.mspx*.

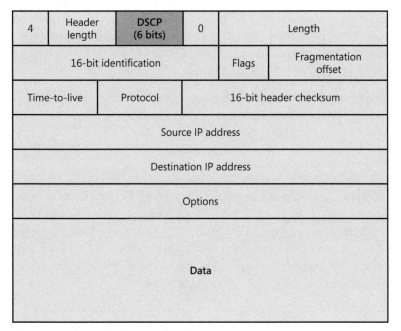

Figure 5-2   DSCP in the IPv4 header

Traffic Throttling

Whereas DSCP allows your routing infrastructure to prioritize traffic, Windows Vista and Windows Server 2008 can also use throttling to limit the amount of bandwidth used by specific applications and protocols. With throttling, a QoS policy limits outgoing network traffic that matches the specified criteria to a given rate.

For example, if you have a 10-Mbps LAN, you could prevent your e-mail servers from consuming all available network bandwidth by placing them into their own organizational unit (OU) and linking a Group Policy Object (GPO) to that OU. In the GPO, configure a QoS policy that throttles e-mail communications (which you can configure using TCP port numbers) to 4 Mbps.

QoS for Inbound Traffic

DSCP values give you some control over how your network infrastructure handles outgoing traffic, whereas traffic throttling directly reduces the outgoing bandwidth used by different applications. Although you cannot directly control the rate of inbound traffic, Windows can adjust the TCP receive window to slow down the rate of incoming traffic.

By default, Windows will optimize the TCP receive window for maximum throughput. However, you can use system-wide QoS settings in computers running Windows Vista or Windows Server 2008 to limit incoming traffic by specifying the maximum size of the TCP receive window. The TCP receive window is the amount of data that a receiver allows a sender to transmit before being required to wait for an acknowledgement. A larger maximum window size means that the sender can send more data at a time, increasing network utilization and throughput. By limiting the maximum size of the TCP receive window, a receiver can indirectly control the incoming throughput for a TCP connection.

For more information about configuring the maximum TCP receive window size, read "How to Configure System-Wide QoS Settings" later in this chapter.

QoS Implementation

On Windows Vista and Windows Server 2008, QoS is implemented in the Pacer.sys NDIS 6.0 lightweight filter driver, located in *%SystemRoot%*\System32\Drivers. Pacer.sys controls QoS packet scheduling for both policy-based QoS and applications that use the Generic QoS (GQoS), Traffic Control (TC), and qWAVE (Quality Windows Audio Video Experience) APIs. Pacer.sys is used only when the QoS Packet Scheduler component of a network connection or adapter is enabled (which it is by default). Pacer.sys replaces Psched.sys, which is used in the Windows Server 2003 and Windows XP operating systems.

> **Note**   Quality Windows Audio Video Experience (qWAVE) is a QoS API designed to improve the performance of audio and video streaming across home networks. On computers running Windows Server 2008, qWAVE provides only rate-of-flow and prioritization services. Because it is designed primarily for home use, it is not discussed further in this chapter.

Planning and Design Considerations

QoS can be deployed to Windows computers with just a few clicks, but without proper planning, you might not realize any performance benefits. This section describes how to identify goals for your QoS implementation, specify DSCP values, plan traffic throttling, verify hardware and software requirements, and design QoS policies.

Setting QoS Goals

When planning QoS policies for your network, determine the applications that require QoS, and set latency and bandwidth goals for each application as follows:

- **Latency goals**   Minimizing latency is critical for VoIP and video conferencing. Although lower latency is always better, the maximum end-to-end delay that humans can tolerate is 150–200 ms. Above 200 ms, people will be irritated by the delay. Conversations with excess latency become awkward, and people frequently begin speaking at the same time.

- **Bandwidth goals**   These goals will depend on your specific applications but might include a minimum number of simultaneous media streams or maximum time to transfer a network backup of a specific size.

After you have implemented QoS, you can use these goals to determine whether the implementation was a success or additional changes are required.

Planning DSCP Values

Table 5-1 lists standard DSCP values for different applications in order from highest to lowest priority. Rows shown in bold are the most commonly used.

Table 5-1   DSCP Interoperability Values

Purpose	Common Uses	DSCP Value
IP routing	Router-to-router communications.	48
VoIP	**VoIP traffic, including signaling and control traffic.**	**46**
Interactive video	**Two-way video conferencing.**	**34**
Streaming video	One-way video streaming. Alternatively, you can classify streaming video as mission critical data.	32
Mission-critical data	**Database queries, line-of-business communications, video streaming.**	**26**
Transactional data	Database queries and transactions. Alternatively, you can classify transactional data as mission-critical data.	28
Call signaling	VoIP control traffic, which can also be classified as VoIP.	24
Network management	Network management protocols such as simple network management protocol (SNMP). Alternatively, you can classify network management traffic as mission-critical data.	16
Best effort	**All other traffic, including e-mail and Web browsing.**	**0**
Bulk data	**Backups, non-business applications, file transfers.**	**10**
Scavenger	Low-priority traffic. Alternatively, you can classify all low-priority traffic as bulk data.	8

> **Note** It's common practice to remove or rewrite DSCP values from traffic originating from remote networks such as the Internet because the DSCP value might have a different meaning, or it might even be part of a denial-of-service (DoS) attack. Therefore, you can't be sure that DSCP values will be retained or respected when sending traffic to networks that you don't manage.

Wireless Multimedia and DSCP Values

Wireless Multimedia (WMM) includes four access categories for prioritizing traffic on 802.11 wireless networks. WMM uses DSCP values to set priority, so you can automatically take advantage of WMM by specifying DSCP values. Table 5-2 shows how DSCP values correspond to WMM access categories.

Table 5-2   DSCP Values and WMM Access Categories

DSCP Value	WMM Access Category
48–63	Voice (VO)
32–47	Video (VI)
24–31, 0–7	Best effort (BE)
8–23	Background (BK)

You do not need to specify a separate DSCP number for every protocol on your network. Instead, you should specify DSCP numbers for a different traffic priority types. For example, a typical DSCP strategy includes the following five queues:

- **Control traffic**   Communications transmitted between routers. Typically these communications require minimal bandwidth, but they should be assigned a high priority because quick transmission can reduce downtime in the event of a hardware failure. You should also use this priority for VoIP control traffic. Use DSCP values of 26 for control traffic.

- **Latency-sensitive traffic**   Traffic, such as VoIP, that must be delivered as quickly as possible. Typically, you should assign this a DSCP value of 46, known as Expedited Forwarding (EF).

- **Business critical traffic, also known as Better than Best Effort (BBE)**   Communications that should receive priority treatment, such as customer service database queries from a line-of-business (LOB) application or streaming video, but that are not highly sensitive to latency. Use a DSCP value of 34.

- **Best effort traffic**   Standard traffic, including any traffic not marked with a DSCP number, that should be handled after either of the preceding two queues. This traffic should have a DSCP value of 0, which is the default if no DSCP value has been specified.

- **Scavenger traffic**   Low-priority traffic, such as backups, downloading of updates, non-critical file synchronization, and non–work-related traffic that employees might generate. Use a DSCP value of 10 or 8.

> **Note**   If you mark traffic from too many applications as high-priority, the high-priority queue on routers can grow long enough to add significant latency. This defeats the purpose of QoS. Therefore, you should reserve the highest priority DSCP marking for real-time communications such as VoIP.

Many networks use an even simpler structure, with only two priorities: one for latency-sensitive traffic and another for best effort traffic. However, if you have third-party tools that can use DSCP values to report on network performance for different types of traffic, it is advantageous to define a larger number of DSCP values even if your network infrastructure isn't configured to handle each DSCP value uniquely.

Planning Traffic Throttling

Ideally, networks should always be fully utilized—even if the traffic is considered low-priority. Prioritizing traffic by using DSCP values supports this philosophy by allowing lower-priority traffic to use all available bandwidth when no higher-priority traffic requires the bandwidth.

If sections of your network do not support prioritizing traffic with DSCP values, you can use traffic throttling to limit the amount of traffic being sent from your computers running Windows Vista and Windows Server 2008. Do not attempt to use traffic throttling to limit the bandwidth of every application or protocol; instead, use traffic throttling to limit only traffic from low-priority applications such as network backups or the downloading of large updates.

Remember, traffic throttling limits traffic on individual computers only. Traffic throttling cannot limit the aggregate bandwidth used by multiple computers. For example, if you have five FTP servers and you want to ensure that they never use more than half of your 500-kilobyte-per-second (KBps) link, you must configure the QoS policy to throttle traffic at 50 KBps for each of the five computers, which would total 250 KBps if all five servers were sending traffic at their throttled maximum.

Hardware and Software Requirements

The sections that follow describe operating system and application support for QoS policies, backwards compatibility for QoS APIs used in earlier versions of Windows, and network infrastructure requirements for QoS support.

Support for QoS Policies

You can apply QoS policies only to Windows Vista and Windows Server 2008. Earlier versions of Windows support QoS APIs that individual applications can use to set DSCP values and traffic throttling; however, they do not support the application of QoS policies through the use of GPOs. To implement QoS policies in a domain, your domain controller can be running Microsoft Windows 2000 Server, Windows Server 2003, or Windows Server 2008.

Applications running on Windows Vista and Windows Server 2008 do not need to support QoS to have their network traffic prioritized. You can use QoS policies to apply QoS to any network traffic, including network traffic generated by core operating system services (such as the Server service).

Backward Compatibility for QoS APIs

Windows 2000, Windows XP, and Windows Server 2003 provide QoS capabilities by using the Generic QoS (GQoS), IP Type Of Service (TOS), and Traffic Control (TC) application programming interfaces (APIs). Developers needed to create an application specifically to take advantage of one of these APIs, and most developers did not add this capability to their applications. Therefore, most applications did not support QoS. If you have an application that uses one of these APIs, the application will still work on Windows Vista and Windows Server 2008.

More Info   For more information about these APIs, see "The MS QoS Components" at *http://www.microsoft.com/technet/prodtechnol/windows2000serv/maintain/featusability/ qoscomp.mspx.*

Note   GQoS, IP TOS, and TC have been deprecated. Although they are still supported in Windows Vista, future versions of Windows might not support them. Therefore, if you have applications that use GQoS, TOS, or TC, you should encourage the developers to use the new QOS2 API instead. Developers can find QOS2 in the QOS2.h header file.

Network Infrastructure Requirements

To fully support QoS policies, your network infrastructure must support the use of multiple queues to prioritize traffic based on DSCP value (as defined in RFC 2474). Traffic throttling does not have any network infrastructure requirements.

Planning GPOs and QoS Policies

With Windows Vista and Windows Server 2008, you can use local or Active Directory GPOs to configure QoS for any application on your network. Combined with the flexibility of Group Policy, this allows you to:

- **Configure QoS policy for organizational units**   Most organizations use Active Directory OUs to organize users and computers. By linking a GPO to an OU and setting the QoS policy in that GPO, you can apply different QoS policies to different computers in your organization. For example, if you have separate OUs for e-mail and Web servers, you could link different GPOs to each OU to configure e-mail traffic (such as Microsoft Office Outlook Web Access or OWA) as a higher priority than standard Web traffic.

- **Configure QoS policy based on user group membership** By configuring GPOs with access control lists (ACLs) that restrict access based on group membership, you can use User Configuration QoS policies to give specific groups a higher priority than other groups. For example, you might assign a higher priority to traffic generated by your customer service team.

- **Configure QoS policy for sites** If different sites have the network infrastructure configured differently (for example, if they use different DSCP values), you can link GPOs to Active Directory sites to apply settings that will work correctly with that site.

- **Configure QoS policy for stand-alone computers** Windows Vista and Windows Server 2008 support multiple local GPOs (MLGPOs). You can use MLGPOs to configure QoS policies on computers that are not a member of your Active Directory domain.

When you configure a QoS policy, you assign a DSCP value or throttle rate and then specify the criteria that Windows will use to identify the traffic that the QoS policy applies to. The criteria you can use are:

- Sending application (by file name, such as *application.exe*)

- Source or destination IPv4 or IPv6 network or address

- Source or destination TCP or UDP port number or range

How it Works: QoS Policy Priorities

If a connection matches the criteria for multiple QoS policies, the most specific QoS policy is applied. For example, if you create a policy for an entire network (such as 192.168.1.0/24) and a second policy for a specific IP address (such as 192.168.1.5), the IP address policy, rather than the network policy, will be applied. The specific rules that Windows follows when applying QoS policies are:

1. User-level QoS policies take precedence over computer-level QoS policies.

2. QoS policies that identify applications take precedence over QoS policies that identify networks or IP addresses.

3. QoS policies that specify IP addresses and more-specific networks take precedence over QoS policies that specify less-specific networks.

4. QoS policies that specify port numbers take precedence over QoS polices that specify port ranges, which take precedence over QoS policies that do not specify a port number.

5. If multiple QoS policies still conflict, policies that specify source IP addresses take precedence over policies that specify destination IP addresses, and policies that specify a source port take precedence over policies that specify a destination port.

> Only one QoS policy can be applied to any given connection. For example, if two traffic throttling policies apply to a single connection, the most specific policy will set the throttle rate—it is not cumulative.

To reduce the number of conflicts and simplify QoS deployment, design your QoS policies to be as specific as possible. For example, instead of applying a QoS policy to all traffic from a computer, apply the QoS policy to traffic with a specific port number from that computer.

QoS Policies for Mobile Computers Running Windows Vista

Computers running Windows Server 2008 always apply QoS policies to all network interfaces. However, computers running Windows Vista operate slightly differently because they are designed to be mobile, so they might connect to networks outside of your organization. Different organizations might use different DSCP numbers or might not use QoS policies at all. Therefore, Windows Vista applies QoS policies only while connected to your internal network. Specifically, Windows Vista applies QoS policies only for domain network types. Windows Vista identifies a network as being part of a domain when it can contact a domain controller across that interface. Therefore, if a user connects to a wireless network at a coffee shop, Windows Vista will not apply your QoS policies. However, if the user connects to your internal network by using a VPN, Windows Vista will apply QoS policies to that VPN.

More Info   For more information about network types in Windows Vista, refer to Chapter 26, "Configuring Windows Networking," in the *Windows Vista Resource Kit* by Mitch Tulloch, Tony Northrup, and Jerry Honeycutt, with the Microsoft Windows Vista Team (Microsoft Press, 2007).

Deployment Steps

After proper planning, it only takes a few minutes to implement QoS policies by using Group Policy settings. This section describes how to use GPOs to configure QoS policies that define DSCP values and traffic throttling. It also describes how to configure system-wide QoS settings such as the inbound TCP throughput level.

How to Configure QoS by Using Group Policy

For QoS to be effective, you should configure as many computers as possible to assign DSCP values to traffic and, when prioritizing traffic is not sufficient, throttling outbound traffic.

To Configure QoS by Using Group Policy

1. In the console tree of the Group Policy Management Editor snap-in for the GPO to which you want to add the policy, open the Computer Configuration\Windows Settings\Policy-based QoS node or the User Configuration\Windows Settings\ Policy-based QoS node.

> **Note**   User QoS policies are applied to user processes only when the user is logged on. For servers, you should almost always configure Computer QoS policies.

2. Right-click the Policy-Based QoS node, and then click Create New Policy.

3. The Policy-Based QoS Wizard appears. On the Create A QoS Policy page, shown in Figure 5-3, specify a unique name for the policy. Then, specify one of the DSCP values shown in Table 5-1 (which your network infrastructure can use to prioritize traffic) and a throttle rate in either KBps or megabytes per second (MBps) (which Windows Vista will use to restrict outgoing bandwidth usage) as needed. Click Next.

> **Note**   Notice that throttle rate must be entered in kilobytes per second (KBps) or megabytes per second (MBps) rather than the more commonly used kilobits per second (Kbps) or megabits per second (Mbps)—notice the lowercase *b*. Eight bits equals one byte. Therefore, if you determine the Kbps or Mbps that you want to throttle at, divide that number by 8 when typing it into the Policy-Based QoS Wizard. For example, if you want to throttle at 128 Kbps, you would type **16 KBps**.

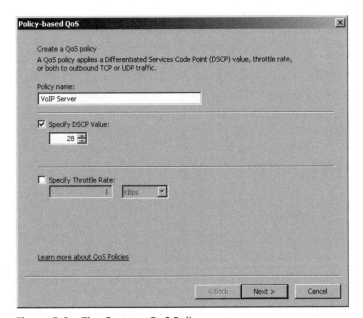

Figure 5-3   The Create a QoS Policy page

4. On the This QoS Policy Applies To page, shown in Figure 5-4, select either All Applications or Only Applications With This Executable Name. If you are specifying an application, Windows Vista will apply the DSCP value or throttle rate to network traffic generated by that application. If you must throttle a service, check the service properties

by viewing them in the Services snap-in. If the service has its own executable file (other than svchost.exe), you can specify that file. Otherwise, you can identify the traffic to apply the policy to by using the next two wizard pages. Click Next.

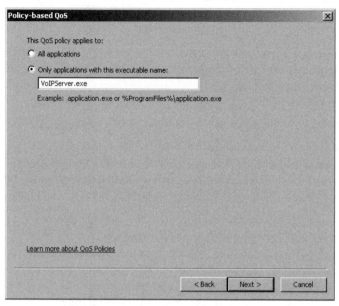

Figure 5-4   The This QoS Policy Applies To page

5. On the Specify The Source And Destination IP Addresses page, shown in Figure 5-5, you can configure the policy to apply to traffic to or from a specific IP address or network. For example, if you want to configure a QoS policy that throttles traffic sent across a VPN, you would select Only For The Following Destination IP Address Or Prefix, and then type the destination network for the VPN. IPv4 and IPv6 addresses will both work, and you can use network prefix length representation to specify networks. With network prefix length representation, you would specify 192.168.1.0/24 to mean the entire 192.168.1.x network or 192.168.0.0/16 to mean the entire 192.168.x.x network. For more information, read "Subnets and Subnet Masks" at *http://www.microsoft.com/ technet/prodtechnol/windows2000serv/reskit/cnet/cnbb_tcp_prux.mspx*. Click Next.

> **Note**   QoS policies apply only to outgoing traffic. So the computer to which you're applying the policy will always be identified by the source address, and the remote computer or network will always be identified by the destination address. Specify a source address if you want to identify the computers to which to apply the policy by using a technique other than the scope of the GPO.

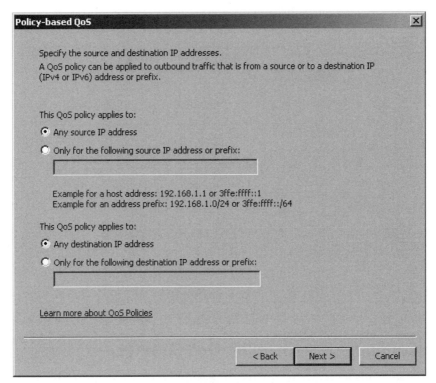

Figure 5-5   The Specify The Source And Destination IP Addresses page

6. On the Specify The Protocol And Port Numbers page, shown in Figure 5-6, you can identify traffic based on TCP or UDP port numbers. For example, if you want to throttle all outgoing Web traffic from a Web server, you would select TCP, select From This Source Port Number Or Range, and then specify port 80 (the port number HTTP Web traffic uses). Click Finish.

> **Note**   When configuring QoS policies for servers, specify the source port number, and allow any destination port number. When configuring QoS policies for clients, specify the destination port number, and allow any source port number.

After creating a policy, you can edit it by right-clicking it in the details pane of the Group Policy Management Editor and then clicking Edit Existing Policy. The Edit An Existing QoS Policy dialog box has tabs that correspond to each of the pages in the Policy-Based QoS Wizard. For more information, see "Editing QoS Policies" and "Removing QoS Policies" later in this chapter.

> **Note**   Currently, using GPOs is the only way to configure QoS policies. Microsoft does not provide tools for configuring QoS policies by using scripts.

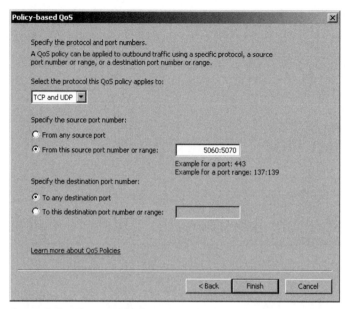

Figure 5-6   The Specify The Protocol And Port Numbers page

How to Configure System-Wide QoS Settings

You can configure system-wide QoS settings within the Computer Configuration\Administrative Templates\Network\QoS Packet Scheduler node of Group Policy. You must modify these settings only if you must limit the outstanding packets, limit the bandwidth that can be reserved, or change the Packet Scheduler timer resolution. The policies available in the QoS Packet Scheduler node are as follows:

- **Limit outstanding packets**   Specifies the maximum number of outstanding packets that can be issued to the network adapter at any given time. When this limit is reached, new packets are queued up in Pacer.sys until the network adapter completes a packet, at which point a previously queued packet is removed from the Pacer.sys queue and sent to the network adapter. This setting is disabled by default, and you should never need to enable this setting.

- **Limit reservable bandwidth**   Controls the percentage of the overall bandwidth that the application can reserve. By default, this is set to 20%, which provides 80 percent of bandwidth to processes that do not have reserved bandwidth.

- **Set timer resolution**   This value is not supported and should not be set.

The QoS Packet Scheduler node also has three sub-nodes that you can use to manually configure the standard DSCP values. The sub-nodes are:

- **DSCP value of conforming packets**   These settings apply to packets that comply with flow specifications.

- **DSCP value of non-conforming packets** These settings apply to packets that do not comply with flow specifications.

- **Layer-2 priority value** These settings specify default link layer priority values for networks that support it.

You would need to change the values contained in these sub-nodes only if you have configured your network infrastructure to use non-standard DSCP values.

You can also configure advanced QoS settings for computers by using Group Policy. Within the Group Policy Management Editor, right-click the Computer Configuration\Windows Settings\Policy-based QoS node, and then click Advanced QoS Settings. You can use the resultant Advanced QoS Settings dialog box to:

- **Specify the inbound TCP throughput level** Most QoS policies relate to outbound traffic that the client computer sends. You can use this setting on the Inbound TCP Traffic tab to configure Windows so that it will attempt to throttle incoming traffic by adjusting the TCP receive window size, as discussed in "QoS for Inbound Traffic" earlier in this chapter. Table 5-3 lists the maximum TCP receive window for each inbound throughput level. By default, Windows will use the level 3 (maximum throughput) for TCP receive window size. Unlike policy-based QoS settings for outgoing traffic, this setting cannot control the rate of incoming traffic on a per-application, per-address, or per-port basis.

Table 5-3 Maximum TCP Receive Windows

Inbound Throughput Level	Maximum
0	64 KB
1	256 KB
2	1 MB
3	16 MB

> **Note** Because UDP traffic is not acknowledged, you cannot throttle UDP traffic from the receiving computer.

- **Control DSCP marking requests from applications** Applications can request their own DSCP values for outgoing network communications, but most applications do not specify a value. By default, Windows will use the DSCP value specified by an application. If you want Windows to ignore the DSCP value specified by the application and rely only on QoS policies to set DSCP values, select the Control DSCP Marking Requests From Applications check box, and then select Ignored, as shown in Figure 5-7.

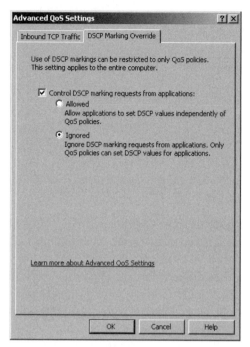

Figure 5-7   Ignoring application-specified DSCP values

Ongoing Maintenance

Ongoing maintenance for QoS consists of updating or removing QoS policies as necessary and monitoring QoS policies to ensure that they are applied and functioning properly. The sections that follow describe ongoing maintenance in more detail.

Removing QoS Policies

You can remove QoS policies by using the Group Policy Management console.

To Remove a Policy

1. In Administrative Tools, open the Group Policy Management console.

2. Right-click the GPO containing the policy, and then click Edit.

3. In the Group Policy Management Editor, expand either User Configuration or Computer Configuration, expand Windows Settings, and then click Policy-Based QoS.

4. In the Details pane, right-click the policy you want to remove, and then click Delete Policy.

5. Click Yes when prompted.

Editing QoS Policies

You can edit QoS policies by using the Group Policy Management console.

To Edit a QoS Policy

1. In Administrative Tools, open the Group Policy Management console.

2. Right-click the GPO that you want to add the policy to, and then click Edit.

3. In the Group Policy Management Editor, expand either User Configuration or Computer Configuration, expand Windows Settings, and then click Policy-Based QoS.

4. In the Details pane, right-click the policy that you want to edit, and then click Edit Existing Policy.

5. Make any required changes, and then click OK.

The changes will be applied the next time computers refresh Group Policy. To immediately refresh Group Policy settings on a computer, run the command **gpupdate /force** from a command prompt with administrative privileges.

Monitoring QoS

You can monitor QoS by using Performance Monitor (built into Windows), Network Monitor (a free download from Microsoft), or third-party monitoring tools. The sections that follow describe each of these tools.

Performance Monitor

The Performance Monitor snap-in (available within the Computer Management console under Reliability And Performance\Monitoring Tools) provide some useful counters for gathering information about network performance:

- **Network Interface\Bytes Sent/sec** and **Network Interface\Packets Sent/sec**   Show the total amount of traffic transmitted, including data that does and does not have QoS policies applied.

- **Pacer Flow\Bytes Transmitted** and **Pacer Flow\Packets Transmitted**   Relative to the Network Interface counters, these counters are useful for gauging the portion of outgoing traffic that has a QoS policy applied.

- **Pacer Pipe\Nonconforming packets scheduled** and **Pacer Pipe\Nonconforming packets scheduled/sec**   If these values are increasing, it means that QoS is enforcing traffic throttling by slowing down the transmission of packets.

Network Monitor

Microsoft Network Monitor is a protocol analyzer, also known as a *sniffer*. Network Monitor captures raw network data and allows you to examine it. As shown in Figure 5-8, you can use

Network Monitor to examine the DSCP values in the IP header. In the figure, notice that the selected IPv4 packet has a DSCP value of 10 (bulk traffic). Therefore, you can use Network Monitor to verify that DSCP values are being applied and to perform detailed troubleshooting.

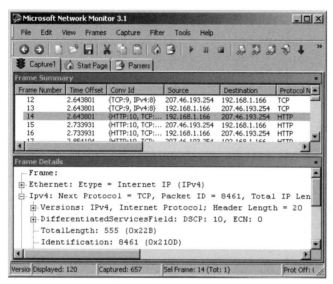

Figure 5-8   Viewing the DSCP value in Network Monitor

You can also use Network Monitor to determine the TCP receive window being used, which you can configure by following the instructions in "How to Configure System-Wide QoS Settings" earlier in this chapter. After capturing traffic, examine the Window value in the TCP header, as shown in Figure 5-9. Windows will dynamically adjust this value, but it should always be below the value shown in Table 5-3 for the configured setting.

To download Network Monitor, visit *http://www.microsoft.com/downloads/*, and search for "Network Monitor." For detailed instructions on how to use Network Monitor to capture and analyze network communications, refer to the Help site.

Third-Party Monitoring Tools

Monitoring individual computers can provide some useful information about how QoS policies are being applied. However, only by monitoring your network infrastructure can you develop a comprehensive view of your network performance and the impact of QoS policies. Contact your network infrastructure provider for information about monitoring tools that provide insight into QoS performance.

You can also use third-party tools to monitor the performance of specific applications. For example, several developers (including Agilent and NetIQ) offer software that monitors VoIP performance. If you are implementing QoS to provide VoIP, use monitoring tools such as these to verify that you are meeting your performance requirements. If performance is low, increase bandwidth, reduce the amount of network traffic that QoS policies label as high priority, or both.

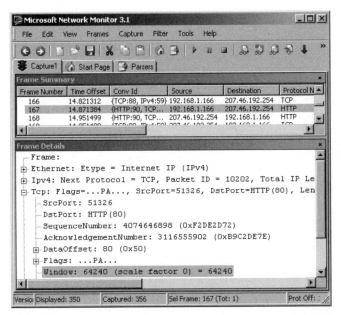

Figure 5-9   Viewing the TCP receive window in Network Monitor

Troubleshooting

QoS policies should never cause outright connectivity problems. However, if QoS does not meet your performance expectations, you can analyze the policies and the configuration of your network infrastructure to verify that your implementation matches your design. The sections that follow describe techniques for troubleshooting problems with QoS policies and network performance.

Analyzing QoS Policies

You can use the Group Policy Results Wizard to generate a report of QoS policies applied to a computer or user.

To Display QoS Policies

1. In Administrative Tools, open the Group Policy Management console.
2. Right-click the Group Policy Results node, and then click Group Policy Results Wizard.
3. On the Welcome To The Group Policy Results Wizard page, click Next.
4. On the Computer Selection page, accept the default setting by clicking Next.
5. On the User Selection page, accept the default setting by clicking Next.
6. On the Summary Of Selections page, click Next.
7. On the Completing The Group Policy Results Wizard page, click Finish.

8. In the Group Policy Management console, press Enter to accept the default name for report.

9. On the Settings tab, under both Computer Configuration and User Configuration, click Show For Policy-Based QoS. Then, click Show For QoS Policies.

10. As shown in Figure 5-10, the Group Policy Management console displays all QoS Polices that are applied to the computer or user.

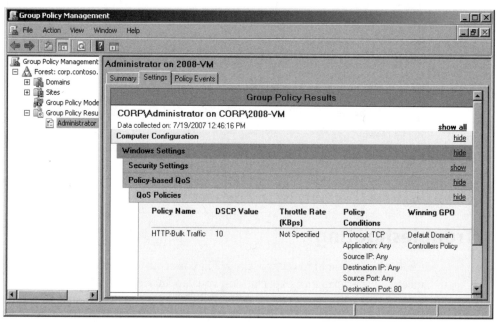

Figure 5-10 Viewing Group Policy Results

The Group Policy Management console shows the QoS policies with their DSCP value, throttle rate, policy conditions, and winning GPO (the GPO with the highest priority). For more information about QoS policy priorities, read "Planning GPOs and QoS Policies" earlier in this chapter.

Direct from the Source: Capturing QoS Tags with Network Monitor

Consider a case where a network application calls Windows QoS APIs to add a layer-2 IEEE 802.1Q UserPriority tag (almost always referred to as 802.1p) to outgoing traffic. Ascertaining whether the tag was actually added to an outgoing packet is not as simple as it seems due to the nature of how the Windows network stack is designed and how framing actually occurs. From an internal implementation perspective, the QoS Packet Scheduler (Pacer.sys in Vista/2008 Server, and Psched.sys in XP/2003 Server) in the network stack merely updates an out-of-band structure (not the actual formed packet) that an 802.1Q UserPriority tag should be added. The specific NDIS structure is NDIS_NET_BUFFER_LIST_8021Q_INFO, which contains member variables for both VlanID and UserPriority and is passed to the NDIS miniport driver for implementing both priority tagging (UserPriority) and VLAN (VlanId). It is up to the NDIS miniport driver to actually insert the 802.1Q tag into the frame based on these values before transmitting on the wire. A miniport driver will only insert this tag if the feature is supported and enabled in the advanced properties of the NIC driver; typically, layer-2 priority tagging is disabled by default.

From a network stack layering perspective, it's important to understand that Pacer.sys is an NDIS Lightweight Filter (LWF) driver and will always be inserted above a miniport driver, which will always be the lowest network software in the stack because it communicates directly with the NIC hardware. Also note that network sniffing applications like Microsoft Network Monitor are also network stack filters, and will always be inserted above the miniport driver. This is important knowledge because it should be clear that taking a network sniff of traffic on the sending computer will never show the tag in a packet (because the tag is added below the sniffing software).

What about trying to do a network sniff on the receiving computer? This is a good question, but it also will not show the layer-2 tag. The reason for this is that NDIS developer documentation clearly states that miniport drivers must strip the tag when received and populate the NDIS_NET_BUFFER_LIST_8021Q_INFO UserPriority and VlanId fields with the values in the tag. This out-of-band structure can then be used by NDIS filter drivers higher up in the stack for implementing these features. The functional reason for stripping the layer-2 tag is because Tcpip.sys will drop any received packet that contains this tag. Therefore, if a misbehaving miniport driver does not strip the tag, the packet will never be received by the user-mode application because it will be dropped internally.

In conclusion:

- A network sniffing app on the sending PC will never see a tag.

- A network sniffing app on the receiving PC will never see a tag.

- Monitoring tagged packets from intermediate network elements (such as a switch) is hard if at all possible.

Gabe Frost, Product Manager

Core Windows Networking

Verifying DSCP Resilience

If you are not experiencing the performance benefit you expect from a QoS policy, first verify that the QoS policy is being applied correctly. Follow the steps in the section titled "Analyzing QoS Policies" earlier in this chapter to verify that the target computer has the appropriate QoS policies applied and that they match the traffic you are attempting to prioritize.

Next, use Network Monitor to verify that outgoing traffic has the correct DSCP value assigned to it. For more information, see "Network Monitor" earlier in this chapter. If the DSCP value is not assigned, the QoS policies are not being applied correctly. Verify that the GPO is being applied to the computer and that the QoS policy matches the traffic by application, port number, or IP address.

Because it's possible for network infrastructure to remove the DSCP value from packets, you also must verify that the DSCP value is intact when packets reach the remote host. If the remote host is a computer running Windows, you can use Network Monitor to verify the DSCP value of the packets as they are received. If the remote host is not a computer running Windows, use another protocol analyzer. If the packets do not have the DSCP value intact when they reach the remote host, the network infrastructure is removing the DSCP value. Contact your network administrators for troubleshooting assistance.

If the DSCP value is intact when it reaches the remote host, the network infrastructure might not be correctly configured to prioritize traffic or might not support QoS. For best results, every router between the client and server should support QoS and be configured to prioritize packets based on their DSCP value. From the client, you can use the PathPing tool to determine a likely path between the client and server, as the following example demonstrates. (Code in bold indicates user input.)

pathping www.contoso.com

```
Tracing route to contoso.com [10.46.196.103]over a maximum of 30 hops:
  0  contoso-test [192.168.1.207]
  1  10.211.240.1
  2  10.128.191.245
  3  10.128.191.73
  4  10.125.39.213
  5  gbr1-p70.cb1ma.ip.contoso.com [10.123.40.98]
  6  tbr2-p013501.cb1ma.ip.contoso.com [10.122.11.201]
  7  tbr2-p012101.cgcil.ip.contoso.com [10.122.10.106]
  8  gbr4-p50.st6wa.ip.contoso.com [10.122.2.54]
  9  gar1-p370.stwwa.ip.contoso.com [10.123.203.177]
 10  10.127.70.6
 11  10.46.33.225
 12  10.46.36.210
 13  10.46.155.17
 14  10.46.129.51
 15  10.46.196.103
```

The performance information that PathPing shows isn't necessarily useful when troubleshooting QoS issues because PathPing uses Internet Control Message Protocol (ICMP) packets that might be assigned a lower or higher priority than the traffic you are troubleshooting. Less frequently, the route between any two paths can vary depending on network conditions, or QoS settings might actually choose a different route for the traffic you are testing than for ICMP traffic.

Once you have used PathPing to identify a possible route between the client and the server, examine each router configuration to verify that it is not removing DSCP values and that it is correctly prioritizing traffic based on DSCP. If possible, use a protocol analyzer to verify that traffic reaching each router still has the DSCP value intact.

Isolating Network Performance Problems

The most common concern with QoS is that high-priority traffic has too much latency or is not receiving sufficient bandwidth. First, follow the steps in "Analyzing QoS Policies" and "Verifying DSCP Resilience" earlier in this chapter to ensure that you have correctly configured QoS policies and your network infrastructure. Then, check for the following common problems:

- **Latency is near physical limits.** As discussed in "Latency" earlier in this chapter, increased distance causes increased latency because of the limitation of the physical speed of the signal. To minimize this impact, ensure that your routing is efficient. For example, if you have two offices on the East Coast and one office on the West Coast, routing traffic sent between the two East Coast offices through the West Coast office would incur a significant latency penalty. To rectify this, you could add a link directly between the East Coast offices. Similarly, routing traffic through a VPN almost always makes a route less efficient.

- **Bandwidth is near realistic limits.** If you cannot achieve throughput near your expectations, verify that your expectations are realistic for your network types. Wired Ethernet networks can achieve only 65 to 80 percent of their theoretical limits, whereas wireless networks are typically capable of only 35 to 50 percent of the stated bandwidth. Internet connections, including VPNs that use the Internet, are highly variable and dependent not only on your Internet service provider (ISP) but every ISP that might handle traffic between the source and destination.

- **The computer is busy.** If a computer has high processor utilization, it may not be able to handle incoming traffic efficiently, or it may reduce the responsiveness of the client or server application. You can eliminate this possible source of problems by stopping services or applications during testing.

- **The high-priority queues on routers are overused.** Most routers that support QoS will allow you to monitor the amount of traffic in each priority queue. The more packets in the queue, the higher the latency. To alleviate this, either increase the bandwidth on the destination network, or reduce the amount of high-priority traffic.

- **Drivers may be inefficient.** Verify that computers have updated versions of network interface drivers. Additionally, verify that router firmware is updated.

Chapter Summary

Used properly, the policy-based QoS built into Windows Vista and Windows Server 2008 can improve efficiency of your network and the quality of network applications such as VoIP. Once you understand the common causes of network performance problems, including latency and jitter, you can create a plan to use QoS to optimize your available bandwidth.

A QoS deployment must include configuring both your network infrastructure and the computers on your network. Fortunately, you can use Group Policy settings to set QoS policies for computers running Windows Vista and computers running Windows Server 2008.

After deployment, you can monitor QoS performance by using Performance Monitor, Network Monitor, or third-party monitoring tools. If necessary, you can edit or remove QoS policies to achieve the QoS goals you set in the planning stage. If you are not achieving your goals, you can troubleshoot the performance problem by analyzing your QoS policies, verifying DSCP resilience, and isolating the specific network links that are introducing the problem.

Additional Information

For additional information about QoS support in Windows, see the following:

- "Quality of Service" at *http://technet.microsoft.com/en-us/network/bb530836.aspx*
- RFC 2474, "Definition of the Differentiated Services Field (DS Field) in the IPv4 and IPv6 Headers," at *http://www.ietf.org/rfc/rfc2474.txt*
- "The MS QoS Components" at *http://www.microsoft.com/technet/prodtechnol/windows2000serv/maintain/featusability/qoscomp.mspx*
- "Quality of Service in Windows Server 'Longhorn' and Windows Vista" at *http://www.microsoft.com/downloads/details.aspx?familyid=0230e025-9549-400b-807e-97e8a0cb9703*
- "Windows Vista Policy-based Quality of Service (QoS)" at *http://www.microsoft.com/downloads/details.aspx?FamilyID=59030735-8fde-47c7-aa96-d4108f779f20*
- "Policy-based QoS Architecture in Windows Server 2008 and Windows Vista: The Cable Guy, March 2006" at *http://www.microsoft.com/technet/community/columns/cableguy/cg0306.mspx*
- Network Quality of Service MSDN community forum at *http://forums.microsoft.com/MSDN/ShowForum.aspx?ForumID=825&SiteID=1*

For additional information about managing Group Policy in Windows, see the following:

- Microsoft Windows Server Group Policy at *http://www.microsoft.com/grouppolicy*
- Enterprise Management with the Group Policy Management Console at *http://go.microsoft.com/fwlink/?LinkID=8630*

Chapter 6
Scalable Networking

This chapter provides information about how to design, deploy, maintain, and troubleshoot networking features in the Windows Server 2008 operating system that are designed to support network throughput of over 1 gigabit while minimizing overhead on the computer's main processors. This chapter assumes that you have a solid understanding of Transmission Control Protocol/Internet Protocol (TCP/IP).

Concepts

As network speeds increase, and applications take advantage of that increased bandwidth, the efficiency of client and server software must also increase. For example, consider a computer running the Windows Server 2003 operating system processing network traffic from several fully utilized gigabit or 10-gigabit Ethernet adapters:

- The large number of interrupts from the network adapters indicating that new packets have arrived can consume a significant amount of processor time.

- Processing of network data is limited to a single CPU core, even though many servers now have eight or more cores, limiting scalability.

- The act of moving data from the network adapter to the operating system requires memory copying, which is performed by the computer's processor and thus increases processor utilization.

- If Internet Protocol security (IPsec) communication is used, even more processing time is required for authentication and encryption.

These technical challenges lead to several real-world problems:

- Storage area networks (SANs) are inefficient because of the high overhead of TCP/IP, which slows storage consolidation efforts.

- Applications that use a significant amount of bandwidth, such as network backups, also incur significant processing overhead, slowing all applications.

- Storage, processing, and bandwidth might allow for server consolidation. However, the increased overhead of the cumulative network utilization, which must be handled by a single processor, would become a bottleneck.

- File and Web servers, which should be able to saturate any speed network, become bottlenecked on the utilization of a single processor. Therefore, multiple servers would be required to work around this performance limitation.

The sections that follow describe important network concepts related to scalable networking.

> **More Info**   TCP Chimney Offload, Receive-Side Scaling (RSS), and NetDMA were first intro-duced with the Windows Server 2003 Scalable Networking Pack. For more information, read "Windows Server 2003 Scalable Networking Pack Overview" at *http://www.microsoft.com/ technet/community/columns/cableguy/cg0606.mspx*. The Microsoft Windows 2000, Windows XP, and Windows Server 2003 operating systems are each capable of supporting IPsec Offload.

TCP Chimney Offload

One of the reasons processor overhead is so significant when processing network communi-cations is that the computer's processors must assemble the data from multiple TCP packets into a single segment. Figure 6-1 shows the TCP Chimney Offload architecture, which allows the network adapter to handle the task of segmenting TCP data for outgoing packets, reassem-bling data from incoming packets, and acknowledging sent and received data.

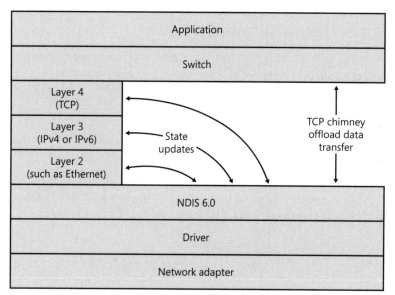

Figure 6-1   TCP Chimney Offload architecture

How It Works: TCP Chimney Offload

With TCP Chimney Offload, the network adapter hands the data directly to a higher layer switch and communicates state updates only to the intermediate protocol layers, offloading much of the TCP overhead from the computer's processor. The switch layer chooses between the conventional software code path (in which data is passed through intermediate protocol layers) and the more efficient chimney. Without TCP Chimney Offload, all data transfer would need to travel through the Layers 2, 3, and 4 protocols.

TCP Chimney Offload supports both 32-bit and 64-bit versions of the Windows Vista and Windows Server 2008 operating systems and both 32-bit and 64-bit input/output (I/O) buses. TCP Chimney Offload is completely transparent to both systems administrators and application developers. TCP Chimney Offload is not compatible with QoS or adapter teaming drivers developed for earlier versions of Windows.

> **Note**   As the name suggests, TCP Chimney Offload does not change how non-TCP packets, including Address Resolution Protocol (ARP), Dynamic Host Configuration Protocol (DHCP), Internet Control Message Protocol (ICMP), and User Datagram Protocol (UDP), are handled.

TCP Chimney Offload still requires the operating system to process every application I/O. Therefore, it primarily benefits large transfers, and chatty applications that transmit small amounts of data will see little benefit. For example, file or streaming media servers can benefit significantly. However, a database server that is sending 100–500 bytes of data to and from the database might see little or no benefit.

> **More Info**   To examine TCP Chimney Offload performance testing data, read "Boosting Data Transfer with TCP Offload Engine Technology" at *http://www.dell.com/downloads/global/ power/ps3q06-20060132-broadcom.pdf* and "Enabling Greater Scalability and Improved File Server Performance with the Windows Server 2003 Scalable Networking Pack and Alacritech Dynamic TCP Offload" at *http://www.alacritech.com/Resources/Files/ File_Serving_White_Paper.pdf*. For more information about TCP Chimney Offload, read "Scalable Networking: Network Protocol Offload—Introducing TCP Chimney" at *http://www.microsoft.com/whdc/device/network/TCP_Chimney.mspx*.

Receive-Side Scaling

As 10-gigabit LAN speeds become more common and we look to even higher speeds in the future, software must avoid becoming the performance bottleneck when it processes traffic it receives. One of the most significant bottlenecks is the processing time required for each packet.

Processing capability in computers has continued to increase over the years. However, instead of continuing to increase the clock speed of processors, computer hardware manufacturers have begun relying on multiple processors and multiple cores per processor. To allow Windows networking components to take advantage of this processing power, the software must avoid any process that is single threaded.

Windows Server 2003 supports Network Driver Interface Specification (NDIS) 5.1, which limits processing of incoming traffic to one processor at a time (though the particular processor used could vary depending on which one handled the interrupt), as shown in Figure 6-2.

With NDIS 6.0 and in Windows Vista and Windows Server 2008, the network interrupt service routine (ISR) can parallelize processing by queuing incoming packets received by an RSS-capable network adapter to multiple processors, as shown in Figure 6-3.

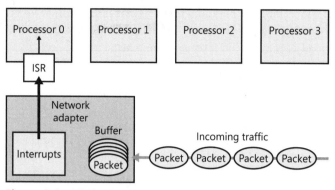

Figure 6-2 NDIS 5.0 receive processing

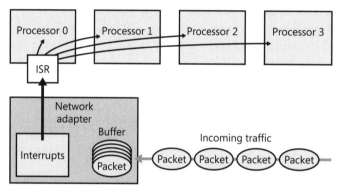

Figure 6-3 NDIS 6.0 receive processing with an RSS-capable network adapter

On PCI-e or PCI-X computers that support MSI or MSI-X, both the queuing and the interrupts can be distributed between multiple processors, as shown in Figure 6-4. Using RSS, applications and services still receive network data in order, but processor utilization in multiprocessor computers is more efficient.

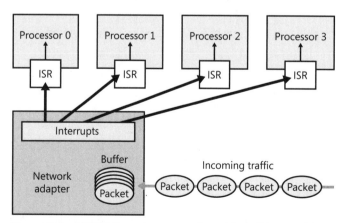

Figure 6-4 NDIS 6.0 receive processing with an RSS-capable network adapter that supports MSI or MSI-X

> ## Direct from the Source: MSI and MSI-X Interrupts
>
> There are two methods for a PCI-e/PCI-X device to generate an interrupt:
>
> - Line based
>
> - MSI or MSI-X based
>
> Line-based interrupts are the "old" way of generating interrupts, and most commonly, all line-based interrupts end up being serviced by a single CPU. However, modern systems that support Message Signaled Interrupts (MSI) enable the hardware device to generate an interrupt on any CPU they choose to. Thus RSS-capable NICs that also support MSI-based interrupts bring optimum performance by distributing both the ISRs across multiple CPUs as well as distributing the actual receive packet processing across multiple CPUs. Also note that Windows Vista and Windows Server 2008 are the first Windows operating systems to have software support for MSI/MSI-X systems and devices.
>
> *Rade Trimceski, Program Manager*
>
> *Windows Networking & Devices*

In addition to load balancing incoming traffic across all processors, Windows Server 2008 can also load-balance transmit processing caused by TCP window updates. In summary, RSS can increase transactions per second, connections per second, and network throughput for all multiprocessor computers, especially Web, file, backup, and database servers.

> **Note**   The default setting for RSS is for RSS to use the first four eligible processors (which is any processor except hyperthreaded virtual processors).

> **More Info**   For detailed information about RSS, read "Scalable Networking: Eliminating the Receive Processing Bottleneck—Introducing RSS" at *http://download.microsoft.com/download/5/D/6/5D6EAF2B-7DDF-476B-93DC-7CF0072878E6/NDIS_RSS.doc*.

NetDMA

NetDMA, co-designed by Intel and Microsoft, is another technique for reducing the processor overhead associated with processing network traffic and increasing network throughput. NetDMA moves data directly from one location in the computer's main memory directly to another location without requiring the data to be moved through the processor.

NetDMA requires the underlying hardware platform to support a technology such as Intel I/O Acceleration Technology (Intel I/OAT), a feature that can be used with Intel Xeon processors and Intel 5000 series chipsets. Intel's tests show that Intel I/OAT with NetDMA reduced processor utilization from 36 to 24 percent when four physical gigabit Ethernet network adapters were fully utilized in both directions, producing close to 8 gigabits per second (Gbps) of traffic. With eight-gigabit Ethernet adapters (producing close to 16 Gbps of traffic), Intel I/OAT and NetDMA increased throughput by more than 20 percent. With two or fewer gigabit Ethernet adapters in a computer (producing 4 Gbps or less of traffic), the improvement was minimal.

 More Info   For more information on Intel I/OAT, see *http://www.intel.com/go/ioat*.

NetDMA and TCP Chimney Offload are not compatible. If a network adapter supports both NetDMA and TCP Chimney Offload, Windows Server 2008 will use TCP Chimney Offload.

 More Info   For more information about NetDMA, read "Introduction to Intel I/O Acceleration Technology and the Windows Server 2003 Scalable Networking Pack" at *http://www.intel.com/technology/ioacceleration/317106.pdf*.

IPsec Offload

IPsec can authenticate and encrypt network traffic without requiring changes to the application. However, authenticating or encrypting each packet requires some processor overhead. On servers that accept a large number of connections and are already processor-limited, the additional processor overhead associated with adding IPsec can cause the processor to become a performance bottleneck.

 Note   Encrypting data within an IPsec session requires processor time because it uses secret key encryption. However, IPsec uses public key encryption when the IPsec session is established to transfer that secret key. It's the public key encryption that takes the most processing time.

IPsec Offload moves IPsec processing to the network adapter, which typically has a processor optimized for handling authentication and encryption tasks. By adding an IPsec Offload card to a server, you can substantially reduce the overhead of using IPsec (which might or might not be significant, depending on the usage and processing capabilities of the server).

For more information about IPsec, see Chapter 4, "Windows Firewall with Advanced Security," and Chapter 16, "IPsec Enforcement."

Planning and Design Considerations

Scalable networking features typically require the use of supported hardware. Some features require trade-offs, such as disabling software firewalls. Because of these costs, you must evaluate whether the benefits of each scalable networking feature outweigh the costs. The sections that follow guide you through the process of evaluating scalable networking features.

Evaluating Network Scalability Technologies

When evaluating specific features, consider the following:

- **TCP Chimney Offload**   TCP Chimney Offload will work only with NDIS 6.0 drivers on Windows Server 2008, NDIS 5.2 drivers on Windows Server 2003 with SP2, and compatible hardware. Therefore, if you have an NDIS 5.1 or earlier driver, or your network adapter does not support TCP Chimney Offload, it will not work. Because the performance benefits of TCP Chimney Offload are significant only with throughputs of about 2 Gbps or more, there is little benefit to using TCP Chimney Offload at network speeds below gigabit Ethernet, and the benefits will be more pronounced at 10-gigabit and faster speeds.

- **RSS and NetDMA**   RSS uses processors more efficiently by distributing load across multiple processors, whereas NetDMA reduces the total amount of processing required for network traffic. In either case, if you need extra budget to purchase hardware that supports RSS or NetDMA, you should use load testing before you purchase the hardware to verify that the processor is limiting the computer's performance and that the server cannot meet your scalability requirements without specialized hardware. If no single processor is fully utilized, RSS and NetDMA will not offer a significant benefit.

- **IPsec Offload**   Like RSS and NetDMA, IPsec Offload will improve performance only if the computer is processor-limited. IPsec Offload hardware does reduce the processing overhead associated with cryptographic functions but does not accelerate filter processing time. When testing IPsec Offload hardware, keep in mind that the Offload hardware typically supports a limited number of security associations (SAs). Above that limit, the computer's processors will handle the cryptographic functions as if the IPsec Offload hardware were not present.

During planning, you should also evaluate whether these scalability features are compatible with your server configuration. TCP Chimney Offload and NetDMA will not work with the following features:

- Windows Firewall
- IPsec
- Network Address Translation (NAT)
- Third-party firewalls

Additionally, RSS is not compatible with NAT drivers and is not effective for IPsec traffic unless it was decrypted with IPsec Offload. Table 6-1 illustrates which scalability technologies can benefit performance depending on the network technologies in use.

Table 6-1   Network Technology Compatibility with Scalability Technologies

Technology	TCP Chimney Offload	RSS	NetDMA	IPsec Offload
Windows Firewall	–	X	X	X
Third-party firewalls	–	X	X	X
IPsec	–	Only if IPsec Offload is in use	X	X
NAT	–	–	–	X

Therefore, if you use any of these features and you determine that processing network communications is consuming too much processor time, you will need to rely on RSS and, if you use IPsec, IPsec Offload. Because using TCP Chimney Offload or NetDMA requires you to disable Windows Firewall and IPsec, you should use these features only on servers that have very high scalability requirements and that rely on external security devices, such as a network firewall, to filter traffic.

Load Testing Servers

Each of the network scalability technologies discussed in this chapter can increase maximum throughput on your servers by decreasing processor utilization. However, if network adapters that support the technology are more costly than standard network adapters, it might not be worthwhile to adopt the technology. Before dedicating part of your hardware budget to these features, you should verify that you require the additional scalability and that network throughput or that the processor is limiting your server's performance.

> **Note**   If you determine that network throughput or the processor is already limiting the performance of a production server, load testing might not be worth the effort. Instead, test the new hardware for compatibility, upgrade the server's network adapter to hardware that supports TCP Chimney Offload, RSS, NetDMA, and, if you use IPsec, IPsec Offload, and monitor the performance in the production environment to determine the benefit.

You can use load testing software to test scalability of servers by simulating a large number of client requests. To avoid impacting your production network, perform the tests in a dedicated lab environment.

Microsoft provides the following tools for different types of servers:

- **Read80Trace and OSTRESS**   Allow you to put stress on database servers. You can download these tools at *http://www.microsoft.com/downloads/details.aspx?familyid=5691ab53-893a-4aaf-b4a6-9a8bb9669a8b.*

- **Web Capacity Analysis Tool**   Allows you to stress Web servers by submitting a large number of queries. This tool is included with the Internet Information Services (IIS) 6.0 Resource Kit Tools, but they will work with any Web server. You can download the tool at *http://www.microsoft.com/downloads/details.aspx?FamilyID=56fc92ee-a71a-4c73-b628-ade629c89499.*

- **Web Application Stress Tool**   Another tool for stressing Web servers, available at *http://www.microsoft.com/downloads/details.aspx?FamilyID=e2c0585a-062a-439e-a67d-75a89aa36495.*

- **Windows Media Load Simulator**   Allows you to stress test streaming media servers. For more information, visit *http://www.microsoft.com/windows/windowsmedia/howto/articles/loadsim.aspx.*

Additionally, third-party developers offer stress testing tools for a variety of different server applications. For internally developed applications, talk with your application development team about creating tools that simulate large numbers of client requests. For detailed information about creating custom load test tools by using Microsoft Visual Studio, read "Working with Load Tests" at *http://msdn2.microsoft.com/en-us/library/ms182561(VS.80).aspx.*

Monitoring Server Performance

It's important that you monitor your server's performance when using a load testing tool so that you can determine the component that is limiting performance (known as the bottleneck). Using the Performance Monitor snap-in, monitor the following counters to determine the limits of your network performance:

- **Processor\% Processor Time**   Add _Total and, if you have multiple processors or multiple cores, add <All Instances>. _Total is useful for measuring the performance benefit of TCP Chimney Offload, NetDMA, and IPsec Offload. <All Instances> shows you the utilization of each processor, which is more useful for determining whether a single processor is bottlenecking performance and whether the server is benefitting from RSS.

- **Process\% Processor Time**   Monitor the System instance (which will indicate the amount of processor time dedicated to processing network traffic, among other activities) and any other instances that might consume processor time. For example, if you are analyzing the performance of a database server, monitor the database process. When load testing file servers, you can assume that the majority of the System processor utilization can be attributed to processing network traffic.

- **Processor\Interrupts/sec**   This number should decrease if you are using TCP Chimney Offload or another form of TCP Offload.

- **Network Interface\Bytes Received/sec and Network Interface\Bytes Sent/sec**   These counters will help you understand the server's current load. When you apply sufficient load to reach the server's performance maximum, these numbers should be higher when network scalability features are enabled.

- **Network Interface\Packets Received/sec and Network Interface\Packets Sent/sec**   When compared to Bytes Received/sec and Bytes Sent/sec, these counters will allow you to calculate the average number of bytes per packet. NetDMA and TCP Chimney Offload offer more significant benefits with larger packets, whereas RSS is effective with packets of any size.

- **TCPv4\Connections Active and TCPv6\Connections Active**   These numbers will show you the current number of active TCP connections, which is helpful for understanding the server's current load.

To Run Performance Monitor and Gather Data in Real-Time

1. Click Start, click Administrative Tools, and then click Reliability And Performance Monitor.

2. Select the Reliability And Performance\Monitoring Tools\Performance Monitor node.

3. Click the Add button (green plus sign) on the toolbar to add counters.

After adding the counters to Performance Monitor, you can create a data collector set to save data to a file for later analysis. This will allow you to compare the performance before and after implementing a scalability technology.

To Create a Data Collector Set

1. In Reliability And Performance Monitor, right-click Performance Monitor, click New, and then click Data Collector Set.

2. Type a name for the data collector set, as shown in Figure 6-5. Then click Next.

3. Select a folder to save the data file in, and then click Next.

4. On the final page, click Finish.

After creating the data collector set, it will be available in the Data Collector Sets\User Defined node. Before you begin your load testing, right-click the data collector set, and then click Start. After you have completed the load test, right-click the data collector set, and then click Stop.

After collecting data, you can analyze it by following these steps:

1. In Reliability And Performance Monitor, right-click Performance Monitor, and then click Properties.

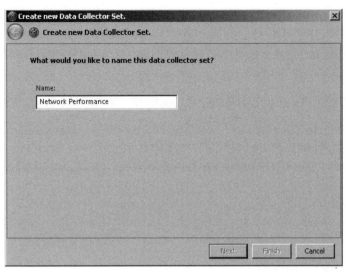

Figure 6-5   The first page of the Create New Data Collector Set Wizard

2. On the Source tab, select Log Files, and then click Add. Select the log file you want to monitor, and then click Open.

3. Click OK to return to Performance Monitor and examine the data.

When examining the data, ask the following questions to evaluate the potential usefulness of scalability features:

■ **Was any single processor fully utilized?**   If the answer to this question is yes and the server has multiple processors, then RSS, TCP Chimney Offload, NetDMA, or, if you are using IPsec, IPsec Offload could improve performance.

■ **Are the Bytes Sent/sec and Bytes Received/sec near the practical limit of the media?**   If the answer is yes, scalability features won't improve network performance, but they can reduce processor utilization and provide more processing cycles to applications. If the answer is no and processors are not near full utilization, another network component is limiting your performance. You might need more load testing clients to fully utilize the server, or your network infrastructure might not be able to handle full speed.

Deployment Steps

Prior to deploying scalable networking features, use load testing software to create a performance baseline of your servers, as discussed in the previous section. After deploying the scalable networking features, rerun the tests and compare the performance to the baseline to verify that you are achieving the expected performance improvements.

Most scalable networking features are enabled by default when compatible network adapters are installed in the computer. Therefore, configuration might not be required. The sections that follow show you how to examine the current configuration and enable or disable each of the scalable networking features.

Configuring TCP Chimney Offload

TCP Chimney Offload is enabled by default. To view the current status, run the following command and examine the Chimney Offload State row:

netsh interface tcp show global

Even if TCP Chimney Offload is enabled, it will be active only when there is a compatible network adapter connected. To explicitly enable TCP Chimney Offload, run the following command:

netsh interface tcp set global chimney=enabled

To disable TCP Chimney Offload, run the following command:

netsh interface tcp set global chimney=disabled

TCP Chimney Offload will be enabled only if all the following is true:

- No firewall, including Windows Firewall, is enabled.
- No IPsec policies are applied.
- NAT is not enabled.

Configuring Receive-Side Scaling

Receive-Side Scaling (RSS) is enabled by default. To view the current status, run the following command:

netsh interface tcp show global

Even if RSS is enabled, it will be active only when you have connected a compatible network adapter. To explicitly enable RSS, run the following command:

netsh interface tcp set global rss=enabled

To disable RSS, run the following command:

netsh interface tcp set global rss=disabled

Configuring NetDMA

Windows does not include tools to configure NetDMA. You should use software provided by the hardware platform provider (such as Intel, in the case of Intel I/OAT) to configure and monitor NetDMA. To download the Intel I/OAT System Check Utility, visit *http://www.intel.com/support/network/adapter/pro100/sb/CS-023725.htm.*

NetDMA will be enabled only if all the following is true:

- The network adapter does not report that it supports TCP Chimney Offload. (The two technologies are not compatible, and TCP Chimney Offload is preferred when both are available.)
- NAT is not enabled.

Configuring IPsec Offload

IPsec Offload is enabled by default. To view whether IPsec Offload and all TCP/IP hardware acceleration are enabled, run the following commands at a command prompt and examine the "Task Offload" row:

netsh interface ipv4 show global

netsh interface ipv6 show global

Additionally, you can run the following commands to view the offload capabilities of the network adapters in more detail:

netsh interface ipv4 show offload

netsh interface ipv6 show offload

To enable or disable IPsec Offload, edit the HKEY_LOCAL_MACHINE\System\Current-ControlSet\Services\Ipsec\EnableOffload registry value. Set it to **0** to disable IPsec Offload, or **1** to enable IPsec Offload.

To explicitly enable IPsec Offload and all TCP/IP hardware acceleration, run the following commands:

netsh interface ipv4 set global taskoffload=enabled

netsh interface ipv6 set global taskoffload=enabled

To disable IPsec Offload and all TCP/IP hardware acceleration, run the following commands:

netsh interface ipv4 set global taskoffload=disabled

netsh interface ipv6 set global taskoffload=disabled

Ongoing Maintenance

Once you have scalable networking features deployed, you should monitor network throughput and processor utilization on servers to verify that the features remain enabled and are functioning properly. If processor utilization increases or network throughput decreases, the scalable networking features might have been disabled. TCP Chimney Offload and NetDMA, in particular, are incompatible with many common network components and might be automatically disabled as an unwanted side effect of applying updates or configuration changes.

After you verify that scalable networking features provide you with performance benefits and work properly in your environment, you should monitor load on your servers to identify other servers that might benefit from these features. If you identify servers with high network and processor utilization, return to the planning and design phase to determine what hardware upgrades are required and whether enabling scalable networking features would be beneficial.

Troubleshooting

If you experience poor network throughput, or network performance decreases after enabling TCP Chimney Offload or RSS, disable those features and test performance to determine whether that solves the problem. For instructions on how to disable those features, refer to "Deployment Steps" earlier in this chapter.

You might also be able to enable, disable, or configure scalability features by changing options in your network adapter driver.

To View and Change the Network Adapter Driver Options

1. Click Start, right-click Computer, and then click Manage.

2. In the Server Manager console, expand Diagnostics, and then click Device Manager.

3. In the Details pane, expand Network Adapters.

4. Right-click your network adapter, and then click Properties.

5. The network adapter properties dialog box appears. Click the Advanced tab.

6. View the advanced properties, and change any settings.

7. Click OK to save your settings.

Troubleshooting TCP Chimney Offload

To determine whether current connections are being offloaded, run the following command at a command prompt:

netstat -t

The output will resemble the following:

```
Active Connections

  Proto  Local Address          Foreign Address        State
Offload State

  TCP    127.0.0.1:27015        d820:49166             ESTABLISHED
InHost
  TCP    127.0.0.1:49166        d820:27015             ESTABLISHED
Offloaded
  TCP    192.168.1.161:49169    by1msg3245816:msnp     ESTABLISHED
InHost
  TCP    192.168.1.161:50279    MCE:5900               ESTABLISHED
Offloaded
  TCP    192.168.1.161:54109    beta:5900              ESTABLISHED
Offloaded
  TCP    192.168.1.161:54880    od-in-f103:http        TIME_WAIT
InHost
  TCP    192.168.1.161:54931    76.9.1.18:http         TIME_WAIT
Offloaded
```

Netstat displays a list of all connections. The last column shows the current offload status. (You might need to increase the width of the command prompt to view the output easily.) The status will be one of the following:

- **In Host**   The network connection is not being offloaded. (The computer's processor is handling it.)

- **Offloaded**   The network connection is being handled by the network adapter.

- **Offloading**   The network connection is in the process of being transferred to the network adapter.

- **Uploading**   The network connection is in the process of being transferred back to the host processor.

To view applications in the TCP Chimney Offload table, run the following command at a command prompt:

netsh interface tcp show chimneyapplications

To view socket information in the TCP Chimney Offload table, run the following command at a command prompt:

netsh interface tcp show chimneyports

Troubleshooting IPsec Offload

If you are using IPsec Offload, Network Monitor will display communications unencrypted, because the IPsec Offload hardware decrypts the data before Network Monitor captures them.

If you experience problems after enabling IPsec Offload, it's possible that the IPsec Offload component is causing compatibility problems. First, verify that you have the latest version of the network adapter driver. If problems persist, disable IPsec Offload by following the steps in "Configuring IPsec Offload" earlier in this chapter. If the problem does not occur with IPsec Offload disabled, you have isolated the cause of the problem as the IPsec Offload capability.

Once you determine that the IPsec Offload adapter is the cause of the problem, collect more information about the problem by doing the following:

- Examine the System event log for IPsec-related events.

- Create a Network Monitor capture, and use IPsec Monitor (Ipsecmon.exe) to analyze each connection attempt. Examine the Confidential Bytes Received counter in Ipsecmon to determine whether packets are being lost on receive.

Contact the IPsec Offload network adapter vendor for additional troubleshooting assistance.

Chapter Summary

As network speeds increase, many enterprises are discovering that the network throughput of a server can be limited by the server's processors. Although you might expect a database server to dedicate a large amount of processing to the database service, in many cases, the server is spending significant processing time simply processing network communications. Typically, the performance impact becomes noticeable on servers that are transmitting and receiving more than 4 Gbps of sustained bandwidth, and the effect becomes significant above 8 Gbps throughput.

To allow servers to scale to multi-gigabit performance, Windows Server 2008 (when paired with compatible network adapters) supports four significant network scalability technologies:

- **TCP Chimney Offload** TCP data is handed directly to higher layers, bypassing Layer 2, 3, and 4 processing.

- **RSS** In a multi-processor computer, network processing can be handled by multiple processors simultaneously while maintaining in-order delivery.

- **NetDMA** Rather than moving network data through the processor, data is moved directly from the network adapter to the computer's memory.

- **IPsec Offload** Authentication and encryption tasks are handled by a dedicated processor on the network adapter, reducing utilization of the server's main processor.

Each of these technologies has trade-offs, however. First, each requires a network adapter that specifically supports the technology. TCP Chimney Offload and NetDMA cannot be used with Windows Firewall, IPsec, or NAT. NetDMA requires a specialized chipset in addition to a supported network adapter, and it cannot be used with TCP Chimney Offload.

To configure the technologies, use the Netsh command-line tool. Maintenance and trouble-shooting requirements should be minimal, because the technologies should function transparently once configured.

Additional Information

For additional information about scalable networking in Windows, see the following:

- "Scalable Networking" at *http://www.microsoft.com/snp*
- "Scalable Networking: Network Protocol Offload—Introducing TCP Chimney" at *http://www.microsoft.com/whdc/device/network/TCP_Chimney.mspx*
- "Scalable Networking: Eliminating the Receive Processing Bottleneck—Introducing RSS" at *http://download.microsoft.com/download/5/D/6/5D6EAF2B-7DDF-476B-93DC-7CF0072878E6/NDIS_RSS.doc*
- "Microsoft Windows Scalable Networking Initiative" at *http://download.microsoft.com/download/5/b/5/5b5bec17-ea71-4653-9539-204a672f11cf/scale.doc*
- "Introduction to Intel I/O Acceleration Technology and the Windows Server 2003 Scalable Networking Pack" at *http://www.intel.com/technology/ioacceleration/317106.pdf*

To examine TCP Chimney Offload performance testing data, see the following:

- "Boosting Data Transfer with TCP Offload Engine Technology" at *http://www.dell.com/downloads/global/power/ps3q06-20060132-broadcom.pdf*
- "Enabling Greater Scalability and Improved File Server Performance with the Windows Server 2003 Scalable Networking Pack and Alacritech Dynamic TCP Offload" at *http://www.alacritech.com/Resources/Files/File_Serving_White_Paper.pdf*

For additional information about load testing, see the following:

- The Read80Trace and OSTRESS tools, available at *http://www.microsoft.com/downloads/details.aspx?familyid=5691ab53-893a-4aaf-b4a6-9a8bb9669a8b*
- The Web Capacity Analysis Tool, part of the Internet Information Services (IIS) 6.0 Resource Kit Tools, at *http://www.microsoft.com/downloads/details.aspx?FamilyID=56fc92ee-a71a-4c73-b628-ade629c89499*
- The Windows Media Load Simulator, available at *http://www.microsoft.com/windows/windowsmedia/howto/articles/loadsim.aspx*
- "Working with Load Tests" at *http://msdn2.microsoft.com/en-us/library/ms182561(VS.80).aspx*
- The Web Application Stress Tool at *http://www.microsoft.com/downloads/details.aspx?FamilyID=e2c0585a-062a-439e-a67d-75a89aa36495*

Part II
Name Resolution Infrastructure

Chapter 7
Domain Name System

This chapter provides information about how to design, deploy, maintain, and troubleshoot the domain name system (DNS) server role in the Windows Server 2008 operating system. This chapter assumes that you have a solid understanding of Active Directory domains, the role of domain controllers, Dynamic Host Configuration Protocol (DHCP), and Transmission Control Protocol/Internet Protocol (TCP/IP).

Concepts

Computers identify each other using IP addresses, but people are more comfortable using host names such as www.microsoft.com. DNS allows computers to translate people-friendly host names into computer-friendly IP addresses. To allow any of the millions of computers on the Internet to be identified with a host name, DNS is hierarchical and distributed.

The sections that follow describe the DNS hierarchy, how DNS zones are used to distribute management, the different types of DNS resource records, how dynamic DNS allows mobile clients to be identified with DNS records, and the process of resolving host names.

DNS Hierarchy

Like the Internet itself, DNS is a very large-scale, distributed, public system. People or organizations register a domain name from a registrar who registers it on the Internet's public, shared, top-level domain DNS servers. Top-level DNS servers resolve name queries such as microsoft.com to Microsoft's authoritative DNS servers. Those DNS servers will then resolve names subordinate to the registered domain (such as support.microsoft.com or windowsupdate.microsoft.com) to IP addresses.

To allow DNS to be scalable and distributed, it has a hierarchical design, as shown in Figure 7-1. There are both generic top-level domains (such as .com, .org, and .net) and country-specific top-level domains (such as .us, .uk, and .tv). Different companies and individuals have different second-level domains (such as microsoft.com or contoso.com), and organizations can create subdomains for their own use (such as corp.microsoft.com). Domains, subdomains, and host names are separated by periods ("."), with host names and lower-level domains appearing first and top-level domains appearing last.

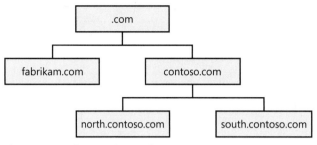

Figure 7-1   The DNS hierarchy

DNS Zones

Each domain name in the DNS hierarchy (such as contoso.com, north.contoso.com, and campus.north.contoso.com) is a distinct zone. Each zone can be managed by a different server, allowing DNS to be distributed. For example, you might host the contoso.com and north.contoso.com zones on DNS servers at your headquarters but host the west.conotoso.com zone on a DNS server at a regional office.

You can configure a server to support a zone in several different ways:

- **Primary zone**   Configures the DNS server to be authoritative for the zone. This means that the DNS server can definitively answer DNS queries for that zone and will allow changes and additions to the DNS database.

- **Secondary zone**   Configures the DNS server to act as a backup server for the domain. This means that the DNS server receives a copy of the zone from a primary server zone and can answer DNS queries for the zone. Secondary zones do not directly allow updates.

- **Stub zone**   Configures the DNS server to forward requests to another name server that is a primary or secondary DNS server for the zone. Stub zones contain only NS, SOA, and A records.

DNS Records

Within a domain, network resources, such as domain controllers, e-mail servers, and client computers, are identified by resource records. For example, in the Fully Qualified Domain Name (FQDN) www.contoso.com, the host name *www* identifies a server in the contoso.com domain.

DNS servers support different types of records for standard host names, mail servers, aliases, reverse IP address lookup, and other resources. Table 7-1 lists the most commonly used DNS resource records.

Table 7-1 **Common DNS Resource Records**

Resource Record	Use
A	The most common way to identify a computer. The A record maps a host name to an IPv4 IP address.
AAAA	An A record for IPv6. Four As are used because an IPv6 address is 128 bits, which is four times longer than required by the 32-bit IPv4 A records.
CNAME	A *canonical name record* that acts as an alias for an existing A or AAAA record. You can use a CNAME record to have more than one host name resolve to a single IP address.
MX	A *mail exchanger record* that identifies the mail server for the domain. You can use multiple MX records to identify backup mail servers.
NS	A *name server record* that identifies a DNS server for a domain. If you have multiple DNS servers for the domain, each server should have an NS record.
PTR	A *pointer record* used to allow clients to look up a host name based on an IP address, which is known as a *reverse DNS lookup*. The top-level domain for IPv4 PTR records is in-addr.arpa. The top-level domain for IPv6 PTR records is ip6.arpa.
SOA	The *start of authority record* specifies the authoritative DNS server and is the required first entry for all forward and reverse lookup zones.
SRV	The SRV record is used to identify Active Directory domain controllers in a domain and can be used to identify other services.

Dynamic DNS Updates

Years ago, when most IP addresses were statically assigned to computers, administrators manually created DNS entries for every computer on the network. Today, most IP addresses are assigned automatically with DHCP. Because DHCP addresses can change, it became impractical to manually update the resource record for each computer.

Dynamic DNS allows clients to update their own DNS resource records. Whereas computers with static IP addresses can use dynamic DNS, it's particularly useful for DHCP clients, which might receive a different IP address when they connect to a new network or when the DHCP lease expires. With dynamic DNS, either the DHCP server or the DHCP client submits an updated resource record to the DNS server when an IP address is assigned to a client.

As described in "DNS Security" later in this chapter, allowing DNS updates introduces a security risk. To minimize this risk, either allow only secure DNS updates or block all dynamic DNS updates.

DNS Name Resolution

Because DNS is distributed across millions of different DNS servers, no single server can answer a query for every host name. For that reason, DNS queries are often *recursive*, which means the DNS server that receives the query must, in turn, query another DNS server for the answer.

A typical DNS query follows this process:

1. A client sends the DNS query to its local DNS server. For example, the client might need to resolve www.microsoft.com to an IP address.

2. That DNS server sends a query to a root DNS server to identify a DNS server for the top-level domain (such as .com).

3. That DNS server then sends a query to the top-level DNS server for the domain. In this example, the local DNS server would query a DNS server that is authoritative for .com.

4. The .com DNS server replies to the client's local DNS server with the IP address of the domain's DNS server as indicated by the domain's NS records. In this example, the .com server would reply with the list of DNS servers for the microsoft.com domain.

5. The local DNS server sends a query to the second-level domain DNS server to resolve the host name. In this example, the local DNS server would query one of the microsoft.com DNS servers to resolve the www.microsoft.com host name.

6. The second-level domain DNS server for microsoft.com replies to the local DNS server with the IP address of the requested host name.

7. The local DNS server forwards the host name's IP address to the client, completing the query process.

> **Note**   Typically, every server at every step of the process caches the results of the query so that it can immediately respond to future requests for the same host name. Additionally, client computers cache host names locally. Because host names might be cached for several hours, changes you make to existing DNS records might not be available to all clients for several hours.

Figure 7-2 illustrates the DNS query process. In this figure, the client's default DNS server already has the IP address of the .com DNS server cached—otherwise, it would need to query a root DNS server to obtain the IP address of the .com DNS server. Although this simplified example involves six steps, in practice, queries can be two steps (if the default DNS server has the host name cached) or many more steps (if the query is for a host name in a subdomain).

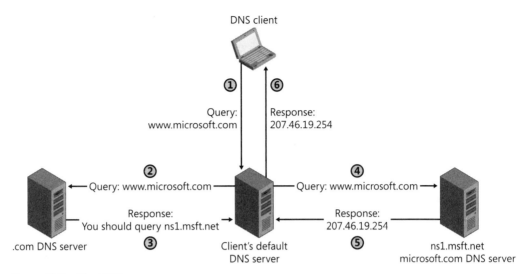

Figure 7-2 The DNS query process

Although DNS can use either TCP or User Datagram Protocol (UDP), DNS queries almost always use UDP to avoid the setup overhead of a TCP connection. Both TCP and UDP use port 53 for DNS traffic.

Planning and Design Considerations

Once deployed, a DNS infrastructure can be difficult to change. Thorough planning is required to minimize the chance that you will need to make major changes to your DNS infrastructure. For example, if you name an intranet server server.contoso.com and later decide to move it to server.north.contoso.com, you would need to update every client application and bookmark that had the original server name stored before the change would take effect. Ultimately, you will save time by planning your DNS infrastructure around the future of your organization, including adding staff, expanding into regional offices, or merging with other organizations. This section describes planning and design considerations for a DNS infrastructure.

DNS Zones

Each zone can have a different primary DNS server, and management of individual zones can be easily delegated to different groups within your organization. Therefore, if your organization has distributed offices and distributed IT departments, you might need to create a separate zone for each office. Alternatively, if you have centralized IT management, a smaller number of zones might be easier to manage. To limit security risks, you might also need separate zones for internal and external names. The sections that follow provide more information about planning your DNS zones.

Internal and External Zones

Many organizations require both internal and external DNS records. For example, Microsoft has external DNS records for public servers such as www.microsoft.com, connect.microsoft.com, and windowsupdate.microsoft.com. Microsoft also has DNS records for each of the thousands of computers on their internal network.

To prevent potential attackers from determining the host names and IP addresses of computers on your internal network, you should create separate zones for internal and external DNS records. You can do this by creating a subdomain within your primary domain (for example, using contoso.com for public addresses and corp.contoso.com for private addresses). Alternatively, you can create a private domain that could be resolved only on your internal network, such as contoso.pvt.

Planning Internal Zones

A single internal zone can be sufficient for a small organization with centralized IT management. For example, you could name your servers file.corp.contoso.com, printer.corp.contoso.com, and mail.corp.contoso.com. However, the complexities of managing a single zone increase as an organization becomes more distributed. Imagine an organization with two offices, each with its own IT department. If they each have a file server, both offices might decide to name the server file.corp.contoso.com, creating a naming conflict. Additionally, an administrator at one office might make a change to the zone that causes problems for an administrator at a different office.

As the number of offices and DNS administrators increases, so do the potential conflicts. You can minimize these conflicts by creating separate zones for each office or IT department. For each zone you create, you must verify that:

- Each zone has one primary DNS server.

- Each zone has at least one secondary DNS server to store a backup of the zone file. Using Active Directory–integrated zones can automatically replicate zone data between domain controllers.

- Each zone can be resolved by all other DNS servers in the organization. This might require creating stub zones (described later in this chapter).

- Each zone has administrators responsible for adding, updating, and removing records.

DNS Server Placement

DNS servers for external domains must be connected to the public Internet. To help limit your exposure to attack, you should connect internal DNS servers only to your private network.

Figure 7-3 demonstrates using two DNS servers to provide both public and private DNS service while minimizing risk. In this sample configuration, the external DNS server is placed on the perimeter network alongside public mail and Web servers. The internal DNS server is placed on the internal network, alongside internal servers and clients. The external DNS server contains records for other external servers. If necessary, the internal DNS server can be configured to forward DNS requests to the external DNS server.

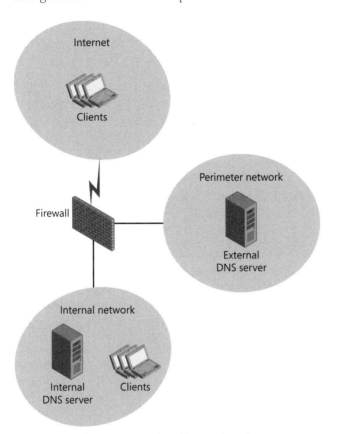

Figure 7-3 Placing external and internal DNS servers

Clients send a DNS request as the first step of establishing almost all outgoing network connections. As a result, slow DNS queries reduce the initial network performance of every network application. Therefore, you should place a DNS server at every regional location to minimize latency even if that region does not require a unique zone.

Note A Microsoft Windows DNS server can handle more than 10,000 queries per second. Large and mission-critical sites should have two DNS servers for the first 20,000 users. For every additional 10,000 users after the first 20,000, add another DNS server. Avoid the tendency to install DNS on every domain controller in a forest unless you need name resolution redundancy in every location.

If you choose to implement regional zones (or regional domains, when using Active Directory–integrated zones), configure DNS servers to act as secondary zones for servers in different regions. This provides geographic redundancy, allowing names in the zone to be resolved even if a network outage or natural disaster impacts a region. Figure 7-4 demonstrates how to use regionally distributed DNS servers to both perform local caching of DNS queries and provide backup of the DNS database of other servers.

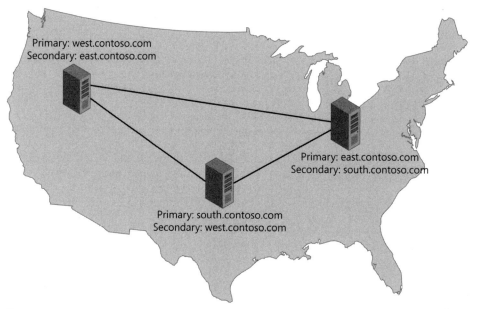

Figure 7-4   Using regional DNS servers

Even if a regional office does not have its own zone, you should configure a caching DNS server at the location. To configure a caching DNS server, simply install the DNS server role without adding any zones. A caching DNS server can be configured to resolve either internal or external DNS records, and it will store a copy of every record after it is resolved so that it can resolve future queries without sending traffic across your WAN. For more information about network performance, read Chapter 5, "Policy-Based Quality of Service."

Regional DNS servers can also be used as primary DNS servers for that region's zone. In Active Directory environments, configure regional domain controllers to act as the regional DNS server to take advantage of improved security and automatic zone replication.

DNS Zone Replication

Other than your routers, there is no network component more critical than the DNS server. Literally every network application depends on DNS servers, and if your DNS servers are offline, almost all network activity will come to a stop. To enable network applications to continue to function if a DNS server fails, you should configure at least one secondary DNS server for each zone.

Zone replication is the process of updating a secondary DNS server with resource records from the primary DNS server. If you have a large number of resource records that are frequently updated (for example, by dynamic DNS clients), you should consider whether you have sufficient bandwidth for the zone replication traffic.

For optimal efficiency, configure your DNS servers as domain controllers, and use Active Directory–integrated zones. Active Directory–integrated zones perform automated, authenticated replication and copy only DNS database changes between servers. The scope of replication can be:

- **To All DNS Servers In This Forest**   All DNS servers in the forest that are domain controllers running the Microsoft Windows Server 2003 or Windows Server 2008 operating systems. Plan to select this type of replication if you have DNS servers in multiple domains within your forest.

- **To All DNS Servers In This Domain**   All DNS servers in the domain that are domain controllers running Windows Server 2003 or Windows Server 2008. This is the default setting for Active Directory–integrated zones.

- **To All Domain Controllers In This Domain**   All domain controllers in the Active Directory domain, including computers running Microsoft Windows 2000 Server. You will need to select this option only if you still have DNS servers running Windows 2000 Server. This will increase the total amount of replication traffic because it will replicate DNS records to domain controllers that do not have the DNS Server service installed, so it should be avoided.

- **To All Domain Controllers In The Scope Of This Directory Partition**   All domain controllers in a specified application directory partition, including computers running Windows 2000 Server. This allows you to replicate DNS data to DNS servers running Windows 2000 Server while limiting the scope of the replication. This option can reduce the amount of replication traffic, but it requires additional configuration. For more information, refer to Windows Server 2008 Help and Support.

You can create Active Directory–integrated zones only on domain controllers; domain member servers or stand-alone computers cannot support Active Directory–integrated zones. If you do not use Active Directory–integrated zones, replication to secondary DNS servers will use traditional zone transfers, which is a standards-based method for updating DNS servers defined in RFC 1034 (available at *http://www.ietf.org/rfc/rfc1034.txt*) and RFC 1035 (available at *http://www.ietf.org/rfc/rfc1035.txt*). The Microsoft DNS server also supports incremental zone transfer as described in RFC 1995 (available at *http://www.ietf.org/rfc/rfc1995.txt*), which will significantly reduce the amount of zone transfer network traffic in many common scenarios.

How It Works: Zone Transfers

While standard DNS queries use UDP port 53, zone transfers use TCP port 53. UDP is more efficient for DNS queries, which typically only require two packets: a one-packet query sent to the DNS server and a one-packet response sent back to the client. Zone transfers can be very large (especially the first zone transfer), and thus they require the reliability and flow control of TCP.

Allowing zone transfers is a significant security vulnerability, because the recipient can immediately identify every computer in your organization, and the processing time required can be used to create a denial-of-service attack. Fortunately, the Windows Server 2008 DNS server will not allow zone transfers from unauthorized servers. To provide an additional layer of protection, use network firewalls and Windows Firewall to block TCP port 53. For more information about firewalls, read Chapter 4, "Windows Firewall with Advanced Security."

If both the primary and secondary DNS server support incremental zone transfers (a feature supported by Windows 2000 Server and later, BIND versions 8.2.1 and later, and many other non-Microsoft DNS servers), only changes to the DNS database will be transferred. If either the primary or secondary DNS server do not support incremental zone transfers, the entire DNS database will be copied each time a zone transfer occurs. With large numbers of resource records, the bandwidth consumed by a zone transfer can be significant.

DNS Security

Security for DNS servers is critical for several reasons. First, DNS clients trust the DNS server to provide the correct IP address for host names. If a malicious attacker can update or add host names to a DNS server, the attacker could redirect traffic and perform a man-in-the-middle attack. For example, if an attacker changed the IP address for www.woodgrovebank.com from its valid IP to the IP address of a malicious server, the malicious server could intercept and record information entered by users, including PIN numbers, passwords, and financial information.

Another reason DNS server security is critical is that DNS servers typically have the host name and IP address of every computer residing in the local DNS zones. An attacker with access to a DNS server database could, therefore, have a list of all computers and IP addresses in your organization, including your domain controllers and their site locations, with which to launch an attack. Some applications, such as Web servers, rely on reverse host name lookup to authenticate users. For example, a Web server might allow requests from all clients that have an IP address that resolves to *.fabrikam.com. Therefore, if an attacker's computer can add its IP address to the reverse host name lookup table for a DNS server, it could impersonate an internal computer.

To minimize these security risks, you should follow these guidelines when planning your DNS server infrastructure:

- Use Active Directory–integrated zones so you can take advantage of the automatic, authenticated DNS database replication between DNS servers.

- Enable only secure dynamic DNS updates. Allowing untrusted clients to register their own DNS records greatly increases the risk that a malicious computer will find a way to use the DNS record to authenticate to a network application or perform a man-in-the-middle attack.

- As with any computer, always install the latest security updates on your DNS servers. Additionally, you should be aware of newly developed security risks and take measures to avoid new attacks.

- For internal DNS servers, configure both Windows Firewall and network firewalls to block requests from external IP addresses.

- Allow zone transfers only to authorized DNS servers on your internal network. If you are using Active Directory, you might be able to disable zone transfers completely.

- Audit changes to your DNS database, and minimize the number of users with permission to make changes.

The GlobalNames Zone

Earlier versions of Windows relied heavily on Windows Internet Name Service (WINS) to resolve NetBIOS computer names to IP addresses on routed networks. WINS name resolution is still supported by the Windows Server 2008 and Windows Vista operating systems. NetBIOS computer names are single-label host names of up to 15 characters, such as CONTOSOSERVER or VISTA342.

DNS is now the preferred method for name resolution. If you do not currently have a WINS infrastructure, you probably do not need to deploy one—DNS can meet all your name resolution requirements. If you do have a WINS infrastructure, you should consider migrating away from it. To facilitate the migration for environments with multiple Active Directory domains, Windows Server 2008 DNS servers support the GlobalNames zone.

 Note   One of the most significant drawbacks to WINS is that it does not support Internet Protocol version 6 (IPv6). DNS fully supports IPv6.

The GlobalNames zone resolves simple, single-label names such as NetBIOS computer names. In other words, the GlobalNames zone could resolve the computer name CONTOSOSERVER without converting it to an FQDN such as contososerver.contoso.com. This would allow clients with different default DNS domains to resolve the same computer names (or other single-label names). Unlike WINS, the GlobalNames zone does not support dynamically registered records, which do not scale sufficiently for enterprise use. However, the Global-Names zone can replace statically registered WINS records for well-known servers.

You should consider replacing your WINS infrastructure with a GlobalNames zone only if you meet all the following requirements:

- You are retiring WINS or you are planning to migrate to a fully IPv6 network.

- You need single-label name resolution only for statically registered names, such as the names of servers or Web sites.

- You cannot rely on clients automatically converting requests for NetBIOS computer names to FQDNs. By default, clients will automatically add the default domain name to any single-label names and attempt to resolve the name by using DNS. Additionally, you can add a list of domain names for clients to attempt to use to resolve single-label names. However, if you have too many different domain names to search, the GlobalNames zone can provide an alternative.

More Info   Read "Configuring DNS Client Settings" at *http://technet2.microsoft.com/ windowsserver/en/library/5fe46cef-db12-4b78-94d2-2a0b62a282711033.mspx?mfr=true.*

- All your authoritative DNS servers are running Windows Server 2008. Earlier versions of Windows do not support the GlobalNames zone.

More Info   For more information about the GlobalNames zone, read "DNS Server GlobalNames Zone Deployment" at *http://www.microsoft.com/downloads/ details.aspx?FamilyID=1c6b31cd-3dd9-4c3f-8acd-3201a57194f1*. For more information about WINS, refer to Chapter 8, "Windows Internet Name Service."

Deployment Steps

Deploying DNS requires adding the DNS server role, configuring the zones that the DNS server will host, configuring your DHCP server with the new DNS server address, and manually configuring DNS clients that have static IP addresses. Fortunately, each of these steps is straightforward and can be accomplished in as little as a few minutes. This section describes these tasks in more detail.

DNS Server Configuration

When configuring a DNS server, first verify that the computer meets the fairly minimal requirements for a DNS server. Then, install the DNS server role. Once the DNS server role is configured, you can test the DNS server, configure the root DNS servers (if necessary), and, optionally, configure a DNS forwarder. Finally, you will configure zones to store resource records on the DNS server.

The sections that follow describe how to configure a computer as a DNS server and how to configure zones.

DNS Server Requirements

The overhead for the DNS Server role is minimal, and any computer capable of running Windows Server 2008 will be able to act as a DNS server. For zones containing thousands of resource records, RAM can become a constraint. In addition to the RAM required by the operating system (about 512 MB) and other installed roles, each DNS record requires about 100 bytes of RAM. Therefore, if a zone contains 10,000 resource records, the server hosting the zone would require about 1MB of memory. If you enable reverse IP address lookups, each computer has at least two resource records: an A record and a PTR record.

Installing the DNS Server Roles

The simplest way to configure a computer running Windows Server 2008 as a DNS server is to add the DNS server role by using Server Manager.

To Configure a Server That Is Not a Domain Controller as a DNS Server

1. Configure the server with a static IP address. Because clients cannot use a host name to look up a DNS server, the IP address of each DNS server must never change.

2. Click Start, and then click Server Manager.

3. In the left pane, click Roles, and then in the right pane, click Add Roles.

4. If the Before You Begin page appears, click Next.

5. On the Server Roles page, select DNS Server, and then click Next.

6. On the DNS Server page, click Next.

7. On the Confirmation page, click Install.

8. On the Results page, click Close.

Windows Server 2008 will spend several minutes installing the DNS Server role. The default configuration includes a list of IP addresses for root DNS servers, enabling the server to immediately be used to resolve public host names and act as a caching DNS server.

Configuring the DNS Server

After installing the DNS Server role, you can configure it by using the DNS Manager snap-in. To open the DNS Manager snap-in from within Server Manager, expand Roles, and then click

DNS Server. The sections that follow describe how to perform different configuration tasks with the DNS Manager open.

Test the DNS Server   You can use Server Manager to verify that your DNS server is correctly resolving names on the Internet. This only verifies that the root servers are configured correctly; it does not test whether your internal zones are set up.

To Test That the DNS Server Is Configured

1. In the left pane, under Server Manager, expand the DNS Server node down to the server name.

2. Right-click your server name, and then click Properties.

3. Click the Monitoring tab.

4. Select one or more check boxes to indicate the type of test you want to perform. The choices are as follows:

   ❑ **A Simple Query Against This DNS Server**   Queries the DNS server for a record the DNS server can resolve locally.

   ❑ **A Recursive Query To Other DNS Servers**   Queries the DNS server for a record that requires it to query a remote DNS server.

   ❑ **Perform Automatic Testing At The Following Interval**   Automatically performs the test on a regular basis, with a minimum interval of 30 seconds. The test continues even if the server properties dialog box is closed.

5. Click Test Now.

The properties dialog box displays the results of the test in the Test Results list. If the simple query test passes, it indicates that the DNS server is running. If the recursive query test passes, the DNS server is running and is able to contact the root DNS servers to resolve public DNS names.

Configure Root DNS Servers   Occasionally (every few years), the Internet Assigned Numbers Authority (IANA) updates the IP address of a root DNS server, or they might add a root DNS server. The IANA would never change more than one or two IP addresses at a time, and as long as one root DNS server is correctly configured on your server, it will be able to resolve public host names. Therefore, you do not need to be too concerned about maintaining the list of root DNS servers. You can obtain the current list of root DNS servers from *http://www.root-servers.org/*.

To Change or Add a Root DNS Server

1. Right-click your server name, and then click Properties.

2. Click the Root Hints tab.

3. To change a root DNS server, select it, and then click Edit. Select the existing IP address, type the new IP address, and then click OK.

4. To add a root DNS server, click Add. Type the name of the DNS server (such as *m.root-servers.net*), and then click Resolve. After the IP address is validated, click OK.

5. Click OK to return to the DNS Manager.

By default, a new DNS server is configured as a caching-only server. The DNS server will be able to resolve host names on the public Internet, and it will cache the results to provide a faster response for subsequent queries.

Direct from the Source: The Difference Between DNS Server Forwarding and Root Hints

A DNS server that uses forwarding will send queries to the specified set of DNS servers and will request recursion. A DNS server that uses root hints will recursively attempt to resolve queries, starting from the specified root hints. The key difference is that root hints can be used only if there is a DNS root that is appropriate for your environment. If you host your own root servers, you can use either forwarding or root hints, but if you do not host your own root servers, you will most likely want to use forwarding exclusively.

For example, if you have a large corporate network and run your own internal root server, you might decide to use root hints. In this case Internet name resolution would not be available inside your corporate network but might be provided by proxy servers. In a smaller environment, especially if you wish to have Internet name resolution on your computers, you should use forwarding since the Internet DNS root servers will not know how to find your Active Directory deployment.

Jeff Westhead, Senior Software Development Engineer

Enterprise Networking Group

Configure a DNS Forwarder   As described earlier in this chapter, DNS servers can send all queries that can't be resolved from the local zone to a DNS forwarder.

To Add a DNS Forwarder

1. Open DNS Manager.

2. Right-click your server name, and then click Properties.

3. Click the Forwarders tab.

4. Click Edit.

   The Edit Forwarders dialog box appears.

5. In the Edit Forwarders dialog box, type the IP address or host name of the DNS server you want the server to send all DNS requests to, and then press Enter.

   The forwarding server will immediately be tested to verify that it can resolve host names.

6. Repeat step 4 to add additional servers, if necessary. Then, use the Up and Down buttons to place the DNS servers in the correct order.

7. Click OK to return to the server properties dialog box.

8. On the Forwarders tab, select the Use Root Hints If No Forwarders Are Available check box if you want the server to attempt to resolve host names by using the public DNS servers if all the forwarders you configure are unresponsive.

9. Click OK to return to DNS Manager.

After configuring forwarders on a DNS server, the DNS server will act as a DNS caching server.

Direct from the Source: Configuring DNS Forwarders

The DNS servers in a non-root Active Directory domain should forward to one or more DNS servers in the immediate parent domain, and so on up the tree of Active Directory domains until the parent is reached. The DNS servers in the parent domain may be configured to forward to your Internet Service Provider's (ISP's) DNS server if you want the computers in your Active Directory deployment to resolve Internet names. If your Active Directory deployment is part of a larger corporate infrastructure, you may instead configure your parent domain DNS servers to forward to DNS servers that host your corporate infrastructure.

It is very important that all DNS servers in the forwarder list have the same view of the DNS namespace. You should not, for instance, forward to both your ISP's DNS servers and to other Active Directory DNS servers in your infrastructure. All forwarders in the list are assumed to be able to resolve all names equally, and since your ISP's DNS server will not be able to resolve your Active Directory names, you cannot mix your ISP's DNS servers with your Active Directory DNS servers when configuring forwarders.

Jeff Westhead, Senior Software Development Engineer

Enterprise Networking Group

Configuring Zones

The sections that follow describe how to configure different types of zones. For information about planning zones, refer to "DNS Zones" earlier in this chapter.

Configure a Primary Forward Lookup Zone   Primary forward lookup zones store the authoritative copy of DNS resource records. You only need to add primary forward lookup zones for zones that you are responsible for maintaining.

To Add a Primary Forward Lookup Zone

1. Open DNS Manager.

2. Expand your server name, right-click Forward Lookup Zones, and then click New Zone. The New Zone Wizard appears.

3. On the Welcome To The New Zone Wizard page, click Next.

4. On the Zone Type page, click Primary Zone. If the DNS server is a domain controller, you have the option of selecting the Store The Zone In Active Directory check box. Click Next.

5. If the Active Directory Zone Replication Scope page appears, select the type of replication you want to use, and then click Next. The Active Directory Zone Replication page appears only when creating a zone that is Active Directory–integrated. For more information about Active Directory zone replication, refer to "DNS Zone Replication" earlier in this chapter.

6. On the Zone Name page, type a name for the zone representing the domain it is managing (such as west.contoso.com), and then click Next.

7. If the Zone File page appears, select whether you want to create a new zone file or use an existing zone file. Click Next. The Zone File page appears only when creating a zone that is not Active Directory–integrated.

8. On the Dynamic Update page, choose one of the following three options, and then click Next:

    ❑ **Allow Only Secure Dynamic Updates**   Available only for Active Directory–integrated zones, this option accepts dynamic updates only from domain members. Whereas servers often have static DNS records, client computers (especially mobile computers) rarely have static DNS records. Therefore, allowing dynamic updates might be the only way for clients to resolve other client host names.

    ❑ **Allow Both Nonsecure And Secure Dynamic Updates**   Available for both standard and Active Directory–integrated zones, this option allows clients to update their own DNS records even if they are not a member of the Active Directory domain. For more information about the security risks of allowing nonsecure dynamic updates, read "DNS Security" earlier in this chapter.

    ❑ **Do Not Allow Dynamic Updates**   Prevents clients (including DHCP servers) from updating DNS records in the zone.

9. On the Completing The New Zone Wizard page, click Finish.

Later, you can change these configuration settings by right-clicking the zone in DNS Manager and clicking Properties. If you choose to allow dynamic updates, read "Maintaining Zones" later in this chapter.

Configure a Secondary Forward Lookup Zone   A secondary forward lookup zone acts as a backup server for a primary lookup zone and can answer DNS queries for the zone. Typically, secondary forward lookup zones are used to provide redundancy for zones that are not Active Directory–integrated.

To Add a Secondary Forward Lookup Zone

1. Open DNS Manager.

2. Expand your server name, right-click Forward Lookup Zones, and then click New Zone. The New Zone Wizard appears.

3. On the Welcome To The New Zone Wizard page, click Next.

4. On the Zone Type page, click Secondary Zone, and then click Next.

5. On the Zone Name page, type a name for the zone representing the domain it is managing (such as west.contoso.com).

6. On the Master DNS Servers page, type the host name or IP address of the master DNS server, and then press Enter. The New Zone Wizard will automatically test the master DNS server.

7. To add more than one master DNS server, repeat step 5. Then, use the Up and Down buttons to place the servers in order. Click Next.

8. On the Completing The New Zone Wizard page, click Finish.

Later, you can change these configuration settings by right-clicking the zone in DNS Manager and clicking Properties.

Configure a WINS Forward Lookup   You can create a WINS forward lookup to allow DNS queries for a zone to be resolved by a WINS server. For example, if a WINS server had a computer named HOST, and a client submitted a DNS query for host.contoso.com that couldn't be resolved by the contoso.com DNS server, the DNS server could query the WINS server to determine the IP address for HOST.

To Add a WINS Forward Lookup

1. Open DNS Manager.

2. Expand your server name, and then expand Forward Lookup Zones.

3. Right-click the zone you want to add WINS forward lookup to, and then click Properties.

4. Click the WINS tab, and then select the Use WINS Forward Lookup check box.

5. Type the IP address of the WINS server, and click Add. Repeat this step for each of your WINS servers, and then use the Up and Down buttons to put them in order of priority. Click OK.

You can also configure a WINS reverse lookup by viewing the properties of a reverse lookup zone and clicking the WINS-R tab.

Configure Replication Scope   As discussed in "DNS Zone Replication" earlier in this chapter, you can configure the scope of replication for Active Directory–integrated zones to replicate to all DNS servers in the forest, all DNS servers in the domain, all domain controllers in the domain, or all domain controllers in the scope of a specific directory. Typically, the default setting is sufficient: standard domains are replicated to all DNS servers in the domain, and the _msdcs subdomain (which contains the SRV records for domain controllers and other related services) is replicated to all DNS servers in the forest.

To Configure the Replication Scope for an Active Directory–Integrated Zone

1. Open DNS Manager.

2. Expand your server name, and then expand Forward Lookup Zones.

3. Right-click the zone you want to configure replication for, and then click Properties.

4. On the General tab, next to Replication, click Change.

5. Click the zone replication type, and then click OK.

6. Click OK again to close the zone properties dialog box.

Allowing Zone Transfers   You should allow zone transfers between primary and secondary DNS servers for zones that are not Active Directory–integrated. However, because an attacker could use a zone transfer to identify hosts on your private network or to perform a denial-of-service attack, you should not allow zone transfers from other computers. In many Active Directory deployments, zone transfers will never be used and should be disabled. Active Directory replication does not use zone transfers.

To Allow a Server to Perform Zone Transfers

1. Open DNS Manager.

2. Expand your server name, and then expand Forward Lookup Zones.

3. Right-click the zone for which you want to configure zone transfers, and then click Properties.

4. Click the Name Servers tab. If the DNS servers to which you want to allow zone transfers are not shown in the list, click Add for each server you want to add. This automatically creates an NS record for the server.

5. Click the Zone Transfers tab, select the Allow Zone Transfers check box, and then select Only To Servers Listed On The Name Servers Tab. Although this is typically the correct option, you have three options to choose from:

    ❑   **Only To Servers Listed On The Name Servers Tab**   Allows all name servers for the zone, as listed on the Name Servers tab, to perform a zone transfer. This is the preferred technique for allowing zone transfers.

> **Note**   You can click the Notify button on the Zone Transfers tab to specify servers to be notified of updated DNS records, which minimizes the time required for all DNS servers to synchronize. However, this is enabled by default for servers listed on the Name Servers tab, so no manual configuration is necessary in most circumstances.

❑ **To Any Server** Avoid selecting this option because it would allow anyone with network access to your DNS server to perform a zone transfer.

❑ **Only To The Following Servers** Select this option to manually configure the IP addresses of servers that can perform zone transfers.

6. Click OK.

Delegate Authority for a Sub-Domain to a Different Zone If a different DNS server will be authoritative for a subdomain, you must delegate authority for that subdomain from the primary DNS server for the parent domain. This delegation allows DNS servers for the parent domain to redirect requests to the name servers for the child domain.

For example, if a new DNS server will be authoritative for south.contoso.com, you should use the DNS Manager console on the contoso.com primary DNS server to delegate authority for the south.contoso.com subdomain to the new DNS server. When a contoso.com DNS server receives queries for the south.contoso.com domain, it will redirect queries to the south.contoso.com DNS servers.

To Delegate Authority for a Subdomain

1. Open DNS Manager

2. Right-click the parent domain, and then click New Delegation.

   The New Delegation Wizard appears.

3. On the Welcome To The New Delegation Wizard page, click Next.

4. On the Delegated Domain Name page, type the name of the new subdomain, and then click Next.

5. On the Name Servers page, click Add to open the New Name Server Record dialog box. Then, type the host name of the DNS server that will be authoritative for the domain. Click OK, click Next, and then click Finish.

Now, follow the steps in "Configure a Primary Forward Lookup Zone" earlier in this section to configure the subdomain on the DNS server.

Configure a Stub Zone Stub zones configure your DNS server to forward requests for a specific domain to a specific server. This is similar to the way a delegating authority directs queries for a subdomain to a different name server; however, stub zones can be used to configure name servers for any domain. Typically, you create stub zones for domains on your internal network that are not listed in your root DNS servers.

To Add a Stub Zone

1. Open DNS Manager

2. Expand your server name, right-click Forward Lookup Zones, and then click New Zone.

   The New Zone Wizard appears.

3. On the Welcome To The New Zone Wizard page, click Next.

4. On the Zone Type page, click Stub Zone. If the DNS server is a domain controller, you have the option of selecting the Store The Zone In Active Directory check box. Click Next.

5. If the Active Directory Zone Replication Scope page appears, select the type of replication you want to use, and then click Next. The Active Directory Zone Replication page appears only when creating a zone that is Active Directory–integrated. For more information about Active Directory zone replication, refer to "DNS Zone Replication" earlier in this chapter.

6. On the Zone Name page, type a name for the zone representing the domain you want the stub zone to handle requests for. Click Next.

7. If the Zone File page appears, click Next. The Zone File page appears only when creating a zone that is not Active Directory–integrated.

8. On the Master DNS Servers page, type the IP addresses of the name servers that handle requests for the zone. Click Next, and then click Finish.

Configure a Conditional Forwarder   Much like a stub zone, a conditional forwarder configures your DNS server to send DNS queries to a specific server for a specific domain. For example, you could configure a conditional forwarder to send all requests for fabrikam.com to a specific name server. Typically, you should use a stub zone instead of a conditional forwarder because a stub zone can be automatically updated if one of the DNS servers for a domain changes. You might need to use a conditional forwarder instead of a stub zone if the DNS requests must pass through a firewall and only some of the remote DNS servers for the zone are accessible.

To Add a Conditional Forwarder

1. Open DNS Manager.

2. Expand your server name, right-click Conditional Forwarder, and then click New Conditional Forwarder.

3. In the New Conditional Forwarder dialog box, in the DNS Domain field, type the zone name. Then type the IP addresses of the DNS servers responsible for that domain, and then click OK.

Configure a Reverse Lookup Zone   Reverse lookup zones allow clients to resolve IP addresses to host names and are often used by server applications such as Microsoft Exchange Server as part of validating a client request.

To Add a Reverse Lookup Zone

1. Open DNS Manager.

2. Expand your server name, right-click Reverse Lookup Zones, and then click New Zone.

3. On the Welcome To The New Zone Wizard page, click Next.

4. On the Zone Type page, click the zone type, and then click Next.

5. If the Active Directory Zone Replication Scope page appears, select how you would like the zone data replicated, and then click Next.

6. On the first Reverse Lookup Zone Name page, select either IPv4 or IPv6, and then click Next.

7. On the second Reverse Lookup Zone Name page, type the network ID of the IP address. In the case of IPv4 addresses, this will typically be the first three octets of the IP address, such as 192.168.1. However, you can use only one or two octets of the IP address. For IPv6 addresses, type the address prefix, such as **2001:DB8::/32**, to have the wizard automatically name the reverse lookup zone. Click Next.

8. If the Zone File page appears, accept the default setting to create a new file unless you have previously created a file that you want to use. Click Next.

9. On the Dynamic Update page, choose one of the three options (as described in "Configure a Primary Forward Lookup Zone" earlier in this chapter), and then click Next.

10. On the Completing The New Zone Wizard page, click Finish.

Using Dnscmd

The DNS Manager console is the easiest way to configure your DNS server when a graphical user interface (GUI) is available. However, if you want to configure a DNS server from a script or when running Windows Server 2008 Server Core, you can use the Dnscmd tool.

> **Note**   In earlier versions of Windows, Dnscmd was part of the Windows Support Tools, which required a separate installation. Dnscmd is now automatically installed in the *%System-Root%*\System32\ directory when you add the DNS Server role.

For complete usage information, run **Dnscmd /?** at a command prompt.

DHCP Server Configuration

This section describes how to configure your DHCP server to provide clients with the addresses of your DNS servers and how to use your DHCP server to provide dynamic DNS updates. For a complete description of DHCP, read Chapter 3, "Dynamic Host Configuration Protocol."

Configuring Your DHCP Server to Provide the DNS Server Addresses

Today, most networks use DHCP to configure client computers. When adding the DHCP Server role to a Windows Server 2008 computer, you can specify the IP addresses of the DNS servers on the Specify IPv4 DNS Server Settings page (as shown in Figure 7-5) and then the Specify IPv6 DNS Server Settings page.

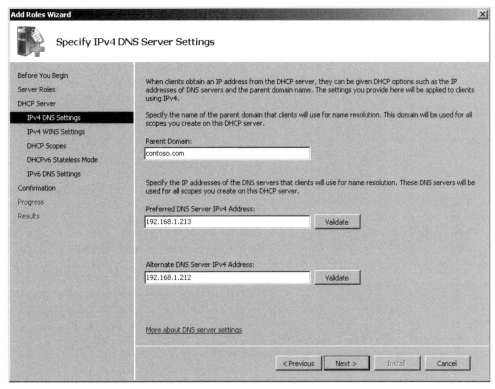

Figure 7-5   Configuring DNS servers while running the DHCP Server Add Roles Wizard

To Update the DNS Server Addresses After Configuring the DHCP Server Role

1. In Server Manager, expand Roles, and then expand DHCP Server.

2. Expand the server name, and then expand either IPv4 or IPv6.

3. Click Server Options.

4. In the right pane, double-click the DNS Servers option. Use the Server Options dialog box to configure the IPv4 or IPv6 IP addresses of your DNS servers. Click OK.

Configuring Your DHCP Server to Perform Dynamic DNS Updates

By default, a Windows Server 2008 DHCP server automatically updates A and PTR records for DHCP clients that request a dynamic DNS update.

To Configure Your DHCP Server to Perform Dynamic DNS Updates

1. In Server Manager, expand Roles, and then expand DHCP Server.

2. Expand the server name, right-click IPv4, and then click Properties.

3. Click the DNS tab. Select Enable DNS Dynamic Updates According To The Settings Below.

4. To allow the DHCP server to remove resource records after a DHCP lease expires, select the Discard A And PTR Records When A Lease Is Deleted check box.

5. To perform dynamic DNS updates for client computers that are not capable of performing their own updates, select the Dynamically Update DNS A And PTR Records For DHCP Clients That Do Not Request Updates check box. Windows 2000 and all later versions of Windows can perform their own dynamic DNS updates. Click OK.

DNS Client Configuration

The sections that follow describe how to configure a DHCP server to provide DHCP clients with the correct IP addresses of your DNS servers and how to manually configure a computer running Windows Vista with DNS server IP addresses.

Direct from the Source: Configuring DNS Clients

All computers running Windows, including DNS servers and domain controllers, act as DNS clients and have a list of DNS servers to which queries are sent. In an Active Directory deployment you should generally point your DNS clients at Active Directory-integrated DNS servers in the local domain. To provide name resolution outside the domain, these DNS servers should forward to either the parent Active Directory domain or your ISP's DNS servers (if you wish to provide Internet name resolution to your clients). All DNS servers in the list are assumed to be able to resolve all names equally.

You should not configure a client to point to DNS servers that cannot resolve the same set of names. For example, because your ISP's DNS server will not be able to resolve your Active Directory names, you cannot mix your ISP's DNS servers with your Active Directory DNS servers when configuring your DNS clients.

Jeff Westhead, Senior Software Development Engineer

Enterprise Networking Group

Manually Configuring Windows Vista or Windows Server 2008

If computers are configured to use DHCP, you need to configure only the DHCP server with the DNS server IP addresses. When clients receive a DHCP lease, they will automatically receive the IP addresses of your DNS servers.

To Configure a Computer with a Manually-Assigned IP Address to Use DHCP

1. Click Start, right-click Network, and then click Properties.

2. Under Tasks, click Manage Network Connections.

3. Right-click the network adapter you want to configure, and then click Properties. Respond to the User Account Control (UAC) prompt that appears.

4. Select Internet Protocol Version 4 (TCP/IPv4) or Internet Protocol Version 6 (TCP/IPv6), and then click Properties.

5. Click Use The Following DNS Server Addresses. Then, in the Preferred DNS Server and Alternate DNS Server boxes, type the IP addresses of your DNS servers. If you have more than two DNS servers, click Advanced, and then add them to the DNS tab.

6. Click OK twice.

The new DNS server settings will take effect within a few seconds.

Configuring Windows Vista or Windows Server 2008 by Using a Script

Use the Netsh tool to configure a computer running Windows Vista or Windows Server 2008 with the IP address of a DNS server, as the following examples demonstrate:

netsh interface ipv4 add dnsserver "Local Area Connection" 192.168.1.213

netsh interface ipv6 add dnsserver "Local Area Connection" fec0:0:0:ffff::1

Configuring Redundant DNS Servers

To configure a redundant DNS server for a zone that is not Active Directory–integrated, follow these general steps. If the zone is Active Directory–integrated, replication is automatic, and you need to complete only the client configuration described in step 3.

1. On the primary server for the zone, in the zone's properties dialog box, on the Name Servers tab, add the secondary server. Verify that zone transfers are allowed.

2. On the new redundant DNS server, follow the steps in "Configure a Secondary Forward Lookup Zone" earlier in this chapter.

3. Configure client computers with the IP address of the secondary server as an alternate DNS server, as described in "DNS Client Configuration," earlier in this chapter.

With this configuration, clients will query the secondary DNS server if the primary DNS server is offline. To load-balance requests between multiple DNS servers, configure half the client computers to use the secondary DNS server as their primary DNS server.

Ongoing Maintenance

Maintaining a DNS server requires keeping the DNS database for all zones up-to-date and occasionally replacing a failed DNS server. The sections that follow describe how to add resource records, how to maintain the accuracy of a zone, and how to perform automated monitoring of your DNS server.

Adding Resource Records

You will need to add A and PTR records for new computers that do not support dynamic DNS. Additionally, you might need to create CNAME records so that a single server can have multiple resource records.

To add a resource record, right-click the zone you want to add it to, and then click the type of record you want to add. DNS Manager will open the New Host or New Resource Record dialog box to prompt you for the record details.

> **Note** Some host names, such as www.microsoft.com, resolve to multiple IP addresses. Your Web browser is smart enough to connect to a different address if the first address isn't working properly, allowing multiple Web servers with different IP addresses to respond to requests for the same host name. This provides both scalability and redundancy. To create a round-robin DNS address when you have multiple servers with identical content, simply create multiple A records with the same host name but different IP addresses. Although Web browsers support round-robin DNS addressing, other applications might not.

To minimize the administrative overhead of adding resource records, configure clients to submit dynamic DNS updates.

Maintaining Zones

Each time a server with a static DNS record is decommissioned and an IP address is deallocated or reassigned, you should remove all resource records, including reverse lookup records, for that server. Additionally, you should verify on a regular basis, such as every six months, that all resource records are current.

If you allow DHCP clients to dynamically update their A and PTR resource records, you can enable the DNS server to automatically remove outdated records by using a process called *scavenging*. If your DHCP server is a computer running Windows Server 2008, the DHCP server will automatically remove the client's resource records when the DHCP lease expires.

To Enable Scavenging on a DNS Server

1. In the DNS Manager console, right-click the zone, and then click Properties.

2. Click the General tab, and then click Aging.

3. In the Zone Aging/Scavenging Properties dialog box, select the Scavenge Stale Resource Records check box. Then specify the No-Refresh Interval and Refresh Interval. Typically, the Refresh Interval should be at least as long as your DHCP lease renewal interval, which is four days by default. For most deployments, the default Refresh and No-Refresh Intervals of seven days each are recommended.

4. Click OK, and then click Yes when warned that the zone file format is incompatible with earlier versions of Windows.

5. Click OK to return to the DNS Manager console.

6. In the DNS Manager console, right-click your server name, and then click Properties. In the server's properties dialog box, on the Advanced tab, select the Enable Automatic Scavenging Of Stale Records check box. For Active Directory–integrated zones, this can be done on all DNS servers or only a subset of centrally located DNS servers because scavenged records will be automatically replicated.

Automated Monitoring

You can perform automated monitoring of your DNS server on the Monitoring tab of the server's properties dialog box. Using the selections on this tab, you can actively test the DNS Server service by submitting DNS queries. The results are then recorded in the Test Results list. For detailed instructions on how to configure automated monitoring, read "Test the DNS Server" earlier in this chapter.

Monitoring tools such as Microsoft System Center Operations Manager 2007 should also be used to monitor your DNS server.

> **More Info**   For more information about Microsoft System Center, visit
> *http://www.microsoft.com/systemcenter/opsmgr/.*

Direct from the Source: Auditing DNS Records (or Deletions)

Some organizations need to audit the addition or deletion of a DNS record. If you look at the DNS Server and DNS Zones, and even the records themselves, you'll notice that object auditing is turned on for these resources by default. It should follow, therefore, that as long as Object Access auditing is turned on for the DNS server, creations, deletions, or other changes would be recorded in the security event log.

It turns out that enabling Object Access auditing does not correspond to DNS zone records being included in the security logs. Instead, you must enable Audit Directory Service Access on the machines where DNS is running. Once working, you will see the following events in the Security log for creating a new DNS record:

```
Event Type: Success Audit
Event Source: Security
Event Category: Directory Service Access
Event ID: 566
Date:   MM/DD/YYYY
Time:   HH:MMM:SS AM|PM
User:   [username]
Computer: [dns server]
```

```
Description:
Object Operation:
  Object Server: DS
  Operation Type: Object Access
  Object Type: dnsZone
  Object Name: DC=[zone].com,CN=MicrosoftDNS,CN=System,DC=[zone],DC=com
  Handle ID: -
  Primary User Name: [machine]$
  Primary Domain: [domain name]
  Primary Logon ID: (0x0,0x3E7)
  Client User Name: administrator
  Client Domain: [domain]
  Client Logon ID: (0x0,0x706012D)
  Accesses: Create Child

  Properties:
 Create Child
 dnsNode    Additional Info:
DC=Testing2,DC=[zone].com,cn=MicrosoftDNS,cn=System,DC=[zone],DC=com
  Additional Info2:
DC=Testing2,DC=[zone].com,CN=MicrosoftDNS,CN=System,DC=[zone],DC=com
  Access Mask: 0x1
```

And for deleting a record:

```
Event Type: Success Audit
Event Source: Security
Event Category: Directory Service Access
Event ID: 566
Date:  8/23/2006
Time:  7:28:30 PM
User:  [perp]
Computer: [dns server]
Description:
Object Operation:
  Object Server: DS
  Operation Type: Object Access
  Object Type: dnsNode
  Object Name: DC=Test,DC=zone.com,CN=MicrosoftDNS,CN=System,DC=zone,DC=com
  Handle ID: -
  Primary User Name: [computer name]$
  Primary Domain: [Domain]
  Primary Logon ID: (0x0,0x3E7)
  Client User Name: administrator
  Client Domain: [domain]
  Client Logon ID: (0x0,0x729EE07)
  Accesses: Write Property

  Properties:
 Write Property
  Default property set
   dnsRecord
   dNSTombstoned
   dnsNode    Additional Info:
```

```
Additional Info2:
Access Mask: 0x20
```

Setting directory access auditing will create a storm of events in your security log. In most production environments, you can expect thousands of "noise" events for every malicious DNS deletion, so this probably needs to be used sparingly. This works only for Active Directory–integrated zones.

Anthony Witecki, Senior Consultant

Microsoft Services, Public Sector

Promoting a Secondary Zone to a Primary Zone

Although traditional backups are important for DNS servers, your primary method for providing availability for DNS data should be Active Directory replication (for Active Directory–integrated zones with multiple domain controllers) or zone transfers (for zones that are not Active Directory–integrated). Replication and zone transfers provide a near real-time backup that can also provide redundancy.

If a primary DNS server for a zone fails, a secondary DNS server will continue to resolve queries for the domain. However, secondary DNS servers do not accept updates. If you are unable to bring the primary DNS server online, you can promote a secondary DNS server to be the primary DNS server so that you can make updates to the zone.

To promote a secondary zone to a primary zone, follow these steps:

1. In the DNS Manager console, right-click the zone, and then click Properties.
2. Click the General tab. Next to Type, click Change.
3. In the Change Zone Type dialog box, click Primary Zone, and then click OK twice.

If you are not planning to bring the former primary DNS server back online, remove its NS records, update the configuration of any secondary zones, and then change any client configurations that have the server's IP address.

If you later bring the former primary DNS server for the zone back online, follow these steps to update the DNS database for the zone from the temporary primary DNS server:

1. On the recovered DNS server, right-click the zone, and then click Properties.
2. Next to Type, click Change. In the Change Zone Type dialog box, click Secondary, and then click OK.
3. Under the Master Servers list, click Edit. In the Edit Master Servers dialog box, add the IP address of the temporary primary DNS server, and then click OK twice to return to the DNS Manager console.

4. Right-click the zone, and then click Transfer From Master. This updates the zone from the temporary primary DNS server, which might take several seconds or minutes, depending on the number of resource records in the zone.

5. Now, promote the secondary zone on the recovered DNS server to primary, and then follow steps 1–4 on the temporary DNS server to convert the zone back to secondary.

Warning If you are not using Active Directory–integrated zones, do not allow two primary DNS servers to coexist. The conflicts between the two primary DNS servers can cause unusual problems that are difficult to troubleshoot.

Troubleshooting

The sections that follow describe tools and techniques for troubleshooting common problems with DNS servers. If the problem is with the DNS server itself (for example, the DNS Server service does not start or zone transfers fail), check the Event Logs. For problems with Active Directory–integrated zones, use the DCDiag tool. If you are still unable to identify the problem, enable debug logging at the server.

If resource records are unavailable or incorrect, you can typically isolate the problem using Nslookup. To troubleshoot more complex problems, use DNSLint or Network Monitor.

Event Logs

By default, the DNS Server service logs both errors and warnings to the Applications and Services\DNS Server event log with a Source of DNS-Server-Service. This log is also available in the DNS Manager console, under *server*\Global Logs\DNS Events. The event log includes a great deal of information that is useful for troubleshooting problems, including:

- Starting and stopping the DNS Server service
- Updates to zone files
- Potential configuration problems, such as missing SOA records
- Zone transfer failures
- Dynamic registration and deregistration failures

Note If you have worked with DNS Servers running on earlier versions of Windows, be aware that some events have new Event IDs in Windows Vista and Windows Server 2008.

To change the logging level (which is typically not necessary), open the DNS Manager, view the server properties, and then click the Event Logging tab.

Using Nslookup

You can use Nslookup to manually submit queries to a DNS server. Nslookup allows you to query for specific types of records, such as MX or SOA records, and allows you to attempt zone transfers.

Performing a Simple Query

To perform a simple DNS query by using the default server, simply specify the record you want to query, as the following example shows:

nslookup contoso.com.
```
Server:  dns.fabrikam.com
Address:  192.168.1.1:53


Non-authoritative answer:
Name:    contoso.com
Addresses:  207.46.232.182, 207.46.197.32
```

Direct from the Source: Dot-Terminating Nslookup Queries

In general, if you are entering an FQDN into Nslookup, you should dot-terminate it. Otherwise, Nslookup may append various search suffixes appropriate in your enterprise, which may give you confusing results. If you wish to have Nslookup resolve an unqualified name, omit the dot termination.

For example, if your computer is a member of the contoso.com domain, you will have contoso.com in your search suffix list. If you try to resolve **www.microsoft.com**, Nslookup will send queries for both www.microsoft.com. and www.microsoft.com.contoso.com. In some cases, the results of these queries may cause confusion, especially if you have multiple search suffixes, so instead use **nslookup www.microsoft.com.** with an explicit terminating period.

Jeff Westhead, Senior Software Development Engineer

Enterprise Networking Group

In the previous example, the client contacted the default DNS server (192.168.1.1) and successfully received a response indicating that contoso.com has two IP addresses: 207.46.232.182 and 207.46.197.32. This indicates that the DNS server is working correctly.

The following response to the same query would indicate that the DNS server could not find an IP address for the contoso.com host name:

```
*** dns.fabrikam.com can't find contoso.com: Non-existent domain
```

If the domain name should exist, verify that the root hints on the DNS server are configured correctly. If the domain is an internal domain, consider adding a stub zone or conditional forwarder for the domain.

The following response indicates that no DNS server is responding:

Server: dns.fabrikam.com
```
Address:  192.168.1.1:53

DNS request timed out.
    timeout was 2 seconds.
DNS request timed out.
    timeout was 2 seconds.
*** Request to dns.fabrikam.com timed-out
```

Verify that the client computer has the correct IP address for the DNS server and that the DNS server is online. Additionally, consider adding a secondary DNS server for redundancy.

Querying for a Specific Record Type

To query for a special DNS record, such as an MX record, set the **type** option, as the following example shows:

nslookup -type=mx contoso.com
```
Server:  dns.contoso.com
Address:  192.168.1.1:53

Non-authoritative answer:
contoso.com     MX preference = 10, mail exchanger =
ail.global.frontbridge.com

mail.global.frontbridge.com     internet address = 10.46.163.22
mail.global.frontbridge.com     internet address = 10.199.154.22
mail.global.frontbridge.com     internet address = 10.209.45.169
Querying a Non-Default DNS Server
```

You can also specify a DNS server to query rather than using the computer's default DNS server. This record demonstrates how to query the DNS server at 192.168.1.213 for the east.contoso.com record:

nslookup east.contoso.com 192.168.1.213
```
Server:  dns.contoso.com
Address:  192.168.1.213:53

Non-authoritative answer:
Name:    east.contoso.com
Addresses:  192.168.13.182
```

This technique is useful for verifying that two DNS servers are returning the same results.

Debug Logging at the Client

For detailed debugging information, enable the **debug** option. The following example shows just part of the debug output for a query for the microsoft.com SOA record:

```
nslookup -debug -type=soa microsoft.com ------------
Got answer:
    HEADER:
        opcode = QUERY, id = 1, rcode = NXDOMAIN
        header flags:  response, want recursion, recursion avail.
        questions = 1,  answers = 0,  authority records = 0,
additional = 0

    QUESTIONS:
        1.1.168.192.in-addr.arpa, type = PTR, class = IN

------------
Server:  dns.contoso.com
Address:  192.168.1.1:53

------------
Got answer:
    HEADER:
        opcode = QUERY, id = 3, rcode = NOERROR
        header flags:  response, want recursion, recursion avail.
        questions = 1,  answers = 1,  authority records = 0,
  additional = 0

    QUESTIONS:
        microsoft.com, type = SOA, class = IN
    ANSWERS:
    ->  microsoft.com
        ttl = 3600 (1 hour)
        primary name server = ns1.msft.net
        responsible mail addr = msnhst.microsoft.com
        serial  = 2007090703
        refresh = 300 (5 mins)
        retry   = 600 (10 mins)
        expire  = 2419200 (28 days)
        default TTL = 3600 (1 hour)
```

For even more flexibility, run **nslookup** in interactive mode by running it with no parameters. Then, while at the nslookup prompt, type the command **?** for complete usage information.

Debug Logging at the Server

If you are unable to resolve a DNS server problem by using the event logs, you can enable debug logging to log incoming, outgoing, or all DNS server traffic.

To Configure Debug Logging

1. Open the DNS Manager console.

2. Right-click your server, and then click Properties.

3. On the Debug Logging tab, as shown in Figure 7-6, select the Log Packets For Debugging check box, and then in the File Path And Name box, type a path and file name.

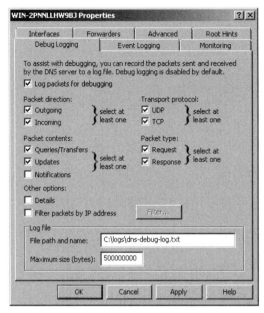

Figure 7-6 The Debug Logging tab

4. If you are having problems with a specific client, select the Filter Packets By IP Address check box, click Filter, specify the IP address, and then click OK twice.

Now that you have enabled debug logging, repeat the steps required to re-create the problem. For example, you might run the **nslookup** command from a client computer to generate a query that the DNS server is not responding correctly to.

To analyze the debug log, open the log file by using a text editor such as Notepad. The debug log contains a description of every packet that matched the criteria you specified on the Debug Logging tab.

Using DNSLint

DNSLint is a Microsoft command-line tool for verifying that specific DNS records are intact and diagnosing some common DNS problems. The following is a portion of the output displayed when examining a domain:

```
DNSLint Report
System Date: Fri Aug 10 15:48:03 2007

Command run:
dnslint /d contoso.com

Domain name tested:
   contoso.com
```

```
The following 5 DNS servers were identified as authoritative for the domain:

DNS server: ns3.msft.net
IP Address: 213.199.161.77
UDP port 53 responding to queries: YES
TCP port 53 responding to queries: Not tested
Answering authoritatively for domain: YES

SOA record data from server:
Authoritative name server: dns.cp.msft.net
Hostmaster: msnhst.microsoft.com
Zone serial number: 2007062601
Zone expires in: 83.33 day(s)
Refresh period: 1800 seconds
Retry delay: 900 seconds
Default (minimum) TTL: 3600 seconds

Additional authoritative (NS) records from server:
ns4.msft.net Unknown
ns5.msft.net Unknown
ns1.msft.net Unknown
ns2.msft.net Unknown
ns3.msft.net Unknown

Host (A) records for domain from server:
207.46.232.182
207.46.197.32
Mail Exchange (MX) records from server (preference/name/IP address):
10 mail.global.contoso.com Unknown
```

In addition to providing a detailed examination of a domain, DNSLint can verify that an Active Directory domain controller is responding to lightweight directory access protocol (LDAP) and DNS requests and that the DNS records required by Active Directory are present. DNSLint can also test connectivity to the e-mail servers in a domain. To download DNSLint, visit *http://support.microsoft.com/?kbid=321045*.

Using DCDiag

DCDiag is a command-line tool included with Windows Server 2008 that you can use to verify that Active Directory domain controllers have the proper DNS configuration (in addition to testing many other aspects of Active Directory configuration). If DCDiag detects a DNS configuration problem, it will display detailed information that you can use to correct the problem.

You can use DCDiag to test only the home server or all domain controllers. Instructions follow:

■   To test the DNS configuration of the home domain controller, run the command **DCDiag /test:DNS**.

■   To test the DNS configuration of all domain controllers, run the command **DCDiag/test:DNS /e**.

The following shows the results of a DCDiag DNS test that passes with several warnings:

```
Directory Server Diagnosis

Performing initial setup:
   Trying to find home server...
   Home Server = 2008-vm
   * Identified AD Forest.
   Done gathering initial info.

Doing initial required tests

   Testing server: Default-First-Site-Name\2008-VM
      Starting test: Connectivity
         Warning during resolution of hostname 2008-vm.corp.contoso.com through IPv6 stack.
         *** Warning: could not confirm the identity of this server
in the directory versus the names returned by DNS servers. If there are
 problems
         accessing this directory server then you may need to check
that this server is correctly registered with DNS.
         ....................... 2008-VM passed test Connectivity

Doing primary tests

   Testing server: Default-First-Site-Name\2008-VM

      Starting test: DNS

         DNS Tests are running and not hung. Please wait a few minutes...
         ....................... 2008-VM passed test DNS

   Running partition tests on : ForestDnsZones

   Running partition tests on : DomainDnsZones

   Running partition tests on : Schema

   Running partition tests on : Configuration

   Running partition tests on : corp

   Running enterprise tests on : corp.contoso.com
      Starting test: DNS
         Test results for domain controllers:

            DC: 2008-vm.corp.contoso.com
            Domain: corp.contoso.com


               TEST: Basic (Basc)
                  Warning: Adapter 00:03:FF:3A:50:8F has dynamic IP
address (can be a misconfiguration)
                  Warning: adapter [00000006] Intel 21140-Based PCI
 Fast Ethernet Adapter (Emulated) has invalid DNS server: 192.168.1.213
```

```
                    (<name unavailable>)
                    Warning: The AAAA record for this DC was not found
            TEST: Records registration (RReg)
               Network Adapter [00000006] Intel 21140-Based PCI
Fast Ethernet Adapter (Emulated):
                  Warning:
                  Missing AAAA record at DNS server ::1:
                  2008-vm.corp.contoso.com

                  Warning:
                  Missing AAAA record at DNS server ::1:
                  gc._msdcs.corp.contoso.com
            Warning: Record Registrations not found in some
network adapters

         Summary of test results for DNS servers used by the above
  domain controllers:

            DNS server: 192.168.1.213 (<name unavailable>)
               1 test failure on this DNS server
               This is not a valid DNS server. PTR record query for
the 1.0.0.127.in-addr.arpa. failed on the DNS server 192.168.1.213
               Name resolution is not functional.
_ldap._tcp.corp.contoso.com. failed on the DNS server 192.168.1.213

            2008-vm                      PASS WARN PASS PASS PASS
   WARN n/a
            ....................... corp.contoso.com passed test DNS
```

To view even more detailed information, add the **/v** switch to enable verbose mode.

Using Network Monitor

Microsoft Network Monitor is a protocol analyzer, also known as a *sniffer*. Network Monitor captures raw network data and allows you to examine it, including every detail of a DNS query and a response. Although debug logging at either the client (by using Nslookup) or the server (by using the DNS Manager console) is typically sufficient, Network Monitor can be used if you need to view raw, uninterpreted packet data.

To download Network Monitor, visit *http://www.microsoft.com/downloads/search.aspx* and search for Network Monitor 3.1. For detailed instructions on how to use Network Monitor to capture and analyze network communications, refer to Help.

Chapter Summary

DNS servers are the one of the most critical components of your network infrastructure. If your DNS servers are not functioning correctly, network applications will not be able to connect to servers, causing e-mail, Web browsing, and any other services to fail.

Fortunately, Windows Server 2008 includes a reliable, scalable, and easy-to-configure DNS server that can provide name resolution for both internal clients and for clients on the public Internet that need to access your Web or e-mail servers. The majority of DNS server configuration can be performed with either the DNS Manager console or the Dnscmd command-line tool. To allow you to quickly troubleshoot problems with DNS servers, Microsoft provides detailed event logs, the Nslookup client-side tool, and server-side debug logging.

Additional Information

For additional information about DNS, see the following resources.

- For a list of Microsoft documentation on the topic of DNS, see "Domain Name System" at *http://www.microsoft.com/dns.*

- For an updated list of root DNS servers, visit *http://www.root-servers.org/.*

- For information about System Center Operations Manager 2007, visit *http://www.microsoft.com/systemcenter/opsmgr/.*

- To download Network Monitor, visit *http://www.microsoft.com/downloads/search.aspx* and search for Network Monitor 3.1.

- To download DNSLint, visit *http://support.microsoft.com/?kbid=321045.*

- For more information about the GlobalNames zone, read "DNS Server GlobalNames Zone Deployment" at *http://www.microsoft.com/downloads/details.aspx?FamilyID= 1c6b31cd-3dd9-4c3f-8acd-3201a57194f1.*

Chapter 8

Windows Internet Name Service

A *Windows Internet Name Service server* (WINS server) is a service that provides centralized name resolution for NetBIOS names. Although Domain Name System (DNS) has replaced WINS as the primary name resolution method for Windows networks, many organizations continue to use WINS for backward compatibility. This chapter provides information about how to design, deploy, maintain, and troubleshoot the WINS server feature in the Windows Server 2008 operating system. This chapter assumes that you have a solid understanding of Transmission Control Protocol/Internet Protocol (TCP/IP), Dynamic Host Configuration Protocol (DHCP), and DNS.

Concepts

This section provides an overview of important WINS and NetBIOS name resolution concepts, including:

- The history of NetBIOS name resolution

- The structure of NetBIOS names

- How clients can use WINS servers to resolve NetBIOS names

- How clients can register their own NetBIOS names by using a WINS server.

For detailed information about NetBIOS and NetBIOS Name Servers (NBNS), read RFC 1001 at *http://www.ietf.org/rfc/rfc1001.txt* and RFC 1002 at *http://www.ietf.org/rfc/rfc1002.txt*. WINS is Microsoft's implementation of NBNS.

History

NetBIOS is an application programming interface (API) designed by IBM to allow computers to easily communicate over a network. Microsoft adopted NetBIOS and a Layer 2 protocol named *NetBIOS Extended User Interface* (NetBEUI) as a way for computers running early versions of Windows to network.

When TCP/IP became widely adopted, Microsoft created NetBIOS over TCP/IP to provide backward compatibility for applications that used the NetBIOS APIs. One of the greatest challenges was extending NetBIOS, a protocol designed to be used on a single local area network (LAN), to work on routed networks that did not support broadcast messages. Specifically, NetBIOS name resolution in NetBEUI required the server to receive a broadcast message from the client, and broadcast messages were not typically forwarded across routers to different network segments on TCP/IP networks.

Microsoft created WINS to allow NetBIOS name resolution to function on routed TCP/IP networks. With WINS, a central WINS server maintains a list of NetBIOS names and IP addresses for every computer on the network. Every client submits a list of NetBIOS names during startup and releases them when shutting down. Clients can query the WINS server to find the IP address for any NetBIOS name.

NetBIOS names are required for participating in Microsoft Windows NT 4.0 and earlier domains. Starting with Microsoft Windows 2000 Server, Active Directory domains relied on DNS for name resolution, and a WINS server was no longer required. However, the Windows 2000 Server, Windows Server 2003, and Windows Server 2008 operating systems all provide a WINS Server service for backward compatibility with earlier versions of Windows. All recent Windows clients support using DNS to resolve NetBIOS names; however, you can also configure them to query a WINS server.

Today, NetBIOS and WINS are almost never required except to support Windows NT 4.0 domains, Windows 95, or earlier versions of Windows. Additionally, Microsoft Exchange 2000 Server and Exchange Server 2003 require WINS for full functionality, as described in Microsoft Knowledge Base article 837391. Whenever possible, you should avoid deploying new WINS servers.

NetBIOS Names

A NetBIOS name is a 16-byte name. NetBIOS names can identify any of the following:

- **Services**   Services running on a computer
- **Users**   Specific users on a computer
- **Groups**   Workgroups or domains

In NetBIOS names, the first 15 bytes are typically the computer, user, workgroup, or domain name, and the sixteenth byte identifies a particular service (in much the same way that a port number identifies a service in TCP/IP networking). Table 8-1 lists common NetBIOS services and the sixteenth byte associated with each.

Table 8-1   Common NetBIOS Service Codes

Name	Sixteenth Character (Hex)	Type	Name Type
ComputerName	00	Unique	Workstation service
ComputerName	01	Unique	Messenger service
ComputerName	03	Unique	Messenger service
UserName	03	Unique	Messenger service
DomainName	1B	Unique	Domain master browser
ComputerName	1D	Unique	Master browser
ComputerName	20	Unique	Server service

Table 8-1 **Common NetBIOS Service Codes**

Name	Sixteenth Character (Hex)	Type	Name Type
DomainName	00	Group	Domain name
.._MSBROWSE_.	01	Group	Master browser
DomainName	1C	Group	Domain controller
DomainName	1Eh	Group	Browser service elections

WINS Name Resolution

WINS queries use the NetBIOS datagram protocol, which uses User Datagram Protocol (UDP) port 137. If the primary WINS server does not respond or responds that the name couldn't be found, the client will send a query to the secondary WINS server.

By default, the Windows Server 2008 and Windows Vista operating systems and most recent versions of Windows use the following process to resolve a simple, single-label name such as a computer name:

1. Check the DNS cache for recently resolved DNS names.

2. Check the local Hosts file for the name, located in the *%SystemRoot%*\System32\Drivers\Etc\ folder. The Hosts file does not have a file extension.

3. Add the default domain to the single-label name, and then query DNS.

   For example, if Windows needs to resolve COMPUTERNAME, and the default domain name is contoso.com, it will query computername.contoso.com. Clients can have multiple domain names configured and will add each domain name to the single-label name that is being queried.

> **More Info** For more information, read "Configuring DNS Client Settings" at *http://technet2.microsoft.com/windowsserver/en/library/5fe46cef-db12-4b78-94d2-2a0b62a282711033.mspx.*

4. Transmit a Linklocal Multicast Name Resolution (LLMNR) query to the local network using Internet Protocol version 4 (IPv4) and Internet Protocol version 6 (IPv6).

> **More Info** For more information about LLMNR, read RFC 4795 at *http://www.ietf.org/rfc/rfc4795.txt* and "The Cable Guy—November 2006, Link Local Multicast Name Resolution" at *http://www.microsoft.com/technet/community/columns/cableguy/cg1106.mspx.*

5. Check the NetBIOS name cache for recently resolved NetBIOS names or names that have been preloaded from the Lmhosts file, located in the *%SystemRoot%*\System32\ Drivers\Etc\ folder. The Lmhosts file does not have a file extension.

6. Transmit a NetBIOS name resolution query to the WINS servers, starting with the primary WINS server and continuing until the name is resolved.

7. Transmit three broadcast NetBIOS name resolution queries to the local network, waiting 750 ms between queries.

8. Check the local *%SystemRoot%*\System32\Drivers\Etc\Lmhosts file for the name.

The process stops if any of these steps successfully resolve the name. If the name is unresolved at the end of the process, the name resolution attempt results in an error. Typically, this process takes 1.5 to 2.5 seconds to time out.

WINS Client Registrations

Like dynamic DNS updates (discussed in Chapter 7, "Domain Name System"), WINS clients register themselves with their configured WINS server during startup. Because clients automatically register themselves, the WINS database stays up to date when computers connect to your network or change IP addresses.

How It Works: Removing WINS Client Registrations

To prevent NetBIOS names from becoming outdated, WINS will delete non-static records after four days if the client does not renew the record. By default, clients re-register NetBIOS names halfway through the time to live (TTL) of the NetBIOS name record, or every two days. When a client shuts down normally, it sends a NetBIOS name release message to the WINS server, and the WINS server deletes the NetBIOS name from the database.

Because WINS uses replication to keep multiple WINS servers synchronized, records are not simply deleted. Instead, WINS records that have expired are tombstoned. Once a record is tombstoned, that status will be replicated to other WINS servers. Eventually, all WINS servers will delete the tombstoned record. If a client queries for a NetBIOS record that has been tombstoned, the WINS server will reply that the NetBIOS record does not exist. Therefore, clients treat a tombstoned record exactly as they would treat a deleted record.

Through WINS replication, WINS records can be automatically copied to other WINS servers and made available throughout your organization.

Planning and Design Considerations

Most large organizations require multiple WINS servers for redundancy, or they need WINS servers in each regional office. To keep these WINS servers synchronized and ensure that all clients can resolve any NetBIOS name, you will need to create replication partnerships between the WINS servers. Properly planned, a distributed WINS infrastructure can operate almost maintenance-free. Without proper planning, a WINS infrastructure can be unreliable, consume excess bandwidth, and be difficult to troubleshoot.

This section describes planning and design considerations for a WINS infrastructure.

WINS Server Placement

A single WINS server can service up to about 10,000 WINS clients. Therefore, most organizations won't need more than a single WINS server to meet their scalability requirements. However, to minimize latency when responding to WINS requests, you should place a WINS server at every regional office, as shown in Figure 8-1.

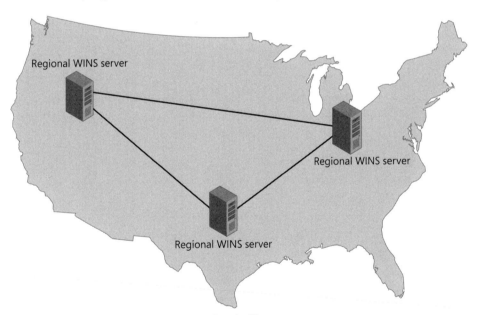

Figure 8-1   Placing WINS servers at regional offices

For simplicity, configure WINS on your Active Directory domain controllers and Windows-based DNS servers. The performance overhead is minimal.

WINS Replication

WINS supports two types of replication:

- **Push**   The WINS server transmits updates to replication partners after a specific number of local updates have occurred. WINS servers determine whether an update is required by comparing the version number of the WINS database (which is updated each time a NetBIOS name is updated).

- **Pull**   WINS servers contact their replication partners and query them to determine whether any updates are necessary. If an update is necessary, the pull replication partner queries the remote WINS server for the updated records.

By default, replication partnerships use push/pull replication together, and you should almost always leave this default setting. You need to stop only one of the two replication methods if you have extremely tight bandwidth requirements and you need to carefully schedule the replication traffic.

All replication updates are incremental. In other words, WINS servers transfer only records that have been updated since the last replication. Administrators can manually initiate replication to ensure that databases are up to date before performing maintenance.

When planning a WINS replication scheme, make an effort to minimize the *convergence time* (a term used to indicate how long it takes for all WINS servers to be synchronized after an update occurs). If the convergence time is too long, clients in one part of the network will not be able to access newly connected network resources that clients using a different WINS server can reach, which complicates troubleshooting.

If your network has only two or three WINS servers, configure them as push/pull replication partners in a full mesh architecture, as shown in Figure 8-2.

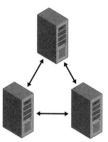

Figure 8-2   The full mesh WINS replication architecture

If you have more than three WINS servers, configure them to replicate in a hub-and-spoke architecture. As shown in Figure 8-3, you can create a redundant hub-and-spoke architecture by configuring two WINS servers as the hub. When configuring the replication, simply configure every WINS server to replicate with the hub computer or computers.

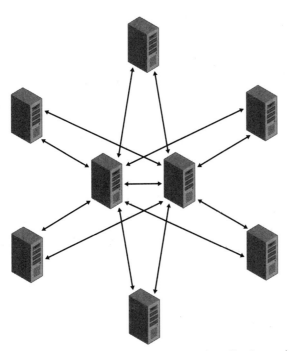

Figure 8-3   The hub-and-spoke WINS replication architecture

Deployment Steps

Configuring WINS is straightforward, and the default settings are the correct choices for most organizations. This section describes the following:

■ How to add the WINS server feature to a computer running Windows Server 2008

■ How to set up WINS replication

■ How to configure WINS clients

Configuring a WINS Server

Before adding the WINS server feature to a computer running Windows Server 2008, you should configure the server with a static IP address. Because clients cannot look up the name of a name resolution server, you must configure clients with the server's IP address. If the server had a dynamic IP address, the address might change, which would require client computers to be reconfigured.

To Configure a WINS Server

1. After configuring the server with a static IP address, click Start, and then click Server Manager.

2. Right-click Features, and then click Add Features.

The Add Features Wizard appears.

3. On the Select Features page, select WINS Server, and then click Next.

4. On the Confirm Installation Selections page, click Install.

5. On the Installation Results page, click Close.

Configuring WINS Replication

To complete the WINS server configuration, configure WINS replication, and then configure WINS clients (including the WINS server itself) with the IP address of the WINS server.

To Configure a WINS Replication Partner

1. Click Start, click Administrative Tools, and then click WINS.

The WINS console appears, as shown in Figure 8-4.

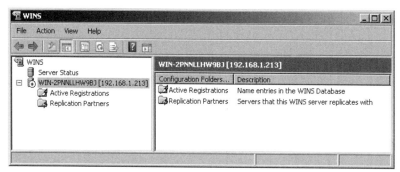

Figure 8-4 The WINS console

2. Expand your WINS server name. Right-click Replication Partners, and then click New Replication Partner.

3. In the New Replication Partner dialog box, type the IP address of the replication partner, and then click OK.

Now repeat these steps at the replication partner so that each partner has a push/pull replication relationship configured with the remote WINS server.

WINS Client Configuration

To register, renew, and resolve NetBIOS names, WINS clients must be configured with the IP address of at least one WINS server. The sections that follow describe how to configure a DHCP server to provide WINS settings to clients, how to manually configure WINS settings on a client computer, and how to configure WINS settings from a script.

> **Note**   If you have early Windows clients that do not support sending queries to a WINS server, such as Windows 3.1, you can configure a WINS proxy on that subnet to intercept the broadcast queries and send a directed query to the WINS server. To configure any version of Windows that supports sending WINS queries as a WINS proxy, set the HKEY_LOCAL_MACHINE\SYSTEM\CurrentControlSet\Services\ Netbt\Parameters\EnableProxy registry value to **1**.

Configuring a DHCP Server to Assign a WINS Server

Today, most networks use DHCP to configure client computers. When adding the DHCP server role to a computer running Windows Server 2008, you can specify the IP addresses of the WINS servers on the IPv4 WINS Settings page.

To Add a WINS Server Address After Configuring a DHCP Server Without a WINS Server

1. Click Start, click Administrative Tools, and then click DHCP.

2. Expand the server name, and then expand either IPv4 or IPv6.

3. Right-click Server Options, and then click Configure Options.

4. Select the 044 WINS/NBNS Server check box, add the IP addresses of your WINS servers, and then click OK.

To Update the WINS Server Addresses After Configuring the DHCP Server Role

1. Click Start, click Administrative Tools, and then click DHCP.

2. Expand the server name, and then expand IPv4.

3. Click Server Options.

4. In the right pane, double-click the WINS/NBNS Server option. Use the Server Options dialog box, shown in Figure 8-5, to configure the IP addresses of your WINS servers, and then click OK.

Manually Configuring a Computer Running Windows Vista or Windows Server 2008

If computers are configured to use DHCP, you need to configure only the DHCP server with the WINS server IP addresses. When clients receive a DHCP lease, they will automatically receive the IP addresses of your WINS servers.

To Configure a Computer That Is Running Windows Vista or Windows Server 2008 and That Has a Manually Assigned IP Address

1. Click Start, right-click Network, and then click Properties.

2. Under Tasks, click Manage Network Connections.

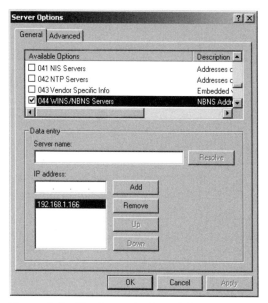

Figure 8-5 The Server Options dialog box

3. Right-click the network adapter you want to configure, and then click Properties. Respond to the UAC prompt that appears.

4. Click Internet Protocol Version 4 (TCP/IPv4), and then click Properties.

5. Click Advanced.

6. Click the WINS tab, and then click Add. Type the IP address of your WINS server, and then click Add. Repeat this step to add multiple, redundant WINS servers.

7. Click OK twice, and then click Close.

> **Note**   Configure WINS servers to be their own WINS client.

Configuring a Computer Running Windows Vista or Windows Server 2008 by Using a Script

Use the Netsh command to configure a computer running Windows Vista or Windows Server 2008 with the IP address of a WINS server, as the following example demonstrates:

netsh interface ipv4 add winsserver "Local Area Connection" 192.168.1.213

Ongoing Maintenance

WINS servers require some ongoing maintenance. Specifically, you should regularly back up the WINS server database (which probably happens automatically as part of your regular server backup process). To optimize performance, you should regularly compact the WINS database and perform consistency checking. To monitor a WINS server, you can use the WINS console or the Performance Monitor console. Additionally, you might need to add or remove WINS records as part of your maintenance. The sections that follow describe each of these tasks in more detail.

Backing Up the WINS Server Database

Standard Windows Server 2008 backup tools will automatically back up the WINS server database, which is located in *%SystemRoot%*\System32\Wins\. You can also back up the WINS server database manually from the WINS console.

To Configure the WINS Server Database Backup Location

1. Click Start, click Administrative Tools, and then click WINS.
2. Right-click the server name, and then click Properties.
3. On the General tab, click Browse. Select a folder to store the backup.
4. Optionally, select the Back Up Database During Server Shutdown check box.
5. Click OK.

To Perform a Backup

1. Click Start, click Administrative Tools, and then click WINS.
2. Right-click the server name, and then click Back Up Database.
3. Select the folder to store the backup, and then click OK. Windows will create a subfolder named wins_bak in the folder you select. Click OK when the backup is confirmed.

Note that you don't necessarily need to back up or restore the WINS database; if you have WINS replication partners that are online, you can follow the steps in "Troubleshooting WINS Database Problems," later in this chapter, to restore the database from a replication partner. Typically, replication partners have a more up-to-date version of the WINS database than would be available from a backup.

Compacting the WINS Database

Every 6 to 12 months, you should compact the WINS database to minimize the disk and memory space it requires. To compact the WINS database, run these commands at a command prompt (or create a batch file to run the commands during off-hours):

net stop wins

compact %systemroot%\system32\wins\wins.mdb

net start wins

Performing Consistency Checking

Occasionally, WINS database corruption can lead to inconsistency between WINS replication partners. Although such problems are rare, the number of incorrect records can grow over time to a significant amount. You can use WINS database consistency checking to cause your WINS servers to regularly verify each record with the WINS server that owns the record. If you have a large number of WINS records, consistency checking can consume a significant amount of both bandwidth and processor time. For that reason, you should schedule consistency checking to occur during periods of low server and network utilization.

To Configure Your WINS Server to Automatically Perform Consistency Checking

1. Click Start, click Administrative Tools, and then click WINS.

2. Right-click your server name, and then click Properties.

3. Click the Database Verification tab. Select the Verify Database Consistency Every check box.

4. As shown in Figure 8-6, set the verification interval to perform verification either daily (24 hours) or weekly (168 hours). Then, specify the amount of time to wait before performing the first verification. In other words, if you want to perform verification at 2:00 A.M. and it is currently 5:00 P.M., you should set the delay to 9 hours.

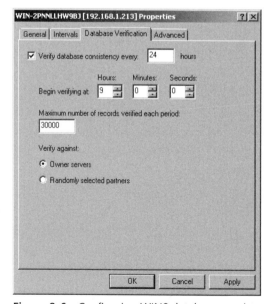

Figure 8-6   Configuring WINS database consistency checking

5. Specify the maximum number of records verified each period. The default of 30000 is typically sufficient.

6. Specify whether the records are verified against the owner servers (meaning the server that accepted the NetBIOS name registration from the client) or a randomly selected partner. Typically, Owner Servers is the best option. However, if a single WINS server is the owner of the majority of your WINS records, and you discover that database consistency checking is placing too heavy a load on that server, you should select Randomly Selected Partners instead.

7. Click OK.

Monitoring a WINS Server

Windows Server 2008 includes two tools for monitoring a WINS server in real-time: the WINS console and the Performance Monitor snap-in. Additionally, you can use Microsoft System Center Operations Manager 2007 to monitor WINS servers.

Viewing Active Registrations

You can use the WINS console to view a list of current WINS registrations.

To View Active WINS Registrations in the WINS Console

1. Click Start, click Administrative Tools, and then click WINS.

2. Expand your WINS server name, right-click Active Registrations, and then click Display Records.

3. In the Display Records dialog box, configure any optional filter options, or leave all filter options at their default setting to view all records. Then, click Find Now.

   The WINS console displays the active WINS registrations that match the criteria you specified.

Monitoring WINS Server Performance

You can monitor the activity on your WINS server by using the Performance Monitor console.

To Monitor the WINS Server Activity in Real-Time

1. Click Start, and then click Server Manager.

2. In Server Manager, expand Diagnostics\Reliability And Performance\Monitoring Tools, and then click Performance Monitor.

3. In the Performance Monitor snap-in, click Add (the green plus sign button) on the toolbar.

   The Add Counter dialog box appears.

4. In the Available Counters list, expand WINS Server. Click the counters that you want to monitor, and then click Add.

5. Click OK to return to the Performance Monitor snap-in.

You can monitor the following WINS-related counters:

- **Queries/Sec, Successful Queries/Sec,** and **Failed Queries/Sec**   Counters that display the current rate of WINS queries

- **Unique Registrations/Sec, Group Registrations/Sec,** and **Total Number Of Registrations/Sec**   Counters that display the current rate of WINS clients registering records

- **Unique Renewals/Sec, Group Renewals/Sec,** and **Total Number Of Renewals/Sec**   Counters that display the current rate of WINS client renewals, which occur every two days by default

- **Unique Conflicts/Sec, Group Conflicts/Sec,** and **Total Number Of Conflicts/Sec**   Counters that display the rate of conflicts from clients attempting to register or renew their WINS records

- **Releases/Sec, Successful Releases/Sec,** and **Failed Releases/Sec**   Counters that display the current rate of WINS clients releasing their records (which clients do when they shut down)

Adding a Static WINS Record

Typically, all the WINS records that you need will be added dynamically when computers start up. You can, however, add static WINS records for servers that are not automatically registered.

To Add Static WINS Records for Servers That Are Not Automatically Registered

1. Click Start, click Administrative Tools, and then click WINS.

2. In the WINS console, expand your server name, right-click Active Registrations, and then click New Static Mapping.

3. In the New Static Mapping dialog box, type the computer name and IP address. For the Type drop-down list, select one of the following:

    ❑ **Unique**   Identifies the Workstation, Messenger, and File Server services on an individual computer. Use this type to identify a client or server computer.

    ❑ **Multihomed**   This type adds the same static mappings as Unique, but it can be applied to multiple IP addresses. Use this static mapping type for computers with multiple network adapters. It's common to use multiple network adapters in a server and configure a multihomed record to allow different clients to connect to different network adapters, distributing bandwidth across the network adapters and increasing scalability.

❑ **Internet Group**   Identifies the Server service on one or more file servers. You can use this static mapping to identify a Distributed File Service (DFS) share that is replicated between multiple file servers.

❑ **Group**   Identifies a workgroup.

❑ **Domain Name**   Identifies one or more domain controllers.

4. Click OK.

The static record will be replicated to all partners, just like any other WINS record.

You can also use Netsh to add static records to a WINS server, using the following syntax:

netsh wins server add name name=*NetBIOS_Name* ip={*IP_Address*}

For example, the following command adds a WINS record with the NetBIOS name "SERVER" and the IP address 192.168.1.10:

netsh wins server add name name=SERVER ip={192.168.1.10}

To specify a service code, as listed in Table 8-1, add the **endchar** parameter to the command, and specify the sixteenth character in hex. The following example demonstrates how to add the NetBIOS name that specifies the Domain Master Browser service (which uses the code 1B):

netsh wins server add name name=DOMAIN ip={192.168.1.10} endchar=1B

Add the **group** parameter with a value from 0–4 to specify the group type for the record. If you do not specify the **group** parameter, WINS assumes the record is unique. The values are:

- **0**   Unique
- **1**   Group
- **2**   Internet
- **3**   Multihomed
- **4**   Domain name

For example, the following command specifies multiple IP addresses for the domain controllers group name, which uses the code **1C**:

netsh wins server add name name=DC ip={192.168.1.10, 192.168.1.11} endchar=1C group=1

For complete usage information, run the following command at a command prompt:

netsh wins server add name ?

Deleting a WINS Record

Under normal circumstances, WINS will automatically remove outdated records. If you need to manually remove a record from all WINS servers in your organization, you should tombstone it. If you need to remove a WINS record from only a single WINS server (without replicating that change to other WINS servers), you should delete it.

To Delete or Tombstone a WINS Record

1. Click Start, click Administrative Tools, and then click WINS.

2. In the WINS console, expand your server name, and then click Active Registrations.

3. Follow the steps in "Viewing Active Registrations," earlier in this chapter, to find the record that you want to delete or tombstone. Then, right-click the record and click Delete.

4. In the Delete Record dialog box, select Replicate Deletion Of The Record To Other Servers to tombstone the record. To simply delete it from that specific server, select Delete The Record Only From This Server. If you delete the record rather than tombstoning it, the record might still exist on other WINS servers.

5. If prompted, click Yes.

6. Click OK.

Troubleshooting

Although early implementations of WINS developed a reputation for replication problems and database corruption, the WINS server included with Windows Server 2008 is much more reliable. Nonetheless, problems can be introduced during client registrations or WINS replication. The sections that follow describe how to troubleshoot problems with WINS servers (such as records that are not removed correctly, replication problems, and database corruption problems) and with WINS clients (including failed WINS queries and registrations).

Troubleshooting WINS Servers

The sections that follow describe how to troubleshoot problems with WINS servers and WINS server databases by:

■   Enabling detailed event logging

■   Deleting the WINS server database

■   Restoring the WINS server database from replication partners

■   Restoring the WINS server database from a backup

Using Event Logs

By default, WINS adds events to the System event log on the WINS server with a source of WINS. If you are experiencing problems with a WINS server, your first troubleshooting step should be to examine the System event log on that WINS server. For detailed information about any event, search *http://support.microsoft.com*.

If you need the WINS server to log more detailed information about a problem, you can enable detailed event logging.

To Enable Detailed Event Logging

1. Click Start, click Administrative Tools, and then click WINS.

2. Right-click your WINS server name, and then click Properties.

3. Click the Advanced tab. Select the Log Detailed Events To Windows Event Log check box, and then click OK.

WINS clients do not add events to the event log when name resolution failures occur.

Troubleshooting WINS Database Problems

Under rare circumstances, a WINS server database can become corrupted. Corrupted databases might have invalid values, fail to update correctly, have missing records, or contain outdated records. If the WINS server has no replication partnerships, you should restore the WINS server database from a backup. If the WINS server has at least one replication partnership, you should delete the server's corrupted database and use replication to restore the WINS database from a replication partnership.

To Delete the WINS Server Database and Copy It from a Replication Partner

1. Click Start, click Administrative Tools, and then click WINS.

2. Right-click your WINS server name, click All Tasks, and then click Stop.

3. Delete the WINS server database by deleting all files from *%SystemRoot%* System32\Wins\.

4. In the WINS console, right-click your WINS server name, and then click Start.

5. Right-click Replication Partners, and then click Replicate Now.

Within a few minutes, the WINS server will receive a copy of the WINS database from its replication partners. This copy includes any records that the corrupted WINS server owned.

If you discover that a WINS server is replicating corrupted data, follow these general steps to troubleshoot the problem:

1. Stop the corrupted WINS server.

2. Open the WINS console on a replication partner, right-click Active Registrations, and then click Delete Owner.

3. In the Delete Owner dialog box, select the corrupted WINS server, click Replicate Deletion To Other Servers, and then click OK.

4. When prompted, click Yes.

5. Force replication to occur by right-clicking Replication Partners and then clicking Replicate Now. Wait several minutes for replication to complete.

6. Delete the WINS server database from the corrupted WINS server. Then restart the corrupted WINS server, and allow it to replicate data from its replication partners.

Restoring the WINS Server Database from a Backup

Whenever possible, you should restore a WINS server database from a replication partner. If that is not possible but you have made a recent backup of your WINS server database, perform the following steps to restore it.

To Restore a WINS Server Database from a Backup

1. Click Start, click Administrative Tools, and then click WINS.

2. Right-click the server name, and then click Stop.

3. After the WINS Server service stops, right-click the server name, and then click Restore Database.

4. Select the folder containing the WINS database backup, and then click OK.

   The WINS console restores the database and automatically starts the WINS server.

5. Click OK when prompted.

Troubleshooting WINS Clients

The sections that follow describe how to troubleshoot problems with WINS clients and problems with WINS queries.

Viewing a WINS Client's Configuration

To quickly view the configuration of a WINS client, run **ipconfig /all** from a command prompt. Examine the Primary WINS Server and Secondary WINS Server lines in bold in the following example output:

```
Windows IP Configuration
    Host Name . . . . . . . . . . . . : WS08
    Primary Dns Suffix  . . . . . . . :
    Node Type . . . . . . . . . . . . : Hybrid
    IP Routing Enabled. . . . . . . . : No
    WINS Proxy Enabled. . . . . . . . : No
    DNS Suffix Search List. . . . . . : hsd1.nh.contoso.com.

Ethernet adapter Local Area Connection:

    Connection-specific DNS Suffix  . : hsd1.nh.contoso.com.
    Description . . . . . . . . . . . : Gigabit Controller
```

```
Physical Address. . . . . . . . . : 00-15-C5-08-82-F3
DHCP Enabled. . . . . . . . . . . : Yes
Autoconfiguration Enabled . . . . : Yes
IPv4 Address. . . . . . . . . . . : 192.168.1.161(Preferred)
Subnet Mask . . . . . . . . . . . : 255.255.255.0
Lease Obtained. . . . . . . . . . : Wednesday, August 15,
2007 7:04:56 AM
Lease Expires . . . . . . . . . . : Thursday, August 16,
2007 7:05:01 AM
Default Gateway . . . . . . . . . : 192.168.1.1
DHCP Server . . . . . . . . . . . : 192.168.1.1
DNS Servers . . . . . . . . . . . : 192.168.1.2
Primary WINS Server . . . . . . . : 192.168.1.2
Secondary WINS Server . . . . . . : 192.168.1.3
NetBIOS over Tcpip. . . . . . . . : Enabled
```

Using NBTStat

You can use the NBTStat tool to perform several different NetBIOS name resolution trouble-shooting tasks, as the following examples demonstrate:

■ View the NetBIOS names registered on the current computer so that you can verify that the names are correctly registered on the WINS server:

nbtstat -n

```
Wireless Network Connection:
Node IpAddress: [192.168.1.142] Scope Id: []

            NetBIOS Local Name Table
       Name              Type        Status
    ---------------------------------------------
    WS08          <00>  UNIQUE      Registered
    MSHOME        <00>  GROUP       Registered
    MSHOME        <1E>  GROUP       Registered
    WS08          <20>  UNIQUE      Registered
    MSHOME        <1D>  UNIQUE      Registered
    .._MSBROWSE_.<01>  GROUP       Registered
```

View recently resolved NetBIOS names to determine the results of recent queries:

nbtstat -r

```
NetBIOS Names Resolution and Registration Statistics
----------------------------------------------------
Resolved By Broadcast     = 16
Resolved By Name Server   = 0
Registered By Broadcast   = 35
Registered By Name Server = 0

NetBIOS Names Resolved By Broadcast
--------------------------------------------
        LAPTOP          <00>
        2003-SERVER     <00>
```

```
LAPTOP          <00>
2003-SERVER     <00>
LAPTOP          <00>
2003-SERVER     <00>
2003-SERVER     <00>
LAPTOP2         <00>
```

View cached NetBIOS names:**nbtstat -c**

```
Wireless Network Connection:
Node IpAddress: [192.168.1.142] Scope Id: []

    No names in cache
```

Clear the NetBIOS name cache (must be run from an administrative command prompt) to ensure that outdated entries are no longer cached:

nbtstat -R

```
    Successful purge and preload of the NBT Remote Cache Name Table.
```

- Release and re-register local NetBIOS names if a computer's NetBIOS names are not registered with the WINS server:

nbtstat -RR

```
    The NetBIOS names registered by this computer have been refreshed.
```

- List the NetBIOS names on a remote computer given the computer's name or IP address:

nbtstat -a *computer_name*

```
Wireless Network Connection:
Node IpAddress: [192.168.1.158] Scope Id: []

        NetBIOS Remote Machine Name Table

    Name               Type         Status
    ---------------------------------------------
    SERVERNAME    <00>  UNIQUE       Registered
    SERVERNAME    <20>  UNIQUE       Registered
    WORKGROUP     <00>  GROUP        Registered
    WORKGROUP     <1E>  GROUP        Registered
    WORKGROUP     <1D>  UNIQUE       Registered
    ..__MSBROWSE__.<01> GROUP        Registered

    MAC Address = 00-13-D3-3B-50-8F
```

Isolating Failed WINS Queries

If a client cannot resolve a NetBIOS name, follow these steps to troubleshoot the problem:

To Determine the Cause of a Failed WINS Query

1. Clear the NetBIOS name cache by running **nbtstat -R** from an administrative command prompt.

2. Verify that the client has the correct WINS server configured. You can view the current WINS server by running **ipconfig /all** at a command prompt.

3. Determine whether the WINS server is online and reachable from the client computer by pinging the WINS server IP address.

4. View the Active Registrations on the WINS server, and verify that the name you are querying has been registered.

Isolating Incorrect Results to NetBIOS Queries

If a client resolves a NetBIOS name incorrectly (for example, if the IP address should be 192.168.1.10, but it is resolving to 192.168.1.11), follow these steps to troubleshoot the problem:

To Isolate the Source of an Invalid NetBIOS Query Response

1. Verify that the *%SystemRoot%*\system32\drivers\etc\lmhosts file, if it exists, does not contain an entry for the NetBIOS name.

2. Clear the WINS cache on the client on the client computer by running the command **nbtstat -R** from an administrative command prompt.

3. Run the command **nbtstat -a** *computer_name* at a command prompt. This command generates a WINS query without first querying DNS or LLMNR.

4. Run **nbtstat -c** to view the NetBIOS name cache and determine the result of the query you performed in the previous step:

   ❑ If the IP address is correct, the previous name resolution attempts that returned incorrect results were the result of DNS or LLMNR queries, rather than a WINS query. Use Nslookup to determine whether a DNS record is incorrect, as described in Chapter 7.

   ❑ If the IP address is incorrect, either the WINS server has an incorrect mapping, or a computer on the local area network is responding incorrectly to a broadcast NetBIOS name resolution request. Check the active registrations on the WINS server, and correct or remove any invalid records.

If you are still unable to isolate the source of the name resolution problem, use Network Monitor to capture and examine the name resolution traffic.

Using Network Monitor

Microsoft Network Monitor is a protocol analyzer, also known as a *sniffer*. Network Monitor captures raw network communications data, including every detail of a WINS query and a response, and allows you to examine it. For detailed instructions on how to use Network Monitor to capture and analyze network communications, refer to Help.

On the Disc   You can link to the download site for Network Monitor from the companion CD-ROM.

Chapter Summary

Although all organizations should be planning to phase WINS out of their infrastructure, many organizations still must support early versions of Windows that require centralized NetBIOS name resolution. To provide that name resolution, Windows Server 2008, like earlier versions of Windows Server, includes the WINS Server service.

When planning a WINS deployment, keep the number of WINS servers to a minimum. If you have two or three WINS servers, configure replication between each of them using a full-mesh architecture. If you need more than three WINS servers, configure push/pull replication partnerships between them with a hub-and-spoke architecture. When deploying WINS, first add the WINS Server feature to your computers running Windows Server 2008, configure replication partnerships if necessary, and then configure your client computers.

Ongoing maintenance for WINS servers is minimal; however, you can back up and restore the WINS server database, compact the database and perform consistency checking, monitor the WINS server, and add or remove WINS records. If problems arise, the WINS server records details are captured in the System event log. Additionally, you can use the NBTStat tool to troubleshoot NetBIOS name resolution problems from client computers.

Additional Information

For additional information about NetBIOS and NetBIOS Name Servers (NBNS), see the following:

- RFC 1001 at *http://www.ietf.org/rfc/rfc1001.txt*
- RFC 1002 at *http://www.ietf.org/rfc/rfc1002.txt*

For additional information about how Windows clients resolve single-label names with DNS, read "Configuring DNS Client Settings" at *http://technet2.microsoft.com/windowsserver/en/ library/5fe46cef-db12-4b78-94d2-2a0b62a282711033.mspx*.

For additional information about LLMNR, see the following:

- RFC 4795 at *http://www.ietf.org/rfc/rfc4795.txt*
- "The Cable Guy—November 2006, Link Local Multicast Name Resolution" at *http://www.microsoft.com/technet/community/columns/cableguy/cg1106.mspx*.

Part III
Network Access Infrastructure

Chapter 9
Authentication Infrastructure

To deploy authenticated or protected network access, you must first deploy elements of a Microsoft Windows–based authentication infrastructure consisting of Active Directory, Group Policy, Remote Authentication Dial-In User Service (RADIUS), and a public key infrastructure (PKI). The set of elements you need to deploy depends on the type of network access and the design choices you make with regard to security, central configuration, and other issues. This chapter provides information about how to design and deploy these elements of an authentication infrastructure that can be used for wireless, wired, remote access, and site-to-site connections. Once deployed, elements of this infrastructure can also be used for Network Access Protection (NAP).

Concepts

The following sections provide technical background on the following technologies that are used in the Windows-based authentication infrastructure:

- Active Directory Domain Services
- Group Policy
- PKI
- RADIUS

Active Directory Domain Services

Active Directory Domain Services in the Windows Server 2008 operating system stores information about objects on the network and makes this information easy for administrators and users to find and use. Active Directory uses a structured data store as the basis for a logical, hierarchical organization of directory information. Active Directory Domain Services can be installed on servers running Windows Server 2008.

This data store, or directory, contains Active Directory objects. These objects typically include shared resources such as servers, volumes, printers, and the network user and computer accounts.

Security is integrated with Active Directory through logon authentication and through access control to objects in the directory. With a single network logon, administrators can manage and organize directory data throughout their network, and authorized users can access resources anywhere on the network. Policy-based administration eases the management of even the most complex network.

Active Directory also includes the following:

- A set of rules (or schema) that defines the classes of objects and attributes contained in the directory, the constraints and limits on instances of these objects, and the format of their names.

- A global catalog that contains information about every object in the directory. This catalog allows users and administrators to find directory information regardless of which domain in the directory actually contains the data.

- A query and index mechanism, which enables objects and their properties to be published and found by network users or applications.

- A replication service that distributes directory data across a network. All domain controllers in a domain participate in replication and contain a complete copy of all directory information for their domain. Any change to directory data is replicated to all domain controllers in the domain.

User Accounts

Active Directory user accounts and computer accounts represent a physical entity such as a person, computer, or device. User accounts can also be used as dedicated service accounts for some applications.

User accounts and computer accounts (and groups) are also referred to as security principals. *Security principals* are directory objects that are automatically assigned security identifiers (SIDs), which can be used to access domain resources. A user or computer account is used to do the following:

- **Authenticate the identity of a user or computer.**   A user account in Active Directory enables a user to log on to computers and domains with an identity that can be authenticated by the domain. Each user who logs on to the network should have his or her own unique user account and password. To maximize security, you should avoid multiple users sharing one account.

- **Authorize or deny access to domain resources.**   When the user is authenticated, the user is authorized or denied access to domain resources based on the explicit permissions assigned to that user on the resource.

- **Administer other security principals.**   Active Directory creates a foreign security principal object in the local domain to represent each security principal from a trusted external domain.

- **Audit actions performed using the user or computer account.**   Auditing can help you monitor account security.

You can manage user or computer accounts by using the Active Directory Users And Computers snap-in.

Each computer that is running the Windows Vista, Windows XP, Windows Server 2008, or Windows Server 2003 operating system and that participates in a domain has an associated computer account. Similar to user accounts, computer accounts provide a means for authenticating and auditing computer access to the network and to domain resources.

User and computer accounts can be added, disabled, reset, and deleted using the Active Directory Users And Computers snap-in. A computer account can also be created when you join a computer to a domain.

Dial-In Properties of an Account

User and computer accounts in Active Directory contain a set of dial-in properties that can be used when allowing or denying a connection attempt. In an Active Directory–based domain, you can set the dial-in properties on the Dial-In tab of the user and computer account properties dialog box in the Active Directory Users And Computers snap-in. Figure 9-1 shows the Dial-In tab for a user account in a Windows Server 2008 functional level domain.

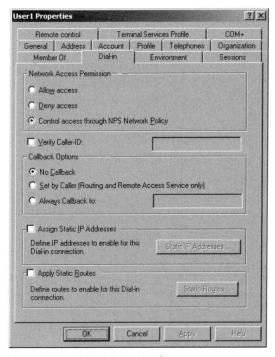

Figure 9-1 The Dial-In tab of a user account properties dialog box in a Windows Server 2008 functional level domain

On the Dial-In tab, you can view and configure the following properties:

- **Network Access Permission** You can use this property to set network access permission to be explicitly allowed, denied, or determined through Network Policy Server (NPS) network policies. NPS network policies are also used to authorize the connection attempt. If access is explicitly allowed, NPS network policy conditions and settings and account properties can still deny the connection attempt. The Control Access Through NPS Network Policy option is available on user and computer accounts in a Windows Server 2008 functional level domain. New accounts that are created for a Windows Server 2008 functional level domain are set to Control Access Through NPS Network Policy.

- **Verify Caller ID** If this property is enabled, the access server verifies the caller's phone number. If the caller's phone number does not match the configured phone number, the connection attempt is denied. This setting is designed for dial-in connections.

- **Callback Options** If this property is enabled, the access server calls the caller back during the connection process. Either the caller or the network administrator sets the phone number that is used by the server. This setting is designed for dial-in connections.

- **Assign Static IP Addresses** You can use this property to assign a specific IP address to a user when a connection is made. This setting is designed for dial-in connections.

- **Apply Static Routes** You can use this property to define a series of static IP routes that are added to the routing table of the server running the Routing and Remote Access service when a connection is made. This setting is designed for demand-dial routing.

Groups

A *group* is a collection of user and computer accounts and other groups that can be managed as a single unit. Users and computers that belong to a particular group are referred to as group members. Using groups can simplify administration by assigning a common set of permissions and rights to many accounts at once rather than assigning permissions and rights to each account individually.

Groups can be either directory-based or local to a particular computer. Active Directory provides a set of default groups upon installation and also allows you to create groups.

Groups in Active Directory allow you to do the following:

- Simplify administration by assigning permissions on a shared resource to a group rather than to individual users. This assigns the same access on the resource to all members of that group.

- Delegate administration by assigning user rights once to a group through Group Policy and then adding to the group members who require the same rights as the group.

Groups have a scope and type. Group *scope* determines the extent to which the group is applied within a domain or forest. Active Directory defines universal, global, and domain local scopes for groups. Group *type* determines whether a group can be used to assign permissions to a shared resource (for security groups); it also determines whether a group can be used for e-mail distribution lists only (for distribution groups).

Nesting allows you to add a group as a member of another group. You nest groups to consolidate member accounts and reduce replication traffic. Nesting options depend on the functional level of your domain. There are usually multiple domain functional levels, allowing for a phased upgrade of an environment, enabling additional domain-native functionality at each progressive level.

When you have decided how to nest groups based on your domain functional level, organize your user and computer accounts into the appropriate logical groups for the organization. For a Windows Server 2008 functional level domain, you can use universal and nested global groups. For example, create a universal group named WirelessUsers that contains global groups of wireless user and computer accounts for wireless intranet access. When you configure your NPS network policy for wireless access, you must specify only the WirelessUsers group name.

 More Info   For more information about the types of groups, group scope, and domain functional levels, see the *Windows Server 2008 Active Directory Resource Kit* (Microsoft Press, 2008), which is available both as a stand-alone title and in the *Windows Server 2008 Resource Kit* (Microsoft Press, 2008); Windows Server 2008 Help and Support; or the resources at *http://www.microsoft.com/ad*.

Public Key Infrastructure

A *public key infrastructure* (PKI) is a system of digital certificates and certification authorities (CAs) that verifies and authenticates the validity of each entity—such as a user, computer, or Windows service—that is participating in secure communications through the use of public key cryptography.

Certification Authorities

When a certificate is presented to an entity as a means of identifying the certificate holder (the subject of the certificate), it is useful only if the entity being presented the certificate trusts the issuing CA. When you trust an issuing CA, it means that you have confidence that the CA has the proper policies in place when evaluating certificate requests and will deny certificates to any entity that does not meet those policies. In addition, you trust that the issuing CA will revoke certificates that should no longer be considered valid and will publish an up-to-date certificate revocation list (CRL). For more information about CRLs, see "Certificate Revocation" later in this chapter.

For Windows users, computers, and services, trust in a CA is established when you have a copy of the self-signed certificate of the root CA of the issuing CA locally installed and there is a valid certification path to the issuing CA. For a certification path to be valid, there cannot be any certificates in the certification path that have been revoked or whose validity periods have expired. The certification path includes every certificate issued to each CA in the certification hierarchy from a subordinate issuing CA to the root CA. For example, for a root CA, the certification path consists of a single certificate: its own self-signed certificate. For a subordinate CA, just below the root CA in the hierarchy, its certification path consists of two certificates: its own certificate and the root CA certificate.

If your organization is using Active Directory, trust in your organization's certification authorities will typically be established automatically based on decisions and settings made during the PKI deployment. For example, when joining a domain, a computer will automatically receive the organization's root CA through Group Policy settings.

Certification Hierarchies

A certification hierarchy provides scalability, ease of administration, and consistency with a growing number of commercial and other CA products. In its simplest form, a certification hierarchy consists of a single CA. However, in general, a hierarchy will contain multiple CAs with clearly defined parent-child relationships. In this model, the subordinate certification authorities are certified by their parent CA–issued certificates, which bind a CA's public key to its identity. The CA at the top of a hierarchy is referred to as the *root authority*, or *root CA*. The child CAs of the root CAs are called *subordinate CAs*.

In Windows Server 2008 and Windows Vista, if you trust a root CA (when you have its certificate in your Trusted Root Certification Authorities certificate store), you trust every subordinate CA in the hierarchy unless a subordinate CA has had its certificate revoked by the issuing CA or has an expired certificate. Thus, any root CA is an important point of trust in an organization and should be secured and maintained accordingly.

Verification of certificates thus requires trust in only a small number of root CAs. At the same time, it provides flexibility in the number of certificate-issuing subordinate CAs. There are several practical reasons for supporting multiple subordinate CAs, including the following:

- **Usage**   Certificates can be issued for a number of purposes, such as securing e-mail and network authentication. The issuing policy for these uses can be distinct, and separation provides a basis for administering these policies.

- **Organizational divisions**   There might be different policies for issuing certificates, depending upon an entity's role in the organization. You can create subordinate CAs for the purpose of separating and administering these policies.

- **Geographic divisions**   Organizations might have entities at multiple physical sites. Network connectivity between these sites might dictate a requirement for multiple subordinate CAs to meet usability requirements.

- **Load balancing**   If your PKI will support the issuing of a large number of certificates, having only one CA issue and manage all these certificates can result in considerable network load for that single CA. Using multiple subordinate certification authorities to issue the same kind of certificates divides the network load among certification authorities.

- **Backup and fault tolerance**   Multiple certification authorities increase the possibility that your network will always have operational certification authorities available to service users.

Such a certificate hierarchy also provides administrative benefits, including the following:

- Flexible configuration of the CA security environment to tailor the balance between security and usability.

  For example, you might choose to employ special-purpose cryptographic hardware on a root CA, operate it in a physically secure area, or operate it offline. These security measures might be unacceptable for subordinate CAs because of cost or usability considerations.

- The ability to deactivate a specific portion of the CA hierarchy without affecting the established trust relationships.

  For example, you can easily shut down and revoke an issuing CA certificate that is associated with a specific geographic site without affecting other parts of the organization.

By using the Certificates snap-in, you can view the certification path for a certificate on the Certification Path tab of the properties dialog box of a certificate.

For a small business environment, a certificate hierarchy consisting of a single root CA that is also the issuing CA is adequate. For a medium-sized organization, a single root CA with a single level of issuing CAs is adequate. For an enterprise network, you can deploy a three-tiered CA hierarchy, consisting of the following:

- A root CA that is offline (not available on the network)
- A layer of intermediate CAs that are offline
- A layer of issuing CAs that are online

This CA hierarchy provides flexibility and insulates the root CA from attempts by malicious users to compromise its private key. The offline root and intermediate CAs are not required to be Windows Server 2008–based or Windows Server 2003–based CAs. Issuing CAs can be subordinates of a third-party intermediate CA. Figure 9-2 shows a three-level enterprise network certificate hierarchy.

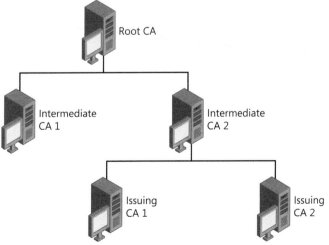

Figure 9-2   Three-level certificate hierarchy for enterprise networks

Certificate Revocation

Revocation of a certificate invalidates that certificate as a trusted security credential prior to the natural expiration of its validity period. There are a number of reasons why a certificate, as a security credential, could become untrustworthy prior to its expiration, including the following:

- Compromise or suspected compromise of the certificate subject's private key
- Compromise or suspected compromise of a CA's private key
- Discovery that a certificate was obtained fraudulently
- Change in the status of the certificate subject as a trusted entity
- Change in the name of the certificate subject

A PKI depends on distributed verification of credentials in which there is no need for direct communication with the central trusted entity that vouches for the credentials. This creates a need to distribute certificate revocation information to individuals, computers, and applications attempting to verify the validity of certificates. The need for revocation information and its timeliness will vary according to the application and its implementation of certificate revocation checking. To effectively support certificate revocation, the validating entity must determine whether the certificate is valid or has been revoked.

Certificate revocation lists (CRLs) are digitally signed lists of unexpired certificates that have been revoked. Clients retrieve this list and can then cache it (based on the configured lifetime of the CRL) and use it to verify certificates presented for use. Because CRLs can become large, depending on the size of the CA, delta CRLs can also be published. *Delta CRLs* contain only the certificates revoked since the last base CRL was published, which allows clients to retrieve the smaller delta CRL and quickly build a complete list of revoked certificates. The use of delta CRLs also allows more frequent publishing because the size of the delta CRL usually does not require as much overhead as a full CRL.

Windows Server 2008 supports industry-standard methods of certificate revocation. These methods include publication of CRLs and delta CRLs in several locations for clients to access in Active Directory and on Web servers and network file shares. Certificate revocation also can be checked by using the Online Certificate Status Protocol (OCSP), which uses the Hypertext Transfer Protocol (HTTP) to obtain a definitive digitally signed response indicating a certificate's revocation status.

Certificate Validation

The certificates that are offered during the negotiation for secure communication must be validated before secure communication can begin. For example, for network access authentication using Extensible Authentication Protocol-Transport Layer Security (EAP-TLS), the authentication server (the RADIUS server) must validate the certificate offered by the IEEE

802.1X or Point-to-Point Protocol (PPP) client. For authentication using either EAP-TLS or Protected EAP (PEAP), the 802.1X or PPP client can be configured to validate the certificate offered by the authentication server.

Windows Certificate Support

Windows has built-in support for certificates as follows:

- Every computer running Windows Vista, Windows Server 2008, Windows XP, or Windows Server 2003 has the ability, subject to Windows security and permissions, to store computer and user certificates and manage them by using the Certificates snap-in.

- Windows Server 2008 includes Active Directory Certificate Services and Windows Server 2003 includes Certificate Services, both of which allow a Windows server to act as a CA.

Certificate Services provides customizable services for issuing and managing certificates used in software security systems employing public key technologies. You can use Certificate Services in Windows Server 2008 and Windows Server 2003 to create a CA that will receive certificate requests, verify both the information in the request and the identity of the requester, issue certificates, revoke certificates, and publish CRLs.

You can also use Certificate Services to do the following:

- Enroll users for certificates from the CA by using a Web page (known as Web enrollment), through the Certificates snap-in, or transparently through autoenrollment.

- Use certificate templates to help simplify the choices that a certificate requester must make when requesting a certificate, depending upon the policy used by the CA.

- Take advantage of Active Directory for publishing trusted root certificates to domain member computers, publishing issued certificates, and publishing CRLs.

- Implement the ability to log on to a Windows domain by using a smart card.

If your organization is using Certificate Services, the CA is one of two types:

- **Enterprise CA** An enterprise CA depends on Active Directory being present. An enterprise CA offers different types of certificates to a requester based on the certificates it is configured to issue in addition to the security permissions of the requester. An enterprise CA uses information available in Active Directory to help verify the requester's identity. An enterprise CA can publish its CRL to Active Directory, a Web site, or a shared directory. You can use the Certificate Request Wizard within the Certificates snap-in, CA Web pages (Web enrollment), and autoenrollment to request certificates from an enterprise CA.

- **Standalone CA** For a user, a Standalone CA is less automated than an enterprise CA because it does not require or depend on the use of Active Directory. Standalone certification authorities that do not use Active Directory generally must request that the certificate requester provide more complete identifying information. A Standalone CA makes its CRL available from a shared folder or from Active Directory if it is available. By default, users can request certificates from a Standalone CA only through Web enrollment.

More Info For more information about PKI support in Windows, see *Windows Server 2008 PKI and Certificate Security* by Brian Komar (Microsoft Press, 2008), Windows Server 2008 Help and Support, or the resources at *http://www.microsoft.com/pki*.

Group Policy

The Group Policy management solution in Windows allows administrators to set configurations for both server and client computers. Local policy settings can be applied to all computers, and for those that are part of a domain, an administrator can use Group Policy to set policies that apply across a given site, domain, or organizational unit (OU) in Active Directory or that apply to a security group. Support for Group Policy is available on computers running Windows Vista, Windows Server 2008, Windows XP, and Windows Server 2003.

Through an Active Directory infrastructure and Group Policy, administrators can take advantage of policy-based management to do the following:

- Enable one-to-many management of users and computers throughout the enterprise.
- Automate enforcement of IT policies.
- Simplify administrative tasks such as system updates and application installations.
- Consistently implement security settings across the enterprise.
- Efficiently implement standard computing environments for groups of users.

Group Policy can be used to specify user-related policies and security, networking, and other policies applied at the computer level for management of domain controllers, member servers, and desktop user computers.

The GPMC snap-in provides a unified graphical user interface for deploying and managing Group Policy settings and enables script-based management of Group Policy operations. You can also use the Group Policy Management Editor snap-in.

On Windows Server 2008, you must install the Group Policy Management feature to use the Group Policy management tools such as the GPMC snap-in and Group Policy Management Editor snap-in.

Group Policy Overview

Administrators can manage computers centrally through Active Directory and Group Policy. Using Group Policy to deliver managed computing environments allows administrators to work more efficiently because of the centralized, one-to-many management it enables. Measurements of total cost of ownership (TCO) associated with administering distributed personal computer networks reveal lost productivity for users as one of the major costs for corporations. Lost productivity is frequently attributed to user errors—such as modifying system configuration files and thus rendering a computer unusable—or to complexity, such as the availability of nonessential applications and features on the desktop. Because Group Policy defines the settings and allowed actions for users and computers, it can create desktops that are tailored to users' job responsibilities and level of experience with computers.

Setting Group Policy   By creating Group Policy settings, administrators use Group Policy to specify configurations for groups of users and computers. These settings are specified through the GPMC snap-in or the Group Policy Management Editor snap-in and are contained in a Group Policy Object (GPO), which is in turn linked to Active Directory containers—such as sites, domains, and OUs—and security groups.

In this way, Group Policy settings are applied to the users and computers in those Active Directory containers or security groups. Administrators can configure the users' work environment once and rely on the user's computer to enforce the policies as set.

Group Policy Capabilities   Through Group Policy, administrators set the policies that determine how applications and operating systems are configured to keep users and systems functional and secure. Group Policies can be used for the following:

- **Registry-based policy**   The most common and the easiest way to provide a policy for an application or operating system component is to implement a registry-based policy. By using the GPMC snap-in or the Group Policy Management Editor snap-in, administrators can create registry-based policies for applications, the operating system, and its components. For example, an administrator can enable a policy setting that removes the Run command from the Start menu for all affected users.

- **Security settings**   Group Policy provides to administrators options for setting security options for computers and users within the scope of a GPO. Local computer, domain, and network security settings can be specified. For added protection, you can apply software restriction policies that prevent users from running files based on the path, URL zone, hash, or publisher criteria. You can make exceptions to this default security level by creating rules for specific software.

Using Group Policy

Administrators use Group Policy and Active Directory together to institute policies across domains, sites, and OUs according to the following rules:

- GPOs are stored on a per-domain basis.

- Multiple GPOs can be associated with a single site, domain, or OU.

- Multiple sites, domains, or OUs can use a single GPO.

- Any site, domain, or OU can be associated with any GPO, even across domains (although doing so slows performance).

- The effect of a GPO can be filtered to target particular groups of users or computers based on their membership in a security group.

Computer and User Configuration   Administrators can configure specific desktop environments and enforce policy settings on groups of computers and users on the network as follows:

- **Computer configuration**   Computer-related policies specify operating system behavior, desktop behavior, application settings, security settings, assigned applications options, and computer startup and shutdown scripts. Computer-related policy settings are applied during the computer startup process and during a periodic refresh of Group Policy.

- **User configuration**   User-related policies specify operating system behavior, desktop settings, application settings, security settings, assigned and published application options, user logon and logoff scripts, and folder redirection options. User-related policy settings are applied when users log on to the computer and during the periodic refresh of Group Policy.

Applying Group Policy   Group Policy is applied in an inherited and cumulative fashion and affects all computers and users in an Active Directory container. Group Policy is applied when the computer starts up and when the user logs on. When a user turns on the computer, the system applies computer-based Group Policy settings. When a user logs on interactively, the system loads the user's profile and then applies user-based Group Policy settings. By default, policy settings are reapplied every 90 minutes. (You can set this period between 0 and 45 days.) You can also locally reapply policy settings on demand by running the **gpupdate** command at a Windows command prompt.

When applying policy, the system queries the directory service for a list of GPOs to process. Active Directory resources that are enforced with Group Policy settings will require read access to the GPOs. If a computer or user is not allowed access to a GPO, the system does not apply the specified policy settings. If access is permitted, the system applies the policy settings specified by the GPO.

The scope of Group Policy can extend from a single computer—the local GPO that all computers include—to Active Directory sites, domains, and OUs. For example, a GPO might be linked to an Active Directory site to specify policy settings for proxy settings and network-related settings that are specific to that site. A GPO becomes useful only after it is linked to a container—the settings in the GPO are then applied according to the scope of the container.

GPOs are processed in the order of local, site, domain, and then OU. As a result, a computer or user receives the policy settings of the last Active Directory container processed—that is, a policy applied later overwrites policy applied earlier.

> **More Info** For more information about Group Policy in Windows, see the *Microsoft Windows Group Policy Resource Kit: Windows Server 2008 and Windows Vista* (Microsoft Press, 2008), Windows Server 2008 Help and Support, or the resources at *http://www.microsoft.com/gp*.

RADIUS

When deploying a network access authentication infrastructure, it is possible to have each network access server store the account information and credentials for authentication and the network access policies for connection authorization. When a connection attempt is made, the access server can authenticate the connection attempt against the locally stored accounts and credentials, evaluate whether the connection attempt is authorized through the local account properties and network access policies, and locally store information about the connection attempt for later analysis. However, this method does not scale, especially in an enterprise environment with a large number of access servers. A scalable and more manageable solution is to offload the authentication and authorization evaluation and the storage of each connection attempt onto a central server that can utilize the existing accounts database.

RADIUS is a widely deployed protocol that allows authentication, authorization, and accounting for network access to be centralized at RADIUS servers. Originally developed for dial-up remote access, RADIUS is now supported by wireless access points (APs), authenticating Ethernet switches, virtual private network (VPN) servers, Digital Subscriber Line (DSL) access servers, and other types of network access servers.

> **More Info**   RADIUS is described in Request for Comments (RFC) 2865, "Remote Authentication Dial-In User Service (RADIUS)," and RFC 2866, "RADIUS Accounting." The listed RFCs can be viewed at *http://www.ietf.org/rfc.html*.

Components of a RADIUS Infrastructure

A RADIUS authentication, authorization, and accounting infrastructure consists of the following components:

- Access clients
- Access servers (RADIUS clients)
- RADIUS servers
- User account databases
- RADIUS proxies

Figure 9-3 shows the components of a RADIUS infrastructure.

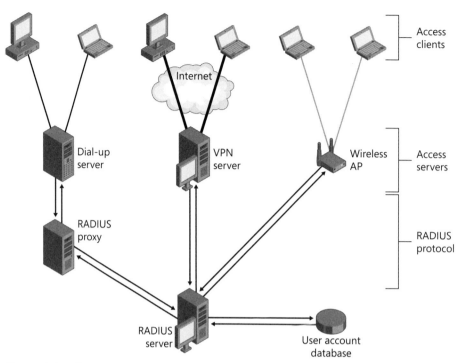

Figure 9-3   The components of a RADIUS infrastructure

These components are described in detail in the following sections.

Access Clients   An access client requires access to a network or another part of the network. Examples of access clients are dial-up or VPN remote access clients, wireless clients, or LAN clients connected to an authenticating switch. Access clients are not RADIUS clients.

Access Servers (RADIUS Clients)   An access server provides access to a network. An access server using a RADIUS infrastructure is also a RADIUS client, which uses the RADIUS protocol to send connection requests and accounting messages to a RADIUS server. Examples of access servers include:

■ Wireless APs that provide physical layer access to an organization's network by using wireless-based transmission and reception technologies.

■ Switches that provide physical layer access to an organization's network by using traditional LAN technologies such as Ethernet.

■ Network access servers (NASs) that provide remote access connectivity to an organization's network or the Internet. An example is a computer running Windows Server 2008 and Routing and Remote Access and providing either traditional dial-up access or VPN-based remote access to an organization's intranet.

■   Network Access Protection (NAP) enforcement points that collect a NAP client's system health status and send it to a Windows Server 2008–based RADIUS server for evaluation. Examples include NAP-enabled Dynamic Host Configuration Protocol (DHCP) servers and Health Registration Authorities (HRAs). For more information about NAP enforcement points, see Chapter 14, "Network Access Protection Overview."

RADIUS Servers   A RADIUS server receives and processes connection requests or accounting messages sent by RADIUS clients or RADIUS proxies. During a connection request, the RADIUS server processes the list of RADIUS attributes in the connection request. Based on a set of rules and the information in the user account database, the RADIUS server authenticates and authorizes the connection and sends back either an accept or reject message. The accept message can contain connection restrictions that are enforced by the access server for the duration of the connection.

> **Note**   The NPS component of Windows Server 2008 is an industry standard–compliant RADIUS server.

User Account Databases   A user account database is a list of user accounts and their properties that can be checked by a RADIUS server to verify authentication credentials and to obtain user account properties containing authorization and connection setting information.

The two user account databases that NPS can use are the local Security Accounts Manager (SAM) and Active Directory. For Active Directory, NPS can provide authentication and authorization for user or computer accounts in the domain in which the NPS server is a member, two-way trusted domains, and trusted forests with domain controllers running Windows Server 2008 or Windows Server 2003.

If the user accounts for authentication reside in a different type of database, you can use a RADIUS proxy to forward the authentication request to another RADIUS server that has access to the user account database.

RADIUS Proxies   A RADIUS proxy routes RADIUS connection requests and accounting messages between RADIUS clients and RADIUS servers. The RADIUS proxy uses information within the RADIUS message to route the RADIUS message to the appropriate RADIUS client or server.

A RADIUS proxy can be used as a forwarding point for RADIUS messages when the authentication, authorization, and accounting must occur at multiple RADIUS servers within an organization or in different organizations.

With the RADIUS proxy, the definitions of *RADIUS client* and *RADIUS server* become blurred. A RADIUS client to a RADIUS proxy can be an access server (that originates connection requests or accounting messages) or another RADIUS proxy (in a chained proxy configuration). There can be multiple RADIUS proxies between the originating RADIUS client and the final RADIUS server using chained RADIUS proxies. In a similar way, a RADIUS server to a RADIUS proxy can be the final RADIUS server (at which the RADIUS message is evaluated for authentication and authorization) or another RADIUS proxy. Therefore, when referring to RADIUS clients and servers from a RADIUS proxy perspective, a RADIUS client is the RADIUS entity that receives RADIUS request messages, and a RADIUS server is the RADIUS entity that forwards RADIUS request messages.

Note   The NPS component of Windows Server 2008 is an industry standard–compliant RADIUS proxy.

How It Works: RADIUS Messages and the RADIUS Authentication, Authorization, and Accounting Process

RADIUS messages are sent as User Datagram Protocol (UDP) messages. RADIUS authentication messages are sent to destination UDP port 1812, and RADIUS accounting messages are sent to UDP port 1813. Legacy access servers might use UDP port 1645 for RADIUS authentication messages and UDP port 1646 for RADIUS accounting messages. Only one RADIUS message is included in the UDP payload of a RADIUS packet.

A RADIUS message consists of a RADIUS header and RADIUS attributes. Each RADIUS attribute contains a specific item of information about the connection. For example, there are RADIUS attributes for the user name, the user password, the type of service requested by the user, the type of access server, and the IP address of the access server.

RADIUS attributes are used to convey information between RADIUS clients, RADIUS proxies, and RADIUS servers. For example, the list of attributes in the RADIUS Access-Request message includes information about the user credentials and the parameters of the connection attempt. In contrast, the list of attributes in the Access-Accept message includes information about the type of connection that can be made, connection constraints, and any vendor-specific attributes (VSAs).

More Info   RADIUS attributes are described in RFCs 2548, 2865, 2866, 2867, 2868, 2869, 3162, and 3579. RFCs and Internet drafts for VSAs define additional RADIUS attributes. The listed RFCs can be viewed at *http://www.ietf.org/rfc.html*.

RFCs 2865 and 2866 define the following RADIUS message types:

- **Access-Request**   Sent by a RADIUS client to request authentication and authorization for a network access connection attempt.

- **Access-Challenge**   Sent by a RADIUS server in response to an Access-Request message. This message is a challenge to the RADIUS client that requires a response. The Access-Challenge message is typically used for challenge-response based authentication protocols to verify the identity of the access client.

■ **Access-Accept**   Sent by a RADIUS server in response to an Access-Request message. This message informs the RADIUS client that the connection attempt is authenticated and authorized.

■ **Access-Reject**   Sent by a RADIUS server in response to an Access-Request message. This message informs the RADIUS client that the connection attempt is rejected. A RADIUS server sends this message if the credentials are not authentic or if the connection attempt is not authorized.

■ **Accounting-Request**   Sent by a RADIUS client to specify accounting information for a connection that was accepted.

■ **Accounting-Response**   Sent by the RADIUS server in response to the Accounting-Request message. This message acknowledges the successful receipt and processing of the Accounting-Request message.

For PPP authentication protocols such as Password Authentication Protocol (PAP), Challenge Handshake Authentication Protocol (CHAP), and Microsoft Challenge Handshake Authentication Protocol version 2 (MS-CHAP v2), the results of the authentication negotiation between the access server and the access client are forwarded to the RADIUS server for verification in the Access-Request message.

For EAP–based authentication, the negotiation occurs between the RADIUS server and the access client. The RADIUS server uses Access-Challenge messages to send EAP messages to the access client. The access server forwards EAP messages sent by the access client to the RADIUS server as Access-Request messages. Within the Access-Challenge and Access-Request messages, EAP messages are encapsulated as the *RADIUS EAP-Message* attribute.

Authentication, authorization, and accounting of network access connections typically use RADIUS messages in the following way. (See Figure 9-3.)

1. Access servers—such as dial-up network access servers, VPN servers, and wireless APs—receive connection requests from access clients.

2. The access server, configured to use RADIUS as the authentication, authorization, and accounting protocol, creates an Access-Request message and sends it to the RADIUS server.

3. The RADIUS server evaluates the Access-Request message.

4. If required (for example, when the authentication protocol is EAP), the RADIUS server sends an Access-Challenge message to the access server. The response to the challenge is sent as a new Access-Request to the RADIUS server. This can occur multiple times during the EAP negotiation.

5. The RADIUS server verifies the user credentials and the authorization of the connection attempt.

6. If the connection attempt is both authenticated and authorized, the RADIUS server sends an Access-Accept message to the access server. If the connection attempt is either not authenticated or not authorized, the RADIUS server sends an Access-Reject message to the access server.

7. Upon receipt of the Access-Accept message, the access server completes the connection process with the access client and sends an Accounting-Request message to the RADIUS server.

8. After the Accounting-Request message is processed, the RADIUS server sends an Accounting-Response message.

Planning and Design Considerations

The following sections describe key planning and design considerations for the following technologies in a Windows-based network access authentication infrastructure:

- Active Directory
- PKI
- Group Policy
- RADIUS

Active Directory

It is beyond the scope of this book to describe in detail the planning and design considerations for deploying Active Directory in an organization of arbitrary size. For detailed information, see the *Windows Server 2008 Active Directory Resource Kit* in the *Windows Server 2008 Resource Kit*, Windows Server 2008 Help and Support, or resources at *http://www.microsoft.com/ad*.

The following sections describe the planning and design considerations for Active Directory that will help you create a manageable Windows-based authentication infrastructure for network access.

Accounts and Groups

Depending on the type of connection, network access authentication can use the credentials and properties of user or computer accounts. For each type, you must ensure that the Network Access Permission on the Dial-In tab is set to either Allow Access or Control Access Through NPS Network Policy (recommended). By default, new computer and user accounts have the Network Access Permission set to Control Access Through NPS Network Policy.

Accounts contain the account name and an encrypted form of the account password that can be used for validation of the client's credentials. Additional account properties determine whether the account is enabled or disabled, locked out, or permitted to log on only during specific hours. If an account is disabled, locked out, or not permitted to log on during the time of the connection, the connection attempt is rejected.

When using groups to manage access, you can use your existing groups and create network policies in NPS that either allow access (with or without restrictions) or reject access based on the group name. For example, you can configure an NPS network policy that specifies the Employees group, which has no network access restrictions for VPN connections. You can also configure another network policy that specifies that the accounts in the Contractors group can create VPN connections only during business hours.

NPS can use Active Directory user principal names (UPNs) and universal groups. In a large domain with thousands of users, create a universal group for all of the users for whom you want to allow access, and then create a network policy that grants access for this universal group. To minimize the processing of group membership for a user account, do not put all of your user accounts directly into the universal group, especially if you have a large number of user accounts. Instead, create separate global groups that are members of the universal group, and add user accounts to those global groups.

Domain and Forest Trust Relationships

The NPS server is an Active Directory domain member and can verify authentication credentials for accounts in the domain of which it is a member and in all other domains that trust the NPS server's domain. Therefore, ensure that all of the domains in your Active Directory infrastructure trust the domain of the NPS server (subject to security restrictions and policies for your organization); otherwise, you must configure the NPS server as a RADIUS proxy to forward the connection request messages to another NPS server that can authenticate the user or computer account that is attempting to connect.

For the NPS server to be able to access the dial-in properties for user and computer accounts, you must add the computer account of the NPS server to the RAS and IAS Servers group for each domain: the domain of the NPS server and all the domains that trust the NPS server's domain.

PKI

It is beyond the scope of this book to describe in detail the planning and design considerations for deploying a PKI in an organization of arbitrary size. For detailed information, see *Windows Server 2008 PKI and Certificate Security* by Brian Komar (Microsoft Press, 2008), Windows Server 2008 Help and Support, or the resources at *http://www.microsoft.com/pki*.

A PKI is needed for the following purposes in a Windows-based network access infrastructure:

- Autoenrollment of computer certificates on domain member computers for computer-level certificate-based network access

- Autoenrollment of user certificates on domain member computers for user-level certificate-based network access

- Automatic provisioning of computer health certificates on domain member computers for Internet Protocol security (IPsec) enforcement when deploying NAP.

Subsequent chapters in this book describe additional PKI requirements for different types of network access and for NAP.

The following planning and design considerations for your PKI are specific to a Windows-based authentication infrastructure for network access:

- When using certificates for computer-level network access authentication, configure Group Policy for autoenrollment of computer certificates.

  Examples are the use of EAP-TLS or Protected EAP-TLS (PEAP-TLS) for computer level wireless authentication.

- When using certificates for user-level network access authentication, configure a certificate template for user certificates, and configure Group Policy for autoenrollment of user certificates.

  Examples are the use of EAP-TLS or PEAP-TLS for user-level wireless authentication.

- When using PEAP-MS-CHAP v2 for network access authentication, configure Group Policy for autoenrollment of computer certificates to install computer certificates on the NPS servers. You can use computer certificates when NPS is not installed on an Active Directory domain controller. Alternatively, you can use the RAS and IAS Server certificate template and configure autoenrollment for members of the RAS and IAS Servers security group.

  Examples are the use of PEAP-MS-CHAP v2 for computer-level or user-level wireless authentication.

- When using IPsec enforcement in NAP, you might need to configure a certificate template for health certificates.

- When using certificates for computer-level or user-level network access authentication, ensure that the CRLs are published in a primary location and in at least one secondary location and that these locations are accessible by all computers, especially the RADIUS servers. The RADIUS servers will first attempt to validate the certificate by using OSCP. If the OSCP validation is not successful, the RADIUS server will attempt to perform a CRL validation of the user or computer certificate. By default, the NPS RADIUS servers will reject all certificate-based connection attempts if they cannot verify the certificate's revocation status.

Direct from the Source: Modifying CLR Checking Behavior

Performing CRL checking is enabled by default for security reasons. It is possible to modify the behavior of NPS for certificate revocation checking. There are special cases in which you might want or need to make this change; three examples are as follows:

- If your PKI environment has a poor or slow CRL distribution infrastructure

- If you are using third-party certificates that do not or are not able to provide CRL distribution points with the most up-to-date CRLs

- If you rely on an external distribution point and do not have redundant external connections

Any of these conditions could lead to problems with the certificate revocation checking, thus causing delays or intermittent authentication failure. If you must modify NPS for your deployment, you will be making changes to values in the following registry key:

HKEY_LOCAL_MACHINE\SYSTEM\CurrentControlSet\Services\RasMan\PPP\EAP\13

The two values you will be most concerned with are:

- **IgnoreNoRevocationCheck**   This is set to 0 by default. When set to 1, NPS allows the clients to connect even when it does not perform or cannot complete a revocation check.

- **NoRevocationCheck**   This is set to 0 by default. When set to 1, NPS does not attempt a revocation check.

If you set either or both of these registry keys to 1, simply revoking someone's certificate won't limit their network access.

Chris Irwin, Premier Field Engineer

Premier Field Engineering Group

Group Policy

It is beyond the scope of this book to describe in detail the planning and design consideration for deploying Group Policy in an organization of arbitrary size. For detailed information, see the *Windows Group Policy Resource Kit: Windows Server 2008 and Windows Vista*, Windows Server 2008 Help and Support, or the resources at *http://www.microsoft.com/gp*.

Group Policy is used for the following purposes in a Windows-based network access authentication infrastructure:

- To deploy settings to install a root certificate on domain member computers in order to validate the computer certificates of the NPS servers

- To deploy settings to autoenroll computer certificates on domain member computers for computer-level certificate-based network access authentication

- To deploy settings to autoenroll user certificates on domain member computers for user-level certificate-based network access authentication

Additionally, Group Policy allows you to deploy configuration settings for the following:

- IEEE 802.11 wireless network profiles

- Wired (Ethernet with 802.1X authentication) network profiles

- Windows Firewall with Advanced Security connection security rules to protect traffic

- NAP client configuration

When planning your Group Policy infrastructure, adhere to the recommendations and best practices for Group Policy configuration within your Active Directory infrastructure, as described in the *Windows Group Policy Resource Kit: Windows Server 2008 and Windows Vista,* Windows Server 2008 Help and Support, or in the resources at *http://www.microsoft.com/gp.* There are no specific planning and design considerations for Group Policy objects that are specific to a Windows-based authentication infrastructure for network access and for NAP. However, you must ensure that the correct Group Policy Objects are being applied to those containers or security groups that contain user or computer accounts for authenticated access or for configuration of wireless or wired network profiles, Windows Firewall with Advanced Security connection security rules, or NAP client settings.

RADIUS

NPS can be used as a RADIUS server, a RADIUS proxy, or both. The following sections describe the planning, design, and security considerations when deploying NPS as a RADIUS server or proxy.

RADIUS Server Planning and Design Considerations

When planning to deploy an NPS-based RADIUS infrastructure for network access authentication or for NAP, consider the following:

- **Domain membership for NPS servers**   You must determine the domain in which to make the NPS server a member. For multiple domain environments, an NPS server can authenticate credentials for user accounts in the domain of which it is a member and all domains that trust its domain. To read the dial-in properties for user and computer accounts, however, you must add the computer account of the NPS server to the RAS and IAS Servers groups for each domain.

■ **UDP ports for RADIUS traffic**   If needed, you can configure the NPS server to receive RADIUS messages that are sent to UDP ports other than the default ports of 1812 and 1645 (for RADIUS authentication) and ports 1813 and 1646 (for RADIUS accounting).

■ **RADIUS clients to configure on the NPS server**   A RADIUS client can be an access server—a network access server (for example, a dial-up or VPN server, a wireless AP, or an Ethernet switch) or a NAP enforcement point—or a RADIUS proxy. NPS supports all access servers and RADIUS proxies that comply with RFC 2865. Configure each access server or RADIUS proxy that sends RADIUS request messages to the NPS server as a RADIUS client on the NPS server.

You can specify IP addresses or DNS names for RADIUS clients. In most cases, it is better to specify IPv4 or IPv6 addresses for RADIUS clients. When you use IP addresses, NPS is not required to resolve host names at startup and will start much more quickly. This is beneficial especially if your network contains a large number of RADIUS clients. Use DNS names to specify RADIUS clients when you require something other than administrative flexibility (for example, the ability to map multiple RADIUS client addresses to a single DNS name).

NPS in Windows Server 2008 allows you to specify a RADIUS client by using an address range. The address range for IPv4-based RADIUS clients is expressed in the network prefix length notation $w.x.y.z/p$, where $w.x.y.z$ is the dotted decimal notation of the address prefix, and p is the prefix length (the number of high order bits that define the network prefix). This is also known as Classless Inter-Domain Routing (CIDR) notation. An example is 192.168.21.0/24. To convert from subnet mask notation to network prefix length notation, p is the number of high order bits in the subnet mask that are set to 1. The address range for IPv6-based RADIUS clients is also expressed in network prefix length notation. An example is 2001:db8:27a1:1c5d::/64.

■ **Wireless APs, switches, and third-party remote access servers**   To determine whether a third-party access server is interoperable with NPS as a RADIUS server, refer to the third-party access server documentation for its RFC 2865 compliance and its use of RADIUS attributes and vendor-specific attributes.

■ **Connection request policy configuration**   Connection request policies determine whether the NPS server is used as a RADIUS server, a RADIUS proxy, or both, depending on the information in the incoming RADIUS request messages. The Use Windows Authentication For All Users default connection request policy is configured for NPS when it is used as a RADIUS server. Additional connection request policies can be used to specify more specific conditions, manipulate attributes, and specify advanced attributes. Connection request policies are processed in order, so place the more specific policies at the top of the list. You use the Network Policy Server snap-in to manage new connection request policies.

- **Realm replacement to convert user name formats**   The *realm* name is the part of the account name that identifies the location of the user account, such as the name of an Active Directory domain. To correctly replace or convert realm names within the user name of a connection request, configure realm name rules for the User-Name RADIUS attribute on the appropriate connection request policy.

- **Network policy configuration**   Network policies are used to grant or deny network access and to set specific conditions for allowed network access, such as dial-in constraints, allowed authentication protocols and encryption strength, and additional RADIUS attributes. Use the Network Policy Server snap-in to manage network policies.

- **Network policies and authorization by user or group**   In small organizations, you can manage authorization by setting the network access permission on each user account. For a large organization, set the network access permission on each user account to be controlled through the settings of an NPS network policy. Then, configure network policies to grant access by using group membership.

- **Additional RADIUS attributes and vendor-specific attributes**   If you plan to return additional RADIUS attributes or vendor-specific attributes (VSAs) with the responses to RADIUS requests, you must add the RADIUS attributes or VSAs to the appropriate network policy.

- **Event logging**   Event logging for authentication events, enabled by default, can assist with troubleshooting connection attempts.

- **Access logging**   Access logging stores the authentication and accounting request messages received from access servers and collects this information in a central location. You can store the information in local log files or a Microsoft SQL Server database.

- **Interim accounting**   Some access servers send interim accounting messages periodically during a connection, in contrast to the accounting message that is sent when the connection attempt is made. To use interim accounting, first verify that your access server supports sending interim accounting messages. Next, add the Acct-Interim-Interval RADIUS attribute as a standard RADIUS attribute from the Settings tab of the appropriate network policy. Configure the Acct-Interim-Interval attribute with the interval (in minutes) to send periodic interim accounting messages.

RADIUS Server Security Considerations

When using NPS as a RADIUS server, consider the following to ensure a protected RADIUS infrastructure:

- **RADIUS shared secrets**   RADIUS shared secrets are used to verify that RADIUS messages, with the exception of the Access-Request message, are sent by a RADIUS-enabled device that is configured with the same shared secret. Shared secrets also verify that the RADIUS message has not been modified in transit (message integrity). The shared secret is also used to encrypt some sensitive RADIUS attributes, such as User-Password and Tunnel-Password. Configure strong shared secrets and change them frequently to prevent dictionary attacks. Strong shared secrets are a long (more than 22 characters) sequence of random letters, numbers, and punctuation. You can use the Network Policy Server snap-in to generate strong RADIUS shared secrets.

■ **Message Authenticator attribute**   To ensure that an incoming RADIUS Access-Request message—for connection requests that use the PAP, CHAP, MS-CHAP, and MS-CHAP v2 authentication protocols—was sent from a RADIUS client configured with the correct shared secret, you can use the RADIUS Message Authenticator attribute (also known as a *digital signature* or the *signature attribute*). You must enable the use of the Message Authenticator attribute on both the NPS server (as part of the configuration of the RADIUS client in the Network Policy Server snap-in) and the RADIUS client (the access server or RADIUS proxy). Ensure that the RADIUS client supports the Message Authenticator attribute before enabling it. The Message Authenticator attribute is always used with EAP-based authentication methods.

For information about enabling the RADIUS Message Authenticator attribute for your access server, see your access server documentation.

■ **Firewall configuration for RADIUS traffic**   If your NPS server is on a perimeter network, configure your Internet firewall (between your perimeter network and the Internet) to allow RADIUS traffic to pass between your NPS server and RADIUS clients on the Internet. You might need to configure an additional firewall that is placed between your perimeter network and your intranet to allow traffic to flow between the NPS server on the perimeter network and domain controllers on the intranet.

■ **Network access authentication protocols**   NPS includes support for several different authentication protocols. The order of included authentication protocols, from the most secure to the least secure, is: PEAP-TLS, EAP-TLS, PEAP-MS-CHAP v2, MS-CHAP v2, CHAP, and PAP. Microsoft recommends using only the strongest authentication protocols that are required for your configuration. For password-based authentication protocols, strong password policies must be enforced to protect from dictionary attacks. The use of PAP is not recommended unless it is required.

Direct from the Source: EAP-MD5 Removed

With the release of Windows Vista, the Microsoft EAP-MD5 implementation has been removed. The decision to remove the Microsoft EAP-MD5 implementation was made in the interest of improving security in Windows Vista. The removal of the Microsoft implementation of EAP-MD5 directly affects remote access services, VPN services, and wired 802.1X deployments. By default, these components can no longer use the Microsoft EAP-MD5 implementation for authentication. The server implementation of EAP-MD5 will continue to ship with Windows Server 2008, but it will be disabled by default. Microsoft will continue to terminate EAP-MD5 connections for legacy network devices but will not initiate them from Microsoft's client operating systems.

Tim Quinn, Support Escalation Engineer

Enterprise Platform Support

■ **Remote access account lockout** To provide protection for online dictionary attacks launched against access servers by using known user names, you can enable remote access account lockout. Remote access account lockout disables remote access for user accounts after a configured number of failed connection attempts has been reached. For more information, see Chapter 12, "Remote Access VPN Connections."

Remote access account lockout can also be used to prevent a malicious user from intentionally locking out a domain account by attempting multiple dial-up or VPN connections with the wrong password. You can set the number of failed attempts for remote access account lockout to a number that is lower than the logon retries for domain account lockout. By doing this, remote access account lockout occurs before domain account lockout, which prevents the domain account from being intentionally locked out.

■ **Certificates to install on NPS servers for network access authentication** When you use the included EAP-TLS, PEAP-TLS, or PEAP-MS-CHAP v2 authentication protocols, by default you must install a computer certificate on the NPS server containing the Server Authentication purpose in the Enhanced Key Usage (EKU) extensions. Other authentication protocols provided by independent software or hardware vendors might also require certificates on NPS servers.

■ **Using Windows Firewall with Advanced Security connection security rules to protect NPS servers** You can configure Windows Firewall with Advanced Security connection security rules to protect RADIUS traffic sent between RADIUS servers and access servers and between RADIUS servers and RADIUS proxies with IPsec. These rules can be configured as part of Group Policy settings and applied to Active Directory containers or filtered for security groups, or they can be created and applied to individual servers.

RADIUS Proxy Planning and Design Considerations

When planning to deploy a RADIUS infrastructure for network access authentication or for NAP, consider the following:

■ **When to use NPS as a RADIUS proxy** The following uses of NPS as a RADIUS proxy are described in this chapter:

❑ When you want to provide authentication and authorization for user accounts that are not members of either the domain in which the NPS server is a member or another domain that has a two-way trust with the domain in which the NPS server is a member. This includes accounts in untrusted domains, one-way trusted domains, and other forests. Instead of configuring your access servers to send their connection requests to an NPS RADIUS server, you can configure them to send their connection requests to an NPS RADIUS proxy. The NPS RADIUS proxy uses the realm name portion of the user name to forward the request to an NPS server in the correct domain or forest. Connection attempts for user accounts in one domain or forest can be authenticated for network access servers that are members of another domain or forest.

❑ When you want to process a large number of connection requests. In this case, instead of configuring your RADIUS clients to attempt to balance their connection and accounting requests across multiple RADIUS servers, you can configure them to send their connection and accounting requests to an NPS RADIUS proxy. The NPS RADIUS proxy dynamically balances the load of connection and accounting requests across multiple RADIUS servers and increases the processing of large numbers of RADIUS clients and authentications per second.

For more information about these configurations, see "Using RADIUS Proxies for Cross-Forest Authentication" and "Using RADIUS Proxies to Scale Authentications" later in this chapter.

■ **Connection request policy configuration** The Use Windows Authentication For All Users default connection request policy uses NPS as a RADIUS server. To create a connection request policy to use NPS as a RADIUS proxy, you must first create a remote RADIUS server group whose members are the set of RADIUS servers to which a RADIUS message is forwarded. Next, create a connection request policy that forwards authentication requests to a remote RADIUS server group. Finally, either delete the Use Windows Authentication For All Users connection request policy or move the new connection request policy higher in the list so that it is evaluated first.

■ **Realm replacement and attribute manipulation** To convert realm names and configure RADIUS message forwarding based on the realm name, you must use realm rules for the User-Name attribute on the appropriate connection request policy. If you are using the MS-CHAP v2 authentication protocol, you cannot manipulate the User Name attribute if the connection request policy is used to forward the RADIUS message. The only exception occurs when a backslash character (\) is used, and the manipulation affects only the information to the left of it. A backslash character is typically used to indicate a domain name (the information to the left of the backslash) and a user account name within the domain (the information to the right of the backslash). In this case, only attribute manipulation rules that modify or replace the domain name are allowed.

■ **The use of additional RADIUS attributes and vendor-specific attributes** If you plan to include additional RADIUS attributes and vendor-specific attributes (VSAs) to RADIUS requests that are being forwarded, you must add the RADIUS attributes and VSAs to the appropriate connection request policy.

■ **Remote RADIUS server group configuration** A remote RADIUS server group contains the set of RADIUS servers to which RADIUS messages matching a connection request policy are forwarded.

■ **Copying logging information at the NPS proxy** The NPS proxy can record all RADIUS accounting information that it receives in the local log file. This creates a central location for all authentication and accounting information for all of the access servers of the NPS proxy.

- **Authentication and accounting ports**   When you configure a server in a remote RADIUS server group, you can configure custom UDP ports to which RADIUS authentication and accounting messages are sent. The default UDP port for authentication requests is 1812. The default UDP port for accounting requests is 1813.

- **Load balancing and failure detection**   When you configure multiple servers in a remote RADIUS server group, you can configure settings that determine how the NPS proxy balances the load of authentication and accounting requests over the RADIUS servers in the group. By default, the RADIUS traffic is balanced equally across the members of the group. You can use additional settings to configure NPS to detect and recover from the failure of a remote RADIUS server group member.

Direct from the Source: RADIUS Proxies and Trusts

It is best to avoid creating arbitrary trusts for cross-domain network authentication. If your goal is to allow domain users the ability to log on to networks in different domains, use RADIUS proxies rather than a transitive trust. With a RADIUS proxy, you are passing only the essential data between the two NPS servers necessary for granting user or computer access. Additionally, this requires at most only two UDP ports to be available between the two domains. With a trust, far more traffic, such as resource access validation, is being passed, and many more ports are required to be opened.

Clay Seymour, Support Escalation Engineer

Enterprise Platform Support

RADIUS Proxy Security Considerations

When using NPS as a RADIUS proxy, consider the following to ensure a protected RADIUS infrastructure:

- **Shared secrets**   Configure strong shared secrets to prevent dictionary attacks, and change them frequently. Strong shared secrets are a long (more than 22 characters) sequence of random letters, numbers, and punctuation.

- **Firewall configuration**   If your NPS proxy is on a perimeter network, configure your Internet firewall (between your perimeter network and the Internet) to allow RADIUS messages to pass between your NPS proxy and RADIUS clients on the Internet. You might need to configure an additional firewall that is placed between your perimeter network and your intranet to allow RADIUS traffic to flow between the NPS proxy on the perimeter network and an NPS server on the intranet.

- **Message Authenticator attribute**   You can use the RADIUS Message Authenticator attribute (also known as a *digital signature* or the *signature attribute*) to ensure that RADIUS Access-Request messages for connection requests were sent from a RADIUS client configured with the correct shared secret. The Message Authenticator attribute is always used with EAP, and you don't have to enable it on the NPS server or access server. For the PAP, CHAP, MS-CHAP, and MS-CHAP v2 authentication protocols, you must enable the use of the Message Authenticator attribute on both the NPS server (as part of the configuration of the RADIUS client) and the RADIUS client (the access server or RADIUS proxy). Ensure that the RADIUS client supports the Message Authenticator attribute before enabling it.

■ **Using Windows Firewall with Advanced Security connection security rules to protect NPS proxies**   You can configure the Windows Firewall with Advanced Security connection security rules to use IPsec to protect RADIUS traffic sent between NPS proxies and access servers and between the NPS proxies and RADIUS servers.

■ **Password Authentication Protocol (PAP)**   The use of PAP is strongly discouraged, especially when using RADIUS proxies.

High Availability for RADIUS Authentication

To provide high availability for RADIUS-based authentication and accounting, you should always use at least two NPS servers. One NPS server is used as the primary RADIUS server, and the other is used as a backup. Access servers or other RADIUS proxies are configured for both NPS servers (a primary and a secondary) and automatically switch to the secondary NPS RADIUS server when the primary NPS RADIUS server becomes unavailable. When using multiple RADIUS servers, failover is based on a RADIUS client switching to another RADIUS server and performing a new authentication transaction. Failover within a transaction is not supported.

High Scalability for RADIUS Authentication

Consider the following for scaling RADIUS authentication to an organization containing a large number of accounts or connection attempt activity:

■ **Use universal groups and group-based network policies**   If you are using network policies to restrict access for all but certain groups, create a universal group for all of the users or computers for whom you want to allow access, and then create a network policy that grants access for this universal group. Do not put all of your user and computer accounts directly into the universal group, especially if you have a large number of them on your network. Instead, create separate groups that are members of the universal group, and add the user and computer accounts to those groups.

■ **Use user principal names**   Use user principal names (UPNs), such as user@contoso.com, to refer to users whenever possible. A user can have the same user principal name regardless of domain membership. This practice provides scalability that might be required in organizations with a large number of domains.

■ **Install NPS on domain controllers** If possible, install NPS on domain controllers for best authentication and authorization performance. When NPS is running on a domain controller, the traffic and processing delays incurred when an NPS RADIUS server contacts a domain controller over the network to verify account credentials and obtain account properties are eliminated.

If the NPS server is on a computer other than a domain controller, and it is receiving a large number of authentication requests per second, you can improve performance by increasing the number of concurrent authentications between the NPS server and the domain controller. To do this, edit the following registry key: HKEY_LOCAL_MACHINE\SYSTEM\CurrentControlSet\Services\Netlogon\ Parameters. Add a new value (REG_DWORD value type) named MaxConcurrentApi, and although the range can be between 0 and 10, assign it a setting from 2 through 5.

This value specifies the maximum number of simultaneous logon calls that can be transmitted to the domain controller over the secure channel at any given time, and the default is 2 for a member server computer. Increasing the setting will allow additional logon calls to be processed simultaneously to improve performance on the NPS server. Avoid setting the MaxConcurrentApi value to a setting higher than 5 because the additional load might cause depletion of resources on the domain controller.

Deployment Steps

This section contains the steps or resources for the steps to deploy the following components of a Windows-based network access authentication infrastructure:

■ Active Directory

■ PKI

■ Group Policy

■ RADIUS

Deploying Active Directory

It is beyond the scope of this book to instruct you on the specific steps to deploy Active Directory for an organization of arbitrary size. For additional information, see the *Windows Server 2008 Active Directory Resource Kit* in the *Windows Server 2008 Resource Kit*, Windows Server 2008 Help and Support, or the resources at *http://www.microsoft.com/ad*.

The elements of configuring Active Directory to best support a Windows-based authentication infrastructure for network access are as follows:

■ Ensure that all users who are making user-level authenticated connections have a corresponding user account that is enabled.

■ Ensure that all computers that are making computer-level authenticated connections have a corresponding computer account that is enabled.

■ Set the network access permission on user and computer accounts to the appropriate setting: either Allow Access or Control Access Through NPS Network Policy (recommended). The network access permission setting is on the Dial-In tab on the properties dialog box of a user or computer account in the Active Directory Users And Computers snap-in.

■ Organize your network access user and computer accounts into the appropriate groups. Use a Windows 2000, Windows Server 2003, or Windows Server 2008 functional-level domain and universal groups and global groups to organize your accounts for a specific type of access into a single group. For example, for wireless access, create a universal group named WirelessUsers that contains global groups of wireless user and computer accounts for intranet access.

Deploying PKI

It is beyond the scope of this book to provide the specific steps to deploy a PKI for an organization of arbitrary size. For additional information, see *Windows Server 2008 PKI and Certificate Security* by Brian Komar (Microsoft Press, 2008), Windows Server 2008 Help and Support, or the resources at *http://www.microsoft.com/pki*.

The elements of configuring a certificate services-based PKI to best support a Windows-based authentication infrastructure for network access are as follows:

■ When using certificates for user-level network access authentication, configure a certificate template for user certificates. If you are running a Windows enterprise CA, you can make a copy of the standard user template. Standalone CAs do not support certificate templates.

■ When using IPsec enforcement in NAP, you might need to configure a certificate template for health certificates.

> **Note** A certificate template for a computer certificate is already configured by default with Windows Certificate Services.

After your PKI has been deployed, there are a set of procedures for deploying certificates that are common to wireless, wired, remote access VPN, and site-to-site VPN connections. These procedures are as follows:

■ Configuring autoenrollment of computer certificates to computers in an Active Directory domain

■ Using the Certificates snap-in to request a computer certificate

- Using the Certificates snap-in to import a computer certificate

- Executing a CAPICOM script that requests a computer or user certificate

- Configuring autoenrollment of user certificates in an Active Directory domain

- Using the Certificates snap-in to request a user certificate

- Using the Certificates snap-in to import a user certificate

- Installing third-party certificate chains by using Group Policy

- Requesting a certificate via the Web

Configuring the Autoenrollment of Computer Certificates to Computers in an Active Directory Domain   If you are using a Windows Server 2008 enterprise CA as an issuing CA, each computer can automatically request a computer certificate from the issuing CA by using a Computer Configuration group policy setting. This method allows a single point of configuration for an entire domain.

To Configure an Active Directory Domain for Automatic Enrollment of Computer Certificates

1. Open the Group Policy Management snap-in.

2. In the console tree, expand Forest, expand Domains, and then click the name of the domain to which your CA belongs.

3. On the Linked Group Policy Objects pane, right-click the appropriate Group Policy Object (the default object is Default Domain Policy), and then click Edit.

4. In the console tree of the Group Policy Management Editor snap-in, expand Computer Configuration, then Windows Settings, then Security Settings, and then Public Key Policies.

5. Right-click Automatic Certificate Request Settings, point to New, and then click Automatic Certificate Request.

6. The Automatic Certificate Request Setup Wizard appears. Click Next.

7. On the Certificate Template page, click Computer, and then click Next.

8. Click Finish.

To immediately obtain an updated Computer Configuration Group Policy to request a computer certificate for a computer running Windows Server 2008, Windows Vista, Windows Server 2003, or Windows XP, restart the computer, or type **gpupdate /target:computer** at a command prompt.

Using the Certificates Snap-In to Request a Computer Certificate   If you are using a Windows Server 2008 enterprise CA as an issuing CA, each computer can separately request a computer certificate from the issuing CA by using the Certificates snap-in.

To Request a Computer Certificate by Using the Certificates Snap-In

1. Log on to the computer using an account that has administrator privileges for that computer.

2. On the Start menu, click Run, type **mmc**, and then press Enter.

3. On the Console menu, click File, and then click Add/Remove Snap-In.

4. In the Add Or Remove Snap-Ins dialog box, under Available Snap-Ins, double-click Certificates. In the Certificates Snap-In dialog box, click Computer Account, and then click Next.

5. Do one of the following:

    ❑   To manage certificates for the local computer, click Local Computer.

    ❑   To manage certificates for a remote computer, click Another Computer and type the name of the computer, or click Browse to select the computer name. Then click OK.

6. Click Finish. Certificates (Local Computer) or Certificates (*computername*) appears on the list of selected snap-ins for the new console. Click OK.

7. In the console tree, expand the Certificates\Personal node.

8. Right-click the Personal node, point to All Tasks, and then click Request New Certificate.

The Certificate Request Wizard guides you through the steps of requesting a certificate. For a Windows-based client computer, the certificate imported into the Local Computer store must have the Client Authentication Enhanced Key Usage (EKU). For the certificate installed on the VPN server or the NPS server, the certificate imported into the Local Computer store must have the Server Authentication EKU.

Using the Certificates Snap-In to Import a Computer Certificate   If you have a certificate file that contains the computer certificate, you can import the computer certificate by using the Certificates snap-in. This must be done when you purchase individual computer certificates for your VPN or RADIUS servers from a third-party CA for PEAP-MS-CHAP v2 authentication or for Secure Socket Tunneling Protocol (SSTP) connections.

To Import a Computer Certificate by Using the Certificates Snap-In

1. Open the Certificates (Local Computer)\Personal node.

2. Right-click the Personal node, point to All Tasks, and then click Import.

The Certificate Import Wizard guides you through the steps of importing a certificate from a certificate file. For a Windows-based client computer, the certificate imported into the Local Computer store must have the Client Authentication EKU. For the certificate installed on the VPN or NPS server, the certificate imported into the Local Computer store must have the Server Authentication EKU.

> **Note**   It is also possible to import a certificate by double-clicking a certificate file that is stored in a folder or sent in an e-mail message. Although this works for certificates created with Windows-based CAs, this method might not work for third-party CAs. The recommended method of importing certificates is to use the Certificates snap-in.

Executing a CAPICOM Script That Requests a Computer or User Certificate   In this method, each computer must execute a CAPICOM script that requests a computer or user certificate from the issuing CA. CAPICOM is a COM client that performs cryptographic functions (the CryptoAPI) by using Microsoft ActiveX and COM objects. CAPICOM can be used with Microsoft Visual Basic, Visual Basic Scripting Edition, and C++. For more information about CAPICOM, visit *http://msdn2.microsoft.com/en-us/library/ms995332.aspx*.

To perform an enterprise deployment of user and computer certificates, a CAPICOM program or script can be distributed through e-mail for execution, or users can be directed to a Web site containing a link to a CAPICOM program or script. Alternately, the CAPICOM program or script can be placed in the user's logon script file for automatic execution. The storage location of the user or computer certificate can be specified using the CAPICOM application programming interfaces (APIs).

Configuring Autoenrollment of User Certificates to Users in an Active Directory Domain   This method allows a single point of configuration for the entire domain. All members of the domain automatically request the user certificate through a User Configuration group policy setting. If you use as an issuing CA an enterprise CA from Windows Server 2008, Windows Server 2003 Enterprise Edition, or Windows Server 2003 Datacenter Edition, you can install user certificates through autoenrollment.

To Configure User Certificate Enrollment for an Enterprise CA

1. On the Start menu, click Run, type **mmc**, and then click OK.

2. On the File menu, click Add/Remove Snap-In.

3. Under Available Snap-Ins, double-click Certificate Templates, and then click OK.

4. In the console tree, click Certificate Templates. All certificate templates appear in the details pane.

5. In the details pane, right-click the User template, and then click Duplicate Template. When prompted for the minimum version of the CA to support the certificate template, click Windows Server 2003, Enterprise Edition, and then click OK.

6. In the Template Display Name field, type the name of the new user certificate template (for example, **VPNAccess**).

    Make sure that the Publish Certificate In Active Directory check box is selected.

7. Click the Security tab.

8. In the Group Or User Names list, click Domain Users.

9. In the Permissions For Domain Users list, select the Read, Enroll, and Autoenroll permission check boxes, and then click OK.

10. Open the Certification Authority snap-in.

11. In the console tree, expand your CA's name, and then click Certificate Templates.

12. On the Action menu, point to New, and then click Certificate Template To Issue.

13. Click the name of the newly created user certificate template (for example, VPNAccess), and then click OK.

14. Open the Group Policy Management snap-in.

15. In the console tree, expand Forest, expand Domains, and then click the name of your domain to which your CA belongs.

16. On the Linked Group Policy Objects pane, right-click the appropriate Group Policy Object (the default object is Default Domain Policy), and then click Edit.

17. In the console tree of the Group Policy Management Editor snap-in, expand Computer Configuration, then Windows Settings, then Security Settings, and then Public Key Policies.

18. In the details pane, double-click Certificate Services Client – Auto–Enrollment.

19. In Configuration Model, select Enabled from the drop-down list.

20. Select the Renew Expired Certificates, Update Pending Certificates, and Remove Revoked Certificates check box.

21. Select the Update Certificates That Use Certificate Templates check box, and then click OK.

Perform steps 15–21 for each domain container, as appropriate. Ensure that all appropriate domain containers are configured for autoenrollment of user certificates, either through the inheritance of group policy settings of a parent container or through explicit configuration.

To immediately update User Configuration group policy and request a user certificate for a computer that is running Windows Server 2008, Windows Vista, Windows Server 2003, or Windows XP and is a member of the domain for which autoenrollment is configured, restart the computer, or at a command prompt, type **gpupdate /target:user**.

Using the Certificates Snap-In to Request a User Certificate   If you are using a Windows Server 2008 enterprise CA as an issuing CA, each computer can separately request a user certificate from the issuing CA by using the Certificates snap-in.

To Request a User Certificate by Using the Certificates Snap-In

1. Log on to the computer using an account that has administrator privileges for that computer.

2. On the Start menu, click Run, type **mmc**, and then press Enter.

3. On the Console menu, click File, and then click Add/Remove Snap-In.

4. In the Add Or Remove Snap-Ins dialog box, under Available Snap-Ins, double-click Certificates. In the Certificates Snap-In dialog box, click My User Account, click Finish, and then click OK.

5. In the console tree, expand the Certificates\Personal node.

6. Right-click the Personal node, point to All Tasks, and then click Request New Certificate.

The Certificate Request Wizard guides you through the steps of requesting a user certificate. For a Windows-based client computer, the imported certificate must have the Client Authentication EKU.

Using the Certificates Snap-In to Import a User Certificate   If you have a certificate file that contains the user certificate, you can import the user certificate by using the Certificates snap-in.

To Import a User Certificate by Using the Certificates Snap-In

1. Open the Certificates (Current User)\Personal node.

2. Right click the Personal node, point to All Tasks, and then click Import.

The Certificate Import Wizard guides you through the steps of importing a certificate from a certificate file. For a Windows-based client computer, the certificate imported into the Local Computer store must have the Client Authentication EKU.

Installing Third-Party Certificate Chains by Using Group Policy   When you are using a third-party CA for the computer certificates that are installed on access servers or RADIUS servers, you might need to install the chain of certificates (the root CA certificate to the issuing CA certificate) for the certificate installed on the access or RADIUS server. If the access client does not trust the certificate chain of the certificate submitted by the access or RADIUS server, certificate validation can fail.

A certificate chain consists of the root CA certificate and the certificate of each intermediate CA, including the issuing CA. The following procedures describe how to deploy a root CA certificate and an intermediate CA certificate to access clients by using Group Policy.

To Install a Root CA Certificate by Using Group Policy

1. In the console tree of the Certificates snap-in for the access or RADIUS server computer account, expand Certificates (Local Computer), expand Trusted Root Certification Authorities, and then click Certificates.

2. In the details pane, right-click the root CA certificate of the issuing CA of the computer certificate on the authentication server, point to All Tasks, and then click Export.

3. In the Certificate Export Wizard, on the Welcome to the Certificate Export Wizard page, click Next.

4. On the Export File Format page, click Cryptographic Message Syntax Standard–PKCS #7 Certificates (.p7b).

5. Click Next. On the File To Export page, type the file name for the exported certificate, or click Browse to specify a location and file name.

6. Click Next. On the Completing The Certificate Export Wizard page, click Finish.

7. Open the Group Policy Management snap-in.

8. In the console tree, expand Forest, expand Domains, and then click the name of your domain to which your CA belongs.

9. On the Linked Group Policy Objects pane, right-click the appropriate Group Policy Object (the default object is Default Domain Policy), and then click Edit.

10. In the console tree of the Group Policy Management Editor snap-in, expand Computer Configuration, Windows Settings, Security Settings, and then Public Key Policies.

11. Right-click Trusted Root Certification Authorities, and then click Import.

12. In the Certificate Import Wizard, specify the file that was saved in step 5.

13. Repeat steps 8–12 for all appropriate domain containers and their Group Policy Objects.

The next time the access client computers update their Computer Configuration group policy, the root CA certificates of the issuing CAs of the authentication server computer certificates are installed in their local certificate store.

To Install an Intermediate CA Certificate by Using Group Policy

1. In the console tree of the Certificates snap-in for the access or RADIUS server computer account, expand Certificates (Local Computer), expand Intermediate Certification Authorities, and then click Certificates.

2. In the details pane, right-click the intermediate CA certificate of the issuing CA of the computer certificate on the authentication server, point to All Tasks, and then click Export.

3. In the Certificate Export Wizard, on the Welcome To The Certificate Export Wizard page, click Next.

4. On the Export File Format page, click Cryptographic Message Syntax Standard–PKCS #7 Certificates (.p7b).

5. Click Next. On the File To Export page, type the file name for the exported certificate, or click Browse to specify a location and file name.

6. Click Next. On the Completing The Certificate Export Wizard page, click Finish.

7. Open the Group Policy Management snap-in.

8. In the console tree, expand Forest, expand Domains, and then click the name of your domain to which your CA belongs.

9. On the Linked Group Policy Objects pane, right-click the appropriate Group Policy Object (the default object is Default Domain Policy), and then click Edit.

10. In the console tree of the Group Policy Management Editor snap-in, expand Computer Configuration, Windows Settings, Security Settings, and then Public Key Policies.

11. Right-click Intermediate Certification Authorities, point to All Tasks, and then click Import.

12. In the Certificate Import Wizard, specify the file that was saved in step 5.

Repeat steps 8–12 for all appropriate domain containers and their Group Policy Objects.

If you cannot use Group Policy, you can manually install root and intermediate certificates on individual access client computers.

To Manually Install a Root or Intermediate CA Certificate on an Access Client

1. Export the root CA certificate of the access or RADIUS server's computer certificate to a .p7b file.

2. On the access client computer, in the console tree of the Certificates (Local Computer) snap-in, expand Certificates (Local Computer), expand Trusted Root Certification Authorities (for a root CA certificate) or Intermediate Certification Authorities (for an intermediate CA certificate), and then click Certificates.

3. Right-click Certificates, point to All Tasks, and then click Import.

4. The Welcome To The Certificate Import Wizard page of the Certificate Import Wizard appears. Click Next.

5. On the File To Import page, in the File Name box, type the file name of the certificate file saved in step 1, or click Browse and use the Browse dialog box to locate it.

6. Click Next. On the Certificate Store page, click Place All Certificates In The Following Store, and then specify the import location.

7. Click Next. On the Completing The Certificate Import Wizard page, click Finish.

Requesting a Certificate via the Web   Requesting a certificate via the Web, also known as Web enrollment, is done with Microsoft Windows Internet Explorer. For the address, type **http://*servername*/certsrv**, where *servername* is the computer name of the Windows Server 2008 or Windows Server 2003 CA that is also running Internet Information Services (IIS). A Web-based wizard takes you through the steps of requesting a certificate. The location where the certificate is stored (whether it is the Current User store or the Local Computer store) is determined by whether the Use Local Machine Store check box was selected when an advanced certificate request was performed. This check box is cleared by default, and certificates are stored in the Current User store. You must have local administrator privileges to store a certificate in the Local Computer store.

You can use Web enrollment with either an enterprise or a Standalone CA.

Direct from the Source: Duplicating Default Certificate Templates

When using certificate templates, you should always make a duplicate of the default template, and if applicable, make your scenario-specific changes to the new template. For example, if you want to change the security groups that can autoenroll for a user certificate, make a duplicate of the user certificate. Then, obtain the properties of the new certificate template, click the Security tab, and add the specific groups that you want to have access to the template.

Clay Seymour, Support Escalation Engineer

Enterprise Platform Support

Group Policy

It is beyond the scope of this book to provide the specific steps to deploy Group Policy for an organization of arbitrary size. For additional information, see the *Windows Group Policy Resource Kit: Windows Server 2008 and Windows Vista*, Windows Server 2008 Help and Support, or resources at *http://www.microsoft.com/gp*.

The elements of configuring Group Policy to best support a Windows-based authentication infrastructure for network access are as follows:

- When using certificates for computer-level network access authentication, configure Group Policy for autoenrollment of computer certificates. This requires deployment of a Windows enterprise CA. Autoenrollment cannot be configured when using a Standalone CA.

- When using certificates for user-level network access authentication, configure a certificate template for user certificates, and configure Group Policy for autoenrollment of user certificates.

- When using PEAP-MS-CHAP v2 for network access authentication, optionally configure Group Policy for autoenrollment of computer certificates to install computer certificates on the NPS servers.

- When you are using PEAP-MS-CHAP v2 for network access authentication and a third-party CA for the computer certificates installed on the NPS RADIUS servers, ensure that the root CA certificate for the NAP RADIUS server's computer certificate is installed on the access clients. If not, configure Group Policy to install the appropriate root CA certificate on domain member computers.

For information about how to configure Group Policy to deploy certificate settings, see "Deploying PKI" earlier in this chapter.

For information about how to configure Group Policy to deploy configuration settings for specific types of network access, see the following:

- Chapter 10, "IEEE 802.11 Wireless Networks"
- Chapter 11, "IEEE 802.1X-Authenticated Wired Networks"
- Chapter 16, "IPsec Enforcement"
- Chapter 17, "802.1X Enforcement"
- Chapter 18, "VPN Enforcement"
- Chapter 19, "DHCP Enforcement"

RADIUS Servers

Configuring a fault-tolerant RADIUS infrastructure requires at a minimum the configuration of at least two NPS RADIUS servers, a primary NPS RADIUS server, and a secondary RADIUS NPS server. You must do the following:

- Configure the primary NPS server.
- Copy the configuration of the primary NPS server to the secondary NPS server.

Because the configuration of the primary NPS server is being copied to the secondary NPS server, you should always make configuration changes to the primary NSP server.

Configuring the Primary NPS Server

To configure the primary NPS server on a computer, complete these steps as discussed in the following sections:

1. Obtain and install a computer certificate.
2. Install NPS and configure NPS server properties.
3. Configure NPS with RADIUS clients.
4. Use IPsec to protect RADIUS traffic.
5. Configure the appropriate policies.

Obtaining and Installing a Computer Certificate   If you have configured computer certificate autoenrollment, force a refresh of computer configuration Group Policy by typing **gpupdate /target:computer** at a command prompt.

If you use a Windows Server 2008 or Windows Server 2003 enterprise CA and you are not using autoenrollment for computer certificates, you can request one, as described in the following procedure.

To Request a Computer Certificate

1. Click Start, click Run, type **mmc**, and then click OK.

2. On the File menu, click Add/Remove Snap-In.

3. Under Available Snap-Ins, double-click Certificates, click Computer Account, and then click Next.

4. Do one of the following:

    ❑ To manage certificates for the local computer, click Local Computer, and then click Finish.

    ❑ To manage certificates for a remote computer, click Another Computer and type the name of the computer, or click Browse to select the computer name. Click Finish.

5. Click OK.

6. In the console tree, expand Certificates (Local Computer or *Computername*), and then click Personal.

7. On the Action menu, point to All Tasks, and then click Request New Certificate to start the Certificate Enrollment Wizard.

8. On the Before You Begin page, click Next.

9. On the Request Certificates page, click Computer, and then click Enroll.

10. Click Finish.

If your PKI does not support autoenrollment of computer certificates, obtain the computer certificate as a saved file, and then use the following procedure to import the computer certificate on the primary NPS server.

> **Note**   To perform the next procedure, you must be a member of the Administrators group on the local computer, or you must have been delegated the appropriate authority.

To Import the Computer Certificate on the Primary NPS Server

1. In the console tree of the Certificates snap-in, expand Certificates (Local Computer or *Computername*).

2. Right-click Personal, point to All Tasks, and then click Import.

3. On the Welcome To The Certificate Import Wizard page, click Next.

4. On the File To Import page, in the File Name box, type the file name of the certificate file provided by the commercial CA. Alternatively, you can click Browse and use the Browse dialog box to locate it.

5. Click Next. On the Certificate Store page, click Place All Certificates In The Following Store. By default, the Personal node should appear as the import location. Click Next, and then click Finish.

Configuring NPS Server Properties   NPS is installed on computers running Windows Server 2008 with the Network Policy and Access Services role through the Initial Configuration Tasks or Server Manager tools. However, the primary NPS server computer must be able to access account properties in the appropriate domains. If NPS is being installed on a domain controller, no additional configuration is required for NPS to access account properties in the domain to which it belongs. If NPS is not installed on a domain controller, you must configure the primary NPS server computer to read the properties of user accounts in the domain, as described in the following procedure:

To Configure the Primary NPS Server Computer to Read the Properties of User Accounts in the Domain

1. In the console tree of the Network Policy Server snap-in, right-click NPS (Local), and then click Register Server In Active Directory.

2. In the Network Policy Server dialog box, click OK twice.

Alternatively, you can do one of the following:

- Use the **netsh nps add registeredserver** command.
- Use the Active Directory Users And Computers snap-in to add the computer account of the NPS server to the RAS and IAS Servers security group.

If the NPS server authenticates and authorizes network access attempts for user accounts in other domains, verify that the other domains have a two-way trust with the domain in which the NPS server computer is a member. Next, configure the NPS server computer to read the properties of user accounts in other domains by using the **netsh nps add registeredserver** command or by using the Active Directory Users And Computers snap-in.

If there are accounts in other domains, and the domains do not have a two-way trust with the domain in which the NPS server computer is a member, you must configure a RADIUS proxy between the two untrusted domains. If there are accounts in other untrusted Active Directory forests, you must configure a RADIUS proxy between the forests. For more information, see "Using RADIUS Proxies for Cross-Forest Authentication" later in this chapter.

If you want to store authentication and accounting information for connection analysis and security investigation purposes, enable logging for accounting and authentication events. Windows Server 2008 NPS can log information to a local file and to a SQL Server database.

To Enable and Configure Local File Logging for NPS

1. In the console tree of the Network Policy Server snap-in, click Accounting.

2. In the details pane, click Configure Local File Logging.

3. On the Settings tab, select one or more check boxes for recording authentication and accounting requests in the NPS log files:

   ❑ To capture accounting requests and responses, select the Accounting Requests check box.

   ❑ To capture authentication requests, access-accept packets, and access-reject packets, select the Authentication Requests check box.

   ❑ To capture periodic status updates, such as interim accounting packets, select the Periodic Accounting Status or Periodic Authentication Status check boxes.

   All these logging options are enabled by default.

4. On the Log File tab, type the log file directory as needed, and then select the log file format and new log time period. The default log file directory is *%SystemRoot%*\System32\ LogFiles.

To Enable and Configure SQL Server Database Logging for NPS

1. In the console tree of the Network Policy Server snap-in, click Accounting.

2. In the details pane, click Configure SQL Server Logging.

3. On the Settings tab, select one or more check boxes for recording authentication and accounting requests. All these logging options are enabled by default.

4. In Maximum Number of Concurrent Sessions, type the maximum number of simultaneous sessions that NPS can create with SQL Server.

5. To configure a SQL data source, click Configure.

6. In the Data Link Properties dialog box, configure the appropriate settings for the SQL Server database.

If needed, configure additional UDP ports for authentication and accounting messages that are sent by RADIUS clients (the access servers). By default, NPS uses UDP ports 1812 and 1645 for authentication messages and UDP ports 1813 and 1646 for accounting messages.

To Configure NPS for Different UDP Ports

1. In the console tree of the Network Policy Server snap-in, right-click NPS, and then click Properties.

2. Click the Ports tab, and then in the Authentication section, type the UDP port numbers for your RADIUS authentication traffic. In the Accounting section, type the UDP port numbers for your RADIUS accounting traffic.

   To use multiple port settings for authentication or accounting traffic, separate the port numbers with commas. You can also specify an IP address to which the RADIUS messages must be sent by typing in the following syntax: ***IPAddress:UDPPort***. For example, if you have multiple network adapters and you want to receive RADIUS authentication messages sent only to the IP address of 10.0.0.99 and UDP port 1812, in the Authentication box, type **10.0.0.99:1812**. However, if you specify IP addresses and copy the configuration of the primary NPS server to the secondary NPS server, you must modify the ports on the secondary NPS server to either remove the IP address of the primary NPS server or change the IP address to that of the secondary NPS server.

Configuring NPS with RADIUS Clients   You must configure the primary NPS server with the access servers or RADIUS proxies as RADIUS clients.

To Add a RADIUS Client for NPS

1. In the console tree of the Network Policy Server snap-in, expand RADIUS Clients And Servers, right-click RADIUS Clients, and then click New RADIUS Client.

2. In the New RADIUS Client dialog box, under Name And Address, in the Friendly Name text box, type a name for the RADIUS client (the access server or RADIUS proxy). In the Address (IP Or DNS) text box, type the IP address or DNS domain name of the RADIUS client. If you type a DNS domain name, click Verify to resolve the name to the correct IP address for the access server.

3. Under Shared Secret, in the Shared Secret and Confirm Shared Secret text boxes, type the shared secret for this combination of NPS server and RADIUS client or click Generate to have the NPS service generate a strong RADIUS shared secret.

4. Under Additional Options, specify whether this RADIUS client will always use the Message-Authenticator attribute in RADIUS messages and whether the RADIUS client is a NAP enforcement point that is running Windows Server 2008 (the RADIUS Client Is NAP-Capable check box), and then click OK.

If you have multiple wireless APs on a single subnet, you can simplify RADIUS client administration by specifying an IPv4 or IPv6 address range instead of specifying the address or DNS name of a single RADIUS client. All of the RADIUS clients in the range must be configured to use the same RADIUS server and shared secret. If you are not using this feature, use a different shared secret for each wireless AP.

Use as many RADIUS shared secrets as you can. Each shared secret should be a random sequence of uppercase and lowercase letters, numbers, and punctuation marks that is at least 22 characters long. To create a strong RADIUS shared secret, use the Generate option when configuring a shared secret with the Network Policy Server snap-in.

Using IPsec to Protect RADIUS Traffic   To ensure maximum security for RADIUS messages, it is recommended that you use IPsec and Encapsulating Security Payload (ESP) to provide data confidentiality, data integrity, and data origin authentication for RADIUS traffic sent between the NPS servers and the RADIUS clients. Computers running Windows Server 2008 and Windows Server 2003 support IPsec. You configure the NPS RADIUS server for IPsec protection of RADIUS traffic through Windows Firewall with Advanced Security connection security rules. To secure RADIUS traffic sent from third-party access servers, the access servers must also support IPsec. For more information about connection security rules, see Chapter 4, "Windows Firewall with Advanced Security."

Configuring the Appropriate Policies   To evaluate authorization and connection constraints for incoming connection requests, you must configure the appropriate policies consisting of connection request policies, network policies, and for NAP, health policies. The Network Policy Server snap-in has a set of wizards to automatically configure a set of policies for common network access and NAP scenarios. The following procedure describes how to run the Network Policy Server wizards.

To Run the Network Policy Server Wizards

1. In the console tree of the Network Policy Server snap-in, click NPS (Local).

2. In the details pane, in the drop-down list select one of the following:

   ❑ Network Access Protection (NAP)

   ❑ RADIUS Server For Dial-up Or VPN Connections

   ❑ RADIUS Server For 802.1X Wireless or Wired Connections

3. If you selected Network Access Protection (NAP), click Configure NAP and use the pages of the Configure NAP Wizard to specify the set of policies for NAP enforcement.

4. If you selected RADIUS Server For Dial-up Or VPN Connections, click Configure VPN Or Dial-up and use the pages of the Configure VPN Or Dial-up Wizard to specify the set of policies for VPN or dial-up–based network access.

5. If you selected RADIUS Server For 802.1X Wireless or Wired Connections, click Configure 802.1X and use the pages of the Configure 802.1X Wizard to specify the set of policies for VPN or dial-up–based network access.

See the following chapters for information about configuring the appropriate policies with the Network Policy Server wizards:

- Chapter 10
- Chapter 11
- Chapter 12
- Chapter 13, "Site-to-Site Connections"
- Chapter 16
- Chapter 17
- Chapter 18
- Chapter 19

If the access servers require vendor-specific attributes (VSAs), you must add the VSAs to the appropriate network policy.

To Add a VSA to a Network Policy

1. In the console tree of the Network Policy Server snap-in, expand Policies, and then click Network Policies.

2. Right-click the NPS network policy to which the VSA will be added, and then click Properties.

3. Click the Settings tab, click Vendor Specific, and then click Add. A list of predefined attributes appears in the Add Vendor Specific Attribute dialog box.

4. Look at the list of available RADIUS attributes to determine whether your vendor-specific attribute is already present. If it is, double-click it and configure it as specified in your access server's documentation.

5. If the vendor-specific attribute is not in the list of available RADIUS attributes, double-click Vendor-Specific. The Attribute Information dialog box appears.

6. Click Add. The Vendor-Specific Attribute Information dialog box appears.

7. To specify the network access server vendor for your access server from the list, click Select From List, and then select the network access vendor for which you are configuring the VSA.

8. If the vendor is not listed, click Enter Vendor Code, and then type the vendor code in the space provided.

> **More Info**   If you do not know the vendor code for your access server, see RFC 1007 for a list of SMI Network Management Private Enterprise Codes. RFC 1007 can be viewed at *http://www.ietf.org/rfc.html*.

9. Specify whether the attribute conforms to the RFC 2865 VSA specification. If you are not sure, see your access server documentation. If your attribute conforms, click Yes. It Conforms, and then click Configure Attribute. The Configure VSA (RFC-Compliant) dialog box appears.

10. In the Vendor-Assigned Attribute Number spin box, type the number that is assigned to the attribute (the numbers available are 0 through 255). In the Attribute Format drop-down list, specify the format for the attribute, and then in the Attribute Value text box, type the value that you are assigning to the attribute. Click OK twice.

11. If the attribute does not conform, click No. It Does Not Conform, and then click Configure Attribute. The Configure VSA (Non-RFC-Compliant) dialog box appears.

12. In the Hexadecimal Attribute Value text box, type the value for the attribute. Click OK twice.

Configuring the Secondary NPS Server

To configure the secondary NPS server on a computer, do the following:

1. Obtain and install a computer certificate.

2. Configure the secondary NPS server computer to read the properties of user accounts in the domain.

3. Copy the configuration of the primary NPS server to the secondary NPS server.

Copying the Configuration of the Primary NPS Server to the Secondary

NPS server   To copy the configuration of the primary NPS server to the secondary NPS server, do the following:

1. On the primary NPS server computer, type **netsh nps export** *path\file* **exportpsk=yes** at a command prompt, which stores the configuration settings, including RADIUS shared secrets, in a text file at *path\file*. The path can be a relative, an absolute, or a network path.

2. Copy the file created in step 1 to the secondary NPS server.

3. On the secondary NPS server computer, type **netsh nps import** *path\file* at a command prompt, which imports all the settings configured on the primary NPS server into the secondary NPS server.

If you must change the NPS server configuration in any way, use the Network Policy Server snap-in to change the configuration of the NPS server that is designated as the primary configuration server, and then use this procedure to synchronize those changes on the secondary NPS server.

Using RADIUS Proxies for Cross-Forest Authentication

Because NPS uses Active Directory to validate credentials and obtain user and computer account properties, a RADIUS proxy must be placed between the access servers and the NPS server computers when the user and computer accounts for access client computers and users exist in the following authentication databases:

- Two different Active Directory forests that do not trust each other

- Two different domains that do not trust each other

- Two different domains that have a one-way trust

Direct from the Source: RADIUS Proxies and EAP-TLS

The use of a RADIUS proxy is required for EAP-TLS because part of the process requires a service principal name (SPN) lookup in Active Directory. However, SPN lookups do not work across trusts. When the NPS server receives the computer identity, it is in the form of an SPN (*host/ComputerName.DNSDomainName*). The NPS server passes the SPN to the local global catalog. If the global catalog is unable to match the SPN to a local domain account, it will fail the request with a No Valid Account Found error condition. SPN requests are not passed to the other domains.

Clay Seymour, Support Escalation Engineer

Enterprise Platform Support

Note You do not need to use a RADIUS proxy if you use PEAP-MS-CHAP v2 and user names like those used prior to Windows 2000 (microsoft\user1, for example).

When an access client sends user credentials, a user name is often included, which includes two elements:

- Identification of the user account name
- Identification of the user account location

For example, for the user name user1@contoso.com, user1 is the user account name, and contoso.com is the location of the user account. The identification of the location of the user account is known as a *realm*, which has different forms:

- **The realm name can be a prefix.** In contoso\user1, *contoso* is the name of a domain like those used prior to Windows 2000.

- **The realm name can be a suffix.** For user1@contoso.com, *contoso.com* is either a DNS domain name or the name of an Active Directory–based domain.

The user name is passed from the access client to the access server during the authentication phase of the connection attempt. This user name becomes the User-Name RADIUS attribute in the Access-Request message sent by the access server to its configured RADIUS server, which is a RADIUS proxy in this configuration. When the RADIUS proxy receives the Access-Request message, connection request policies on the RADIUS proxy determine the RADIUS server to which the Access-Request message is forwarded based on the realm name.

Figure 9-4 shows NPS RADIUS proxies forwarding RADIUS messages between access servers and multiple NPS RADIUS servers in two different Active Directory forests.

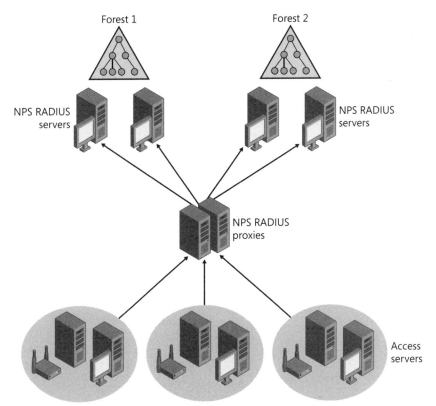

Figure 9-4   Using NPS RADIUS proxies for cross-forest authentication

The following configuration is for an organization that uses the following:

- **Active Directory domains**   Active Directory domains contain the user accounts, passwords, and dial-in properties that each NPS RADIUS server requires to authenticate user credentials and evaluate authorization.

- **At least two NPS RADIUS servers in each forest**   At least two NPS RADIUS servers (one primary and one secondary) can provide fault tolerance for RADIUS-based authentication, authorization, and accounting in each forest. If only one NPS RADIUS server is configured and it becomes unavailable, access clients for that forest cannot be authenticated. By using at least two NPS RADIUS servers and configuring the NPS RADIUS proxies for both the primary and secondary NPS RADIUS servers, the NPS RADIUS proxies can detect when the primary NPS RADIUS server is unavailable and then automatically fail over to the secondary NPS RADIUS server.

- **A network policy for network access**   A network policy is configured on the NPS RADIUS servers to authorize network connections based on group membership.

- **At least two NPS RADIUS proxies**   At least two NPS RADIUS proxies can provide fault tolerance for RADIUS requests that are sent from the access servers.

To deploy the configuration just described, do the following:

1. Configure the certificate infrastructure.

2. Configure the Active Directory forests for accounts and groups.

3. Configure the primary NPS RADIUS server on a computer in the first forest.

4. Configure the secondary NPS RADIUS server on another computer in the first forest.

5. Configure the primary NPS RADIUS server on a computer in the second forest.

6. Configure the secondary NPS RADIUS server on another computer in the second forest.

7. Configure the primary NPS RADIUS proxy.

8. Configure the secondary NPS RADIUS proxy.

9. Configure RADIUS authentication and accounting on the access servers.

Configuring the Certificate Infrastructure

Follow the instructions in the "Deploying PKI" subsection of "Deployment Steps" earlier in this chapter.

Configuring the Active Directory Forests for Accounts and Groups

Follow the instructions in the "Deploying Active Directory" subsection of "Deployment Steps" earlier in this chapter.

Configuring the Primary NPS Server on a Computer in the First Forest

To configure the primary NPS RADIUS server on a computer in the first forest, perform on a computer in the first forest the steps described in the following subsections of "Configuring the Primary NPS Server" earlier in this chapter:

- ■ "Obtaining and Installing a Computer Certificate"
- ■ "Configuring NPS Server Properties"
- ■ "Configuring Appropriate Policies"

Next, configure the primary NPS RADIUS server in the first forest with the primary and secondary NPS RADIUS proxies as RADIUS clients. To do this, perform the steps in the "Configuring NPS with RADIUS Clients" subsection of "Configuring the Primary NPS Server" earlier in this chapter. (Instead of the access servers, add the primary and secondary NPS RADIUS proxies as RADIUS clients.)

Configuring the Secondary NPS Server on Another Computer in the First Forest

To configure the secondary NPS RADIUS server on another computer in the first forest, follow the instructions in "Configuring the Secondary NPS Server" earlier in this chapter.

Configuring the Primary NPS Server on a Computer in the Second Forest

To configure the primary NPS RADIUS server on a computer in the second forest, perform the steps in the following subsections of "Configuring the Primary NPS Server" earlier in this chapter on a computer in the second forest:

- "Obtaining and Installing a Computer Certificate"
- "Configuring NPS Server Properties"
- "Configuring Appropriate Policies"

Next, configure the primary NPS RADIUS server in the second forest with the primary and secondary NPS RADIUS proxies as RADIUS clients. To do this, follow the instructions in the "Configuring NPS with RADIUS Clients" subsection of "Configuring the Primary NPS Server" earlier in this chapter (instead of the access servers, add the primary and secondary NPS RADIUS proxies as RADIUS clients).

Configuring the Secondary NPS Server on Another Computer in the Second Forest

To configure the secondary NPS RADIUS server on another computer in the second forest, perform the steps in "Configuring the Secondary NPS Server" earlier in this chapter.

Configuring the Primary NPS RADIUS Proxy

The computer acting as the primary NPS RADIUS proxy is not required to be dedicated to forwarding RADIUS messages. For example, you can install NPS on a file server. Because the primary NPS RADIUS proxy computer is not performing authentication or authorization of network access connections, it can be a member of a domain of either forest.

To Configure the Primary NPS RADIUS Proxy for RADIUS Ports and Clients

1. In the Network Policy Server snap-in for the primary NPS RADIUS proxy, configure additional UDP ports for RADIUS messages that are sent by the access servers as needed. By default, NPS uses UDP ports 1812 and 1645 for authentication and UDP ports 1813 and 1646 for accounting.

2. Add the access servers as RADIUS clients by using the instructions in the "Configuring NPS with RADIUS Clients" section of "Configuring the Primary NPS Server" earlier in this chapter.

To Configure the Primary NPS RADIUS Proxy for a Remote RADIUS Server Group Corresponding to the NPS RADIUS Servers in the First Forest

1. In the console tree of the Network Policy Server snap-in, expand RADIUS Clients And Servers.

2. Right-click Remote RADIUS Server Groups, and then click New.

3. In the New Remote RADIUS Server Group dialog box, in the Group Name field, type the group name for the NPS RADIUS servers in the first forest (for example: RADIUS Servers in Forest1). Click Add.

4. On the Address tab, type the DNS name, IPv4 address, or IPv6 address of the primary NPS RADIUS server in the first forest. If you specify a name, click Verify to resolve the name to an IP address.

5. On the Authentication/Accounting tab, type the shared secret between the primary and secondary NPS RADIUS proxies and the primary NPS server in the first forest.

6. Click OK to add the server to the list of servers in the group.

7. In the New Remote RADIUS Server Group dialog box, click Add.

8. On the Address tab, type the DNS name, IPv4 address, or IPv6 address of the secondary NPS RADIUS server in the first forest.

9. On the Authentication/Accounting tab, type the shared secret between the primary and secondary NPS RADIUS proxies and the secondary NPS server in the first forest.

10. Click OK to add the server to the list of servers in the group, and then click OK again.

To Configure the Primary NPS RADIUS Proxy for a Remote RADIUS Server Group Corresponding to the NPS RADIUS Servers in the Second Forest

1. In the console tree of the Network Policy Server snap-in, expand RADIUS Clients And Servers.

2. Right-click Remote RADIUS Server Groups, and then click New.

3. In the New Remote RADIUS Server Group dialog box, in the Group Name field, type the group name for the NPS RADIUS servers in the second forest (for example: RADIUS Servers in Forest2). Click Add.

4. On the Address tab, type the DNS name, IPv4 address, or IPv6 address of the primary NPS RADIUS server in the second forest. If you specify a name, click Verify to resolve the name to an IP address.

5. On the Authentication/Accounting tab, type the shared secret between the primary and secondary NPS RADIUS proxies and the primary NPS RADIUS server in the second forest.

6. Click OK to add the server to the list of servers in the group.

7. In the New Remote RADIUS Server Group dialog box, click Add.

8. On the Address tab, type the DNS name, IPv4 address, or IPv6 address of the secondary NPS RADIUS server in the second forest.

9. On the Authentication/Accounting tab, type the shared secret between the primary and secondary NPS RADIUS proxies and the secondary NPS RADIUS server in the second forest.

10. Click OK to add the server to the list of servers in the group, and then click OK again.

To Configure the Primary NPS RADIUS Proxy for a Connection Request Policy to Forward RADIUS Request Messages to the NPS RADIUS Servers in the First Forest

1. In the console tree of the Network Policy Server snap-in, expand Polices, right-click Connection Request Policies, and then click New.

2. On the Specify Connection Request Policy Name And Connection Type page, in the Policy Name box, type the name for the connection request policy (for example: Forward Requests to RADIUS Servers in Forest1). Click Next.

3. On the Specify Conditions page, click Add.

4. In the Select Conditions dialog box, double-click User Name.

5. In the User Name dialog box, type the realm name for all names in the first forest (for example: forest1.example.com), click OK, and then click Next.

6. On the Specify Connection Request Forwarding page, select Forward Requests To The Following Remote RADIUS Server Group For Authentication, and then in the drop-down list, select the remote RADIUS server group for the NPS RADIUS servers in the first forest (for example: RADIUS Servers in Forest1). Click Next.

7. On the Configure Settings page, click Next,

8. On the Completing Connection Request Policy Wizard page, click Finish.

To Configure the Primary NPS RADIUS Proxy for a Connection Request Policy to Forward RADIUS Request Messages to the NPS RADIUS Servers in the Second Forest

1. In the console tree of the Network Policy Server snap-in, expand Policies, right-click Connection Request Policies, and then click New.

2. On the Specify Connection Request Policy Name And Connection Type page, in the Policy Name box, type the name for the connection request policy (for example: Forward Requests to RADIUS Servers in Forest2). Click Next.

3. On the Specify Conditions page, click Add.

4. In the Select Conditions dialog box, double-click User Name.

5. In the User Name dialog box, type the realm name for all names in the second forest (for example: forest2.example.com), click OK, and then click Next.

6. On the Specify Connection Request Forwarding page, select Forward Requests To The Following Remote RADIUS Server Group For Authentication, and then, in the drop-down list, select the remote RADIUS server group for the NPS RADIUS servers in the second forest (for example: RADIUS Servers in Forest2). Click Next.

7. On the Configure Settings page, click Next,

8. On the Completing Connection Request Policy Wizard page, click Finish.

Configuring the Secondary NPS RADIUS Proxy

The computer acting as the secondary NPS RADIUS proxy is not required to be dedicated to forwarding RADIUS messages. For example, you can install NPS on a file server. Like the primary NPS RADIUS proxy, the secondary NPS RADIUS proxy computer can be a member of a domain of either forest because it is not performing authentication or authorization of network access connections.

To Configure the Secondary NPS RADIUS Proxy on Another Computer

1. On the primary NPS RADIUS proxy computer, type **netsh nps export** *path\file* **exportpsk=yes** at a command prompt.

    This command stores the configuration settings, including RADIUS shared secrets, in a text file. The path can be relative, absolute, or a network path.

2. Copy the file created in step 1 to the secondary NPS RADIUS proxy.

3. On the secondary NPS RADIUS proxy computer, type **netsh nps import** *path\file* at a command prompt.

    This command imports all the settings configured on the primary NPS RADIUS proxy into the secondary NPS RADIUS proxy.

Based on the default load-balancing settings of the RADIUS servers in the two remote RADIUS server groups, each NPS RADIUS proxy will distribute the authentication request load equally to the two NPS servers in each forest.

Configuring RADIUS Authentication on the Access Servers

Configure the RADIUS client on your access servers with the following settings:

-   The IP address or name of a primary RADIUS server, the shared secret, UDP ports for authentication and accounting, and failure-detection settings.

-   The IP address or name of a secondary RADIUS server, the shared secret, UDP ports for authentication and accounting, and failure-detection settings.

To balance the load of RADIUS traffic between the primary and secondary NPS RADIUS proxies, configure half of the access servers with the primary NPS RADIUS proxy as their primary RADIUS server and the secondary NPS RADIUS proxy as their secondary RADIUS server. Configure the other half of the access servers with the secondary NPS RADIUS proxy as their primary RADIUS server and the primary NPS RADIUS proxy as their secondary RADIUS server.

Using RADIUS Proxies to Scale Authentications

When performing authentication for a large number of access clients by using certificate-based authentication or for a large NAP deployment, the volume of RADIUS authentication traffic necessary to keep access clients connected can be substantial. In a large deployment, it is best to spread the load of authentication traffic among multiple NPS server computers. Because you cannot rely on the access servers to consistently or adequately spread their authentication traffic among multiple RADIUS servers, intermediate NPS RADIUS proxies can provide this function.

Without the RADIUS proxies, each access server sends its RADIUS requests to one or multiple RADIUS servers and detects unavailable RADIUS servers. The access server might or might not be balancing the load of RADIUS traffic across multiple RADIUS servers. By using NPS RADIUS proxies, consistent load balancing spreads the load of authentication, authorization, and accounting traffic across all the NPS servers in the organization. Additionally, there is a consistent scheme for failure detection and RADIUS server failover (the detection of an unavailable RADIUS server and avoidance of its use for future authentication requests) and failback (the detection that a previously unavailable RADIUS server is available).

The following configuration is for an organization that uses the following:

- **Active Directory domains**   Active Directory domains contain the user accounts, passwords, and dial-in properties that each NPS server requires to authenticate user credentials and evaluate authorization.
- **Multiple NPS servers**   To balance a large load of RADIUS authentication, authorization, and accounting traffic, there are multiple NPS servers.
- **Network policies**   Network policies are configured to authenticate and authorize network access based on group membership.
- **Two NPS RADIUS proxies**   Two NPS RADIUS proxies provide fault tolerance for RADIUS requests that are sent from the access servers.

Figure 9-5 shows the use of NPS RADIUS proxies to balance the load of RADIUS traffic from access servers across multiple NPS servers.

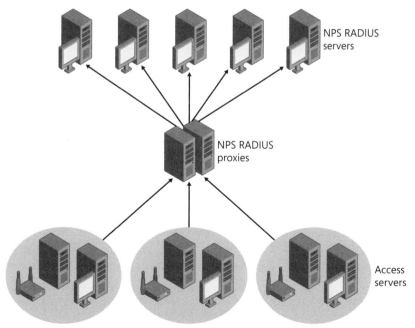

Figure 9-5   Using NPS RADIUS proxies to load-balance RADIUS traffic

To deploy this configuration, do the following:

1. Configure the certificate infrastructure.

2. Configure Active Directory for accounts and groups.

3. Configure NPS as a RADIUS server on multiple computers.

4. Configure the primary NPS RADIUS proxy.

5. Configure the secondary NPS RADIUS proxy.

6. Configure RADIUS authentication and accounting on access servers.

Configuring the Certificate Infrastructure

Follow the instructions in the "Deploying PKI" subsection of "Deployment Steps" earlier in this chapter.

Configuring Active Directory for Accounts and Groups

Follow the instructions in the "Deploying Active Directory" subsection of "Deployment Steps" earlier in this chapter.

Configuring NPS as a RADIUS Server on Multiple Computers

To configure NPS on each NPS server computer, perform on each NPS server computer the steps described in the following subsections of "Configuring the Primary NPS Server" earlier in this chapter:

- "Obtaining and Installing a Computer Certificate"
- "Configuring NPS Server Properties"
- "Configuring Appropriate Policies"

Next, configure each NPS server computer with the primary and secondary NPS RADIUS proxies as RADIUS clients. To do this, perform the steps in the "Configuring NPS with RADIUS Clients" subsection of "Configuring the Primary NPS Server" earlier in this chapter. (Instead of the access servers, add the primary and secondary NPS RADIUS proxies as RADIUS clients.)

Note You can configure each NPS RADIUS server separately rather than configuring an initial NPS RADIUS server and copying its configuration to other NPS RADIUS server computers. This is done so that different RADIUS shared secrets can be used between the NPS RADIUS proxies and the NPS RADIUS server.

Configuring the Primary NPS RADIUS Proxy

The computer acting as the primary NPS RADIUS proxy need not be dedicated to forwarding RADIUS messages. For example, you can install NPS on a file server.

To Configure the Primary NPS RADIUS Proxy

1. In the Network Policy Server snap-in, configure additional UDP ports for RADIUS messages that are sent by the access servers if needed.

    By default, NPS uses UDP ports 1812 and 1645 for authentication and UDP ports 1813 and 1646 for accounting.

2. Add the access servers as RADIUS clients of the NPS RADIUS proxy by following the steps in the "Configuring NPS with RADIUS Clients" subsection of "Configuring the Primary NPS Server" earlier in this chapter.

3. In the console tree of the Network Policy Server snap-in, expand RADIUS Clients and Servers.

4. Right-click Remote RADIUS Server Groups, and then click New.

5. In the New Remote RADIUS Server Group box, type the group name for all of the NPS RADIUS servers (for example: RADIUS Servers in the contoso.com Domain).

6. Click Add.

7. On the Address tab, type the DNS name, IPv4 address, or IPv6 address of an NPS RADIUS server. If you specify a name, click Verify to resolve the name to an IP address.

8. On the Authentication/Accounting tab, type the shared secret between the primary and secondary NPS RADIUS proxies and the NPS RADIUS server.

9. Click OK to add the server to the list of servers in the group.

10. Repeat steps 6–9 for each NPS RADIUS server, and then click OK.

11. In the console tree of the Network Policy Server snap-in, expand Policies, right-click Connection Request Policies, and then click New.

12. On the Specify Connection Request Policy Name And Connection Type page, in the Policy Name box, type the name for the connection request policy (for example: Forward Requests to RADIUS Servers in the contoso.com Domain). Click Next.

13. On the Specify Conditions page, click Add.

14. In the Select Conditions dialog box, double-click User Name.

15. In the User Name dialog box, type the realm name for all names in the second forest (for example: forest2.example.com), click OK, and then click Next.

16. On the Specify Connection Request Forwarding page, select Forward Requests To The Following Remote RADIUS Server Group For Authentication, and then in the drop-down list, select the remote RADIUS server group for all of the NPS RADIUS servers in the domain. Click Next.

17. On the Configure Settings page, click Next,

18. On the Completing Connection Request Policy Wizard page, click Finish.

Configuring the Secondary NPS RADIUS Proxy

The computer acting as the secondary NPS RADIUS proxy need not be dedicated to forwarding RADIUS messages. For example, you can install NPS on a file server.

To Configure the Secondary NPS RADIUS Proxy on Another Computer

1. On the primary NPS RADIUS proxy computer, type **netsh nps export** *path\file* **exportpsk=yes** at a command prompt.

   This command stores the configuration settings, including RADIUS shared secrets, in a text file. The path can be relative, absolute, or a network path.

2. Copy the file created in step 1 to the secondary NPS RADIUS proxy computer.

3. On the secondary NPS RADIUS proxy computer, type **netsh nps import** *path\file* at a command prompt. This command imports all the settings configured on the primary NPS RADIUS proxy into the secondary NPS RADIUS proxy.

Based on the default load-balancing settings of the RADIUS servers in the remote RADIUS server group, each NPS RADIUS proxy distributes the authentication request load equally to all of the NPS RADIUS servers.

Configuring RADIUS Authentication on the Access Servers

Configure the RADIUS client on your access servers with the following settings:

- The IP address or name of a primary RADIUS server, the shared secret, UDP ports for authentication and accounting, and failure-detection settings

- The IP address or name of a secondary RADIUS server, the shared secret, UDP ports for authentication and accounting, and failure-detection settings

To balance the load of RADIUS traffic between the primary and secondary NPS RADIUS proxies, configure half of the access servers with the primary NPS RADIUS proxy as their primary RADIUS server and the secondary NPS RADIUS proxy as their secondary RADIUS server. Configure the other half of the access servers with the secondary NPS RADIUS proxy as their primary RADIUS server and the primary NPS RADIUS proxy as their secondary RADIUS server.

Ongoing Maintenance

This section describes the ongoing maintenance for the following components of a Windows authentication infrastructure for network access:

- Active Directory

- PKI

- Group Policy
- RADIUS

Active Directory

It is beyond the scope of this book to describe the ongoing maintenance of an Active Directory infrastructure for an organization of an arbitrary size. For detailed information, see the *Windows Server 2008 Active Directory Resource Kit* in the *Windows Server 2008 Resource Kit*, Windows Server 2008 Help and Support, or the resources at *http://www.microsoft.com/ad*.

The elements of maintaining Active Directory to best support a Windows-based authentication infrastructure for network access are as follows:

- When adding user or computer accounts, ensure that the new accounts have the appropriate security group membership to allow network access. For example, if wireless access is being granted through membership in the WirelessUsers group, add new user or computer accounts to this group or to a group that is a member of this group.

- When adding new domains or forests, ensure that the appropriate trust relationships are created to allow NPS RADIUS servers to authenticate account credentials. Additionally, add the computer accounts of the NPS RADIUS servers to the RAS and IAS Servers security groups of the new domains. If the new domains or forests do not have a trust relationship, use NPS RADIUS proxies to provide cross-domain or cross-forest authentication. For more information, see "Using RADIUS Proxies for Cross-Forest Authentication" earlier in this chapter.

PKI

It is beyond the scope of this book to describe the ongoing maintenance of a PKI for an organization of an arbitrary size. For detailed information, see Windows Server 2008 Help and Support or the resources at *http://www.microsoft.com/pki*.

Group Policy

It is beyond the scope of this book to describe the ongoing maintenance of Group Policy for an organization of an arbitrary size. For detailed information, see the *Windows Group Policy Resource Kit: Windows Server 2008 and Windows Vista*, Windows Server 2008 Help and Support, or the resources at *http://www.microsoft.com/gp*.

The elements of maintaining Group Policy to best support a Windows-based authentication infrastructure for network access are as follows:

- When adding new domains or forests, ensure that the appropriate Group Policy objects are applied to the appropriate Active Directory containers to propagate settings for autoenrollment of certificates or configuration settings.

RADIUS

The following sections describe how to maintain the RADIUS component of the network access infrastructure.

Adding a New NPS RADIUS Server to the RADIUS Infrastructure

When you add a new NPS RADIUS server to the RADIUS infrastructure, you must do the following:

1. Register the new NPS server in its default domain.

2. Register the new NPS server in other domains.

3. If the new NPS server is a secondary RADIUS server, obtain and install a computer certificate if needed, and copy the configuration of the primary RADIUS server to the new NPS server.

4. If the new NPS server is a primary RADIUS server, do the following:

    ❏ Obtain and install a computer certificate.

    ❏ Configure NPS server properties.

    ❏ Configure NPS with RADIUS clients.

    ❏ Configure NPS with the appropriate network policies.

5. Configure access servers (RADIUS clients) to use the new NPS server.

6. If IPsec is being used to protect RADIUS traffic, update Windows Firewall with Advanced Security connection security rules to include protection for RADIUS traffic to and from the new NPS server.

Instructions for these procedures can be found in the "RADIUS Servers" subsection of "Deployment Steps" earlier in this chapter.

Removing an NPS RADIUS Server from the RADIUS Infrastructure

When you remove an NPS RADIUS server from the RADIUS infrastructure, you must do the following:

1. Reconfigure your access servers to remove references to the NPS server that is being removed.

2. Remove the computer account of the NPS server that is being removed from the RAS and IAS Servers security group of its default domain.

3. Remove the computer account of the NPS server that is being removed from the RAS and IAS Servers security group of other domains.

4. If IPsec is being used to protect RADIUS traffic to and from the NPS server that is being removed, update Windows Firewall with Advanced Security connection security rules to remove protection for the NPS server.

Maintaining RADIUS Clients

When you deploy a new access server, such as a new wireless AP for your wireless network, you must do the following:

1. Add the access server as a RADIUS client to either your NPS RADIUS servers or your NPS RADIUS proxies.

2. Configure the access server to use your NPS RADIUS servers or your NPS RADIUS proxies.

3. If IPsec is being used to protect traffic between your RADIUS servers or proxies and the access server, update Windows Firewall with Advanced Security connection security rules to include protection for RADIUS traffic to and from the new access server.

When you remove an access server, you must do the following:

1. Delete the access server as a RADIUS client on either your NPS RADIUS servers or your NPS RADIUS proxies.

2. If IPsec is being used to protect traffic between your RADIUS servers and the access server, update Windows Firewall with Advanced Security connection security rules to remove protection for RADIUS traffic between the access server and the NPS RADIUS servers or proxies.

Troubleshooting Tools

This section describes the troubleshooting tools or the resources that describe troubleshooting tools for the following components of a Windows authentication infrastructure for network access:

- Active Directory
- PKI
- Group Policy
- RADIUS

Active Directory

It is beyond the scope of this book to describe in detail the troubleshooting tools for Active Directory. For additional information, see the *Windows Server 2008 Active Directory Resource Kit* in the *Windows Server 2008 Resource Kit*, Windows Server 2008 Help and Support, or the resources at *http://www.microsoft.com/ad*.

Active Directory–specific troubleshooting issues are described as needed in subsequent chapters to troubleshoot network access or NAP.

PKI

It is beyond the scope of this book to describe in detail the troubleshooting tools for a Windows-based PKI. For additional information, see *Windows Server 2008 PKI and Certificate Security* by Brian Komar (Microsoft Press, 2008), Windows Server 2008 Help and Support, or the resources at *http://www.microsoft.com/pki*.

Digital certificate and PKI-specific troubleshooting issues are described as needed in subsequent chapters to troubleshoot network access or NAP.

Group Policy

It is beyond the scope of this book to describe in detail the troubleshooting tools for Group Policy. For additional information, see the *Windows Group Policy Resource Kit: Windows Server 2008 and Windows Vista* by Derek Melber, Group Policy MVP, with the Windows Group Policy Team (Microsoft Press, 2008) Windows Server 2008 Help and Support, or the resources at *http://www.microsoft.com/gp*.

Group Policy–specific troubleshooting issues are described as needed in subsequent chapters to troubleshoot network access or NAP.

RADIUS

To help you gather information to troubleshoot problems with NPS, Microsoft provides the following troubleshooting tools:

- NPS event logging and Windows Event Viewer
- Network Monitor 3.1
- Performance Monitor counters
- SNMP Service

NPS Event Logging and Windows Event Viewer

Use Event Viewer, available from the Administrative Tools program group, to obtain information about hardware and software problems and to monitor all security events, including informational, warning, and error events.

To troubleshoot NPS authentication attempts, view the NPS events in Windows Logs\Security. Viewing the authentication attempts in this log is useful in troubleshooting network policies. When you have multiple network policies configured, you can use the security event log to determine the name of the network policy that either accepted or rejected the connection attempt. Enabling NPS event logging and reading the text of NPS authentication events in the security event log is the most useful tool for troubleshooting failed NPS authentications.

To view the NPS events, configure a filter with the Event Sources option set to Microsoft Windows Security Auditing and the Task Category option set to Network Policy Server.

Both types of logging (rejected authentication requests and successful authentication requests) are enabled by default.

To Configure NPS for Event Logging

1. In the console tree of the Network Policy Server snap-in, right-click NPS, and then click Properties.

2. On the General tab, select each required check box, and then click OK.

Network Monitor 3.1

You can use Network Monitor 3.1 (or later) or a commercial packet analyzer (also known as a *network sniffer*), to capture and view RADIUS authentication and accounting messages that are sent to and from the NPS server. Network Monitor 3.1 includes a RADIUS parser, which you can use to view the attributes of a RADIUS message and troubleshoot network access or NAP issues.

> **On the Disc**   You can link to the download site for Network Monitor from the companion CD-ROM.

Reliability and Performance Counters

You can use the Reliability and Performance snap-in to monitor the resource use of specific components and program processes. With Performance Monitor, which is in the Reliability and Performance snap-in, you can use charts and reports to determine how efficiently your server uses NPS and both identify and troubleshoot potential problems.

You can use Performance Monitor to monitor the following NPS-related performance objects:

- NPS Accounting Clients
- NPS Accounting Server
- NPS Authentication Clients
- NPS Authentication Server

SNMP Service

You can use the Simple Network Management Protocol (SNMP) service to monitor status information for your NPS server. NPS supports the RADIUS Authentication Server Management Information Base (MIB), as specified in RFC 2619, and the RADIUS Accounting Server MIB, as specified in RFC 2621.

Chapter Summary

A Windows-based network access infrastructure consists of Active Directory, PKI, Group Policy, and RADIUS components. Active Directory stores user and computer account credentials and properties and provides an infrastructure to deploy centrally configured user and computer configuration Group Policy settings. A PKI issues and validates digital certificates used in different types of network access scenarios or NAP enforcement methods. Group Policy settings can instruct computers to automatically request specific types of certificates or configure network access and protection settings. RADIUS provides a standard protocol and centralized management of network access authorization, authentication, and accounting.

The combination of Active Directory, PKI, Group Policy, and RADIUS creates a Windows-based infrastructure that provides centralized authentication for 802.11 wireless access, 802.1X wired access, dial-up or VPN-based remote access connections, and dial-up or VPN-based site-to-site connections. The combination of PKI, Group Policy, and RADIUS creates a Windows-based infrastructure that provides centralized configuration and validation of system health status for NAP.

Additional Information

For additional information about Active Directory, see the following:

- *Windows Server 2008 Active Directory Resource Kit* in the *Windows Server 2008 Resource Kit* (both from Microsoft Press, 2008)
- Windows Server 2008 Technical Library at *http://technet.microsoft.com/windowsserver/2008*
- Windows Server 2008 Help and Support
- Microsoft Windows Server Active Directory (*http://www.microsoft.com/ad*)

For additional information about PKI, see the following:

- Windows Server 2008 Technical Library at *http://technet.microsoft.com/windowsserver/2008*
- Windows Server 2008 Help and Support
- Microsoft Public Key Infrastructure for Windows Server (*http://www.microsoft.com/pki*)
- *Windows Server 2008 PKI and Certificate Security* by Brian Komar (Microsoft Press, 2008)

For additional information about Group Policy, see the following:

- *Windows Group Policy Resource Kit: Windows Server 2008 and Windows Vista* (Microsoft Press, 2008)
- Windows Server 2008 Technical Library at *http://technet.microsoft.com/windowsserver/2008*
- Windows Server 2008 Help and Support
- Microsoft Windows Server Group Policy (*http://www.microsoft.com/gp*)

For additional information about RADIUS and NPS, see the following:

- Windows Server 2008 Technical Library at *http://technet.microsoft.com/windowsserver/2008*
- Windows Server 2008 Help and Support
- Network Policy Server (*http://www.microsoft.com/nps*)
- RFC 2548, "Microsoft Vendor-Specific RADIUS Attributes"
- RFC 2619, "RADIUS Authentication Server MIB"
- RFC 2621, "RADIUS Accounting Server MIB"
- RFC 2865, "Remote Authentication Dial-In User Service (RADIUS)"
- RFC 2866, "RADIUS Accounting"
- RFC 2867, "RADIUS Accounting Modifications for Tunnel Protocol Support"
- RFC 2868, "RADIUS Attributes for Tunnel Protocol Support"
- RFC 2869, "RADIUS Extensions"
- RFC 3162, "RADIUS and IPv6"
- RFC 3579, "RADIUS (Remote Authentication Dial In User Service) Support For Extensible Authentication Protocol (EAP)"

For additional information about Windows-based network access, see the following:

- Chapter 10, "IEEE 802.11 Wireless Networks"
- Chapter 11, "IEEE 802.1X-Authenticated Wired Networks"
- Chapter 12, "Remote Access VPN Connections"
- Chapter 13, "Site-to-Site VPN Connections"

For additional information about NAP, see the following:

- Chapter 14, "Network Access Protection Overview"
- Chapter 15, "Preparing for Network Access Protection"
- Chapter 16, "IPsec Enforcement"
- Chapter 17, "802.1X Enforcement"
- Chapter 18, "VPN Enforcement"
- Chapter 19, "DHCP Enforcement"
- The Windows Server 2008 Technical Library at *http://technet.microsoft.com/windowsserver/2008*
- Windows Server 2008 Help and Support
- Microsoft Network Access Protection (*http://www.microsoft.com/nap*)

Chapter 10

IEEE 802.11 Wireless Networks

This chapter provides information about how to design, deploy, maintain, and troubleshoot Institute of Electrical and Electronic Engineers (IEEE) 802.11 wireless networks. Once deployed, the protected wireless network solution can be modified for the 802.1X Enforcement method of Network Access Protection (NAP) as described in Chapter 17, "802.1X Enforcement."

This chapter assumes that you understand the role of Active Directory, public key infrastructure (PKI), Group Policy, and Remote Authentication Dial-In User Service (RADIUS) elements of a Microsoft Windows–based authentication infrastructure for network access. For more information, see Chapter 9, "Authentication Infrastructure."

Concepts

IEEE 802.11 wireless local area network (LAN) networking provides the following benefits:

- Wireless connections can extend or replace a wired infrastructure in situations where it is costly, inconvenient, or impossible to lay cables. This benefit includes the following:

  - To connect the networks in two buildings separated by a physical, legal, or financial obstacle, you can either use a link provided by a telecommunications vendor (for a fixed installation cost and ongoing recurring costs), or you can create a point-to-point wireless link using wireless LAN technology (for a fixed installation cost but no recurring costs). Eliminating recurring telecommunications charges can provide significant cost savings to organizations.

  - Wireless LAN technologies can be used to create a temporary network, which is in place for only a specific amount of time. For example, you can set up a wireless network for a convention or trade show rather than deploying the physical cabling required for a traditional Ethernet network.

  - Some types of buildings, such as historical buildings, might be governed by building codes that prohibit the use of wiring, making wireless networking an important alternative.

- The wiring-free aspect of wireless LAN networking is also attractive to homeowners who want to connect the various computers in their home together without having to drill holes and pull network cables through walls and ceilings.

- Increased productivity for the mobile employee. This benefit includes the following:

    ❑ The mobile user whose primary computer is a laptop or notebook computer can change location and always remain connected to the network. This enables the mobile user to travel to various places—meeting rooms, hallways, lobbies, cafeterias, classrooms, and so forth—and still have access to networked data. Without wireless access, the user has to carry cabling and is restricted to working near a network jack.

    ❑ Wireless LAN networking is well suited for environments where movement is required. For example, retail environments can benefit when employees use a wireless laptop or palmtop computer to enter inventory information directly into the store database from the sales floor.

    ❑ Even if no wireless infrastructure is present, wireless laptop computers can still form their own ad-hoc networks to communicate and share data with each other.

- Easy access to the Internet in public places. Beyond the corporate campus, access to the Internet and even corporate sites can be made available through public wireless "hot spot" networks. Airports, restaurants, rail stations, and common areas throughout cities can be provisioned to provide this service. When the traveling worker reaches his or her destination, perhaps meeting a client at the client's corporate office, limited access can be provided to the traveling worker through the local wireless network. The network can recognize that a user is from another corporation and create a connection that is isolated from the local corporate network but provides Internet access to the visiting user. Wireless infrastructure providers are enabling wireless connectivity in public areas around the world. Many airports, conference centers, and hotels provide wireless access to the Internet for their visitors.

Support for IEEE 802.11 Standards

The Windows Server 2008, Windows Vista, Windows XP, and Windows Server 2003 operating systems provide built-in support for 802.11 wireless LAN networking. An installed 802.11 wireless LAN network adapter appears as a wireless network connection in the Network Connections folder. Although there is built-in support for 802.11 wireless LAN networking, the wireless components of Windows are dependent upon the following:

- **The capabilities of the wireless network adapter**   The installed wireless network adapter must support the wireless LAN or wireless security standards that you require. For example, Windows Vista supports configuration options for the Wi-Fi Protected Access (WPA) security standard. However, if the wireless network adapter does not support WPA, you cannot enable or configure WPA security options.

- **The capabilities of the wireless network adapter driver**   To allow you to configure wireless network options, the driver for the wireless network adapter must support the reporting of all of its capabilities to Windows. Verify that the driver for your wireless network adapter was written for the capabilities of Windows Vista or Windows XP and is the most current version by checking Microsoft Update or the Web site of the wireless network adapter vendor.

Table 10-1 lists the IEEE wireless standards supported by Windows and by wireless network adapters, their maximum bit rate, range of frequencies, and their typical usage.

Table 10-1   802.11 Standards

Standard	Maximum Bit Rate	Range of Frequencies	Usage
802.11	2 megabits per second (Mbps)	S-Band Industrial, Scientific, and Medical (ISM) frequency range (2.4 to 2.5 GHz)	Obsolete. Not widely used.
802.11b	11 Mbps	S-Band ISM	Widely used.
802.11a	54 Mbps	C-Band ISM (5.725 to 5.875 GHz)	Not widely used due to expense and limited range.
802.11g	54 Mbps	S-Band ISM	Widely used. 802.11g devices are backward-compatible with 802.11b devices.
802.11n (standards development in progress)	250 Mbps	C-Band and S-Band ISM	Pre-standard ratification devices are available starting in August 2007. 802.11n devices can be backward-compatible with 802.11a, b, and g devices.

Note   The S-Band ISM uses the same frequency range as microwave ovens, cordless phones, baby monitors, wireless video cameras, and Bluetooth devices. The C-Band ISM uses the same frequency range as newer cordless phones and other devices. Due to this overlapping use, there might be contention when multiple devices are active at the same time.

802.11 Operating Modes

Wireless LAN networks for all the IEEE 802.11 standards use the following operating modes:

- **Infrastructure mode**   The wireless network contains at least one wireless access point (AP), a device that bridges wireless-based computers to each other and to a wired network such as the Internet or an intranet.

- **Ad-hoc mode**   The wireless network contains no wireless APs. Wireless-based computers connect and communicate directly with each other. This chapter does not describe ad-hoc mode wireless networks.

Regardless of the operating mode, a *Service Set Identifier* (SSID), also known as the wireless network name, identifies a specific wireless network. You configure the SSID on the wireless AP for infrastructure mode or the initial wireless client for ad-hoc mode. The wireless AP or the initial wireless client periodically advertises the SSID so that other wireless nodes can discover and join the wireless network.

Wireless Security

Although IEEE 802.11 wireless LAN technologies provide the benefits previously described, they introduce security issues that do not exist for wired networks. Unlike the closed cabling system of an Ethernet network, which can be physically secured, wireless frames are sent as radio transmissions that propagate beyond the physical confines of your office. Any computer within range of the wireless network can receive wireless frames and send its own. Without protecting your wireless network, malicious users can use your wireless network to access your private information or launch attacks against your computers or other computers across the Internet.

To protect your wireless network, you must use authentication and encryption, described as follows:

- Authentication requires that computers provide either valid account credentials (such as a user name and password) or proof that they have been configured with a specific authentication key before being allowed to send data frames on the wireless network. Authentication prevents malicious users from being able to join your wireless network.

- Encryption requires that the content of all wireless data frames be encrypted so that only the designated receiver can interpret its contents. Encryption prevents malicious users from capturing wireless frames sent on your wireless network and determining sensitive data. Encryption also helps prevent malicious users from sending valid frames and accessing your private resources or the Internet.

IEEE 802.11 wireless LANs support the following security standards:

- IEEE 802.11
- IEEE 802.1X
- Wi-Fi Protected Access (WPA)
- Wi-Fi Protected Access 2 (WPA2)

IEEE 802.11

The original IEEE 802.11 standard defined the open system and shared key authentication methods for authentication and Wired Equivalent Privacy (WEP) for encryption. WEP can use either 40-bit or 104-bit encryption keys. However, the original IEEE 802.11 security standard has proven to be relatively weak and because there was no specified method for WEP encryption key management, cumbersome for widespread public and private deployment. Because of its susceptibility to attack and the widespread support of newer security standards, such as WPA and WPA2, its use is highly discouraged.

IEEE 802.1X

IEEE 802.1X was a standard that existed for Ethernet switches and was adapted to 802.11 wireless LANs to provide much stronger authentication than the original 802.11 standard. IEEE 802.1X authentication is designed for medium and large wireless LANs that contain an authentication infrastructure consisting of Remote Authentication Dial-In User Service (RADIUS) servers and account databases, such as the Active Directory domain service.

IEEE 802.1X prevents a wireless node from joining a wireless network until the node is successfully authenticated and authorized. Authentication verifies that wireless clients have valid account credentials and prevents users without valid credentials from being able to join your wireless network. Authorization verifies that the wireless client is allowed to make a connection to the wireless AP. IEEE 802.1X uses the Extensible Authentication Protocol (EAP) to exchange authentication credentials. IEEE 802.1X authentication can be based on different EAP authentication methods, such as those using user name and password credentials or a digital certificate.

To address the key management issues of the original 802.11 standard, 802.1X authentication can produce dynamic WEP keys, which are mutually determined by the wireless client and RADIUS server. The RADIUS server sends the WEP key to the wireless AP after authentication completes. The combination of WEP encryption and dynamic keys determined for each 802.1X authentication is known as dynamic WEP.

WPA

Although 802.1X addresses the weak authentication and key management issues of the original 802.11 standard, it provides no solution to the weaknesses of the WEP encryption algorithm. While the IEEE 802.11i wireless LAN security standard, which will be discussed in the section titled "WPA2" later in this chapter, was being finalized, the Wi-Fi Alliance, an organization of wireless equipment vendors, created an interim standard known as Wi-Fi Protected Access (WPA). WPA replaces WEP with a much stronger encryption method known as the Temporal Key Integrity Protocol (TKIP). WPA also allows the optional use of the Advanced Encryption Standard (AES) for encryption.

WPA is available in two different modes:

- **WPA-Enterprise**   Uses 802.1X authentication and is designed for medium and large infrastructure mode networks

- **WPA-Personal**   Uses a preshared key (PSK) for authentication and is designed for small office/home office (SOHO) infrastructure mode networks

WPA2

The IEEE 802.11i standard formally replaces WEP and the other security features of the original IEEE 802.11 standard. Wi-Fi Protected Access 2 (WPA2) is a product certification available through the Wi-Fi Alliance that certifies wireless equipment as being compatible with the IEEE 802.11i standard. The goal of WPA2 certification is to support the additional mandatory security features of the IEEE 802.11i standard that are not already included for products that support WPA. For example, WPA2 requires support for both TKIP and AES encryption. WPA2 includes fast roaming techniques, such as Pairwise Master Key (PMK) caching and pre-authentication.

How It Works: Fast Roaming for WPA2

When a wireless client authenticates using 802.1X, there are a series of messages sent between the wireless client and the wireless AP to exchange credentials (802.1X authentication) and to determine the pairwise transient keys (the 4-way handshake). The pairwise transient keys are used for encryption and data integrity of WPA2-protected wireless data frames. This message exchange introduces a delay in the connection process. When a wireless client roams from one wireless AP to another, the delay to perform 802.1X authentication can cause noticeable interruptions in network connectivity, especially for time-dependent traffic, such as voice-based or video-based data streams. To minimize the delay associated with roaming to another wireless AP, WPA2 wireless equipment can optionally support PMK caching and preauthentication.

PMK Caching

As a wireless client roams from one wireless AP to another, it must perform a full 802.1X authentication with each wireless AP. WPA2 allows the wireless client and the wireless AP to cache the results of a full 802.1X authentication so that if a client roams back to a wireless AP with which it has previously authenticated, the wireless client needs to perform only the 4-way handshake and determine new pairwise transient keys. In the Association Request frame, the wireless client includes a PMK identifier that was determined during the initial authentication and stored with both the wireless client and wireless AP's PMK cache entries. PMK cache entries are stored for a finite amount of time as configured on the wireless client and the wireless AP.

To make the transition faster for wireless networking infrastructures that use a switch that acts as the 802.1X authenticator, Windows Server 2008 and Windows Vista calculate the PMK identifier value so that the PMK as determined by the 802.1X authentication with the switch can be reused when roaming between wireless APs that are attached to the same switch. This practice is known as *opportunistic PMK caching*.

Preauthentication

With preauthentication, a WPA2 wireless client can optionally perform 802.1X authentications with other wireless APs within its range while connected to its current wireless

AP. The wireless client sends preauthentication traffic to the additional wireless AP over its existing wireless connection. After preauthenticating with a wireless AP and storing the PMK and its associated information in the PMK cache, a wireless client that connects to a wireless AP with which it has preauthenticated needs to perform only the 4-way handshake.

WPA2 clients that support preauthentication can preauthenticate only with wireless APs that advertise their preauthentication capability in Beacon and Probe Response frames.

WPA2 is available in two different modes:

- **WPA2-Enterprise**   Uses 802.1X authentication and is designed for medium and large infrastructure mode networks

- **WPA2-Personal**   Uses a PSK for authentication and is designed for SOHO infrastructure mode networks

Table 10-2 summarizes the 802.11 wireless LAN security standards.

Table 10-2   802.11 Wireless LAN Security Standards

Security Standard	Authentication Methods	Encryption Methods	Encryption Key Size (bits)	Comments
IEEE 802.11	Open system and shared key	WEP	40 and 104	Weak authentication and encryption. Use is highly discouraged.
IEEE 802.1X	EAP authentication methods	N/A	N/A	Strong EAP methods provide strong authentication.
WPA-Enterprise	802.1X	TKIP and AES (optional)	128	Strong authentication (with strong EAP method) and strong (TKIP) or very strong (AES) encryption.
WPA-Personal	PSK	TKIP and AES (optional)	128	Strong authentication (with strong PSK) and strong (TKIP) or very strong (AES) encryption.
WPA2-Enterprise	802.1X	TKIP and AES	128	Strong authentication (with strong EAP method) and strong (TKIP) or very strong (AES) encryption.
WPA2-Personal	PSK	TKIP and AES	128	Strong authentication (with strong PSK) and strong (TKIP) or very strong (AES) encryption.

Windows Server 2008 and Windows Vista support the following security standards for 802.11 wireless LAN networking (the wireless network adapter and driver must also support the standard):

- 802.11 with WEP
- 802.1X
- WPA-Enterprise
- WPA-Personal
- WPA2-Enterprise
- WPA2-Personal

Note Unless stated otherwise, all subsequent references to WPA2 refer to WPA2-Enterprise, and references to WPA refer to WPA-Enterprise.

Components of 802.11 Wireless Networks

Figure 10-1 shows the components of Windows-based 802.11 protected wireless networks.

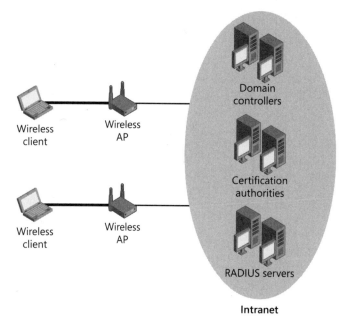

Figure 10-1 Components of Windows-based 802.11 protected wireless networks

The components are:

- **Wireless clients**   Initiate wireless connections to wireless APs and communicate with intranet resources or other wireless clients once connected

- **Wireless APs**   Listen for wireless connection attempts, enforce authentication and connection requirements, and forward frames between wireless clients and intranet resources

- **RADIUS servers**   Provide centralized authentication and authorization processing and accounting for network access attempts from wireless APs and other types of access servers

- **Active Directory domain controllers**   Validate user credentials for authentication and provide account information to the RADIUS servers to evaluate authorization

- **Certification authorities**   Part of the PKI that issues computer or user certificates to wireless clients and computer certificates to RADIUS servers

Planning and Design Considerations

When deploying a protected 802.11 wireless network solution, you must consider the following for planning and design issues:

- Wireless security technologies

- Wireless authentication modes

- Intranet infrastructure

- Wireless AP placement

- Authentication infrastructure

- Wireless clients

- PKI

- 802.1X Enforcement with NAP

Wireless Security Technologies

Wireless security technologies are a combination of a wireless security standard (WPA2 or WPA) and an EAP authentication method. To authenticate the computer or the user that is attempting to make a protected wireless connection, Windows Server 2008 and Windows Vista support the following EAP authentication methods:

- EAP-TLS

- Protected EAP (PEAP)-TLS

- PEAP-Microsoft Challenge Handshake Authentication Protocol version 2 (PEAP-MS-CHAP v2)

EAP-TLS and PEAP-TLS are used in conjunction with a PKI and computer certificates, user certificates, or smart cards. With EAP-TLS, the wireless client sends its computer certificate, user certificate, or smart card certificate for authentication, and the RADIUS server sends its computer certificate for authentication. By default, the wireless client validates the RADIUS server's certificate. With PEAP-TLS, the wireless client and RADIUS server create an encrypted TLS session, and then the wireless client and RADIUS server exchange certificates. PEAP-TLS is the strongest authentication method because the certificate exchange between the wireless client and the RADIUS server is encrypted.

In the absence of computer certificates, user certificates, or smart cards, use PEAP-MS-CHAP v2. PEAP-MS-CHAP v2 is a password-based authentication method in which the exchange of authentication messages is protected with an encrypted TLS session, making it much more difficult for a malicious user to determine the password of a captured authentication exchange with an offline dictionary attack.

Despite the encrypted TLS session, however, both EAP-TLS and PEAP-TLS are much stronger than PEAP-MS-CHAP v2 because they do not rely on passwords.

Design Choices for Wireless Security Technologies

Microsoft recommends that you use one of the following combinations of wireless security technologies (in order of most to least secure):

- WPA2 with AES encryption, PEAP-TLS or EAP-TLS authentication, and both user and computer certificates

- WPA2 with AES encryption, PEAP-MS-CHAP v2 authentication, and a requirement for users to create strong user passwords

- WPA with EAP-TLS or PEAP-TLS authentication and both user and computer certificates

- WPA with PEAP-MS-CHAP v2 authentication and a requirement for users to create strong user passwords

Requirements for Wireless Security Technologies

The requirements for wireless security technologies are the following:

- For a protected wireless network, you must use either WPA or WPA2. If you use WEP, even dynamic WEP, your wireless network will not be secure. Dynamic WEP should not be used except temporarily when transitioning to a WPA2 or WPA-based security configuration.

- EAP-TLS or PEAP-TLS requires the installation of a computer certificate on the RADIUS server and a computer certificate, user certificate, or smart card on all wireless client computers. To validate the RADIUS servers' computer certificates, the root certification authority (CA) certificate of the issuing CA of the RADIUS server computer certificates must be installed on all wireless client computers. To validate the wireless clients' computer or user certificates, the root CA certificate of the issuing CA of the wireless client certificates must be installed on each of the RADIUS servers.

■ PEAP-MS-CHAP v2 requires the installation of computer certificates on each of the RADIUS servers. It also requires that the root CA certificates of the RADIUS server computer certificates be installed on each of the wireless client computers.

■ For WPA2, some wireless equipment might need to be replaced. Older wireless equipment that supports only 802.11 can typically be upgraded to support WPA but not WPA2.

■ If you are planning to eventually deploy the 802.1X Enforcement method of NAP, you should use a PEAP-based authentication method, such as PEAP-MS-CHAP v2 or PEAP-TLS.

Best Practices for Wireless Security Technologies

The best practices for wireless security technologies are as follows:

■ Do not configure your wireless APs to use SSID suppression. The SSID (also known as the wireless network name) is by default included in the Beacon frames sent by wireless APs. Configuring your wireless APs to suppress the advertising of the SSID information element in Beacon frames does prevent the casual wireless client from discovering your wireless network. However, SSID suppression does not prevent a more sophisticated hacker from capturing other types of wireless management frames sent by your wireless AP and determining your SSID. Wireless networks with SSID suppression enabled are known as *non-broadcast* or *hidden* networks.

Besides being a weak form of wireless network name privacy, non-broadcast wireless networks also create problems for authorized wireless clients that want to automatically connect to the non-broadcast wireless network. For example, because the wireless network name is not being advertised, the wireless client must send Probe-Request messages containing the wireless network name in an attempt to locate a wireless AP for the wireless network. These messages advertise the name of the wireless network, reducing the privacy of the wireless configuration of the wireless client.

■ Do not use media access control (MAC) address filtering. MAC address filtering allows you to configure your wireless APs with the set of MAC addresses for allowed wireless clients. MAC address filtering adds administrative overhead in order to keep the list of allowed MAC addresses current and does not prevent a hacker from spoofing an allowed MAC address.

■ If you must use PEAP-MS-CHAP v2, require the use of strong passwords on your network. Strong passwords are long (longer than 8 characters) and contain a mixture of upper and lower case letters, numbers, and punctuation. In an Active Directory domain, use Group Policy settings in Computer Configuration\Windows Settings\Security Settings\Account Policies\Password Policy to enforce strong user passwords requirements.

Wireless Authentication Modes

Windows-based wireless clients can perform authentication using the following modes:

- **Computer-only**   Windows performs 802.1X authentication with computer credentials before displaying the Windows logon screen. This allows the wireless client to have access to networking resources, such as Active Directory domain controllers, before the user logs on. Windows does not attempt authentication with user credentials after the user logs on.

- **User-only**   By default, Windows performs 802.1X authentication with user credentials after the user logon process has completed. Windows does not attempt authentication with computer credentials before the user logon.

- **Computer-or-user**   Windows performs an 802.1X authentication with computer credentials before displaying the Windows logon screen. Windows performs another 802.1X authentication with user credentials either after the user has logged on or when the wireless client roams to a new wireless AP.

Problems with the default behavior of user-only authentication mode are as follows:

- A user cannot perform an initial domain logon to a computer because locally cached credentials for the user's user account are not available and there is no connectivity to the domain controller to authenticate new logon credentials.

- Domain logon operations will not be successful because there is no connectivity to the domain controllers of the Active Directory domain during the user logon process. Logon scripts, Group Policy updates, and user profile updates will fail, resulting in Windows event log errors.

Some network infrastructures use different virtual LANs (VLANs) to separate wireless clients that have authenticated with computer credentials from wireless clients that have authenticated with user credentials. If the user-level authentication to the wireless network and the switch to the user-authenticated VLAN occurs after the user logon process, a Windows wireless client will not have access to resources on the user-authenticated VLAN—such as Active Directory domain controllers—during the user logon process. This can lead to unsuccessful initial logons and domain logon operations such as logon scripts, Group Policy updates, and user profile updates.

To address the availability of network connectivity when performing user logon in user-only authentication mode and user-or-computer authentication mode when using separate VLANs, Windows Server 2008 and Windows Vista wireless clients support Single Sign On. With Single Sign On, you can specify that wireless network authentication with user credentials occur before the user logon process. To enable and configure Single Sign On, you can use the Wireless Network (IEEE 802.11) Policies Group Policy extension to configure a Windows Vista policy, or you can run **netsh wlan** with the appropriate parameters. For more information, see the section titled "Configuring Wireless Clients" later in this chapter.

Requirements for Wireless Authentication Modes

Only wireless clients running Windows Server 2008 or Windows Vista support Single Sign On.

Best Practices for Wireless Authentication Modes

Best practices for wireless authentication modes are as follows:

■ Use user-or-computer authentication mode; user authentication occurs after user logon. This is the default authentication mode.

■ If you are using user-only authentication mode, configure your wireless profiles to enable Single Sign On and perform wireless authentication with user credentials before user logon to prevent initial and domain logon problems.

■ If you are using different VLANs for computer-authenticated and user-authenticated wireless clients and computer-or-user authentication mode, configure your wireless profiles to enable Single Sign On and perform wireless authentication with user credentials before user logon to prevent initial and domain logon problems.

Intranet Infrastructure

Wireless clients need the same Transmission Control Protocol/Internet Protocol (TCP/IP) configuration settings and connectivity as wired clients, but there are differences in how you should configure wireless clients because of their inherent mobility. For this reason, place your wireless clients on different subnets than your wired clients rather than have a mixture of wired and wireless clients on the same subnet.

Subnet Design for Wireless Clients

Creating separate subnets for your wireless clients provides the following benefits:

■ Wired network components do not need to draw from the same pool of existing IPv4 addresses as your wireless clients.

■ Wireless clients are easier to identify from their IPv4 and IPv6 address prefixes, which makes it easier to manage and troubleshoot wireless clients.

■ Separate IPv4 subnets give you increased control over DHCP lease times.

■ You can associate each of your physical subnets (both wireless and wired) with sites within Active Directory, which allows you to assign Group Policy settings to specific subnets.

■ If all of your wireless APs are on the same subnet, your wireless clients can seamlessly perform network-layer roaming.

Network-layer roaming occurs when a wireless client connects to a different wireless AP for the same wireless network within the same subnet. For network-layer roaming, the wireless client renews its current DHCP configuration. When a wireless client connects to a different wireless AP for the same wireless network that is on a different subnet, the wireless client gets a new DHCP configuration that is relevant to that new subnet. When you cross a subnet boundary, applications that cannot handle a change of IPv4 or IPv6 address, such as some e-mail applications, might fail.

When creating an IPv4 subnet prefix for your wireless clients, consider that you need at least one IPv4 address for the following:

- Each wireless AP's LAN interface that is connected to the wireless subnet.

- Each router interface that is connected to the wireless subnet.

- Any other TCP/IP-capable host or device that is attached to the wireless subnet.

- Each wireless client that can connect to the wireless network. If you underestimate this number, Windows wireless clients that connect after all of the available IPv4 addresses have been assigned through DHCP to connected wireless clients will automatically configure an IP address with no default gateway using Automatic Private IP Addressing (APIPA). This configuration does not allow connectivity to the intranet. Wireless clients with APIPA configurations will periodically attempt to obtain a DHCP configuration.

Because each IPv6 subnet can support a very large number of hosts, you do not need to determine the number of IPv6 addresses needed for the IPv6 subnet prefix.

DHCP Design for Wireless Clients

With different subnets for wired and wireless clients, you must configure separate DHCP scopes. Because wireless clients can easily roam from one wireless subnet to another, you should configure the lease for the DHCP scopes to have a shorter duration for wireless subnets than for wired subnets.

The typical lease duration for a DHCP scope for wired networks is a specified number of days. Because wireless clients do not release their addresses when roaming to a new subnet, you should shorten the lease duration to several hours for DHCP scopes corresponding to wireless subnets. By setting a shorter lease duration for wireless subnets, the DHCP server will automatically make IPv4 addresses that are no longer being used by wireless clients available for reuse throughout the day instead of leaving the addresses unavailable for days. When determining the optimal lease duration for the wireless clients in your environment, keep in mind the additional processing load that the shorter lease duration places on your DHCP server.

For more information about configuring DHCP scopes, see Chapter 3, "Dynamic Host Configuration Protocol."

Wireless AP Placement

An important and time-consuming task in deploying a wireless LAN is determining where to place the wireless APs in your organization. Wireless APs must be placed to provide seamless coverage across the floor, building, or campus. With seamless coverage, wireless users can roam from one location to another without experiencing an interruption in network connectivity, except for a change in IPv4 and IPv6 addresses when crossing a subnet boundary. Determining where to place your wireless APs is not as simple as installing them and turning them on. Wireless LAN technologies are based on propagation of a radio signal, which can be obstructed, reflected, shielded, and interfered with.

When planning the deployment of wireless APs in an organization, you should take the following design elements into consideration (as described in the following sections):

- Wireless AP requirements
- Channel separation
- Signal propagation modifiers
- Sources of interference
- Number of wireless APs

 Note   For additional specifications and guidelines for placing wireless APs, see the manufacturer's documentation for the wireless APs and the antennas used with them.

Wireless AP Requirements

You must identify the requirements for your wireless APs, which might include the following features:

- WPA
- WPA2
- 802.1X and RADIUS
- 802.11a, b, g, and n

Depending on your budget and bandwidth requirements, you might need wireless APs that support 802.11b, 802.11a, 802.11g, 802.11n, or a combination of technologies.

- **Building or fire code compliance**   The plenum area (the space between the suspended ceiling and the ceiling) is regulated by building and fire codes. Therefore, for plenum placement of APs and associated wiring, you must purchase wireless APs that are fire-rated and in compliance with building and fire codes. If you place your wireless APs in the plenum area, you must determine the best method for powering the wireless

APs. Consult with the wireless AP manufacturer to determine how to meet the power requirements for the wireless APs. Some wireless APs can receive electrical power through the Ethernet cable that connects them to the wired network.

- **Preconfiguration and remote configuration**   Preconfiguring the wireless APs before installing them on location can speed up the deployment process and can save labor costs because less-skilled workers can perform the physical installation. You can preconfigure wireless APs by using the console port (serial port), Telnet, or a Web server that is integrated with the wireless AP. Regardless of whether you decide to preconfigure the wireless APs, make sure that you can access them remotely, configure the wireless APs remotely through a vendor-supplied configuration tool, or upgrade the wireless APs by using scripts.

- **Antenna types**   Verify that the wireless AP supports different types of antennas. For example, in a building with multiple floors, a loop antenna—which propagates the signal equally in all directions except vertically—might work best.

> **Note**   For information about which type of antenna will work best for your wireless WLAN deployment, see the documentation for your wireless APs.

- **IPsec support**   Although not a requirement, if possible, choose wireless APs that use Internet Protocol security (IPsec) and Encapsulating Security Payload (ESP) with encryption to provide data confidentiality for RADIUS traffic sent between wireless APs and RADIUS servers. Use Triple Data Encryption Standard (3DES) encryption and, if possible, certificates for Internet Key Exchange (IKE) main mode authentication.

Channel Separation

Direct communication between an 802.11b or 802.11g wireless network adapter and a wireless AP occurs over a common channel, which corresponds to a frequency range in the S-Band ISM. You configure the wireless AP for a specific channel, and the wireless network adapter automatically configures itself to the channel of the wireless AP with the strongest signal.

To reduce interference between 802.11b wireless APs, ensure that wireless APs with overlapping coverage volumes use unique frequency channels. The 802.11b or 802.11g standards reserve 14 channels for use with wireless APs. Within the United States, the Federal Communications Commission (FCC) allows channels 1 through 11. In most of Europe, you can use channels 1 through 13. In Japan, you have only one choice: channel 14. Figure 10-2 shows the channel overlap for 802.11b and 802.11g wireless APs in the United States.

To prevent signals from adjacent wireless APs from interfering with one another, you must set their channel numbers so that they are at least five channels apart. To get the most usable channels in the United States, you can set your wireless APs to use one of three channels: 1, 6, or 11. If you need fewer than three usable channels, ensure that the channels you choose maintain the five-channel separation.

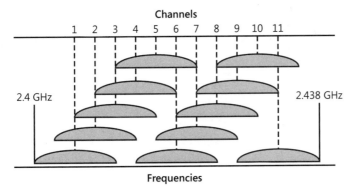

Figure 10-2   Channel overlap for 802.11b and 802.11g wireless APs in the United States

Figure 10-3 shows an example of a set of wireless APs deployed in multiple floors of a building so that overlapping signals from adjacent wireless APs use different usable channel numbers.

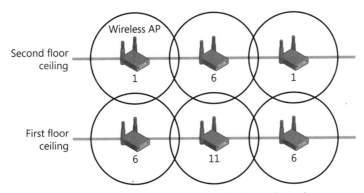

Figure 10-3   Example of assigning 802.11b channel numbers

Signal Propagation Modifiers

The wireless AP is a radio transmitter and receiver that has a limited range. The volume around the wireless AP for which you can send and receive wireless data for any of the supported bit rates is known as the *coverage volume*. (Many wireless references use the term *coverage area*; however, wireless signals propagate in three dimensions.) The shape of the coverage volume depends on the type of antenna used by the wireless AP and the presence of signal propagation modifiers and other interference sources.

With an idealized omnidirectional antenna, the coverage volume is a series of concentric spherical shells of signal strengths corresponding to the different supported bit rates. Figure 10-4 shows an example of the idealized coverage volume for 802.11b and an omnidirectional antenna.

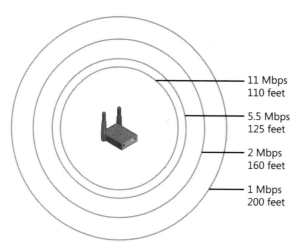

11 Mbps
110 feet

5.5 Mbps
125 feet

2 Mbps
160 feet

1 Mbps
200 feet

Figure 10-4   Idealized coverage volume example

Signal propagation modifiers change the shape of the ideal coverage volume through radio frequency (RF) attenuation (the reduction of signal strength), shielding, and reflection, which can affect how you deploy your wireless APs. Metal objects within a building or used in the construction of a building can affect the wireless signal. Examples of such objects include:

- Support beams

- Elevator shafts

- Steel reinforcement in concrete

- Heating and air-conditioning ventilation ducts

- Wire mesh that reinforces plaster or stucco in walls

- Walls that contain metal, cinder blocks, and concrete

- Cabinets, metal desks, or other types of large metal equipment

Sources of Interference

Any device that operates on the same frequencies as your wireless devices (in the S-Band ISM, which operates in the frequency range of 2.4 gigahertz [GHz] to 2.5 GHz, or the C-Band ISM, which operates in the frequency range of 5.725 GHz to 5.875 GHz) might interfere with the wireless signals. Sources of interference also change the shape of a wireless AP's ideal coverage volume.

Devices that operate in the S-Band ISM include the following:

- Bluetooth-enabled devices

- Microwave ovens

- 2.4-GHz cordless phones

- Wireless video cameras

- Medical equipment

- Elevator motors

Devices that operate in the C-Band ISM include the following:

- 5-GHz cordless phones

- Wireless video cameras

- Medical equipment

Number of Wireless APs

To determine how many wireless APs to deploy, follow these guidelines:

- Include enough wireless APs to ensure that wireless users have sufficient signal strength from anywhere in the coverage volume.

  Typical wireless APs use antennas that produce a vertically flattened sphere of signal that propagates across the floor of a building. Wireless APs typically have indoor coverage within a 200-foot radius. Include enough wireless APs to ensure signal overlap between the wireless APs.

- Determine the maximum number of simultaneous wireless users per coverage volume.

- Estimate the data throughput that the average wireless user requires. If needed, add more wireless APs, which will:

  ❑ Improve wireless client network bandwidth capacity.

  ❑ Increase the number of wireless users supported within a coverage area.

  ❑ Based on the total data throughput of all users, determine the number of users who can connect to a wireless AP. Obtain a clear picture of throughput before deploying the network or making changes. Some wireless vendors provide an 802.11 simulation tool, which you can use to model traffic in a network and view throughput levels under various conditions.

  ❑ Ensure redundancy in case a wireless AP fails.

- When designing wireless AP placement for performance, use the following best practices:

  ❑ Do not overload your wireless APs with too many connected wireless clients. Although most wireless APs can support hundreds of wireless connections, the practical limit is 20 to 25 connected clients. An average of 2 to 4 users per wireless AP is a good average to maximize the performance while still effectively utilizing the wireless LAN.

  ❑ For higher density situations, lower the signal strength of the wireless APs to reduce the coverage area, thereby allowing more wireless APs to fit in a specific space and more wireless bandwidth to be distributed to more wireless clients.

Authentication Infrastructure

The authentication infrastructure exists to:

- Authenticate the credentials of wireless clients.
- Authorize the wireless connection.
- Inform wireless APs of wireless connection restrictions.
- Record the wireless connection creation and termination for accounting purposes.

The authentication infrastructure for protected wireless connections consists of:

- Wireless APs
- RADIUS servers
- Active Directory domain controllers
- Issuing CAs of a PKI (optional)

If you are using a Windows domain as the user account database for verification of user or computer credentials and for obtaining dial-in properties, use Network Policy Server (NPS) in Windows Server 2008. NPS is a full-featured RADIUS server and proxy that is tightly integrated with Active Directory. See Chapter 9 for additional design and planning considerations for NPS-based RADIUS servers.

NPS performs the authentication of the wireless connection by communicating with a domain controller over a protected remote procedure call (RPC) channel. NPS performs authorization of the connection attempt through the dial-in properties of the user or computer account and network policies configured on the NPS server.

By default, NPS logs all RADIUS accounting information in a local log file (*%SystemRoot%*System32\Logfiles*Logfile*.log by default) based on settings configured in the Accounting node in the Network Policy Server snap-in.

Best Practices for Authentication Infrastructure

Best practices to follow for the authentication infrastructure are the following:

- To better manage authorization for wireless connections, create a universal group in Active Directory for wireless access that contains global groups for the user and computer accounts that are allowed to make wireless connections. For example, create a universal group named WirelessAccounts that contains the global groups based on your organization's regions or departments. Each global group contains allowed user and computer accounts for wireless access. When you configure your NPS policies for wireless connections, specify the WirelessAccounts group name.

- From the NPS node of the Network Policy Server snap-in, use the Configure 802.1X Wizard to create a set of policies for 802.1X-authenticated wireless connections. For example, create a set of policies for wireless clients that are members of a specific group and to use a specific authentication method.

Wireless Clients

A Windows-based wireless client is one that is running Windows Server 2008, Windows Vista, Windows XP with Service Pack 2, or Windows Server 2003. You can configure wireless connections on Windows-based wireless clients in the following ways:

- **Group Policy**   The Wireless Network (IEEE 802.11) Policies Group Policy extension is part of a Computer Configuration Group Policy Object that can specify wireless network settings in an Active Directory environment.

- **Command line**   You can configure wireless settings by using Netsh.exe (running the command **netsh wlan** with the desired parameters). These commands apply only to wireless clients running Windows Vista or Windows Server 2008.

> **Note**   To run **netsh wlan** commands on computers running Windows Server 2008, you must add the Wireless LAN Service feature with the Server Manager tool.

- **Wireless XML profiles**   Wireless Extensible Markup Language (XML) profiles are XML files that contain wireless network settings. You can use either the Netsh tool or the Wireless Network (IEEE 802.11) Policies Group Policy extension to export and import XML-based wireless profiles.

- **Manually**   For a Windows Vista–based or Windows Server 2008–based wireless client, connect to the wireless network when prompted or use the Connect to a Network Wizard from the Network and Sharing Center. For a Windows XP with SP2–based or Windows Server 2003–based wireless client, connect to the wireless network when prompted, or use the Wireless Network Setup Wizard from the Network Connections folder.

Wireless Network (IEEE 802.11) Policies Group Policy Extension

To automate the configuration of wireless network settings for Windows wireless client computers, Windows Server 2008 and Windows Server 2003 Active Directory domains support a Wireless Network (IEEE 802.11) Policies Group Policy extension. This extension allows you to configure wireless network settings as part of Computer Configuration Group Policy for a domain-based Group Policy Object. By using the Wireless Network (IEEE 802.11) Policies Group Policy extension, you can specify a list of preferred networks and their settings to automatically configure wireless LAN settings for wireless clients running Windows Server 2008, Windows Vista, Windows XP with SP2, Windows XP with SP1, or Windows Server 2003.

For each preferred network, you can specify the following:

■ Connection settings, such as the wireless network name and whether the wireless network is a non-broadcast network

■ Security settings, such as the authentication and encryption method, the EAP type, and the authentication mode

■ Advanced 802.1X security settings, such as Single Sign On (for Windows Server 2008 and Windows Vista wireless clients)

These settings are automatically applied to wireless clients running Windows Server 2008, Windows Vista, Windows XP with SP2, and Windows Server 2003 that are members of a Windows Server 2008 or Windows Server 2003 Active Directory domain. You can configure wireless policies by using the Computer Configuration\Windows Settings\Security Settings\Wireless Network (IEEE 802.11) Policies node in the Group Policy Management Editor snap-in.

Note   To modify Group Policy settings from a computer running Windows Server 2008, you might need to install the Group Policy Management feature using the Server Manager tool.

By default, there are no Wireless Network (IEEE 802.11) policies. To create a new policy for a Windows Server 2008–based Active Directory domain, right-click Wireless Network (IEEE 802.11) Policies in the Group Policy Management Editor snap-in console tree, and then click Create A New Windows Vista Policy or Create A New Windows XP Policy. For each type of policy, you can create only a single policy. A Windows XP Policy can contain profiles with settings for multiple wireless networks, and each network must have a unique SSID. A Windows Vista policy can also contain profiles with settings for multiple wireless networks with unique SSIDs. Additionally, different profiles can contain multiple instances of the same SSID, each with unique settings. This allows you to configure profiles for mixed-mode deployments in which some clients are using different security technologies, such as WPA and WPA2.

The Windows Vista–based wireless policy contains policy settings specific to Windows Server 2008 and Windows Vista wireless clients. If both types of wireless policies are configured, Windows XP with SP2–based and Windows Server 2003–based wireless clients will use only the Windows XP policy settings, and the Windows Server 2008 and Windows Vista wireless clients will use only the Windows Vista policy settings. If there are no Windows Vista policy settings, Windows Server 2008 and Windows Vista wireless clients will use the Windows XP policy settings.

Windows Vista Wireless Policy   The properties dialog box of a Windows Vista wireless policy consists of a General tab and a Network Permissions tab. Figure 10-5 shows the General tab.

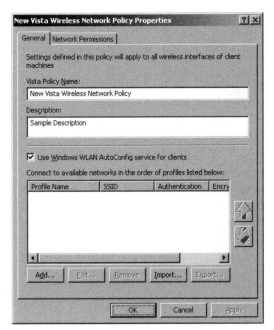

Figure 10-5   The General tab of a Windows Vista wireless policy

On the General tab, you can configure a name and description for the policy, specify whether to enable the WLAN AutoConfig service (Wireless Auto Configuration), and configure the list of wireless networks and their settings (known as *profiles*) in preferred order. On the General tab, you can import and export profiles as files in XML format. To export a profile to an XML file, select the profile and click Export. To import an XML file as a wireless profile, click Import, and then specify the file's location.

Figure 10-6 shows the Network Permissions tab for a Windows Vista wireless network policy.

The Network Permissions tab is new for Windows Server 2008 and Windows Vista and allows you to specify wireless networks by name that are either allowed or denied access. For example, you can create allow or deny lists.

With an allow list, you can specify the set of wireless networks by name to which a Windows Server 2008 or Windows Vista wireless client is allowed to connect. This is useful for network administrators who want an organization's laptop computers to connect to a specific set of wireless networks, which might include the organization's wireless network in addition to wireless Internet service providers.

With a deny list, you can specify the set of wireless networks by name to which the wireless clients are not allowed to connect. This is useful to prevent managed laptop computers from connecting to other wireless networks that are within range of the organization's wireless network—for example, when an organization occupies a floor of a building and there are other wireless networks of other organization on adjoining floors—or to prevent managed laptop computers from connecting to known unsecured wireless networks.

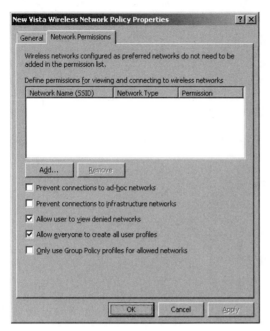

Figure 10-6   The Network Permissions tab of a Windows Vista wireless policy

On the Network Permissions tab, there are also settings to prevent connections to either ad-hoc or infrastructure mode wireless networks, to allow the user to view the wireless networks in the list of available networks that have been configured as denied, and to allow any user to create an all-user profile. An *all-user profile* can be used to connect to a specific wireless network by any user with an account on the computer. If this setting is disabled, only users in the Domain Admins or Network Configuration Operators groups can create all-user wireless profiles on the computer. Last, there is a setting to require that the wireless client use Group Policy–based profiles for allowed profiles, rather than local profiles of the same name.

To manage a wireless network profile, in the New Windows Vista Wireless Policy Properties dialog box, on the General tab, either select an existing profile and click Edit, or click Add and then specify whether the new wireless profile is for an infrastructure or ad-hoc mode wireless network. The profile properties dialog box of a Windows Vista wireless network profile consists of a Connection tab and a Security tab. Figure 10-7 shows the default Connection tab for a Windows Vista wireless network profile.

On the Connection tab, you can configure a name for the profile and a list of wireless network names to which this profile applies. You can add new names by typing the name in the Network Name(s) (SSID) box and clicking Add. You can also specify whether the wireless client using this profile will automatically attempt to connect to the wireless networks named in the profile when in range (subject to the preference order of the list of wireless profiles on the General tab for the Windows Vista policy), whether to automatically disconnect from this wireless network if a more preferred wireless network comes within range, and to indicate that the wireless networks in this profile are non-broadcast networks (also known as hidden networks).

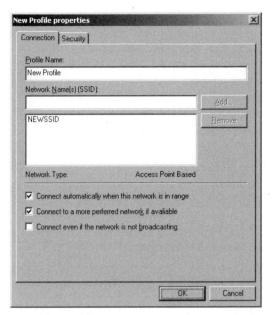

Figure 10-7   The Connection tab for a Windows Vista wireless network profile

Figure 10-8 shows the Security tab for a Windows Vista wireless network profile.

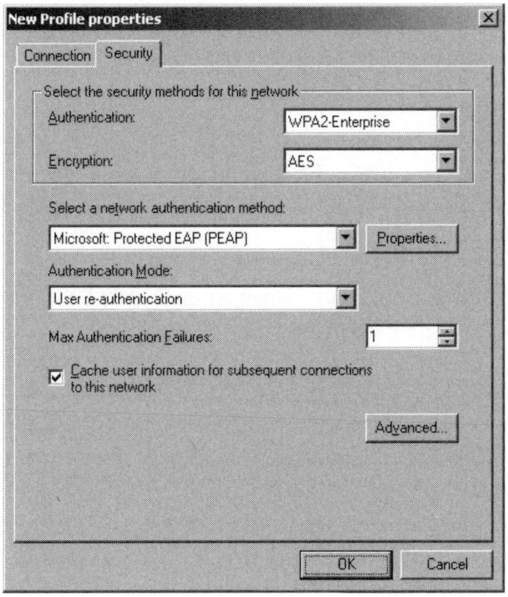

Figure 10-8   The Security tab for a Windows Vista wireless network profile

On the Security tab, you can configure the authentication and encryption methods for the wireless networks in the profile. For authentication methods, you can select Open, Shared, Wi-Fi Protected Access (WPA)–Personal, WPA-Enterprise, WPA2-Personal, WPA2-Enterprise, and Open with 802.1X. For encryption methods, you can select Wired Equivalent Privacy (WEP), Temporal Key Integrity Protocol (TKIP), and Advanced Encryption Standard (AES). The choice of encryption methods depends on your choice of authentication method.

If you select Open with 802.1X, WPA-Enterprise, or WPA2-Enterprise as the authentication method, you can also configure the network authentication method (the EAP type), the authentication mode (user reauthentication, computer authentication, user authentication, or guest authentication), the number of times authentication attempts can fail before authentication is abandoned, and whether to cache user information for subsequent connections. If you configure this last setting not to cache the user information, when the user logs off, the user credential data is removed from the registry. The result is that when the next user logs on, that user will be prompted for credentials (such as user name and password).

Direct from the Source: Locations of Cached Credentials

For wireless clients running Windows Server 2008 or Windows Vista, the cached credentials are stored at:

HKEY_CURRENT_USER\Software\Microsoft\Wlansvc\UserData\Profiles*Profile-GUID*\MSMUserdata

For wireless clients running Windows XP or Windows Server 2003, the cached credentials are stored at:

HKEY_CURRENT_USER\Software\Microsoft\Eapol\UserEapInfo

Clay Seymour, Support Escalation Engineer

Enterprise Platform Support

To configure advanced security settings for the WPA-Enterprise, WPA2-Enterprise, or Open with 802.1X authentication methods, in the New Profile Properties Dialog Box, on the Security tab, click Advanced. Figure 10-9 shows the default Advanced Security Settings dialog box.

In the IEEE 802.1X section, there are settings to specify the number of successive EAP over LAN (EAPOL)-Start messages that are sent out when no response to the initial EAPOL-Start messages is received, the time interval between the retransmission of EAPOL-Start messages when no response to the previously sent EAPOL-Start message is received, the period for which the authenticating client will not perform any 802.1X authentication activity after it has received an authentication failure indication from the authenticator, and the interval for which the authenticating client will wait before retransmitting any 802.1X requests after end-to-end 802.1X authentication has been initiated.

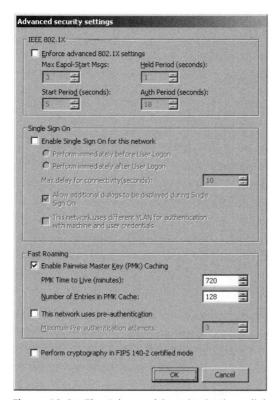

Figure 10-9   The Advanced Security Settings dialog box

In the Single Sign On section, there are settings to perform wireless authentication immediately before or after the user logon process, specify the number of seconds of delay for connectivity before the user logon process begins, choose whether to prompt the user for additional dialog boxes, and choose whether the wireless networks for this profile use a different virtual LAN (VLAN) for computer or user authentication and to perform a DHCP renewal when switching from the computer-authenticated VLAN to the user-authenticated VLAN. For information about when to use Single Sign On, see "Wireless Authentication Modes" earlier in this chapter.

In the Fast Roaming section, you can configure Pairwise Master Key (PMK) caching and preauthentication options. The Fast Roaming section appears only when you select WPA2-Enterprise as the authentication method on the Security tab. With PMK caching, wireless clients and wireless APs cache the results of 802.1X authentications. Therefore, access is much faster when a wireless client roams back to a wireless AP to which the client already authenticated. You can configure a maximum time to keep an entry in the PMK cache and the maximum number of entries. With preauthentication, a wireless client can perform an 802.1X authentication with other wireless APs in its range while it is still connected to its current wireless AP. If the wireless client roams to a wireless AP with which it has preauthenticated, access time is substantially decreased. You can configure the maximum number of times to attempt preauthentication with a wireless AP.

> **Note** Fast roaming for WPA2 is different than fast reconnect. Fast reconnect minimizes the connection delay in wireless environments when a wireless client roams from one wireless AP to another when using PEAP. With fast reconnect, the Network Policy Server service caches information about the PEAP TLS session so that when reauthenticating, the wireless client does not need to perform PEAP authentication, only MS-CHAP v2 (for PEAP-MS-CHAP v2) or TLS (for PEAP-TLS) authentication. Fast reconnect is enabled by default for Windows wireless clients and for NPS network policies.

A final check box allows you to specify whether to perform AES encryption in a Federal Information Processing Standard (FIPS) 140-2 certified mode. FIPS 140-2 is a U.S. government computer security standard that specifies design and implementation requirements for cryptographic modules. Windows Server 2008 and Windows Vista are FIPS 140-2 certified. When you enable FIPS 140-2 certified mode, Windows Server 2008 or Windows Vista will perform the AES encryption in software, rather than relying on the wireless network adapter. This check box only appears when you select WPA2-Enterprise as the authentication method on the Security tab.

Windows XP Wireless Policy   To create a new Windows XP wireless policy, in the Group Policy Management Editor snap-in, in the console tree, right-click Wireless Network (IEEE 802.11) Policies, and then click Create A New Windows XP Policy. The properties dialog box of a Windows XP wireless policy consists of a General tab and a Preferred Networks tab.

Figure 10-10 shows the General tab for a Windows XP wireless network policy.

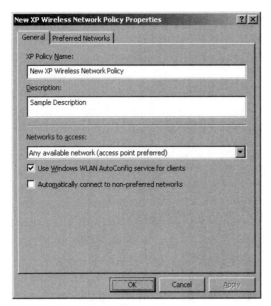

Figure 10-10   The General tab for a Windows XP wireless network policy

On the General tab, you can configure a name and description for the policy, specify whether the Wireless Zero Configuration service is enabled, select the types of wireless networks to access (any available, infrastructure, or ad-hoc networks), and specify whether to automatically connect to non-preferred networks.

~~~ure 10-11 shows the Preferred Networks tab for a Windows XP wireless policy.

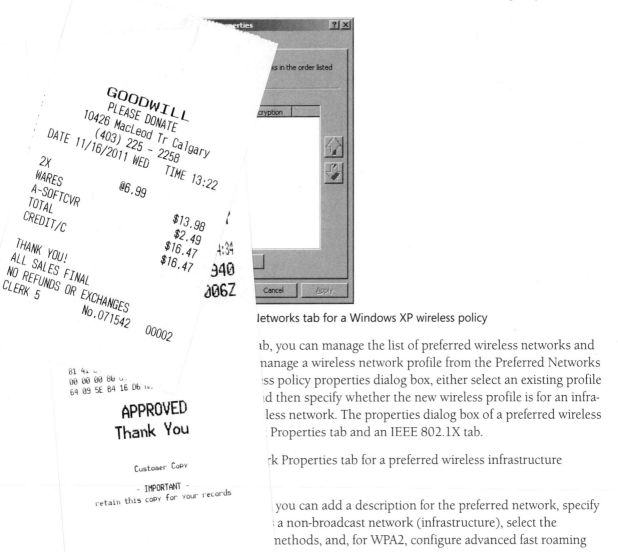

letworks tab for a Windows XP wireless policy

ib, you can manage the list of preferred wireless networks and
nanage a wireless network profile from the Preferred Networks
ss policy properties dialog box, either select an existing profile
d then specify whether the new wireless profile is for an infra-
less network. The properties dialog box of a preferred wireless
Properties tab and an IEEE 802.1X tab.

rk Properties tab for a preferred wireless infrastructure

you can add a description for the preferred network, specify
a non-broadcast network (infrastructure), select the
nethods, and, for WPA2, configure advanced fast roaming

Figure 10-13 shows the default IEEE 802.1X tab for a preferred wireless network.

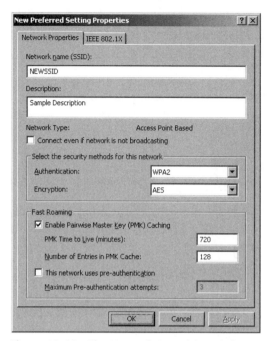

Figure 10-12   The Network Properties tab for a preferred wireless infrastructure network

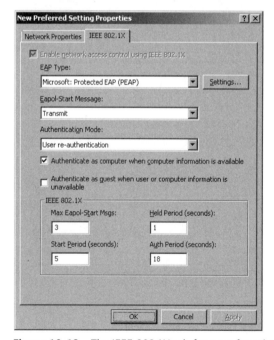

Figure 10-13   The IEEE 802.1X tab for a preferred wireless network

On the IEEE 802.1X tab, you can specify the EAP type and configure its settings, specify when to send the EAPOL-Start message, choose the authentication mode, specify whether to authenticate with computer credentials or as a guest, and set advanced 802.1X settings.

Command-Line Configuration

Windows Vista supports a command-line interface that allows you to configure some of the wireless settings that are available from the wireless dialog boxes in the Network Connections folder or through the Wireless Network (IEEE 802.11) Policies Group Policy extension. Command-line configuration of wireless settings can help deployment of wireless networks in the following situations:

- **Automated script support for wireless settings without using Group Policy**   The Wireless Network (IEEE 802.11) Policies Group Policy extension applies only in an Active Directory domain. For an environment without a Group Policy infrastructure, a script that automates the configuration of wireless connections can be run either manually or automatically, such as part of the logon script.

- **Bootstrap of a wireless client onto the organization's protected wireless network**   A wireless client computer that is not a member of the domain cannot connect to the organization's protected wireless network. Additionally, a computer cannot join the domain until it has successfully connected to the organization's protected wireless network. A command-line script provides a method to connect to the organization's secure wireless network to join the domain.

To perform command-line configuration of Windows Vista–based and Windows Server 2008–based wireless clients, run the **netsh wlan** command with the appropriate parameters.

> **More Info**   For more information about **netsh wlan** command syntax, see Netsh Commands for Wireless Local Area Network (WLAN) at *http://go.microsoft.com/fwlink/ ?LinkID=81751.*

XML-Based Wireless Profiles

To simplify command-line configuration of Windows Vista or Windows Server 2008 wireless clients, you can export the configuration of a wireless profile to an XML file that can be imported on other wireless clients. You can export a wireless profile from a wireless client by running the **netsh wlan export profile** command or by using the General tab of the Windows Vista wireless policy properties dialog box. To import a wireless profile, run **netsh wlan add profile**.

Design Choices for Wireless Clients

The design choices for wireless clients are the following:

- To prevent your Windows Vista or Windows Server 2008 wireless clients from connecting to certain wireless networks, configure a list of denied wireless networks on the Network Permissions tab of the Windows Vista wireless policy properties dialog box, or run the **netsh wlan add filter** command.

- To configure your Windows Vista or Windows Server 2008 wireless clients to connect to only specific wireless networks, configure a list of allowed wireless networks on the Network Permissions tab of the Windows Vista wireless policy dialog box, or run the **netsh wlan add filter** command.

Requirements for Wireless Clients

The requirements for wireless clients are the following:

- To use WPA2, wireless clients must be running Windows XP with SP2 and the Wireless Client Update for Windows XP with Service Pack 2, Windows Vista, or Windows Server 2008.

- Command-line configuration using the **netsh wlan** command, export and import of wireless XML profiles, and Single Sign On are supported by wireless clients running only Windows Vista or Windows Server 2008.

- To deploy 802.1X enforcement with Network Access Protection, you must configure your wireless clients to use a PEAP-based authentication method.

Best Practices for Wireless Clients

Best practices for wireless clients are the following:

- For a small number of wireless clients, configure each wireless client manually.

- For enterprise deployment of wireless configuration in an Active Directory environment, use the Wireless Network (IEEE 802.11) Wireless Policies Group Policy extension.

- For enterprise deployment of wireless configuration through the use of scripts, create wireless XML profiles and configure wireless clients with a script containing the **netsh wlan add profile** command.

PKI

To perform authentication for wireless connections using PEAP-TLS or EAP-TLS, a PKI must be in place to issue computer or user certificates to wireless clients and computer certificates to RADIUS servers. For PEAP-MS-CHAP v2–based authentication, a PKI is not required. It is possible to purchase certificates from a third-party CA to install on your NPS servers. You might also need to distribute the root CA certificate of third-party computer certificates to your wireless client computers.

PKI for Smart Cards

The use of smart cards for user authentication is the strongest form of user authentication in Windows. For wireless connections, you can use smart cards with the EAP-TLS or PEAP-TLS authentication method. The individual smart cards are distributed to users who have a computer with a smart card reader. To log on to the computer, you must insert the smart card into the smart card reader and type the smart card personal identification number (PIN). When the user attempts to make a wireless connection, the smart card certificate is sent during the connection negotiation process.

PKI for User Certificates

User certificates that are stored in the Windows registry for user authentication can be used in place of smart cards. However, it is not as strong a form of authentication. With smart cards, the user certificate issued during the authentication process is made available only when the user possesses the smart card and has knowledge of the PIN to log on to the computer. With user certificates, the user certificate issued during the authentication process is made available when the user logs on to the computer using a domain-based user name and password. Just as with smart cards, authentication using user certificates for wireless connections uses the EAP-TLS or PEAP-TLS authentication methods.

To deploy user certificates in your organization, first deploy a PKI. You'll then need to install a user certificate for each user. The easiest way to accomplish this is if Windows Certificate Services is installed as an enterprise CA. Then configure Group Policy settings for user certificate autoenrollment. For more information, see the section titled "Deploying Certificates" later in this chapter.

When the wireless client attempts user-level authentication for a wireless connection, the wireless client computer sends the user certificate during the authentication process.

PKI for Computer Certificates

Computer certificates are stored in the Windows registry for computer-level authentication for wireless access with the EAP-TLS or PEAP-TLS authentication methods. To deploy computer certificates in your organization, first deploy a PKI. You'll then need to install a computer certificate for each computer. The easiest way to accomplish this is if Windows Active Directory Certificate Services or Certificate Services is installed as an enterprise CA. Then, configure Group Policy settings for computer certificate autoenrollment. For more information, see "Deploying Certificates" later in this chapter.

When the wireless client attempts computer-level authentication for a wireless connection, the wireless client computer sends the computer certificate during the authentication process.

Requirements for PKI

Requirements for PKI for a protected wireless network are the following:

- For computer-level authentication with EAP-TLS or PEAP-TLS, you must install computer certificates, also known as *machine* certificates, on each wireless client.

  The computer certificates of the wireless clients must be valid and verifiable by the NPS servers; the NPS servers must have a root CA certificate for the CA that issued the computer certificates of the wireless client.

- For user-level authentication with EAP-TLS or PEAP-TLS, you must use a smart card, or you must install a user certificate on each wireless client.

  The smart card or user certificates of the wireless clients must be valid and verifiable by the NPS servers; the NPS servers must have the root CA certificates of the issuing CAs of the smart card or user certificates of the wireless clients.

- You must install the root CA certificates of the issuing CA of the NPS server computer certificates on each wireless client.

  The computer certificates of the NPS servers must be valid and verifiable by each wireless client; the wireless clients must have a root CA certificates for the CAs that issued the computer certificates of the NPS servers.

- For EAP-TLS authentication, the requirements for the user certificate, smart card certificate, or computer certificate of the wireless client are as follows:

  - The certificate must contain a private key.

  - The certificate must be issued by an enterprise CA or mapped to a user or computer account in Active Directory.

  - The certificate must be chained to a trusted root CA on the NPS server and must not fail any of the checks that are performed by CryptoAPI and specified in the network policy for wireless connections.

  - The certificate must be configured with the Client Authentication purpose in the Enhanced Key Usage field (the object identifier for Client Authentication is 1.3.6.1.5.5.7.3.2).

  - The Subject Alternative Name field must contain the user principal name (UPN) of the user or computer account.

- For EAP-TLS authentication, the requirements for the computer certificate of the NPS server are as follows:

  - The certificate must contain a private key.

❑ The Subject field must contain a value.

❑ The certificate must be chained to a trusted root CA on the wireless clients and must not fail any of the checks that are performed by CryptoAPI and specified in the network policy for wireless connections.

❑ The certificate must be configured with the Server Authentication purpose in the Enhanced Key Usage field (the object identifier for Server Authentication is 1.3.6.1.5.5.7.3.1).

❑ The certificate must be configured with a required cryptographic service provider (CSP) value of Microsoft RSA SChannel Cryptographic provider.

❑ The Subject Alternative Name field of the certificate, if used, must contain the DNS name of the NPS server.

Best Practices for PKI

Best practices for the PKI for protected wireless access are the following:

■ For computer certificates with EAP-TLS or PEAP-TLS, if you are using a Windows Server 2008 enterprise CA as an issuing CA, configure your Active Directory domain for autoenrollment of computer certificates using a Computer Configuration Group Policy. Each computer that is a member of the domain automatically requests a computer certificate when the Computer Configuration Group Policy is updated.

■ For registry-based user certificates for EAP-TLS or PEAP-TLS, if you are using a Windows Server 2008 enterprise CA as an issuing CA, use a User Configuration Group Policy to configure your Active Directory domain for autoenrollment of user certificates. Each user who successfully logs on to the domain automatically requests a user certificate when the User Configuration Group Policy is updated.

■ If you have purchased third-party computer certificates for your NPS servers for PEAP-MS-CHAP v2 authentication, and the wireless clients do not have the root CA certificate of the issuing CA of the NPS server computer certificates installed, use Group Policy to install the root CA certificate of the issuing CA of the NPS server computer certificates on your wireless clients. Each computer that is a member of the domain automatically receives and installs the root CA certificate when the Computer Configuration Group Policy is updated.

■ For EAP-TLS, PEAP-TLS, and PEAP-MS-CHAP v2 authentication, it is possible to configure the wireless clients so that they do not validate the certificate of the NPS server. If so, it is not required to have computer certificates on the NPS servers and their root CA certificates on wireless clients. However, having the wireless clients validate the certificate of the NPS server is recommended for mutual authentication of the wireless client and NPS server. With mutual authentication, you can protect your wireless clients from connecting to rogue wireless APs with spoofed authentication servers.

802.1X Enforcement with NAP

NAP for Windows Server 2008, Windows Vista, and Windows XP with Service Pack 3 provides components and an application programming interface (API) set that help you enforce compliance with health policies for network access or communication. Developers and network administrators can create solutions for validating computers that connect to their networks, can provide needed updates or access to needed resources, and can limit the access of noncompliant computers.

802.1X Enforcement is one of the NAP enforcement methods included with Windows Server 2008, Windows Vista, and Windows XP. With 802.1X Enforcement, an 802.1X-authenticated wireless client must prove that it is compliant with system health requirements before being allowed full access to the intranet. If the wireless client is not compliant with system health requirements, the wireless AP places the wireless client on a restricted network containing servers that have resources to bring the wireless client back into compliance. The wireless AP enforces the restricted access through packet filters or a VLAN ID that are assigned to the wireless connection. After correcting its health state, the wireless client validates its health state again, and if compliant, the constraints on the wireless connection that confine the access to the restricted network are removed.

In order for 802.1X Enforcement to work, you must already have a working protected wireless deployment that uses a PEAP-based authentication method. For the details on deploying 802.1X Enforcement after successfully deploying a protected wireless network solution, see Chapter 17.

Deploying Protected Wireless Access

To deploy a protected wireless network using Windows Server 2008 and Windows Vista, follow these steps:

1. Deploy certificates.
2. Configure Active Directory for user accounts and groups.
3. Configure NPS servers.
4. Deploy wireless APs.
5. Configure wireless clients.

Deploying Certificates

Each wireless client in the following authentication configurations needs a computer certificate:

- **Computer authentication with EAP-TLS or PEAP-TLS and computer certificates** Each wireless client computer needs a computer certificate.

- **User authentication with EAP-TLS or PEAP-TLS and either smart cards or registry-based user certificates**   Each wireless user needs a smart card, or each wireless client computer needs a user certificate.

- **User or computer authentication with PEAP-MS-CHAP v2**   Each wireless client needs the root CA of the issuing CA of the NPS server's computer certificate.

Deploying Computer Certificates

To install computer certificates for EAP-TLS or PEAP-TLS authentication, a PKI must be present to issue certificates. Once the PKI is in place, you can install a computer certificate on wireless clients and NPS servers in the following ways:

- By configuring autoenrollment of computer certificates to computers in an Active Directory domain (recommended)

- By using the Certificates snap-in to request a computer certificate

- By using the Certificates snap-in to import a computer certificate

- By executing a CAPICOM script that requests a computer certificate

For more information, see "Deploying PKI" in Chapter 9.

Deploying User Certificates

You can install a user certificate on wireless clients in the following ways:

- By configuring autoenrollment of user certificates to users in an Active Directory domain (recommended)

- By using the Certificates snap-in to request a user certificate

- By using the Certificates snap-in to import a user certificate

- By requesting a certificate over the Web

- By executing a CAPICOM script that requests a user certificate

For more information, see "Deploying PKI" in Chapter 9.

Deploying Root CA Certificates

If you use PEAP-MS-CHAP v2 authentication, you might need to install the root CA certificates of the computer certificates that are installed on your NPS servers on your wireless clients. If the root CA certificate of the issuer of the computer certificates that are installed on the NPS servers is already installed as a root CA certificate on your wireless clients, no other configuration is necessary. For example, if your root CA is a Windows Server 2008–based online root enterprise CA, the root CA certificate is automatically installed on each domain member computer through Group Policy.

To verify whether the correct root CA certificate is installed on your wireless clients, you need to determine:

- The root CA of the computer certificates installed on the NPS servers

- Whether a certificate for the root CA is installed on your wireless clients

To Determine the Root CA of the Computer Certificates Installed on the NPS Servers

1. In the console tree of the Certificates snap-in for the NPS server computer account, expand Certificates (Local Computer or *Computername*), expand Personal, and then click Certificates.

2. In the details pane, double-click the computer certificate that is being used by the NPS server for PEAP-MS-CHAP v2 authentication.

3. In the Certificate properties dialog box, on the Certification Path tab, note the name at the top of the certification path. This is the name of the root CA.

To Determine Whether a Certificate for the Root CA Is Installed on Your Wireless Client

1. In the console tree of the Certificates snap-in for the wireless client computer account, expand Certificates (Local Computer or *Computername*), expand Trusted Root Certification Authorities, and then click Certificates.

2. Examine the list of certificates in the details pane for a name matching the root CA for the computer certificates issued to the NPS servers.

You must install the root CA certificates of the issuers of the computer certificates of the NPS servers on each wireless client that does not contain them. The easiest way to install a root CA certificate on all your wireless clients is through Group Policy. For more information, see "Deploying PKI" in Chapter 9.

Configuring Active Directory for Accounts and Groups

To configure Active Directory for wireless access, do the following for the user and computer accounts that will be used to authenticate wireless connections:

- On the Dial-in tab, set the network access permission to Allow Access or Control Access Through NPS Network Policy. With this setting, the permission for access to the network is set by the Access Permission in the NPS network policy. By default, in native-mode domains, new user accounts and computer accounts have the network access permission set to Control Access Through NPS Network Policy.

- Organize the computer and user accounts into the appropriate universal and global groups to take advantage of group-based network policies.

Configuring NPS Servers

Configure and deploy your NPS servers as described in Chapter 9, taking the following steps:

1. Install a computer certificate on each NPS server.

2. Install the root CA certificates of the computer or user certificates of the wireless clients on each NPS server (if needed).

3. Configure logging on the primary NPS server.

4. Add RADIUS clients to the primary NPS server corresponding to each wireless AP.

5. Create on the primary NPS server a set of policies that are customized for wireless connections using the universal group name for your wireless accounts.

For the details of steps 1–4, see Chapter 9.

To Create a Set of Policies for Wireless Connections

1. In the console tree of the Network Policy Server snap-in, click NPS.

2. In the details pane, under Standard Configuration, select RADIUS Server For 802.1X Wireless Or Wired Connections from the drop-down list, and then click Configure 802.1X.

3. In the Configure 802.1X Wizard, on the Select 802.1X Connections Type page, click Secure Wireless Connections from the drop-down list, and then in the Policy Name box, type a name (or use the name created by the wizard). Click Next.

4. On the Specify 802.1X Switches page, add RADIUS clients as needed that correspond to your wireless APs. Click Next.

5. On the Configure An Authentication Method page, configure the EAP type to use for wireless connections.

   To configure EAP-TLS, in the Type drop-down list, select Microsoft: Smart Card Or Other Certificate, and then click Configure. In the Smart Card Or Other Certificate Properties dialog box, select the computer certificate to use for wireless connections, and then click OK. If you cannot select the certificate, the cryptographic service provider for the certificate does not support Secure Channel (SChannel). SChannel support is required for NPS to use the certificate for EAP-TLS authentication.

   To configure PEAP-MS-CHAP v2, in the Type drop-down list, select Protected EAP (PEAP), and then click Configure. In the Edit Protected EAP Properties dialog box, select the computer certificate to use for wireless connections, and then click OK. If you cannot select the certificate, the cryptographic service provider for the certificate does not support SChannel. SChannel support is required for NPS to use the certificate for PEAP authentication.

To configure PEAP-TLS, in the Type drop-down list, select Protected EAP (PEAP), and then click Configure. In the Edit Protected EAP Properties dialog box, select the computer certificate to use for wireless connections. If you cannot select the certificate, the cryptographic service provider for the certificate does not support SChannel. Under EAP Types, click Secured Password (EAP-MSCHAP v2), and then click Remove. Click Add. In the Add EAP dialog box, click Smart Card Or Other Certificate, and then click OK. In the Edit Protected EAP Properties dialog box, under EAP Types, click Smart Card Or Other Certificate, and then click Edit. In the Smart Card Or Other Certificate Properties dialog box, select the computer certificate to use for wireless connections, and then click OK. If you cannot select the certificate, the cryptographic service provider for the certificate does not support Secure Channel (SChannel). Click OK twice.

6. Click Next. On the Specify User Groups page, add the groups containing the wireless computer and user accounts (for example, WirelessAccounts).

7. On the Configure A Virtual LAN (VLAN) page, click Configure if needed to specify the RADIUS attributes and their values that configure your wireless APs for the appropriate VLAN. Click Next.

8. On the Completing New IEEE 802.1X Secure Wired And Wireless Connections And RADIUS Clients page, click Finish.

After you have configured the primary NPS server with the appropriate logging, RADIUS client, and policy settings, copy the configuration to the secondary or other NPS servers. For more information, see Chapter 9.

Deploying Wireless APs

To deploy your wireless APs, do the following:

1. Perform an analysis of wireless AP locations based on plans of floors and buildings.

2. Temporarily install your wireless APs.

3. Perform a site survey analyzing signal strength in all areas.

4. Relocate wireless APs or sources of RF attenuation or interference.

5. Verify the coverage volume.

6. Update the architectural drawings to reflect the final number and placement of the wireless APs.

7. Configure TCP/IP, security, and RADIUS settings.

These steps are discussed in more detail in the following sections.

Note An alternate method of performing a site survey is to move a single wireless AP around to various locations within your site to discover interference issues and identify the eventual locations of your wireless APs. This method allows you to determine the feasibility of a wireless network within your site before you install numerous wireless APs.

Perform an Analysis of Wireless AP Locations

Obtain or create scaled architectural drawings of each floor for each building for which wireless access is being planned. On the drawing for each floor, identify the offices, conference rooms, lobbies, or other areas where you want to provide wireless coverage.

It might be useful to enable wireless coverage for a building in its entirety rather than for specific locations within the building. This type of coverage can prevent connectivity problems that might result from undocking a laptop from an office for use in a different part of your building.

On the plans, indicate the devices that interfere with the wireless signals, and mark the building construction materials or objects that might attenuate, reflect, or shield wireless signals. Then indicate the locations of wireless APs so that each wireless AP is no farther than 200 feet from an adjacent wireless AP.

After you have determined the initial locations of the wireless APs, you must determine their channels and then assign those channel numbers to each wireless AP.

To Select the Channels for the Wireless APs

1. Identify the wireless networks owned by other organizations in the same building. Find out the placement of their wireless APs and the assigned channel.

   Wireless network signal waves travel through floors and ceilings, so wireless APs located near each other on different floors need to be set to non-overlapping channels. If another organization located on a floor adjacent to your organization's offices has a wireless network, the wireless APs for that organization might interfere with the wireless APs in your network. Contact the other organization to determine the placement and channel numbers of their wireless APs to ensure that your own wireless APs that provide overlapping coverage use a different channel number.

2. Identify overlapping wireless signals on adjacent floors within your own organization.

3. After identifying overlapping coverage volumes outside and within your organization, assign channel numbers to your wireless APs.

To Assign the Channel Numbers to the Wireless APs

1. Assign channel 1 to the first wireless AP.

2. Assign channels 6 and 11 to the wireless APs that overlap coverage volumes with the first wireless AP ensuring that those wireless APs do not also interfere with other coverage volumes with the same channel.

3. Continue assigning channel numbers to the wireless APs ensuring that any two wireless APs with overlapping coverage are assigned different channel numbers that are separated by at least five channels.

Temporarily Install Your Wireless APs

Based on the locations and channel configurations indicated in your plan-based analysis of wireless AP locations, temporarily install your wireless APs.

Perform a Site Survey

Perform a site survey by walking around the building and its floors with a laptop computer equipped with an 802.11 wireless adapter and site survey software. (Site survey software ships with most wireless adapters and wireless APs.) Determine the signal strength and bit rate for the coverage volume for each installed wireless AP.

Relocate Wireless APs or Sources of RF Attenuation or Interference

In locations where signal strength is low, you can make any of the following adjustments to improve the signal:

- Reposition the temporarily installed wireless APs to increase the signal strength for that coverage volume.

- Reposition or eliminate devices that interfere with signal strength (such as Bluetooth devices or microwave ovens).

- Reposition or eliminate metal obstructions that interfere with signal propagation (such as filing cabinets and appliances).

- Add more wireless APs to compensate for the weak signal strength.

> **Note** If you add a wireless AP, you might have to change the channel numbers of adjacent wireless APs.

- Purchase antennas to meet the requirements of your building infrastructure.

For example, to eliminate interference between wireless APs located on adjoining floors in your building, you can purchase directional antennas that flatten the signal (forming a donut-shaped coverage volume) to increase the horizontal range and further decrease the vertical range.

Verify Coverage Volume

Perform another site survey to verify that the changes made to the configuration or placement of the wireless APs eliminated the locations with low signal strength.

Update Your Plans

Update the architectural drawings to reflect the final number and placement of the wireless APs. Indicate the boundaries of the coverage volume and where the data rate changes for each wireless AP.

Configure TCP/IP, Security, and RADIUS Settings

Configure your wireless APs with the following:

- A new wireless network name and strong administrator password

- A static IPv4 address, subnet mask, and default gateway for the wireless subnet on which it is placed

- WPA2 or WPA with 802.1X authentication (WPA2-Enterprise or WPA-Enterprise).

  Configure the following RADIUS settings:

  - ❑ The IP address or name of a primary RADIUS server, the RADIUS shared secret, UDP ports for authentication and accounting, and failure detection settings

  - ❑ The IP address or name of a secondary RADIUS server, the RADIUS shared secret, UDP ports for authentication and accounting, and failure detection settings

To balance the load of RADIUS traffic between the two NPS servers, configure half of the wireless APs with the primary NPS server as the primary RADIUS server and the secondary NPS server as the secondary RADIUS server. Then, configure the other half of the wireless APs with the secondary NPS server as the primary RADIUS server and the primary NPS server as the secondary RADIUS server.

If the wireless APs require vendor-specific attributes (VSAs) or additional RADIUS attributes, you must add the VSAs or attributes to the wireless network policy of the NPS servers. If you add VSAs or RADIUS attributes to the wireless network policy on the primary NPS server, copy the primary NPS server configuration to the secondary NPS server.

Configuring Wireless Clients

You can configure wireless clients in the following three ways:

- Through Group Policy
- By configuring and deploying wireless XML profiles
- Manually

Configuring Wireless Clients Through Group Policy

To configure Wireless Network (IEEE 802.11) Policies Group Policy settings, perform the following steps:

1. From a computer running Windows Server 2008 that is a member of your Active Directory domain, open the Group Policy Management snap-in.

2. In the console tree, expand Forest, expand Domains, and then click the name of the domain to which your wireless clients belong.

3. On the Linked Group Policy Objects pane, right-click the appropriate Group Policy Object (the default object is Default Domain Policy), and then click Edit.

4. In the console tree of the Group Policy Management Editor snap-in, expand the Group Policy Object, then Computer Configuration, then Windows Settings, then Security Settings, and then Wireless Network (IEEE 802.11) Policies.

5. Right-click Wireless Network (IEEE 802.11) Policies, and then click either Create a New Windows Vista Policy or Create a New Windows XP Policy.

For a new Windows Vista wireless policy, perform the following steps:

1. For the newly created Windows Vista wireless network policy, on the General tab, type a name for the policy and a description.

2. On the Network Permissions tab, add allowed and denied wireless networks by name as needed.

3. On the General tab, click Add to add a wireless network profile, and then click Infrastructure to specify an infrastructure mode wireless network.

4. On the Connection tab, type the wireless network name (SSID) and a description (optional), and then specify connection settings as needed.

5. On the Security tab, specify the authentication and encryption security methods.

   ❑ For WPA2, in the Authentication section, select WPA2, and then in the Encryption area, select AES.

   ❑ For WPA, select WPA in Authentication and either TKIP or AES in Encryption. Select AES only if both your wireless clients and wireless APs support WPA with AES encryption.

6. In the Select A Network Authentication Method drop-down list, specify the EAP type.

   ❑ For EAP-TLS:

      a. Select Smart Card Or Other Certificate, and then click Properties.

      b. In the Smart Card Or Other Certificate Properties dialog box, configure EAP-TLS settings as needed, and then click OK. By default, EAP-TLS uses a registry-based certificate and validates the server certificate.

   ❑ For PEAP-MS-CHAP v2, no additional configuration is required. PEAP-MS-CHAP v2 is the default authentication method.

   Specify the authentication mode and other settings as needed.

7. To configure advanced settings for 802.1X, including Single Sign On and Fast Roaming, click Advanced and specify settings as needed. Click OK when complete.

8. Click OK twice to save the changes.

For a new Windows XP wireless policy, perform the following steps:

1. For the newly created Windows XP wireless network policy, on the General tab, change settings as needed.

2. On the Preferred Networks tab, click Add to add a preferred network, and then click Infrastructure to specify an infrastructure mode wireless network.

3. On the Network Properties tab, type the wireless network name (SSID), a description (optional), specify whether this wireless network is non-broadcast, and then specify the security methods.

   ❑ For WPA2, in the Authentication drop-down list, select WPA2, and then in the Encryption drop-down list, select AES.

   ❑ For WPA, in the Authentication drop-down list, select WPA, and then in the Encryption drop-down list, select TKIP. Select AES only if both your wireless clients and wireless APs support WPA with AES encryption.

4. On the IEEE 802.1X tab, specify the EAP type.

   ❑ For EAP-TLS:

      a. In the EAP Type drop-down list, select Smart Card Or Other Certificate, and then click Settings.

      b. In the Smart Card Or Other Certificate Properties dialog box, configure EAP-TLS settings as needed, and then click OK. By default, EAP-TLS uses a registry-based certificate and validates the server certificate.

   ❑ For PEAP-MS-CHAP v2, no additional configuration is required. PEAP-MS-CHAP v2 is the default authentication method.

5. Also on the IEEE 802.1X tab, specify the authentication mode and other settings as needed.

6. Click OK twice to save changes.

> **Note**   To obtain help information for the dialog boxes of the Wireless Network (IEEE 802.11) Policies Group Policy extension, press the F1 key.

The next time your Windows Server 2008, Windows Vista, Windows XP with SP2, Windows XP with SP1, or Windows Server 2003 wireless clients update the Computer Configuration Group Policy, the wireless network settings in the Group Policy Object will be automatically applied.

Configuring and Deploying Wireless Profiles

You can also manually configure wireless clients running Windows Vista or Windows Server 2008 on a wireless network by importing a wireless profile in XML format by running the **netsh wlan add profile** command. To create an XML-based wireless profile, configure a Windows Vista or Windows Server 2008 wireless client with a wireless network that has all the appropriate settings including the authentication method, encryption methods, and EAP type. Then, run the **netsh wlan export profile** command to write the wireless network profile to an XML file. You can also create, configure, and export an XML profile from a Windows Vista wireless policy.

Manually Configuring Wireless Clients

If you have a small number of wireless clients, you can manually configure wireless connections for each wireless client. For Windows Server 2008 and Windows Vista wireless clients, run the Set Up a Connection Wizard or the Network Wizard. For Windows XP with SP2 wireless clients, run the New Connection Wizard. The following sections describe how to manually configure the EAP-TLS, PEAP-TLS, and PEAP-MS-CHAP v2 authentication methods for Windows wireless clients.

EAP-TLS   To manually configure EAP-TLS authentication on a wireless client running Windows Server 2008 or Windows Vista, do the following:

1. In the Network and Sharing Center, click the Manage Wireless Networks task. In the Manage Wireless Networks window, double-click your wireless network name.

2. On the Security tab, in the Security Type box, select WPA-Enterprise or WPA2-Enterprise. In the Choose A Network Authentication Method drop-down list, select Smart Card Or Other Certificate, and then click Settings.

3. In the Smart Card Or Other Certificate Properties dialog box, to use a registry-based user certificate, select Use A Certificate On This Computer. For a smart card–based user certificate, select Use My Smart Card.

    If you want to validate the computer certificate of the NPS server, select Validate Server Certificate (recommended and enabled by default). If you want to specify the names of the NPS servers that must perform the TLS authentication, select Connect To These Servers, and then type the names. Click OK twice.

To manually configure EAP-TLS authentication on a wireless client running Windows XP with SP2, Windows XP with SP1, or Windows Server 2003, do the following:

1. Obtain properties of the wireless connection in the Network Connections folder. On the Wireless Networks tab, in the list of preferred networks, click the name of the wireless network, and then click Properties.

2. On the Authentication tab, select Enable Network Access Control Using IEEE 802.1X and the Smart Card Or Other Certificate EAP type. This is enabled by default.

3. Click Properties. In the properties dialog box of the Smart Card or other Certificate EAP type, to use a registry-based user certificate, select Use A Certificate On This Computer. For a smart card–based user certificate, select Use My Smart Card.

   If you want to validate the computer certificate of the NPS server, select Validate Server Certificate (recommended and enabled by default). If you want to specify the names of the authentication servers that must perform the TLS authentication, select Connect To These Servers, and then type the names.

4. Click OK to save changes to the Smart Card or other Certificate EAP type.

PEAP-TLS   To manually configure PEAP-TLS authentication on a wireless client running Windows Server 2008 or Windows Vista, do the following:

1. In the Network and Sharing Center, click the Manage Wireless Networks task. In the Manage Wireless Networks window, double-click your wireless network name.

2. On the Security tab, in the Security Type drop-down list, select WPA-Enterprise or WPA2-Enterprise. In Choose A Network Authentication Method, select Protected EAP (PEAP), and then click Settings.

3. In the Protected EAP Properties dialog box, if you want to validate the computer certificate of the NPS server for the PEAP authentication, select Validate Server Certificate (recommended and enabled by default). If you want to specify the names of the NPS servers that must perform the PEAP authentication, select Connect To These Servers, and then type the names.

4. In the Select Authentication Method drop-down list, click Smart Card Or Other Certificate. Click Configure. To use a registry-based user certificate, in the Smart Card Or Other Certificate Properties dialog box, select Use A Certificate On This Computer. For a smart card–based user certificate, select Use My Smart Card.

   If you want to validate the computer certificate of the NPS server for the user-level authentication, select the Validate Server Certificate check box (recommended and enabled by default). If you want to specify the names of the NPS servers that must perform the TLS authentication, select Connect To These Servers, and then type the names.

5. Click OK to save changes to the Smart Card or other Certificate PEAP type. Click OK to save the changes to the Protected EAP type. Click OK to save the changes to the wireless network configuration.

To manually configure PEAP-TLS authentication on a wireless client running Windows XP with SP2, Windows XP with SP1, or Windows Server 2003, do the following:

1. Obtain properties of the wireless connection in the Network Connections folder. On the Wireless Networks tab, in the list of preferred networks, click the name of the wireless network, and then click Properties. The Wireless Network's properties dialog box appears.

2. On the Authentication tab, select Enable Network Access Control Using IEEE 802.1X and the Protected EAP (PEAP) type.

3. Click Properties. In the Protected EAP Properties dialog box, select the Validate Server Certificate check box to validate the computer certificate of the NPS server for the PEAP authentication (recommended and enabled by default). If you want to specify the names of the authentication servers that must perform PEAP authentication, select Connect To These Servers, and then type the names. In the Select Authentication Method drop-down list, click Smart Card Or Other Certificate.

4. Click Configure. In the Smart Card Or Other Certificate Properties dialog box, to use a registry-based user certificate, select Use A Certificate On This Computer. For a smart card–based user certificate, select Use My Smart Card.

   If you want to validate the computer certificate of the NPS server for the user-level authentication, select Validate Server Certificate (recommended and enabled by default). If you want to specify the names of the NPS servers that must perform the TLS authentication, select Connect To These Servers, and then type the names.

5. Click OK to save changes to the Smart Card or other Certificate PEAP type. Click OK to save the changes to the Protected EAP type. Click OK to save the changes to the wireless network configuration.

PEAP-MS-CHAP v2   To manually configure PEAP-MS-CHAP v2 authentication on a wireless client running Windows Server 2008 or Windows Vista, do the following:

1. In the Network and Sharing Center, click the Manage Wireless Networks task. In the Manage Wireless Networks window, double-click your wireless network name.

2. On the Security tab, in the Security Type drop-down list, select WPA-Enterprise or WPA2-Enterprise. In the Choose a network authentication method drop-down list, select Protected EAP (PEAP), and then click Settings.

3. In the Protected EAP Properties dialog box, if you want to validate the computer certificate of the NPS server for the PEAP authentication, select the Validate Server Certificate check box (recommended and enabled by default). If you want to specify the names of the NPS servers that must perform the PEAP authentication, select Connect To These Servers, and then type the names.

4. In Select Authentication Method, select Secured Password (EAP-MS-CHAP v2), and then click OK twice.

To manually configure PEAP-MS-CHAP v2 authentication on a wireless client running Windows XP with SP2, Windows XP with SP1, or Windows Server 2003, do the following:

1. Obtain properties of the wireless connection in the Network Connections folder. Click the Wireless Networks tab, click the name of the wireless network in the list of preferred networks, and then click Properties. The wireless network's properties dialog box appears.

2. On the Authentication tab, select Enable Network Access Control Using IEEE 802.1X and the Protected EAP (PEAP) EAP type.

3. Click Properties. In the Protected EAP Properties dialog box, select Validate Server Certificate to validate the computer certificate of the NPS server (enabled by default). If you want to specify the names of the authentication servers that must perform validation, select Connect To These Servers, and then type the names. In Select Authentication Method, click Secured Password (EAP-MSCHAP v2), and then click OK twice.

Ongoing Maintenance

The areas of maintenance for a protected wireless solution are as follows:

- Management of user and computer accounts
- Management of wireless APs
- Updating of wireless profiles

Managing User and Computer Accounts

When a new user or computer account is created in Active Directory, and that user or computer is allowed wireless access, add the new account to the appropriate group for wireless connections. For example, add the new account to the WirelessAccounts security group, which is specified in the network policy for wireless connections.

When user or computer accounts are deleted in Active Directory, no additional action is necessary to prevent wireless connections.

As needed, you can create additional universal groups and network policies to set wireless network access for different sets of users. For example, you can create a global WirelessAccessContractors group and a network policy that allows wireless connections to members of the WirelessAccessContractors group only during normal business hours or for access to specific intranet resources.

Managing Wireless APs

Once deployed, wireless APs do not need a lot of ongoing maintenance. Most of the ongoing changes to wireless AP configuration are due to managing wireless network capacity and changes in network infrastructure.

Adding a Wireless AP

To add a wireless AP, do the following:

1. Follow the design points and deployment steps in "Deploying Wireless APs" earlier in this chapter to add a new wireless AP to your wireless network.

2. Add the wireless AP as a RADIUS client to your NPS servers.

Removing a Wireless AP

When removing a wireless AP, update the configuration of your NPS servers to remove the wireless AP as a RADIUS client.

Configuration for Changes in NPS Servers

If the NPS servers change (for example, because of additions or removals of NPS servers on the intranet), you will need to do the following:

1. Ensure that new NPS servers are configured with RADIUS clients corresponding to the wireless APs and with the appropriate network policies for wireless access.

2. Update the configuration of the wireless APs for the new NPS server configuration as needed.

Updating Wireless XML Profiles

To update a wireless XML profile and apply it to your Windows Vista or Windows Server 2008 wireless clients, do the following:

1. If you are using a Windows Vista or Windows Server 2008 wireless client or if you have a Windows Vista wireless policy, create an updated XML profile with the Group Policy Editor snap-in or by running the **netsh wlan export profile** command.

2. Execute the **netsh wlan add profile** command to import the XML profile on your wireless clients through a script or other method.

Troubleshooting

Because of the different components and processes involved, troubleshooting wireless connections can be a difficult task. This section describes the following:

- The tools that are provided with Windows Server 2008 and Windows Vista to troubleshoot wireless connections

- How to troubleshoot wireless connection problems from the wireless client

- How to troubleshoot wireless connection problems from the wireless AP

- How to troubleshoot wireless connection problems from the NPS server

---

Direct from the Source: Wireless Troubleshooting Tips

One of the most difficult aspects of troubleshooting wireless connectivity is knowing where to start. Generally, the client is the device that shows the symptom, but it is only one piece in a chain of devices and technologies that could fail.

As a general rule to follow, if the wireless client fails to see the wireless network or establish an association, the issue lies between the wireless client and the wireless AP. Most of these issues are resolved by driver or firmware updates for the wireless network adapter and the wireless AP. Having the latest drivers and firmware installed is a required first step in the troubleshooting process.

If authentication is failing, you most likely can rule out hardware as an issue. First review your client-side System event logs. Windows XP and Windows Server 2003 do not have any diagnostic logs, but Windows Server 2008 and Windows Vista log quite a bit of useful information that might point you to a configuration issue such as a missing certificate.

After reviewing these logs, review the Windows Logs\Security event log on the NPS server. If you have a failed authentication, there will be an NPS event with the keyword Audit Failure. If, however, you do not see any log entries related to the wireless authentication attempt, this is a strong indicator that NPS did not receive the authentication attempt or the process timed out. Take a look at the wireless AP to confirm that its RADIUS settings are appropriate for the NPS server.

Clay Seymour, Support Escalation Engineer

Enterprise Platform Support

Wireless Troubleshooting Tools in Windows

Microsoft provides the following tools to troubleshoot wireless connections:

- TCP/IP troubleshooting tools
- The Network Connections folder
- **Netsh wlan** commands
- Network Diagnostics Framework support for wireless connections
- Wireless diagnostics tracing
- NPS authentication and accounting logging
- NPS event logging
- SChannel logging
- SNMP agent
- Reliability and Performance snap-in
- Network Monitor 3.1

TCP/IP Troubleshooting Tools

The Ping, Tracert, and Pathping tools use Internet Control Message Protocol (ICMP) Echo and Echo Reply and ICMPv6 Echo Request and Echo Reply messages to verify connectivity, display the path to a destination, and test path integrity. The Route tool can be used to display the IPv4 and IPv6 routing tables. The Nslookup tool can be used to troubleshoot domain name system (DNS) name resolution issues.

The Network Connections Folder

When you obtain status on the wireless connection in the Network Connection folder, you can view information such as the signal speed, which is shown on the General tab. Click Details to view the TCP/IP configuration.

If the wireless adapter is assigned an Automatic Private IP Addressing (APIPA) address in the range 169.254.0.0/16 or the configured alternate IP address, the wireless client is still associated with the wireless AP, but either authentication has failed or the DHCP server is not available. If the authentication fails and the association is still in place, the wireless adapter is enabled and TCP/IP performs its normal configuration process. If a DHCP server is not found (either authenticated or not), Windows Vista automatically configures an APIPA address unless there is an alternate address configured.

Direct from the Source: APIPA in Windows Vista

You might notice that a Windows Vista wireless client will automatically configure an APIPA address sooner or more frequently than in previous versions of Windows. A computer running Windows Vista will wait only six seconds to contact a DHCP server before using an APIPA address and will then continue to attempt to contact a DHCP server. By contrast, a computer running Windows XP will wait a full minute before using an APIPA address. This change in behavior is by design and is meant to facilitate ad-hoc connectivity when there are no DHCP servers available.

Tim Quinn, Support Escalation Engineer

Enterprise Platform Support

Netsh Wlan Commands

You can run the **netsh wlan** command with the following parameters to gather information for troubleshooting wireless issues:

- **netsh wlan show autoconfig**   Displays whether the WLAN Autoconfig service is enabled

- **netsh wlan show blockednetworks**   Displays whether blocked networks are visible in the list of available networks

- **netsh wlan show createalluserprofile**   Displays whether everyone is allowed to create all-user profiles

- **netsh wlan show drivers**   Displays the properties of the drivers for the installed wireless network adapters

- **netsh wlan show filters**   Displays the allowed and blocked wireless networks lists

- **netsh wlan show interfaces**   Displays properties for the installed wireless network adapters

- **netsh wlan show networks**   Displays the list and properties of the available wireless networks

- **netsh wlan show profiles**   Displays the list of Group Policy and local wireless profiles

- **netsh wlan show settings**   Displays the global wireless settings, which includes the state of Wireless Auto Configuration and whether everyone is allowed to create all-user profiles.

- **netsh wlan show tracing**   Displays the state of tracing and the location of the wireless tracing logs (by default in *%SystemRoot%*\Tracing\Wireless)

- **netsh wlan show all**   Displays complete wireless network adapter information and information on available wireless networks

Network Diagnostics Framework Support for Wireless Connections

To provide a better user experience when encountering network connectivity issues, Windows Vista includes the Network Diagnostics Framework (NDF), a set of technologies and guidelines that allows a set of troubleshooters (also known as *helper classes*) to assist in the diagnosis and possible automatic correction of networking problems. When a user experiences a networking problem in Windows Vista, NDF will provide the user the ability to diagnose and repair the problem within the context of that problem. This means that the diagnostics assessment and resolution steps are presented to the user within the application or dialog box that they were using when the problem occurred or based on the failed network operation.

Windows Vista includes a troubleshooter to diagnose failed wireless connections. If a wireless connection fails, Windows displays a dialog box with information about the error. The dialog box includes a Diagnose button that launches the wireless NDF troubleshooter. In the diagnosis session, users can repair their wireless connection problem without needing to involve IT support staff. The wireless NDF troubleshooter will help users resolve many common issues that arise with wireless network connectivity, such as:

- The network adapter radio being turned off
- The wireless AP not being powered

- A missing or mismatched configuration of security options, encryption types, or network keys between the wireless AP and wireless client

- Disconnected media

- Missing certificates

Windows logs all wireless connection attempts in the System event log. When Windows Network Diagnostics runs, it creates additional events in the System event log that contain the following information:

- The name of the wireless network adapter and whether its driver is designed for Windows Vista.

- A list of visible wireless networks with the signal strength, channel, protocol (such as 802.11b or 802.11g), and operating mode (infrastructure or ad hoc) for each.

- The list of preferred wireless networks and each network's configuration settings.

- The diagnostic conclusions, such as, "The wireless connection on this computer appears to be working correctly," "The Internet connection on the wireless router or access point might not be working correctly," and "The computer has a low signal strength from ContosoWLAN."

- The repair options offered to the user, such as, "Try moving the computer to a different location, eliminating any sources of possible interference, and then try connecting to ContosoWLAN again."

- The repair options chosen by the user and whether the repair solved the problem.

You can view these events in the Event Viewer snap-in to understand the network environment at the time the problem occurred without needing to re-create the scenario, and you need no longer rely on users to explain the symptoms of the problem.

To obtain additional information about the diagnostics process, Windows creates a detailed diagnostic log that is separate from the System event log.

To Access The Diagnostics Log

1. In the Event Viewer snap-in, in the tree view, expand Applications and Services Logs\Microsoft\Windows\Diagnostics-Networking.

2. Click Operational.

3. In the contents pane, view the events for the wireless diagnostics session.

Wireless Diagnostics Tracing

Occasionally, you might need to escalate a wireless networking problem to Microsoft or another support specialist in your organization. To perform a detailed analysis, Microsoft or your support specialists need in-depth information about the computer's state and wireless components in Windows and their interaction when the problem occurred. You can obtain this information from wireless diagnostics tracing in Windows Vista. To use wireless diagnostics tracing, you must start tracing, reproduce the problem, stop tracing, and then collect the tracing report.

To start wireless diagnostics tracing, do one of the following:

- Type the **netsh wlan set tracing mode=yes** command at a command prompt.

- In the console tree of the Reliability and Performance Monitor snap-in, expand Data Collector Sets\System. Right-click Wireless Diagnostics, and then click Start.

After you have reproduced the problem and want to stop wireless diagnostics tracing, do one of the following:

- Type the **netsh wlan set tracing mode=no** command.

- In the console tree of the Reliability and Performance Monitor snap-in, expand Data Collector Sets\System. Right-click Wireless Diagnostics, and then click Stop.

Note   It is important to stop the wireless diagnostics tracing prior to viewing or gathering the trace logs to initiate a process that converts the trace files into a readable format.

To view the report generated by wireless diagnostics tracing, in the console tree of the Reliability and Performance Monitor snap-in, expand Reports\System\Wireless Diagnostics.

The report includes the following information:

- Wireless configuration, including allowed and blocked wireless networks

- Current TCP/IP configuration (including data provided by the **ipconfig /all** command)

- A list of all connection attempts and detailed information about each step of the connection process

- A detailed list of all Windows Network Diagnostics events

- Wireless client certificate configuration

- Wireless profiles and their locations

- Wireless network adapter driver information

- Wireless networking system files and versions

- Raw network tracing information

- Computer make and model

- Operating system version

- A list of all services, their current states, and their process identifiers

This report and its associated files are stored by default in the *%SystemRoot%*\Tracing\Wireless folder.

In addition to wireless diagnostic tracing, Windows Server 2008 and Windows Vista support tracing for components of the Remote Access Connection Manager and Routing and Remote Access services, which are also used for wireless connections. Like the wireless diagnostic tracing, tracing for these components creates information that you can use to troubleshoot complex problems for specific components. The information in these additional tracing files is typically useful only to Microsoft support engineers, who might request that you create trace files for a connection attempt during their investigation of a support issue. You can enable this additional tracing by using the Netsh tool.

To enable and disable tracing for a specific component of the Remote Access Connection Manager and Routing and Remote Access services, the command is:

netsh ras diagnostics set rastracing *component* enabled | disabled

in which *component* is a component in the list of components found in the registry under HKEY_LOCAL_MACHINE\SOFTWARE\Microsoft\Tracing.

To enable tracing for all components, the command is:

netsh ras diagnostics set rastracing * enabled

To disable tracing for all components, the command is:

netsh ras diagnostics set rastracing * disabled

The tracing log files are stored in the *%SystemRoot%*\Tracing folder. The most interesting log files for wireless authentication are the following:

- **Svchost_rastls.log** TLS authentication activity
- **Svchost_raschap.log** MS-CHAP v2 authentication activity

NPS Authentication and Accounting Logging

By default, NPS supports the logging of authentication and accounting information for wireless connections in local log files. This logging is separate from the events recorded in the Windows Logs\Security. You can use the information in the logs to track wireless usage and authentication attempts. Authentication and accounting logging is especially useful for troubleshooting network policy issues. For each authentication attempt, the name of the network policy that either accepted or rejected the connection attempt is recorded. You can configure authentication and accounting logging options in the Accounting node in the Network Policy Server snap-in.

The authentication and accounting information is stored in a configurable log file or files stored in the *%SystemRoot%*\System32\LogFiles folder. The log files are saved in Internet

Authentication Service (IAS) or database-compatible format, meaning that any database program can read the log file directly for analysis. NPS can also send authentication and accounting information to a SQL Server database.

NPS Event Logging

Check the Windows Logs\Security event log on the NPS server for NPS events corresponding to rejected (event ID 6273) or accepted (event ID 6272) connection attempts. NPS event log entries contain a lot of information on the connection attempt, including the name of the connection request policy that matched the connection attempt (the Proxy Policy Name in the description of the event) and the network policy that accepted or rejected the connection attempt (the Network Policy Name field in the description of the event). NPS event logging for rejected or accepted connection attempts is enabled by default. You can configure it in the Network Policy Server snap-in, in the properties dialog box of an NPS server, on the General tab.

NPS events can be viewed from the Event Viewer snap-in. Viewing the NPS events in the Windows Logs\Security event log is one of the most useful troubleshooting methods to obtain information about failed authentications.

SChannel Logging

Secure channel (SChannel) logging is the logging of detailed information for SChannel events in the System event log. By default, only SChannel error messages are recorded. To log errors, warnings, and informational and successful events, set the HKEY_LOCAL_MACHINE\System\CurrentControlSet\Control\SecurityProviders\SCHANNEL\EventLogging registry value to **4** (DWORD value type). With SChannel logging recording all events, it is possible to obtain more information about the certificate exchange and validation process on the NPS server.

SNMP Agent

You can use the Simple Network Management Protocol (SNMP) agent software included with Windows Server 2008 to monitor status information for your NPS server from an SNMP console. NPS supports the RADIUS Authentication Server MIB (RFC 2619) and the RADIUS Accounting Server MIB (RFC 2621). Use Features in the Server Manager console to install the optional SNMP service.

The SNMP service can be used in conjunction with your existing SNMP-based network management infrastructure to monitor your NPS RADIUS servers or proxies.

Reliability and Performance Snap-In

You can use the Reliability and Performance snap-in to monitor counters, create logs, and set alerts for specific NPS components and program processes. You can also use charts and reports to determine how efficiently your server uses NPS and to both identify and troubleshoot potential problems.

You can use the Reliability and Performance snap-in to monitor counters within the following NPS-related performance objects:

- NPS Accounting Clients
- NPS Accounting Proxy
- NPS Accounting Server
- NPS Authentication Clients
- NPS Authentication Proxy
- NPS Authentication Server
- NPS Policy Engine
- NPS Remote Accounting Servers
- NPS Remote Authentication Servers

> **More Info**   For more information about how to use the Reliability and Performance snap-in, see the Help And Support Center in Windows Server 2008.

Network Monitor 3.1

You can use Microsoft Network Monitor 3.1 (or later) or a commercial packet analyzer (also known as a network sniffer), to capture and view the authentication and data traffic sent on a network. Network Monitor 3.1 includes RADIUS, 802.1X, EAPOL, and EAP parsers. A *parser* is a component included with Network Monitor that can separate the fields of a protocol header and display their structure and values. Without a parser, Network Monitor 3.1 displays the hexadecimal bytes of a header, which you must parse manually.

> **On the Disc**   You can link to the download site for Network Monitor from the companion CD-ROM.

For Windows wireless client authentications, you can use Network Monitor 3.1 to capture the set of frames exchanged between the wireless client computer and the wireless AP during the wireless authentication process. You can then use Network Monitor 3.1 to view the individual frames and determine why the authentication failed. Network Monitor 3.1 is also useful for capturing the RADIUS messages that are exchanged between a wireless AP and its RADIUS server and for determining the RADIUS attributes of each message.

The proper interpretation of wireless traffic with Network Monitor 3.1 requires an in-depth understanding of EAPOL, RADIUS, and other protocols. Network Monitor 3.1 captures can be saved as files and sent to Microsoft support for analysis.

Troubleshooting the Windows Wireless Client

When troubleshooting wireless connectivity, it is important to first determine whether some or all of your wireless clients are experiencing problems. If all your wireless clients are experiencing problems, issues might exist in your authentication infrastructure. If some of your wireless clients are experiencing problems, issues might exist for your wireless APs or individual wireless clients.

The following are some common problems with wireless connectivity and authentication that are encountered by a Windows wireless client:

■ **Wireless network is not found.** Verify that you are within range of the wireless AP for the wireless network by using tools provided by the wireless adapter vendor. You can move the wireless AP or the wireless client, adjust the transmission power level on the wireless AP, or reposition or remove sources of radio frequency attenuation or interference.

■ **Unable to authenticate.** Some wireless network adapters have a link light that indicates sent or received data frames. However, because IEEE 802.1X authentication occurs before the wireless network adapter begins sending or receiving data frames, the link light does not reflect 802.1X authentication activity. If the link light does not indicate any wireless traffic, the cause could be a failed 802.1X authentication.

Verify that the user or computer account for the wireless client exists, is enabled, and is not locked out (via account properties or remote access account lockout), and that the connection is being attempted during allowed logon times.

Verify that the connection attempt for the user or computer account matches a network policy. For example, if you are using a group-based network policy, verify that the user or computer account is a member of the group specified in the Windows Groups condition of the appropriate network policy.

Verify that the root CA certificates for the issuing CAs of the NPS server certificates are installed in the Trusted Root Certification Authorities Local Computer store on the wireless client computer.

For an EAP-TLS–based or PEAP-TLS–based wireless client, verify that the computer or user certificate meets the conditions described in the section titled "Validating the Wireless Client's Certificate" later in this chapter.

For a PEAP-MS-CHAP v2–based wireless client, investigate whether the wireless client's account password has expired, and verify that the Allow Client to Change Password After It Has Expired check box in the EAP MS-CHAP v2 Properties dialog box is enabled on the NPS servers.

■ **Unable to authenticate with a certificate.** The most typical cause for this message is that you do not have either a user or computer certificate installed. Depending on the configured authentication mode, you might need to have both installed. Verify that you have a computer certificate, a user certificate, or both installed by using the Certificates snap-in.

Another possible cause for this message is that you have certificates installed, but they either cannot be used for wireless authentication, or they cannot be validated by all of your NPS servers. For more information, see "Troubleshooting Certificate-Based Validation" later in this chapter.

Troubleshooting the Wireless AP

If you have multiple wireless APs and are unable to connect or authenticate with one of them, you might have a problem with that specific wireless AP. This section describes the common troubleshooting tools of wireless APs and the common problems of connecting and authenticating with a wireless AP.

Wireless AP Troubleshooting Tools

Although the set of troubleshooting tools for wireless APs varies with each manufacturer and with each model, some of the more common troubleshooting tools are the following:

- Panel indicators
- Site survey software
- SNMP support
- Diagnostics

These tools are described in the following sections. Consult your wireless AP documentation for information about the set of troubleshooting tools provided with your wireless AP.

Panel Indicators   Most wireless APs have one or more indicators, which are status lights that are visible on the housing of the wireless AP, from which you can obtain a quick assessment of the wireless AP's hardware status. For example, you might see the following:

- An indicator to show that the wireless AP has electrical power.
- An indicator to show general operation status. For example, the indicator might show whether the wireless AP is associated with any wireless clients.
- An indicator to show wireless network traffic. This indicator might blink for each frame received on the wireless network.
- An indicator to show data collisions. If the blinking of this indicator seems excessive, evaluate the performance of the link by using the methods suggested by the wireless AP vendor.
- An indicator to show wired network traffic. This indicator might blink for each frame received on the wired network.

Alternatively, the wireless AP might have a liquid crystal display (LCD) panel that shows icons that indicate its current status. Consult your wireless AP documentation for information about panel indicators and their interpretation.

Site Survey Software   Site survey software, which you use during the deployment of wireless APs to determine their optimal placement, is typically installed on a wireless-capable laptop computer from a CD-ROM provided by the wireless AP or wireless network adapter vendor.

As described in "Deploying Wireless APs," earlier in this chapter, the site survey software is used to determine the coverage volume and where the data rate changes for each wireless AP. If wireless clients cannot connect to a specific wireless AP, use the site survey software to perform a site survey for that wireless AP. There might have been a change in the devices that create interference and objects that interfere with signal propagation since the original site survey and AP placement were done.

SNMP Support   Many wireless APs include a Simple Network Management Protocol (SNMP) agent with support for the following SNMP Management Information Bases (MIBs):

- IEEE 802.11 MIB
- IEEE 802.1 PAE (Port Access Entity) MIB
- SNMP Management MIB (described in RFC 1157)
- SNMP MIB II (described in RFC 1213)
- Bridge MIB (described in RFC 1286)
- Ethernet Interface MIB (described in RFC 1398)
- IETF Bridge MIB (described in RFC 1493)
- Remote Monitoring (RMON) MIB (described in RFC 1757)
- RADIUS Client Authentication MIB (described in RFC 2618)

The SNMP agent on the wireless AP can be used in conjunction with your existing SNMP-based network management infrastructure to configure your wireless APs, set trap conditions, and monitor loads on your wireless APs.

Diagnostics   Diagnostics for wireless APs can be in the following forms:

- Diagnostic facilities that are available through the main wireless AP configuration program, such as a Windows program provided on the wireless AP vendor product CD-ROM or a series of Web pages.
- Diagnostic facilities that are available through a command-line tool or facility, such as terminal access to the wireless AP.

The exact diagnostic facilities of a wireless AP vary from one wireless AP to another; however, the purpose of the diagnostics is to ensure that the wireless AP is operating properly (from a hardware standpoint) and to validate its current configuration.

Common Wireless AP Problems

The following are common problems with wireless APs:

- Inability to see the wireless AP
- Inability to authenticate with the wireless AP
- Inability to communicate beyond the wireless AP

These common problems are discussed in detail in the following sections.

Inability to See the Wireless AP   If wireless clients are unable to see the wireless AP in a scan of wireless networks, one or more of the following might be happening:

- **The wireless AP is not beaconing.**   All wireless APs should be sending periodic beacon messages that contain the SSID—unless the wireless AP has been configured to suppress the SSID in the beacon message—and the wireless AP's capabilities (such as supported bit rates and security options). To verify that the wireless AP is beaconing, you can use the site survey software or a packet sniffer that can capture wireless beacon frames. A simple packet sniffer that can capture beacon frames and other types of wireless management frames might be included on the CD-ROM provided by your wireless AP vendor.

- **The wireless AP is not configured for the correct channel.**   If the wireless AP is using the same channel as an adjacent wireless AP, signal interference might be impairing the wireless clients' ability to connect. Change the wireless AP channel if needed.

- **The wireless AP is not advertising the correct set of capabilities.**   Confirm that the wireless AP is configured to operate for the correct technology (such as 802.11b, 802.11a, or 802.11g) and with the correct bit rates and security options (WPA or WPA2). By capturing the beacon frame with a network sniffer, you can compare the configured wireless options to those being advertised in the beacon frame.

- **The wireless AP has inadequate signal strength in the anticipated coverage volume.**   Use your site survey software to confirm that the coverage volume of the wireless AP is as described in your plans after initially deploying the wireless APs. If there are new sources of signal attenuation, reflection, or interference, make the appropriate changes to the locations of either interfering equipment or the wireless AP.

Inability to Authenticate with the Wireless AP   If you have multiple wireless APs, and your wireless clients cannot authenticate with any of them, you might have a problem with your authentication infrastructure. See "Troubleshooting the Authentication Infrastructure" later in this chapter for instructions on how to troubleshoot this situation. If you have multiple wireless APs, and the wireless clients cannot authenticate with an individual wireless AP, you need to troubleshoot the authentication-related configuration of the wireless AP. The three areas of authentication configuration you need to investigate are as follows:

- 802.1X configuration

- RADIUS configuration
- WPA configuration

802.1X Configuration   Ensure that the wireless AP has 802.1X authentication enabled. Some wireless APs might refer to 802.1X authentication as EAP authentication.

RADIUS Configuration   The RADIUS configuration consists of the following elements:

- **Wireless AP RADIUS configuration**   Ensure that the wireless AP has been properly configured for RADIUS. The wireless AP should contain the following configuration information:

    - The IPv4 or IPv6 address of a primary RADIUS server (one of your NPS servers)

    - The destination User Datagram Protocol (UDP) ports for RADIUS traffic sent to the primary RADIUS server (UDP port 1812 for RADIUS authentication traffic and UDP port 1813 for RADIUS accounting traffic)

    - The RADIUS shared secret for the primary RADIUS server

    - The IPv4 or IPv6 address of a secondary RADIUS server (another of your NPS servers)

    - The destination UDP ports for RADIUS traffic sent to the secondary RADIUS server

    - The RADIUS shared secret for the secondary RADIUS server

- **NPS server reachability**   Ensure that the primary and secondary NPS servers are reachable from the wireless AP by doing the following:

    - If the wireless AP has a ping facility—the capability to send an Internet Control Message Protocol (ICMP) Echo message to an arbitrary unicast IPv4 destination—try pinging the IPv4 address of the primary and secondary NPS servers.

    - If the wireless AP does not have a ping facility, try pinging the IPv4 address of the primary and secondary NPS servers from a network node that is attached to the same subnet as the wireless AP.

If the ping from the network node succeeds and the ping from the wireless AP does not, examine the IPv4 configuration of the wireless AP to ensure that it has been configured with the correct IPv4 address, subnet mask, and default gateway for the attached wired subnet. If neither ping works, troubleshoot the lack of IPv4 connectivity between the attached subnet and the RADIUS servers.

Note   The ping test is not necessarily a definitive test of IPv4 reachability. There might be routers in the path between the wireless AP and the RADIUS server that are filtering ICMP traffic, or the NPS server might be configured with packet filters to discard ICMP traffic.

To ensure that RADIUS traffic is reaching the primary and secondary NPS servers, use a network sniffer such as Network Monitor 3.1 on the NPS servers to capture the RADIUS traffic sent from and to the wireless AP during an authentication attempt.

- **NPS server configuration**   If RADIUS traffic is reaching the primary and secondary NPS servers, verify that the primary and secondary NPS servers are configured with a RADIUS client that corresponds to the wireless AP, including the following:

  - ❑ The IPv4 address of the wireless AP's wired interface

  - ❑ The destination UDP ports for RADIUS traffic sent by the wireless AP (UDP port 1812 for RADIUS authentication traffic and UDP port 1813 for RADIUS accounting traffic)

  - ❑ The RADIUS shared secret configured at the wireless AP

  Check the Windows Logs\Security event log for authentication failure events corresponding to connection attempts to the wireless AP. To view the failed authentication events, use the Event Viewer to view the events in the Security event log with the event ID of 6273.

- **IPsec for RADIUS traffic**   If you are using IPsec to encrypt the RADIUS traffic sent between the wireless AP and the NPS server, check the IPsec settings on both the wireless AP and NPS server to ensure that they can successfully negotiate security associations and authenticate each other.

> **Note**   For more information about how to configure IPsec policies in Windows Server 2008 to provide protection for RADIUS traffic, see Chapter 4, "Windows Firewall with Advanced Security." For more information about how to configure IPsec settings for a wireless AP, see your wireless AP's product documentation.

WPA or WPA2 Configuration   If your wireless AP is WPA-capable or WPA2-capable and you want to use WPA or WPA2 for wireless security, ensure that WPA or WPA2 is enabled.

Inability to Communicate Beyond the Wireless AP   The wireless AP is a transparent bridge and Layer 2 switching device, forwarding packets between the wired network to which it is attached and the connected wireless clients. If wireless clients can connect and authenticate but cannot reach locations beyond the wireless AP, one or more of the following might be happening.

- **The wireless AP is not forwarding frames as a bridge.**   All transparent bridges support the spanning tree protocol, which is used to prevent loops in a bridged section of the network. The spanning tree protocol uses a series of multicast messages to communicate bridge configuration information and automatically configure bridge interfaces to forward frames or block forwarding to prevent loops. While the spanning tree algorithm is determining forwarding and blocking interfaces, the bridge is not forwarding frames. Check the wireless AP's forwarding status and bridge configuration.

■ **The wireless AP is not configured with the correct VLAN IDs.**   Many wireless APs support VLANs, which are switch ports grouped so that they appear on the same link or subnet. Each group is assigned a separate VLAN ID. Verify that the VLAN IDs for your wireless client and your wired interfaces are correctly configured. For example, you might use one VLAN ID for authenticated wireless clients (that connects them to the organization intranet) and a separate VLAN ID for guest wireless clients (that connects them to an alternate subnet or the Internet).

Troubleshooting the Authentication Infrastructure

If you have multiple wireless APs and are unable to authenticate with any of them, you might have a problem with your authentication infrastructure, which consists of your NPS servers, PKI, and Active Directory accounts. In this section we examine common issues with NPS authentication and authorization, and validation of certificate-based and password-based authentications.

Troubleshooting NPS Authentication and Authorization

To troubleshoot the most common issues with NPS authentication and authorization, verify the following:

■ **That the wireless AP can reach the NPS servers**   To test this, try to ping the IP address of the wireless AP's interface on the wired network from each of the NPS servers. Additionally, ensure that IPsec policies, IP packet filters, and other mechanisms that restrict network traffic are not preventing the exchange of RADIUS messages between the wireless AP and its configured NPS servers. RADIUS traffic to the NPS servers uses a source IPv4 or IPv6 address of the wireless AP, a destination IPv4 or IPv6 address of the NPS server, and a UDP destination port of 1812 for authentication messages and UDP destination port 1813 for accounting messages. RADIUS traffic from the NPS servers uses a source IPv4 or IPv6 address of the NPS server, a destination IPv4 or IPv6 address of the wireless AP, a UDP source port of 1812 for authentication messages, and UDP source port 1813 for accounting messages. These examples assume that you are using the RADIUS UDP ports defined in RFC 2865 and 2866 for RADIUS authentication and accounting traffic.

■ **That each NPS server/wireless AP pair is configured with a common RADIUS shared secret**   Each NPS server/wireless AP pair is not necessarily required to use a unique RADIUS shared secret, but it must use the same value for the RADIUS shared secret for the members of the pair. For example, when you copy the NPS configuration from one NPS server to another, verify all of the shared secret pairs between the NPS servers and the wireless APs.

■ **That the NPS servers can reach a global catalog server and an Active Directory domain controller**   The NPS server uses a global catalog server to resolve the user principal name (UPN) of the computer or user certificate or the MS-CHAP v2 account name to the distinguished name of the corresponding account in Active Directory. The NPS server uses an Active Directory domain controller to validate the credentials of the computer and user account and obtain account properties to evaluate authorization.

- **That the computer accounts of the NPS servers are members of the RAS and IAS Servers security group for the appropriate domains** Adding the NPS server computer accounts to the RAS and IAS Servers security group for the appropriate domains is normally done during the initial configuration of the NPS server. To add the NPS server computer account to the appropriate domains, you can run the **netsh nps add registeredserver** command.

- **That there are no configured restrictions blocking access** Ensure that the user or computer account is not locked out, expired, or disabled or that the time the connection is being made corresponds to the permitted logon hours.

- **That the user account has not been locked out by remote access account lock-out** Remote access account lockout is an authentication counting and lockout mechanism designed to prevent an online dictionary attack against a user's password. If remote access account lockout is enabled, you can reset account lockout for the account by deleting the HKEY_LOCAL_MACHINE\SYSTEM\CurrentControlSet\Services\ RemoteAccess\Parameters\AccountLockout*DomainName:AccountName* registry value on the NPS server.

- **That the connection is authorized** For authorization, the parameters of the connection attempt must:

  - ❏ Match all the conditions of at least one network policy. If there is no matching policy, all wireless authentication requests are rejected.

  - ❏ Be granted network access permission through the user account (set to Allow Access), or if the user account has the Control Access Through NPS Network Policy option selected, the access permission of the first matching network policy must be set to Grant Access.

  - ❏ Match all the settings of the profile. Verify that the authentication settings of the profile have EAP-TLS or PEAP-MS-CHAP v2 enabled and properly configured.

  - ❏ Match all the settings of the dial-in properties of the user or computer account.

  To obtain the name of the network policy that rejected the connection attempt, ensure that NPS event logging is enabled for rejected authentication attempts, and use the Event Viewer to view the events in the Windows Logs\Security event log that have the event ID of 6273. In the text of the event for the connection attempt, look for the network policy name in the Network Policy Name field.

- **That you have not changed the mode of your domain from mixed mode to native mode** If you have just changed your Active Directory domain from mixed mode to native mode, NPS servers can no longer authenticate valid connection requests. You must restart every domain controller in the domain for the change to replicate.

Troubleshooting Certificate-Based Validation

Troubleshooting certificate validation for EAP-TLS or PEAP-TLS authentication consists of verifying the wireless client's computer and user certificates and the computer certificates of the NPS servers.

Validating the Wireless Client's Certificate   For an NPS server to validate the certificate of a wireless client, the following must be true for each certificate in the certificate chain sent by the wireless client:

- **The current date is within the validity dates of the certificate.**   When certificates are issued, they are issued with a valid date range, before which they cannot be used and after which they are considered expired.

- **The certificate has not been revoked.**   Issued certificates can be revoked at any time. Each issuing CA maintains a list of certificates that should no longer be considered valid by publishing an up-to-date certificate revocation list (CRL). The server will first attempt to validate the certificate using the Online Certificate Status Protocol (OSCP). If the OSCP validation is successful, the validation verification is satisfied; otherwise, it will then attempt to perform a CRL validation of the user or computer certificate. By default, the NPS server checks all the certificates in the wireless client's certificate chain (the series of certificates from the wireless client certificate to the root CA) for revocation. If any of the certificates in the chain have been revoked, certificate validation fails. This behavior can be modified by changing registry settings as described later in this chapter.

  To view the CRL distribution points for a certificate in the Certificates snap-in, in the contents pane, double-click the certificate, click the Details tab, and then click the CRL Distribution Points field. To perform a revocation check, the NPS server must be able to reach the CRL distribution points.

  The certificate revocation check works only as well as the CRL publishing and distribution system. If the CRL is not updated often, a certificate that has been revoked can still be used and considered valid because the published CRL that the NPS server is checking is out of date. Verify that the CRLs available to the NPS servers have not expired. If the CRLs available to the NPS servers have expired, EAP-TLS and PEAP-TLS authentication fails.

- **The certificate has a valid digital signature.**   CAs digitally sign certificates they issue. The NPS server verifies the digital signature of each certificate in the chain (with the exception of the root CA certificate) by obtaining the public key from the certificate's issuing CA and mathematically validating the digital signature.

  The wireless client certificate must also have the Client Authentication certificate purpose (also known as Enhanced Key Usage, or EKU) and must contain either a UPN of a valid user account or a Fully Qualified Domain Name (FQDN) of a valid computer account in the Subject Alternative Name field of the certificate.

  To view the EKU for a certificate in the Certificates snap-in, double-click the certificate in the contents pane, and then on the Details tab, click the Enhanced Key Usage field.

To view the Subject Alternative Name field for a certificate in the Certificates snap-in, in the contents pane, double-click the certificate, click the Details tab, and then click the Subject Alternative Name field.

- **The NPS server must have the appropriate certificate installed correctly.** To trust the certificate chain offered by the wireless client, the NPS server must have the root CA certificate of the issuing CA of the wireless client certificate installed in its Trusted Root Certification Authorities Local Computer store.

> **Note** In addition to performing normal certificate validation, the NPS server verifies that the identity sent in the initial EAP-Response/Identity message is the same as the name in the Subject Alternative Name property of the received certificate. This prevents a malicious user from masquerading as a different user or computer from that specified in the EAP-Response/Identity message.

For additional requirements for the wireless client's certificate, see "Requirements for PKI" earlier in this chapter.

By default, NPS performs certificate revocation checking on the certificate received from the wireless clients. You can use the following registry values in HKEY_LOCAL_MACHINE\ SYSTEM\CurrentControlSet\Services\RasMan\PPP\EAP\13 on the NPS server to modify certificate revocation checking behavior:

- **IgnoreNoRevocationCheck** When set to 1, NPS accepts EAP-TLS authentications, even when it does not perform or cannot complete a revocation check of the client's certificate chain (excluding the root certificate). Typically, revocation checks fail because the certificate does not include CRL information.

- **IgnoreNoRevocationCheck is set to 0 (disabled) by default. NPS rejects an EAP-TLS or PEAP-TLS authentication unless it can complete a revocation check of the client's certificate chain (including the root certificate) and verify that none of the certificates has been revoked.** Set IgnoreNoRevocationCheck to 1 to accept EAP-TLS or PEAP-TLS authentications when the certificate does not include CRL distribution points, such as those from third-party CAs.

- **IgnoreRevocationOffline** When set to 1, NPS accepts EAP-TLS or PEAP-TLS authentications even when a server that stores a CRL is not available on the network. IgnoreRevocationOffline is set to 0 by default. NPS rejects an EAP-TLS or PEAP-TLS authentication unless it can access CRLs and complete a revocation check of their certificate chain and verify that none of the certificates has been revoked. When it cannot connect to a location that stores a CRL, EAP-TLS or PEAP-TLS considers the certificate to have failed the revocation check.

Set IgnoreRevocationOffline to 1 to prevent certificate validation failure because of poor network conditions that inhibit revocation checks from completing successfully.

- **NoRevocationCheck**   When set to 1, NPS does not perform a revocation check on the wireless client's certificate. The revocation check verifies that the wireless client's certificate and the certificates in its certificate chain have not been revoked. NoRevocationCheck is set to 0 by default.

- **NoRootRevocationCheck**   When set to 1, NPS does not perform a revocation check of the wireless client's root CA certificate. This entry eliminates only the revocation check of the client's root CA certificate. A revocation check is still performed on the remainder of the wireless client's certificate chain. NoRootRevocationCheck is set to 0 by default.

  You can use NoRootRevocationCheck to authenticate clients when the root CA certificate does not include CRL distribution points, such as those from third-party CAs. Also, this entry can prevent certification-related delays that occur when a certificate revocation list is offline or is expired.

All these registry values must be added as a DWORD type (a registry data type composed of hexadecimal data with a maximum allotted space of 4 bytes) and set to 0 or 1. The Windows wireless client does not use these values.

Validating the NPS Server's Certificate   For the wireless client to validate the certificate of the NPS server, the following must be true for each certificate in the certificate chain sent by the NPS server:

- **The current date must be within the validity dates of the certificate.**   When certificates are issued, they are issued with a range of valid dates before which they cannot be used and after which they are considered expired.

- **The certificate has a valid digital signature.**   CAs digitally sign certificates they issue. The wireless client verifies the digital signature of each certificate in the chain with the exception of the root CA certificate by obtaining the public key from the certificate's issuing CA and mathematically validating the digital signature.

Additionally, the NPS server computer certificate must have the Server Authentication EKU, which has the object identifier (OID) 1.3.6.1.5.5.7.3.1. To view the EKU for a certificate in the Certificates snap-in, in the contents pane, double-click the certificate, click the Details tab, and then click the Enhanced Key Usage field.

Finally, to trust the certificate chain offered by the NPS server, the wireless client must have the root CA certificate of the issuing CA of the NPS server certificate installed in its Trusted Root Certification Authorities Local Computer store.

For additional requirements for the computer certificate of the NPS server, see "Requirements for PKI" earlier in this chapter.

Notice that the wireless client does not perform certificate revocation checking for the certificates in the certificate chain of the NPS server's computer certificate. The assumption is that the wireless client does not yet have a connection to the network and therefore cannot access a Web page or other resource in order to check for certificate revocation.

Troubleshooting Password-Based Validation

Troubleshooting password validation with PEAP-MS-CHAP v2 authentication consists of verifying the wireless client's user name and password credentials and the computer certificates of the NPS servers.

Validating the Wireless Client's Credentials   When you are using PEAP-MS-CHAP v2 for authentication, the name and password as sent by the wireless client must match the credentials of a valid account. The successful validation of the MS-CHAP v2 credentials by the NPS server depends on the following:

- The domain portion of the name corresponds to a domain that is either the domain of the NPS server or a domain that has a two-way trust with the domain of the NPS server.

- The account portion of the name corresponds to a valid account in the domain.

- The password is the correct password for the account.

To verify user account credentials, have the user of the wireless client log on to his or her domain using a computer that is already connected to the network, such as with an Ethernet connection (if possible). This process demonstrates whether there is a problem with the user's credentials or if the problem lies in the configuration of the authentication infrastructure.

Validating the NPS Server's Certificate   For the wireless client to validate the certificate of the NPS server for PEAP-MS-CHAP v2 authentication, the following must be true for each certificate in the certificate chain sent by the NPS server:

- **The current date must be within the validity dates of the certificate.**   When certificates are issued, they are issued with a valid date range before which they cannot be used and after which they are considered expired.

- **The certificate has a valid digital signature.**   CAs digitally sign certificates they issue. The wireless client verifies the digital signature of each certificate in the chain, with the exception of the root CA certificate, by obtaining the public key from the certificate's issuing CA and mathematically validating the digital signature.

Additionally, the NPS server computer certificate must have the Server Authentication EKU (OID 1.3.6.1.5.5.7.3.1). To view the EKU for a certificate in the Certificates snap-in, in the contents pane, double-click the certificate, and then on the Details tab, click the Enhanced Key Usage field.

Finally, to trust the certificate chain offered by the NPS server, the wireless client must have the root CA certificate of the issuing CA of the NPS server certificate installed in its Trusted Root Certification Authorities Local Computer store.

For additional requirements for the computer certificate of the NPS server, see "Requirements for PKI" earlier in this chapter.

Chapter Summary

Deploying a protected wireless network solution involves configuration of Active Directory, PKI, Group Policy, and RADIUS elements of a Windows-based authentication infrastructure and wireless APs and wireless clients. Once deployed, ongoing maintenance consists of managing wireless APs and their configuration for changes in infrastructure servers and updating and deploying wireless profiles. Common problems with wireless connections include the inability to connect due to an authentication or authorization failure and the inability to reach intranet resources from the wireless client.

Additional Information

For additional information about wireless support in Windows Server 2008 and Windows Vista, see the following:

- Windows Server 2008 Technical Library at *http://technet.microsoft.com/windowsserver/2008*
- Windows Server 2008 Help and Support
- Microsoft Wireless Networking (*http://www.microsoft.com/wifi*)

For additional information about Active Directory, see the following:

- Chapter 9, "Authentication Infrastructure"
- *Windows Server 2008 Active Directory Resource Kit*, available as a stand-alone title or in the *Windows Server 2008 Resource Kit* (both Microsoft Press, 2008)
- Windows Server 2008 Technical Library at *http://technet.microsoft.com/windowsserver/2008*
- Windows Server 2008 Help and Support

For additional information about PKI, see the following:

- Chapter 9, "Authentication Infrastructure"
- Windows Server 2008 Technical Library at *http://technet.microsoft.com/windowsserver/2008*
- Windows Server 2008 Help and Support
- Public Key Infrastructure for Microsoft Windows Server (*http://www.microsoft.com/pki*)
- *Windows Server 2008 PKI and Certificate Security* by Brian Komar (Microsoft Press, 2008)

For additional information about Group Policy, see the following:

- Chapter 9, "Authentication Infrastructure"
- *Windows Group Policy Resource Kit: Windows Server 2008 and Windows Vista* (Microsoft Press, 2008)
- Windows Server 2008 Technical Library at *http://technet.microsoft.com/windowsserver/2008*
- Windows Server 2008 Help and Support
- Microsoft Windows Server Group Policy (*http://www.microsoft.com/gp*)

For additional information about RADIUS and NPS, see the following:

- Chapter 9, "Authentication Infrastructure"
- Windows Server 2008 Technical Library at *http://technet.microsoft.com/windowsserver/2008*
- Windows Server 2008 Help and Support
- Microsoft Network Policy Server (*http://www.microsoft.com/nps*)

For additional information about NAP and 802.1X Enforcement, see the following:

- Chapter 14, "Network Access Protection Overview"
- Chapter 15, "Preparing for Network Access Protection"
- Chapter 17, "802.1X Enforcement"
- Windows Server 2008 Technical Library at *http://technet.microsoft.com/windowsserver/2008*
- Windows Server 2008 Help and Support
- Network Access Protection (*http://www.microsoft.com/nap*)

Chapter 11

IEEE 802.1X–Authenticated Wired Networks

This chapter provides information about how to design, deploy, maintain, and troubleshoot wired networks that use IEEE 802.1X authentication. Once deployed, the protected wired network solution can be modified for the 802.1X Enforcement method of Network Access Protection (NAP) as described in Chapter 17, "802.1X Enforcement."

This chapter assumes that you understand the role of Active Directory, public key infrastructure (PKI), Group Policy, and Remote Authentication Dial-In User Service (RADIUS) elements of a Microsoft Windows–based authentication infrastructure for network access. For more information, see Chapter 9, "Authentication Infrastructure."

Concepts

Many modern Ethernet switches support port-based network access control, a technology that prevents communication on a switch port until the computer accessing the port has been authenticated and authorized. The standard used to perform the authentication for the use of the port is IEEE 802.1X. IEEE 802.1X authentication is designed for medium and large wired LANs that contain an authentication infrastructure consisting of RADIUS servers and account databases such as Active Directory. IEEE 802.1X prevents a wired node from sending or receiving frames on a wired network until the node is successfully authenticated and authorized.

Authentication verifies that wired nodes have valid account credentials. Authentication prevents users without valid credentials from being able to join your wired network. Authorization verifies that the wired node meets the conditions required to make a connection to the switch. IEEE 802.1X uses the Extensible Authentication Protocol (EAP) to exchange authentication credentials. IEEE 802.1X authentication can be based on different EAP authentication methods such as those using user name and password credentials or a digital certificate.

Components of Wired Networks With 802.1X Authentication

Figure 11-1 shows the components of Windows-based wired networks with 802.1X authentication.

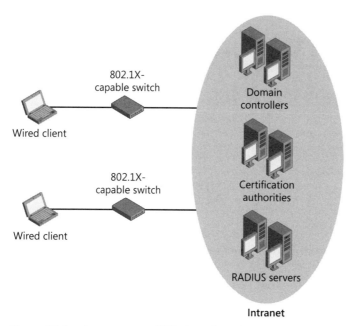

Figure 11-1   Components of Windows-based wired networks with 802.1X authentication

The components are:

- **Wired clients**   Nodes that support 802.1X authentication for LAN connections and connect to 802.1X-capable wired switches

- **802.1X-capable switches**   Switches that enforce 802.1X authentication and connection requirements on switch ports and forward frames between wired clients and intranet resources

- **RADIUS servers**   Computers that provide centralized authentication and authorization processing and accounting for network access attempts for 802.1X-capable switches and other types of access servers

- **Active Directory domain controllers**   Computers that validate user and computer credentials for authentication and provide account information to the RADIUS servers to evaluate authorization

- **Certification authorities**   Part of the PKI that issues computer or user certificates to wired clients and computer certificates to RADIUS servers

Planning and Design Considerations

When deploying an 802.1X-authenticated wired network solution, you need to consider the following for planning and design issues:

- Wired authentication methods

- Wired authentication modes
- Authentication infrastructure
- Wired clients
- PKI
- 802.1X Enforcement with NAP

Wired Authentication Methods

Windows Server 2008 and Windows Vista support the following EAP authentication methods for wired authentication:

- EAP-Transport Layer Security (TLS)
- Protected PEAP-Microsoft Challenge Handshake Authentication Protocol version 2 (PEAP-MS-CHAP v2)
- PEAP-TLS

EAP-TLS and PEAP-TLS are used in conjunction with a PKI and computer certificates, user certificates, and smart cards. With EAP-TLS, the wired client sends its computer certificate, user certificate, or smart card certificate for authentication, and the RADIUS server sends a computer certificate for authentication. By default, the wired client validates the RADIUS server's certificate.

In the absence of computer certificates, user certificates, or smart cards, you can use PEAP-MS-CHAP v2. PEAP-MS-CHAP v2 is a password-based authentication method in which the exchange of authentication messages is protected with an encrypted TLS session. Use of the encrypted TLS session makes it much more difficult for a malicious user to determine the password of a captured authentication exchange through an offline dictionary attack.

EAP-TLS and PEAP-TLS are much stronger than PEAP-MS-CHAP v2 because they do not rely on passwords.

How It Works: PEAP-MS-CHAP v2

MS-CHAP v2 is a password-based, challenge-response, mutual authentication protocol that uses the industry-standard Message Digest 4 (MD4) and Data Encryption Standard (DES) algorithms to encrypt responses. The authenticating server challenges the access client, and the access client challenges the authenticating server. If either challenge is not correctly answered, the connection is rejected. Microsoft originally developed MS-CHAP v2 as a Point-to-Point Protocol (PPP) authentication protocol to provide better protection for dial-up and virtual private network (VPN) connections.

Although MS-CHAP v2 provides better protection than other PPP-based challenge-response authentication protocols, it is still susceptible to an offline dictionary attack.

A malicious user can capture a successful MS-CHAP v2 exchange and methodically guess passwords until the correct one is determined. Using the combination of PEAP with MS-CHAP v2, the MS-CHAP v2 exchange is protected with the strong security of a TLS session.

The PEAP-MS-CHAP v2 authentication process occurs in two parts: the first part uses PEAP to create an encrypted TLS session, and the second part uses MS-CHAP v2 as an EAP type to exchange credentials for network access authentication.

PEAP Part 1: Creating the TLS Session

1. The 802.1X-capable switch sends an EAP-Request/Identity message to the wired client.

2. The wired client responds with an EAP-Response/Identity message that contains the identity (user name or computer name) of the wired client.

3. The switch sends the EAP-Response/Identity message to the RADIUS server. From this point on, the logical communication occurs between the RADIUS server and the wired client by using the switch as a pass-through device.

4. The RADIUS server sends an EAP-Request/Start PEAP message to the wired client.

5. The wired client and the RADIUS server exchange a series of TLS messages in which the RADIUS server sends its computer certificate and certificate chain to the wired client for validation, and the wired client and RADIUS server determine encryption keys and the encryption method for the TLS session.

At the end of the PEAP negotiation, the RADIUS server has validated itself to the wired client. Both nodes have determined mutual encryption keys for the TLS session by using public key cryptography, not passwords. All subsequent EAP messages sent between the wired client and the RADIUS server are encrypted within the PEAP TLS session.

PEAP Part 2: Authenticating with MS-CHAP v2

1. The RADIUS server sends an EAP-Request/Identity message.

2. The wired client responds with an EAP-Response/Identity message that contains the identity (user or computer name) of the wired client.

3. The RADIUS server sends an EAP-Request/EAP-MS-CHAP v2 Challenge message that contains a challenge string.

4. The wired client responds with an EAP-Response/EAP-MS-CHAP v2 Response message that contains both the response to the RADIUS server challenge string and a challenge string for the RADIUS server.

5. The RADIUS server sends an EAP-Request/EAP-MS-CHAP v2 Success message, indicating that the wired client's response is correct and containing the response to the wired client challenge string.

6. The wired client responds with an EAP-Response/EAP-MS-CHAP v2 Ack message, indicating that the RADIUS server response is correct.

7. The RADIUS server sends an EAP-Success message.

By the end of this mutual authentication exchange, the following has occurred:

- The wired client has provided proof of knowledge of the correct password (the response to the RADIUS server challenge string).

- The RADIUS server has provided proof of knowledge of the correct password (the response to the wired client challenge string).

The entire exchange has been encrypted with the TLS session created in the first part of the PEAP authentication. To perform an offline dictionary attack, an attacker would first have to decrypt the TLS-encrypted messages, a daunting task of cryptanalysis.

Requirements for Authentication Methods

Requirements for wired authentication methods are the following:

- EAP-TLS requires the installation of a computer certificate on each RADIUS server and a computer certificate, user certificate, or smart card on all wired client computers. To validate the RADIUS servers' computer certificates, the root certification authority (CA) certificates of the issuing CAs of the RADIUS server computer certificates must be installed on all wired client computers. To validate the wired clients' computer certificate, user certificate, or smart card, the root CA certificates of the issuing CAs of the wired client certificates must be installed on each RADIUS server.

- PEAP-MS-CHAP v2 requires the installation of a computer certificate on each RADIUS server, and for validation of the RADIUS servers' computer certificates, the root CA certificates of the issuing CAs of the RADIUS server computer certificates on each of the wired client computers.

- If you are planning to eventually deploy the 802.1X Enforcement method of NAP, you should use a PEAP-based authentication method, such as PEAP-MS-CHAP v2 or PEAP-TLS.

Best Practices for Wired Authentication Methods

Best practices for wired authentication methods are the following:

- If you must use PEAP-MS-CHAP v2, require the use of strong passwords on your network. Strong passwords are long (longer than eight characters) and contain a mixture of uppercase and lowercase letters, numbers, and punctuation. In an Active Directory domain, use Group Policy settings to enforce strong user passwords requirements in Computer Configuration\Windows Settings\Security Settings\Account Policies\Password Policy.

Wired Authentication Modes

Windows-based wired clients can perform authentication using the following modes:

- **Computer-only** Windows performs 802.1X authentication with computer credentials before displaying the Windows logon screen. This allows the wired client to have access to networking resources such as Active Directory domain controllers before the user logs on. Windows does not attempt authentication with user credentials after the user logs on.

- **User-only** Windows performs 802.1X authentication with user credentials after the user logon process has completed. Windows does not attempt authentication with computer credentials before or after the user logon.

- **Computer-or-user** Windows performs an 802.1X authentication with computer credentials before displaying the Windows logon screen. Windows performs another 802.1X authentication with user credentials after the user has logged on.

In computer-only or computer-or-user authentication modes, an additional benefit is that the resources of the authenticating computer, such as shared folders, are available to other computers without requiring a user to log on.

Problems with the behavior of user-only authentication mode include the following:

- A user cannot perform an initial domain logon to a computer because locally cached credentials for the user's account are not available and there is no connectivity to the domain controller to authenticate new logon credentials.

- Domain logon operations will not be successful because there is no connectivity to the domain controllers of the Active Directory domain during the user logon process. Logon scripts, Group Policy updates, and user profile updates will fail, resulting in Windows event log error entries.

Additionally, some network infrastructures use different virtual LANs (VLANs) to separate wired clients that have authenticated with computer credentials from wired clients that have authenticated with user credentials. If the user-level authentication to the wired network and the change to the user-authenticated VLAN occurs after the user logon process, a Windows wired client will not have access to resources on the user-authenticated VLAN–such as Active Directory domain controllers–during the user logon process. This can lead to unsuccessful initial logons and domain logon operations, such as logon scripts, Group Policy updates, and user profile updates.

To address the availability of network connectivity when performing user logon for the user-only authentication mode and the user-or-computer authentication mode when using separate VLANs, wired clients running Windows Vista with Service Pack 1 and Windows Server 2008 support Single Sign On. With Single Sign On, you can specify that wired network authentication with user credentials occurs before the user logon process. To enable and configure Single Sign On, you can use the Wired Network (IEEE 802.3) Policies Group Policy extension or **netsh lan** commands with the appropriate parameters. For more information, see "Configuring Wired Clients" later in this chapter.

Best Practices for Wired Authentication Modes

Best practices for wired authentication modes are the following:

- Use user-or-computer authentication mode in which the user authentication occurs after user logon. This is the default authentication mode.

- If you are using the user-only authentication mode, configure your wired profiles to enable Single Sign On and perform wired authentication with user credentials before user logon to prevent initial and domain logon problems.

- If you are using different VLANs for computer and user-authenticated wired clients and the computer-or-user authentication mode, configure your wired profiles to enable Single Sign On and perform wired authentication with user credentials before user logon to prevent initial and domain logon problems.

Authentication Infrastructure

The authentication infrastructure exists to:

- Authenticate the credentials of wired clients

- Authorize the wired connection

- Inform 802.1X-capable switches of wired connection restrictions

- Record the wired connection creation and termination times for accounting purposes

The authentication infrastructure for 802.1X-authenticated wired connections consists of:

- 802.1X-capable switches

- RADIUS servers

- Active Directory domain controllers

- Issuing CAs of a PKI (optional)

If you are using a Windows domain as the user account database to verify user or computer credentials and store dial-in properties, use Network Policy Server (NPS) in Windows Server 2008. NPS is a full-featured RADIUS server and proxy that replaces Internet Authentication Service (IAS), which was included in Windows Server 2003 and is tightly integrated with Active Directory. See Chapter 9 for additional design and planning considerations for NPS-based RADIUS servers.

NPS performs the authentication of the wired connection by communicating with a domain controller through a protected remote procedure call (RPC) channel. NPS performs authorization of the connection attempt through the dial-in properties of the user or computer account and network policies configured on the NPS server.

NPS by default logs all RADIUS accounting information in a local log file (*%System-Root%\System32\Logfiles\Logfile.log* by default) based on settings configured in the Accounting node in the Network Policy Server snap-in.

Best Practices for Authentication Infrastructure

Best practices for the authentication infrastructure for protected wired access are the following:

- To better manage authorization for wired connections, create a universal group in Active Directory for wired access that contains global groups for the user and computer accounts that are allowed to make 802.1X-authenticated wired connections. For example, create a universal group named WiredAccounts that contains the global groups based on your organization's regions or departments. Each global group contains user and computer accounts allowed for wired access. When you configure your NPS policies for wired connections, specify the WiredAccounts group name.

- From the NPS node of the Network Policy Server snap-in, use the Configure 802.1X Wizard to create a set of policies for 802.1X-authenticated wired connections. For example, create a set of policies for wired clients that are members of a specific group and to use a specific authentication method.

Wired Clients

A Windows-based wired client runs Windows Vista, Windows Server 2008, Windows XP with SP2, or Windows Server 2003. You can configure wired connections on Windows Vista-based and Windows Server 2008–based wired clients in the following ways:

- **Group Policy** The Wired Network (IEEE 802.3) Policies Group Policy extension is part of a Computer Configuration Group Policy Object that can specify wired network settings in an Active Directory environment. This Group Policy extension applies only to computers running Windows Server 2008 or Windows Vista.

- **Command line** Wired settings can be configured by running **netsh lan** commands with the appropriate parameters.

- **Wired XML profiles** Wired XML profiles are XML files that contain wired network settings. These settings can be exported from a Windows Server 2008 or Windows Vista wired client and then imported to a Windows Server 2008 or Windows Vista wired client by using the Netsh tool.

You can also configure Windows wired clients manually in the following ways:

- For an individual Windows Vista–based or Windows Server 2008–based wired client, you can use the Services snap-in to start the Wired AutoConfig service and configure it for automatic startup. You must then configure 802.1X authentication settings on the Authentication tab of the properties dialog box of a LAN connection in the Network Connections folder.

For an Active Directory domain, you can use Group Policy to start the Wired AutoConfig service and configure it for automatic startup. Configure the Computer Configuration\Windows Settings\Security Settings\System Services\Wired AutoConfig setting to Enabled and Automatic start.

■ For a Windows XP–based or Windows Server 2003–based wired client, you must configure 802.1X authentication settings from the Authentication tab of the properties dialog box of a LAN connection in the Network Connections folder.

Wired Network (IEEE 802.3) Policies Group Policy Extension

To automate the configuration of wired network settings for Windows wired client computers, Windows Server 2008 and Windows Server 2003 Active Directory domains support a Wired Network (IEEE 802.3) Policies Group Policy extension. This extension allows you to configure wired network settings as part of Computer Configuration Group Policy for a domain-based Group Policy Object. By using the Wired Network (IEEE 802.3) Policies Group Policy extension, you can specify the EAP authentication method and other settings for wired clients running Windows Server 2008 or Windows Vista.

These settings are downloaded and applied to wired clients running Windows Server 2008 or Windows Vista that are members of a Windows Server 2008 or Windows Server 2003 Active Directory domain. A Windows Server 2003 Active Directory domain must be extended to support the new extension.

> **More Info**   For information about how to extend a Windows Server 2003 Active Directory domain, see "Active Directory Schema Extensions for Windows Vista Wireless and Wired Group Policy Enhancements" at *http://technet.microsoft.com/en-us/library/bb727029.aspx*.

You can configure wired policies from the Computer Configuration\Windows Settings\Security Settings\Wired Network (IEEE 802.3) Policies node in the Group Policy Object Management Editor snap-in. By default, there are no Wired Network (IEEE 802.3) Policies. To create a new policy, right-click Wired Network (IEEE 802.3) Policies in the console tree of the Group Policy Object Editor snap-in, and then click Create A New Windows Vista Policy.

> **Note**   To modify Group Policy settings from a computer running Windows Server 2008, you might need to install the Group Policy Management feature by using the Server Manager tool.

The properties dialog box of a Windows Vista wired policy consists of a General tab and a Security tab. Figure 11-2 shows the default General tab.

On the General tab, you can configure a name and description for the policy and specify whether to enable the Wired AutoConfig service.

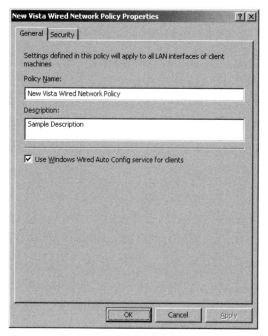

Figure 11-2   The General tab of a Windows Vista wired policy

Figure 11-3 shows the default Security tab for a Windows Vista wired policy.

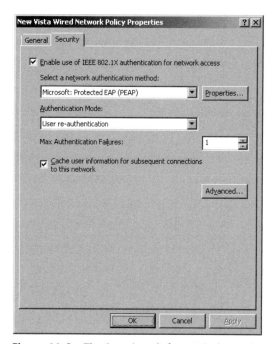

Figure 11-3   The Security tab for a Windows Vista wired policy

On the Security tab, you can enable or disable 802.1X authentication; select and configure the PEAP-MS-CHAP v2 or EAP-TLS authentication methods, the authentication mode (user reauthentication, computer only, user authentication, or guest authentication), and the number of times authentication attempts can fail before authentication is abandoned; and choose whether to cache user information for subsequent connections. This last setting, if the check box is cleared, specifies that when the user logs off, the user credential data is removed from the registry. The result is that the next user will be prompted for credentials (such as user name and password) at logon.

By clicking the Advanced button on the Security tab, you can configure the following advanced settings for 802.1X and Single Sign On. Figure 11-4 shows the default Advanced Security Settings dialog box for a Windows Vista wired policy.

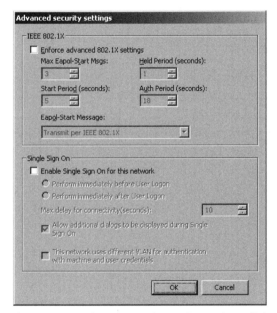

Figure 11-4   The Advanced Security Settings dialog box for a Windows Vista wired policy

From the Advanced Security Settings dialog box, you can configure the following 802.1X settings:

- **Max Start**   The number of successive EAP over LAN (EAPOL)-Start messages that are sent out when no response to the initial EAPOL-Start messages is received

- **Held Period**   The time interval between the retransmission of EAPOL-Start messages when no response to the previously sent EAPOL-Start message is received

- **Start Period**   The period during which the authenticating client will not perform any 802.1X authentication activity after it has received an authentication failure indication from the authenticator

- **Auth Period**   The amount of time the authenticating client will wait before retransmitting any 802.1X requests after end-to-end 802.1X authentication has been initiated

Wired clients running Windows Vista with SP1 or Windows Server 2008 support Single Sign On for wired connections. There are Single Sign On settings in the Wired Network (IEEE 802.3) Policies extension for the following:

- **Perform Immediately Before User Logon**   Perform user-level 802.1X authentication prior to the user logon process.

- **Perform Immediately After User Logon**   Perform user-level 802.1X authentication after the user logon process.

- **Max. Delay For Connectivity (Seconds)**   Wait the configured number of seconds for user-level 802.1X authentication to complete before starting the user logon process.

- **Allow Additional Dialogs To Be Displayed During Single Sign On**   Display dialog boxes for user-level authentication beyond the consolidation of input fields on the Windows logon screen. For example, if an EAP type wants the user to confirm the certificate sent from the RADIUS server during authentication, the EAP type can display the dialog box.

- **This Network Uses Different VLAN For Authentication With Machine And User Credentials**   After performing user-level authentication, initiate a Dynamic Host Configuration Protocol (DHCP) renewal of the Transmission Control Protocol/Internet Protocol (TCP/IP) configuration of the wired adapter. Select this option if there are separate VLANs for computer-level and user-level authenticated wired clients and those VLANs are different Internet Protocol version 4 (IPv4) or Internet Protocol version 6 (IPv6) subnets.

For information about when to use Single Sign On, see "Wired Authentication Modes" earlier in this chapter.

Command-Line Configuration

Windows Server 2008 and Windows Vista support a command-line interface that allows you to configure some of the wired settings that are available from the wired dialog boxes in the Network Connections folder or through the Wired Network (IEEE 802.3) Policies Group Policy extension. Command-line configuration of wired settings can help deployment of wired networks in the following situations:

- **Automated script support for wired settings without using Group Policy**   The Wired Network (IEEE 802.3) Policies Group Policy extension applies only in an Active Directory domain. For an environment without a Group Policy infrastructure, a script that automates the configuration of wired connections can be run either manually or automatically, such as part of the logon script.

- **Bootstrap of a wired client onto the organization's 802.1X-authenticated wired network**   A wired client computer that is not a member of the domain cannot connect to the organization's 802.1X-authenticated wired network. Additionally, a computer cannot join the domain until it has successfully connected to the organization's secure wired network. A command-line script provides a method to connect to the organization's wired network and join the domain.

To perform command-line configuration of Windows Vista–based and Windows Server 2008–based wired clients, run **netsh lan** commands with the appropriate parameters.

> **More Info**   For more information about **netsh lan** command syntax, see "Netsh Commands for Wired Local Area Network (lan)" at *http://technet.microsoft.com/en-us/windowsvista/ aa905084.aspx*.

XML-Based Wired Profiles

To simplify command-line configuration of Windows Vista–based and Windows Server 2008–based wired clients, you can export the configuration of a wired profile to an XML file that can be imported on other wired clients. You can export a wired profile from a wired client by running the **netsh lan export profile** command. To import a wired profile, run the **netsh lan add profile** command.

> **More Info**   For examples of wired profiles, see Wired Profile Samples at *http://msdn2.microsoft.com/en-us/library/aa816372.aspx*.

Requirements for Wired Clients

Requirements for wired clients are the following:

- The Wired Network (IEEE 802.3) Policies Group Policy extension applies only to computers running Windows Server 2008 or Windows Vista. Unlike the Wireless Network (IEEE 802.11) Policies Group Policy extension, computers running Windows XP or Windows Server 2003 do not support Group Policy–based configuration of wired authentication settings.

- Single Sign On configuration is supported only by wired clients running Windows Vista with SP1 or Windows Server 2008.

- To deploy 802.1X enforcement with NAP, you must configure your wired clients to use a PEAP-based authentication method.

Best Practices for Wired Clients

Best practices for wired clients are the following:

- For a small number of wired clients, either manually configure each wired client or use the Wired Network (IEEE 802.3) Wired Policies Group Policy extension.

- For deployment of wired configuration in an Active Directory environment for a medium or large organization, use the Wired Network (IEEE 802.3) Wired Policies Group Policy extension.

- For deployment of wired configuration using scripts for a medium or large organization, create wired XML profiles, and configure wired clients with a script containing the **netsh lan add profile** command.

PKI

To perform authentication for wired connections using EAP-TLS, a PKI must be in place to issue computer certificates, user certificates, or smart cards to wired clients and computer certificates to RADIUS servers. For PEAP-MS-CHAP v2–based authentication, a PKI is not required to issue computer certificates to RADIUS servers. It is possible to purchase certificates from a third-party CA to install on your NPS servers. However, you might also need to distribute the root CA certificate of third-party computer certificates to your wired client computers.

PKI for Smart Cards

The use of smart cards for user authentication is the strongest form of user authentication in Windows. For wired connections, you can use smart cards with the EAP-TLS authentication method. The individual smart cards are distributed to users whose computer has a smart card reader. To log on to the computer, the user must insert the smart card into the smart card reader and then type the personal identification number (PIN). When the user attempts to make a wired connection, the smart card certificate is sent during the connection negotiation process. For more information on how to deploy smart cards, see Windows Server 2008 Help and Support.

PKI for User Certificates

User certificates that are stored in the Windows registry for user-level authentication can be used in place of smart cards. However, this is not as strong a form of authentication. With smart cards, the user certificate issued during the authentication process is made available only when the user possesses the smart card and has knowledge of the PIN to log on to the computer. With user certificates, the user certificate issued during the authentication process is made available when the user logs on to the computer using a domain-based user name and password. Just as with smart cards, authentication using user certificates for wired connections uses the EAP-TLS authentication method.

To deploy user certificates in your organization, perform the following steps:

1. Deploy a PKI.

2. Install a user certificate for each user. This is most easily accomplished when you have Windows Certificate Services installed as an enterprise CA and configuring Group Policy settings for user certificate autoenrollment. For more information, see "Deploying Certificates" later in this chapter.

When the wired client attempts user-level authentication for a wired connection, the wired client computer sends the user certificate during the authentication process.

PKI for Computer Certificates

Computer certificates are stored in the Windows registry for computer-level authentication for wired access with the EAP-TLS authentication method. To deploy computer certificates in your organization, take the following steps:

1. Deploy a PKI.

2. Install a computer certificate on each wired client computer. This is most easily accomplished when you have Windows Active Directory Certificate Services or Certificate Services installed as an enterprise CA and configuring Group Policy settings for computer certificate autoenrollment. For more information, see "Deploying Certificates" later in this chapter.

When the wired client attempts computer-level authentication for a wired connection, the wired client computer sends the computer certificate during the authentication process.

Requirements for PKI

Requirements for the PKI for protected wired access are the following:

- For computer-level authentication with EAP-TLS, you must install computer certificates, also known as machine certificates, on each wired client.

  The computer certificates of the wired clients must be valid and verifiable by the NPS servers; the NPS servers must have a root CA certificate for the CA that issued the computer certificates of the wired client.

- For user-level authentication with EAP-TLS, you must use a smart card, or you must install a user certificate on each wired client.

  The smart card or user certificates of the wired clients must be valid and verifiable by the NPS servers; the NPS servers must have the root CA certificates of the issuing CAs of the smart card or user certificates of the wired clients.

- You must install the root CA certificates of the issuing CA of the NPS server computer certificates on each wired client.

  The computer certificates of the NPS servers must be verifiable by the wired clients; the wired clients must have the root CA certificate of the issuing CAs of the computer certificates of the NPS servers.

- For EAP-TLS authentication, the requirements for the user certificate, smart card certificate, or computer certificate of the wired client are as follows:

  ❑ The certificate must contain a private key.

  ❑ The certificate must be issued by an enterprise CA or be mapped to a user or computer account in Active Directory.

- ❑ The certificate must be chained to a trusted root CA on the NPS server and must not fail any of the checks that are performed by CryptoAPI and specified in the network policy for wired connections.

- ❑ The certificate is configured with the Client Authentication purpose in the Enhanced Key Usage field. (The object identifier for Client Authentication is 1.3.6.1.5.5.7.3.2.)

- ❑ The Subject Alternative Name field contains the user principal name (UPN) of the user or computer account.

- For EAP-TLS authentication, the requirements for the computer certificate of the NPS server are as follows:

  - ❑ The certificate must contain a private key.

  - ❑ The Subject field must contain a value.

  - ❑ The certificate must be chained to a trusted root CA on the wired clients and must not fail any of the checks that are performed by CryptoAPI and specified in the network policy for wired connections.

  - ❑ The certificate is configured with the Server Authentication purpose in the Enhanced Key Usage field. (The object identifier for Server Authentication is 1.3.6.1.5.5.7.3.1.)

  - ❑ The certificate is configured with a required cryptographic service provider (CSP) value of Microsoft RSA) SChannel Cryptographic provider.

  - ❑ The Subject Alternative Name field of the certificate, if used, must contain the DNS name of the NPS server.

Best Practices for PKI

Best practices for the PKI for protected wired access are the following:

- For computer certificates with EAP-TLS, if you are using a Windows Server 2008 enterprise CA as an issuing CA, configure your Active Directory domain for autoenrollment of computer certificates by using Computer Configuration Group Policy. Each computer that is a member of the domain automatically requests a computer certificate when Computer Configuration Group Policy is updated.

- For registry-based user certificates for EAP-TLS, if you are using a Windows Server 2008 enterprise CA as an issuing CA, configure your Active Directory domain for autoenrollment of user certificates by using User Configuration Group Policy. Each user that successfully logs on to the domain automatically requests a user certificate when User Configuration Group Policy is updated.

- If you have purchased third-party computer certificates for your NPS servers for PEAP-MS-CHAP v2 authentication and the wired clients do not have the root CA certificate of the issuing CA of the NPS server computer certificates installed, use Group Policy to install the root CA certificate of the issuing CA of the NPS server computer certificates on your wired clients. Each computer that is a member of the domain automatically receives and installs the root CA certificate when Computer Configuration Group Policy is updated.

- For EAP-TLS and PEAP-MS-CHAP v2 authentication, it is possible to configure the wired clients so that they do not validate the certificate of the NPS server. In this configuration, computer certificates on the NPS servers and their root CA certificates on wired clients are not required. However, having the wired clients validate the certificate of the NPS server is highly recommended for mutual authentication of the wired client and NPS server. With mutual authentication, you can protect your wired clients from connecting to rogue switches with spoofed authentication servers.

802.1X Enforcement with NAP

Network Access Protection (NAP) for Windows Server 2008, Windows Vista, and Windows XP with Service Pack 3 provides components and an application programming interface (API) set that help you enforce compliance with health policies for network access or communication. Developers and network administrators can create solutions for validating computers that connect to their networks, can provide needed updates or access to needed resources, and can limit the access of noncompliant computers.

802.1X Enforcement is one of the NAP enforcement methods included with Windows Server 2008, Windows Vista, and Windows XP. With 802.1X Enforcement, an 802.1X-authenticated wired client must prove that it is compliant with system health requirements before it is allowed full access to the intranet. An example of a system health requirement is the use of an antivirus program. If the wired client is not compliant with system health requirements, the 802.1X-capable switch can place the wired client on a restricted network containing servers that have resources to bring the wired client back into compliance. The switch enforces the restricted access through packet filters or a VLAN ID that are assigned to the wired connection. After correcting its health state, the wired client validates its health state again, and if compliant, the constraints on the wired connection that confine the access to the restricted network are removed.

In order for 802.1X Enforcement to work, you must already have a working 802.1X-authenticated wired deployment that uses a PEAP-based authentication method. For the details of deploying 802.1X Enforcement after successfully deploying an 802.1X-authenticated wired network solution, see Chapter 17.

Deploying 802.1X-Authenticated Wired Access

To deploy an 802.1X-authenticated wired network using Windows Server 2008 and Windows Vista, perform the following tasks:

- Deploy certificates.
- Configure Active Directory for accounts and groups.
- Configure NPS servers.
- Configure 802.1X-capable switches.
- Configure wired clients.

Deploying Certificates

You must deploy certificates if you are doing the following:

- **Computer-level authentication with EAP-TLS and computer certificates**   Each wired client computer needs a computer certificate.

- **User-level authentication with EAP-TLS and either smart cards or registry-based user certificates**   Either each wired user needs a smart card, or each wired client computer needs a user certificate.

- **User or computer-level authentication with PEAP-MS-CHAP v2**   Each wired client needs the root CA of the issuing CA of the NPS servers' computer certificates.

For all of these configurations, each NPS server needs a computer certificate.

Deploying Computer Certificates

To install computer certificates for EAP-TLS authentication, a PKI must be present to issue certificates. Once the PKI is in place, you can install a computer certificate on wired clients and NPS servers in the following ways:

- By configuring autoenrollment of computer certificates to computers in an Active Directory domain (recommended)
- By using the Certificates snap-in to request a computer certificate
- By using the Certificates snap-in to import a computer certificate
- By executing a CAPICOM script that requests a computer certificate

For more information, see the section titled "Deploying PKI" in Chapter 9.

Deploying User Certificates

You can install a registry-based user certificate on wired clients in the following ways:

- By configuring autoenrollment of user certificates to users in an Active Directory domain (recommended)

- By using the Certificates snap-in to request a user certificate

- By using the Certificates snap-in to import a user certificate

- By requesting a certificate over the Web

- By executing a CAPICOM script that requests a user certificate

For more information, see the section titled "Deploying PKI" in Chapter 9.

Deploying Root CA Certificates

If you use PEAP-MS-CHAP v2 authentication, you might need to install the root CA certificates of the computer certificates that are installed on your NPS servers on your wired clients. If the root CA certificate of the issuer of the computer certificates that are installed on the NPS servers is already installed as a root CA certificate on your wired clients, no other configuration is necessary. For example, if your root CA is a Windows Server 2008–based online root enterprise CA, the root CA certificate is automatically installed on each domain member computer through Group Policy.

To verify whether the correct root CA certificate is installed on your wired clients, you need to determine:

1. The root CA of the computer certificates installed on the NPS servers

2. Whether a certificate for the root CA is installed on your wired clients

To Determine the Root CA of the Computer Certificates Installed on the NPS Servers

1. In the console tree of the Certificates snap-in for the NPS server computer account, expand Certificates (Local Computer or *Computername*), expand Personal, and then click Certificates.

2. In the details pane, double-click the computer certificate that is being used by the NPS server for PEAP-MS-CHAP v2 authentication.

3. On the Certification Path tab of the Certificate dialog box, note the name at the top of the certification path. This is the name of the root CA.

To Determine Whether a Certificate for the Root CA Is Installed on Your Wired Client

1. In the console tree of the Certificates snap-in for the wired client computer account, expand Certificates (Local Computer or *Computername*), expand Trusted Root Certification Authorities, and then click Certificates.

2. Examine the list of certificates in the details pane for a name matching the root CA for the computer certificates issued to the NPS servers.

You must install the root CA certificates of the issuers of the computer certificates of the NPS servers on each wired client that does not contain them. The easiest way to install a root CA certificate on all your wired clients is through Group Policy. For more information, see the section titled "Deploying PKI" in Chapter 9.

Configuring Active Directory for Accounts and Groups

To configure Active Directory for wired access, do the following for the user and computer accounts that will be used to authenticate wired connections:

- On the Dial-in tab, set the network access permission to Allow Access or Control Access Through NPS Network Policy. When you use the Control Access Through NPS Network Policy setting, the permission for access to the network is set by the Policy Type setting on the Overview tab of the wired NPS network policy. By default, in native-mode domains, new user and computer accounts have the network access permission set to Control Access Through NPS Network Policy.

- Organize the computer and user accounts into the appropriate universal and global security groups to take advantage of group-based network policies.

Configuring NPS Servers

Configure and deploy your NPS servers as described in Chapter 9, including the following steps:

1. Install a computer certificate on each NPS server.

2. Install the root CA certificates of the computer certificates, user certificates, or smart cards of the wired clients on each NPS server (if needed).

3. If you are using an EAP method that is not provided with Windows Server 2008, install it on each NPS server.

4. Configure logging on the primary NPS server.

5. Add RADIUS clients to the primary NPS server corresponding to each 802.1X-capable switch.

6. Create a set of network policies on the primary NPS server that are customized for wired connections and that use the universal security group name for your wired accounts.

For the details of steps 1–4, see Chapter 9.

To Create a Set of Policies for Wired Connections

1. In the console tree of the Network Policy Server snap-in, click NPS.

2. In the details pane, under Standard Configuration, in the drop-down list, select RADIUS Server For 802.1X Wireless Or Wired Connections, and then click Configure 802.1X.

3. In the Configure 802.1X Wizard, on the Select 802.1X Connections Type page, click Secure Wired (Ethernet) Connections, and then in the Policy Name box, type a name (or use the name created by the wizard). Click Next.

4. On the Specify 802.1X Switches page, add RADIUS clients as needed that correspond to your 802.1X-capable switches. Click Next.

5. On the Configure An Authentication Method page, configure the EAP type to use for wired connections.

    To configure EAP-TLS, in the Type drop-down list, select Microsoft: Smart Card Or Other Certificate, and then click Configure. In the Smart Card Or Other Certificate Properties dialog box, select the computer certificate to use for wired connections, and then click OK. If you cannot select the certificate, the cryptographic service provider for the certificate does not support Secure Channel (SChannel). SChannel support is required for NPS to use the certificate for EAP-TLS authentication.

    To configure PEAP-MS-CHAP v2, in the Type drop-down list, select Microsoft: Protected EAP (PEAP), and then click Configure. In the Edit Protected EAP Properties dialog box, select the computer certificate to use for wired connections, and then click OK. If you cannot select the certificate, the cryptographic service provider for the certificate does not support SChannel. SChannel support is required for NPS to use the certificate for PEAP authentication.

    To configure PEAP-TLS, in the Type drop-down list, select Microsoft: Protected EAP (PEAP), and then click Configure. In the Edit Protected EAP Properties dialog box, select the computer certificate to use for wired connections. If you cannot select the certificate, the cryptographic service provider for the certificate does not support SChannel. Under EAP Types, click Secured Password (EAP-MSCHAP v2) and then click Remove. Click Add. In the Add EAP dialog box, click Smart Card Or Other Certificate, and then click OK. In the Edit Protected EAP Properties dialog box, under EAP Types, click Smart Card Or Other Certificate, and then click Edit. In the Smart Card Or Other Certificate Properties dialog box, select the computer certificate to use for wired connections, and then click OK. If you cannot select the certificate, the cryptographic service provider for the certificate does not support Secure Channel (SChannel). Click OK twice.

6. Click Next. On the Specify User Groups page, add the groups containing the wired computer and user accounts (for example, WiredAccounts).

7. On the Configure A Virtual LAN (VLAN) page, click Configure if needed to specify the RADIUS attributes and their values that configure your 802.1X-capable switches for the appropriate VLAN. Click Next.

8. On the Completing New IEEE 802.1X Secure Wired And Wireless Connections And RADIUS Clients page, click Finish.

The Configure 802.1X Wizard creates a connection request policy and a network policy for wired connections. The Configure 802.1X Wizard configures the wired network policy with a single EAP method. For additional EAP methods, you can configure additional methods from the Settings tab for the properties of the network policy.

After you have configured the primary NPS server with the appropriate logging, RADIUS client, and policy settings, copy the configuration to the secondary or other NPS servers. For more information, see Chapter 9.

Configuring 802.1X-Capable Switches

Configure your 802.1X-capable switches with the following:

- A static IPv4 address, subnet mask, and default gateway for the subnet on which it is placed
- VLANs as needed
- The following RADIUS settings:
    - The IPv4 address, IPv6 address, or DNS name of a primary RADIUS server, the RADIUS shared secret, UDP ports for authentication and accounting, and failure detection settings
    - The IPv4 address, IPv6 address, or DNS name of a secondary RADIUS server, the RADIUS shared secret, UDP ports for authentication and accounting, and failure detection settings

To balance the load of RADIUS traffic between two NPS servers, configure half of the 802.1X-capable switches with the primary NPS server as the primary RADIUS server and the secondary NPS server as the secondary RADIUS server. Then, configure the other half of the 802.1X-capable switches with the secondary NPS server as the primary RADIUS server and the primary NPS server as the secondary RADIUS server.

If the 802.1X-capable switches require vendor-specific attributes (VSAs) or additional RADIUS attributes for special features or customized configuration of the switch, you must add the VSAs or RADIUS attributes to the wired NPS network policy on the NPS servers. If you add VSAs or RADIUS attributes to the wired NPS network policy on the primary NPS server, copy the primary NPS server configuration to the secondary NPS server.

Direct from the Source: RADIUS Attributes for VLANs

When you use virtual local area network (VLAN)–aware network hardware—such as routers, switches, and access controllers—you can configure NPS network policy to instruct the access servers to place members of Active Directory groups on VLANs.

Before configuring network policy in NPS for VLANs, create groups of users in Active Directory that you want to assign to specific VLANs. Then when you create the wired NPS network policy, add the Active Directory group as a condition of the network policy. You can create a separate NPS network policy for each group that you want to assign to a VLAN.

When you configure network policy for use with VLANs, you must configure the RADIUS standard attributes Tunnel-Medium-Type, Tunnel-Pvt-Group-ID, and Tunnel-Type. Some hardware vendors also require the use of the RADIUS standard attribute Tunnel-Tag.

To configure these attributes in an NPS network policy, use the Configure A Virtual LAN (VLAN) page of the Configure 802.1X Wizard. You can add the attributes to the NPS network policy settings while running the wizard or after you have successfully created a policy by using the wizard.

On the Configure A Virtual LAN (VLAN) page of the Configure 802.1X Wizard, add and configure the following RADIUS standard and vendor-specific attributes:

- **Tunnel-Medium-Type**   Select Value: 802 (includes all 802 media plus Ethernet canonical format).

- **Tunnel-Pvt-Group-ID**   Type the integer that represents the VLAN number to which the group members will be assigned. For example, if your Sales VLAN is on VLAN 4, type the number 4.

- **Tunnel-Type**   Select the value Virtual LANs (VLAN).

- **Tunnel-Tag**   Some hardware devices do not require this attribute. If your hardware device does require this attribute, obtain this value from your hardware documentation.

> **Note**   To add the attributes after you have created the network policy with the wizard, double-click the policy in the Policies\Network Policies node of the NPS console. Right-click the policy, click Properties, and then in the policy properties dialog box, click the Settings tab. Ensure that RADIUS Attributes - Standard is selected, and then click Add. In the Add Standard Attribute dialog box, add the Tunnel-Medium-Type, Tunnel-Pvt-Group-ID, and Tunnel-Type attributes. Select RADIUS Attributes - Vendor Specific, and then click Add. In the Add Vendor Specific Attribute dialog box, add the Tunnel-Tag attribute.

James McIllece, Technical Writer

Windows Server User Assistance

Configuring Wired Clients

You can configure wired clients by using the following:

- Group Policy
- Wired XML profiles
- Manual configuration

Configuring Wired Clients Through Group Policy

To configure Wired Network (IEEE 802.3) Policies Group Policy settings, perform the following steps:

1. From a computer that is running Windows Server 2008 and is a member of your Active Directory domain, open the Group Policy Management snap-in.

2. In the console tree, expand Forest, expand Domains, and then click the name of your domain to which your wired clients belong.

3. On the Linked Group Policy Objects pane, right-click the appropriate Group Policy Object. (The default object is Default Domain Policy.) Then click Edit.

4. In the console tree of the Group Policy Management Editor snap-in, expand the Group Policy Object, and then navigate to Computer Configuration\Windows Settings\ Security Settings\System Services. In the details pane, double-click Wired AutoConfig. In the Wired AutoConfig Properties dialog box, select the Define This Policy Setting check box, select Automatic, and then click OK.

5. In the console tree, navigate to Computer Configuration\Windows Settings\Security Settings\Wired Network (IEEE 802.3) Policies.

6. Right-click Wired Network (IEEE 802.3) Policies, and then click Create A New Windows Vista Policy.

7. On the General tab, type a name for the policy and a description. To view help information, press F1.

8. On the Security tab, specify the EAP type, authentication mode, and other settings as needed. To view help information, press F1.

   For EAP-TLS authentication, select Smart Card Or Other Certificate, and then click Properties. In the Smart Card Or Other Certificate Properties dialog box, configure EAP-TLS settings as needed, and then click OK. By default, EAP-TLS uses a registry-based certificate and validates the server certificate.

   For PEAP-MS-CHAP v2, no additional configuration is required. PEAP-MS-CHAP v2 is the default authentication method.

9. Click OK.

The next time your Windows Server 2008 or Windows Vista wired clients update Computer Configuration Group Policy for this Group Policy Object, the wired network settings in the Group Policy Object will be automatically applied. You can manually force an update of an existing Group Policy Object by running the **gpupdate** command at a command prompt. For a new Group Policy Object, you must restart the wired client.

After the wired network settings are applied, the Authentication tab of the properties dialog box of LAN connections in the Network Connections folder will display the message "These settings are managed by your system administrator," and users will not be able to modify settings on the Authentication tab.

Configuring and Deploying Wired Profiles

You can also manually configure wired clients running Windows Vista with a wired network by importing a wired profile in XML format by running the **netsh lan add profile** command. To create an XML-based wired profile, configure a Windows Vista wired client with a wired network that has all the appropriate settings including the authentication method. Then, run the **netsh lan export profile** command to write the wired network profile to an XML file.

Direct from the Source: Controlling Authentication and Supplicant Modes

In Windows XP, we controlled some of the authentication behavior and supplicant behavior with the AuthMode and SupplicantMode registry values. With Windows Vista, we now manage all these behaviors in the profiles themselves so there are no equivalent AuthMode and SupplicantMode values in the registry in Windows Vista. For the supplicant mode in Windows XP, we would change the value to help an 802.1X-capable client initiate authentication to a passive switch. With Windows Vista, the default setting is to initiate all 802.1X authentication attempts, so there is no reason to change this setting in Windows Vista. The AuthMode registry value in Windows XP is used to control the behavior of the computer authentication and primarily to restrict user authentications when appropriate. To change this in Windows Vista, you need to export the appropriate profile and edit the resulting XML output. For a default profile, you should change the following line in the OneX element from:

```
<authMode>machineOrUser</authMode>
to
<authMode>machine</authMode>
```

Clay Seymour, Support Escalation Engineer

Enterprise Platform Support

Manually Configuring Wired Clients

If you have a small number of wired clients, you can manually configure LAN connections for each wired client. For Windows Server 2008 and Windows Vista wired clients, the Authentication tab is enabled through the Wired AutoConfig service. Because the Wired AutoConfig service is not started by default, the Authentication tab for LAN connection does not appear by default. You must use the Services snap-in to start the Wired AutoConfig service and configure it for automatic startup. For Windows XP and Windows Server 2003 wired clients, the Authentication tab is enabled through the Wireless Zero Configuration service, which is started by default.

The following sections describe how to manually configure EAP-TLS and PEAP-MS-CHAP v2 authentication for Windows wired clients.

EAP-TLS To manually configure EAP-TLS authentication on a wired client running Windows Server 2008 or Windows Vista, perform the following steps:

1. In the Network Connections folder, right-click your LAN connection, and then click Properties.

2. Click the Authentication tab, and then click Enable IEEE 802.1X Authentication. In Choose A Network Authentication Method drop-down list, select Smart Card Or Other Certificate, and then click Settings.

3. In the Smart Card Or Other Certificate Properties dialog box, select Use A Certificate On This Computer to use a registry-based user certificate or Use My Smart Card for a smart card–based user certificate.

    If you want to validate the computer certificate of the NPS server, select Validate Server Certificate (recommended and enabled by default). If you want to specify the names of the NPS servers that must perform the TLS authentication, select Connect To These Servers, and then type the names. Click OK twice.

To manually configure EAP-TLS authentication on a wired client running Windows XP with SP2, Windows XP with SP1, or Windows Server 2003, perform the following steps:

1. In the Network Connections folder, obtain properties of the LAN connection.

2. Click the Authentication tab, and then ensure that Enable IEEE 802.1X Authentication For This Network and Smart Card Or Other Certificate EAP type are selected. (These are selected by default.)

3. Click Properties. In the properties dialog box of the Smart Card Or Other Certificate EAP type, to use a registry-based computer and user certificates, select Use A Certificate On This Computer or for a smart card–based user certificate, select Use My Smart Card.

    If you want to validate the computer certificate of the NPS server, select Validate Server Certificate (recommended and enabled by default). If you want to specify the names of the authentication servers that must perform the TLS authentication, select Connect To These Servers, and then type the names. Click OK twice.

PEAP-MS-CHAP v2   To manually configure PEAP-MS-CHAP v2 authentication on a wired client running Windows Server 2008 or Windows Vista, do the following:

1. In the Network Connections folder, right-click your LAN connection, and then click Properties.

2. Click the Authentication tab, and then select the Enable IEEE 802.1X Authentication check box. PEAP-MS-CHAP v2 is the default authentication method. Click OK.

To manually configure PEAP-MS-CHAP v2 authentication on a wired client running Windows XP with SP2, Windows XP with SP1, or Windows Server 2003, perform the following steps:

1. In the Network Connections folder, obtain properties of the LAN connection.

2. Click the Authentication tab, select the Enable IEEE 802.1X Authentication check box, and on the drop-down list, choose Protected EAP (PEAP) as the authentication type.

3. Click Settings. In the Protected EAP Properties dialog box, select Validate Server Certificate to validate the computer certificate of the NPS server (enabled by default). If you want to specify the names of the authentication servers that must perform validation, select Connect To These Servers, and then type the names. In the Select Authentication Method drop-down list, click Secured Password (EAP-MSCHAP v2) (selected by default). Click OK twice.

Ongoing Maintenance

The three general categories of maintenance for an 802.1X-authenticated wired solution are as follows:

- Management of user and computer accounts
- Management of 802.1X-capable switches
- Updating of wired profiles

Managing User and Computer Accounts

When a new user or computer account is created in Active Directory and that user or computer is allowed wired access, add the new account to the appropriate group for wired connections. For example, add the new account to the WiredAccounts security group, which is specified in the network policy for wired connections.

When user or computer accounts are deleted in Active Directory, no additional action is necessary to prevent those user or computer accounts from making wired connections.

As needed, you can create additional universal security groups and network policies to configure wired network access for different sets of users. For example, you can create a global

WiredAccessContractors group and a network policy that allows wired connections to members of the WiredAccessContractors group only during normal business hours or for access to specific intranet resources.

Managing 802.1X-Capable Switches

Once deployed, 802.1X-capable switches do not require a lot of maintenance. Most of the ongoing changes to 802.1X-capable switch configuration are because of wired network capacity management and changes in network infrastructure.

Adding an 802.1X-Capable Switch

To add an 802.1X-capable switch:

1. Follow the deployment steps in "Configuring 802.1X-Capable Switches," earlier in this chapter, to add a new 802.1X-capable switch to your wired network.

2. Add the 802.1X-capable switch as a RADIUS client to your NPS servers.

Removing an 802.1X-Capable Switch

When removing an 802.1X-capable switch, update the configuration of your NPS servers to remove the 802.1X-capable switch as a RADIUS client.

Configuration for Changes in NPS Servers

If the NPS servers change (for example, because of additions or removals of NPS servers on the intranet), you will need to do the following:

1. Ensure that new NPS servers are configured with RADIUS clients corresponding to the 802.1X-capable switches and with the appropriate network policies for wired access.

2. Update the configuration of the 802.1X-capable switches for the new NPS server configuration as needed.

Updating Wired XML Profiles

To update a wired XML profile and import it on your Windows Server 2008 or Windows Vista wired clients, perform the following steps:

1. Create an updated XML profile by running the **netsh lan export profile** command using a Windows Server 2008 or Windows Vista wired client.

2. Execute the **netsh lan add profile** command to import the XML profile on your wired clients through a script or other method.

Troubleshooting

This section describes the following:

- The tools that are provided with Windows Server 2008 and Windows Vista to trouble-shoot wired connections

- How to troubleshoot wired connection problems from the wired client

- How to troubleshoot wired connection problems from the 802.1X-capable switch

- How to troubleshoot wired connection problems from the NPS server

Wired Troubleshooting Tools in Windows

Microsoft provides the following tools to troubleshoot wired connections:

- TCP/IP troubleshooting tools

- The Network Connections folder

- **Netsh lan** commands

- Network Diagnostics Framework support for wired connections

- Wired diagnostics tracing

- NPS authentication and accounting logging

- NPS event logging

- SChannel logging

- SNMP agent

- Reliability and Performance snap-in

- Network Monitor 3.1

TCP/IP Troubleshooting Tools

The Ping, Tracert, and Pathping tools use ICMP Echo and Echo Reply and ICMPv6 Echo Request and Echo Reply messages to verify connectivity, display the path to a destination, and test path integrity. The Route tool can be used to display the IPv4 and IPv6 routing tables. The Nslookup tool can be used to troubleshoot DNS name resolution issues.

The Network Connections Folder

When you double-click on a wired connection in the Network Connections folder, you can view information such as the link speed on the General tab. Click Details to view the TCP/IP configuration.

If the wired adapter is assigned an Automatic Private IP Addressing (APIPA) address in the range 169.254.0.0/16 or the configured alternate IPv4 address, the wired client is connected to the 802.1X-capable switch, but either authentication has failed or the DHCP server is not available. If the authentication fails, TCP/IP performs its normal configuration process. If a DHCP server is not found (either authenticated or not), Windows Vista automatically configures an APIPA address unless there is an alternate address configured.

Netsh Lan Commands

You can run the following **netsh lan** commands to gather information for troubleshooting wired issues:

- **netsh lan show interfaces** Displays information about the installed LAN adapters and whether the devices to which they are connected support 802.1X authentication
- **netsh lan show profiles** Displays the Group Policy and local wired profiles
- **netsh lan show settings** Displays the state of Wired AutoConfig service
- **netsh lan show tracing** Displays the state of wired tracing

To obtain additional information about the diagnostics process, Windows creates a detailed diagnostic log that is separate from the System event log.

To Access the Wired Diagnostics Log

1. In the Event Viewer snap-in, in the tree view, expand Applications And Services Logs\Microsoft\Windows\Wired-AutoConfig.

2. Click Operational.

3. In the contents pane, view the events for the wired diagnostics session.

Generating Microsoft Wired Diagnostics Report and Wired Trace Files

Generating the Microsoft Wired Diagnostics Report is a three-step process: enable tracing, reproduce the connectivity error, and then stop the wired tracing.

When tracing is enabled, it runs silently in the background while the problem is re-created. When the logging is turned off, a process will run that will automatically compile the Microsoft Wired Diagnostics Report.

To Generate a Microsoft Wired Diagnostics Report

1. In the Administrative Tools folder, click Computer Management.

2. In the Computer Management console, expand Reliability and Performance\Data Collector Sets\System\LAN Diagnostics.

3. Right-click LAN Diagnostics, and then click Start.

4. Log off and log back on to the network, or otherwise reproduce the error condition.

5. Return to the Computer Management console and expand Reliability and Performance\ Data Collector Sets\System\LAN Diagnostics, right-click LAN Diagnostics, and then click Stop to stop the wired diagnostic tracing.

6. In Reliability and Performance, expand Reports\System\LAN Diagnostics, and then click Wired to open the top level of the Microsoft Wired Diagnostics Report.

Occasionally, you might need to escalate a wired networking problem to Microsoft or another support specialist in your organization. To perform a detailed analysis, Microsoft or your support specialists need in-depth information about the computer's state and wired components in Windows and their interaction when the problem occurred. You can obtain this information from the wired trace logs that are generated in the Microsoft Wired Diagnostics Report. These are a set of files that contain highly detailed information about specific aspects of wired service-related components.

To Open Wired Trace Logs

1. In the Microsoft Wired Diagnostics Report, expand Wired Networking Troubleshooting Information.

2. Open Wired Trace.

The most useful logs are:

- OneX Trace

- Msmsec Trace

- Wired Auto-Configuration Service Trace

In addition to wired diagnostic tracing, Windows Server 2008 and Windows Vista support tracing for components of the Remote Access Connection Manager and Routing and Remote Access services, which are also used for 802.1X-authenticated wired connections. Like the wired diagnostic tracing, tracing for these components creates information that you can use to troubleshoot complex problems for specific components. The information in these additional tracing files is typically useful only to Microsoft support engineers, who might request that you create trace files for a connection attempt during their investigation of a support issue. You can enable this additional tracing by using the Netsh tool.

To enable and disable tracing for a specific component of the Remote Access Connection Manager and Routing and Remote Access services, the command is:

netsh ras diagnostics set rastracing *component* enabled|disabled

in which *component* is a component in the list of components found in the registry under HKEY_LOCAL_MACHINE\SOFTWARE\Microsoft\Tracing.

To enable tracing for all components, the command is:

netsh ras diagnostics set rastracing * enabled

To disable tracing for all components, the command is:

netsh ras diagnostics set rastracing * disabled

The tracing log files are stored in the *%SystemRoot%*\Tracing folder. The most interesting log files for wired authentication are the following:

- **Svchost_rastls.log**   Records TLS authentication activity
- **Svchost_raschap.log**   Records MS-CHAP v2 authentication activity

NPS Authentication and Accounting Logging

By default, NPS supports the logging of authentication and accounting information for wired connections in local log files. This logging is separate from the events recorded in the Windows Logs\Security event log. You can use the information that is logged to track wired usage and authentication attempts. Authentication and accounting logging is especially useful for troubleshooting network policy issues. For each authentication attempt, the name of the network policy that either accepted or rejected the connection attempt is recorded. You can configure NPS authentication and accounting logging options in the Accounting node in the Network Policy Server snap-in.

The authentication and accounting information is stored in a configurable log file or files stored in the *%SystemRoot%*\System32\LogFiles folder. The log files are saved in Internet Authentication Service (IAS) or database-compatible format, meaning that any database program can read the log file directly for analysis. NPS can also send authentication and accounting information to a Microsoft SQL Server database.

NPS Event Logging

Check the Windows Logs\Security event log on the NPS server for NPS events corresponding to rejected (event ID 6273) or accepted (event ID 6272) connection attempts. NPS event log entries contain a lot of information on the connection attempt, including the name of the connection request policy that matched the connection attempt (the Proxy Policy Name field in the description of the event) and the network policy that accepted or rejected the connection attempt (the Network Policy Name field in the description of the event). NPS event logging for rejected or accepted connection attempts is enabled by default and configured in the Network Policy Server snap-in, in the properties dialog box of an NPS server, on the Service tab.

NPS events can be viewed from the Event Viewer snap-in. Viewing the NPS events in the Windows Logs\Security event log is one of the most useful troubleshooting methods to obtain information about failed authentications.

SChannel Logging

Secure channel (SChannel) logging is the logging of detailed information for SChannel events in the system event log. By default, only SChannel error messages are recorded. To log errors,

warnings, and informational and successful events, set the HKEY_LOCAL_MACHINE\
System\CurrentControlSet\Control\SecurityProviders\SCHANNEL\EventLogging registry
value to 4 (as a DWORD value type). With SChannel logging recording all events, it is possible
to obtain more information about the certificate exchange and validation process on the NPS
server.

SNMP Agent

You can use the Simple Network Management Protocol (SNMP) agent software included with
Windows Server 2008 to monitor status information for your NPS server from an SNMP console. NPS supports the RADIUS Authentication Server MIB (RFC 2619) and the RADIUS
Accounting Server MIB (RFC 2621). Use Features in the Server Manager console to install the
optional SNMP service.

The SNMP agent can be used in conjunction with your existing SNMP-based network management infrastructure to monitor your NPS RADIUS servers or proxies.

Reliability and Performance Snap-In

You can use the Reliability and Performance snap-in to monitor counters, create logs, and set
alerts for specific NPS components and program processes. You can also use charts and
reports to determine how efficiently your server uses NPS and to both identify and troubleshoot potential problems.

You can use the Reliability and Performance snap-in to monitor counters within the following
NPS-related performance objects:

- NPS Accounting Clients
- NPS Accounting Proxy
- NPS Accounting Server
- NPS Authentication Clients
- NPS Authentication Proxy
- NPS Authentication Server
- NPS Policy Engine
- NPS Remote Accounting Servers
- NPS Remote Authentication Servers

More Info   For more information about how to use the Reliability and Performance snap-in,
see Help and Support in Windows Server 2008.

Network Monitor 3.1

You can use Microsoft Network Monitor 3.1 or a commercial packet analyzer (also known as a network sniffer), to capture and view the authentication and data traffic sent on a network. Network Monitor 3.1 includes RADIUS, 802.1X, EAPOL, and EAP parsers. A *parser* is a component included with Network Monitor 3.1 that can separate the fields of a protocol header and display their structure and values. Without a parser, Network Monitor 3.1 displays the hexadecimal bytes of a header, which you must parse manually.

> **On the Disc**   You can link to the download site for Network Monitor from the companion CD-ROM.

For Windows wired client authentications, you can use Network Monitor 3.1 to capture the set of frames exchanged between the wired client computer and the 802.1X-capable switch during the wired authentication process. You can then use Network Monitor 3.1 to view the individual frames and determine why the authentication failed. Network Monitor 3.1 is also useful for capturing the RADIUS messages that are being exchanged between an 802.1X-capable switch and its RADIUS server and for determining the RADIUS attributes of each message.

The proper interpretation of wired traffic with Network Monitor 3.1 requires an in-depth understanding of EAPOL, RADIUS, and other protocols. Network Monitor 3.1 captures can be saved as files and sent to Microsoft support for analysis.

Troubleshooting the Windows Wired Client

When troubleshooting wired connectivity, it is important to first determine the scope of the problem. If all your wired clients are experiencing problems, issues might exist in your authentication infrastructure. If all your wired clients that are connected to a specific switch are experiencing problems, issues might exist in the configuration of the switch or its RADIUS servers. If only specific wired clients are experiencing problems, issues might exist for those individual wired clients.

The following are some common problems with wired connectivity and authentication that are encountered by a Windows wired client:

Unable to Authenticate

- Verify that the user or computer account for the wired client exists, is enabled, and is not locked out (via account properties or remote access account lockout); and that the connection is being attempted during allowed logon times.

- Verify that the connection attempt for the user or computer account matches a network policy. For example, if you are using a group-based network policy, verify that the user or computer account is a member of the group specified in the Windows Groups condition of the appropriate network policy.

■ Verify that the root CA certificates for the issuing CAs of the NPS server certificates are installed in the Trusted Root Certification Authorities Local Computer store on the wired client computer.

■ For an EAP-TLS-based wired client, verify that the computer or user certificate meets the conditions described in the section titled "Validating the Wired Client's Certificate" later in this chapter.

■ For a PEAP-MS-CHAP v2–based wired client, investigate whether the wired client's account password has expired and verify that the Allow Client To Change Password After It Has Expired check box in the EAP MS-CHAP v2 Properties dialog box is selected on the NPS servers.

Unable to Authenticate with a Certificate

■ The most typical cause for this problem is that you do not have either a user or computer certificate installed. Depending on the authentication mode configured through wired Group Policy, you might need to have both installed. Using the Certificates snap-in, verify that you have a computer certificate, a user certificate, or both installed.

■ Another possible cause is that you have certificates installed, but they either cannot be used for wired authentication or they cannot be validated by your NPS servers. For more information, see "Troubleshooting Certificate-Based Validation" later in this chapter.

Troubleshooting the 802.1X-Capable Switch

If you have multiple 802.1X-capable switches and are unable to connect or authenticate with one of them, you might have a problem with that specific switch. This section describes the common troubleshooting tools of 802.1X-capable switches and the common problems of connecting and authenticating with such a switch.

Switch Troubleshooting Tools

Although the set of troubleshooting tools for 802.1X-capable switches varies with each manufacturer and with each model, some of the more common troubleshooting tools include the following:

■ Panel indicators

■ SNMP support

■ Diagnostics

These tools are described in the following sections. Consult your 802.1X-capable switch documentation for information about the set of troubleshooting tools provided with it.

Panel Indicators   Most 802.1X-capable switches have one or more indicators, which are status lights that are visible on the housing of the switch, from which you can obtain a quick assessment of the switch's hardware status. For example, you might see the following:

- An indicator to show that the 802.1X-capable switch has electrical power.

- An indicator to show general operation status. For example, the indicator might show whether the 802.1X-capable switch has any authenticated wired clients.

- An indicator to show wired network traffic. This indicator might blink for each frame sent or received.

- An indicator to show data collisions. If the blinking of this indicator seems excessive, evaluate the performance of the link using the methods suggested by the 802.1X-capable switch vendor.

Alternatively, it might have a liquid crystal display (LCD) panel that shows icons indicating its current status. Consult your 802.1X-capable switch documentation for information about panel indicators and their meaning.

SNMP Support   Many 802.1X-capable switches include a Simple Network Management Protocol (SNMP) agent with support for the following SNMP Management Information Bases (MIBs):

- IEEE 802.1 PAE (Port Access Entity) MIB

- SNMP Management MIB (described in RFC 1157)

- SNMP MIB II (described in RFC 1213)

- Bridge MIB (described in RFC 1286)

- Ethernet Interface MIB (described in RFC 1398)

- IETF Bridge MIB (described in RFC 1493)

- Remote Monitoring (RMON) MIB (described in RFC 1757)

- RADIUS Client Authentication MIB (described in RFC 2618)

The SNMP agent can be used in conjunction with your existing SNMP-based network management infrastructure to configure your 802.1X-capable switches, set trap conditions, and monitor loads on your switches.

Diagnostics   Diagnostics for 802.1X-capable switches can be of the following forms:

- Diagnostic facilities that are available through the switch's main configuration program, such as a Windows program provided on the CD-ROM included with the switch, or a series of Web pages

- Diagnostic facilities that are available through a command-line tool or facility, such as terminal access to the 802.1X-capable switch

The exact diagnostic facilities of an 802.1X-capable switch vary from one switch to another; however, the purpose of the diagnostics is to ensure that the switch is operating properly (from a hardware standpoint) and to validate its current configuration.

Common 802.1X-Capable Switch Problems

The following are common problems with 802.1X-capable switches:

- Clients are unable to authenticate with the switch.
- Clients are unable to communicate beyond the switch.

These common problems are discussed in detail in the following sections.

Inability to Authenticate with the 802.1X-Capable Switch   If you have multiple 802.1X-capable switches, and your wired clients cannot authenticate with any of them, you might have a problem with your authentication infrastructure. See "Troubleshooting the Authentication Infrastructure," later in this chapter, for instructions on how to troubleshoot this situation. If you have multiple 802.1X-capable switches, and the wired clients cannot authenticate with an individual switch, you must troubleshoot the authentication-related configuration of the switch. You must investigate the following areas of authentication configuration:

- 802.1X configuration
- RADIUS configuration

802.1X Configuration   Ensure that the switch has 802.1X authentication enabled.

RADIUS Configuration   The RADIUS configuration consists of the following elements:

- **802.1X-capable switch RADIUS configuration**   Ensure that the 802.1X-capable switch has been properly configured for RADIUS settings as a RADIUS client. The switch should contain the following configuration information:
  - ❑ The IPv4 or IPv6 address of a primary RADIUS server (one of your NPS servers)
  - ❑ The destination UDP ports for RADIUS traffic sent to the primary RADIUS server (UDP port 1812 for RADIUS authentication traffic and UDP port 1813 for RADIUS accounting traffic)
  - ❑ The RADIUS shared secret for a primary RADIUS server
  - ❑ The IPv4 or IPv6 address of a secondary RADIUS server (another of your NPS servers)
  - ❑ The destination UDP ports for RADIUS traffic sent to the secondary RADIUS server
  - ❑ The shared secret for the secondary RADIUS server

- **NPS server reachability** Ensure that the primary and secondary NPS servers are reachable from the 802.1X-capable switch by doing the following:

  ❑ If the switch has a ping facility—the capability to send an Internet Control Message Protocol (ICMP) Echo or an ICMP for IPv6 (ICMPv6) message to an arbitrary unicast IPv4 destination—try pinging the IPv4 or IPv6 addresses of the configured primary and secondary RADIUS servers.

  ❑ If the switch does not have a ping facility, try pinging the IPv4 or IPv6 addresses of the configured primary and secondary RADIUS servers from a network node that is attached to the same subnet as the switch.

If the IPv4-based ping from the network node succeeds and the ping from the 802.1X-capable switch does not, examine the IPv4 configuration of the switch to ensure that it has been configured with the correct IPv4 address, subnet mask, and default gateway for the attached wired subnet. If neither ping works, troubleshoot the lack of IPv4 connectivity between the attached subnet and the NPS servers.

> **Note** The ping test is not necessarily a definitive test of IPv4 reachability. There might be routers in the path between the 802.1X-capable switch and the NPS server that are filtering ICMP traffic, or the NPS servers might be configured with packet filters to discard ICMP traffic.

To ensure that RADIUS traffic is reaching the NPS servers, use a network sniffer such as Network Monitor 3.1 on the NPS servers to capture the RADIUS traffic sent from and to the 802.1X-capable switch during an authentication attempt.

- **NPS server configuration** If RADIUS traffic is reaching the primary and secondary NPS servers, verify that the NPS servers corresponding to the configured primary and secondary RADIUS servers of the 802.1X-capable switch are configured with a RADIUS client that corresponds to the switch, including the following:

  ❑ The IPv4 or IPv6 address of the switch's interface

  ❑ The destination UDP ports for RADIUS traffic sent by the (UDP port 1812 for RADIUS authentication traffic and UDP port 1813 for RADIUS accounting traffic)

  ❑ The shared secret configured at the switch

Check the System event log for authentication failure events corresponding to connection attempts to the switch. To view the failed authentication events, use the Event Viewer to view the events in the System event log with the Source of NPS and the Event ID of 2.

- **IPsec for RADIUS traffic** If you are using IPsec to encrypt the RADIUS traffic sent between the 802.1X-capable switch and the NPS server, check the IPsec settings on both the 802.1X-capable switch and NPS server to ensure that they can successfully negotiate security associations and authenticate each other.

> **More Info**   For more information about how to configure IPsec policies in Windows Server 2008 to provide protection for RADIUS traffic, see Chapter 4, "Windows Firewall with Advanced Security." For more information about how to configure IPsec settings for an 802.1X-capable switch, see your switch's product documentation.

Inability to Communicate Beyond the 802.1X-Capable Switch   The 802.1X-capable switch is a transparent bridge and Layer 2 switching device that forwards packets between the connected wired clients and the wired network to which it is attached. If wired clients can connect and authenticate but cannot reach locations beyond the switch, one or more of the following might be happening:

- **The switch is not forwarding frames as a bridge.**   All transparent bridges support the spanning tree protocol, which is used to prevent loops in a bridged section of the network. The spanning tree protocol uses a series of multicast messages to communicate bridge configuration information and automatically configure bridge interfaces to forward frames or block forwarding to prevent loops. While the spanning tree algorithm is determining forwarding and blocking interfaces, the bridge is not forwarding frames. Check the switch's forwarding status and bridge configuration.

- **The 802.1X-capable switch is not configured with the correct VLAN IDs.**   Many 802.1X-capable switches support VLANs, which are switch ports that are administratively grouped so that they appear on the same link or subnet. Each group is assigned a separate VLAN ID. Verify that the VLAN IDs for your wired clients are correctly configured on the switch and in the NPS network policy. For example, you might use one VLAN ID for authenticated wired clients (that connects them to the organization intranet) and a separate VLAN ID for guest wired clients (that connects them to an alternate subnet or the Internet).

Troubleshooting the Authentication Infrastructure

If you have multiple 802.1X-capable switches and are unable to authenticate with any of them, then you might have a problem with your authentication infrastructure, which consists of your NPS servers, PKI, and Active Directory accounts. In this section, we examine common issues with NPS authentication and authorization and validation of certificate and password-based authentications.

Troubleshooting NPS Authentication and Authorization

To troubleshoot the most common issues with NPS authentication and authorization, verify the following:

- **That the switch can reach the NPS servers**   To test this, try to ping the IP address of the switch's interface on the wired network from each of the NPS servers. Additionally, ensure that IPsec policies, IP packet filters, and other mechanisms that restrict network traffic are not preventing the exchange of RADIUS messages between the switch and its configured NPS servers. RADIUS traffic to the NPS servers uses a source IPv4 or IPv6 address of the switch, a destination IPv4 or IPv6 address of the NPS server, and a UDP destination port of 1812 for authentication messages and UDP destination port 1813 for accounting messages. RADIUS traffic from the NPS servers uses a source IPv4 or IPv6 address of the NPS server, a destination IPv4 or IPv6 address of the switch, and a UDP source port of 1812 for authentication messages and UDP source port 1813 for accounting messages. These examples assume that you are using the RADIUS UDP ports defined in RFC 2865 and 2866 for RADIUS authentication and accounting traffic.

- **That each NPS server/switch pair is configured with a common RADIUS shared secret** The RADIUS shared secret does not necessarily need to be unique, but each member of the pair must have the same RADIUS shared secret. For example, when you copy the NPS configuration from one NPS server to another, the shared secret must be the same for the NPS server/802.1X-capable switch pair for the NPS server that the configuration is being copied from to each server/switch pair for the NPS servers the configuration is being copied to.

- **That the NPS servers can reach a global catalog server and an Active Directory domain controller** The NPS server uses a global catalog server to resolve the user principal name (UPN) of the computer certificate, user certificate, smart card, or the MS-CHAP v2 account name to the distinguished name of the corresponding account in Active Directory. The NPS server uses an Active Directory domain controller to validate the credentials of the computer and user account and obtain account properties to evaluate authorization.

- **That the computer accounts of the NPS servers are members of the RAS and IAS Servers security group for the appropriate domains** Adding the NPS server computer accounts to the RAS and IAS Servers security group for the appropriate domains is normally done during the initial configuration of the NPS server. To add the NPS server computer account to the appropriate domains, you can run the **netsh nps add registeredserver** command. For more information, see Chapter 9.

- **That there are no configured restrictions blocking access** The user or computer account is not locked out, expired, or disabled; or the time the connection is being made corresponds to the permitted logon hours.

- **That the user account has not been locked out by remote access account lockout** Remote access account lockout is an authentication counting and lockout mechanism designed to prevent an online dictionary attack against a user's password. If remote access account lockout is enabled, you can reset account lockout for the account by deleting the HKEY_LOCAL_MACHINE\SYSTEM\CurrentControlSet\ Services\RemoteAccess\Parameters\AccountLockout*DomainName:AccountName* registry value on the NPS server.

- **That the connection is authorized**   For authorization, the parameters of the connection attempt must:

    ❏ Match all the conditions of at least one network policy. If there is no matching policy, all wired authentication requests are rejected.

    ❏ Be granted network access permission through the user account (set to Allow Access), or if the user account has the Control Access Through NPS Network Policy option selected, the policy type of the first matching network policy must be set to Grant Access.

    ❏ Match all the settings of the profile. Verify that the authentication settings of the profile have EAP-TLS or PEAP-MS-CHAP v2 enabled and properly configured.

    ❏ Match all the settings of the dial-in properties of the user or computer account.

    To obtain the name of the network policy that rejected the connection attempt, ensure that NPS event logging is enabled for rejected authentication attempts, and use the Event Viewer to view the events in the Windows Logs\Security event log that have the event ID of 6273. In the text of the event for the connection attempt, look for the network policy name in the Network Policy Name field.

- **That you have not changed the mode of your domain from mixed mode to native mode**   If you have just changed your Active Directory domain from mixed-mode to native-mode, NPS servers can no longer authenticate valid connection requests. You must restart every domain controller in the domain for the change to replicate.

Troubleshooting Certificate-Based Validation

Troubleshooting certificate validation for EAP-TLS authentication consists of verifying the wired client's computer and user certificates and the computer certificates of the NPS servers.

Validating the Wired Client's Certificate   For an NPS server to validate the certificate of a wired client, the following must be true for each certificate in the certificate chain sent by the wired client:

- **The current date is within the validity dates of the certificate.**   When certificates are issued, they are issued with a range of valid dates before which they cannot be used and after which they are considered expired.

- **The certificate has not been revoked.**   Issued certificates can be revoked at any time. Each issuing CA maintains a list of certificates that should no longer be considered valid by publishing an up-to-date certificate revocation list (CRL). The NPS server will first attempt to validate the certificate by using OSCP. If the OSCP validation is successful, the validation verification is satisfied; otherwise, it will then attempt to perform a CRL validation of the user or computer certificate. By default, the NPS server checks all the certificates in the wired client's certificate chain (the series of certificates from the wired client certificate to the root CA) for revocation. If any of the certificates in the chain have been revoked, certificate validation fails. This behavior can be modified by changing the registry settings as described later in this chapter.

To view the CRL distribution points for a certificate in the Certificates snap-in, in the contents pane, double-click the certificate, click the Details tab, and then click the CRL Distribution Points field. To perform a revocation check, the NPS server must be able to reach the CRL distribution points.

The certificate revocation check works only as well as the CRL publishing and distribution system. If the CRL is not updated often, a certificate that has been revoked can still be used and considered valid because the published CRL that the NPS server is checking is out of date. Verify that the CRLs available to the NPS servers have not expired. If the CRLs available to the NPS servers have expired, EAP-TLS authentication fails.

- **The certificate has a valid digital signature.**   CAs digitally sign certificates they issue. The NPS server verifies the digital signature of each certificate in the chain (with the exception of the root CA certificate) by obtaining the public key from the certificate's issuing CA and mathematically validating the digital signature.

  The wired client certificate must also have the Client Authentication certificate purpose (also known as Enhanced Key Usage or EKU) and must contain either a UPN of a valid user account or a Fully Qualified Domain Name (FQDN) of a valid computer account in the Subject Alternative Name field of the certificate.

  To view the EKU for a certificate, in the Certificates snap-in, in the contents pane, double-click the certificate, click the Details tab, and then click the Enhanced Key Usage field. To view the Subject Alternative Name field, click the Subject Alternative Name field.

Finally, to trust the certificate chain offered by the wired client, the NPS server must have the root CA certificate of the issuing CA of the wired client certificate installed in its Trusted Root Certification Authorities Local Computer store.

> **Note**   In addition to performing normal certificate validation, the NPS server verifies that the identity sent in the initial EAP-Response/Identity message is the same as the name in the Subject Alternative Name property of the received certificate. This prevents a malicious user from masquerading as a different user or computer from that specified in the EAP-Response/ Identity message.

For additional requirements for the wired client's certificate, see "Requirements for PKI," earlier in this chapter.

By default, NPS performs certificate revocation checking on the certificate received from the wired clients. You can use the following registry values in HKEY_LOCAL_MACHINE\ SYSTEM\CurrentControlSet\Services\RasMan\PPP\E AP\13 on the NPS server to modify certificate revocation checking behavior:

■ **IgnoreNoRevocationCheck**   When set to 1, NPS accepts EAP-TLS authentications, even when it does not perform or cannot complete a revocation check of the client's certificate chain (excluding the root certificate). Typically, revocation checks fail because the certificate does not include CRL information.

IgnoreNoRevocationCheck is set to 0 (disabled) by default. NPS rejects an EAP-TLS authentication unless it can complete a revocation check of the client's certificate chain (including the root certificate) and verify that none of the certificates has been revoked.

Set IgnoreNoRevocationCheck to 1 to accept EAP-TLS authentications when the certificate does not include CRL distribution points, such as those from third-party CAs.

■ **IgnoreRevocationOffline**   When set to 1, NPS accepts EAP-TLS authentications, even when a server that stores a CRL is not available on the network. IgnoreRevocation-Offline is set to 0 by default. NPS rejects an EAP-TLS authentication unless it can access CRLs and complete a revocation check of their certificate chain and verify that none of the certificates has been revoked. When it cannot connect to a location that stores a CRL, EAP-TLS considers the certificate to have failed the revocation check.

Set IgnoreRevocationOffline to 1 to prevent certificate validation failure due to poor network conditions that inhibit revocation checks from completing successfully.

■ **NoRevocationCheck**   When set to 1, NPS does not perform a revocation check on the wired client's certificate. The revocation check verifies that the wired client's certificate and the certificates in its certificate chain have not been revoked. NoRevocationCheck is set to 0 by default.

■ **NoRootRevocationCheck**   When set to 1, NPS does not perform a revocation check of the wired client's root CA certificate. This entry eliminates only the revocation check of the client's root CA certificate. A revocation check is still performed on the remainder of the wired client's certificate chain. NoRootRevocationCheck is set to 0 by default.

You can use NoRootRevocationCheck to authenticate clients when the root CA certificate does not include CRL distribution points, such as those from third-party CAs. Also, this entry can prevent certification-related delays that occur when a certificate revocation list is offline or is expired.

All these registry values must be added as a DWORD type (a registry data type composed of hexadecimal data with a maximum allotted space of 4 bytes) and set to 0 or 1. The Windows wired client does not use these values.

Validating the NPS Server's Certificate   For the wired client to validate the certificate of the NPS server, the following must be true for each certificate in the certificate chain sent by the NPS server:

■ **The current date must be within the validity dates of the certificate.**   When certificates are issued, they are issued with a range of valid dates before which they cannot be used and after which they are considered expired.

■ **The certificate has a valid digital signature.** CAs digitally sign certificates they issue. The wired client verifies the digital signature of each certificate in the chain, with the exception of the root CA certificate, by obtaining the public key from the certificate's issuing CA and mathematically validating the digital signature.

Additionally, the NPS server computer certificate must have the Server Authentication EKU (object identifier or OID 1.3.6.1.5.5.7.3.1). To view the EKU for a certificate in the Certificates snap-in, double-click the certificate in the contents pane, click the Details tab, and then click the Enhanced Key Usage field.

Finally, to trust the certificate chain offered by the NPS server, the wired client must have the root CA certificate of the issuing CA of the NPS server certificate installed in its Trusted Root Certification Authorities Local Computer store.

For additional requirements for the computer certificate of the NPS server, see "Requirements for PKI," earlier in this chapter.

Notice that the wired client does not perform certificate revocation checking for the certificates in the certificate chain of the NPS server's computer certificate. The assumption is that the wired client does not yet have a connection to the network and therefore cannot access a Web page or other resource for it to be able to check for certificate revocation.

Troubleshooting Password-Based Validation

Troubleshooting password validation with PEAP-MS-CHAP v2 authentication consists of verifying the wired client's user name and password credentials and the computer certificates of the NPS servers.

Validating the Wired Client's Credentials   When you are using PEAP-MS-CHAP v2 for authentication, the name and password as sent by the wired client must match the credentials of a valid account. The successful validation of the MS-CHAP v2 credentials by the NPS server depends on the following:

■ The domain portion of the name must correspond to a domain that is either the domain of the NPS server or a domain that has a two-way trust with the domain of the NPS server.

■ The account portion of the name must correspond to a valid account in the domain.

■ The password must be the correct password for the account.

To verify user account credentials, have the user of the wired client log on to the domain using a computer that is already connected to the network, such as with an unauthenticated wired connection (if possible). This process demonstrates whether the problem is with the user's credentials or if the problem lies in the configuration of the authentication infrastructure.

Validating the NPS Server's Certificate   For the wired client to validate the certificate of the NPS server for PEAP-MS-CHAP v2 authentication, the following must be true for each certificate in the certificate chain sent by the NPS server:

- **The current date must be within the validity dates of the certificate.**   When certificates are issued, they are issued with a valid date range before which they cannot be used and after which they are considered expired.

- **The certificate has a valid digital signature.**   CAs digitally sign certificates they issue. The wired client verifies the digital signature of each certificate in the chain, with the exception of the root CA certificate, by obtaining the public key from the certificate's issuing CA and mathematically validating the digital signature.

Additionally, the NPS server computer certificate must have the Server Authentication EKU (OID 1.3.6.1.5.5.7.3.1). To view the EKU for a certificate in the Certificates snap-in, in the contents pane, double-click the certificate, click the Details tab, and then click the Enhanced Key Usage field.

Finally, to trust the certificate chain offered by the NPS server, the wired client must have the root CA certificate of the issuing CA of the NPS server certificate installed in its Trusted Root Certification Authorities Local Computer store.

Chapter Summary

Deploying a protected wired network solution involves configuration of Active Directory, PKI, Group Policy, and RADIUS elements of a Windows-based authentication infrastructure. Once deployed, ongoing maintenance consists of managing 802.1X-capable switches and their configuration for changes in infrastructure servers and updating and deploying wired profiles. Common problems with wired connections include the inability to connect because of an authentication or authorization failure and the inability to reach intranet resources from the wired client.

Additional Information

For additional information about wired support in Windows Server 2008 and Windows Vista, see the following:

- Windows Server 2008 Technical Library at *http://technet.microsoft.com/windowsserver/2008*

- Windows Server 2008 Help and Support

- "Wired Networking with 802.1X Authentication" (*http://technet.microsoft.com/en-us/network/bb545365.aspx*)

For additional information about Active Directory, see the following:

- Chapter 9, "Authentication Infrastructure"
- *Windows Server 2008 Active Directory Resource Kit* (Microsoft Press, 2008)
- Windows Server 2008 Technical Library at *http://technet.microsoft.com/windowsserver/2008*
- Windows Server 2008 Help and Support

For additional information about PKI, see the following:

- Chapter 9, "Authentication Infrastructure"
- Windows Server 2008 Technical Library at *http://technet.microsoft.com/windowsserver/2008*
- Windows Server 2008 Help and Support
- "Public Key Infrastructure for Windows Server" (*http://www.microsoft.com/pki*)
- *Windows Server 2008 PKI and Certificate Security* by Brian Komar (Microsoft Press, 2008)

For additional information about Group Policy, see the following:

- Chapter 9, "Authentication Infrastructure"
- *Windows Group Policy Resource Kit: Windows Server 2008 and Windows Vista* (Microsoft Press, 2008)
- Windows Server 2008 Technical Library at *http://technet.microsoft.com/windowsserver/2008*
- Windows Server 2008 Help and Support
- "Microsoft Windows Server Group Policy" (*http://www.microsoft.com/gp*)

For additional information about RADIUS and NPS, see the following:

- Chapter 9, "Authentication Infrastructure"
- Windows Server 2008 Technical Library at *http://technet.microsoft.com/windowsserver/2008*
- Windows Server 2008 Help and Support
- "Network Policy Server" (*http://www.microsoft.com/nps*)

For additional information about NAP and 802.1X Enforcement, see the following:

- Chapter 14, "Network Access Protection Overview"
- Chapter 15, "Preparing for Network Access Protection"
- Chapter 17, "802.1X Enforcement"
- Windows Server 2008 Technical Library at *http://technet.microsoft.com/ windowsserver/2008*
- Windows Server 2008 Help and Support
- "Network Access Protection" (*http://www.microsoft.com/nap*)

Chapter 12

Remote Access VPN Connections

This chapter provides information about how to design, deploy, maintain, and troubleshoot remote access virtual private network (VPN) connections. Once deployed, the remote access VPN solution can be modified for the VPN Enforcement method of Network Access Protection (NAP), as described in Chapter 18, "VPN Enforcement."

This chapter assumes that you understand the role of Active Directory, public key infrastructure (PKI), Group Policy, and Remote Authentication Dial-up User Service (RADIUS) elements of a Windows-based authentication infrastructure for network access, as described in Chapter 9, "Authentication Infrastructure."

 More Info This chapter does not describe the deployment planning and steps for dial-up remote access. For more information on those topics, see Windows Server 2008 Help and Support or the Windows Server 2008 Technical Library at *http://technet.microsoft.com/windowsserver/2008*.

Concepts

A VPN is the extension of a private network that encompasses links across shared or public networks such as the Internet. With a VPN, you can send data between two computers across a shared or public network in a manner that emulates a point-to-point private link, such as a long-haul T-Carrier–based wide area network (WAN) link. Virtual private networking is the act of creating and configuring a virtual private network.

To emulate a point-to-point link, data is encapsulated, or wrapped, with a header that provides routing information, which allows the data to traverse the shared or public network to reach its endpoint. To emulate a private link, the data is encrypted for confidentiality. The link in which the private data is encapsulated and encrypted is the VPN connection.

Users working at home or on the road can use VPN connections to establish a remote access connection to an organization's server by using the infrastructure provided by a public network such as the Internet. From the user's perspective, the VPN connection is a point-to-point connection between the computer (the VPN client) and an organization server (the VPN server). The exact infrastructure of the shared or public network is irrelevant because it appears logically as if the data is sent over a dedicated private link.

Organizations can also use VPN connections to establish routed connections with geographically separate offices or with other organizations over a public network such as the Internet while maintaining secure communications. A routed VPN connection across the Internet logically operates as a dedicated WAN link. For more information about routed VPN connections, see Chapter 13, "Site-to-Site VPN Connections."

With both remote access and routed connections, an organization can use VPN connections in place of long-distance dial-up or leased lines for connecting to an Internet service provider (ISP).

There are three types of remote access VPN technologies in the Windows Server 2008 and Windows Vista operating systems:

- **Point-to-Point Tunneling Protocol (PPTP)** PPTP uses Point-to-Point Protocol (PPP) authentication methods for user-level authentication and Microsoft Point-to-Point Encryption (MPPE) for data encryption.

- **Layer Two Tunneling Protocol with Internet Protocol security (L2TP/IPsec)** L2TP/IPsec uses PPP authentication methods for user-level authentication and IPsec for computer-level peer authentication, data authentication, data integrity, and data encryption.

- **Secure Socket Tunneling Protocol (SSTP)** SSTP uses PPP authentication methods for user-level authentication and Hypertext Transfer Protocol (HTTP) encapsulation over a Secure Sockets Layer (SSL) channel (also known as a Transport Layer Security or TLS channel) for data authentication, data integrity, and data encryption.

A remote access client (a single user computer) makes a remote access VPN connection to a private network through a VPN server. The VPN server can provide access to the entire network to which the VPN server is attached. The packets sent from the remote client across the VPN connection originate at the remote access client computer.

During the connection process, the remote access client (the VPN client) authenticates itself to the remote access server (the VPN server), and for authentication methods that support mutual authentication, the server authenticates itself to the client.

Note Using IPsec tunnel mode as a remote access VPN technology is not supported by Windows-based VPN clients or servers because of the lack of an industry standard method of performing user authentication and IP address configuration over an IPsec tunnel. IPsec tunnel mode is described in Requests for Comments (RFCs) 2401, 2402, and 2406.

Direct from the Source: Enhancements to PPTP and L2TP/IPsec

In Windows Server 2008 and Windows Vista, VPN security has been enhanced for the following:

■ **PPTP**   MPPE encryption with a 40-bit and 56-bit key has been disabled by default in Windows Server 2008 and Windows Vista. PPTP connections now support only 128-bit MPPE keys by default. If a Windows Vista–based VPN client is connecting to a Windows Server 2003–based VPN server, or if a Windows XP–based VPN client is connecting to a Windows Server 2008–based VPN server, connections will be successful only if both the VPN client and VPN server are configured to use 128-bit MPPE encryption.

You can configure Windows Server 2008 and Windows Vista to use 40-bit and 56-bit MPPE keys for PPTP connections by setting the HKEY_LOCAL_MACHINE\System\CurrentControlSet\Services\Rasman\Parameters\AllowPPTPWeakCrypto registry value to 1 and then restarting the computer. However, this is not recommended.

■ **L2TP/IPsec**   In L2TP connections, use of IPsec with the Data Encryption Standard (DES) and the Message Digest 5 (MD5) hashed message authentication code (HMAC) in Windows Server 2008 and Windows Vista has been disabled by default. L2TP/IPsec connections now support only 3DES encryption and the Secure Hash Algorithm-1 (SHA1) HMAC by default. If a Windows Vista–based VPN client is connecting to a Windows Server 2003–based VPN server, or if a Windows XP–based VPN client is connecting to a Windows Server 2008–based VPN server, connections will be successful only if both the VPN client and VPN server are configured to use 3DES encryption and the SHA1 HMAC. However, support for the Advanced Encryption Standard (AES) using 128-bit or 256-bit keys has been added.

You can configure Windows Server 2008 and Windows Vista to use DES encryption and the MD5 HMAC for L2TP/IPsec connections by setting the HKEY_LOCAL_MACHINE\System\CurrentControlSet\Services\Rasman\Parameters\AllowL2TPWeakCrypto registry value to 1 and then restarting the computer. However, this is not recommended.

Samir Jain, Lead Program Manager

India Development Center

Components of Windows Remote Access VPNs

Figure 12-1 shows the components of Windows-based remote access VPNs.

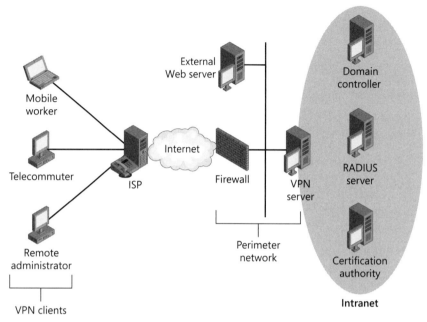

Figure 12-1 Components of Windows-based remote access VPNs

The components are:

- **VPN clients** VPN clients initiate remote access VPN connections to VPN servers and communicate with intranet resources once connected.

- **VPN servers** VPN servers listen for remote access VPN connection attempts, enforce authentication and connection requirements, and route packets between VPN clients and intranet resources.

- **RADIUS servers** RADIUS servers provide centralized authentication and authorization processing and accounting for network access attempts from multiple VPN servers (and other types of access servers).

- **Active Directory domain controllers** Active Directory domain controllers validate user credentials for authentication and provide user account information to evaluate authorization.

- **Certification authorities (CAs)** CAs are part of the PKI, and they issue computer or user certificates to VPN clients and computer certificates to VPN servers and RADIUS servers for computer-level and user-level authentication of VPN connections.

> **More Info**   *Computer certificates* are certificates that are stored in the local computer certificate store and have the appropriate properties to perform PPP-based, SSL-based, or IPsec-based authentication. For more details about certificate requirements for PPP-based or SSL-based authentication, see "Network Access Authentication and Certificates" at *http://go.microsoft.com/fwlink/?LinkID=20016*. For more details about certificate requirements for IPsec-based authentication, see "How IPSec Works" at *http://go.microsoft.com/fwlink/?LinkID=67907*.

Typical users of remote access VPN connections are:

- Laptop users who connect to an intranet to access e-mail and other resources while traveling
- Telecommuters who use the Internet to access intranet resources from home
- Remote administrators who use the Internet to connect to a private network and configure network or application services

Planning and Design Considerations

When deploying a remote access VPN solution, you must consider the following planning and design issues:

- VPN protocols
- Authentication methods
- VPN servers
- Internet infrastructure
- Intranet infrastructure
- Concurrent intranet and Internet access for VPN clients
- Authentication infrastructure
- VPN clients
- PKI
- VPN enforcement with NAP

VPN Protocols

Windows Server 2008 includes support for the following remote access VPN protocols:

- **PPTP**   PPTP uses PPP user authentication and MPPE encryption. When Microsoft Challenge Handshake Authentication Protocol (MS-CHAP v2) or Protected EAP (PEAP)-MS-CHAP v2 is used with strong passwords, PPTP is a secure VPN technology. For certificate-based authentication, Extensible Authentication Protocol-Transport Layer

Security (EAP-TLS) can be used with registry-based certificates or smart cards. PPTP is widely supported, easily deployed, and can be used across most network address translators (NATs). PPTP is supported by the Windows Server 2008, Windows Vista, Windows Server 2003, and Windows XP operating systems.

- **L2TP/IPsec**   L2TP utilizes PPP user authentication and IPsec packet protection. L2TP/IPsec uses certificates (by default) and the IPsec computer-level authentication process to negotiate the protected IPsec session and then PPP-based user authentication to authenticate the user of the VPN client computer. By using IPsec, L2TP/IPsec provides data confidentiality (encryption), data integrity (proof that the data was not modified in transit), and data origin authentication (proof that the data was sent by the authorized user) for each packet. However, L2TP/IPsec requires a PKI to allocate computer certificates to each L2TP/IPsec-based VPN client. L2TP/IPsec is supported by Windows Server 2008, Windows Vista, Windows Server 2003, and Windows XP.

- **SSTP**   SSTP utilizes PPP user authentication and an HTTP-over-SSL channel for encapsulation and encryption. Because SSTP uses SSL traffic (using TCP port 443), SSTP can be used in many different network configurations, such as when VPN clients or servers are behind network address translations (NATs), firewalls, or proxy servers that can block or are not designed to forward PPTP or L2TP/IPsec traffic. SSTP is supported only by Windows Server 2008 and Windows Vista SP1.

Design Choices for VPN Protocols

- When using PEAP-MS-CHAP v2, EAP-MS-CHAP v2, or MS-CHAP v2 for authentication, PPTP does not require a certificate infrastructure to issue certificates to each VPN client.

- PPTP-based VPN connections provide data confidentiality (encryption) for packets. PPTP-based VPN connections do not provide data integrity or data origin authentication.

- By using IPsec, L2TP/IPsec-based VPN connections provide data confidentiality, data integrity, and data origin authentication.

- SSTP-based VPN clients and servers can be behind NATs, firewalls, or Web proxies. However, SSTP does not support VPN clients or servers that are located behind authenticating Web proxies.

- By default, a VPN server running Windows Server 2008 supports all three types of VPN connections simultaneously. You can use PPTP for some remote access VPN connections (for example, from VPN clients that do not have an installed computer certificate), L2TP/IPsec for other remote access VPN connections (for example, from VPN clients that have an installed computer certificate), and SSTP for VPN clients running Windows Vista SP1.

- If you are using a combination of VPN protocols, you can create separate network policies that define different connection settings for PPTP, L2TP/IPsec, or SSTP-based connections.

■ In Windows Server 2008 and Windows Vista, IPv6 traffic can be sent over a PPTP-based VPN connection as IPv4-tunneled traffic or as native IPv6 traffic inside the VPN tunnel. For more information, see "How It Works: IPv6 and VPN Connections" later in this chapter.

■ In Windows Server 2008 and Windows Vista, L2TP/IPsec and SSTP-based VPN connections support IPv6 traffic as IPv4-tunneled traffic, as native IPv6 traffic inside the VPN tunnel, and for VPN connections over IPv6. For more information, see "How It Works: IPv6 and VPN Connections" later in this chapter.

Requirements for VPN Protocols

■ PPTP-based VPN clients can be located behind a NAT if the NAT includes a NAT editor that knows how to properly translate PPTP tunneled data. For example, both the Internet Connection Sharing (ICS) feature of the Network Connections folder and the NAT routing protocol component of Routing and Remote Access include a NAT editor that translates PPTP traffic to and from PPTP clients located behind the NAT. VPN servers cannot be behind a NAT unless there are multiple public IP addresses and there is a one-to-one mapping of a public IP address to the private IP address of the VPN server. If there is only one public address, the NAT must be configured to translate and forward the PPTP tunneled data to the VPN server. Most NATs using a single public IPv4 address, including ICS and the NAT routing protocol component, can be configured to allow inbound traffic based on IPv4 addresses and TCP and UDP ports. However, PPTP tunneled data does not use TCP or UDP headers. Therefore, a VPN server cannot be located behind a computer using ICS or the NAT routing protocol component when using a single public IPv4 address.

■ L2TP/IPsec-based VPN clients or servers cannot be behind a NAT unless both the client and server support IPsec NAT Traversal (NAT-T). IPsec NAT-T is supported by Windows Server 2008, Windows Vista, Windows Server 2003, and Windows XP SP2.

■ L2TP/IPsec supports computer certificates as the default and recommended authentication method for IPsec. Although you can configure a preshared key to authenticate L2TP/IPsec connections, this is not recommended except as a transition authentication method when deploying a PKI. Computer certificate authentication requires a PKI to issue computer certificates to the VPN server computer and all VPN client computers.

■ SSTP is supported only by Windows Server 2008 (as a VPN server or client) and Windows Vista SP1 (as a VPN client).

■ SSTP uses an encrypted SSL channel to protect all data sent across the VPN connection. To create this encrypted channel, the VPN server must have a computer certificate, and the VPN client computer must be able to validate the computer certificate of the VPN server. This means that the VPN clients must have the root CA certificate of the issuing CA of the VPN server's computer certificate installed.

- If you want to send native IPv6 traffic inside the VPN tunnel across a demand-dial VPN connection, you must use L2TP/IPsec. For more information, see "How It Works: IPv6 and VPN Connections."

- If you want to use demand-dial VPN connections across the IPv6 Internet, you must use L2TP/IPsec.

Best Practices for VPN Protocols

- If you already have a PKI in place, use L2TP/IPsec instead of PPTP.

- If you are not using all the VPN protocols, configure the Ports node in the Routing and Remote Access snap-in to set the number of ports for unused VPN protocols to 0.

How It Works: IPv6 and VPN Connections

For VPN connections, Windows Server 2008 and Windows Vista support IPv6 in the following ways:

- IPv4-tunneled IPv6 traffic
- Native IPv6 traffic inside the VPN tunnel
- VPN connections over IPv6

IPv4-Tunneled IPv6 Traffic

In Windows XP and Windows Server 2003, you could send IPv6 traffic over a VPN connection, but only if it was already wrapped in an IPv4 header (IPv4 tunneling). With IPv4-tunneled IPv6 traffic support, a remote access client can create a VPN connection across the IPv4 Internet and then use IPv4-tunneled IPv6 traffic to communicate with IPv6/IPv4 nodes or IPv6 nodes on the intranet.

IPv4-tunneled IPv6 traffic sent over a VPN connection consist of IPv6 packets that are wrapped with an IPv4 header (this is the IPv4 tunneling), which are wrapped with a PPP header and a VPN protocol header (such as PPTP or L2TP/IPsec), which are wrapped with a final IPv4 header to allow the packet to traverse the IPv4 Internet.

PPTP, L2TP/IPsec, and SSTP in Windows Server 2008 and Windows Vista support IPv4-tunneled IPv6 traffic. IPv4-tunneled IPv6 traffic sent over a VPN connection requires Internet Protocol Control Protocol (IPCP) support on the VPN client and VPN server, IPv6 transition technology support on the VPN client, and an IPv6 transition technology infrastructure (such as ISATAP) on the intranet. IPCP is a PPP network control protocol that allows PPP hosts to configure settings for using IPv4 over a PPP link.

Native IPv6 Traffic Inside the VPN Tunnel

Windows Server 2008 and Windows Vista support VPN connections with native IPv6 traffic inside the VPN tunnel. The VPN client creates a VPN connection with a VPN server over the IPv4 Internet and then negotiates the use of IPv6 over the PPP link. IPv6 packets are encapsulated by the VPN protocol inside of the VPN tunnel. With native support for IPv6 traffic inside the VPN tunnel, a remote access client can create a VPN connection across the IPv4 Internet and then use native IPv6 traffic to communicate with IPv6 nodes on the intranet.

Native IPv6 traffic inside the VPN tunnel consists of IPv6 packets that are wrapped with a PPP header and a VPN protocol header, which are wrapped with a final IPv4 header to allow the packet to traverse the IPv4 Internet.

Native IPv6 traffic inside the VPN tunnel requires IPv6 Control Protocol (IPV6CP) support on the VPN client and VPN server, IPv6 routing support on the VPN server, and a native IPv6 routing infrastructure on the intranet. PPTP, L2TP/IPsec, and SSTP in Windows Server 2008 and Windows Vista support native IPv6 traffic inside the VPN tunnel. IPV6CP is a PPP network control protocol that allows PPP hosts to configure settings for using IPv6 over a PPP link.

> **Note**   Windows XP and Windows Server 2003 do not support native IPv6 traffic inside the VPN tunnel.

VPN Connections Over IPv6

Windows Server 2008 and Windows Vista also support VPN connections over IPv6. The VPN client creates a VPN connection with a VPN server over the IPv6 Internet and then negotiates the use of either IPv6 or IPv4 over the PPP link. With VPN connections over IPv6 support, a remote access client can create a VPN connection across the IPv6 Internet and then use either native IPv6 or IPv4 traffic to communicate with nodes on the intranet.

Traffic for VPN connections over IPv6 consist of IPv6 or IPv4 packets that are wrapped with a PPP header and a VPN protocol header, which are wrapped with a final IPv6 header to allow the packet to traverse the IPv6 Internet.

SSTP and L2TP/IPsec in Windows Server 2008 and Window Vista support VPN connections over IPv6. VPN connections over IPv6 require native IPv6 support for VPN protocols on the VPN client and VPN server, IPv6 routing support on the VPN server, and connections to the IPv6 Internet.

Native IPv6 capability for VPN connections, which is the ability to send native IPv6 packets over a VPN connection, is possible with native IPv6 traffic inside the VPN tunnel and with VPN connections over IPv6.

> **Note**   Windows XP and Windows Server 2003 do not support VPN connections over IPv6 or native IPv6 capability for VPN connections.

Authentication Methods

To authenticate the user who is attempting a VPN connection, Windows Server 2008 supports a wide variety of authentication protocols, including the following:

- MS-CHAP v2
- EAP-MS-CHAP v2
- EAP-TLS
- PEAP-MS-CHAP v2
- PEAP-TLS

> **Note** In Windows Server 2008 and Windows Vista, support for the Microsoft Challenge Handshake Authentication Protocol (MS-CHAP and also known as MS-CHAP v1), Shiva Password Authentication Protocol (SPAP), and EAP-Message Digest 5 (EAP-MD5) protocols has been removed because of security considerations.

EAP-TLS and PEAP-TLS are used in conjunction with a PKI and either user certificates or smart cards. With EAP-TLS, the VPN client sends its user certificate for authentication, and the authentication server sends a computer certificate for authentication. By default, the VPN client validates the VPN server's certificate. With PEAP-TLS, the VPN client and authentication server create an encrypted TLS channel, and then the VPN client and authentication server exchange certificates. Both EAP-TLS and PEAP-TLS are much stronger than either PEAP-MS-CHAP v2 or MS-CHAP v2 because they do not rely on passwords. PEAP-TLS is the strongest authentication method because the certificate exchange between the VPN client and the authentication server is encrypted.

In the absence of user certificates or smart cards, use PEAP-MS-CHAP v2, EAP-MS-CHAP v2, or MS-CHAP v2. PEAP-MS-CHAP v2 is recommended over either MS-CHAP v2 or EAP-MS-CHAP v2 because the MS-CHAP v2 exchange of messages is protected with an encrypted TLS channel, making it much more difficult for a malicious user to capture the message exchange and determine the user's password through an offline dictionary attack.

Design Choices for Authentication Protocols

- MS-CHAP v2, EAP-MS-CHAP v2, and PEAP-MS-CHAP v2 are password-based authentication protocols.

- EAP-TLS and PEAP-TLS are certificate-based authentication protocols.

- For L2TP/IPsec-based connections, any user-level authentication protocol can be used because the authentication occurs after the VPN client and VPN server have established an IPsec-protected channel. However, the use of PEAP-MS-CHAP v2, MS-CHAP v2,

EAP-MS-CHAP v2, EAP-TLS, or PEAP-TLS is recommended to provide strong user authentication and mutual authentication with the authentication server.

Requirements for Authentication Protocols

- For encrypted PPTP-based connections, you must use MS-CHAP v2, EAP-MS-CHAP v2, PEAP-MS-CHAP v2, EAP-TLS, or PEAP-TLS. Only these authentication protocols provide a mechanism to generate a per-session initial encryption key that is used by both the VPN client and the VPN server to encrypt PPTP data sent on the VPN connection.

- PEAP-MS-CHAP v2 and EAP-MS-CHAP v2 are supported by VPN clients running Windows Server 2008 and Windows Vista. MS-CHAP v2 is supported by VPN clients running Windows Server 2008, Windows Vista, Windows Server 2003, or Windows XP.

- PEAP-MS-CHAP v2 requires the installation of a computer certificate on the authentication server (either the VPN server or, more typically, a RADIUS server) and the root CA certificate of the issuing CA of the computer certificate on each of the VPN client computers. PEAP-MS-CHAP v2 is supported only by VPN clients running Windows Server 2008 or Windows Vista.

- For SSTP-based connections, you must use MS-CHAP v2, EAP-MS-CHAP v2, PEAP-MS-CHAP v2, EAP-TLS, or PEAP-TLS. Only these authentication protocols provide a mechanism to generate a per-session initial encryption key that is used by both the VPN client and the VPN server to avoid attacks on the SSTP-based VPN connection by malicious users between the VPN client and server.

- To deploy VPN enforcement with NAP, you must use a PEAP-based authentication method.

Best Practices for Authentication Protocols

- Use the strongest authentication scheme that is possible for your remote access VPN configuration. The strongest authentication scheme is the use of PEAP-TLS or EAP-TLS with certificates. Otherwise, use PEAP-MS-CHAP v2, MS-CHAP v2, or EAP-MS-CHAP v2 authentication.

- If you are using smart cards or have a PKI that issues user certificates, use PEAP-TLS or EAP-TLS for your VPN connections. PEAP-TLS is supported by VPN clients running Windows Server 2008 or Windows Vista. EAP-TLS is supported by VPN clients running Windows Server 2008, Windows Vista, Windows Server 2003, or Windows XP.

- If you must use a password-based authentication protocol such as PEAP-MS-CHAP v2, MS-CHAP v2, or EAP-MS-CHAP v2, require the use of strong passwords on your network. Strong passwords are long (longer than eight characters) and contain a mixture of uppercase and lowercase letters, numbers, and punctuation. In an Active Directory domain, use the Computer Configuration\Windows Settings\Security Settings\Account Policies\Password Policy node in Group Policy settings to enforce strong user password requirements.

VPN Servers

A VPN server is a computer running Windows Server 2008 and Routing and Remote Access that does the following:

- Listens for PPTP connection attempts, IPsec negotiations for L2TP connection attempts, and SSL negotiations for SSTP connection attempts

- Requires authentication and authorization of VPN connections before allowing intranet data to flow to and from VPN clients

- Acts as a router forwarding packets between VPN clients and resources on the intranet

A VPN server typically has two or more installed network adapters: one or more network adapters connected to the Internet and one or more network adapters connected to the intranet.

Configuring Routing and Remote Access

When you configure and enable Routing and Remote Access, the Routing and Remote Access Server Setup Wizard prompts you to select the role that the computer will fill. For VPN servers, you should select the Remote Access (Dial-Up Or VPN) configuration option. For more information about the Routing and Remote Access Server Setup Wizard, see "Deploying VPN Servers" later in this chapter. With the Remote Access (Dial-Up Or VPN) option, the Routing and Remote Access server operates in the role of a dial-up or VPN server that supports remote access VPN connections.

When you select the Remote Access (Dial-Up Or VPN) option in the Routing and Remote Access Server Setup Wizard, the following occurs:

1. You are first prompted to specify whether VPN, dial-up, or both types of access are needed.

2. Next, you are prompted to select the network interface that is connected to the Internet. By default, the interface that you select will be automatically configured with IPv4 and IPv6 packet filters that allow only VPN-related traffic. All other traffic is silently discarded.

   For example, you will no longer be able to ping the Internet interface of the VPN server. If you are running other services on the VPN server (such as Internet Information Services), you must manually add packet filters and exceptions for Windows Firewall to allow the traffic to and from the other services.

3. Next, if you have multiple network adapters that are connected to the intranet, you are prompted to select an interface over which DHCP, DNS, and WINS configuration is obtained.

4. Next, you are prompted to decide whether you want to obtain IPv4 addresses to assign to remote access clients by using either DHCP or a specified range of addresses. If you select a specified range of addresses, you are prompted to add the address ranges.

5. Next, you are prompted to specify whether you want to use RADIUS for authentication and accounting of VPN connections. If you select RADIUS, you are prompted to configure primary and alternate RADIUS servers and the RADIUS shared secret.

When you select and configure the Remote Access (Dial-Up Or VPN) option in the Routing and Remote Access Server Setup Wizard, the configuration results are as follows:

- The Routing and Remote Access service is enabled as an IPv4-based remote access server and LAN and demand-dial router, which performs authentication and accounting either locally or through RADIUS. If there is only one network adapter connected to the intranet, that network adapter is automatically selected as the interface from which to obtain DHCP, DNS, and WINS configuration. Otherwise, the network adapter specified in the wizard is selected to obtain DHCP, DNS, and WINS configuration. If specified, the static IPv4 address ranges are configured.

- Depending on the version of Windows Server 2008, up to 128 PPTP ports, 128 L2TP ports, and 128 SSTP ports are created. Each port represents a possible remote access VPN connection. All of them are enabled for both inbound remote access connections and inbound and outbound demand-dial connections (used for site-to-site VPN connections).

- The selected Internet interface is configured with input and output IPv4 and IPv6 packet filters that allow only VPN traffic.

- The DHCP Relay Agent component is added with the Internal interface. The Internal interface is a logical interface that represents the connection to all other authenticated remote access clients. If the VPN server is a DHCP client at the time the wizard is run, the DHCP Relay Agent is automatically configured with the IPv4 address of a DHCP server. Otherwise, you must manually configure the properties of the DHCP Relay Agent with an IPv4 address of a DHCP server on your intranet. IPv4-based remote access clients send a DHCPInform message to obtain additional configuration settings, such as DNS settings and static routes. The DHCP Relay Agent forwards DHCPInform messages between VPN remote access clients and an intranet DHCP server.

- The IGMP component is added and the Internal interface is configured for Internet Group Management Protocol (IGMP) router mode. All other LAN interfaces are configured for IGMP proxy mode. If your intranet is IPv4 multicast-enabled, this allows VPN remote access clients to send and receive IPv4 multicast traffic.

Design Choices for VPN Servers

- The VPN server can be configured to obtain IPv4 addresses from DHCP or from a manually configured set of address ranges (known as *static pools* of addresses). Using

DHCP to obtain IPv4 addresses simplifies configuration; however, you must ensure that the DHCP scope for the subnet to which the intranet connection of the VPN server is attached has enough addresses for all the computers physically connected to the subnet and the maximum number of remote access clients.

If you are configuring a static pool of addresses, there might be additional routing considerations. For more information, see "Configuring Intranet Network Infrastructure" later in this chapter.

- The VPN server can either evaluate authentication and authorization for VPN connections itself or rely on a RADIUS server. When configuring the VPN server, you can choose to use Windows or RADIUS for authentication or accounting.

  When configured to use Windows for authentication and accounting, the VPN server is a member of an Active Directory domain and communicates with an Active Directory domain controller to validate the credentials of the VPN client and obtain the VPN client's user-account dial-in properties. The VPN server uses the user-account properties and locally configured network policies to authorize the VPN connection. The VPN server by default logs VPN connection accounting information in local accounting log files.

  When configured to use RADIUS for authentication and accounting, the VPN server uses a configured RADIUS server to validate the credentials of the VPN client, authorize the connection attempt, and log VPN connection accounting information. In this configuration, the VPN server need not be a member of an Active Directory domain. If the RADIUS server is a computer running Windows Server 2008 and Network Policy Server (NPS), it must be a member of an Active Directory domain.

- The Routing and Remote Access Server Setup Wizard does not automatically enable IPv6 support for remote access VPN connections. For more information, see "Deploying VPN Servers" later in this chapter.

Requirements for VPN Servers

- The VPN server must have a manual TCP/IP (IPv4) configuration for its Internet interface and intranet interfaces. Because of possible default route conflicts, you should manually configure your intranet interfaces with an IPv4 address, subnet mask, DNS servers, and WINS servers. However, do not configure a default gateway on the VPN server's intranet interfaces. It is possible for the VPN server to have a manual TCP/IP configuration and use DHCP to obtain IPv4 addresses that are assigned to VPN clients.

- For VPN connections that use the PEAP-MS-CHAP v2, EAP-TLS, or PEAP-TLS authentication protocols, you must install on the authentication server (either the VPN server or the RADIUS server) a computer certificate that can be validated by the VPN client. You might also need to install the root CA certificate of the issuing CA of the authentication server's computer certificate on your VPN client.

- For SSTP-based VPN connections, you must install on the VPN server a computer certificate that can be validated by the VPN client. You might also need to install the root CA certificate of the issuing CA of the VPN server's computer certificate on your VPN client.

- For L2TP/IPsec-based VPN connections, you must install on the VPN server a computer certificate that can be validated by the VPN client.

- If you configure the VPN server for local authentication or for RADIUS authentication, and the RADIUS server is a computer running NPS, the default network policy named Connections to Microsoft Routing and Remote Access server rejects all types of connection attempts unless the remote access permission of the user account's dial-in properties is set to Allow Access. If you want to use this network policy for your VPN connections, set the policy type to Allow Access. If you want to manage authorization and connection settings for VPN connections by group or by type of connection, you must configure additional NPS policies. For more information, see "Configuring RADIUS Servers" later in this chapter.

Best Practices for VPN Servers

- Determine the connection of the VPN server that will be connected to the Internet. Typical Internet-connected VPN servers have at least two LAN connections: one connected to the Internet (either directly or connected to a perimeter network) and one connected to the organization intranet. To make this distinction easier to see when using the Routing and Remote Access Server Setup Wizard, in the Network Connections folder, rename the connections to a name that describes their purpose or role. For example, rename the connection named "Local Area Connection 2" that is connected to the Internet with the name "Internet."

Internet Infrastructure

For a VPN client to successfully exchange traffic with a VPN server over the Internet, the following must be true:

- The VPN server's DNS name or IP address is reachable.

- The VPN server is reachable.

- VPN traffic is allowed to and from the VPN server.

VPN Server Name Resolvability

In most cases, you will refer to the VPN server by its fully qualified domain name (FQDN) rather than its IPv4 or IPv6 address. You can use an FQDN (for example, vpn.example.microsoft.com) as long as the name can be resolved to an IPv4 or IPv6 address. Therefore, you must ensure that whatever name you are using for your VPN servers when configuring a VPN connection is resolvable to an IPv4 or IPv6 address using Internet-based DNS servers.

When you use names rather than addresses, you can also take advantage of DNS round-robin load balancing if you have multiple VPN servers with the same DNS host name. Within DNS, you can create multiple records that resolve a specific host name to different IPv4 addresses. In this situation, DNS servers send back all the addresses in response to a DNS name query and typically randomize the order of the addresses for successive queries. Because most DNS clients use the first address in the DNS query response, the result is that VPN client connections are, on average, spread across the VPN servers, as long as both VPN servers are available. To ensure availability of the VPN servers, you can use Network Load Balancing.

VPN Server Reachability

To be reachable, the VPN server must be assigned a public IPv4 address or a global IPv6 address to which packets are forwarded by the routing infrastructure of the IPv6 or IPv6 Internet. If you have been assigned a static public IPv4 address or global IPv6 address prefix from an ISP or an Internet registry, this is typically not an issue. In some IPv4 configurations, the VPN server is actually configured with a private IPv4 address and has a published static IPv4 address by which it is known on the Internet. A device between the Internet and the VPN server translates the published and actual IPv4 addresses of the VPN server in packets to and from the VPN server.

Although the routing infrastructure might provide reachability, the VPN server might be unreachable because of the placement of firewalls, packet filtering routers, NATs, security gateways, or other types of devices that prevent packets from either being sent to or received from the VPN server computer.

VPN Servers and Firewall Configuration

There are two approaches to using a firewall with a VPN server:

- **The VPN server is attached directly to the Internet, and the firewall is between the VPN server and the intranet.** In this configuration, the VPN server must be configured with packet filters that allow VPN traffic in and out of its Internet interface only. The firewall can be configured to allow specific types of remote access traffic.

- **The firewall is attached to the Internet, and the VPN server is between the firewall and the intranet.** In this configuration, both the firewall and the VPN server are attached to a subnet known as the *perimeter network* (also known as a *screened subnet*). Both the firewall and the VPN server must be configured with packet filters that allow only VPN traffic to and from the Internet.

For the details of configuring packet filters for the VPN server and the firewall for both of these configurations, see "Firewall Packet Filtering for VPN Traffic" later in this chapter.

Requirements for Internet Infrastructure

■ Ensure that the FQDNs of your VPN servers are resolvable from the Internet by placing either appropriate DNS address (A) or IPv6 address (AAAA) records in your Internet DNS server or the DNS server of your ISP. Test the resolvability by using the Ping tool to ping the name of each of your VPN servers when directly connected to the IPv4 or IPv6 Internet.

Because of packet filtering, the ping command might display the result "Request timed out," but check to ensure that the name specified was resolved by the Ping tool to the proper address. To force the Ping tool to use an IPv4 address, use the **-4** command-line switch. To force the Ping tool to use an IPv6 address, use the **-6** command-line switch. You can also use the Nslookup tool to test name resolution.

■ Ensure that the IPv4 or IPv6 addresses of your VPN servers are reachable from the Internet by using the Ping tool to ping the FQDN or address of your VPN server with a 5-second timeout (using the **-w 5** command-line switch) when directly connected to the Internet. If you see a "Destination unreachable" error message, the VPN server is not reachable.

Best Practices for Internet Infrastructure

Configure packet filtering for PPTP traffic, L2TP traffic, SSTP traffic, or all types of traffic on the appropriate firewall and VPN server interfaces connecting to the Internet and the perimeter network. For more information, see "Firewall Packet Filtering for VPN Traffic" later in this chapter.

Intranet Infrastructure

The intranet infrastructure ensures that the VPN client can exchange packets with nodes on the intranet using the VPN server as an IPv4 or IPv6 router. Without proper intranet infrastructure design, VPN clients might be unable to do the following:

■ Resolve intranet names

■ Obtain an IPv4 address or IPv6 subnet prefix that is reachable from the intranet

■ Reach intranet locations

Intranet Name Resolution

Ensure that each VPN server is configured with the IPv4 or IPv6 addresses of your intranet DNS servers and, if you are using WINS to resolve intranet NetBIOS names, the IPv4 addresses of your intranet WINS servers. The VPN server should be manually configured with DNS and WINS servers.

As part of the PPP connection negotiation process for IPv4, the VPN clients receive IPv4 addresses of DNS and WINS servers. By default, the VPN clients inherit the DNS and WINS server addresses configured on the VPN server. After the PPP connection negotiation is complete, a VPN client running Windows Server 2008, Windows Vista, Windows Server 2003, or Windows XP sends a DHCPInform message to the VPN server. If properly configured, the VPN server forwards the DHCPInform message to a DHCP server, which responds with a DHCPAck message. The VPN server sends the DHCPAck message to the VPN client, which can contain a DNS domain name, additional DNS server addresses for DNS servers (which are queried before the DNS servers configured through the PPP negotiation), and WINS server addresses (which replace the WINS server addresses configured through the PPP negotiation). The relaying of DHCP messages is facilitated by the DHCP Relay Agent routing protocol component of Routing and Remote Access, which is automatically added by the Routing and Remote Access Server Setup Wizard.

If the VPN server is using DHCP to configure its intranet interfaces (not recommended), the VPN server relays the DHCPInform messages to the DHCP server that was in use when the Routing and Remote Access Server Wizard was run. If the VPN server has a static TCP/IP configuration on its intranet interface (recommended), the DHCP Relay Agent routing protocol component must be configured with the IPv4 address of at least one DHCP server on your intranet. You can add DHCP server IPv4 addresses to the DHCP Relay Agent routing protocol component in Routing and Remote Access snap-in from the General tab for the properties of the DHCP Relay Agent item under IPv4 Routing.

To dynamically configure the IPv6 addresses of DNS servers for VPN connections that support native IPv6 traffic, the Windows Vista–based or Windows Server 2008–based VPN client relies on the Router Advertisement message sent by the VPN server after IPV6CP negotiation completes. If the Router Advertisement message has the Other Stateful Configuration flag (the O flag) set, the VPN client sends a DHCPv6 Information-Request message to the VPN server. If the Windows Server 2008 VPN server is properly configured with the DHCPv6 Relay Agent, it will forward the Information-Request message to a DHCPv6 server. The DHCPv6 Reply message is forwarded back to the VPN client and can contain the IPv6 addresses of DNS servers on the intranet.

Requirements for Intranet Name Resolution

- Using the Ping and Net tools, test DNS and WINS name resolution for intranet resources from the VPN server computer. If name resolution does not work from the VPN server, it might not work for VPN clients. Troubleshoot and fix all name resolution problems of the VPN server before testing VPN connections.

- Because the intranet interfaces of the VPN server are manually configured with a TCP/IP configuration, the Routing and Remote Access Server Setup Wizard cannot automatically configure the DHCP Relay Agent routing protocol component. You must manually add the IPv4 address of at least one DHCP server on your intranet to the DHCP Relay

Agent component. If you do not, the VPN server discards DHCPInform messages sent by VPN clients, and the VPN clients do not receive the updated DNS and WINS server addresses or the DNS domain name.

- If you have a single-subnet small office/home office (SOHO) with no DHCP, DNS, or WINS server, you must either configure a DNS server or WINS server to resolve names for computers on the SOHO subnet and VPN clients or enable NetBIOS broadcast name resolution, which enables NetBIOS over TCP/IP name resolution between connected VPN clients and computers on the SOHO network. To enable NetBIOS broadcast name resolution, in the Routing and Remote Access snap-in, in the properties dialog box of a VPN server, on the IPv4 tab, select the Enable Broadcast Name Resolution check box.

- To forward DHCPv6 messages between IPv6-capable VPN clients and a DHCPv6 intranet server, you must add and configure the DHCPv6 Relay Agent routing protocol component. For more information, see "Deploying VPN Servers" later in this chapter.

Best Practices for Intranet Name Resolution   To ensure that VPN clients obtain the most current list of DNS and WINS server IPv4 addresses, manually configure the DHCP Relay Agent component of Routing and Remote Access rather than relying on the VPN server to configure VPN clients with its own DNS and WINS server IPv4 addresses.

VPN Server Routing to the Internet and the Intranet

The VPN server is an IPv4 and IPv6 router that forwards packets between VPN clients and nodes on the intranet. Therefore, it must be configured with the proper set of routes to be able to reach any Internet location (because a VPN client can connect from anywhere on the Internet) and any intranet location. For both IPv4 and IPv6 traffic, the VPN server needs the following:

- A default route that points to a firewall or router directly connected to the Internet. This route makes all the locations on the Internet reachable.

- One or more routes that summarize the addresses used on your intranet and point to a neighboring intranet router. These routes make all the locations on your intranet reachable from the VPN server. Without these routes, all intranet hosts not connected to the same intranet subnet as the VPN server are unreachable.

For a default route that points to the Internet, configure the Internet interface of the VPN server with a default gateway, but do not configure the intranet interfaces with a default gateway. If you configure your intranet interfaces with default gateways, you will have multiple default routes in the IPv4 and IPv6 routing tables of the VPN server. Because of the way that the TCP/IP protocol selects the default route for forwarding default route traffic, having multiple default routes can result in default route traffic being forwarded to the intranet, rather than the Internet, making Internet locations unreachable.

To add intranet routes to the routing table of the VPN server, you can:

- Add IPv4 and IPv6 static routes by using the Routing and Remote Access snap-in. You do not necessarily need to add a route for each subnet in your intranet. At a minimum, you need to add the routes that summarize the IPv4 or IPv6 address space used on your intranet.

  For example, if your intranet uses the private IPv4 address space 10.0.0.0/8 to number its subnets and hosts, you do not need to add a route for each subnet. Just add a route for 10.0.0.0 with the subnet mask 255.0.0.0 that points to a neighboring router on the intranet subnet to which your VPN server is attached.

- If you are using Routing Information Protocol (RIP) in your intranet, you can add and configure the RIP component of the Routing and Remote Access service so that the VPN server participates in the propagation of intranet routing information as a RIP-based router.

If your intranet has only a single subnet, no further configuration is required.

VPN Client Routing to the Intranet

The reachability of VPN clients from the intranet for IPv4 traffic depends on how you configure the VPN server to obtain IPv4 addresses to assign to VPN clients. The IPv4 addresses assigned to VPN clients as they connect can be from either of the following:

- An *on-subnet address range*, which is an address range of the intranet subnet to which the VPN server is attached.

  An on-subnet address range is used whenever the VPN server is configured to use DHCP to obtain IP addresses for VPN clients or when the manually configured pools of IPv4 addresses are within the range of addresses of the attached subnet.

- An *off-subnet address range*, which is an address range that represents a different subnet that is logically attached to the VPN server.

  An off-subnet address range is used whenever the VPN server is manually configured with pools of IPv4 addresses for a separate subnet.

If you are using an on-subnet address range, no additional routing configuration is required because the VPN server acts as an Address Resolution Protocol (ARP) proxy for all packets destined for VPN clients. Routers and hosts on the VPN server subnet forward packets destined to VPN clients to the VPN server, which sends them the appropriate VPN client.

If you are using an off-subnet address range, you must add the route(s) that summarize the off-subnet address range to the intranet routing infrastructure so that traffic destined for VPN clients is forwarded to the VPN server and then sent by the VPN server to the appropriate VPN client. To provide the best summarization of address ranges for routes, choose address ranges that can be expressed using a single prefix and subnet mask.

To add the routes that summarize the off-subnet address range to the routing infrastructure of the intranet, add static routes to a neighboring router of the VPN server for the off-subnet address range that point to the VPN server's intranet interface. Configure the neighboring router to propagate this static route to other routers in the intranet using the dynamic routing protocol used in your intranet.

If your intranet consists of a single subnet, you must either configure each intranet host for persistent route(s) of the off-subnet address range that point to the VPN server's intranet interface or configure each intranet host with the VPN server as its default gateway. Therefore, it is recommended that you use an on-subnet address pool for a SOHO network consisting of a single subnet.

For IPv6-based VPN connections, the subnet prefix assigned to VPN clients in the Router Advertisement message is always for a subnet separate from the subnet to which the VPN server is connected. All the VPN clients are assigned the same subnet prefix, which is always an off-subnet prefix. To make the VPN clients reachable from the intranet, you must add the subnet prefix as a route pointing to the VPN server to your IPv6 routing infrastructure.

Requirements for Intranet Routing Infrastructure

■ Configure the Internet interface of the VPN server with a default gateway, but do *not* configure the intranet interfaces of the VPN server with a default gateway.

■ Add static IPv4 and IPv6 routes that summarize the addresses used in your intranet to the VPN server. Alternatively, if you use RIP for your IPv4 dynamic routing protocol, configure and enable RIP on the VPN server. If you use a routing protocol other than RIP, you might be able to use route redistribution. For example, if you use Interior Gateway Routing Protocol (IGRP), you might configure the VPN server's neighboring intranet router to use RIP on the interface connected to the subnet to which the VPN server is attached and IGRP on all other interfaces.

■ Add the IPv6 subnet prefix for IPv6-capable VPN clients as a route pointing to the VPN server to your IPv6 routing infrastructure.

Best Practices for Intranet Routing Infrastructure

If possible, configure the VPN server with an on-subnet address range either by obtaining IPv4 addresses through DHCP or by manually configuring on-subnet address pools.

Concurrent Intranet and Internet Access for VPN Clients

By default, when a Windows-based VPN client makes a VPN connection, it automatically adds a new default route for the VPN connection and modifies the existing default route to have a higher metric. Adding the new default route means that all Internet locations except the IPv4 address of the VPN server and locations based on other routes are not reachable for the duration of the VPN connection.

To prevent the default route from being created, you can configure the VPN connection to not use the default gateway of the remote network. For VPN connections in the Network Connections folder, do the following:

1. Obtain properties of the Internet Protocol (TCP/IP) or Internet Protocol Version 4 (TCP/IPv4) component from the Networking tab for the properties of the VPN connection.

2. Click Advanced.

3. In the Advanced TCP/IP Settings dialog box, on the General tab, clear the Use Default Gateway On Remote Network check box.

When the Use Default Gateway On Remote Network check box is cleared, a default route is not created when the connection is made. However, a route corresponding to the Internet address class of the assigned IPv4 address is created. For example, if the address assigned during the connection process is 10.0.12.119, the Windows-based VPN client creates a route for the class-based address prefix 10.0.0.0 with the subnet mask 255.0.0.0.

Based on the Use Default Gateway On Remote Network setting, one of the following occurs when the VPN connection is active:

■   Internet locations are reachable and intranet locations are not reachable except those matching the address class of the assigned IP address. (The Use Default Gateway On Remote Network check box is cleared.)

■   All intranet locations are reachable and Internet locations are not reachable except the address of the VPN server and locations available through other routes. (The Use Default Gateway On Remote Network check box is selected.)

For most Internet-connected VPN clients, this behavior does not represent a problem because they are typically engaged in either intranet or Internet communication, not both.

For VPN clients who want concurrent access to intranet and Internet resources when the VPN connection is active (also known as *split tunneling*), you can do one of the following:

■   Select the Use Default Gateway On Remote Network check box (the default setting), and allow Internet access through the organization intranet. Internet traffic between the VPN client and Internet hosts would pass though firewalls or proxy servers as if the VPN client is physically connected to the organization intranet. Although there is an impact on performance, this method allows Internet access to be filtered and monitored according to the organization's network policies while the VPN client is connected to the organization network.

■   If the IPv4 addressing within your intranet is based on a single class-based address prefix, clear the Use Default Gateway On Remote Network check box. An example is when your intranet is using the private IPv4 address prefix 10.0.0.0/8.

- If the IPv4 addressing within your intranet is not based on a single class-based address prefix, you can use the following solutions:

    ❑ The Classless Static Routes DHCP option

    ❑ The Connection Manager Administration Kit

    ❑ A command (.cmd) file on the VPN client

For more information about these methods, see the section "Configuring Concurrent Access to the Internet and Intranet" later in this chapter.

> **Note**   For native IPv6-based VPN clients, the default route is added based on the receipt of the Router Advertisement from the VPN server. If the Use Default Gateway On Remote Network check box is selected for the TCP/IPv6 protocol, the interface metric of the VPN connection—which becomes the metric of the default IPv6 route that uses the VPN connection—is set to a low value so that the default route over the VPN connection has the lowest metric. If the Use Default Gateway On Remote Network check box is cleared, the interface metric of the VPN connection is set to a static value or to an automatic metric, but it is not guaranteed to be lowest. Therefore, the default route over the VPN connection might not have the lowest metric.

Authentication Infrastructure

The authentication infrastructure exists to:

- Authenticate the credentials of VPN clients

- Authorize the VPN connection

- Record the VPN connection creation and termination for accounting purposes

The authentication infrastructure for remote access VPN connections consists of:

- The VPN server computer

- A RADIUS server computer

- A domain controller

- An issuing CA of a PKI (optional)

Using Windows or RADIUS for Authentication

A Windows Server 2008–based VPN server can be configured to use either Windows or RADIUS for authentication or accounting. RADIUS provides a centralized authentication, authorization, and accounting service when you have multiple VPN servers or a mix of heterogeneous dial-up and VPN equipment or other types of access servers such as wireless access points.

When the VPN server uses Windows for authentication, it performs the authentication of the VPN connection by communicating with a domain controller using a protected remote procedure call (RPC) channel and performs authorization of the connection attempt through the dial-in properties of the user account and locally configured network policies. When the VPN server uses RADIUS for authentication, it relies on a RADIUS server to perform both the authentication and authorization.

When the VPN server uses Windows for authentication, it logs VPN connection information in a local log file (*%SystemRoot%*\System32\Logfiles\Logfile.log by default) based on settings configured in the Accounting node in the Network Policy Server snap-in. When the VPN server uses Windows for authentication, it relies on the RADIUS server to record the accounting information.

If you are using RADIUS and a Windows domain as the user account database from which to verify user credentials and obtain dial-in properties, you should use NPS in Windows Server 2008. NPS is a full-featured RADIUS server and proxy that is tightly integrated with Active Directory and Routing and Remote Access.

When NPS is used as the RADIUS server, it does the following:

- NPS performs the authentication of the VPN connection by communicating with a domain controller over a protected RPC channel. NPS performs authorization of the connection attempt through the dial-in properties of the user account and network policies configured on the NPS server.

- NPS by default logs all RADIUS accounting information in a local log file (*%SystemRoot%*\System32\Logfiles\Logfile.log by default) based on settings configured in the Accounting node in the Network Policy Server snap-in.

Best Practices for Authentication Infrastructure

- If you have multiple VPN servers and you want to centralize authentication, authorization, and accounting services, or you have a heterogeneous mixture of network access equipment, use a RADIUS server and configure the VPN server to use RADIUS for authentication and accounting.

- If your user account database is the Active Directory domain service, use NPS as your RADIUS server. See Chapter 9 for additional design and planning considerations for NPS-based RADIUS servers.

- To better manage authorization for remote access VPN connections, create a universal group in Active Directory for VPN access that contains global groups for the user accounts that are allowed to make remote access VPN connections. For example, create a universal group named VPNUsers that contains the global groups based on your organization's regions or departments. Each global group contains allowed user accounts for VPN remote access. When you configure your NPS policies for VPN connections, you specify the VPNUsers group name.

- Whether the VPN server is configured for local or RADIUS–based authentication, use a VPN-specific network policy to authorize VPN connections and specify connection constraints and requirements. For example, use network policies to grant access based on group membership, to require strong encryption, to require the use of specific authentication methods (such as PEAP-MS-CHAP v2 or EAP-TLS), or to limit traffic by using IP packet filtering.

VPN Clients

The VPN client can be any computer that is capable of creating a PPTP connection using MPPE encryption, an L2TP connection using IPsec encryption, or an SSTP connection using SSL encryption. A Windows-based VPN client running Windows Vista, Windows Server 2008, Windows Server 2003, or Windows XP can create PPTP or L2TP/IPsec-based VPN connections. A Windows-based VPN client running Windows Vista SP1 or Windows Server 2008 can create SSTP-based VPN connections.

You can configure VPN connections on the Windows-based VPN client either manually or by using the Connection Manager components available in Windows Server 2008. The exact method for manually configuring VPN connections varies in Windows. The methods for different versions are as follows:

- For a Windows Vista–based or Windows Server 2008–based VPN client, in the Network and Sharing Center, click Connect to a Network. To create a VPN connection, you must specify the IP address or DNS name of the VPN server on the Internet.

- For a Windows XP–based or Windows Server 2003–based VPN client, use the New Connection Wizard in the Network Connections folder.

Connection Manager

When scaling the configuration of VPN connections for an enterprise network, you might encounter the following issues:

- The exact procedure to configure a VPN connection varies depending on the version of Windows running on the client computer.

- To prevent configuration errors, it is preferable to have the IT staff, rather than users, configure the VPN connection.

- A configuration method must be able to scale to hundreds or thousands of client computers in a large organization.

- A VPN connection might need a double-dial configuration, in which a user must obtain a dial-up connection to the Internet before creating a VPN connection with the organization intranet.

The solution to these issues of configuring VPN connections across an enterprise is Connection Manager. Connection Manager consists of the following components:

- Connection Manager client dialer
- Connection Manager Administration Kit
- Connection Point Services

Connection Manager Client Dialer   The Connection Manager (CM) client dialer is software that is installed on each VPN client. It includes advanced features that make it a superset of basic remote access networking. At the same time, the CM client dialer presents a simplified connection experience to the user. It limits the number of configuration options that a user can change, ensuring that the user can always connect successfully. For example, a CM client dialer can:

- Use customized graphics, icons, messages, and help
- Automatically create a dial-up connection before the VPN connection is made
- Run custom actions during various parts of the connection process, such as pre-connect and post-connect actions (executed before or after the dial-up or VPN connection is completed)
- For dial-up connections, select from a list of phone numbers to use, based on physical location

A *customized CM client dialer profile*, also known as a *package*, is a self-extracting executable file that is created by a network administrator using the Connection Manager Administration Kit (CMAK). The CM profile is distributed to VPN users via CD-ROM, e-mail, Web site, or file share. When the user runs the CM profile, it automatically configures the customized dial-up or VPN connection. The CM profile does not require a specific version of Windows; it configures connections for computers running Windows Server 2008, Windows Vista, Windows Server 2003, or Windows XP.

Connection Manager Administration Kit   You create a customized CM profile by using the CMAK. With the CMAK, you can develop client dialer and connection software that allows your users to connect to the network by using only the connection features that you specify for them. The CM profile supports a variety of features that both simplify and enhance implementation of connection support for you and your users, most of which can be incorporated using the CMAK. The CMAK allows you to build CM profiles customizing the CM client dialer so that connection reflects the identity of your organization. It allows you to determine which functions and features you want to include and how the dial-up or VPN connection appears to your users.

Connection Point Services   For dial-up CM profiles, Connection Point Services (CPS) allows you to automatically distribute and update custom phone books. These phone books contain one or more Point of Presence (POP) entries, with each POP supplying a telephone number that provides dial-up access to an intranet, or more commonly, to an Internet access point. The phone books give users complete POP information so that when they travel, they can connect to different Internet access points rather than being restricted to a single POP.

Without the ability to update phone books (a task CPS handles automatically), users would need to contact their organization's technical support staff to be informed of changes in POP information and to reconfigure their client dialer software.

CPS has two components:

- **Phone Book Administrator**   A tool to create and maintain the phone book database and to publish new phone book information to the Phone Book Service.

- **Phone Book Service**   A Microsoft Internet Information Services (IIS) 7.0 extension. A CM profile can be configured to check the Phone Book Service running on a specified IIS server to ensure that it is using the latest phone book. If not, the remote access client automatically downloads a phone book update.

Design Choices for VPN Clients

- If you have a small number of VPN clients, you can perform manual configuration of VPN connections on each computer.

- If you have a large number of VPN clients or they are running different versions of Windows, use the Connection Manager components of Windows Server 2008 to create a CM profile containing customized VPN configuration settings, and for dial-up connections, to maintain the phone book database.

Requirements for VPN Clients

- For L2TP/IPsec connections, you must install a computer certificate on the VPN client computer.

- For the PEAP-TLS or EAP-TLS authentication methods, you must either install a user certificate on the VPN client computer or issue smart cards to your users.

- For SSTP connections, you must ensure that the VPN clients have the root CA certificate of the issuing CA of the VPN server's computer certificate installed.

- For the PEAP-MS-CHAP v2 or PEAP-TLS authentication methods, if your VPN clients are validating the certificate of the authentication server (recommended), you must ensure that the VPN clients have the root CA certificate of the issuing CA of the authentication server's computer certificate installed.

Design Choices for Connection Manager Profiles

- The name of the CM profile should reflect its purpose and use because it will be the name of the connection in the Network Connections folder after it is installed on the VPN client.

- You can merge settings from existing profiles into new profiles. The new profiles inherit the settings of the merged profiles.

- The VPN client computer might need to make a dial-up connection to obtain Internet access before attempting the VPN connection.

- If VPN clients need concurrent access to the Internet and the intranet, you can configure the CM profile to add static routes to the VPN client's routing table for intranet locations. For more information, see "Configuring Concurrent Access to the Internet and Intranet" later in this chapter.

- The CM profile can be configured to automatically configure the VPN client with the Internet Explorer proxy settings for the intranet proxy servers.

- If you need to run programs such as disabling certain services or launching a Windows program (known as *actions*) during various phases of the VPN connection setup, you can configure custom actions. For example, you can configure actions that run before the connection is made (a pre-connect action) or after the connection is made (a post-connect action).

- If you want to specify a custom logon picture for your organization's logo that appears when your users activate the VPN connection, create a bitmap file that is 330 by 140 pixels.

- If you want to specify a custom picture for your organization's logo that appears when your users access the phone book, create a bitmap file that is 114 by 309 pixels.

- If you want to specify a custom program and title bar icons for the VPN connection in the Network and Sharing Center or Network Connections folder, create bitmap files that are 32 by 32 pixels and 16 by 16 pixels, respectively.

- If you want to provide your users with customized help for the VPN connection, create a custom help file in compiled help module (CHM) format.

- You can add files that are installed with the CM profile, such as organization information, support, or troubleshooting tools.

- You must determine how to distribute the CM profile to your users. For more information, see "Distributing Your CM Profiles" later in this chapter.

Requirements for Connection Manager Profiles

- If you have a mixture of VPN clients running Windows Vista, Windows Server 2008, Windows Server 2003, and/or Windows XP, you will need to create separate CM profiles for VPN clients running Window Vista or Windows Server 2008 and for VPN clients running Windows Server 2003 and/or Windows XP.

PKI

To perform certificate-based authentication for L2TP connections and smart card or user certificate–based authentication for VPN connections using PEAP-TLS or EAP-TLS, a PKI must be in place to issue the proper certificates to VPN clients, VPN servers, and RADIUS servers to submit during the authentication process and to validate the certificate being submitted.

For PEAP-MS-CHAP v2–based authentication and SSTP-based VPN connections, a PKI is not required. It is possible to purchase certificates from a third-party certification authority (CA) to install on your authentication server (for PEAP-MS-CHAP v2) or VPN server (for SSTP). You might also need to distribute the root CA and intermediate CA certificates of the third-party computer certificates to your VPN client computers.

Computer Certificates for L2TP/IPsec Connections

When you are using the certificate authentication method for L2TP/IPsec connections, the list of certification authorities (CAs) is not configurable. Instead, each IPsec peer sends a list of root CAs from which it accepts a certificate for authentication. The root CAs in this list correspond to the root CAs that issued computer certificates to the computer. For example, if Computer A is issued computer certificates by root CAs CertAuth1 and CertAuth2, it notifies its IPsec peer that it will accept certificates for authentication from only CertAuth1 and CertAuth2. If the IPsec peer, Computer B, does not have a valid computer certificate issued from either CertAuth1 or CertAuth2, IPsec negotiation fails.

The VPN client must have a valid computer certificate installed that was issued by a CA that follows a valid certificate chain from the issuing CA up to a root CA that the VPN server trusts. Additionally, the VPN server must have a valid computer certificate installed that was issued by a CA that follows a valid certificate chain from the issuing CA up to a root CA that the VPN client trusts.

For example, if the VPN client is issued computer certificates by root CAs CertAuth1 and CertAuth2, it notifies the VPN server during IPsec security negotiation that it will accept certificates for authentication from only CertAuth1 and CertAuth2. If the VPN server does not have a valid computer certificate issued from a CA that follows a certificate chain to either CertAuth1 or CertAuth2, IPsec negotiation fails.

An organization typically has a single root CA and one or multiple issuing CAs of the root CA that issue computer certificates. Because of this, all computers within the organization have both computer certificates from an issuing CA of the single root CA *and* request certificates for authentication from issuing CAs of the same single root CA.

To deploy computer certificates for L2TP/IPsec connections in your organization, perform the following actions:

1. Deploy a PKI.

2. Install a computer certificate on each computer. This is most easily accomplished with Windows Active Directory Certificate Services or Certificate Services installed as an enterprise CA and by configuring Group Policy settings for computer certificate auto-enrollment. For more information, see "Deploying Certificates" later in this chapter.

PKI for Smart Cards

The use of smart cards is the strongest form of user authentication in Windows Server 2008. For remote access VPN connections, you can use smart cards with the EAP-TLS or PEAP-TLS authentication method.

The individual smart cards are distributed to users who have a computer with a smart card reader. To log on to the computer, the user must insert the smart card into the smart card reader and type the smart card personal identification number (PIN). When the user attempts to make a VPN connection, the smart card certificate is sent during the connection negotiation process.

To manually configure EAP-TLS for smart cards on the VPN client:

- The VPN connection must be configured to use EAP with the Smart Card Or Other Certificate EAP type. In the properties dialog box of the Smart Card Or Other Certificate EAP type, select Use My Smart Card.

- For VPN clients running Windows Server 2008, Windows Vista, Windows Server 2003, Windows XP SP2, or Windows XP SP1, if you want to validate the computer certificate of the authentication server, select Validate Server Certificate (enabled by default). If you want to configure the names of the authentication servers, select Connect To These Servers, and then type the server names. To require the server's computer certificate to have been issued a certificate from a specific set of trusted root CAs, in the Trusted Root Certification Authorities section, select the appropriate CAs.

For instructions on configuring the Connection Manager Administration Kit so that EAP-TLS uses smart cards, see "Configuring and Deploying CM Profiles by Using the CMAK" later in this chapter.

EAP is enabled as an authentication type by default, but if it isn't enabled, in the Routing and Remote Access snap-in, in the properties dialog box of the VPN server, on the Security tab, click Authentication Methods to open its dialog box, and then enable EAP.

To configure EAP-TLS authentication in the NPS network policy for remote access VPN connections, in the properties dialog box of the network policy, ensure that EAP is enabled. On the Constraints tab, add the Smart Card Or Other Certificate EAP type to the list of EAP types for the Authentication Methods constraint. If the authentication server has multiple computer certificates installed, configure the properties of the Smart Card Or Other Certificate EAP type, and then select the appropriate computer certificate to submit during EAP-TLS authentication.

PKI for User Certificates

User certificates that are stored in the Windows registry for user authentication can be used in place of smart cards. However, it is not as strong a form of authentication. With smart cards, the user certificate issued during the authentication process is made available only when the user possesses the smart card and has knowledge of the PIN to log on to the computer. With user certificates, the user certificate issued during the authentication process is made available when the user logs on to the computer using a domain-based user name and password.

Just as with smart cards, authentication using user certificates for remote access VPN connections use the EAP-TLS or PEAP-TLS authentication methods.

To deploy user certificates in your organization, perform the following steps:

1. Deploy a PKI.
2. Install a user certificate for each user. This is most easily accomplished with Windows Certificate Services installed as an enterprise CA and configuring Group Policy settings for user certificate autoenrollment. For more information, see "Deploying Certificates" later in this chapter.

When the user attempts a VPN connection, the VPN client computer sends the user certificate during the authentication process.

Requirements for PKI

- For L2TP/IPsec remote access VPN connections using computer certificate authentication for IPsec, you must install computer certificates, also known as *machine certificates*, on each VPN client and VPN server.

  The computer certificate of the VPN client must be valid and verifiable by the VPN server; the VPN server must have a root CA certificate for the CA that issued the computer certificate of the VPN client.

  The computer certificate of the VPN server must be valid and verifiable by the VPN client; the VPN client must have a root CA certificate for the CA that issued the computer certificate of the VPN server.

- To authenticate VPN connections using a smart card or user certificate with EAP-TLS or PEAP-TLS, the VPN client must have a smart card or registry-based user certificate installed, and the authentication server must have a computer certificate installed.

  The smart card or user certificate of the VPN client must be valid and verifiable by the authentication server; the authentication server must have the root CA certificate of the issuing CA of the certificate of the VPN client.

The computer certificate of the authentication server must be verifiable by the VPN client; the VPN client must have the root CA certificate of the issuing CA of the computer certificate of the authentication server.

- To authenticate VPN connections using PEAP-TLS, the authentication server must have a computer certificate installed.

  The computer certificate of the authentication server must be verifiable by the VPN client; the VPN client must have the root CA certificate of the issuing CA for the computer certificate of the authentication server.

- For SSTP-based VPN connections, you must install a computer certificate on the VPN server.

  The computer certificate of the VPN server must be valid and verifiable by the VPN client. The VPN client must have the root CA certificate of the issuing CA of the computer certificate that is installed on the VPN server.

Best Practices for PKI

- For computer certificates for L2TP/IPsec, if you are using a Windows Server 2008 enterprise CA as an issuing CA, use Computer Configuration Group Policy to configure your Active Directory domain for autoenrollment of computer certificates. Each computer that is a member of the domain automatically requests a computer certificate when Computer Configuration Group Policy is updated.

- For registry-based user certificates for EAP-TLS or PEAP-TLS, if you are using a Windows Server 2008 enterprise CA as an issuing CA, use Computer Configuration Group Policy to configure your Active Directory domain for autoenrollment of computer certificates. Each user that successfully logs on to the domain automatically requests a user certificate when User Configuration Group Policy is updated.

VPN Enforcement with NAP

Network Access Protection (NAP) for Windows Server 2008, Windows Vista, and Windows XP with Service Pack 3 provides components and an application programming interface (API) set that help you enforce compliance with health policies for network access or communication. Developers and network administrators can create solutions for validating computers that connect to their networks, can provide needed updates or access to needed resources, and can limit the access of noncompliant computers.

VPN Enforcement is one of the NAP enforcement methods included with Windows Server 2008, Windows Vista, and Windows XP with Service Pack 3. With VPN Enforcement, a VPN-based remote access client must prove that it is compliant with system health requirements before being allowed full access to the intranet. If the VPN client is not compliant with system health requirements, the VPN server places the VPN client on a restricted network containing servers that have resources to bring the VPN client back into compliance. The VPN server enforces the restricted access through IP packet filters that are placed on the VPN connection. After correcting its health state, the VPN client validates its health state again, and if compliant, the IP packet filters on the VPN connection that confine the access to the restricted network are removed.

For VPN Enforcement to work, you must already have a working VPN deployment with Windows Server 2008–based VPN servers that uses a PEAP-based authentication method. For the details of deploying VPN Enforcement after successfully deploying a remote access VPN solution, see Chapter 18, "VPN Enforcement."

Additional Security Considerations

When deploying a remote access VPN solution, you must consider the following additional security considerations:

- Strong link encryption
- Packet filtering on the VPN server
- Firewall packet filtering for VPN traffic
- Multi-use VPN servers
- Preventing traffic routed from VPN clients
- Concurrent access
- Unused VPN protocols

Strong Link Encryption

For encryption, you can use link encryption or both end-to-end encryption and link encryption, described as follows:

- *Link encryption* encrypts the data only on the link between the VPN client and the VPN server across the Internet. For PPTP connections, you must use MPPE in conjunction with MS-CHAP v2, PEAP-MS-CHAP v2, EAP-TLS, or PEAP-TLS authentication. For L2TP/IPsec connections, IPsec provides encryption. For SSTP connections, SSL provides encryption.

- *End-to-end encryption* encrypts the data between the source host and its final destination. You can use IPsec after the VPN connection is made to encrypt data between the VPN client on the Internet and the node on the intranet. For more information about IPsec and end-to-end protection of IP traffic, see Chapter 4, "Windows Firewall with Advanced Security."

To configure the VPN server to require link encryption, select the appropriate encryption strengths for the Encryption settings on the network policy that is used for remote access VPN connections. Do not select the No Encryption check box.

VPN Traffic Packet Filtering on the VPN Server

To prevent the VPN server from sending or receiving any traffic on its Internet interface except VPN traffic (assuming that the VPN server is not hosting other services accessible from the Internet), you must ensure that IPv4 and IPv6 input and output packet filters for PPTP, L2TP/IPsec, and SSTP traffic are configured on the Internet interface of the VPN server. Because a VPN server is an IPv4 and IPv6 router, if the VPN traffic filters are not configured on the Internet interface, the VPN server might forward unwanted Internet traffic to your intranet. These filters are automatically added when you run the Routing and Remote Access Server Setup Wizard using the options described in "Deploying VPN Servers" later in this chapter.

Firewall Packet Filtering for VPN Traffic

It is a common practice to use a firewall to provide protection for intranet hosts, such as a VPN server, from Internet hosts. If you have a firewall, you must configure packet filters on the firewall to allow traffic to and from VPN clients on the Internet and the VPN server.

The following are common configurations of firewalls with a VPN server:

- The VPN server is directly attached to the Internet, and the firewall is between the VPN server and the intranet.

- The firewall is directly attached to the Internet, and the VPN server is between the firewall and the intranet.

- Two firewalls are used—one between the VPN server and the intranet and one between the VPN server and the Internet.

VPN Server in Front of the Firewall

To prevent the VPN server from sending or receiving any traffic on its Internet interface except VPN traffic, you must configure PPTP, L2TP/IPsec, and SSTP input and output filters on the interface that corresponds to the connection to the Internet. Because IPv4 and IPv6 routing is enabled by default on the Internet interface by the Routing and Remote Access Server Setup Wizard, if VPN packet filters are not configured on the Internet interface, traffic received on the Internet interface is forwarded.

When the VPN server is in front of the firewall attached to the Internet, you must add to the Internet interface packet filters that allow only VPN traffic to and from the IPv4 or IPv6 address of the VPN server's Internet interface.

For inbound traffic, the VPN server decrypts the tunneled data and forwards it to the firewall. The firewall in this configuration is acting as a filter for intranet traffic and can prevent specific resources from being accessed, scan data for viruses, and perform intrusion detection, among other functions. Figure 12-2 shows the VPN server in front of the firewall.

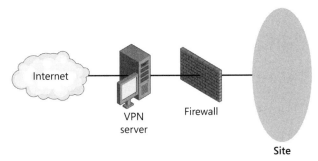

Figure 12-2   The VPN server in front of the firewall

The firewall is configured for the appropriate rules for intranet traffic to and from VPN clients according to your network security policies.

For the Internet interface on the VPN server, you can configure the VPN traffic input and output filters for both IPv4 and IPv6 using the Routing and Remote Access snap-in. These filters are automatically configured when you run the Routing and Remote Access Server Setup Wizard and choose the Remote Access (Dial-up or VPN) configuration, the VPN remote access type, select the correct Internet interface, and leave the Enable Security On The Selected Interface By Setting Up Packet Filters check box on the VPN Connection page selected (enabled by default). Additionally, the Routing and Remote Access Server Setup Wizard will automatically add and enable the same ports in the Windows Firewall.

The following sections describe these filters in detail in case you must manually configure them.

PPTP Traffic Filters   The following are IPv4 input filters (also known as *inbound filters*) for PPTP traffic with the filter action set to Drop All Packets Except Those That Meet The Criteria Below:

- Destination IPv4 address of the VPN server's Internet interface, subnet mask of 255.255.255.255, and TCP destination port of 1723

    This filter allows PPTP tunnel management traffic to the VPN server.

- Destination IPv4 address of the VPN server's Internet interface, subnet mask of 255.255.255.255, and IP Protocol ID of 47

    This filter allows PPTP tunneled data to the VPN server.

- Destination IPv4 address of the VPN server's Internet interface, subnet mask of 255.255.255.255, and TCP [established] source port of 1723

This filter is required only when the VPN server is acting as a calling router in a site-to-site (also known as router-to-router) VPN connection. TCP [established] traffic is accepted only when the VPN server initiated the TCP connection.

The following are IPv4 output filters (also known as *outbound filters*) for PPTP traffic with the filter action set to Drop All Packets Except Those That Meet The Criteria Below:

- Source IPv4 address of the VPN server's Internet interface, subnet mask of 255.255.255.255, and TCP source port of 1723

  This filter allows PPTP tunnel management traffic from the VPN server.

- Source IPv4 address of the VPN server's Internet interface, subnet mask of 255.255.255.255, and IP Protocol ID of 47

  This filter allows PPTP tunneled data from the VPN server.

- Source IPv4 address of the VPN server's Internet interface, subnet mask of 255.255.255.255, and TCP [established] destination port of 1723

  This filter is required only when the VPN server is acting as a VPN client (a calling router) in a site-to-site VPN connection. TCP [established] traffic is sent only when the VPN server initiated the TCP connection.

The following are IPv6 input filters for PPTP traffic with the filter action set to Drop All Packets Except Those That Meet The Criteria Below:

- Destination IPv6 address of the VPN server's Internet interface, prefix length of 128, and TCP destination port of 1723

- Destination IPv6 address of the VPN server's Internet interface, prefix length of 128, and IP Protocol ID of 47

- Destination IPv6 address of the VPN server's Internet interface, prefix length of 128, and TCP [established] source port of 1723

The following are IPv6 output filters for PPTP traffic with the filter action set to Drop All Packets Except Those That Meet The Criteria Below:

- Source IPv6 address of the VPN server's Internet interface, prefix length of 128, and TCP source port of 1723

- Source IPv6 address of the VPN server's Internet interface, prefix length of 128, and IP Protocol ID of 47

- Source IPv6 address of the VPN server's Internet interface, prefix length of 128, and TCP [established] destination port of 1723

L2TP/IPsec Traffic Filters   The following are IPv4 input filters for L2TP/IPsec traffic with the filter action set to Drop All Packets Except Those That Meet The Criteria Below:

- Destination IPv4 address of the VPN server's Internet interface, subnet mask of 255.255.255.255, and UDP destination port of 500

  This filter allows Internet Key Exchange (IKE) traffic to the VPN server.

- Destination IPv4 address of the VPN server's Internet interface, subnet mask of 255.255.255.255, and UDP destination port of 4500

  This filter allows IPsec NAT-T traffic to the VPN server.

- Destination IPv4 address of the VPN server's Internet interface, subnet mask of 255.255.255.255, and UDP destination port of 1701

  This filter allows L2TP traffic to the VPN server.

The following are IPv4 output filters for L2TP/IPsec traffic with the filter action set to Drop All Packets Except Those That Meet The Criteria Below:

- Source IPv4 address of the VPN server's Internet interface, subnet mask of 255.255.255.255, and UDP source port of 500

  This filter allows IKE traffic from the VPN server.

- Source IPv4 address of the VPN server's Internet interface, subnet mask of 255.255.255.255, and UDP source port of 4500.

  This filter allows IPsec NAT-T traffic from the VPN server.

- Source IPv4 address of the VPN server's Internet interface, subnet mask of 255.255.255.255, and UDP source port of 1701

  This filter allows L2TP traffic from the VPN server.

There are no filters required for IPsec Encapsulating Security Protocol (ESP) traffic for the IP protocol of 50. The Routing and Remote Access service filters are applied after the IPsec components remove the ESP header.

The following are IPv6 input filters for L2TP/IPsec traffic with the filter action set to Drop All Packets Except Those That Meet The Criteria Below:

- Destination IPv6 address of the VPN server's Internet interface, prefix length of 128, and UDP destination port of 500

- Destination IPv6 address of the VPN server's Internet interface, prefix length of 128, and UDP destination port of 4500

- Destination IPv6 address of the VPN server's Internet interface, prefix length of 128, and UDP destination port of 1701

The following are IPv6 output filters for L2TP/IPsec traffic with the filter action set to Drop All Packets Except Those That Meet The Criteria Below:

- Source IPv6 address of the VPN server's Internet interface, prefix length of 128, and UDP source port of 500

- Source IPv6 address of the VPN server's Internet interface, prefix length of 128, and UDP source port of 4500

- Source IPv6 address of the VPN server's Internet interface, prefix length of 128, and UDP source port of 1701

SSTP Traffic Filters   The following is an IPv4 input filter for SSTP traffic with the filter action set to Drop All Packets Except Those That Meet The Criteria Below:

- Destination IPv4 address of the VPN server's Internet interface, subnet mask of 255.255.255.255, and TCP destination port of 443

   This filter allows SSTP traffic to the VPN server.

The following is an IPv4 output filter for SSTP traffic with the filter action set to Drop All Packets Except Those That Meet The Criteria Below:

- Source IPv4 address of the VPN server's Internet interface, subnet mask of 255.255.255.255, and TCP source port of 443

   This filter allows SSTP traffic from the VPN server.

The following is an IPv6 input filter for SSTP traffic with the filter action set to Drop All Packets Except Those That Meet The Criteria Below:

- Destination IPv6 address of the VPN server's Internet interface, prefix length of 128, and TCP destination port of 443

The following is an IPv6 output filter for SSTP traffic with the filter action set to Drop All Packets Except Those That Meet The Criteria Below:

- Source IPv6 address of the VPN server's Internet interface, prefix length of 128, and TCP source port of 443

VPN Server Behind the Firewall

In the more common configuration, the firewall is connected to the Internet, and the VPN server is an intranet resource that is connected to the perimeter network, also known as a screened subnet. The perimeter network is a subnet that contains resources that are available to Internet users, such as Web and FTP servers. The VPN server has an interface on both the perimeter network and the intranet. In this approach, the firewall must be configured with input and output filters on its Internet interface that allow the passing of tunnel maintenance traffic and tunneled data to the VPN server. Additional filters can allow the passing of traffic to Web, FTP, and other types of servers on the perimeter network. For an added layer of security, the VPN server should also be configured with VPN traffic packet filters on its perimeter network interface.

The firewall in this configuration is acting as a filter for Internet traffic and can confine the incoming and outgoing traffic to the specific resources on the perimeter network, perform intrusion attempt detection, prevent denial of service attacks, and perform other functions.

Because the firewall does not have the encryption keys for each VPN connection, it can filter only on the plaintext headers of the tunneled data. In other words, all tunneled data passes through the firewall. This is not a security concern, however, because the VPN connection requires an authentication process that prevents unauthorized access beyond the VPN server. Figure 12-3 shows the VPN server behind the firewall on the perimeter network.

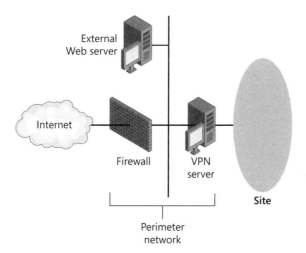

Figure 12-3   The VPN server behind the firewall on the perimeter network

For both the Internet and network perimeter interfaces on the firewall, configure VPN traffic input and output filters by using the firewall's configuration software. Separate input and output packet filters can be configured on the Internet interface and the perimeter network interface.

Tables 12-1 and 12-2 summarize the packet filters that should be configured on the Internet and perimeter network interfaces of the firewall.

Table 12-1 Packet Filters on the Internet Interface

Filter Type	IP Version	VPN Protocol	Traffic
Input	IPv4	PPTP	Destination IPv4 address of the VPN server's perimeter network interface and TCP destination port of 1723 (0x6BB)
Input	IPv4	PPTP	Destination IPv4 address of the VPN server's perimeter network interface and IP Protocol ID of 47 (0x2F)
Input	IPv4	PPTP	Destination IPv4 address of the VPN server's perimeter network interface and TCP source port of 1723 (0x6BB)*
Input	IPv4	L2TP/IPsec	Destination IPv4 address of the VPN server's perimeter network interface and UDP destination port of 500 (0x1F4)
Input	IPv4	L2TP/IPsec	Destination IPv4 address of the VPN server's perimeter network interface and UDP destination port of 4500 (0x1194)
Input	IPv4	L2TP/IPsec	Destination IPv4 address of the VPN server's perimeter network interface and IP Protocol ID of 50 (0x32)
Input	IPv6	L2TP/IPsec	Destination IPv6 address of the VPN server's perimeter network interface and UDP destination port of 500 (0x1F4)
Input	IPv6	L2TP/IPsec	Destination IPv6 address of the VPN server's perimeter network interface and UDP destination port of 4500 (0x1194)
Input	IPv6	L2TP/IPsec	Destination IPv6 address of the VPN server's perimeter network interface and IP Protocol ID of 50 (0x32)
Input	IPv4	SSTP	Destination IPv4 address of the VPN server's perimeter network interface and TCP destination port of 443 (0x1BB)
Input	IPv6	SSTP	Destination IPv6 address of the VPN server's perimeter network interface and TCP destination port of 443 (0x1BB)
Output	IPv4	PPTP	Source IPv4 address of the VPN server's perimeter network interface and TCP source port of 1723 (0x6BB)
Output	IPv4	PPTP	Source IPv4 address of the VPN server's perimeter network interface and IP Protocol ID of 47 (0x2F)
Output	IPv4	PPTP	Source IPv4 address of the VPN server's perimeter network interface and TCP source port of 1723 (0x6BB)*

Table 12-1   Packet Filters on the Internet Interface

Filter Type	IP Version	VPN Protocol	Traffic
Output	IPv4	L2TP/IPsec	Source IPv4 address of the VPN server's perimeter network interface and UDP source port of 500 (0x1F4)
Output	IPv4	L2TP/IPsec	Source IPv4 address of the VPN server's perimeter network interface and UDP source port of 4500 (0x1194)
Output	IPv4	L2TP/IPsec	Source IPv4 address of the VPN server's perimeter network interface and IP Protocol ID of 50 (0x32)
Output	IPv6	L2TP/IPsec	Source IPv6 address of the VPN server's perimeter network interface and UDP source port of 500 (0x1F4)
Output	IPv6	L2TP/IPsec	Source IPv6 address of the VPN server's perimeter network interface and UDP source port of 4500 (0x1194)
Output	IPv6	L2TP/IPsec	Source IPv6 address of the VPN server's perimeter network interface and IP Protocol ID of 50 (0x32)
Output	IPv4	SSTP	Source IPv4 address of the VPN server's perimeter network interface and TCP source port of 443 (0x1BB)
Output	IPv6	SSTP	Source IPv6 address of the VPN server's perimeter network interface and TCP source port of 443 (0x1BB)

*These filters are required only when the VPN server is acting as a calling router in a site-to-site VPN connection. These filters should be used only in conjunction with PPTP packet filters described in "VPN Server in Front of the Firewall" earlier in this chapter and configured on the VPN server's network perimeter interface. By allowing all traffic to the VPN server from TCP port 1723, there exists the possibility of network attacks from sources on the Internet that use this port.

Table 12-2   Packet Filters on the Perimeter Network Interface

Filter Type	IP Version	VPN Protocol	Traffic
Input	IPv4	PPTP	Source IPv4 address of the VPN server's perimeter network interface and TCP source port of 1723 (0x6BB)
Input	IPv4	PPTP	Source IPv4 address of the VPN server's perimeter network interface and IP Protocol ID of 47 (0x2F)
Input	IPv4	PPTP	Source IPv4 address of the VPN server's perimeter network interface and TCP source port of 1723 (0x6BB)*
Input	IPv6	PPTP	Source IPv6 address of the VPN server's perimeter network interface and TCP source port of 1723 (0x6BB)
Input	IPv6	PPTP	Source IPv6 address of the VPN server's perimeter network interface and IP Protocol ID of 47 (0x2F)

Table 12-2   Packet Filters on the Perimeter Network Interface

Filter Type	IP Version	VPN Protocol	Traffic
Input	IPv6	PPTP	Source IPv6 address of the VPN server's perimeter network interface and TCP source port of 1723 (0x6BB)*
Input	IPv4	L2TP/IPsec	Source IPv4 address of the VPN server's perimeter network interface and UDP source port of 500 (0x1F4)
Input	IPv4	L2TP/IPsec	Source IPv4 address of the VPN server's perimeter network interface and UDP source port of 4500 (0x1194)
Input	IPv4	L2TP/IPsec	Source IPv4 address of the VPN server's perimeter network interface and IP Protocol ID of 50 (0x32)
Input	IPv6	L2TP/IPsec	Source IPv6 address of the VPN server's perimeter network interface and UDP source port of 500 (0x1F4)
Input	IPv6	L2TP/IPsec	Source IPv6 address of the VPN server's perimeter network interface and UDP source port of 4500 (0x1194)
Input	IPv6	L2TP/IPsec	Source IPv6 address of the VPN server's perimeter network interface and IP Protocol ID of 50 (0x32)
Input	IPv4	SSTP	Source IPv4 address of the VPN server's perimeter network interface and TCP source port of 443 (0x1BB)
Input	IPv6	SSTP	Source IPv6 address of the VPN server's perimeter network interface and TCP source port of 443 (0x1BB)
Output	IPv4	PPTP	Destination IPv4 address of the VPN server's perimeter network interface and TCP destination port of 1723 (0x6BB)
Output	IPv4	PPTP	Destination IPv4 address of the VPN server's perimeter network interface and IP Protocol ID of 47 (0x2F)
Output	IPv4	PPTP	Destination IPv4 address of the VPN server's perimeter network interface and TCP destination port of 1723 (0x6BB)*
Output	IPv6	PPTP	Destination IPv6 address of the VPN server's perimeter network interface and TCP destination port of 1723 (0x6BB)
Output	IPv6	PPTP	Destination IPv6 address of the VPN server's perimeter network interface and IP Protocol ID of 47 (0x2F)
Output	IPv6	PPTP	Destination IPv6 address of the VPN server's perimeter network interface and TCP destination port of 1723 (0x6BB)*

Table 12-2   Packet Filters on the Perimeter Network Interface

Filter Type	IP Version	VPN Protocol	Traffic
Output	IPv4	L2TP/IPsec	Destination IPv4 address of the VPN server's perimeter network interface and UDP destination port of 500 (0x1F4)
Output	IPv4	L2TP/IPsec	Destination IPv4 address of the VPN server's perimeter network interface and UDP destination port of 4500 (0x1194)
Output	IPv4	L2TP/IPsec	Destination IPv4 address of the VPN server's perimeter network interface and IP Protocol ID of 50 (0x32)
Output	IPv6	L2TP/IPsec	Destination IPv6 address of the VPN server's perimeter network interface and UDP destination port of 500 (0x1F4)
Output	IPv6	L2TP/IPsec	Destination IPv6 address of the VPN server's perimeter network interface and UDP destination port of 4500 (0x1194)
Output	IPv6	L2TP/IPsec	Destination IPv6 address of the VPN server's perimeter network interface and IP Protocol ID of 50 (0x32)
Output	IPv4	SSTP	Destination IPv4 address of the VPN server's perimeter network interface and TCP destination port of 443 (0x1BB)
Output	IPv6	SSTP	Destination IPv6 address of the VPN server's perimeter network interface and TCP destination port of 443 (0x1BB)

*These filters are required only when the VPN server is acting as a calling router in a site-to-site VPN connection. These filters should be used only in conjunction with PPTP packet filters described in "VPN Server in Front of the Firewall" earlier in this chapter and configured on the VPN server's network perimeter interface. By allowing all traffic to the VPN server from TCP port 1723, there exists the possibility of network attacks from sources on the Internet that use this port.

There are no filters required for L2TP traffic at the UDP port of 1701. All L2TP traffic at the firewall, including tunnel maintenance and tunneled data, is encrypted as an IPsec ESP payload.

There are no IPv6 filters for PPTP traffic because Routing and Remote Access does not support IPv6 over PPTP connections.

VPN Server Between Two Firewalls

Another configuration is when the VPN server computer in placed on the perimeter network between two firewalls. The Internet firewall, which is the firewall between the Internet and the VPN server, filters all Internet traffic from all Internet clients. The intranet firewall, which is the firewall between the VPN server and the intranet, filters intranet traffic from VPN clients. Figure 12-4 shows the VPN server between two firewalls on the perimeter network.

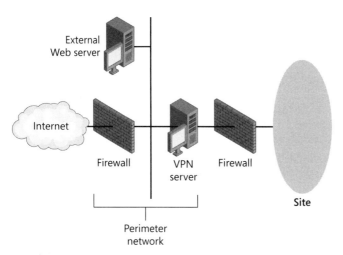

Figure 12-4   The VPN server between two firewalls on the perimeter network

In this configuration, you should do the following:

- Configure your Internet firewall and VPN server with the packet filters as described in "VPN Server Behind the Firewall" earlier in this chapter.

- Configure your intranet firewall for the appropriate rules for intranet traffic to and from VPN clients according to your network security policies.

Multi-Use VPN Servers

Because of the routes that are automatically created on VPN remote access clients, it is possible for the VPN client to send some unencrypted traffic to the VPN server rather than through the encrypted tunnel of the VPN connection. For example, the VPN client might connect to other services running on the VPN server without sending the traffic across the VPN connection. Only traffic that is destined to the public IP address of the VPN server is sent in the clear. If traffic from the client uses the IPv4 address of the Internal interface of the VPN server, however, it will be encrypted.

When a remote access VPN client creates a VPN connection with a VPN server, it creates a series of routes in the IPv4 routing table on the VPN client, including the following:

- **A default route that uses the VPN connection**   The new default route for the VPN connection effectively replaces the existing default route for the duration of the connection. After the connection is made, all traffic that does not match an address on the directly connected network or the address of the VPN server is sent encrypted over the VPN connection.

- **A host route to the VPN server's Internet IPv4 address**   The host route for the address of the VPN server is created so that the VPN server is reachable. If the host route is not present, VPN traffic to the VPN server cannot be sent.

The result of having the host route for the VPN server is that all traffic that is sent to applications or services running on the VPN server to the VPN server's Internet IPv4 address is not sent across the VPN connection but is instead sent unencrypted across the Internet.

For example, when a remote access VPN client creates a VPN connection with a VPN server and then accesses a shared file on the VPN server computer using the VPN server's Internet address, that traffic is not sent using the VPN connection. The file sharing traffic is sent in plaintext over the Internet.

Additionally, if packet filters that allow VPN connection traffic only on the Internet interface are configured on the VPN server, all other traffic sent to the VPN server is discarded. All attempts to connect to applications or services running on the VPN server will fail because traffic attempting to connect to those services is not sent over the VPN connection.

The IPv4 address that is used by the VPN client to access services running on the VPN server depends on the way that the name of the VPN server is resolved. Typical users and applications refer to network resources using names rather than IPv4 addresses. The name must be resolved to an IPv4 address using either DNS or WINS. If the intranet DNS and WINS infrastructures do not contain a record mapping the name of the VPN server to the public IPv4 address of the VPN server's interface on the Internet, traffic to services running on the VPN server will always be sent across the VPN connection.

To prevent the VPN server from registering the public IPv4 address of its Internet interface in the intranet DNS, do the following:

1. In the Network Connections folder, obtain properties of the Internet Protocol Version 4 (TCP/IPv4) component of the Internet connection.

2. On the General tab, click Advanced.

3. In the Advanced TCP/IP Settings dialog box, on the DNS tab, clear the Register This Connection's Addresses In DNS check box, and then click OK three times.

If you are using NetBIOS over TCP/IP on your intranet, to prevent the VPN server from registering the public IPv4 address of its Internet interface with intranet WINS servers, do the following:

1. In the Network Connections folder, obtain properties of the Internet Protocol Version 4 (TCP/IPv4) component of the Internet connection.

2. On the General tab, click Advanced.

3. In the Advanced TCP/IP Settings dialog box, on the WINS tab, click Disable NetBIOS Over TCP/IP, and then click OK three times.

Before the VPN connection is made, the VPN client uses the Internet DNS infrastructure to resolve the name of the VPN server computer to its public IPv4 addresses. After the VPN connection is made, assuming that intranet DNS and WINS servers are configured either during the PPP connection process or through the relaying of the DHCPInform message, the VPN client uses the intranet DNS and WINS infrastructures to resolve the name of the VPN server computer to its intranet IPv4 addresses.

Blocking Traffic Routed from VPN Clients

After a VPN client successfully establishes a VPN connection, by default, any packet sent over the connection is received by the VPN server and forwarded. Packets sent over the connection can include:

- Packets originated by the VPN client computer
- Packets forwarded by the VPN client computer that are received from other computers

When the client computer makes the VPN connection, it creates by default a default route so that all traffic that matches the default route is sent over the VPN connection. If other computers are forwarding traffic to the VPN client, treating the VPN client computer as a router, that traffic is also forwarded across the VPN connection. This is a security problem because the VPN server has not authenticated the computer that is forwarding its traffic to the VPN client computer. The computer forwarding traffic to the VPN client computer has the same ability to send packets to the intranet as the authenticated VPN client computer.

To prevent the VPN server from forwarding traffic across the VPN connection for computers other than authenticated VPN client computers, configure IPv4 input packet filters on the network policy that is used for your VPN connections to discard all traffic except that originating from VPN clients. The default network policy named Connections to Microsoft Routing and Remote Access Server has a single IPv4 input filter with the filter action to Permit Only The Packets Listed Below and with the settings listed in Table 12-3.

Table 12-3 Input Filter Settings

IP Packet Filter Field	Setting
Source Address	User's Address
Source Network Mask	User's Mask
Destination Address	Any
Destination Mask	Any
Protocol	Any

Note Although the Routing and Remote Access snap-in displays User's Address and User's Mask, the actual filter that is created for each remote access client is for the client's assigned IPv4 address and a subnet mask of 255.255.255.255.

With this IPv4 input packet filter, the VPN server discards all traffic sent across the VPN connection except traffic that originates from VPN clients.

Concurrent Access

When a VPN client computer has concurrent access to both the Internet and your intranet and has routes that allow reachability to both networks, the possibility exists that a malicious Internet user might use the connected VPN client computer to reach the private intranet through the authenticated VPN connection. This is possible if the VPN client computer has IPv4 routing enabled. IPv4 routing can be manually enabled on Windows-based computers by setting the HKEY_LOCAL_MACHINE\SYSTEM\CurrentControlSet\Services\Tcpip \Parameters\IPEnableRouter registry entry to **1** (data type is REG_DWORD).

If your VPN clients must use concurrent access, you can help block unwanted traffic from the Internet by doing the following:

- Use an IPv4 packet filter on your network policies for VPN connections to discard inbound traffic on the VPN connection that has not been sent from the VPN client. The default network policy named Connections To Microsoft Routing And Remote Access Server has this IPv4 packet filter configured by default.

- Use the Network Access Protection feature in Windows Server 2008, Windows Vista, and Windows XP with Service Pack 3 to check whether connecting VPN clients have IPv4 routing enabled. If they do, do not allow unlimited remote access until it has been disabled.

Unused VPN Protocols

If you not using all the VPN protocols, configure the Ports node in the Routing and Remote Access snap-in to set the number of ports for unused VPN protocols to 0. This prevents connections to the VPN server through protocols other than those being used for remote access VPN connections.

Deploying VPN-Based Remote Access

To deploy VPN-based remote access by using Windows Server 2008, take the following steps:

- Deploy certificates.
- Configure Internet infrastructure.
- Configure RADIUS servers.
- Deploy VPN servers.
- Configure intranet infrastructure.
- Deploy VPN clients.

Deploying Certificates

You must deploy certificates if you are using the following:

- **L2TP/IPsec connections with certificate authentication** Each VPN client computer and VPN server requires a computer certificate.

  The Routing and Remote Access service supports the configuration of a preshared key for IPsec authentication of L2TP/IPsec connections. In the Routing and Remote Access snap-in, in the properties dialog box of a VPN server, on the Security tab, you can enable a custom IPsec policy and type the preshared key. VPN clients running Windows Server 2008, Windows Vista, Windows XP, or Windows Server 2003 also support the configuration of an IPsec preshared key. (In the properties dialog box of a VPN connection, on the Security tab, click IPsec Settings.) However, preshared key authentication for L2TP/IPsec connections is a weak form of authentication and is not recommended.

- **EAP-TLS or PEAP-TLS authentication with either smart cards or registry-based user certificates** Each VPN client computer needs either a smart card or a user certificate, and each authentication server needs a computer certificate.

  It is possible to configure the VPN clients so that they do not validate the certificate of the authentication server, in which case computer certificates would not be required on the authentication servers. However, having the VPN clients validate the certificate of the authentication server is recommended for mutual authentication of the VPN client and authentication server, which helps prevent the VPN client from authenticating with an impersonating authentication server.

- **PEAP-MS-CHAP v2 authentication** Each authentication server needs a computer certificate, and each VPN client needs the certificate chain of the authentication server's computer certificate installed.

  It is possible to configure the VPN clients so that they do not validate the certificate of the authentication server, in which case computer certificates on the authentication servers and the root CA certificate of the issuing CA on the VPN client is not required. However, having the VPN clients validate the certificate of the authentication server is recommended for mutual authentication of the VPN client and authentication server.

- **SSTP connections** Each VPN server needs a computer certificate, and each VPN client needs the root CA certificate of the issuing CA of the VPN server's computer certificate.

  The VPN server computer certificate can have the Server Authentication or All Purpose usage in the Enhanced Key Usage (EKU) property of the certificate. The computer certificate should be valid, not expired, and have a certification revocation list (CRL) distribution point that is accessible from the Internet. The VPN client verifies that the computer certificate has not been revoked during the SSL authentication by checking the CRL at the distribution point stored in the computer certificate. Certificate revocation can also be checked by using the Online Certificate Status Protocol (OCSP), which uses HTTP to return a definitive digitally signed response of a certificate's status.

Additionally, the name of the Subject property of the VPN server's computer certificate must match the name of the VPN server in the properties dialog box of the VPN connection in the Network Connections folder on the VPN client. This name must match whether you are using DNS host names, IPv4 addresses, or IPv6 addresses for the VPN server.

Deploying Computer Certificates

To install a computer certificate, a PKI must be present to issue certificates. Once the PKI is in place, you can install a computer certificate on VPN clients, VPN servers, or authentication servers in the following ways:

- By configuring autoenrollment of computer certificates to computers in an Active Directory domain
- By using the Certificates snap-in to request a computer certificate
- By using the Certificates snap-in to import a computer certificate
- By requesting a certificate over the Web
- By executing a CAPICOM script that requests a computer certificate

For more information, see "Deploying PKI" in Chapter 9.

Deploying Root CA Certificates

You might need to deploy root CA certificates under the following circumstances:

- You are using PEAP-MS-CHAP v2 authentication.
- You are using SSTP connections.

Root CA Certificates for PEAP-MS-CHAP v2   If you use PEAP-MS-CHAP v2 authentication, you might need to install the root CA certificates on your VPN clients for the computer certificate that your authentication servers (the VPN servers or the RADIUS servers) have been configured to use. If the root CA certificate of the issuer of the computer certificates that are installed on the authentication servers is already installed as a root CA certificate on your VPN clients, no other configuration is necessary. For example, if your root CA is a Windows Server 2008–based or Windows Server 2003–based online root enterprise CA, the root CA certificate is automatically installed on each domain member computer through Group Policy.

To verify whether the correct root CA certificate is installed on your VPN clients, you must:

1. Determine the root CA from the computer certificates installed on the authentication servers
2. Determine whether a certificate for the root CA is installed on your VPN clients

To Determine the Root CA from the Computer Certificates Installed on the Authentication Servers

1. In the console tree of the Certificates snap-in for the authentication server computer account, expand Certificates (Local Computer or *Computername*), expand Personal, and then click Certificates.

2. In the details pane, double-click the computer certificate used for PEAP-MS-CHAP v2 authentication.

3. On the Certification Path tab for the properties of the certificate, note the name at the top of the certification path. This is the name of the root CA.

To Determine Whether a Certificate for the Root CA Is Installed on Your VPN Client

1. In the console tree of the Certificates snap-in for the VPN client computer account, expand Certificates (Local Computer or *Computername*), expand Trusted Root Certification Authorities, and then click Certificates.

2. Examine the list of certificates in the details pane for a name matching the root CA for the computer certificates issued to the authentication servers.

You must install the root CA certificates of the issuers of the computer certificates of the authentication servers on each VPN client that does not contain them. The easiest way to install a root CA certificate on all your VPN clients is through Group Policy. For more information, see "Deploying PKI" in Chapter 9.

Root CA Certificates for SSTP Connections   If you use SSTP connections, you might need to install the root CA certificate of the issuing CA of the computer certificates that are installed on your VPN servers. If the root CA certificate of the issuer of the computer certificates installed on the VPN servers is already installed as a root CA certificate on your VPN clients, no other configuration is necessary. If your root CA is a Windows Server 2008–based or Windows Server 2003–based online root enterprise CA, the root CA certificate is automatically installed on each domain member computer through Group Policy.

To verify whether the correct root CA certificate is installed on your VPN clients, you must:

1. Determine the root CA from the computer certificates installed on the VPN servers

2. Determine whether a certificate for the root CA is installed on your VPN clients

To Determine the Root CA from the Computer Certificates Installed on the VPN Servers

1. In the console tree of the Certificates snap-in for the VPN server computer account, expand Certificates (Local Computer or *Computername*), expand Personal, and then click Certificates.

2. In the details pane, double-click the computer certificate used for SSL authentication.

3. On the Certification Path tab, note the name at the top of the certification path. This is the name of the root CA.

To Determine Whether a Certificate for the Root CA Is Installed on Your VPN Client

1. In the console tree of the Certificates snap-in for the VPN client computer account, expand Certificates (Local Computer or *Computername*), expand Trusted Root Certification Authorities, and then click Certificates.

2. Examine the list of certificates in the details pane for a name or names matching the root CA for the computer certificate issued to the VPN servers.

You must install the root CA certificates of the issuers of the computer certificates of the VPN servers on each Windows Server 2008 or Windows Vista SP1–based VPN client that does not contain them. The easiest way to install a root CA certificate on all your VPN clients is through Group Policy. For more information, see "Deploying PKI" in Chapter 9.

Deploying User Certificates

You can deploy user certificates to VPN client computers in the following ways:

- By configuring autoenrollment of user certificates to users in an Active Directory domain
- By using the Certificates snap-in to request a user certificate
- By using the Certificates snap-in to import a user certificate
- By requesting a certificate over the Web
- By executing a CAPICOM script that requests a user certificate

For more information, see "Deploying PKI" in Chapter 9.

Configuring Internet Infrastructure

To configuring the Internet infrastructure for remote access VPN connections, perform the following:

- Place VPN servers in the perimeter network or on the Internet.
- Install Windows Server 2008 on VPN servers and configure Internet interfaces.
- Add address records to Internet DNS servers.

Placing VPN Servers in the Perimeter Network or on the Internet

Decide where to place the VPN servers in relation to your Internet firewall. In the most common configuration, the VPN servers are placed behind the firewall on the perimeter network between the Internet and your intranet. If so, configure packet filters on the firewall to allow VPN traffic to and from the IPv4 or IPv6 address of the VPN servers' perimeter network interfaces. For more information, see "Firewall Packet Filtering for VPN Traffic" earlier in this chapter.

Installing Windows Server 2008 on VPN Servers and Configuring Internet Interfaces

Install Windows Server 2008 on the VPN server computer. Name the interfaces in the Network Connections folder with names that identify the network to which they are connecting. Connect the VPN server to either the Internet or to the perimeter network with one network adapter, and connect it to the intranet with another network adapter. Prior to running the Routing and Remote Access Server Setup Wizard, the VPN server computer will not forward IPv4 or IPv6 packets between the Internet and the intranet.

For the connection attached to the IPv4 Internet or the perimeter network, configure the TCP/IP (IPv4) protocol with a public IPv4 address, a subnet mask, and the default gateway of either the firewall (if the VPN server is connected to a perimeter network) or an ISP router (if the VPN server is directly connected to the Internet). Do not configure the connection with DNS server or WINS server IPv4 addresses.

For the connection attached to the IPv6 Internet or the perimeter network, configure the TCP/IP (IPv6) protocol with a global IPv6 address, a 64-bit prefix length, and the default gateway of either the firewall (if the VPN server is connected to a perimeter network) or an ISP router (if the VPN server is directly connected to the IPv6 Internet). Do not configure the connection with DNS server IPv6 addresses.

Adding Address Records to Internet DNS Servers

To ensure that the name of the VPN server (for example, vpn.example.microsoft.com) can be resolved to its public IPv4 address or global IPv6 address, either add DNS address (A) or IPv6 address (AAAA) records to your Internet DNS server (if you are providing DNS name resolution for Internet users) or have your ISP add A or AAAA records to their DNS server(s) (if your ISP is providing DNS name resolution for Internet users). Verify that the name of the VPN server can be resolved to its public IPv4 address or global IPv6 address when connected to the Internet.

Configuring Active Directory for User Accounts and Groups

To configure Active Directory for user accounts and groups, do the following:

1. Ensure that all users of VPN client computers have a corresponding user account.

2. Set the remote access permission on VPN client user accounts to Allow Access or Deny Access to manage remote access by user. Or, to manage access by group, set the remote access permission on user accounts to Control Access Through NPS Network Policy.

3. Organize VPN client user accounts into the appropriate universal and nested groups to take advantage of group-based network policies.

Configuring RADIUS Servers

If you are using RADIUS for authentication, authorization, and accounting of VPN connections, configure and deploy your NPS-based RADIUS servers as described in Chapter 9, including the following steps:

1. Install a computer certificate on the NPS servers (for EAP-TLS, PEAP-TLS, or PEAP-MS-CHAP v2 authentication).

2. Configure logging.

3. Add RADIUS clients to the NPS server corresponding to each VPN server.

The NPS server uses a network policy to authorize remote access VPN connections. The default network policy named Connections To Microsoft Routing And Remote Access Server can be used for remote access VPN connections. However, by default, this network policy has its policy type set to Deny Access.

To use this network policy to accept remote access VPN connections, do the following:

1. In the console tree of the Network Policy Server snap-in, under Policies, click Network Policies.

2. Double-click the network policy named Connections To Microsoft Routing And Remote Access Server.

3. On the Overview tab, under Access Permission, click Grant Access, and then click OK.

You can also use the Configure VPN Or Dial-Up Wizard to create a set of policies that are customized for remote access VPN connections.

To Create a Set of Policies for Remote Access VPN Connections

1. In the console tree of the Network Policy Server snap-in, click NPS.

2. In the details pane, under Standard Configuration, select RADIUS Server For Dial-Up Or VPN Connections from the drop-down list, and then click Configure VPN Or Dial-Up.

3. In the Configure VPN Or Dial-Up Wizard, on the Select Dial-Up or Virtual Private Network Connections Type page, click Virtual Private Network (VPN) Connections, and then type the name of the new NPS network policy (or use the name supplied by the wizard). Click Next.

4. On the Specify Dial-Up Or VPN Server page, add RADIUS clients as needed that correspond to your VPN servers. Click Next.

5. On the Configure Authentication Methods page, MS-CHAP v2 is already enabled. To enable and configure an EAP authentication type, select the Extensible Authentication Protocol check box, click an EAP type in the drop-down list, and then click Configure as needed (for example, to select the specific computer certificate to use for EAP-TLS, PEAP-TLS, or PEAP-MS-CHAP v2 authentication). Click Next.

6. On the Specify User Groups page, add the groups containing the user accounts allowed to make VPN remote access connections (for example, VPNUsers), and then click Next.

7. On the Specify IP Filters page, add IPv4 and IPv6 input and output packet filters to apply to all remote access VPN connections as needed. Click Next.

8. On the Specify Encryption Settings page, enable the allowed encryption strengths, and then click Next.

9. On the Specify A Realm Name page, specify the realm name and select the Before Authentication check box as needed. For more information about realm names, see Chapter 9. Click Next.

10. On the Completing New Dial-Up Or Virtual Private Network Connections And RADIUS Clients page, click Finish.

The Configure VPN Or Dial-Up Wizard creates a connection request policy and a network policy for remote access VPN connections. The Configure VPN Or Dial-Up Wizard configures the network policy with a single EAP method. For additional EAP methods, you can configure additional methods from the Settings tab for the properties of the network policy.

After you have configured the primary NPS server with the appropriate logging, RADIUS client, and policy settings, copy the configuration to the secondary or other NPS servers. For more information, see Chapter 9.

Deploying VPN Servers

To deploy the VPN servers for remote access VPN connections, perform the following steps:

1. Install computer certificates.

2. Configure the VPN server's connection to the intranet.

3. Install the Network Access Services role.

4. Run the Routing and Remote Access Server Setup Wizard.

5. Add native IPv6 capability (optional).

Installing Computer Certificates

For L2TP/IPsec or SSTP-based connections, or if the VPN server is the authentication server and you are using PEAP-MS-CHAP v2, EAP-TLS, or PEAP-TLS authentication, you must install a computer certificate on the VPN server. You can install a computer certificate using the methods described in "Deploying Certificates" earlier in this chapter.

Configuring the VPN Server's Connection to the Intranet

For IPv4, configure the VPN server's connection to the intranet with a manual TCP/IP (IPv4) configuration consisting of IPv4 address, subnet mask, intranet DNS servers, and intranet

WINS servers. For IPv6, configure the VPN server's connection to the intranet with a manual TCP/IP (IPv6) configuration consisting of IPv6 address, 64-bit prefix length, and intranet DNS servers. In both cases, to prevent default route conflicts with the default route pointing to the IPv4 or IPv6 Internet, you must not configure the default gateway on the intranet connection.

Installing the Network Access Services Role

To install Routing and Remote Access and the Connection Manager Administration Kit, use the Server Manager tool to install the Network Access and Policy Services role and the Connection Manager Administration Kit feature.

Running the Routing and Remote Access Server Setup Wizard

The Routing and Remote Access Server Setup Wizard automates the configuration of many elements of the VPN server. The resulting default configuration can then be customized to fit your specific deployment needs.

To Run the Routing and Remote Access Server Setup Wizard

1. On the Start menu, point to Administrative Tools, and then click Routing and Remote Access.

2. Right-click your server name, and then click Configure And Enable Routing And Remote Access. In the Routing and Remote Access Server Setup Wizard, on the Welcome page, click Next.

3. On the Configuration page, select Remote Access (Dial-up Or VPN), and then click Next.

4. On the Remote Access page, select VPN. If you also want the VPN server to support dial-up remote access connections, click Dial-up. Click Next.

5. On the VPN Connection page, click the connection that is connected to the Internet or your perimeter network. Ensure that the Enable Security On The Selected Interface By Setting Up Static Packet Filters check box is selected, and then click Next. Figure 12-5 shows an example.

6. On the Network Selection page (displayed only if you have multiple network adapters attached to the site), select the connection from which you want Routing and Remote Access to obtain DHCP, DNS, and WINS configuration for remote access VPN clients. Click Next if this page appeared.

7. On the IP Address Assignment page, select Automatically if the VPN server should use DHCP to obtain IPv4 addresses for remote access VPN clients. Alternatively, select From A Specified Range Of Addresses to use one or more static ranges of addresses. If any of the static address ranges is an off-subnet address range, routes must be added to the routing infrastructure for the VPN clients to be reachable. When you have completed IPv4 address assignment, click Next.

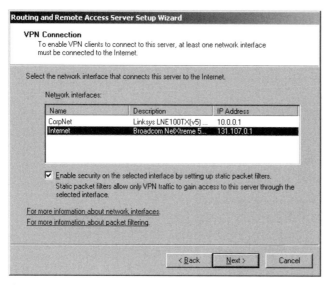

Figure 12-5   VPN Connection page

8.   On the Managing Multiple Remote Access Servers page, if you are using the VPN server for authentication and authorization, select No, Use Routing And Remote Access To Authenticate Connection Requests. If you are using RADIUS for authentication and authorization, select Yes, Set Up This Server To Work With A RADIUS Server. Click Next.

9.   If you selected RADIUS in step 8, on the RADIUS Server Selection page, configure the primary (mandatory) and alternate (optional) RADIUS servers and the RADIUS shared secret, and then click Next. Figure 12-6 shows an example.

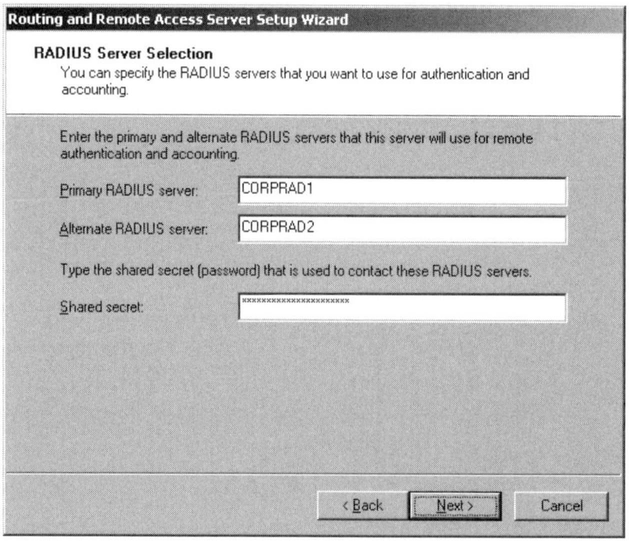

Figure 12-6   RADIUS Server Selection page

10. On the Completing The Routing and Remote Access Server Setup Wizard page, click Finish.

11. If the Routing and Remote Access Server Setup Wizard cannot automatically configure the DHCP Relay Agent component with the IPv4 addresses of DHCP servers on the intranet, you are prompted with a message. Click OK, or click Help for more information.

If your VPN server is not acting as a site-to-site VPN router, you can disable demand-dial routing to create a dedicated remote access VPN server.

To Disable Demand-Dial Routing for Site-to-Site VPN Connections

1. From the console tree of the Routing and Remote Access snap-in, right-click the name of the server, and then click Properties.

2. On the General tab, under IPv4 Router, click Local Area Network (LAN) Routing Only, and then click OK.

Enabling Native IPv6 Capability

Native IPv6 capability for remote access VPN connections—IPv6 packets either inside the VPN tunnel or over a native IPv6 VPN connection—is not a current requirement for many intranets. For this reason, the Routing and Remote Access Server Setup Wizard does not automatically enable native IPv6 capability for remote access VPN connections over the IPv4 or IPv6 Internet.

To configure native IPv6 capability for remote access VPN connections in Routing and Remote Access, you need to do the following:

- Enable IPv6 routing for remote access connections.

- Configure router advertisement behavior.

- Configure the DHCPv6 Relay Agent to relay DHCPv6 messages between VPN clients and DHCPv6 servers on the intranet.

To Configure the VPN Server to Support Native IPv6 Traffic Over VPN Connections

1. In the console tree of the Routing and Remote Access snap-in, right-click the name of the VPN server, and then click Properties.

2. On the General tab, select IPv6 Remote Access Server, and then click Apply.

3. On the IPv6 tab, ensure that the Enable IPv6 Forwarding and Enable Default Route Advertisement check boxes are selected. Type the subnet prefix that will be assigned to IPv6-based VPN clients as they connect. You do not need to specify the prefix length. For example, for the subnet prefix 2001:db8:4a2c:29::/64, type **2001:db8:4a2c:29::**. Figure 12-7 shows an example.

4. Click OK. You will be prompted to restart the Routing and Remote Access service.

5. In the console tree of the Routing and Remote Access snap-in, expand the IPv6 node.

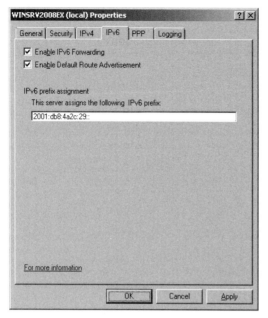

Figure 12-7 The IPv6 tab of the Routing and Remote Access Server Properties page

6. Right-click General, and then click New Routing Protocol.

7. In the New Routing Protocol dialog box, click OK to add the DHCPv6 Relay Agent component.

8. In the console tree, right-click DHCPv6 Relay Agent, click New Interface, select Internal, and then click OK twice.

9. Right-click DHCPv6 Relay Agent, and then click Properties.

10. On the Servers tab, type the global addresses of your DHCPv6 servers on the intranet, and then click OK.

Configuring Intranet Network Infrastructure

To deploy the intranet network infrastructure for remote access VPN connections, perform the following steps:

1. Configure routing on the VPN server.

2. Verify name resolution and intranet reachability from the VPN server.

3. Configure routing for off-subnet address pools (if needed).

4. Configure routing for the IPv6 subnet prefix for remote access clients.

Configuring Routing on the VPN Server

For your VPN servers to properly forward traffic to locations on the intranet, you must do one of the following:

- Add static routes that summarize the IPv4 and IPv6 address space used on the intranet.

- If you are using a RIP-capable IPv4 router on the intranet subnet connected to the VPN server, add the RIP routing protocol so that the VPN server can exchange routes with neighboring RIP routers and automatically add routes for intranet subnets to its routing table.

To Add IPv4 Static Routes

1. In the console tree of the Routing and Remote Access snap-in, expand the IPv4 node.

2. Right-click Static Routes, and then click New Static Route.

3. In the IPv4 Static Route dialog box, shown in Figure 12-8, select the appropriate interface, and then type the destination, network mask, gateway, and metric for the static route. Click OK.

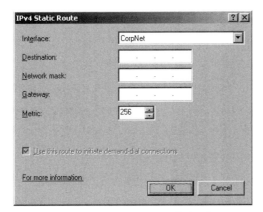

Figure 12-8   IPv4 Static Route dialog box

4. Repeat steps 2 and 3 for additional IPv4 static routes.

To Add IPv6 Static Routes

1. In the console tree of the Routing and Remote Access snap-in, expand the IPv6 node.

2. Right-click Static Routes, and then click New Static Route.

3. In the IPv6 Static Route dialog box, shown in Figure 12-9, select the appropriate interface and type the destination, prefix length, gateway, and metric for the static route. Click OK.

4. Repeat steps 2 and 3 for additional IPv6 static routes.

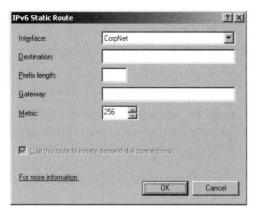

Figure 12-9 IPv6 Static Route dialog box

> **Note** You must add IPv6 static routes only if you have configured your VPN server for native IPv6 capability.

To Configure the VPN Server as a RIP Router

1. In the console tree of the Routing and Remote Access snap-in, expand the IPv4 node.

2. Right-click General, and then click New Routing Protocol.

3. In the New Routing Protocols dialog box, click RIP Version 2 For Internet Protocol, and then click OK.

4. Right-click RIP, and then click New Interface.

5. Select the intranet interface of the VPN server, and then click OK.

6. In the RIP Properties dialog box, configure the RIP routing protocol as used by the neighboring RIP router on the intranet subnet of the VPN server, and then click OK.

Verifying Name Resolution and Reachability from the VPN Server

Verify that the VPN server can resolve names and successfully communicate with intranet resources by using the Ping command, Windows Internet Explorer, and making drive and printer connections to known intranet servers.

Configuring Routing for Off-Subnet Address Pools

If you configured the VPN server with IPv4 address pools, and any of the pools are off-subnet, you must ensure that the routes representing the off-subnet address pools are present in your intranet IPv4 routing infrastructure. You can add static routes representing the off-subnet address pools to the neighboring routers of the VPN server and then propagate the routes to other routers by using the routing protocol of your intranet. When you add the static routes, you must specify that the gateway or next hop address is the intranet interface of the VPN server.

Configuring Routing for the IPv6 Subnet Prefix for Remote Access Clients

To ensure that IPv6-capable remote access clients are reachable from the intranet, you must add a static route representing the subnet prefix for remote access clients to the neighboring IPv6 routers of the VPN server and then propagate the routes to other routers by using the routing protocol of your intranet. When you add the static routes, you must specify that the gateway or next hop address is the link-local address of the intranet interface of the VPN server.

Deploying VPN Clients

To deploy VPN clients for remote access VPN connections, do the following as needed:

- Manually configure VPN clients.
- Configure and deploy CM profiles by using the CMAK.
- Configure concurrent access to the Internet and intranet.

Manually Configuring VPN clients

If you have a small number of VPN clients, you can manually configure VPN connections for each VPN client. For Windows Server 2008 and Windows Vista VPN clients, use the Set Up A Connection Or Network Wizard. For Windows XP and Windows 2003 VPN clients, use the New Connection Wizard.

Configuring and Deploying CM Profiles by Using the CMAK

For a large number of VPN clients running different versions of Windows, you should use the CMAK to create a CM profile for your users. After it is created, you must distribute the CM profile (a self-extracting executable file) to your users. Each user must execute the CM profile, which automatically creates a VPN connection in that user's Network Connections folder.

To Configure a CM Profile for a VPN Connection

1. On the Start menu, click Administrative Tools, and then click Connection Manager Administration Kit. If the CMAK is not already installed, you can install it by clicking Add Features in Server Manager and selecting it from the Features list.

2. On the Welcome page of the CMAK Wizard, click Next.

3. On the Select The Target Operating System page, select either Windows Vista or Windows Server 2003, Windows XP, Or Windows 2000, depending on which set of VPN client computers this CM profile will be distributed. Click Next.

4. On the Create Or Modify A Connection Manager Profile page, click Next to create a new profile.

5. On the Specify The Service Name And The File Name page, type the name of the profile as it will appear in the Network Connections folder and the name of the profile as it will be stored on the disk. Click Next.

6. On the Specify A Realm Name page, configure a realm name and where it will appear relative to the user name if needed. A realm name typically indicates where the user account is stored, as identified by a domain or an organization name. If you do not need to specify a realm name, click Next.

7. On the Merge Information From Other Profiles page, specify which existing profiles need to be merged into this new profile as needed, and then click Next.

8. On the Add Support For VPN Connections page, shown in Figure 12-10, select Phone Book From This Profile. In the VPN Server Name Or IP Address section, type the fully qualified domain name (FQDN), the public IPv4 address, or the global IPv6 address of the VPN server's Internet interface. Alternatively, select Allow The User To Choose A VPN Server Before Connecting, and then specify a text file containing a list of names or addresses of your VPN servers. Click Next.

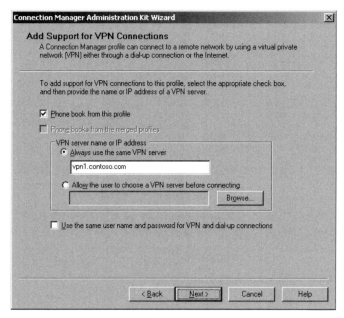

Figure 12-10 Add Support For VPN Connections page

9. On the Create Or Modify A VPN Entry page, click Edit to modify the settings of the default VPN entry. In the Edit VPN Entry dialog box, specify appropriate settings on the General, IPv4, IPv6, Security (authentication protocols and encryption requirements), and Advanced tabs. Figure 12-11 shows the default settings on the Security tab for a new entry. Click OK, and then click Next.

10. On the Add a Custom Phone Book page, clear the Automatically Download Phone Book Updates check box. (The VPN connection does not need to automatically create a dial-up connection.) Click Next.

11. On the Configure Dial-up Networking Entries page, click Next.

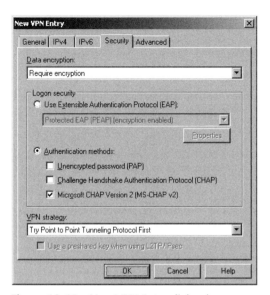

Figure 12-11   New VPN Entry dialog box

12. On the Specify Routing Table Updates page, if you are using the CM profile to add routes to the VPN clients for concurrent Internet and intranet access, select Define A Routing Table Update, and then specify the file containing the routes or a URL that contains the routes. Click Next.

13. On the Configure Proxy Settings For Internet Explorer page, if you want to configure the VPN clients with a proxy server on the intranet, select either Automatically Copy The Internet Explorer Proxy Settings For The Current Use To The Tunnel Interface or Automatically Configure Proxy Settings, and then specify the file containing the proxy settings. Click Next.

14. On the Add Custom Actions page, configure custom actions as needed. Click Next.

15. On the Display A Custom Logon Bitmap page, if you want to use a custom bitmap for the user logon dialog box, click Custom Graphic, and then specify the location of the bitmap file that is 330 by 140 pixels. Click Next.

16. On the Display A Custom Phone Book Bitmap page, if you want to use a custom bitmap for the phone book dialog box, click Custom Graphic, and then specify the location of the bitmap file that is 114 by 309 pixels. Click Next.

17. On the Display Custom Icons page, if you want to use custom bitmaps in the Network and Sharing Center or Network Connections folder, click Custom Icons, and then specify the location of the bitmap files that are 32 by 32 and 16 by 16 pixels. Click Next.

18. On the Include A Custom Help File page, if you want to include a custom help file with the profile, click Custom Help File, and then specify the location of the CHM file. Click Next.

19. On the Display Custom Support Information page, if you want to include standard support text that appears in the logon dialog box, in the Support Information text box, type the desired text. Click Next.

20. On the Display A Custom License Agreement page, if you want to display a custom license agreement during the installation of the CM profile, specify the file containing the license agreement text. Click Next.

21. On the Install Additional Files With The Connection Manager Profile page, if you want to include with the CM profile additional files that are installed on the user's computer with the profile, specify their locations. Click Next.

22. On the Build The Connection Manager Profile And Its Installation Program page, click Next.

23. On the Your Connection Manager Profile Is Complete And Ready To Distribute page, click Finish.

Direct from the Source: Enhancements to CM Profiles

Remote access connections using CM profiles made with Windows Server 2003 do not support DNS dynamic updates by the remote access clients. As a workaround, it is necessary to specify a post-connect action script within the CM profile to register with the intranet DNS server after the VPN connection has been established. The new version of Connection Manager included with Windows Server 2008 adds client DNS dynamic update registration functionality. You can configure DNS dynamic update from the Advanced tab for a dial-up or VPN entry on the Dial-Up Or VPN Entry Page within the CMAK Wizard. CM profiles for Windows Vista also includes support for profile authoring with IPv6 configuration options.

Tim Quinn, Support Escalation Engineer

Enterprise Platform Support

Distributing Your CM Profiles

There are several ways to distribute your CM profile. Choose one of the following methods, or provide more than one method to give your users a choice.

Distributing CM Profiles on CD or Disk   You can distribute CDs or disks containing your self-installing CM profile. A disk can include a floppy disk or, more commonly with new computers that do not include floppy disk drives, a Universal Serial Bus (USB) flash drive (UFD).

The benefit of distributing this way is that you can physically give a copy to all users or send them easily through the mail. However, this solution might be costly and has little inherent security.

Distributing CM Profiles by E-Mail   You can send a CM profile through e-mail to your users. If you choose to send the CM profile through e-mail, ensure that users are able to receive .exe files, because not all e-mail systems allow executable files as attachments. A workaround is to compress the CM profile in a Zip format before sending.

Distributing CM Profiles by Download   You can set up a Web site from which users can download the CM profile. Desktop users and portable-computer users can download directly to their computers from a Web site on your intranet.

It is also possible to make the CM profile available by download from a Web site over the Internet. However, identify any security risks to your organization before posting your CM profile on an Internet site.

Pre-Installing CM Profiles   You can pre-install the CM profile on each client computer individually. The benefit of this method is that users are not required to install anything themselves, which can reduce user frustration and calls to your help desk. However, this method requires administrator or help desk resources during the initial installation, which might be a large resource hit during the rollout phase of your deployment. This method is useful when there are a small number of client computers or when all the client computers and devices are controlled by your organization.

Combining Distribution Methods   You can also use a combination of distribution methods. For example, a company could distribute the CM profiles on CD to users who work from their own computers from remote locations, provide downloads for local employees who have portable computers, and pre-install the CM profile on any new portable computers before distribution.

Configuring Concurrent Access to the Internet and Intranet

To configure concurrent access to the IPv4 Internet and your intranet, you can use the following:

- Classless Static Routes DHCP option
- Connection Manager Administration Kit

Using the Classless Static Routes DHCP Option   VPN clients running Windows Server 2008, Windows Vista, Windows XP, or Windows Server 2003 send a DHCPInform message to the VPN server after the PPP negotiation is complete, requesting a set of DHCP options. This is done so that the VPN client can obtain an updated list of DNS and WINS servers and a DNS domain name that is assigned to the VPN connection. The DHCPInform message is forwarded to a DHCP server on the intranet by the VPN server, and the response is sent back to the VPN client.

The DHCPInform message includes a request for the Classless Static Routes DHCP option. For concurrent access, the Classless Static Routes DHCP option contains a set of routes that represent the address space of your intranet and that are automatically added to the routing table of the requesting VPN client and automatically removed when the VPN connection is terminated. The Classless Static Routes DHCP option (option number 121) must be manually configured on a DHCP server running Windows Server 2008 or Windows Server 2003.

To use the Classless Static Routes option for concurrent access, configure this option for the scope that corresponds to the intranet subnet to which the VPN server is connected, and add the set of routes that correspond to the summarized IPv4 address space of your organization intranet. For example, if you use the private IPv4 address space for your organization intranet, the Classless Static Routes option would have the following three routes:

- 10.0.0.0 with the subnet mask of 255.0.0.0
- 172.16.0.0 with the subnet mask of 255.240.0.0
- 192.168.0.0 with the subnet mask of 255.255.0.0

The Router IP address for each route added to the Classless Static Routes option should be set to the IPv4 address of a router interface on the intranet subnet to which the VPN server is connected. For example, if the VPN server is connected to the intranet subnet 10.89.192.0/20, and the IPv4 address of the intranet router on this subnet is 10.89.192.1, set the Router IP address for each route to 10.89.192.1.

Using the Connection Manager Administration Kit   You can use the Connection Manager Administration Kit (CMAK) for Windows Server 2008 to configure specific routes as part of the CM profile that is distributed to VPN clients. For more information about the CMAK and CM profiles, see "VPN Clients" earlier in this chapter.

> **More Info**   For more information about configuring concurrent access with the CMAK, see "Split Tunneling for Concurrent Access to the Internet and an Intranet" at *http://technet.microsoft.com/en-us/library/bb878117.aspx*.

Ongoing Maintenance

The areas of maintenance for a remote access VPN solution are as follows:

- Management of user accounts
- Management of VPN servers
- Updating of CM profiles

Managing User Accounts

When a new user account is created in Active Directory and that user is allowed to create remote access VPN connections, add the new user account to the appropriate group for VPN access. For example, add the account to the Wcoast_VPNUsers security group, which is a member of the VPNUsers universal group. The network policy for VPN connections is configured to use membership in the VPNUsers group as a condition for granting access.

When user accounts are deleted in Active Directory, no additional action is necessary to prevent remote access VPN connections.

As needed, you can create additional universal groups and network policies to define remote access for different sets of users. For example, you can create a global Contractors group and a network policy that allows remote access VPN connections to members of the Contractors group only during normal business hours or for access to specific intranet resources.

Managing VPN Servers

You might need to manage VPN servers when adding or removing a VPN server from your remote access VPN solution. Once deployed, VPN servers do not need a lot of ongoing maintenance. Most of the ongoing changes to VPN server configuration are because of capacity and changes in network infrastructure.

Adding a VPN Server

1. Follow the design points and deployment steps in this chapter to create a new VPN server on the Internet.

2. Update or add the FQDN in the Internet DNS for the IPv4 or IPv6 address of the new VPN server.

3. Update your RADIUS server configuration to add the VPN server as a RADIUS client.

Removing a VPN Server

To remove a VPN server:

1. Update or remove the FQDN in the Internet DNS for the IPv4 or IPv6 address of the VPN server.

2. Update your RADIUS server configuration to remove the VPN server as a RADIUS client.

3. Shut down and remove the VPN server.

Adding Possible Connections

By default, the Routing and Remote Access Server Setup Wizard configures Routing and Remote Access with up to the following ports (each port can support a single VPN connection):

- 128 PPTP ports
- 128 L2TP ports
- 128 SSTP ports

To increase the maximum number of connections for a VPN protocol, do the following:

1. In the console tree of the Routing and Remote Access snap-in, right-click Ports, and then click Properties.

2. In the Ports Properties dialog box, double-click the WAN Miniport device corresponding to the VPN protocol.

3. In the Configure Device dialog box, in the Maximum Ports spin-box, type the maximum number of ports, and then click OK twice.

Configuration for Changes in Infrastructure Servers

Infrastructure servers include DHCP, DNS, WINS, and RADIUS (NPS) servers. If the changes to these types of infrastructure servers affect the configuration of the VPN server, you will need to change the configuration of the VPN server for the new infrastructure.

DHCP   The Routing and Remote Access service on the VPN server uses the DHCP Relay Agent and DHCPv6 Relay Agent routing protocol components to forward DHCP and DHCPv6 messages between VPN clients and DHCP or DHCPv6 servers on the intranet. If the IPv4 or IPv6 addresses of the configured DHCP or DHCPv6 servers change (for example, because of additions or removals of DHCP or DHCPv6 servers on the intranet), you must change the list of DHCP and DHCPv6 addresses for the DHCP Relay Agent and DHCPv6 Relay Agent routing protocol components on the VPN server.

DNS   The VPN server sends the IPv4 addresses of its configured DNS servers to VPN clients during the PPP negotiation. Additional IPv4 addresses of DNS servers might be configured on the VPN client from the response to the DHCPInform message. If the IPv4 addresses of the configured DNS servers change (for example, because of additions or removals of DNS servers on the intranet), you must change the DNS server configuration on the VPN server and the DNS server option on the DHCP server to prevent VPN clients from configuring incorrect DNS server IPv4 addresses.

For native IPv6-based VPN connections, VPN clients obtain the IPv6 addresses from the response to the DHCPv6 Information-Request message. If the IPv6 addresses of the configured DNS servers change (for example, because of additions or removals of DNS servers on the intranet), you must change the IPv6 DNS server option on the DHCPv6 server to prevent it from configuring VPN clients with incorrect DNS server IPv6 addresses.

WINS   The VPN server sends the IPv4 addresses of its configured WINS servers to VPN clients during the PPP negotiation. Additional IPv4 addresses of WINS servers might be configured on the VPN client based on the response to the DHCPInform message. If the IPv4 addresses of the configured WINS servers change (for example, because of additions or removals of WINS servers on the intranet), you must change the WINS server configuration on the VPN server and the NetBIOS name server option on the DHCP server to prevent VPN clients from configuring an incorrect WINS server IPv4 address.

RADIUS   If the VPN server is configured to use RADIUS authentication, and the IPv4 addresses of the RADIUS servers change (for example, because of additions or removals of RADIUS servers on the intranet), you must do the following:

1. Ensure that the new RADIUS servers are configured with a RADIUS client corresponding to the VPN servers.

2. Update the configuration of the VPN servers to include the IPv4 addresses of the new RADIUS servers.

Updating CM Profiles

To update a CM profile, do the following:

1. Create an updated CM profile by using the CMAK.

2. Distribute the updated CM profile to your VPN client users through e-mail, a file share, or other means with the instructions or automated process to execute the profile and update their VPN connection settings.

Troubleshooting

Because of the different components and processes involved, troubleshooting remote access VPN connections can be a difficult task. This section describes the many tools that are provided with Windows Server 2008 and Windows Vista to troubleshoot remote access VPN connections and the most common problems with remote access VPN connections.

Troubleshooting Tools

Microsoft provides the following tools to troubleshoot VPN connections from the VPN server:

- TCP/IP troubleshooting tools
- Authentication and accounting logging
- Event logging
- NPS event logging
- PPP logging
- Tracing
- Network Monitor 3.1

Additionally, Windows Server 2008 and Windows Vista provide the following tools to troubleshoot VPN connections from the VPN client:

- TCP/IP troubleshooting tools
- Network Diagnostics Framework support for remote access connections

TCP/IP Troubleshooting Tools

The Ping, Tracert, and Pathping tools use ICMP Echo and Echo Reply and ICMPv6 Echo Request and Echo Reply messages to verify connectivity, display the path to a destination, and test path integrity. The **route print** command can be used to display the IPv4 and IPv6 routing tables. Alternatively, on the VPN server, you can use the **netsh routing ip show rtmroutes** command or the Routing and Remote Access snap-in to display routes. The Nslookup tool can be used to troubleshoot DNS and name resolution issues.

Authentication and Accounting Logging

A VPN server running Windows Server 2008 supports the logging of authentication and accounting information for remote access VPN connections in local logging files when Routing and Remote Access is configured to perform authentication and accounting locally. This logging is separate from the events recorded in the Windows Logs\Security event log. You can use the information that is logged to track remote access usage and authentication attempts. Authentication and accounting logging is especially useful for troubleshooting network policy issues. For each authentication attempt, the name of the network policy that either accepted or rejected the connection attempt is recorded.

To enable authentication and accounting logging, open the Network Policy Server snap-in, click Accounting, and then click Configure Local File Logging. On the Settings tab, configure the appropriate settings.

The authentication and accounting information is stored in a configurable log file or files stored in the *%SystemRoot%*\System32\LogFiles folder. The log files are saved in Internet Authentication Service (IAS) or database-compatible format, meaning that any database program can read the log file directly for analysis. Routing and Remote Access can also send authentication and accounting information to a Structured Query Language (SQL) database.

If the VPN server is configured for RADIUS authentication and accounting, and the RADIUS server is a computer running Windows Server 2008 and NPS, the authentication and accounting logs are stored in the *%SystemRoot%*\System32\LogFiles folder on the NPS server computer. NPS for Windows Server 2008 can also send authentication and accounting information to a Microsoft SQL Server database.

Event Logging

In the Routing and Remote Access snap-in, in the properties dialog box of a VPN server, on the Logging tab, there are four levels of logging for creating entries in the Windows Logs\System event log. To obtain the maximum amount of information, select Log All Events, and then try to complete the connection again. When the connection fails, check the Windows Logs\System event log for events with the event sources of RasServer, Remote-Access, or RasSSTP that were logged during the connection process. After you are finished viewing the events, on the Logging tab, select Log Errors And Warnings to conserve system resources.

NPS Event Logging

If your VPN servers are configured for RADIUS authentication, and your RADIUS servers are computers running Windows Server 2008 and NPS, check the Windows Logs\Security event log for NPS events corresponding to rejected (event ID 6273) or accepted (event ID 6272) connection attempts. NPS event log entries contain a lot of information on the connection attempt, including the name of the connection request policy that matched the connection attempt (the Proxy Policy Name field in the description of the event) and the network policy that accepted or rejected the connection attempt (the Network Policy Name field in the description of the event). NPS event logging for rejected or accepted connection attempts is enabled by default and configured in the Network Policy Server snap-in, in the properties dialog box of an NPS server, on the Service tab.

PPP Logging

PPP logging records the series of programming functions and PPP control messages during a PPP connection and is a valuable source of information when you are troubleshooting the failure of a PPP connection. To enable PPP logging, in the Routing and Remote Access snap-in, in the properties dialog box of a VPN server, on the Logging tab, select the Log Additional Routing And Remote Access Information check box.

By default, the PPP log is stored as the Ppp.log file in the *%SystemRoot%*\Tracing folder.

Tracing

The Routing and Remote Access service has an extensive tracing capability that you can use to troubleshoot complex network problems. You can enable components of Windows Server 2008 to log tracing information to files by using the Netsh tool or by setting registry values.

Enabling Tracing with Netsh   You can use the Netsh tool to enable and disable tracing for specific components or for all components. To enable and disable tracing for a specific component, use the following syntax:

netsh ras diagnostics set rastracing *Component* enabled|disabled

where ***Component*** is a component in the list of Routing and Remote Access service components found in the Windows Server 2008 registry under HKEY_LOCAL_MACHINE\ SOFTWARE\Microsoft\Tracing. For example, to enable tracing for the RASAUTH component, the command is:

netsh ras diagnostics set rastracing rasauth enabled

To enable tracing for all components, run the following command:

netsh ras diagnostics set rastracing * enabled

Enabling Tracing Through the Registry   You can configure the tracing function by changing settings in the Windows registry under HKEY_LOCAL_MACHINE\SOFTWARE\Microsoft\Tracing.

You can enable tracing for each Routing and Remote Access service component by setting the registry values described later. You can enable and disable tracing for components while the Routing and Remote Access service is running. Each component is capable of tracing and appears as a subkey under the Tracing registry key.

To enable tracing for each component, you can configure the following registry value entries for each protocol key:

- **EnableFileTracing (REG_DWORD) Flag**   You can enable logging tracing information to a file by setting EnableFileTracing to **1**. The default value is 0.

- **FileDirectory (REG_EXPAND_SZ) Path**   You can change the default location of the tracing files by setting FileDirectory to the path you want. The file name for the log file is the name of the component for which tracing is enabled. By default, log files are placed in the *%SystemRoot%*\Tracing folder.

- **FileTracingMask (REG_DWORD) LevelOfTracingInformationLogged**   FileTracingMask determines how much tracing information is logged to the file. The default value is 0xFFFF0000.

- **MaxFileSize (REG_DWORD) SizeOfLogFile**   You can change the size of the log file by setting different values for MaxFileSize. The default value is 0x10000 (64K).

> **Note**   Tracing consumes system resources and should be used sparingly to help identify network problems. After the trace is captured or the problem is identified, you should immediately disable tracing. Do not leave tracing enabled on multiprocessor computers.
>
> Tracing information can be complex and detailed. Most of the time, this information is useful only to Microsoft support professionals or to network administrators who are experienced with Routing and Remote Access. The tracing log files can be sent to Microsoft support for analysis if necessary.

Network Monitor 3.1

You can use Microsoft Network Monitor 3.1 or a commercial packet analyzer (also known as a *network sniffer*) to capture and view the traffic sent between a VPN server and VPN client during the VPN connection process and during data transfer or the RADIUS traffic sent between a VPN server and a RADIUS server. Network Monitor 3.1 includes RADIUS, PPTP, PPP, L2TP, IPsec, HTTP, SSL, and EAP parsers. A *parser* is a component included with Network Monitor 3.1 that can separate the fields of a protocol header and display their structure and values. Without a parser, Network Monitor 3.1 displays the hexadecimal bytes of a header, which you must parse manually.

On the Disc   You can link to the download site for Network Monitor from the companion CD-ROM.

The proper interpretation of the remote access and VPN traffic with Network Monitor 3.1 requires an in-depth understanding of PPP, PPTP, IPsec, SSL, RADIUS, and other protocols. You can save Network Monitor 3.1 captures as files and send them to Microsoft support for analysis.

Network Diagnostics Framework Support for Remote Access Connections

To provide a better user experience when encountering network connectivity issues, Windows Vista includes the Network Diagnostics Framework (NDF), a set of technologies and guidelines that enable a set of troubleshooters (also known as a *helper classes*) to assist in the diagnosis and possible automatic correction of networking problems. When a user experiences a networking problem in Windows Vista, NDF will provide the user the ability to diagnose and repair the problem within the context of that problem. This means that the diagnostics assessment and resolution steps are presented to the users within the application or dialog box that they were using when the problem occurred or based on the failed network operation.

With NDF, when the user tries to complete a task that depends on network connectivity, such as browsing to a Web site or sending an e-mail message, an error message might appear indicating failure to complete the task (such as "Page cannot be displayed" or "Server is not available"). With NDF, the error message might include an option to diagnose the problem. During the diagnosis, NDF will analyze why the user's task has failed and present a solution to the problem or possible list of causes and corrections in clear language, allowing the user to take action to fix the problem.

Windows Vista includes a troubleshooter to diagnose failed remote access connections. If a remote access connection fails, Windows displays a dialog box with information about the error. The dialog box includes a Diagnose button that launches the remote access NDF troubleshooter. From the diagnosis session, users can repair their remote access connection problem without needing to involve IT support staff.

Troubleshooting Remote Access VPNs

Remote access VPN problems typically fall into the following categories:

- Connection attempt is rejected when it should be accepted.
- L2TP/IPsec authentication issues.
- SSTP authentication issues.
- Connection attempt is accepted when it should be rejected.

- Unable to reach locations beyond the VPN server.

- Unable to establish a tunnel.

Use the following troubleshooting tips to isolate the configuration or infrastructure issue that is causing the problem.

Connection Attempt Is Rejected When It Should Be Accepted

If a connection attempt is being rejected when it should be accepted, check the following:

- Using the Ping command, verify that the FQDN of the VPN server is being resolved to its correct IPv4 address. The ping itself might not be successful because of packet filtering that is preventing the delivery of ICMP messages to and from the VPN server.

- For password-based authentication, verify that the VPN client's user credentials—consisting of user name, password, and domain name—are correct and can be validated by the authentication server (the VPN server or the RADIUS server).

- Verify that the user account of the VPN client is not locked out, expired, or disabled, and that the time the connection is being made corresponds to the configured logon hours. If the password on the account has expired, verify that the remote access VPN client is using PEAP-MS-CHAP v2 or MS-CHAP v2. PEAP-MS-CHAP v2 and MS-CHAP v2 are the only authentication protocols provided with Windows Server 2008 that allow you to change an expired password during the connection process.

  For an administrator-level account whose password has expired, reset the password using another administrator-level account.

- Verify that the user account has not been locked out because of remote access account lockout.

- Verify that the Routing and Remote Access service is running on the VPN server.

- For SSTP based VPN connections, verify that the Secure Socket Tunneling Protocol Service is running on the VPN server.

- In the Routing and Remote Access snap-in, in the properties dialog box of a VPN server, on the General tab, verify that the VPN server is enabled as an IPv4 or IPv6 remote access server.

- In the Routing and Remote Access snap-in, in the properties dialog box of the Ports node, verify that the WAN Miniport (PPTP), WAN Miniport (L2TP), and WAN Miniport (SSTP) devices are enabled for inbound remote access.

- Verify that the VPN client, the VPN server, and the network policy for VPN connections are configured to use at least one common authentication method.

- Verify that the VPN client and the network policy for VPN connections are configured to use at least one common encryption strength.

- Verify that the parameters of the connection have permission through network policies. For the connection to be accepted, the parameters of the connection attempt must:

  - Match all the conditions of at least one network policy.

  - Be granted remote access permission through the user account (set to Allow Access), or if the user account has the Control Access Through NPS Network Policy option selected, the matching network policy must have the Grant Access policy type selected.

  - Match all the settings of the network policy.

  - Match all the settings of the dial-in properties of the user account.

  To obtain the name of the network policy that rejected the connection attempt, scan the Windows Logs\Security event log for events corresponding to rejected (event ID 6273) or accepted (event ID 6272) connection attempts. The network policy that accepted or rejected the connection attempt is the Network Policy Name field in the description of the event.

- If you are logged on using an account with domain administrator permissions when you run the Routing and Remote Access Server Setup Wizard and configure Routing and Remote Access to perform authentication locally, the wizard automatically adds the computer account of the VPN server to the RAS and IAS Servers domain-local security group. This group membership allows the VPN server computer to access user account information. If the VPN server is unable to access user account information, verify that:

- The computer account of the VPN server computer is a member of the RAS and IAS Servers security group for all the domains that contain user accounts for which the VPN server is authenticating remote access. You can run the **netsh nps show registered-server** command at a command prompt to view the current registration. You can run the **netsh nps add registeredserver** command to register the server in a domain in which the VPN server is a member or other domains. Alternatively, you or your domain administrator can add the computer account of the VPN server computer to the RAS and IAS Servers security group of all the domains that contain user accounts for which the VPN server is authenticating remote access.

- If you add or remove the VPN server computer to the RAS and IAS Servers security group, the change does not take effect immediately (because of the way that Windows Server 2008 caches Active Directory information). For the change to take effect immediately, you must restart the VPN server computer.

- Verify that all the PPTP, L2TP, or SSTP ports on the VPN server are not already being used. If necessary to allow more connections, in the Routing and Remote Access snap-in, in the properties dialog box of the Ports object, increase the number of PPTP, L2TP, or SSTP ports.

- Verify that the VPN server supports the VPN protocol of the VPN client.

By default, a VPN client running Windows Server 2008, Windows Vista, Windows Server 2003, or Windows XP has the Automatic VPN Type option selected. If the PPTP, L2TP IPsec, or SSTP VPN type is selected, verify that the VPN server supports the selected tunneling protocol.

When you run the Routing and Remote Access Server Setup Wizard and configure a VPN server, a Windows Server 2008–based computer running the Routing and Remote Access service is a PPTP, L2TP, and SSTP server with 128 PPTP ports, 128 L2TP ports, and 128 SSTP ports. To create a PPTP-only server, set the number of L2TP and SSTP ports to zero. To create an L2TP-only server, set the number of SSTP ports to 0 and the PPTP ports to 1, and disable remote access inbound connections and demand-dial connections for the WAN Miniport (PPTP) device. Do this in the Routing and Remote Access snap-in, in the Ports object dialog box. To create an SSTP-only server, set the number of L2TP ports to 0 and the PPTP ports to 1 and disable remote access inbound connections and demand-dial connections for the WAN Miniport (PPTP) device.

■ If the VPN server is configured with static IPv4 address pools, verify that there are enough addresses for all the possible connections. If all the addresses in the static pools have been allocated to connected VPN clients, the VPN server will be unable to assign an IPv4 address for TCP/IP-based connections, and the connection attempt will be rejected.

■ Verify how the VPN server is performing authentication. The VPN server can be configured to authenticate the credentials of the VPN client either locally or use RADIUS.

   ❑ For RADIUS-based authentication, verify that the VPN server computer can communicate with the RADIUS server.

   ❑ For local authentication, verify that the VPN server has joined the Active Directory domain and that the computer account of the VPN server computer has been added to the RAS and IAS Servers security group.

L2TP/IPsec Authentication Issues

The following are the most common problems that cause L2TP/IPsec connections to fail:

■ **No certificate** By default, L2TP/IPsec connections require that the VPN server and VPN client exchange computer certificates for IPsec peer authentication. Use the Certificates snap-in to check the local computer certificate stores of both the VPN client and VPN server to ensure that a suitable certificate exists.

■ **Incorrect certificate** If certificates exist, they must be verifiable. Unlike manually configuring IPsec rules, the list of certification authorities (CAs) for L2TP/IPsec connections is not configurable. Instead, each computer in the L2TP connection sends a list of root CAs to its IPsec peer from which it accepts a certificate for authentication. The root CAs in this list correspond to the root CAs that issued computer certificates to the computer. For example, if Computer A is issued computer certificates by root CAs

CertAuth1 and CertAuth2, it notifies its IPsec peer during main mode negotiation that it will accept certificates for authentication from only CertAuth1 and CertAuth2. If the IPsec peer, Computer B, does not have a valid computer certificate issued from either CertAuth1 or CertAuth2, IPsec security negotiation fails.

The VPN client must have a valid computer certificate for IPsec authenticate installed that was issued by a CA that follows a valid certificate chain from the issuing CA up to a root CA that the VPN server trusts. Additionally, the VPN server must have a valid computer certificate installed that was issued by a CA that follows a valid certificate chain from the issuing CA up to a root CA that the VPN client trusts.

- **A NAT is between the remote access client and remote access server**   If there is a NAT between the VPN client and the VPN server, both computers must support IPsec NAT-T. VPN clients running Windows Server 2008, Windows Vista, Windows Server 2003, or Windows XP SP2 support IPsec NAT-T. VPN servers running Windows Server 2008 or Windows Server 2003 support IPsec NAT-T.

- **A firewall is between the remote access client and remote access server**   If there is a firewall between a Windows VPN client and a Windows Server 2008 VPN server and you cannot establish an L2TP/IPsec connection, verify that the firewall allows L2TP/IPsec traffic to be forwarded. For more information, see "Firewall Packet Filtering for VPN Traffic" earlier in this chapter.

SSTP Authentication Issues

The following are the most common problems that cause SSTP connections to fail:

- **No certificate**   SSTP connections require that the VPN server send a computer certificate to the VPN client during the SSL authentication. Using the Certificates snap-in, verify that the VPN server has a suitable computer certificate installed.

- **Certificate validation fails**   The VPN client must have the root CA certificate for the issuing CA of the VPN server's computer certificate installed. Obtain the name of the root CA certificate of the VPN server's computer certificate, and then verify that it is installed on your VPN clients. Also, do the following:

- Verify that the computer certificate of the VPN server has not expired or been revoked.

- Verify that the CRL distribution points listed in the CRL Distribution Points property of the VPN server's computer certificate are reachable on the Internet.

- Verify that the name of the VPN server, on the General tab in the properties dialog box of the VPN connection in the Network Connections folder, on the VPN client matches the Subject property of the VPN server's computer certificate. This name must match whether you are using DNS host names, IPv4 addresses, or IPv6 addresses for the VPN server.

Connection Attempt Is Accepted When It Should Be Rejected

If a connection attempt is being accepted when it should be rejected, check the following:

- Verify that the remote access permission on the user account is set to either Deny access or Control Access Through NPS Network Policy. If set to the latter, verify that the first matching network policy's type is set to Deny Access. To obtain the name of the network policy that accepted the connection attempt, scan the Windows Logs\Security event log for an event that corresponds to the connection attempt. The text of the event contains the policy name. The network policy that accepted or rejected the connection attempt is the Network Policy Name field in the description of the event

- If you have created a network policy to explicitly reject all connections, verify the policy conditions, type, and settings, and its location in the list of network policies.

Unable to Reach Locations Beyond the VPN Server

If a VPN client cannot reach locations on the intranet beyond the VPN server, check the following:

- In the Routing and Remote Access snap-in, in the properties dialog box of a VPN server, on the General tab, verify that the IPv4 Remote Access Server and IPv6 Remote Access Server check boxes are selected.

- Verify that the IPv4 or IPv6 protocol is enabled for forwarding on the IPv4 and IPv6 tabs for the properties of a VPN server in the Routing and Remote Access snap-in.

- Verify the IPv4 address pools of the VPN server.

  If the VPN server is configured to use an off-subnet IPv4 address pool, verify that the range of addresses set by the IPv4 address pool are reachable by the hosts and routers of the intranet. If not, you must either add the IPv4 routes for the VPN server's IPv4 address pools to the routers of the intranet or, if you are using the RIP routing protocol, enable RIP on the VPN server. If the routes for the off-subnet address pools are not present, remote access VPN clients cannot receive traffic from locations on the intranet.

  If the VPN server is configured to use DHCP to obtain IPv4 addresses for remote access clients, and no DHCP server is available, the VPN server assigns addresses from the Automatic Private IP Addressing (APIPA) address range from 169.254.0.1 through 169.254.255.254. Allocating APIPA addresses for remote access clients works only if the network to which the VPN server is attached is also using APIPA addresses.

  If the VPN server is using APIPA addresses when a DHCP server is available, verify that the proper adapter is selected from which to obtain DHCP-allocated IPv4 addresses. This selection is done through the Routing and Remote Access Server Setup Wizard. In the Routing and Remote Access snap-in, in the properties dialog box of a VPN server, on the IPv4 tab, you can manually choose a LAN adapter from the Adapter list.

If the IPv4 address pools are on-subnet—a range of IPv4 addresses that are a subset of the range of IP addresses for the network to which the VPN server is attached—verify that the range of IPv4 addresses in the IPv4 address pools are not assigned to other TCP/IP nodes either through manual configuration or through DHCP.

■   Verify that the IPv6 subnet prefix that is being assigned to IPv6-capable VPN clients is a route in your IPv6 routing infrastructure that points back to the intranet interface of the VPN server.

■   Verify that there are no IPv4 or IPv6 input or output packet filters in the settings of the network policy for VPN connections that are preventing the sending or receiving of traffic.

Unable to Establish Tunnel

If a VPN client cannot create a tunnel to the VPN server, check the following:

■   Verify that packet filtering on a router interface between the VPN client and the VPN server is not preventing the forwarding of VPN traffic. See "Firewall Packet Filtering for VPN Traffic" earlier in this chapter for information about the types of traffic that must be allowed for VPN connections.

On a Windows Server 2008–based VPN server, IPv4 packet filtering can be separately configured on the Windows Firewall with Advanced Security and the Routing and Remote Access snap-in. Check both places for filters that might be excluding VPN connection traffic.

■   Verify that the Winsock Proxy client is not currently running on the VPN client.

When the Winsock Proxy client is active, Windows Sockets (Winsock) API calls such as those used to create tunnels and send tunneled data are intercepted and forwarded to a configured proxy server.

A proxy server–based computer allows an organization to access specific types of Internet resources (typically Web and FTP) without directly connecting that organization to the Internet. The organization can instead use private IP address prefixes such as 10.0.0.0/8, 172.16.0.0/12, and 192.168.0.0/16.

Proxy servers are typically used so that private users in an organization can have access to public Internet resources as if they were directly attached to the Internet. VPN connections are typically used so that authorized public Internet users can gain access to private organization resources as if they were directly attached to the private network. A single computer can act as a proxy server (for private users) and a VPN server (for authorized Internet users) to facilitate both exchanges of information.

Chapter Summary

Deploying a remote access VPN solution involves configuration of Active Directory, PKI, Group Policy, and RADIUS elements of a Windows-based authentication infrastructure and planning and deployment of VPN servers on the Internet. Once deployed, ongoing maintenance of a remote access VPN solution consists of managing VPN servers and their configuration for changes in infrastructure servers and updating and deploying CM profiles. Common problems with VPN connections include the inability to connect because of an authentication or authorization failure and the inability to reach intranet resources from the VPN client.

Additional Information

For additional information about VPN support in Windows, see the following:

- Windows Server 2008 Technical Library at *http://technet.microsoft.com/windowsserver/2008*
- Windows Server 2008 Help and Support
- "Virtual Private Networks" (*http://www.microsoft.com/vpn*)

For additional information about VPN Internet standards, see the following:

- RFC 2637, "Point-to-Point Tunneling Protocol (PPTP)"
- RFC 2661, "Layer Two Tunneling Protocol (L2TP)"
- RFC 3193, "Securing L2TP using IPsec"

For additional information about Active Directory, see the following:

- Chapter 9, "Authentication Infrastructure"
- *Windows Server 2008 Active Directory Resource Kit* by Stan Reimer, Mike Mulcare, Conan Kezema, and Byron Wright, with the Microsoft Active Directory Team (Microsoft Press, 2008)
- Windows Server 2008 Technical Library at *http://technet.microsoft.com/windowsserver/2008*
- Windows Server 2008 Help and Support

For additional information about PKI, see the following:

- Chapter 9, "Authentication Infrastructure"
- Windows Server 2008 Technical Library at *http://technet.microsoft.com/windowsserver/2008*

- Windows Server 2008 Help and Support

- "Public Key Infrastructure for Windows Server" (*http://www.microsoft.com/pki*)

- *Windows Server 2008 PKI and Certificate Security* by Brian Komar (Microsoft Press, 2008)

For additional information about Group Policy, see the following:

- Chapter 9, "Authentication Infrastructure"

- *Windows Group Policy Resource Kit: Windows Server 2008 and Windows Vista* by Derek Melber, Group Policy MVP, with the Windows Group Policy Team (Microsoft Press, 2008)

- Windows Server 2008 Technical Library at *http://technet.microsoft.com/windowsserver/ 2008*

- Windows Server 2008 Help and Support

- "Microsoft Windows Server Group Policy" (*http://www.microsoft.com/gp*)

For additional information about RADIUS and NPS, see the following:

- Chapter 9, "Authentication Infrastructure"

- Windows Server 2008 Technical Library at *http://technet.microsoft.com/windowsserver/ 2008*

- Windows Server 2008 Help and Support

- "Network Policy Server" (*http://www.microsoft.com/nps*)

For additional information about NAP and VPN Enforcement, see the following:

- Chapter 14, "Network Access Protection Overview"

- Chapter 15, "Preparing for Network Access Protection"

- Chapter 18, "VPN Enforcement"

- Windows Server 2008 Technical Library at *http://technet.microsoft.com/windowsserver/ 2008*

- Windows Server 2008 Help and Support

- "Network Access Protection" (*http://www.microsoft.com/nap*)

Chapter 13

Site-to-Site VPN Connections

This chapter provides information about how to design, deploy, maintain, and troubleshoot site-to-site virtual private network (VPN) connections. This chapter assumes that you understand the role of Active Directory, public key infrastructure (PKI), Group Policy, and Remote Authentication Dial-In User Service (RADIUS) elements of a Microsoft Windows–based authentication infrastructure for network access, as described in Chapter 9, "Authentication Infrastructure."

 More Info This chapter does not describe the deployment planning and steps for site-to-site dial-up connections. For more information, see Windows Server 2008 Help and Support or the Windows Server 2008 Technical Library at *http://technet.microsoft.com/windowsserver/2008*.

Concepts

As described in Chapter 12, "Remote Access VPN Connections," a VPN is the extension of a private network that encompasses links across shared or public networks such as the Internet. Organizations can use VPN connections to establish routed connections, also known as *site-to-site* or *router-to-router* connections, with geographically separate offices or with other organizations across the Internet while maintaining protected communications.

A site-to-site VPN connection across the Internet logically operates as a dedicated WAN link. With a site-to-site VPN connection, an organization can use low-cost broadband or leased-line connections to an Internet service provider (ISP) rather than high-cost, long-distance dial-up or leased lines. Computers that use site-to-site VPN connections are known as VPN routers.

There are two types of site-to-site VPN technology in the Windows Server 2008 operating system:

- **Point-to-Point Tunneling Protocol (PPTP)** PPTP uses user-level Point-to-Point Protocol (PPP) authentication methods and Microsoft Point-to-Point Encryption (MPPE) for data encryption.

- **Layer Two Tunneling Protocol with Internet Protocol security (L2TP/IPsec)** L2TP/IPsec uses user-level PPP authentication methods and IPsec for computer-level IPsec peer authentication and data authentication, integrity, and encryption.

 Note The Secure Socket Tunneling Protocol (SSTP) in the Windows Server 2008 and Windows Vista with Service Pack 1 operating systems can be used only for remote access VPN connections.

VPN routers can also be any computer that is capable of creating a routed PPTP connection using MPPE or a routed L2TP connection using IPsec encryption.

A VPN router that initiates a site-to-site VPN connection is known as a *calling router*. A VPN router that is listening for incoming site-to-site connections is known as an *answering router*. During the connection process, the calling router authenticates itself to the answering router, and for authentication methods that support mutual authentication, the answering router authenticates itself to the calling router.

Note   Using IPsec tunnel mode is not a site-to-site VPN technology supported by Windows-based VPN routers because of the lack of an industry standard method of performing user authentication and IP address configuration over an IPsec tunnel. IPsec tunnel mode is described in Requests for Comments (RFCs) 4301, 4302, and 4303.

Demand-Dial Routing Overview

The Windows Server 2008 Routing and Remote Access service includes support for demand-dial routing (also known as *dial-on-demand routing*) over dial-up connections (such as analog phone lines or ISDN), VPN connections, and PPP over Ethernet (PPPoE) connections. Demand-dial routing is the forwarding of packets across a Point-to-Point Protocol (PPP) link. The PPP link is represented inside Routing and Remote Access as a demand-dial interface, which can be used to create on-demand connections across dial-up or non-permanent media or consistent connections across persistent media. Demand-dial connections allow you to use dial-up telephone lines instead of leased lines for low-traffic situations and to utilize the connectivity of the Internet to connect branch offices with VPN connections.

Demand-dial routing is not the same as remote access. Whereas remote access connects a single computer to a network, demand-dial routing connects two portions of a network. However, both use PPP as the protocol through which to negotiate and authenticate the connection and encapsulate the data sent over it. As implemented in Routing and Remote Access, both remote access and demand-dial connections can be enabled separately or together and share the following properties:

- Behavior for the dial-in properties of user accounts
- Security (authentication protocols and encryption)
- Use of Windows or Remote Authentication Dial-In User Service (RADIUS) for authentication, authorization, and accounting
- Use of network policies for authorization
- IPv4 address assignment and configuration
- Troubleshooting facilities, including event logging, Windows or RADIUS authentication and accounting logging, and tracing

Whereas the concept of demand-dial routing is fairly simple, configuration of demand-dial routing can be complex. This complexity is because of the following factors:

- **Connection endpoint addressing**   The connection must be made over public data networks such as the Internet. A fully qualified domain name, IPv4 address, or IPv6 address must identify the endpoint of the connection.

- **Authentication and authorization of demand-dial connections**   Incoming connections to the answering router must be authenticated and authorized. Authentication is based on the calling router's set of credentials that are passed during the connection establishment process. The credentials that are passed must correspond to an account. Authorization is granted based on the dial-in properties of the account and network policies.

- **Differentiation between remote access clients and calling routers**   Both demand-dial routing and remote access capabilities can coexist on the same computer running Windows Server 2008. Both remote access clients and demand-dial routers can initiate a connection. The computer running Windows Server 2008 that answers a connection attempt can distinguish a remote access client from a demand-dial router by checking the user name, which is included in the authentication credentials sent by the calling router. If the user name matches the name of a demand-dial interface on the answering router, the connection is a demand-dial connection. Otherwise, the incoming connection is a remote access connection.

- **Configuration of both ends of the connection**   Both ends of the connection must be configured, even if only one end of the connection always initiates the demand-dial connection. If you configure only one side of the connection, packets can be successfully routed only in one direction. Communication typically requires that information travel in both directions.

- **Configuration of static routes**   You should not use dynamic routing protocols over temporary demand-dial connections. Therefore, routes for IPv4 or IPv6 address prefixes that are available across the demand-dial interface must be added as static routes to the routing tables of the demand-dial routers. You can add static routes manually or by using auto-static updates. Additionally, those routes need to be added to your routing infrastructure to provide reachability to remote sites.

To summarize, a site-to-site VPN connection is a demand-dial connection that uses a VPN protocol such as PPTP or L2TP/IPsec to connect two portions of a private network. The calling router initiates the connection by using a demand-dial interface. The answering router listens for connection attempts, receives the connection attempt from the calling router, and completes the connection by using a demand-dial interface. After the connection is successfully made, both calling and answering routers act as IPv4 or IPv6 routers, forwarding packets between the two sites of an organization network across the VPN connection.

Direct from the Source: Matching Demand-Dial Interface and User Names

A common mistake made in setting up demand-dial site-to-site VPN connections between VPN routers is the failure to have the user name match the name of the demand-dial interface on the answering router. Two separate tunnels will be established if the user name of the calling router does not match the answering router's demand-dial interface. Routing and Remote Access uses the user name to determine whether a local demand-dial interface should be associated with the tunnel. If a match is found, the two interfaces are associated, and both enter a connected state. Traffic can then be routed in both directions over one VPN tunnel. If the user name does not match, two tunnels are established as separate remote access client connections, one in each direction. Frequently, there is an intermediate router that does not support more than a single concurrent VPN tunnel. The symptom of this issue will manifest itself by the ability to establish a demand-dial connection from VPNRouter1 to VPNRouter2 and from VPNRouter2 to VPNRouter1, but not both at the same time. If one is connected, the other demand-dial attempt will fail, regardless of the direction. This is seen most often with routers intended for home use deployed in small branch office scenarios and can be resolved by correcting the demand-dial account configuration.

Tim Quinn, Support Escalation Engineer

Enterprise Platform Support

Demand-Dial Routing Updates

Typical routing protocols rely on a periodic advertising process to communicate routing information. For example, Routing Information Protocol (RIP) for IPv4 advertises the contents of its routing table every 30 seconds on all interfaces. This behavior is not a problem for permanently connected LAN or WAN lines. For usage-sensitive dial-up WAN lines, this type of periodic behavior could cause the router to call another router every 30 seconds, which might result in an undesirable phone bill. Therefore, you should not run routing protocols across temporary dial-up WAN lines.

If you do not use routing protocols to update the routing tables of the VPN routers, you must add the routes as static routes. The static routes that correspond to the IPv4 or IPv6 address prefixes available across a demand-dial interface can be configured manually or automatically. The automatic entering of IPv4 static routes for demand-dial interfaces is known as an *auto-static update* and is supported when you use RIP for IPv4 with Routing and Remote Access.

When instructed, a demand-dial interface that is configured for auto-static updates sends a RIP for IPv4 request across an active connection to request all the routes of the router on the other side of the connection. Based on the response to the request, the IPv4 routes of the requested router are automatically added as static routes in the routing table of the requesting router. The static routes are persistent; they are kept in the routing table even if the interface becomes disconnected or the router is restarted. An auto-static update is a one-time, one-way exchange of routing information.

For more information, see "Configuring Intersite Network Infrastructure" later in this chapter.

> **Note**   The *auto* in *auto-static* refers to the automatic adding of the requested routes as static routes in the routing table. The sending of the request for routes is performed through an explicit action—either through the Routing and Remote Access snap-in or with a **Netsh** command while the demand-dial interface is in a connected state. Auto-static updates are not automatically performed every time a demand-dial connection is made.

On-Demand vs. Persistent Connections

A site-to-site VPN connection can be on-demand or persistent:

- An on-demand site-to-site connection is initiated when traffic must be forwarded across the connection and the connection has not already been established. A connection can be initiated automatically by configuring static routes on the calling router to initiate a demand-dial connection. When traffic matching the route must be forwarded, the connection is made and the traffic is forwarded. On-demand connections are terminated after a configured amount of idle time. For more information about configuring idle disconnect behavior, see "Deploying the Calling Routers" later in this chapter.

- A persistent site-to-site connection is always connected. If the connection is dropped, it is immediately retried. For more information about configuring a persistent connection, see "Deploying the Calling Routers" later in this chapter.

By default, demand-dial interfaces use on-demand connections with a five-minute idle timeout.

Restricting the Initiation of On-Demand Connections

To prevent the calling router from making unnecessary on-demand connections, you can restrict the calling router from initiating site-to-site VPN connections in the following ways:

- **Demand-dial filtering**   You can use demand-dial filtering to configure the types of IPv4 or IPv6 traffic that do not cause a demand-dial connection to be initiated or the types of IPv4 or IPv6 traffic that cause a connection to be initiated. For more information, see "Deploying the Calling Routers" later in this chapter.

- **Dial-out hours**   You can use dial-out hours to configure the hours that a calling router is either permitted or not allowed to make a site-to-site VPN connection. For more information, see "Deploying the Calling Routers" later in this chapter.

You can also use network policies to configure the times when incoming demand-dial connections at the answering router are allowed.

Two-Way vs. One-Way Initiated Connections

With two-way initiated connections, either VPN router can be the calling router or answering router depending on who is initiating the connection. Both VPN routers must be configured to both initiate and accept a site-to-site VPN connection. You can use two-way initiated connections when the site-to-site VPN connection is not active 24 hours a day and traffic from either router is used to create an on-demand connection. Two-way initiated site-to-site VPN connections have the following requirements:

- Both VPN routers must be connected to the Internet via a permanent WAN link.

- Both VPN routers must be configured as LAN and demand-dial routers.

- User accounts must be added for both VPN routers so that the authentication credentials of the calling router can be validated by the answering router.

- Demand-dial interfaces, with the same name as the user account that is used by the calling router, must be fully configured at both routers, including settings for the host name, user account credentials, and the IPv4 or IPv6 address of the answering router.

Table 13-1 lists a correct example configuration for two-way initiated demand-dial routing between Router 1, a demand-dial router in the Seattle site of an organization, and Router 2, a demand-dial router in the New York site of an organization.

Table 13-1   Example Configuration for Two-Way Initiated Demand-Dial Routing

Router	Demand-Dial Interface Name	User Account Name in User Credentials
Router 1	DD_NewYork	DD_Seattle
Router 2	DD_Seattle	DD_NewYork

Notice how the user account name in the user credentials of the demand-dial interface of one router matches the name of a demand-dial interface on the other router.

With one-way initiated connections, one VPN router is always the calling router, and the other VPN router is the always the answering router. One-way initiated connections are well suited to a permanent connection spoke-and-hub topology in which the branch office router is the only router that initiates the connection to a hub office router. One-way initiated connections have the following requirements:

- Both VPN routers must be configured as LAN and demand-dial routers.

- A user account that can be validated by the answering router must be added for the authentication credentials of the calling router.

- A demand-dial interface is configured at the answering router with the same name as the user account that is used by the calling router. This demand-dial interface is not used to initiate a connection, so it does not need to be configured with the host name, user account credentials, or the IPv4 or IPv6 address of the calling router.

Components of Windows Site-to-Site VPNs

Figure 13-1 shows the components of Windows-based site-to-site VPNs.

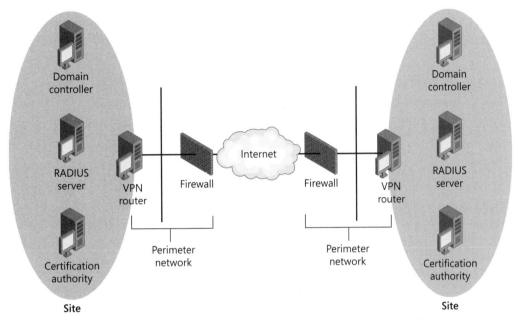

Figure 13-1   Components of Windows-based site-to-site VPNs

The components are:

- **VPN routers**   VPN routers either initiate site-to-site VPN connections to answering routers and forward packets across a VPN-based demand-dial connection (calling routers) or listen for site-to-site VPN connection attempts, enforce authentication and connection requirements, and forward packets across a VPN-based demand-dial connection (answering routers).

- **RADIUS servers**   RADIUS servers provide centralized authentication and authorization processing and accounting for network access attempts for answering routers, remote access VPN servers, and other types of access servers.

- **Active Directory domain controllers**   Active Directory domain controllers validate user credentials for authentication and provide user account information to evaluate authorization for answering routers.

- **Certification authorities (CAs)**   CAs are part of the PKI, and they issue computer or user certificates to calling routers and computer certificates to answering routers and RADIUS servers for authentication of site-to-site VPN connections.

Planning and Design Considerations

When deploying a site-to-site VPN solution, you must consider the following planning and design issues:

- VPN protocols
- Authentication methods
- VPN routers
- Internet infrastructure
- Site network infrastructure
- Authentication infrastructure
- PKI

VPN Protocols

Windows Server 2008 includes support for the following site-to-site VPN protocols:

- **PPTP**   PPTP uses PPP user authentication and MPPE encryption. When Microsoft Challenge Handshake Authentication Protocol (MS-CHAP v2) is used with strong passwords, PPTP is a secure VPN technology. For certificate-based authentication, EAP-TLS can be used with registry-based user certificates. PPTP is easily deployed and can be used across most network address translators (NATs).

- **L2TP/IPsec**   L2TP utilizes PPP user authentication and IPsec encryption. L2TP/IPsec by default uses certificates and the IPsec computer-level authentication process to negotiate the protected IPsec session and then PPP-based user authentication. L2TP/IPsec is more secure than PPTP.

  A new feature of L2TP/IPsec in Windows Server 2008 is the verification of the Subject Alternative Name and Enhanced Key Usage fields of the computer certificate of the answering router to help detect man-in-the-middle attacks. This feature is enabled by default in the properties dialog box of a demand-dial connection on the Networking tab in the IPsec Settings dialog box.

Design Choices for VPN Protocols

- When using MS-CHAP v2 for authentication, PPTP does not require a PKI to issue certificates to each VPN router.

- PPTP provides data confidentiality for packets. PPTP-based VPN connections do not provide data integrity or data origin authentication.

- L2TP/IPsec provides data confidentiality (encryption), data integrity (proof that the data was not modified in transit), and data origin authentication (proof that the data was sent by the authorized user) for each packet. L2TP/IPsec provides much better protection of VPN packets than PPTP.

- By default, a Windows Server 2008 VPN router supports PPTP and L2TP/IPsec for site-to-site VPN connections. You can use PPTP for some VPN connections (for example, from calling routers that do not have an installed computer certificate) and L2TP/IPsec for other connections (for example, from calling routers that have an installed computer certificate).

- If you are using both VPN protocols, you can create separate network policies that define different connection settings for PPTP or L2TP/IPsec-based connections.

Requirements for VPN Protocols

- Encrypted PPTP-based demand dial connections require the MS-CHAP v2 or EAP-TLS authentication protocols.

- PPTP-based calling routers can be located behind a NAT if the NAT includes a NAT editor that knows how to properly translate PPTP tunneled data. For example, both the Internet Connection Sharing (ICS) feature of the Network Connections folder and the NAT routing protocol component of Routing and Remote Access include a NAT editor that translates PPTP traffic to and from PPTP clients located behind the NAT. Answering routers cannot be behind a NAT unless there are multiple public IP addresses and there is a one-to-one mapping of a public IP address to the private IP address of the answering router. If there is only one public address, the NAT must be configured to translate and forward the PPTP tunneled data to the answering router. Most NATs using a single public IP address, including ICS and the NAT routing protocol component, can be configured to allow inbound traffic based on IP addresses and TCP and UDP ports. However, PPTP tunneled data does not use TCP or UDP headers. Therefore, an answering router cannot be located behind a computer using ICS or the NAT routing protocol component when using a single IP address.

- L2TP/IPsec-based calling routers cannot be behind a NAT unless both routers support IPsec NAT Traversal (NAT-T). IPsec NAT-T is supported by the Windows Server 2008 and Windows Server 2003 operating systems. L2TP/IPsec-based answering routers cannot be behind a NAT.

- L2TP/IPsec supports computer certificates as the default and recommended authentication method for IPsec. Computer certificate authentication requires a PKI to issue computer certificates to the VPN router computers.

- If you want to use demand-dial VPN connections across the IPv6 Internet, you must use L2TP/IPsec. For more information, see "How It Works: IPv6 and VPN Connections" later in this chapter.

Best Practices for VPN Protocols

- If you already have a PKI in place, use L2TP/IPsec.

- L2TP/IPsec connections also support preshared key authentication. A preshared key is a string of text that is configured on both the calling and answering routers. Preshared key is a weak authentication method. Therefore, it is recommended that you use preshared key authentication only while your PKI is being deployed or when preshared key authentication is required for third-party VPN routers. You can enable preshared key authentication for the calling router in the properties dialog box of a demand-dial connection, on the Networking tab, in the IPsec Settings dialog box. You can enable preshared key authentication for the answering router in the Routing and Remote Access snap-in, in the properties dialog box of a server, on the Security tab.

How It Works: IPv6 and VPN Connections

Windows Server 2008 and Windows Vista have enhanced support for IPv6, which is installed and enabled by default. Native IPv6 operation is supported by almost all the networking applications and services included with Windows Server 2008 and Windows Vista. For site-to-site VPN connections, Windows Server 2008 and Windows Vista support IPv6 traffic in the following ways:

- IPv4-tunneled IPv6 traffic
- Native IPv6 traffic inside the VPN tunnel
- VPN connections over IPv6

IPv4-Tunneled IPv6 Traffic

Using Windows Server 2003, you can send IPv6 traffic over a site-to-site VPN connection but only if it has already been wrapped in an IPv4 header. IPv4 tunneling of IPv6 traffic is a mechanism used by IPv6 transition technologies, such as the Intra-Site Automatic Tunnel Addressing Protocol (ISATAP), to provide IPv6 connectivity between IPv6/IPv4 hosts across an intranet that supports only IPv4 routing.

With IPv4-tunneled IPv6 traffic support, a calling router can create a site-to-site VPN connection across the IPv4 Internet and then forward IPv4-tunneled IPv6 traffic. IPv4-tunneled IPv6 traffic sent over a site-to-site VPN connection has the following structure:

- An IPv6 packet is wrapped with an IPv4 header (this is the IPv4 tunneling), which is wrapped with a PPP header and a VPN protocol header (such as PPTP or L2TP/IPsec), which is wrapped with a final IPv4 header to allow the packet to traverse the IPv4 Internet.

PPTP and L2TP/IPsec in Windows Server 2008 support IPv4-tunneled IPv6 traffic. IPv4-tunneled IPv6 traffic sent over a VPN connection requires Internet Protocol Control Protocol (IPCP) support on the VPN routers and an IPv6 transition technology infrastructure (such as ISATAP) on the intranet. IPCP is a PPP network control protocol that allows PPP hosts to configure settings for using IPv4 over a PPP link.

Native IPv6 Traffic Inside the VPN Tunnel

Windows Server 2008 supports VPN connections with native IPv6 traffic inside the VPN tunnel. The calling router creates a site-to-site VPN connection with an answering router over the IPv4 Internet and then negotiates the use of IPv6 over the PPP link. IPv6 packets are encapsulated by the VPN protocol inside of the VPN tunnel. With native IPv6 traffic inside the VPN tunnel support, VPN routers can create a site-to-site VPN connection across the IPv4 Internet and then forward native IPv6 traffic across the VPN connection.

Native IPv6 traffic inside the VPN tunnel has the following structure:

- An IPv6 packet is wrapped with a PPP header and a VPN protocol header and is wrapped with a final IPv4 header to allow the packet to traverse the IPv4 Internet.

Native IPv6 traffic inside the VPN tunnel requires IPv6 routing and Internet Protocol version 6 Control Protocol (IPV6CP) support on the VPN routers and a native IPv6 routing infrastructure on the intranet. PPTP and L2TP/IPsec in Windows Server 2008 supports native IPv6 traffic inside the VPN tunnel. IPV6CP is a PPP network control protocol that allows PPP hosts to configure settings for using IPv6 over a PPP link.

> **Note**   Windows Server 2003 does not support native IPv6 traffic inside the VPN tunnel.

VPN Connections Over IPv6

Windows Server 2008 also supports site-to-site VPN connections over IPv6. The VPN client creates a VPN connection with a VPN server over the IPv6 Internet and then negotiates the use of either IPv6 or IPv4 over the PPP link. With VPN connections over IPv6 support, VPN routers can create site-to-site VPN connections across the IPv6 Internet and then forward either native IPv6 or IPv4 traffic across the connection.

Packets for VPN connections over IPv6 have the following structure:

- An IPv6 or IPv4 packet is wrapped with a PPP header and a VPN protocol header, which is wrapped with a final IPv6 header to allow the packet to traverse the IPv6 Internet.

L2TP/IPsec in Windows Server 2008 supports site-to-site VPN connections over IPv6. VPN connections over IPv6 requires native IPv6 support for VPN protocols on the VPN routers, IPv6 routing support on the VPN routers, and connections to the IPv6 Internet.

Native IPv6 capability for site-to-site VPN connections, which is the ability to send native IPv6 packets over a site-to-site VPN connection, is possible with native IPv6 traffic inside the VPN tunnel and with VPN connections over IPv6.

> **Note**   Windows Server 2003 does not support VPN connections over IPv6 or native IPv6 capability for site-to-site VPN connections.

Authentication Methods

To authenticate the calling router that is attempting a VPN connection, Windows Server 2008 supports a variety of authentication protocols, including the following:

- **MS-CHAP v2**   MS-CHAP v2 is a password-based authentication method that provides mutual authentication.

- **EAP-TLS**   EAP-TLS is a certificate-based authentication method that is used in conjunction with a PKI. EAP-TLS also provides mutual authentication. With EAP-TLS, the calling router sends its user certificate for authentication, and the authentication server (either the answering router or a RADIUS server) sends a computer certificate for authentication.

> **Note**   In Windows Server 2008, support for the Microsoft Challenge Handshake Authentication Protocol (MS-CHAP) (also known as MS-CHAP v1), Shiva Password Authentication Protocol (SPAP), and EAP-Message Digest 5 (EAP-MD5) protocols has been removed because of security considerations. Unlike remote access VPN connections, Windows Server 2008 does not support the use of the EAP-MS-CHAP v2, Protected EAP (PEAP)-TLS, or PEAP-MS-CHAP v2 authentication protocols for site-to-site VPN connections.

Design Choices for Authentication Protocols

- If you have a PKI, use EAP-TLS for your site-to-site VPN connections. If a PKI is not deployed or is not practical for your network, use MS-CHAP v2.

- EAP-TLS is much stronger than MS-CHAP v2 because it does not rely on passwords and is resistant to offline dictionary attacks.

Requirements for Authentication Protocols

- For encrypted PPTP-based connections, you must use MS-CHAP v2 or EAP-TLS. Only these authentication protocols provide a mechanism to generate a per-session initial encryption key that is used by both VPN routers to encrypt PPTP data sent on the VPN connection.

- EAP-TLS requires a PKI to issue user and computer certificates.

Best Practices for Authentication Protocols

- If you must use MS-CHAP v2, require the use of strong passwords on your network. Strong passwords are long (greater than 8 characters) and contain a mixture of uppercase and lowercase letters plus numbers and punctuation. An example of a strong password for a calling router user account is f3L*q02~>xR3w#4o. In an Active Directory domain, use Group Policy settings in Computer Configuration\Windows Settings\Security Settings\Account Policies\Password Policy to enforce strong user passwords requirements.

- For EAP-TLS, the calling router by default validates the answering router's computer certificate. It is possible to configure the calling routers so that they do not validate the certificate of the authentication server, in which case computer certificates would not be required on the authentication servers. However, having the calling routers validate the certificate of the authentication server is recommended for mutual authentication of the calling router and authentication server, which helps prevent the calling router from authenticating with an impersonating authentication server.

- For L2TP/IPsec-based connections, any user-level authentication protocol can be used because the authentication occurs after the VPN routers have established an IPsec-protected channel. However, the use of EAP-TLS or MS-CHAP v2 is recommended to provide strong user authentication and mutual authentication with the authentication server.

VPN Routers

VPN routers either initiate or receive VPN-based demand-dial connections. A calling router does the following:

- Initiates VPN connections based on connection persistence, an administrator action, or when a packet being forwarded matches a route using a VPN-based demand-dial interface

- Waits for authentication and authorization before forwarding packets

- Acts as a router, forwarding packets between nodes in its site and nodes in the site of the answering router

An answering router does the following:

- Listens for VPN connection attempts

- Authenticates and authorizes VPN connections before allowing data to flow

- Acts as a router, forwarding packets between nodes in its site and nodes in the site of the calling router

Configuring Routing and Remote Access

When you configure and enable Routing and Remote Access, the Routing and Remote Access Server Setup Wizard prompts you to select the role that the computer will fill. For VPN routers, you should select the Remote Access (Dial-Up Or VPN) option. With the Remote Access (Dial-Up Or VPN) option, the Routing and Remote Access server is configured to support both remote access and site-to-site VPN connections.

> **Note**   Microsoft recommends the choice of the Remote Access (Dial-Up Or VPN) option over the Secure Connection Between Two Private Networks option in the Routing and Remote Access Server Setup Wizard because the Secure Connection Between Two Private Networks option does not prompt you to select an Internet interface over which to automatically configure VPN traffic packet filters, does not prompt you to configure RADIUS servers, and creates a limited number of PPTP and L2TP ports.

When you select the Remote Access (Dial-Up Or VPN) option in the Routing and Remote Access Server Setup Wizard, the following events occur:

1. You are first prompted to specify whether VPN, dial-up, or both types of access are needed.

2. Next, you are prompted to select the interface that is connected to the Internet. By default, the interface that you select will be automatically configured with packet filters that allow only VPN traffic. All other traffic is silently discarded. For example, you will no longer be able to ping the Internet interface of the VPN router.

3. Next, if you have multiple network adapters that are connected to the intranet, you are prompted to select an interface over which DHCP, DNS, and WINS configuration is obtained.

4. Next, you are prompted to determine whether you want to obtain IPv4 addresses to assign to calling routers and remote access clients by using either DHCP or a specified range of addresses. If you select a specified range of addresses, you are prompted to add the address ranges.

5. Next, you are prompted to specify whether you want to use RADIUS for authentication and accounting of VPN connections. If you select RADIUS, you are prompted to configure the names, IPv4 addresses, or IPv6 addresses of the primary and alternate RADIUS servers and the RADIUS shared secret.

When you select and configure the Remote Access (Dial-Up Or VPN) option in the Routing and Remote Access Server Setup Wizard, the configuration results are as follows:

- The Routing and Remote Access service is enabled as an IPv4-based remote access server and LAN and demand-dial router, which performs authentication and accounting either locally or through RADIUS.

- If there is only one network adapter connected to the intranet, that network adapter is automatically selected as the interface from which to obtain DHCP, DNS, and WINS configuration. Otherwise, the network adapter you specified in the wizard fills that role.

- If specified, the IPv4 address ranges to assign to the VPN interfaces of calling routers are configured.

- Either Windows or RADIUS is configured to provide authentication and accounting of VPN connection attempts.

- Depending on the version of Windows Server 2008, up to 128 PPTP and 128 L2TP ports are created for demand-dial connections. Each port represents a possible VPN connection. All of them are enabled for both inbound remote access connections and inbound and outbound demand-dial connections (used for site-to-site VPN connections).

- The selected Internet interface is configured with input and output IPv4 and IPv6 packet filters that allow only VPN traffic.

- The DHCP Relay Agent component is added with the Internal interface. The *Internal interface* is a logical interface that represents the connection to all other authenticated remote access clients. The DHCP Relay Agent is not used for site-to-site VPN connections.

- The IGMP component is added, and the Internal interface is configured for Internet Group Management Protocol (IGMP) router mode. All other LAN interfaces are configured for IGMP proxy mode. This allows VPN routers to forward IPv4 multicast traffic across demand-dial interfaces.

> **More Info**   For more information, see the Windows Server 2008 Technical Library at *http://technet.microsoft.com/windowsserver/2008*.

Design Choices for VPN Routers

- The VPN router can be configured to obtain IPv4 addresses from DHCP or from a manually configured set of address ranges (known as *static pools of addresses*). Using DHCP to obtain IPv4 addresses simplifies configuration; however, you should ensure that the DHCP scope for the subnet to which the intranet connection of the VPN router is attached has enough addresses for all the computers physically connected to the subnet and has the maximum number of PPTP and L2TP ports.

  If there are not enough addresses in your static pool, calling routers will still be able to connect. Calling and answering routers request an IPv4 address from each other during the connection establishment process. But if one of the routers does not have an address to assign, both routers continue with the connection establishment process. The VPN interface on the point-to-point connection does not have an assigned IPv4 address. This is known as an *unnumbered connection*. Although Windows Server 2008 VPN routers support unnumbered connections, the RIP for IPv4 routing protocol component of Routing and Remote Access does not work over an unnumbered connection.

- The answering router can either evaluate authentication and authorization for VPN connections itself or rely on a RADIUS server. When configuring an answering router, you can choose to use Windows or RADIUS for authentication or accounting.

  When configured to use Windows for authentication and accounting, an answering router communicates with an Active Directory domain controller to validate the credentials of the calling router and obtain the calling router's user account dial-in properties. The answering router uses the user account properties and locally configured network policies to authorize the VPN connection. The answering router by default logs VPN connection accounting information in local accounting log files.

  When configured to use RADIUS for authentication and accounting, the answering router uses a configured RADIUS server to validate the credentials of the calling router, authorize the connection attempt, and log VPN connection accounting information.

- The Routing and Remote Access Server Setup Wizard does not automatically enable IPv6 support for site-to-site VPN connections. For more information, see "Deploying the Answering Routers" and "Deploying the Calling Routers" later in this chapter.

- For on-demand connections, if you want to prevent connections from occurring during certain times of the day during the week or for certain types of traffic, configure dial-out hours or demand-dial filters, accessible by right-clicking the demand-dial network interface of the calling router.

  Demand-dial filters are applied before the connection is made. IPv4 or IPv6 packet filters are applied after the connection is made. To prevent the demand-dial connection from being established for traffic that is discarded by the IPv4 or IPv6 packet filters, you should match your IPv4 or IPv6 packet filters to the demand-dial filters. For more information, see "Deploying the Calling Routers" later in this chapter.

Requirements for VPN Routers

- The VPN router must have a manual TCP/IP (IPv4) configuration for its Internet interface and for its intranet interface(s). Because of possible default route conflicts, you should manually configure the intranet interfaces with an IPv4 address, subnet mask, DNS server(s), and WINS server(s). However, do not configure a default gateway on the VPN router's intranet interfaces. It is possible for the VPN router to have a manual TCP/IP configuration and use DHCP to obtain IPv4 addresses that are assigned to calling routers.

- For VPN connections that use the EAP-TLS authentication protocol, you must install a computer certificate on the authentication server (either the answering router or the RADIUS server) that can be validated by the calling router and a user certificate on the calling router that can be validated by the authentication server.

> **Note** *Computer certificates* are certificates that are stored in the local computer certificate store and have the appropriate properties to perform TLS-based or IPsec-based authentication. For more details about certificate requirements for TLS-based authentication, see *http://go.microsoft.com/fwlink/?LinkID=20016*. For more details about certificate requirements for IPsec-based authentication, see *http://go.microsoft.com/fwlink/?LinkID=67907*.

- For L2TP/IPsec connections that use certificate authentication (recommended), you must install computer certificates on both the answering router and the calling router.

- If you configure the answering router to perform its own authentication or for RADIUS authentication, and the RADIUS server is a computer running the Network Policy Server (NPS), the default network policy named Connections to Microsoft Routing and Remote Access Server rejects all types of connection attempts unless the network access permission of the user account's dial-in properties is set to Allow Access. If you want to use this network policy for your site-to-site VPN connections, set the policy type to Allow Access. If you want to manage authorization and connection settings for site-to-site VPN connections by group or by type of connection, you must configure additional NPS policies. For more information, see "Authentication Infrastructure" later in this chapter.

Best Practices for VPN Servers

■   Determine the connection of the VPN router that will be connected to the Internet. Typical VPN routers have at least two LAN connections: one connected to the Internet (either directly or connected to a perimeter network) and one connected to the organization intranet. To make this distinction easier to see when running the Routing and Remote Access Server Setup Wizard, rename the connections within the Network Connections folder. For example, rename the connection named Local Area Connection that is connected to the site *Site* and the connection named Local Area Connection 2 that is connected to the Internet *Internet*.

Internet Infrastructure

In order for a calling router to successfully exchange traffic with an answering router over the Internet, the following conditions must be met:

■   The answering router's DNS name must be resolvable.

■   The answering router must be reachable.

■   VPN traffic must be allowed to and from both VPN routers.

Answering Router Name Resolvability

In the demand-dial interface of the calling router, you will refer to the answering router by its Fully Qualified Domain Name (FQDN) rather than its IPv4 or IPv6 address. You can use an FQDN (for example, vpn.example.microsoft.com) as long as the name can be resolved to an IPv4 or IPv6 address. Therefore, you must ensure that whatever name you are using for your answering routers when configuring a demand-dial connection is resolvable to its IPv4 or IPv6 address.

Answering Router Reachability

To be reachable, the answering router must be assigned a public IPv4 address or a global IPv6 address to which packets are forwarded by the routing infrastructure of the IPv4 or IPv6 Internet. If you have been assigned a static public IPv4 address from an ISP or an Internet registry, this is typically not an issue. In some configurations, the answering router is actually configured with a private IPv4 address and has a published static IPv4 address by which it is known on the Internet. A device between the Internet and the answering router translates the published and actual IPv4 addresses of the answering router in packets to and from the answering router.

Although the routing infrastructure of the IPv4 or IPv6 Internet might provide reachability, the answering router might be unreachable because of the placement of firewalls, packet filtering routers, NATs, security gateways, or other types of devices that prevent packets from being either sent to or received from the answering router computer.

VPN Routers and Firewall Configuration

The following are common configurations of firewalls with a VPN router:

- **The VPN router is attached directly to the Internet, and the firewall is between the VPN router and the intranet.**   In this configuration, there is no separate firewall between the VPN server and the Internet, and the VPN server is performing its own packet filtering. The VPN router must be configured with packet filters that allow only VPN traffic in and out of its Internet interface. The firewall on the intranet can be configured to allow specific types of intersite traffic.

    This is the firewall configuration if you use Microsoft Internet Security and Acceleration Server on the VPN router.

- **A firewall is attached to the Internet, and the VPN router is between the firewall and the intranet.**   In this configuration, both the firewall and the VPN router are attached to a subnet known as the *perimeter network* (also known as a *screened subnet*). Both the firewall and the VPN router must be configured with packet filters that allow only VPN traffic to and from the Internet.

- **Two firewalls are used—one between the VPN server and the intranet and one between the VPN server and the Internet.**   In this configuration, there is a firewall filtering the traffic between the Internet and the perimeter network and a firewall filtering the traffic between the computers on the perimeter network and the intranet. The Internet firewall and the VPN router must be configured with packet filters that allow only VPN traffic to and from the Internet. The intranet firewall can be configured to allow specific types of intersite traffic.

For the details of configuring packet filters for the VPN router and the firewall for these configurations, see "Firewall Packet Filtering for VPN Traffic" in Chapter 12.

Requirements for Internet Infrastructure

- Wherever possible, configure your demand-dial interfaces with the IPv4 or IPv6 addresses of answering routers. If you are using names, ensure that the FQDNs of your answering routers are resolvable through Hosts file entries or by placing appropriate DNS address (A) or IPv6 address (AAAA) records in either your Internet DNS server or the DNS server of your ISP. Test the resolvability by using the Ping tool to ping the name of each of your answering routers when directly connected to the Internet.

    Because of packet filtering, the **ping** command might display the result Request Timed Out, but check to ensure that the name specified was resolved by the Ping tool to the proper address. To force the Ping tool to use an IPv4 address, use the **-4** switch. To force the Ping tool to use an IPv6 address, use the **-6** switch. You can also use the Nslookup tool to test name resolution.

■ Ensure that the IPv4 or IPv6 addresses of your answering routers are reachable from the Internet by using the Ping tool to ping the FQDN or address of your answering router with a five-second timeout (using the **-w 5** switch) when directly connected to the Internet. If you see a Destination Unreachable message, the answering router is not reachable.

Best Practices for Internet Infrastructure

For site-to-site VPN connections, configure packet filtering for PPTP traffic, L2TP/IPsec traffic, or both types of traffic on the appropriate firewall and VPN router interfaces connecting to the Internet and the perimeter network. For more information, see "Firewall Packet Filtering for VPN Traffic" in Chapter 12.

Site Network Infrastructure

The network infrastructure of the site is an important element of VPN design. Without proper site network infrastructure design, VPN routers might be unable to do the following:

■ Resolve intranet names

■ Obtain an IPv4 address that is reachable from the intranet

■ Reach intranet locations

Intranet Name Resolution

If the calling router is configured with the IP addresses of Domain Name System (DNS) or Windows Internet Name Service (WINS) servers, DNS and WINS server IPv4 addresses are not requested from the answering router during the PPP connection negotiation. If the calling router is not configured with the IPv4 addresses of DNS and WINS servers, DNS and WINS servers are requested. The answering router never requests DNS and WINS server IPv4 addresses from the calling router.

Unlike Windows-based remote access clients, the calling router does not send a DHCPInform message to the answering router to discover additional TCP/IP configuration information.

By default, the calling router does not register itself with the DNS or WINS servers obtained from the answering router. To change this behavior, set the registry value HKEY_LOCAL_MACHINE\System\CurrentControlSet\Services\Rasman\PPP\ControlProtocols\BuiltIn\RegisterRoutersWithNameServers to **1**.

VPN Router Routing to the Internet and the Intranet

Each VPN router is an IPv4 or IPv6 router and must be properly configured with the set of IPv4 and IPv6 routes that makes all locations on the Internet and the site of the VPN router reachable. Each VPN router needs the following:

- **A default route that points to a firewall or router directly connected to the IPv4 or IPv6 Internet**   This route makes all the locations on the IPv4 or IPv6 Internet reachable.

- **One or more routes that summarize the IPv4 and IPv6 address space used within the site of the VPN router that point to a neighboring site router**   These routes make all the locations within the site of the VPN router reachable from the VPN router. Without these routes, nodes in the site of the VPN router that are not connected to the same subnet as the VPN router are unreachable.

For a single default route that points to the Internet, configure the Internet interface with a default gateway, and then manually configure the site interface without a default gateway.

To add site routes to the routing table of each VPN router, you can:

- Add static IPv4 or IPv6 routes by using the Routing and Remote Access snap-in. You do not necessarily need to add a route for each subnet in your site. At a minimum, you need to add just the routes that summarize all the possible addresses in your site. For example, if your site uses the private IPv4 address space 10.0.0.0/8 to number its subnets and hosts, you do not need to add a route for each subnet. Just add a route for 10.0.0.0 with the subnet mask 255.0.0.0 that points to a neighboring router on the site subnet to which your VPN router is attached. Similarly, if your site uses the 2001:db8:5ef2::/48 IPv6 address prefix for a site, you must add only a single route with this prefix as a static IPv6 route.

- If you are using the RIP for IPv4 routing protocol in your site, you can add and configure the RIP routing protocol component of Routing and Remote Access so that the VPN router participates in the propagation of IPv4 routing information as a dynamic router.

If your site has only a single subnet, no further configuration is required.

When a site-to-site VPN connection is made, each router sends traffic using a logical VPN interface that corresponds to the PPTP or L2TP port of the demand-dial connection. During the PPP negotiation, IPv4 and IPv6 addresses might be assigned to these VPN interfaces. Ensuring the reachability of the VPN interfaces of VPN routers depends on how you configure each VPN router to obtain IPv4 and IPv6 addresses for remote access clients and calling routers.

The IPv6 address assigned to VPN routers are based on a common IPv6 subnet prefix that represents the IPv6 subnet for all remote access and site-to-site VPN connections. For more information, see "Deploying the Answering Routers" and "Deploying the Calling Routers" later in this chapter.

The IPv4 addresses assigned to VPN routers as they connect can be from:

- **An on-subnet address range, which is an address range of the site subnet to which the VPN router is attached**   An on-subnet address range is used whenever the VPN router is configured to use DHCP to obtain IPv4 addresses and when the manually configured pool(s) of IPv4 addresses are within the range of addresses of the attached site subnet.

- **An off-subnet address range, which is an address range that represents a different subnet that is logically attached to the VPN router**   An off-subnet address range is used whenever the VPN router is manually configured with a pool of IP addresses for a separate subnet.

On-Subnet Address Range   If you are using an on-subnet address range, no additional routing configuration is required because the VPN router acts as an Address Resolution Protocol (ARP) proxy for all packets destined for the VPN interfaces of the other connected VPN routers. Routers and hosts on the site subnet forward packets destined for the VPN interfaces of connected VPN routers, and the VPN router relays them to the correct VPN routers.

Off-Subnet Address Range   If you are using an off-subnet address range, you must add the routes that summarize the off-subnet address range to the site's routing infrastructure so that traffic destined for the VPN interfaces of connected VPN routers are forwarded to the VPN router and then sent by the VPN router to the appropriate connected VPN router at another site. To provide the best summarization of address ranges for routes, choose address ranges that can be expressed using a single prefix and subnet mask.

You can add the routes that summarize the off-subnet address range to the routing infrastructure of the site by adding to the neighboring router for the off-subnet address range static IPv4 routes that point to the VPN router's site interface. Use the dynamic routing protocol used in your site to configure the neighboring router to propagate this static route to other routers in the site.

If your site consists of a single subnet, you must either configure each site host for persistent routes of the off-subnet address range that point to the VPN router's site interface or configure each site host with the VPN router as its default gateway. Because routing for off-subnet address ranges requires additional host configuration, it is recommended that you use an on-subnet address pool for a small office/home office (SOHO) network consisting of a single subnet.

Requirements for Site Network Infrastructure

- Configure the Internet interface of the VPN router with a default gateway. Do not configure the site interface of the VPN router with a default gateway.

- Add to the VPN router static IPv4 and IPv6 routes that summarize the address space used in the site in which the VPN router is located. Alternatively, if you use RIP for IPv4 as your dynamic IPv4 routing protocol, configure and enable RIP on the VPN router. If you use a routing protocol other than RIP, you might be able to use route redistribution. For example, if you use Interior Gateway Routing Protocol (IGRP), you might configure the VPN router's neighboring intranet router to use RIP on the interface connected to the subnet to which the VPN router is attached and IGRP on all other interfaces.

■ Add to your IPv6 routing infrastructure the IPv6 subnet prefix for your VPN connections as a route pointing to the VPN router.

Best Practice for Site Network Infrastructure

Configure the VPN router with an on-subnet IPv4 address range either by obtaining IPv4 addresses through DHCP or by manually configuring on-subnet address pools.

Authentication Infrastructure

The authentication infrastructure exists to:

■ Authenticate the credentials of calling routers

■ Authorize the VPN connection

■ Record the VPN connection creation and termination for accounting purposes

The authentication infrastructure for site-to-site VPN connections consists of:

■ The answering router or a RADIUS server

■ A domain controller

A Windows Server 2008–based VPN router can be configured to use either Windows or RADIUS for authentication or accounting. When you configure Routing and Remote Access to use Windows for authentication, the answering router authenticates the VPN connection by communicating with a domain controller through a protected remote procedure call (RPC) channel and authorizes the connection attempt through the dial-in properties of the user account and locally configured network policies. When you configure the VPN router to use RADIUS, the answering router relies on a RADIUS server to perform the authentication and authorization.

When you configure Windows for accounting, the answering router by default logs VPN connection information in a local log file based on settings configured for Local File Logging in the Accounting node in the Network Policy Server snap-in. When you configure RADIUS for accounting, the answering router sends RADIUS accounting messages for VPN connections to a RADIUS server, which records the accounting information.

If you are using RADIUS, you should use Network Policy Server (NPS) in Windows Server 2008. NPS is a full-featured RADIUS server and proxy that is tightly integrated with Active Directory and Routing and Remote Access.

When NPS is used as the RADIUS server, the following occurs:

- NPS performs the authentication of the VPN connection by communicating with a domain controller through a protected RPC channel. NPS authorizes the connection attempt through the dial-in properties of the user account and network policies configured on the NPS server.

- By default, NPS logs all RADIUS accounting information in a local log file (*%System-Root%*\System32\Logfiles\Logfile.log by default) based on settings configured for Local File Logging in the Accounting node in the Network Policy Server snap-in.

Domain User Accounts and Groups

Active Directory domains contain the user accounts and groups used by Routing and Remote Access or NPS to authenticate and authorize VPN connection attempts. User accounts contain the user name and a cryptographic form of the user's password that can be used for validation of the calling router's user credentials. Additional account properties determine whether the user account is enabled or disabled, locked out, or permitted to log on only during specific hours. If the user account is disabled, locked out, or not permitted to log on during the time of the VPN connection, the site-to-site VPN connection attempt is denied. Additionally, if the user account of the calling router is configured to change the password at the next logon the site-to-site VPN connection attempt will fail because changing the password while attempting to make the connection is an interactive process.

Demand-dial routers must be able to make connections as needed without requiring human intervention. Therefore, the user accounts for calling routers must be configured in the user account properties dialog box on the Account tab. Ensure that the User Must Change Password at Next Logon check box is cleared and the Password Never Expires check box is selected. When you use the Demand-Dial Interface Wizard to create dial-in accounts, these account settings are automatically configured.

You should use a separate user account for each calling router. Each user account should have a name that matches a demand-dial interface configured on the answering router. When you use the Demand-Dial Interface Wizard to create dial-in accounts, this relationship between user accounts used by calling routers in separate sites and demand-dial interfaces is automatically created.

Best Practices for Authentication Infrastructure

- If you have multiple VPN servers and routers and you want to centralize authentication, authorization, and accounting services, or you have a heterogeneous mixture of network access equipment, use a RADIUS server, and configure the VPN router to use RADIUS for authentication and accounting.

- If your user account database is a Windows domain, use NPS as your RADIUS server. See Chapter 9 for additional design and planning considerations for NPS-based RADIUS servers.

- To better manage authorization for site-to-site VPN connections, create a universal group in Active Directory that contains global groups for the user accounts that are allowed to make site-to-site VPN connections. For example, create a universal group named VPNRouters that contains the global groups based on your organization's regions or departments. Each global group should contain allowed user accounts for site-to-site VPN connections. When you configure your network policy for site-to-site VPN connections, you specify the VPNRouters group name.

- Whether configured locally or on an NPS server, use a VPN-specific network policy to authorize VPN connections and specify connection constraints and requirements. For example, use NPS policies to grant access for VPN connections based on group membership, to require strong encryption, or to require the use of specific authentication methods (such as MS-CHAP v2 or EAP-TLS).

PKI

To perform certificate-based authentication for L2TP connections and EAP-TLS authentication for site-to-site VPN connections, a certificate infrastructure must be in place to issue the proper certificates to submit during the authentication process and to validate the certificate being submitted.

Computer Certificates for L2TP/IPsec Connections

If you manually configure the certificate authentication method for a rule of an IPsec policy in Windows, you can specify the list of root certification authorities (CAs) from which a certificate is accepted for authentication. For L2TP connections, the IPsec rule for L2TP traffic is automatically configured, and the list of root CAs is not configurable. Instead, each computer in the L2TP connection sends a list of root CAs to its IPsec peer, from which it accepts a certificate for authentication. The root CAs in this list correspond to the root CAs that issued certificates that are stored in the computer certificate store. For example, if Computer A is issued computer certificates by root CAs CertAuth1 and CertAuth2, it notifies its IPsec peer during main mode negotiation that it will accept certificates for authentication from only CertAuth1 and CertAuth2. If the IPsec peer, Computer B, does not have a valid certificate in its computer certificate store issued from CertAuth1 or CertAuth2, IPsec security negotiation fails.

Ensure that one of the following is true before attempting an L2TP/IPsec connection:

- Both the calling router and answering router were issued computer certificates from the same CA.

- Both the calling router and answering router were issued computer certificates from CAs that follow a valid certificate chain up to the same root CA.

In general, the calling router must have a valid computer certificate installed that was issued by a CA that follows a valid certificate chain from the issuing CA up to a root CA that the answering router trusts. Additionally, the answering router must have a valid computer certificate installed that was issued by a CA that follows a valid certificate chain from the issuing CA up to a root CA that the calling router trusts.

A single CA commonly issues computer certificates to all computers in an organization. Because of this, all computers within the organization both have computer certificates from a single CA and request certificates for authentication from the same single CA.

For information about installing computer certificates on VPN routers for L2TP connections, see Chapter 12.

Note   Routing and Remote Access supports the configuration of a preshared key for IPsec authentication of L2TP/IPsec connections. To configure the answering router, in the Routing and Remote Access snap-in, in the properties dialog box of a VPN router, on the Security tab, select Allow Custom IPsec Policy for L2TP Connection, and then type the preshared key. To configure the calling router, in the properties dialog box of a demand-dial interface, on the Security tab, click IPsec Settings, and then type the preshared key. However, note that pre-shared key authentication for L2TP/IPsec connections is not secure and is not recommended except either as a temporary solution while deploying a certificate infrastructure or to connect to third-party VPN routers that do not support certificate authentication.

PKI for EAP-TLS

To perform EAP-TLS authentication for a site-to-site VPN connection, the following requirements must be met:

- The calling router must be configured with a user certificate to submit during the EAP-TLS authentication process.

- The authentication server (the answering router or a RADIUS server) must be configured with a computer certificate to submit during the EAP-TLS authentication process.

EAP-TLS authentication is successful when the following conditions are met:

- The calling router submits a valid user certificate that was issued by a CA that follows a valid certificate chain from the issuing CA up to a root CA that the answering router trusts.

- The authentication server submits a valid computer certificate that was issued by a CA that follows a valid certificate chain from the issuing CA up to a root CA that the calling router trusts.

For a Windows Server 2008 or Windows Server 2003 CA, a *Router (Offline Request) certificate* is a special type of user certificate for demand-dial connections. A Router (Offline Request) certificate must be obtained and mapped to an Active Directory user account. When the calling router attempts a VPN connection, the Router (Offline Request) certificate is sent during the authentication process. If the Router (Offline Request) certificate is valid, the authentication server can determine the appropriate user account from which to obtain dial-in properties.

For information about configuring user and computer certificates for EAP-TLS authentication, see "Deploying Certificates" later in this chapter.

Requirements for PKI

- For L2TP/IPsec site-to-site VPN connections that use certificates for IPsec authentication, you must install a computer certificate on the calling router and the answering router.

- To authenticate site-to-site VPN connections using EAP-TLS, the calling router must have a user certificate installed, and the authentication server (either the answering router or the RADIUS server) must have a computer certificate installed.

- For EAP-TLS authentication, the requirements for the user certificate of the calling router are as follows:

  - The certificate must contain a private key.

  - The certificate must be issued by an enterprise CA or mapped to a user account in Active Directory.

  - The certificate must chain to a trusted root CA on the NPS server and must not fail any of the checks that are performed by CryptoAPI and specified in the network policy for site-to-site VPN connections.

  - The certificate must be configured with the Client Authentication purpose in the Enhanced Key Usage field. (The object identifier for Client Authentication is 1.3.6.1.5.5.7.3.2.)

  - The Subject Alternative Name field must contain the user principal name (UPN) of the user account.

- For EAP-TLS authentication, the requirements for the computer certificate of the answering router or the NPS server are as follows:

  - The certificate must contain a private key.

  - The Subject field must contain a value.

  - The certificate must chain to a trusted root CA on the calling router and must not fail any of the checks that are performed by CryptoAPI and specified in the network policy for site-to-site VPN connections.

  - The certificate must be configured with the Server Authentication purpose in the Enhanced Key Usage field. (The object identifier for Server Authentication is 1.3.6.1.5.5.7.3.1.)

  - The certificate must be configured with a required cryptographic service provider (CSP) value of Microsoft RSA SChannel Cryptographic provider.

❑   The Subject Alternative Name field of the certificate, if used, must contain the FQDN of the server.

Best Practices for PKI

For computer certificates for L2TP/IPsec, if you are using a Windows Server 2008 enterprise CA as an issuing CA, use Computer Configuration Group Policy to configure your Active Directory domain for autoenrollment of computer certificates. Each computer that is a member of the domain automatically requests a computer certificate when Computer Configuration Group Policy is updated. For more information, see "Deploying Certificates" later in this chapter.

Deploying Site-to-Site VPN Connections

The deployment of site-to-site VPN connections using Windows Server 2008 consists of the following tasks:

- Deploying certificates
- Configuring Internet infrastructure
- Configuring Active Directory for user accounts and groups
- Configuring RADIUS servers
- Deploying the answering routers
- Deploying the calling routers
- Configuring site network infrastructure
- Configuring intersite network infrastructure

Deploying Certificates

You must deploy certificates if you are using the following:

- **L2TP/IPsec connections with certificate authentication**   Each VPN router computer needs a computer certificate.
- **EAP-TLS authentication with registry-based user certificates**   Each calling router needs a user certificate, and each authentication server needs a computer certificate.

Deploying Computer Certificates

For you to be able to install a computer certificate, a PKI must be present to issue certificates. Once the PKI is in place, you can install a computer certificate on VPN routers or authentication servers in the following ways:

- By configuring autoenrollment of computer certificates to computers in an Active Directory domain

- By using the Certificates snap-in to request a computer certificate

- By using the Certificates snap-in to import a computer certificate

- By requesting a certificate over the Web

- By executing a CAPICOM script that requests a computer certificate

For more information, see "Deploying PKI" in Chapter 9.

Deploying User Certificates for Calling Routers

If you are using a Windows Server 2008 CA, calling routers can use a Router (Offline request) certificate. The certificate must be obtained and mapped to an Active Directory user account that is used by the calling router. To deploy a Router (Offline request) certificate for a calling router, do the following:

1. Create a user account for the calling router. You can do this by using the New Demand-Dial Interface Wizard and the Active Directory User and Groups snap-in. The recommended method is to use the New Demand-Dial Interface Wizard.

2. Configure the Windows Server 2008 CA to issue Router (Offline request) certificates. See the "To Configure the Windows Server 2008 CA to Issue Router (Offline Request) Certificates" procedure in this section.

3. Request a Router (Offline request) certificate. See the "To Request a Router (Offline Request) Certificate" procedure in this section.

4. Export the Router (Offline request) certificate to a .CER file. See the "To Map the .CER Certificate File to the Appropriate User Account" procedure in this section.

5. Map the .CER certificate file to the appropriate user account. See the "To Export the Router (Offline Request) Certificate to a .CER File" procedure in this section.

6. Export the Router (Offline request) certificate to a .PFX file. See the "To Export the Router (Offline Request) Certificate to a .PFX File" procedure in this section.

7. Send the Router (Offline request) .PFX certificate file to the network administrator of the calling router.

8. Import the Router (Offline request) .PFX certificate file on the calling router. See the "To Import the Router (Offline Request) .PFX Certificate File on the Calling Router" procedure in this section.

To Configure the Windows Server 2008 CA to Issue Router (Offline Request) Certificates

1. In the console tree of the Certification Authority snap-in, expand the CA name.

2. Right-click Certificate Templates, point to New, and then click Certificate Template To Issue.

3. In the Enable Certificate Templates dialog box, click Router (Offline Request). This is shown in Figure 13-2. Click OK.

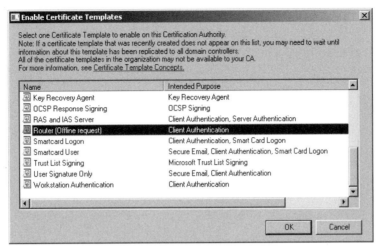

Figure 13-2 Enable Certificate Templates dialog box

To Request a Router (Offline Request) Certificate

1. Open Windows Internet Explorer.

2. In the Address bar, type the address of the CA that issues computer certificates. The address is the name of the server followed by "/certsrv," for example, **http://ca1/certsrv**.

3. On the Welcome page, click Request A Certificate, click Advanced Certificate Request, and then click Create And Submit A Request To This CA.

4. In the Certificate Template area, select Router (Offline Request) or the name of the template that the CA administrator directed you to choose.

5. In the Name box, type the user account name that is used by the calling router.

6. Under Key Options, select the Mark Keys As Exportable and Store Certificate In The Local Computer Certificate Store check boxes.

7. Confirm the other options that you want, and then click Submit.

8. A message appears that asks you to confirm that you trust this Web site and that you want to request a certificate. Click Yes.

9. On the Certificate Issued page, click Install This Certificate.

   A message informs you that a new certificate has been successfully installed.

Note   To request a Router (Offline Request) certificate through Web enrollment, a Windows Server 2008–based CA must have the Certification Authority Web Enrollment role service for the Active Directory Certificate Services role installed.

To Export the Router (Offline Request) Certificate to a .CER File

1. Open an MMC console containing Certificates - Local Computer.

2. Open Personal, and then open Certificates.

3. In the details pane, right-click the Router (Offline request) certificate obtained through Web enrollment, point to All Tasks, and then click Export.

4. On the Welcome page, click Next.

5. In the Certificate Export Wizard, click No, Do Not Export The Private Key. Click Next.

6. Select DER Encoded Binary X.509 (.CER) as the export file format, and then click Next.

7. Type the name for the certificate file, click Next, and then click Finish.

To Map the .CER Certificate File to the Appropriate User Account

1. From the Active Directory Users and Computers snap-in, on the View menu, click Advanced Features.

2. In the console tree, expand the appropriate domain system container and folder that contains the user account for the calling router.

3. In the details pane, right-click the user account to which you want to map a certificate, and then click Name Mappings.

4. On the X.509 Certificates tab, click Add.

5. In the Add Certificate dialog box, navigate to and select the .CER certificate file, click Open, and then click OK.

To Export the Router (Offline Request) Certificate to a .PFX File

1. Open an MMC console containing Certificates - Local Computer.

2. Expand Personal, and then Certificates.

3. In the details pane, right-click the Router (Offline Request) certificate obtained through Web enrollment, point to All Tasks, and then click Export.

4. On the Welcome page of the Certificate Export Wizard, click Next.

5. On the Export Private Key page, click Yes, Export The Private Key. Click Next.

6. On the Export File Format page, Select Personal Information Exchange - PKCS #12 (.PFX) as the export file format. Select Include All Certificates In The Certification Path If Possible, and then click Next.

7. On the Password page, in the Password and Confirm Password fields, type a password that protects the private key of the certificate and that is needed to import the certificate. Click Next.

8. On the File To Export page, type the name of the certificate file, and then click Next.

9. On the Completing The Certificate Export Wizard page, click Finish.

To Import the Router (Offline Request) .PFX Certificate File on the Calling Router

1. Open an MMC console containing Certificates - Current User.

2. Open Personal.

3. Right-click the Personal folder, point to All Tasks, and then click Import.

4. In the Certificate Import Wizard, on the Welcome page, click Next.

5. On the File To Import page, type the file name containing the certificate to be imported, and then click Next. (You can also click Browse and navigate to the file.)

6. Type the password used to protect the private key, and then click Next.

7. At this point, do one of the following:

    ❑ If the certificate should be automatically placed in a certificate store based on the type of certificate, select Automatically Select The Certificate Store Based On The Type Of Certificate.

    ❑ If you want to specify where the certificate is stored, select Place All Certificates In The Following Store, click Browse, and then select the certificate store to use.

8. Click Next, and then click Finish.

Configuring Internet Infrastructure

To configure the Internet infrastructure for site-to-site VPN connections, perform the following:

  ❑ Place the VPN routers in the perimeter network or on the Internet.

  ❑ Install Windows Server 2008 on VPN router computers, and configure Internet interfaces.

  ❑ Add address records to Internet DNS servers (as needed).

Placing VPN Routers on the Perimeter Network or on the Internet

Decide where to place the VPN routers in relation to your Internet firewall. In the most common configuration, the VPN routers are placed behind a firewall on the perimeter network between your site and the Internet. If that is the case, configure packet filters on the firewall to allow PPTP and L2TP/IPsec traffic to and from the IPv4 or IPv6 address of the VPN routers' perimeter network interface. For more information, see "Firewall Packet Filtering for VPN Traffic" in Chapter 12.

Installing Windows Server 2008 on VPN Routers and Configuring Internet Interfaces

Install Windows Server 2008 on VPN router computers, and connect them to either the Internet or to the perimeter network with one network adapter. Then connect the router computers to the site with another network adapter. Without running the Routing and Remote Access

Server Setup Wizard, the VPN router computer will not forward IPv4 or IPv6 packets between the Internet and the site.

For the connection attached to the IPv4 Internet or the perimeter network, configure the TCP/IP (IPv4) protocol with a public IPv4 address, a subnet mask, and the default gateway of either the firewall (if the router is connected to a perimeter network) or an ISP router (if the router is directly connected to the Internet). Do not configure the connection with DNS server or WINS server IPv4 addresses.

For the connection attached to the IPv6 Internet or the perimeter network, configure the TCP/IP (IPv6) protocol with a global IPv6 address, a 64-bit prefix length, and the default gateway of either the firewall (if the VPN server is connected to a perimeter network) or an ISP router (if the VPN server is directly connected to the IPv6 Internet). Do not configure the connection with DNS server IPv6 addresses.

Adding Address Records to Internet DNS Servers

If you are using names for answering routers, either add DNS address (A) or IPv6 address (AAAA) records to your Internet DNS servers (if you are providing DNS name resolution for Internet users), or have your ISP add DNS A and AAAA records to their DNS servers (if your ISP is providing DNS name resolution for Internet users). Verify that the name of the answering router can be resolved to its public IPv4 address or global IPv6 address when connected to the Internet.

Configuring Active Directory for User Accounts and Groups

If you configure the settings in the Demand-Dial Interface Wizard to automatically add user accounts for calling routers, the accounts are automatically configured with the correct user account settings for demand-dial connections. If you manually create user accounts for calling routers, ensure that they have the following settings:

- On the Dial-in tab, the network access permission must be set to Allow Access or Control Access Through NPS Network Policy.

- On the Account tab, the User Must Change Password at Next Logon check box must be cleared, and the Password Never Expires check box must be selected.

Organize your calling router user accounts into the appropriate universal and global security groups to take advantage of group-based network policies.

Configuring RADIUS Servers

If you are using RADIUS for authentication, authorization, and accounting of site-to-site VPN connections, configure and deploy your NPS-based RADIUS servers as described in Chapter 9, including the following tasks:

- For EAP-TLS authentication, install a computer certificate on the NPS servers.

- Configure logging.

- Add RADIUS clients to the NPS server corresponding to each answering router.

The NPS server uses a network policy to authorize VPN connections. The default network policy named Connections to Microsoft Routing and Remote Access Server can be used for site-to-site VPN connections. However, by default, this network policy has its policy type set to Deny Access.

To Use the Connections to Microsoft Routing and Remote Access Server Network Policy

1. In the console tree of the Network Policy Server snap-in, under Policies, click Network Policies.

2. Double-click the Connections to Microsoft Routing and Remote Access Server policy.

3. On the Overview tab, under Policy State, select the Policy Enabled check box, and then click OK.

You can also use the Configure VPN Or Dial-Up Wizard to create a set of policies that are customized for site-to-site VPN connections using the universal group name for your VPN routers.

To Create a Set of Policies for Site-To-Site VPN Connections

1. In the console tree of the Network Policy Server snap-in, click NPS.

2. In the details pane, under Standard Configuration, select RADIUS Server For Dial-Up Or VPN Connections from the drop-down list, and then click Configure VPN Or Dial-Up.

3. In the Configure VPN Or Dial-Up Wizard, on the Select Dial-Up or Virtual Private Network Connections Type page, click Virtual Private Network (VPN) Connections, and then type the name of the new NPS network policy (or use the name of the policy supplied by the wizard). Click Next.

4. On the Specify Dial-Up Or VPN Server page, add RADIUS clients as needed that correspond to your answering routers. Click Next.

5. On the Configure Authentication Methods page, MS-CHAP v2 is already enabled. To enable and configure an EAP authentication type, select the Extensible Authentication Protocol check box, click an EAP type from the drop-down list, and then click Configure as needed (for example, to select the specific computer certificate to use for EAP-TLS authentication).

   To enable and configure EAP-TLS, select Extensible Authentication Protocol. In the Types drop-down list, select Smart Card Or Other Certificate, and then click Configure. In the Smart Card Or Other Certificate Properties dialog box, select the computer certificate to use for site-to-site VPN connections, and then click OK. If you cannot select the certificate, the cryptographic service provider for the certificate does not support

Secure Channel (SChannel). SChannel support is required for NPS to use the certificate for EAP-TLS authentication.

6. Click Next. On the Specify User Groups page, add the groups containing the user accounts allowed to make site-to-site VPN connections (for example, VPNRouters). Click Next.

7. On the Specify IP Filters page, click Next.

8. On the Specify Encryption Settings page, enable the allowed encryption strengths, and then click Next.

9. On the Specify A Realm Name page, click Next.

10. On the Completing New Dial-Up Or Virtual Private Network Connections And RADIUS Clients page, click Finish.

The Configure VPN Or Dial-Up Wizard creates a connection request policy and a network policy for VPN connections. The Configure VPN Or Dial-Up Wizard configures the network policy with a single EAP method. You can configure additional EAP methods from the Settings tab for the properties of the network policy.

After you have configured the primary NPS server with the appropriate logging, RADIUS client, and policy settings, copy the configuration to the secondary or other NPS servers. For more information, see Chapter 9.

Deploying the Answering Routers

To deploy an answering router for a site-to-site VPN connection, perform the following tasks:

- Install computer certificates.
- Configure the answering router's connection to the site.
- Install the Network Policy and Access Services role.
- Run the Routing and Remote Access Server Setup Wizard.
- Add native IPv6 capability.
- Configure a demand-dial interface.

Installing Computer Certificates

For L2TP/IPsec-based connections or if the answering router is the authentication server and you are using EAP-TLS authentication, you must install a computer certificate on the answering router. You can install a computer certificate using the methods described in "Deploying Certificates" earlier in this chapter.

Configuring the Answering Router's Connection to the Site

For IPv4, configure the answering router's connection to the intranet with a manual TCP/IP (IPv4) configuration consisting of IPv4 address, subnet mask, intranet DNS servers, and intranet WINS servers. For IPv6, configure the answering router's connection to the intranet with a manual TCP/IP (IPv6) configuration consisting of IPv6 address, 64-bit prefix length, and intranet DNS servers.

In both cases, you must not configure the default gateway on the intranet connection to prevent default route conflicts with the default route pointing to the IPv4 or IPv6 Internet.

Installing the Network Access and Policy Services Role

To install Routing and Remote Access, use the Server Manager tool to install the Network Policy and Access Services role.

Running the Routing and Remote Access Server Setup Wizard

The Routing and Remote Access Server Setup Wizard automates the configuration of many elements of the answering router. The resulting default configuration can then be customized to fit your specific deployment needs.

To Run the Routing and Remote Access Server Setup Wizard

1. In the console tree of the Routing and Remote Access snap-in, right-click your server name, and then click Configure and Enable Routing and Remote Access.

2. In the Routing and Remote Access Server Setup Wizard, on the Welcome page, click Next.

3. On the Configuration page, click Remote Access (Dial-up Or VPN), and then click Next.

4. On the Remote Access page, select VPN, and then click Next.

5. On the VPN Connection page, click the connection that is connected to the Internet or your perimeter network. Ensure that the Enable Security On The Selected Interface By Setting Up Packet Filters check box is selected, and then click Next. Figure 13-3 shows an example.

6. On the Network Selection page (displayed only if you have multiple network adapters attached to the site), click the connection from which you want Routing and Remote Access to obtain DHCP, DNS, and WINS configuration for calling routers or remote access VPN clients.

7. On the IP Address Assignment page, click Automatically if the answering router should use DHCP to obtain IPv4 addresses for calling routers and remote access VPN clients. Alternatively, click From A Specified Range Of Addresses to use one or more ranges of IPv4 addresses. When IPv4 address assignment is complete, click Next.

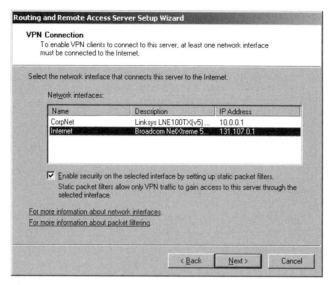

Figure 13-3 VPN Connection page

8. On the Managing Multiple Remote Access Servers page, if the answering router is performing authentication and authorization for incoming VPN connection requests, click No, Use Routing And Remote Access To Authenticate Connection Requests. If you are using RADIUS for authentication and authorization, click Yes, Set Up This Server To Work With A RADIUS Server, and then click Next.

9. If you selected RADIUS in step 8, on the RADIUS Server Selection page shown in Figure 13-4, configure the name, IPv4 address, or IPv6 addresses of primary (mandatory) and alternate (optional) RADIUS servers and the RADIUS shared secret, and then click Next.

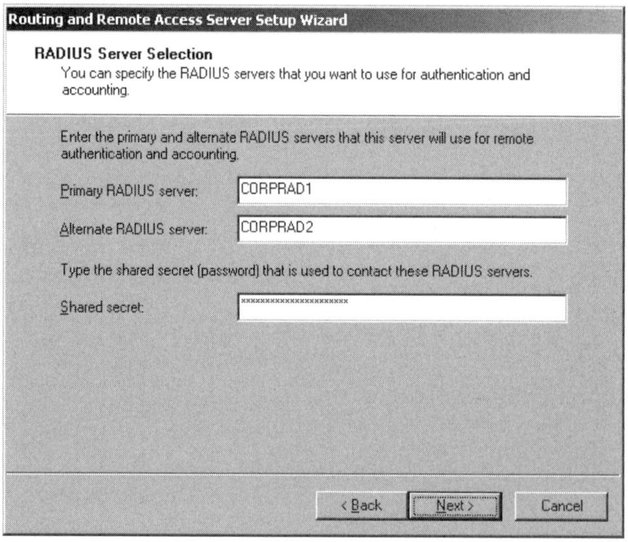

Figure 13-4 RADIUS Server Selection page

10.   On the Completing The Routing And Remote Access Server Setup Wizard page, click Finish.

11.   If the Routing and Remote Access Server Setup Wizard could not automatically configure the DHCP Relay Agent component with the IPv4 addresses of DHCP servers on the intranet, you are prompted with a message box. Click OK, or click Help for more information.

Adding Native IPv6 Capability

Native IPv6 capability for site-to-site VPN connections—IPv6 packets either inside the VPN tunnel or over a native IPv6 VPN connection—is not a current requirement for many intranets. For this reason, the Routing and Remote Access Server Setup Wizard does not automatically enable native IPv6 capability for site-to-site VPN connections over the IPv4 or IPv6 Internet.

To configure Routing and Remote Access for native IPv6 capability for site-to-site VPN connections, you need to do the following:

■   Enable IPv6 routing for LAN and demand-dial connections.

■   Configure router advertisement behavior.

To Configure the Answering Router to Support Native IPv6 Traffic

1.   In the console tree of the Routing and Remote Access snap-in, right-click the name of the VPN server, and then click Properties.

2.   On the General tab, select IPv6 Router, select LAN And Demand-Dial Routing.

3.   On the IPv6 tab, ensure that the Enable IPv6 Forwarding and Enable Default Route Advertisement check boxes are selected. Type the subnet prefix that will be assigned to IPv6-based VPN routers that perform router discovery. You do not need to specify the prefix length. For example, for the subnet prefix 2001:db8:4a2c:29::/64, type **2001:db8:4a2c:29::**. Figure 13-5 shows an example. Click OK. When prompted to restart the router, click OK.

Configuring a Demand-Dial Interface

To create and configure a demand-dial interface, in the Routing and Remote Access snap-in on the answering router, do the following:

1.   In the console tree of the Routing and Remote Access snap-in, right-click Network Interfaces, and then click New Demand-Dial Interface.

2.   In the Demand-Dial Interface Wizard, on the Welcome page, click Next.

3.   On the Interface Name page, type the name of the demand-dial interface. For a two-way initiated connection, this is the same name as the user name in the user credentials used by the calling router. Click Next.

4.   On the Connection Type page, click Connect Using Virtual Private Networking (VPN), and then click Next.

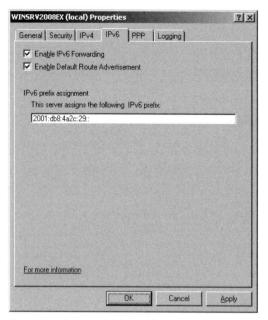

Figure 13-5   IPv6 tab of the VPN server Properties page

5. On the VPN Type page, click Automatic Selection, Point To Point Tunneling Protocol (PPTP), or Layer 2 Tunneling Protocol (L2TP) as needed, and then click Next.

6. On the Destination Address page, type the name, IPv4 address, or IPv6 address of the calling router. For a one-way initiated site-to-site VPN connection, you can skip this step because the answering router never uses this interface to initiate a connection to the calling router.

7. On the Protocols And Security page, if you have not already created user accounts for the calling routers, select the Add A User Account So That A Remote Router Can Dial In check box. Click Next.

8. On the Static Routes for Remote Networks page, click Add to add a static route assigned to the demand-dial interface. Figure 13-6 shows an example.

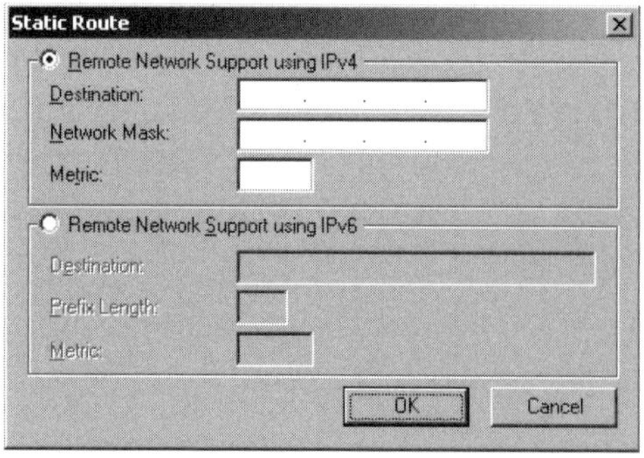

Figure 13-6   The Static Route dialog box

Add the IPv4 and IPv6 static routes that summarize the IPv4 and IPv6 address space of the site of the calling router. Click Next.

9. If you selected the Add A User Account So A Remote Router Can Dial In check box on the Protocols And Security page, the Dial-In Credentials page appears, as shown in Figure 13-7.

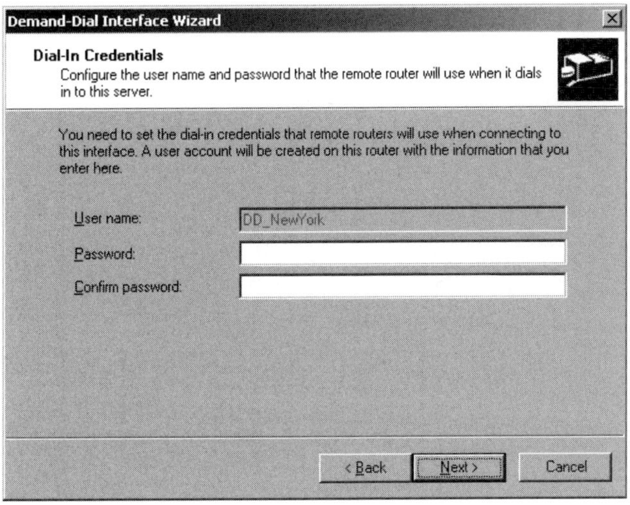

Figure 13-7   The Dial-In Credentials page

In the Password and Confirm Password fields, type the password of the user account used by the calling router, and then click Next. The password must comply with the password complexity requirements for your domain.

This step automatically creates a user account with the same name as the demand-dial interface that is being created. This is done so that when a calling router initiates a connection to this answering router, it is using a user account name that matches the name of a demand-dial interface. Therefore, the answering router can determine that the incoming connection from the calling router is a demand-dial connection rather than a remote access connection.

10. On the Dial Out Credentials page, type the user name in the User Name field, the account domain name in the Domain field, and the account password in both Password and Confirm Password fields. Figure 13-8 shows an example.

For a one-way initiated site-to-site VPN connection, you can type any name in User Name and skip the rest of the fields because this router never uses this interface to initiate a connection to another router. Click Next.

11. On the Completing the Demand-Dial Interface Wizard page, click Finish.

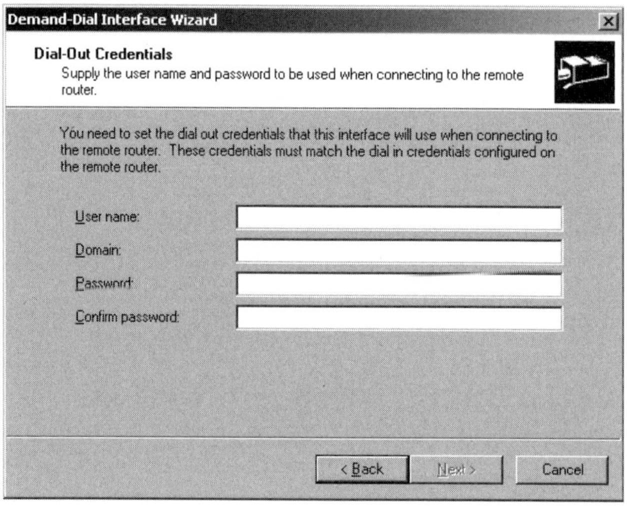

Figure 13-8   Dial-Out Credentials page

The result of this configuration is a VPN-based demand-dial interface in the Network Interfaces node of the Routing and Remote Access snap-in over which IPv4 and IPv6 routing is enabled. If you selected the Add A User Account So A Remote Router Can Dial In check box on the Protocols And Security page, a user account with the same name as the demand-dial interface is automatically added with correct account and dial-in settings.

Deploying the Calling Routers

To deploy a calling router for a site-to-site VPN connection, perform the following tasks:

- Install computer certificates.
- Install user certificates.
- Configure the calling router's connection to the site.
- Install the Network Policy and Access Services role.
- Run the Routing and Remote Access Server Setup Wizard.
- Add native IPv6 capability.
- Configure a demand-dial interface.
- Configure idle timeouts or connection persistence.
- Configure demand-dial filters.
- Configure dial-out hours.
- Configure EAP-TLS authentication.

Installing Computer Certificates

For L2TP/IPsec-based connections, you must install a computer certificate on the calling router. You can install a computer certificate by using the methods described in "Deploying Certificates" earlier in this chapter.

Installing User Certificates

For EAP-TLS authenticated connections, you must install a user certificate on the calling router. You can install a user certificate by using the methods described in "Deploying Certificates" earlier in this chapter.

Configuring the Calling Router's Connection to the Site

For IPv4, configure the calling router's connection to the intranet with a manual TCP/IP (IPv4) configuration consisting of IPv4 address, subnet mask, intranet DNS servers, and intranet WINS servers. For IPv6, configure the calling router's connection to the intranet with a manual TCP/IP (IPv6) configuration consisting of IPv6 address, 64-bit prefix length, and intranet DNS servers. In both cases, you must not configure the default gateway on the intranet connection to prevent default route conflicts with the default route pointing to the IPv4 or IPv6 Internet.

Installing the Network Access and Policy Services Role

To install Routing and Remote Access, use the Server Manager tool to install the Network Policy and Access Services role.

Running the Routing and Remote Access Server Setup Wizard

To install Routing and Remote Access on the calling router, use the Server Manager tool to install the Network Policy and Access Services role. After the Network Policy and Access Services role is installed, run the Routing and Remote Access Server Setup Wizard to configure the Windows Server 2008 calling router.

To Run the Routing and Remote Access Server Setup Wizard

1. In the console tree of the Routing and Remote Access snap-in, right-click your server name, and then click Configure and Enable Routing and Remote Access.

2. In the Routing and Remote Access Server Setup Wizard, on the Welcome page, click Next.

3. On the Configuration page, click Remote Access (Dial-up Or VPN), and then click Next.

4. On the Remote Access page, select VPN, and then click Next.

5. On the VPN Connection page, click the connection that is attached to the Internet or your perimeter network, and then click Next.

6. On the Network Selection page (displayed only if you have multiple network adapters attached to the site), click the connection from which you want Routing and Remote Access to obtain DHCP, DNS, and WINS configuration for other calling routers or remote access VPN clients.

7. On the IP Address Assignment page, click Automatically if the calling router should use DHCP to obtain IPv4 addresses for other calling routers and remote access VPN clients. Alternatively, click From A Specified Range Of Addresses to use one or more ranges of IPv4 addresses. When IPv4 address assignment is complete, click Next.

8. On the Managing Multiple Remote Access Servers page, if the calling router is performing authentication and authorization for other calling routers, click No, Use Routing And Remote Access To Authenticate Connection Requests. If you are using RADIUS for authentication and authorization, click Yes, Set Up This Server To Work With A RADIUS Server, and then click Next.

9. If you selected RADIUS in step 8, on the RADIUS Server Selection page, configure the names, IPv4 addresses, or IPv6 addresses of the primary (mandatory) and alternate (optional) RADIUS servers and the RADIUS shared secret, and then click Next.

10. On the Completing The Routing And Remote Access Server Setup Wizard page, click Finish.

11. If the Routing and Remote Access Server Setup Wizard could not automatically configure the DHCP Relay Agent component with the IPv4 addresses of DHCP servers on the intranet, you are prompted with a message. Click OK, or click Help for more information.

Adding Native IPv6 Capability

Native IPv6 capability for site-to-site VPN connections—IPv6 packets either inside the VPN tunnel or over a native IPv6 VPN connection—is not a current requirement for many intranets. For this reason, the Routing and Remote Access Server Setup Wizard does not automatically enable native IPv6 capability for site-to-site VPN connections over the IPv4 or IPv6 Internet.

To configure native IPv6 capability for site-to-site VPN connections in Routing and Remote Access, perform the following additional tasks:

- Enable IPv6 routing for LAN and demand-dial connections.
- Configure router advertisement behavior.

To Configure the Calling Router to Support Native IPv6 Traffic

1. In the console tree of the Routing and Remote Access snap-in, right-click the name of the VPN server, and then click Properties.

2. On the General tab, select IPv6 Router, select LAN and Demand-Dial Routing.

3. On the IPv6 tab, ensure that the Enable IPv6 Forwarding and Enable Default Route Advertisement check boxes are selected. Type the same subnet prefix that was configured on the answering router. You do not need to specify the prefix length. Click OK. When prompted to restart the router, click OK.

Configuring a Demand-Dial Interface

To create and configure a demand-dial interface, in the Routing and Remote Access snap-in on the calling router, do the following:

1. In the console tree of the Routing and Remote Access snap-in, right-click Network Interfaces, and then click New Demand-Dial Interface.

2. In the Demand-Dial Interface Wizard, on the Welcome page, click Next.

3. On the Interface Name page, type the name of the demand-dial interface. For a two-way initiated connection, this is the same name as the user name in the user credentials used by another calling router. Click Next.

4. On the Connection Type page, click Connect Using Virtual Private Networking (VPN), and then click Next.

5. On the VPN Type page, click Automatic Selection, Point to Point Tunneling Protocol (PPTP), or Layer 2 Tunneling Protocol (L2TP) as needed, and then click Next.

6. On the Destination Address page, type the name, IPv4 address, or IPv6 address of the answering router.

7. On the Protocols And Security page, for a two-way initiated connection, if you have not already created user accounts for other calling routers, select the Add A User Account So That A Remote Router Can Dial In check box, and then click Next.

8. On the Static Routes for Remote Networks page, click Add to add a static route assigned to the demand-dial interface. Add all the IPv4 and IPv6 static routes that summarize the IPv4 and IPv6 address space of the site of the answering router. Click Next.

9. If you selected the Add A User Account So A Remote Router Can Dial In check box on the Protocols And Security page, in the Dial In Credentials page, in the Password and Confirm Password fields, type the password of the user account used by another calling router, and then click Next. The password must comply with the password complexity requirements for your domain.

   This step automatically creates a user account with the same name as the demand-dial interface that is being created. This is done so that when another calling router initiates a connection to this router, it is using a user account name that matches the name of a demand-dial interface. Therefore, this router can determine that the incoming connection is a demand-dial connection rather than a remote access connection.

10. On the Dial Out Credentials page, type the user name in the User Name field, the user account domain name in the Domain field, and the user account password in both the Password and Confirm Password fields. Click Next.

11. On the Completing The Demand-Dial Interface Wizard page, click Finish.

The result of this configuration is a demand-dial interface over which IPv4 and IPv6 routing is enabled. If you selected the Add A User Account So A Remote Router Can Dial In check box on the Protocols And Security page, a user account with the same name as the demand-dial interface is automatically added with correct account and dial-in settings.

Configuring Idle Timeouts or Connection Persistence

By default, the Demand-Dial Interface Wizard configures a demand-dial interface with a five-minute idle disconnect time. You can configure idle disconnect behavior for the calling router in the Routing and Remote Access snap-in, in the Network Interfaces node, in the properties dialog box of the demand-dial interface, on the Options tab.

To configure an idle disconnect for an answering router, in the Network Policy Server snap-in, in the properties dialog box of the network policy for site-to-site VPN connections, on the Constraints tab, configure the Idle Timeout setting.

To configure the calling router for connection persistence, in the Routing and Remote Access snap-in, in the properties dialog box of the demand-dial interface, on the Options tab, select Persistent Connection.

To configure the answering router for connection persistence, in the Network Policy Server snap-in, in the properties dialog box of the network policy for site-to-site VPN connections, click the Constraints tab, click Idle Timeout, and then clear the Disconnect After The Maximum Idle Time check box.

Configuring Demand-Dial Filters

To configure demand-dial filtering for IPv4 or IPv6 traffic, in the Routing and Remote Access snap-in, in the Network Interfaces node, right-click the demand-dial interface, and then click Set IP Demand-Dial Filters or Set IPv6 Demand-Dial Filters.

To prevent the calling router from initiating a connection for traffic that is not allowed across the demand-dial interface, do the following:

■ If you have configured a set of output IPv4 or IPv6 packet filters on the demand-dial interface in the IPv4\General or IPv6\General node of the Routing and Remote Access snap-in with the Transmit All Packets Except Those That Meet The Criteria Below option, configure the same set of filters as demand-dial filters with Initiate Connection set to For All Traffic Except.

■ If you have configured a set of output IPv4 or IPv6 packet filters on the demand-dial interface in the IPv4\General or IPv6\General node of the Routing and Remote Access snap-in with the Drop All Packets Except Those That Meet the Criteria Below option, configure the same set of filters as demand-dial filters with Initiate Connection set to Only For The Following Traffic.

Configuring Dial-Out Hours

To configure dial-out hours, in the Routing and Remote Access snap-in, in the Network Interfaces node, right-click the demand-dial interface, and then click Dial-Out Hours. Specify the permitted and denied hours during which a demand-dial connection can be made, and then click OK.

To configure the answering router for allowed hours for incoming demand-dial connections, in the Network Policy Server snap-in, in the properties dialog box of network policy for site-to-site VPN connections, on the Constraints tab, configure the Day And Time Restrictions setting.

Configuring EAP-TLS Authentication

To configure EAP-TLS for user certificates on the calling router, do the following:

1. In the Routing and Remote Access snap-in, in the Network Interfaces node, double-click the demand-dial interface.

2. In the properties dialog box, click the Security tab, select Advanced (Custom Settings), and then click Settings.

3. Under Logon Security, click Use Extensible Authentication Protocol (EAP), select Smart Card Or Other Certificate (Encryption Enabled) from the drop-down list, and then click Properties.

4. In the Smart Card Or Other Certificate properties dialog box, select Use A Certificate On This Computer. Validation of the computer certificate of the authentication server is enabled by default. If you want to configure the names of the authentication servers (such as the RADIUS servers), select Connect To These Servers, and then type the server names. To require the server's computer certificate to have been issued a certificate from a specific trusted root CA, in the Trusted Root Certification Authorities list, select the CA.

5. Click OK three times.

To select the correct certificate to submit during EAP-TLS authentication, right-click the demand-dial interface, and then click Set Credentials. In the Interface Credentials dialog box, in the User Name On Certificate box, select the correct user or Router (Offline request) certificate, and then click OK.

Configuring Site Network Infrastructure

To deploy the network infrastructure of a site for site-to-site VPN connections, perform the following tasks:

- Configure routing on the VPN routers.
- Verify reachability from each VPN router.
- Configure routing for off-subnet address pools.
- Configuring routing for the IPv6 subnet prefix for VPN routers.

Configuring Routing on the VPN Routers

For your VPN routers to properly forward traffic to locations within the site in which they are located, you must configure them with static IPv4 and IPv6 routes that summarize the IPv4 and IPv6 address spaces used within the site. For IPv4, you can use the RIP for IPv4 routing protocol so that the VPN router can automatically add IPv4 routes for site subnets to its routing table.

To Add Static IPv4 Routes for Intrasite Traffic

1. In the console tree of the Routing and Remote Access snap-in, expand IPv4.

2. Right-click Static Routes, and then click New Static Route.

3. In the IPv4 Static Route dialog box shown in Figure 13-9, select the site interface and type the destination, network mask, gateway, and metric for the static route, and then click OK.

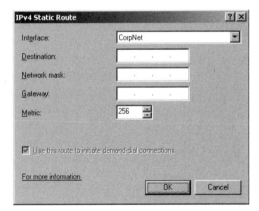

Figure 13-9   The IPv4 Static Route dialog box

4. Repeat steps 2 and 3 for additional IPv4 static routes.

To Add a Static IPv6 Route for Intrasite Traffic

1. In the console tree of the Routing and Remote Access snap-in, expand IPv6.

2. Right-click Static Routes, and then click New Static Route.

3. In the IPv6 Static Route dialog box shown in Figure 13-10:

   a. Select the site interface.

   b. In the Destination field, type the address prefix.

   c. In the Prefix Length field, type the prefix length for the address prefix. For subnet address prefixes, the prefix length is 64.

   d. In the Gateway field, type the link-local address of a neighboring intranet IPv6 router.

   e. In the Metric spin-box, type the metric for the route.

4. Click OK.

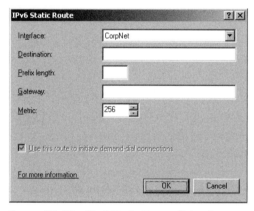

Figure 13-10   IPv6 Static Route dialog box

5. Repeat steps 2–4 for additional IPv6 static routes.

> **Note**   You must add IPv6 static routes for the site only if you have configured your VPN router for native IPv6 capability.

To Configure the VPN Router as a RIP for IPv4 Router

1. In the console tree of the Routing and Remote Access snap-in, expand the IPv4 node.

2. Right-click General, and then click New Routing Protocol.

3. In the Routing Protocols list, click RIP Version 2 For Internet Protocol, and then click OK.

4. In the console tree, right-click RIP, and then click New Interface.

5. Click the site interface of the VPN router, and then click OK.

6. In the RIP properties dialog box, configure the RIP routing protocol as used by the neighboring RIP router on the intranet subnet of the VPN router, and then click OK.

Verifying Reachability from Each VPN Router

From each VPN router, verify that the VPN router computer can successfully communicate with resources within the VPN router's site by using the Ping tool, Internet Explorer, and making drive and printer connections to known servers within the site.

Configuring Routing for Off-Subnet Address Pools

If you configured any of the VPN routers with IPv4 address pools, and any of the ranges within the pools are off-subnet, you must ensure that the IPv4 routes representing the off-subnet address ranges are present in your site routing infrastructure to reach the VPN interfaces of calling routers. You can ensure this by adding routes representing the off-subnet address ranges as static routes to the neighboring routers of the VPN routers and then using the routing protocol of your site to propagate the routes to other routers. When you add the static routes, you must specify that the gateway or next hop address is the IPv4 address of the site interface of the VPN router.

Configuring Routing for the IPv6 Subnet Prefix for VPN Routers

To ensure that the VPN interfaces of IPv6-capable VPN routers are reachable from the intranet, you must add a static route representing the subnet prefix for calling routers to the neighboring IPv6 routers of the VPN server and then propagate the routes to other routers using the routing protocol of your intranet. When you add the static routes, you must specify that the gateway or next hop address is the link-local IPv6 address of the intranet interface of the VPN router.

Configuring Intersite Network Infrastructure

Deploying the intersite network infrastructure consists of configuring each VPN router with the set of routes for the IPv4 and IPv6 address space that is available in the other sites (across the site-to-site VPN connection). In the Demand-Dial Interface Wizard, on the Static Routes for Remote Networks page, you can add static IPv4 or IPv6 routes assigned to the demand-dial interface. These routes summarize the IPv4 and IPv6 address space of the site of the other VPN router. If you need to add more routes, you can do the following:

- Manually configure static routes on each VPN router.
- Perform auto-static updates on each VPN router.
- Configure routing protocols to operate over the site-to-site VPN connection.

Manually Configuring Static Routes on Each VPN Router

You can manually configure additional IPv4 or IPv6 static routes.

To Add Static IPv4 Routes for Intersite Traffic

1. In the console tree of the Routing and Remote Access snap-in, expand IPv4.

2. Right-click Static Routes, and then click New Static Route.

3. In the IPv4 Static Route dialog box, select the demand-dial interface, and then type the destination, network mask, and metric for the static route for the site across the demand-dial connection. You can also select the Use This Route To Initiate Demand-Dial Connections check box to initiate a demand-dial connection for traffic that matches the route. Click OK.

4. Repeat steps 2 and 3 for additional IPv4 static routes.

> **Note** Because the demand-dial connection is a point-to-point connection, the Gateway field for routes associated with demand-dial interfaces is not configurable.

To Add IPv6 Static Routes for Intersite Traffic

1. In the console tree of the Routing and Remote Access snap-in, expand IPv6.

2. Right-click Static Routes, and then click New Static Route.

3. In the IPv6 Static Route dialog box, select the demand-dial interface, and then type the destination, prefix length, and metric for the static route for the site across the demand-dial connection. You can also select the Use This Route To Initiate Demand-Dial Connections check box to initiate a demand-dial connection for traffic that matches the route. Click OK.

4. Repeat steps 2 and 3 to add additional IPv6 static routes.

> **Note** You must add intersite IPv6 static routes only if you have configured your VPN router for native IPv6 capability.

Performing Auto-Static Updates on Each VPN Router

If RIP for IPv4 is enabled on the demand-dial interfaces of both VPN routers, you can use auto-static updates to automatically configure IPv4 static routes when the VPN connection is in a connected state.

To Initiate an Auto-Static Update

1. In the console tree of the Routing and Remote Access snap-in, expand IPv4, and then click General.

2. In the details pane, check the Operational Status column for the appropriate demand-dial interface to ensure that it is in a Connected state.

3. Right-click the demand-dial interface, and then click Update Routes.

You can also run the Netsh commands to perform an auto-static update at a command prompt. You can automate scheduled updates by using a combination of Netsh scripts and Task Scheduler. To perform an automated auto-static update by using RIP for IP for a specific demand-dial interface, run the following netsh commands:

netsh interface set interface name=*DemandDialInterfaceName* **connect=CONNECTED**

netsh routing ip rip update name=*DemandDialInterfaceName*

netsh interface set interface name=*DemandDialInterfaceName* **connect=DISCONNECTED**

For example, to automatically update the IP routes by using a demand-dial connection named CorpHub, you type the following netsh commands:

netsh interface set interface name=CorpHub connect=CONNECTED

netsh routing ip rip update name=CorpHub

netsh interface set interface name=CorpHub connect=DISCONNECTED

You can run these commands from a batch file, or you can place them in a Netsh script file. For example, the script file Corphub.scp runs the following Netsh commands for CorpHub:

```
interface set interface name=CorpHub connect=CONNECTED
routing ip rip update name=CorpHub
interface set interface name=CorpHub connect=DISCONNECTED
```

To run the Corphub.scp script, type the following at a command prompt:

netsh -f corphub.scp

After the batch file or Netsh script file is created, you can execute the batch file or Netsh script on a scheduled basis by using Task Scheduler.

Configuring Routing Protocols

If the site-to-site VPN connection is persistent, you can also configure the RIP for IPv4 routing protocol on the demand-dial interfaces on both VPN routers to automatically update each VPN router with IPv4 routes.

Ongoing Maintenance

The areas of maintenance for a site-to-site VPN solution are as follows:

- Management of user accounts
- Management of VPN routers

Managing User Accounts

When a new user account for a calling router is created in Active Directory, either manually or using the Demand-Dial Interface Wizard, add the new user account to the appropriate group for site-to-site VPN connections. For example, add the new account to the VPNRouters security group, which is specified in the network policy for site-to-site VPN connections.

When user accounts are deleted in Active Directory, no additional action is necessary to prevent site-to-site VPN connections.

Managing VPN Routers

You might need to manage VPN routers when adding or removing a VPN router from your site-to-site VPN solution. Once deployed, VPN routers do not need a lot of ongoing maintenance. Most of the ongoing changes to configuration are related to increased capacity demand and changes in network infrastructure.

Adding a VPN Router

To add a VPN router:

1. Follow the design points and deployment steps in this chapter to create a new VPN router on the Internet.

2. To ensure that calling routers that are using names for answering routers can reach a new answering router by its name, update or add the appropriate A and AAAA records in the Internet DNS for the IPv4 or IPv6 address of the new answering router.

3. Update your RADIUS server configuration to add the new answering router as a RADIUS client.

Removing a VPN Router

To remove a VPN router:

1. If needed, update or remove the FQDN in the Internet DNS for the IPv4 or IPv6 address of an answering router.

2. Update your RADIUS server configuration to remove the answering router as a RADIUS client.

3. Shut down and remove the VPN router.

4. For the calling routers of an answering router that is removed, update or delete the demand-dial interfaces that are configured to connect to the removed answering router.

Adding Possible Connections

By default, the Routing and Remote Access Server Setup Wizard configures Routing and Remote Access with an initial number of PPTP and L2TP ports. To increase the maximum number of ports for a VPN protocol, do the following:

1. In the console tree of the Routing and Remote Access snap-in, right-click Ports, and then click Properties.

2. In the Ports properties dialog box, double-click the WAN Miniport device corresponding to the VPN protocol.

3. In the Configure Device dialog box, in the Maximum Ports spin-box, specify the maximum number of ports, and then click OK twice.

Configuration for Changes in Infrastructure Servers

Infrastructure servers include DNS, WINS, and RADIUS (NPS) servers. If the changes to these types of infrastructure servers impact the configuration of the VPN router, you might need to change the configuration of the VPN router for the new infrastructure.

DNS and WINS   If requested by the calling router, the answering router sends the IPv4 addresses of its configured DNS and WINS servers to the calling router during the PPP negotiation. If the IPv4 addresses of the configured DNS or WINS servers change (for example, because of addition or removal of DNS or WINS servers on the intranet), you must change the DNS or WINS server configuration on the answering router to prevent it from configuring the calling router with an incorrect DNS or WINS server IPv4 address.

RADIUS   If an answering router is configured to use RADIUS authentication, and the IPv4 or IPv6 addresses of the RADIUS servers change (for example, because of additions or removals of RADIUS servers on the intranet), you must do the following:

1. Ensure that the new RADIUS servers are configured with RADIUS clients that correspond to the answering routers.

2. Update the configuration of the answering routers to include the names, IPv4 addresses, or IPv6 addresses of the new RADIUS servers.

Adding Site or Remote Site Routes

If the address space of a site to which a VPN router is attached changes and requires either additions or deletions to the routes that use the site interface in the routing table of the VPN router, in the Routing and Remote Access snap-in, in the IPv4\Static Routes node or the IPv6\Static Routes node, add or remove routes as needed.

Similarly, if the address space of a remote site to which a VPN router is connecting changes and requires either additions or deletions to the routes that use the demand-dial interface in the routing table of the VPN router, in the Routing and Remote Access snap-in, in the IPv4\Static Routes node or the IPv6\Static Routes node, add or remove routes as needed.

Troubleshooting

Because of the different components and processes involved, troubleshooting site-to-site VPN connections can be a difficult task. This section describes the tools that are provided with Windows Server 2008 to troubleshoot site-to-site VPN connections and the most common problems with site-to-site VPN connections.

Troubleshooting Tools

Microsoft provides the following tools to troubleshoot VPN connections from the VPN router:

- TCP/IP troubleshooting tools
- Authentication and accounting logging
- Event logging
- NPS event logging
- PPP logging
- Tracing
- Network Monitor 3.1

For information about these tools, see Chapter 12.

For site-to-site VPN connections, you can also use the unreachability reason facility. When a demand-dial interface fails to make a connection, the interface is left in an unreachable state, and Routing and Remote Access records the reason why the connection attempt failed.

To View the Unreachable Reason

1. In the console tree in the Routing and Remote Access snap-in, click Network Interfaces.

2. In the details pane, right-click the demand-dial interface, and then click Unreachability Reason. Routing and Remote Access displays a message with information about the connection failure.

Troubleshooting Site-to-Site VPN Connections

Site-to-site VPN connection problems typically fall into the following categories:

- Inability to connect
- Inability to reach locations beyond the VPN routers

- Inability to reach the VPN interfaces of VPN routers

- On-demand connection is not made automatically

Use the following troubleshooting tips to isolate the configuration or infrastructure issue that is causing the problem.

Inability to Connect

When a calling router is unable to connect to an answering router, check the following:

- If the calling router demand-dial interface is using a name for the answering router, use the Ping tool when connected to the Internet to verify that the host name for the answering router is being resolved to its correct IPv4 or IPv6 address. The ping itself might not be successful because of packet filtering that is blocking Internet Control Message Protocol (ICMP) or ICMP for IPv6 (ICMPv6) messages to and from the answering router.

- If you are using password-based credentials, verify that the calling router's credentials, consisting of user name, password, and domain name, are correct and can be validated by the answering router.

- Verify that the user account of the calling router is not locked out, expired, or disabled, and check whether the time the connection is being made corresponds to the configured logon hours.

- Verify that the user account of the calling router is not configured to change its password at the next logon or that the password has not expired. A calling router cannot change an expired password during the connection process, so such a connection attempt is rejected.

- Verify that the user account has not been locked out because of remote access account lockout.

- Verify that the Routing and Remote Access service is running on the answering router.

- In the Routing and Remote Access snap-in, in the properties dialog box of an answering router, on the General tab, verify that the answering router is enabled for LAN And Demand-Dial Routing.

- On both the calling and answering routers, in the Routing and Remote Access snap-in, in the properties dialog box of the Ports node, verify that the WAN Miniport (PPTP) and WAN Miniport (L2TP) devices are enabled for Demand-Dial Routing Connections (Inbound And Outbound).

- Verify that the calling router, the answering router, and the network policy corresponding to site-to-site VPN connections are configured to use at least one common authentication method.

- Verify that the calling router and the network policy corresponding to VPN connections are configured to use at least one common encryption strength.

- Verify that the parameters of the connection are authorized through network policies.

  For the connection to be accepted, the parameters of the connection attempt must:

  - Match all the conditions of at least one network policy.

  - Be granted network access permission through the user account (set to Allow Access), or if the user account has the Control Access Through NPS Network Policy option selected, the network access permission of the matching network policy must have the Grant Access option selected.

  - Match all the settings of the policy.

  - Match all the settings of the dial-in properties of the user account.

  To obtain the name of the network policy that rejected the connection attempt, scan the Windows Logs\Security event log for NPS events corresponding to rejected (event ID 6273) or accepted (event ID 6272) connection attempts. The network policy that accepted or rejected the connection attempt is the Network Policy Name field in the description of the event.

- If you are logged on using an account with domain administrator permissions when you run the Routing and Remote Access Server Setup Wizard, it automatically adds the computer account of the VPN router to the RAS and IAS Servers security group. This group membership allows the answering router computer to access user account information if it is configured to perform authentication locally, rather than use a RADIUS server. If the answering router is unable to access user account information, verify that:

  - The computer account of the answering router computer is a member of the RAS and IAS Servers security group for all the domains that contain user accounts for which the answering router is authenticating. You can run the **netsh nps show registeredserver** command at a command prompt to view the current registration. You can run the **netsh nps add registeredserver** command to register the server in a domain in which the answering router is a member or in other domains. Alternatively, you can add the computer account of the answering router computer to the RAS and IAS Servers security group of all the domains that contain user accounts for which the answering router is authenticating site-to-site VPN connections.

  - If you add or remove the answering router computer to the RAS and IAS Servers security group, the change does not take effect immediately (because of the way that Windows Server 2008 caches Active Directory information). For the change to take effect immediately, you must restart the answering router computer.

- In the Routing and Remote Access snap-in for both the calling router and answering router, in the server properties dialog box, on the General tab, verify that IPv4 or IPv6 is enabled for LAN And Demand-Dial Routing.

- Verify that all the PPTP or L2TP ports on the calling router and answering router are not already being used. If necessary, in the Routing and Remote Access snap-in, the properties dialog box of the Ports node, change the number of PPTP to L2TP ports to allow more concurrent connections.

- Verify that the answering router supports the tunneling protocol of the calling router.

  By default, a Windows Server 2008 demand-dial interface with the VPN Type set to Automatic will try to establish a PPTP-based VPN connection first and then try an L2TP/IPsec-based VPN connection. If either the Point-to-Point Tunneling Protocol (PPTP) or Layer-2 Tunneling Protocol (L2TP) server type option is selected, verify that the answering router supports the selected tunneling protocol.

- Verify how the answering router is performing authentication. The answering router can be configured to authenticate the credentials of the calling router locally or use RADIUS.

  - For local authentication, verify that the answering router has joined the Active Directory domain and that the computer account of the answering router has been added to the RAS and IAS Servers security group.

  - For RADIUS-based authentication, verify that the answering router computer can communicate with the RADIUS server.

- Verify that packet filtering on a router or firewall interface between the calling router and the answering router is not preventing the forwarding of VPN traffic. For the details of packet filters for VPN traffic on the VPN router and the firewall, see "Firewall Packet Filtering for VPN Traffic" in Chapter 12.

L2TP/IPsec Authentication Issues

The following are the most common problems that prevent site-to-site L2TP/IPsec connections:

- **No certificate**   By default, site-to-site L2TP/IPsec connections require that the calling and answering router exchange computer certificates for IPsec peer authentication. Use the Certificates snap-in to check the Local Computer certificate stores of both the calling and answering router to ensure that a suitable certificate exists.

- **Incorrect certificate**   If certificates exist, they must be verifiable. Unlike manually configuring IPsec rules, the list of CAs for L2TP/IPsec connections is not configurable. Instead, each router in the L2TP/IPsec connection sends a list of root CAs to its IPsec peer from which it accepts a certificate for authentication. The root CAs in this list correspond to the root CAs that issued computer certificates to the computer. For example, if Router A is issued computer certificates by root CAs CertAuth1 and

CertAuth2, it notifies its IPsec peer during main mode negotiation that it will accept certificates for authentication only from CertAuth1 and CertAuth2. If the IPsec peer, Router B, does not have a valid computer certificate issued from either CertAuth1 or CertAuth2, IPsec security negotiation fails.

The calling router must have a valid computer certificate installed that was issued by a CA that follows a valid certificate chain from the issuing CA up to a root CA that the answering router trusts. Additionally, the answering router must have a valid computer certificate installed that was issued by a CA that follows a valid certificate chain from the issuing CA up to a root CA that the calling router trusts.

EAP-TLS Authentication Issues

When EAP-TLS is used for authentication, the calling router submits a user certificate, which is a Router (Offline request) certificate with Windows Certificate Services, and the authentication server (the answering router or the RADIUS server) submits a computer certificate.

Verify that the calling router and answering router are correctly configured by doing the following:

■ On the calling router, on the Security tab for the properties of the demand-dial interface, in the Advanced Security Settings dialog box of the demand-dial interface, verify that EAP is configured as the authentication protocol. Verify the settings of the properties of the Smart Card or other Certificate EAP type. Verify that the correct certificate is selected when configuring the credentials of the demand-dial interface.

■ On the answering router, verify that EAP is enabled as an authentication method on the answering router and that EAP-TLS is enabled on the matching network policy. Verify that the correct computer certificate of the authentication server (the answering router or NPS server) is selected from the Authentication Method settings of the Smart Card Or Other Certificate EAP type in the network policy for site-to-site VPN connections.

In order for the authentication server, the answering router or the NPS server, to validate the certificate of the calling router, the following must be true for each certificate in the certificate chain sent by the calling router:

■ **The current date must be within the validity dates of the certificate.**   When certificates are issued, they are issued with a valid date range before which they cannot be used and after which they are considered expired.

■ **The certificate must not have been revoked.**   Issued certificates can be revoked at any time. Certificate revocation can be checked by using the Online Certificate Status Protocol (OCSP), which uses HTTP to return a definitive digitally signed response of a certificate's status. Each issuing CA also publishes an up-to-date certificate revocation list (CRL), which is, in effect, a list of certificates that should no longer be considered valid. By default, the authentication server checks all the certificates in the calling router's certificate chain (the series of certificates from the calling router certificate to the root CA) for revocation. If any of the certificates in the chain have been revoked, certificate validation fails.

For CRL checking, if the CRL is locally available, it can be checked. In some configurations, the CRL cannot be checked until after the connection is made. For example, if the CRL is stored on the root CA, an authentication server in a site that does not have existing connectivity to the site that contains the root CA cannot access the CRL. There are two solutions to this configuration's problem:

❑ Publish the CRL in Active Directory. Once the CRL is published in Active Directory, the local domain controller in the site will have the latest CRL after Active Directory synchronization.

❑ On the VPN router, set the HKEY_LOCAL_MACHINE\System\CurrentControlSet\Services\Rasman\PPP\EAP\13\IgnoreRevocationOffline registry value to **1**.

To view the CRL distribution points for a certificate, in the Certificates snap-in, obtain the certificate properties, click the Details tab, and then click the CRL Distribution Points field.

The certificate revocation validation using CRLs works only as well as the CRL publishing and distribution system. If the CRL in a certificate is not updated often, a certificate that has been revoked can still be used and considered valid because the published CRL that the authentication server is checking is out of date.

■ **The certificate must have a valid digital signature.** CAs digitally sign certificates they issue. The authentication server verifies the digital signature of each certificate in the chain, with the exception of the root CA certificate, by obtaining the public key from the certificate's issuing CA and mathematically validating the digital signature.

The calling router certificate must also have the Client Authentication certificate purpose, also known as Enhanced Key Usage (EKU) OID 1.3.6.1.5.5.7.3.2, and must contain a UPN of a valid user account for the Subject Alternative Name field of the certificate.

To view the EKU for a certificate in the Certificates snap-in, in the contents pane, double-click the certificate, and then on the Details tab, click the Enhanced Key Usage field. To view the Subject Alternative Name field, select it.

Finally, to trust the certificate chain offered by the calling router, the authentication server must have the root CA certificate of the issuing CA of the calling router certificate installed in its Trusted Root Certification Authorities store.

The authentication server also verifies that the identity sent in the EAP-Response/Identity message is the same as the name in the Subject Alternative Name property of the certificate. This prevents a malicious user from masquerading as a different user from that specified in the EAP-Response/Identity message.

For additional requirements for the user certificate of the calling router, see "Requirements for PKI" earlier in this chapter.

If the authentication server is a Windows Server 2008 answering router or an NPS server, the following registry values in HKEY_LOCAL_MACHINE\SYSTEM\CurrentControlSet\ Services\Rasman\PPP\EAP\13 can modify the behavior of EAP-TLS when performing certificate revocation checking:

- **IgnoreNoRevocationCheck**   When set to 1, the authentication server allows EAP-TLS clients to connect even when it does not perform or cannot complete a revocation check of the calling router's certificate chain (excluding the root certificate). Typically, revocation checks fail because the certificate doesn't include CRL information.

  IgnoreNoRevocationCheck is set to 0 (disabled) by default. An EAP-TLS client cannot connect unless the server completes a revocation check of the client's certificate chain (including the root certificate) and verifies that none of the certificates has been revoked.

  You can use this entry to authenticate clients when the certificate does not include CRL distribution points, such as those from third parties.

- **IgnoreRevocationOffline**   When set to 1, the authentication server allows EAP-TLS clients to connect even when a server that stores a CRL is not available on the network. IgnoreRevocationOffline is set to 0 by default. The authentication server does not allow clients to connect unless it can complete a revocation check of their certificate chain and verify that none of the certificates has been revoked. When it cannot connect to a server that stores a revocation list, EAP-TLS considers the certificate to have failed the revocation check.

  Set IgnoreRevocationOffline to **1** to prevent certificate validation failure due to poor network conditions that prevent revocation checks from completing successfully.

- **NoRevocationCheck**   When set to 1, the authentication server prevents EAP-TLS from performing a revocation check of the calling router's certificate. The revocation check verifies that the calling router's certificate and the certificates in its certificate chain have not been revoked. NoRevocationCheck is set to 0 by default.

- **NoRootRevocationCheck**   When set to 1, the authentication server prevents EAP-TLS from performing a revocation check of the calling router's root CA certificate. NoRootRevocationCheck is set to 0 by default. This entry eliminates the revocation check of the client's root CA certificate only. A revocation check is still performed on the remainder of the calling router's certificate chain.

  You can use NoRootRevocationCheck to authenticate clients when the certificate does not include CRL distribution points, such as those from third parties. Also, NoRoot-RevocationCheck can prevent certification-related delays that occur when a certificate revocation list is offline or is expired.

All these registry values must be added as a DWORD type and have the valid values of 0 or 1. The calling router does not use these values.

In order for the calling router to validate the certificate of the authentication server for EAP-TLS authentication, the following must be true for each certificate in the certificate chain sent by the authentication server:

- The current date must be within the validity dates of the certificate.
- The certificate must have a valid digital signature.

Additionally, the authentication server computer certificate must have the Server Authentication EKU (OID 1.3.6.1.5.5.7.3.1). To view the EKU for a certificate, in the Certificates snap-in, double-click the certificate in the contents pane, and then on the Details tab, select the Enhanced Key Usage field.

Finally, to trust the certificate chain offered by the authentication server, the calling router must have the root CA certificate of the issuing CA of the authentication server certificate installed in its Trusted Root Certification Authorities Local Computer store.

For additional requirements for the computer certificate of the authentication server, see "Requirements for PKI" earlier in this chapter.

Notice that the calling router does not perform certificate revocation checking for the certificates in the certificate chain of the authentication server's computer certificate. The assumption is that the calling router does not yet have a connection to the network and therefore might not have access to a Web page or other resource to be able to check for certificate revocation.

Unable to Reach Locations Beyond the VPN Router

If traffic cannot be sent and received between locations in sites that are beyond the VPN routers, check the following:

- In the Routing and Remote Access snap-for both the calling router and answering router, in the properties dialog box of a server, on the General tab, verify that IPv4 or IPv6 is enabled for LAN And Demand-Dial Routing.
- Verify that the demand-dial interface over which traffic is being sent has been added to the IPv4\General or IPv6\General nodes in the Routing and Remote Access snap-in. This is done automatically when you create the interface by using the New Demand-Dial Interface Wizard.
- Verify that there are routes in the calling router's and answering router's sites so that all locations on both networks are reachable. Unlike a remote access connection, a demand-dial connection does not automatically create a default route. You must create routes on both sides of the demand-dial connection so that traffic can be routed to and from the other side of the demand-dial connection.

You can manually add IPv4 or IPv6 static routes during the creation of the demand-dial interface or by using the Routing and Remote Access snap-in. For persistent demand-dial connections, you can enable RIP for IPv4 across the demand-dial connection. For on-demand demand-dial connections, you can automatically update routes through an auto-static RIP for IPv4 update.

- For two-way initiated site-to-site VPN connections, verify that the answering router is not interpreting the site-to-site VPN connection as a remote access connection.

  For two-way initiated connections, either router can be the calling router or the answering router. The user names and demand-dial interface names must be properly matched. For example, two-way initiated connections would work under the following configuration:

  ❏ Router 1 has a demand-dial interface named NEW-YORK that is configured to use SEATTLE as the user name when sending authentication credentials.

  ❏ Router 2 has a demand-dial interface named SEATTLE that is configured to use NEW-YORK as the user name when sending authentication credentials.

  This example assumes that Router 2 can validate the SEATTLE user name and that Router 1 can validate the NEW-YORK user name.

  If the connection is a demand-dial connection, the port on which the connection was received shows a status of Active, and the corresponding demand-dial interface is in a Connected state. If the user account name in the credentials of the calling router appears under Remote Access Clients in the Routing and Remote Access snap-in, the answering router has interpreted the calling router as a remote access client.

- Verify that there are no IPv4 or IPv6 packet filters on the demand-dial interfaces of the calling router and answering router that prevent the sending or receiving of traffic.

  You can configure each demand-dial interface with IPv4 or IPv6 input and output filters to control the exact nature of the traffic that is allowed into and out of the demand-dial interface.

Unable to Reach the VPN Interfaces of VPN Routers

The VPN interfaces of the VPN routers are those interfaces on either side of the site-to-site VPN connection that represent the ends of the VPN tunnel. If traffic cannot be sent and received between the VPN interfaces, check the following:

- **Verify the IPv4 address pools of the calling router and answering router.**   If the VPN router is configured to use an IPv4 address pool, verify that the routes to the range of addresses specified by the IPv4 address pools are reachable by the hosts and routers of the site. If not, add IPv4 routes consisting of the VPN router static IP address pools, as specified by the IPv4 address and mask of the range, to the routers of the site, or enable RIP for IPv4 on the VPN router.

If the VPN router is configured to use Dynamic Host Configuration Protocol (DHCP) for IPv4 address allocation, but no DHCP server is available, the VPN router assigns addresses from the Automatic Private IP Addressing (APIPA) address range from 169.254.0.1 through 169.254.255.254. Assigning APIPA addresses to VPN routers works only if the network to which the VPN router is attached is also using APIPA addresses.

If the VPN router is using APIPA addresses when a DHCP server is available, verify that the proper adapter is selected from which to obtain DHCP-allocated IPv4 addresses. By default, the VPN router chooses the adapter to use to obtain IPv4 addresses through DHCP based on your selections in the Routing and Remote Access Server Setup Wizard. You can manually choose a LAN adapter in the Routing and Remote Access snap-in, in the properties dialog box of the VPN router, on the IPv4 tab, in the Adapter drop-down list.

If the IPv4 address pools are a subset of the range of IP addresses for the site subnet to which the VPN router is attached, verify that the range of IPv4 addresses in the IPv4 address pool are not assigned to other TCP/IP nodes either through static configuration or through DHCP.

- **Verify the IPv6 subnet prefix advertised by the calling router and answering router.**   The IPv6 subnet prefix should be the same for both the calling router and the answering router and reachable through a route in the routing infrastructures of both sites.

On-Demand Connection Is Not Made Automatically

If an on-demand connection is not being made automatically, check the following:

- In the properties dialog box of the calling router, on the General tab, verify that IPv4 or IPv6 LAN And Demand-Dial Routing is enabled.

- Verify that the correct static routes exist and are configured with the appropriate demand-dial interface. For the static routes that use a demand-dial interface, in the properties dialog box of the demand-dial interface, verify that the Use This Route To Initiate Demand-Dial Connections check box is selected.

- Verify that the demand-dial interface is not in an unreachable state.

- Verify that the demand-dial interface is not in a disabled state.

  To enable a demand-dial interface that is in a disabled state, in the Routing and Remote Access snap-in, in the Network Interfaces node, right-click the demand-dial interface, and then click Enable.

- Verify that the dial-out hours configured on the demand-dial interface are not preventing the connection attempt.

To configure dial-out hours, in the Routing and Remote Access snap-in, in the Network Interfaces node, right-click the demand-dial interface, and then click Dial-Out Hours.

- Verify that the demand-dial filters for the demand-dial interface are not preventing the connection attempt.

  To configure demand-dial filters, in the Routing and Remote Access snap-in, in the Network Interfaces node, right-click the demand-dial interface, and then click Set IP Demand-Dial Filters or Set IPv6 Demand-Dial Filters.

Chapter Summary

Deploying a site-to-site VPN solution involves configuration of Active Directory, PKI, Group Policy, and RADIUS elements of a Windows-based authentication infrastructure and planning and deployment of calling and answering VPN routers on the Internet. Once deployed, ongoing maintenance of a site-to-site VPN solution consists of managing calling and answering routers and their configuration for changes in infrastructure servers and routes. Common problems with site-to-site VPN connections include the inability to connect because of an authentication or authorization failure and the inability to reach site resources beyond a VPN router.

Additional Information

For additional information about VPN support in Windows, see the following:

- Chapter 12, "Remote Access VPN Connections"
- Windows Server 2008 Technical Library at *http://technet.microsoft.com/windowsserver/2008*
- Windows Server 2008 Help and Support
- "Virtual Private Networks" (*http://www.microsoft.com/vpn*)

For additional information about VPN Internet standards, see the following:

- RFC 2637, "Point-to-Point Tunneling Protocol (PPTP)"
- RFC 2661, "Layer Two Tunneling Protocol (L2TP)"
- RFC 3193, "Securing L2TP Using IPsec"

For additional information about Active Directory, see the following:

- Chapter 9, "Authentication Infrastructure"
- *Windows Server 2008 Active Directory Resource Kit* by Stan Reimer, Mike Mulcare, Conan Kezema, and Byron Wright, with the Microsoft Active Directory Team, available both as a stand-alone title and in the *Windows Server 2008 Resource Kit* (both from Microsoft Press, 2008)

- Windows Server 2008 Technical Library at *http://technet.microsoft.com/windowsserver/2008*
- Windows Server 2008 Help and Support

For additional information about PKI, see the following:

- Chapter 9, "Authentication Infrastructure"
- Windows Server 2008 Technical Library at *http://technet.microsoft.com/windowsserver/2008*
- Windows Server 2008 Help and Support
- "Public Key Infrastructure for Microsoft Windows Server" (*http://www.microsoft.com/pki*)
- *Windows Server 2008 PKI and Certificate Security* by Brian Komar (Microsoft Press, 2008)

For additional information about Group Policy, see the following:

- Chapter 9, "Authentication Infrastructure"
- *Windows Group Policy Resource Kit: Windows Server 2008 and Windows Vista* (Microsoft Press, 2008)
- Windows Server 2008 Technical Library at *http://technet.microsoft.com/windowsserver/2008*
- Windows Server 2008 Help and Support
- "Microsoft Windows Server Group Policy" (*http://www.microsoft.com/gp*)

For additional information about RADIUS and NPS, see the following:

- Chapter 9, "Authentication Infrastructure"
- Windows Server 2008 Technical Library at *http://technet.microsoft.com/windowsserver/2008*
- Windows Server 2008 Help and Support
- "Network Policy Server" (*http://www.microsoft.com/nps*)

Part IV
Network Access Protection Infrastructure

Chapter 14
Network Access Protection Overview

This chapter describes the need for the new Network Access Protection (NAP) platform in the Windows Server 2008, Windows Vista, and Windows XP SP3 operating systems, the components of NAP on an example intranet, and how NAP works for different types of NAP enforcement methods.

This chapter assumes that you understand the role of Active Directory, public key infrastructure (PKI), Group Policy, and Remote Authentication Dial-In User Service (RADIUS) elements of a Microsoft Windows–based authentication infrastructure for network access. For more information, see Chapter 9, "Authentication Infrastructure."

The Need for Network Access Protection

To understand the need for NAP, it is important to review the measures that must be taken to prevent the spread of malicious software (malware). This section provides an overview of malware threats and methods, malware prevention technologies, and how NAP provides centralized definition, integration, and enforcement of system health requirements to help prevent the exposure to malware on a private network.

Malware and Its Impact on Enterprise Computing

It is an unfortunate fact of life that modern computer networks are hostile environments. The same computer networking technologies that allow seamless communication between computers for e-mail, file transfers, Web access, and real-time collaboration are also used by malware to access and infect vulnerable computers. Malware is designed to install on a computer without the knowledge or consent of the computer user for the purposes of damage, data access, to report on the activities of the computer, or to allow the computer to be controlled by other computers. Malware can take the form of computer viruses (programs that propagate from one computer to another through media exchange or automatically over a network), Trojan horses (malware concealed inside programs that have another primary purpose), spyware (malware that records and reports on how the computer is being used), or adware (malware that displays advertising material to the user).

The Internet is an especially hostile environment, where a vulnerable computer can be attacked and infected in minutes by address and port scanning malware. Home networks also can be hostile environments because home computers are more likely to be vulnerable not only to address-scanning and port-scanning malware but also to malware that is installed on home computers through Trojan horse techniques such as e-mail attachments, Web controls, and free software exchanged through the computer enthusiast community.

Private organization networks, also known as intranets, are less hostile because they are typically not directly connected to the Internet. Additionally, at least for enterprise networks, an information technology (IT) staff has typically deployed malware prevention software. However, enterprise networks are still vulnerable to infection by Trojan horse–based malware that is downloaded and installed by users from the Internet.

How Malware Enters the Enterprise Network

Typical enterprise networking environments are not directly connected to the Internet. There is a small set of computers that are directly connected to the Internet to provide Internet services to customers or business partners. Most intranet computers are separated from the Internet by perimeter systems such as firewalls and proxy servers. Therefore, the computers of the enterprise network are typically protected from scanning attacks by network-level viruses emanating from the Internet.

However, the following can circumvent the perimeter security provided by firewalls or proxy servers:

- **Trojan horse–based viruses that are installed through code that is executed on a computer** Users on the enterprise network can inadvertently obtain viruses from e-mail, Web pages, and other types of files that are downloaded from the Internet. E-mail attachments are a common method of delivering Trojan horse–based viruses. Web pages are another common method because the proxy server for Internet Web access is designed to transfer the files that comprise a Web page. Enterprise network users can obtain viruses from Web pages and their associated files.

- **Mobile computers that can be moved and connected to other networks** The obvious example of a mobile computer is a laptop computer. A user takes a laptop home, on business trips, and to other public network locations such as wireless hot spots. Each time the user connects the laptop computer to a network that is not the enterprise network, the laptop runs the risk of being exposed to network-level viruses.

- **Employee remote access** When employees use remote access connections to connect to an enterprise network, they are logically connected to the enterprise network as if there were an Ethernet cable from the employee's location to a switch port on the enterprise network. Through this logical connection, the organization network can be exposed to network-level viruses.

- **Guest computers** When guests of the organization—such as consultants, vendors, or business partners—connect their computers to the organization network, they can expose it to network-level viruses.

Malware Impact

Malware can have a direct financial impact on networking operations for both the Internet and private networks because of exposure of confidential information, loss of intellectual property, bandwidth consumed, lost productivity to computers that have become unusable because of the malware, and the time required to remove the malware from all the infected computers. Malware has disrupted networking communications in the past and has the potential of doing so in the future.

Preventing Malware on Enterprise Networks

Based on previous malware infections (such as Love Bug in 2000 and Code Red in 2001), the IT industry began to work to prevent future infections. The result is a set of malware prevention technologies and techniques that many organization networks and end users employ today.

Malware Prevention Technologies

Because malware is inherently software, malware prevention software has evolved to prevent its installation and spread. Malware prevention software has the following forms:

- **Antivirus**   Software that monitors for known malware in files copied or downloaded to a computer. Antivirus software typically uses a local database of known signatures that identify malware stored in files and e-mail. If malware is detected, the antivirus software can remove the malware or prevent the file from being stored or executed. Because new viruses are created and distributed, the database of known antivirus signatures must be periodically updated.

- **Antispam**   Software that prevents unwanted e-mail messages from being stored in your e-mail inbox. Spam is a very common way to spread viruses or spyware.

- **Antispyware**   Software that detects and removes known spyware and adware from your computer. Just like antivirus software, antispyware software must be periodically updated to prevent new spyware from being installed. An example of antispyware software is Windows Defender from Microsoft, included with Windows Vista.

In addition to malware prevention software, the following technologies also help prevent malware:

- **Automatic updates for Windows-based computers**   For computers running a version of Windows, some types of viruses are designed to exploit a known security issue that has been identified by Microsoft and for which a security update is available. The virus attempts to infect those computers that have not yet been updated. To automate the installation of security updates from Microsoft before virus writers have a chance to write malware and spread it across the Internet, current versions of Windows support automatic updates. Based on a user-specified schedule, a computer running the

Windows Vista, Windows Server 2008, Windows XP, or Windows Server 2003 operating systems can poll the Windows Update Web site and download the latest security updates and automatically install them. Windows Update reduces the administrative burden on IT administrators to keep their computers current with the latest operating system updates.

■ **Host-based stateful firewalls**   A host-based stateful firewall runs on a computer and monitors network traffic at the packet level to help prevent malicious traffic from being either received or sent by the computer. Some viruses attempt to automatically propagate themselves by scanning the local subnet for available computers and then attacking the computers that are found. If successful, the virus automatically propagates from one computer to another. If an infected computer is moved, the virus begins attacking the computers on the newly attached subnet. An example is when a laptop computer that was infected on a home network is plugged into an organization's private network.

A stateful host-based firewall, such as Windows Firewall included with Windows Vista, Windows Server 2008, Windows XP SP2, and Windows Server 2003 SP1 or SP2, discards all unsolicited incoming traffic that does not correspond to either traffic sent in response to a request of the computer (solicited traffic) or unsolicited traffic that has been specified as allowed (excepted traffic). An example of solicited incoming traffic is the traffic corresponding to a Web page requested by a user of the computer. An example of excepted traffic is traffic that is allowed because the computer is running a server service, such as a Web server, and must receive unsolicited requests.

Because typical network-based viruses rely on unsolicited incoming traffic to scan and attack computers, enabling a host-based stateful firewall on all computers connected to the Internet and an intranet can help prevent the spread of these types of viruses.

To prevent malware from entering and spreading on an enterprise network, IT administrators should do the following:

■ Ensure that your host computers are using the correct privilege levels for network services and user accounts. By minimizing the privilege level, you can help prevent malware from installing itself on and exploiting a host computer. For example, computers running Windows Vista use User Account Control (UAC) to reduce the risk of exposure by limiting administrator-level access to processes requiring authorization.

■ Use malware prevention software and keep it updated.

■ Enable automatic update to install Windows updates as they become available. An organization network can also deploy approved updates through a central server, such as through Windows Server Updates Services (WSUS).

■ Use a host-based stateful firewall, such as Windows Firewall, to help prevent infection by network-level viruses that depend on unsolicited incoming traffic.

Computer System Health and Monitoring

The use of malware prevention technologies brings to light a new issue for IT administrators to determine and monitor: the system health of computers on the intranet. The system health is defined by a computer's current configuration state, which includes the set of installed malware prevention technologies, their current state (such as *enabled* or *disabled* and *current* or *delinquent* with the latest updates), and other configuration settings.

Determining System Health Requirements   The definition of system health will vary based on an organization's installed malware prevention technologies, computer configuration settings, and other security requirements. To help set the parameters of required system health, an IT administrator should consider the following:

- Antivirus software
    - ❏ Is an antivirus program deployed throughout the organization network?
    - ❏ If so, how current must the antivirus signature file or other updates be for a computer to be considered healthy?
- Antispam software
    - ❏ Is an antispam program deployed throughout the organization network?
    - ❏ If so, how current should the antispam updates be for a computer to be considered healthy?
- Antispyware software
    - ❏ Is an antispyware program deployed throughout the organization network?
    - ❏ If so, how current should the antispyware updates be for a computer to be considered healthy?
- Automatic operating system updates
    - ❏ Is Windows Automatic Update used throughout the organization network?
    - ❏ If so, must automatic updates be enabled for a computer to be considered healthy?
    - ❏ How current do the installed updates have to be for a computer to be considered healthy?
- Host-based stateful firewall
    - ❏ Is a host-based stateful firewall deployed throughout the organization network?
    - ❏ If so, must the firewall be enabled for a computer to be considered healthy? Which exceptions can be configured for a computer to be considered healthy?
- Other configuration settings
    - ❏ Are there other configuration settings required for adherence to the organization's security policies?
    - ❏ If so, which settings are required for a computer to be considered healthy?

For example, an IT administrator can create a system health policy that requires that all computers meet all the following requirements:

- All critical operating system updates must have been installed as of a specific date.

- The antivirus software must have been installed and be running to monitor incoming and outgoing files.

- The most recent signature for the antivirus software must have been installed.

- The antispyware software must have been installed and be running to monitor running services and incoming files.

- The most recent updates to the antispyware software must have been installed.

- The antispam software must have been installed and be running to monitor incoming e-mail messages.

- The most recent updates to the antispam software must have been installed.

- The host-based stateful firewall has been installed and is enabled.

- The host-based firewall must have an approved list of exceptions.

- The Transmission Control Protocol/Internet Protocol (TCP/IP) protocol stack on the computer must have IP routing disabled.

- The TCP/IP protocol stack on the computer must have automatic configuration enabled.

However, the biggest problem facing IT administrators is not in setting the requirements for system health but ensuring that all the computers on the organization network meet those requirements and implementing an enforcement mechanism for those computers that do not meet the requirements.

Enforcing System Health Requirements Coupled with the problem of determining whether the requirements for system health are being met is enforcing system health requirements for the computers on an organization network. In other words, if a computer on the organization network does not meet the requirements for system health, there should be consequences. For example, a computer that is not compliant with system health requirements should not be allowed to communicate with other computers on the network.

Although most malware prevention software has its own mechanisms for keeping current, there is no enforcement of system health requirements. For example, if an antivirus program does not have the latest updates, there are no consequences for the computer and the user of the computer.

To make system health enforceable, there must be a central computer on the intranet that evaluates system health and is configured with the organization's system health requirements. Client computers that attempt to connect to communicate on the network must have their system health evaluated so that noncompliant computers can be detected. The central system health evaluation computer must impose a consequence on noncompliant computers. An obvious consequence for a noncompliant computer is that it is refused a connection to the network. However, this dire consequence does not allow the noncompliant computer an opportunity to correct its configuration state.

Rather than preventing all access to the intranet, a solution that allows the noncompliant computer to correct its state, an action known as *remediation,* is to allow limited access to a subset of intranet servers that contain the needed updates, software, scripts, or other resources. Examples of servers on this limited access logical network can include antivirus or software update servers. By using these resources and instructions from the central computer that is evaluating system health, a noncompliant computer can automatically correct its configuration.

The Role of NAP

NAP for Windows Server 2008, Windows Vista, and Windows XP SP3 provides components and an application programming interface (API) set that can help IT administrators enforce compliance with health requirement policies for network access or communication. With NAP, developers and administrators can create solutions for validating computers that connect to their networks, provide needed updates or access to required health update resources, and limit the access or communication of noncompliant computers. Third-party vendors can leverage the powerful capabilities of NAP to create custom solutions for enforcing system health requirements. Administrators can customize the health maintenance solution they develop and deploy, whether for monitoring the computers accessing the network for health policy compliance, automatically updating computers with software updates to meet health policy requirements, or limiting the access of computers that do not meet health policy requirements.

With NAP, Windows-based networks now have an infrastructure that allows the following:

- IT administrators can configure system health requirements for NAP-capable computers.

- IT administrators can specify access enforcement behaviors for NAP-capable and non-NAP-capable computers, which include the following:

  - Monitoring of the access and communication attempts of computers and recording the access attempts in server event logs for ongoing or forensic analysis

  - Enforcement of network access restrictions for noncompliant or non-NAP-capable computers

- NAP-capable computers can automatically update themselves to become compliant (upon initial network access or communication) and remain compliant (automatically download updates or change settings on an ongoing basis).

Aspects of NAP

NAP has three important and distinct aspects:

- **Health state validation**   When a computer attempts to connect to the network, the computer's health state is validated against the health requirement policies as specified by the administrator. Administrators can also specify what to do if a computer is not compliant. In a monitoring-only environment, all computers have their health state evaluated, and the compliance state of each computer is logged for analysis. In a limited access environment, computers that comply with the health requirement policies are allowed unlimited access to the network. Computers that do not comply with health requirement policies can have their access limited.

- **Health policy compliance**   Administrators can help ensure compliance with health requirement policies by configuring settings to automatically update noncompliant computers with missing software updates or configuration changes through separate management software products, such as Microsoft Systems Management Server or Microsoft System Center Configuration Manager 2007. In a monitoring-only environment, computers will have access to the network before they are updated with required updates or configuration changes. In a limited access environment, noncompliant computers have limited access until the updates and configuration changes are completed. In both environments, computers that are compatible with NAP can automatically become compliant, and administrators can specify exceptions for computers that are not compatible with NAP.

- **Limited access**   Administrators can protect their networks by limiting the access of noncompliant computers, as specified by the administrator. Administrators can create a restricted network containing health update resources and other servers, and noncompliant computers can only access the restricted network. Administrators can also configure exceptions so that computers that are not compatible with NAP do not have their network access limited.

Typical NAP Scenarios

NAP helps provide a solution for the following common needs:

- **Verification of the health state of roaming laptops**   Portability and flexibility are two primary advantages of laptops, but these features also present a health threat. Company laptops frequently leave and return to the company network. While laptops are away from the company, they might not receive the most recent software updates or configuration changes. Laptops might also become infected while they are exposed to unprotected networks such as the Internet. By using NAP, network administrators can check the health state of any laptop when it reconnects to the company network, whether by creating a virtual private network (VPN) connection to the company network or by physically returning to the office.

- **Verification of the health state of desktop computers**   Although desktop computers do not usually leave the premises, they still can present a threat to a network. To minimize this threat, administrators must maintain these computers with the most recent updates and required software. Otherwise, these computers are at higher risk of infection from Web sites, e-mail, files from shared folders, and other publicly accessible resources. By using NAP, network administrators can automate health state checks to verify each desktop computer's compliance with health requirement policies. Administrators can check log files to determine which computers do not comply. With the addition of management software, administrators can generate automatic reports and automatically update noncompliant computers. When administrators change health requirement policies, computers can be automatically provided with the most recent updates.

- **Verification of the health state of visiting laptops**   Organizations sometimes must allow consultants, business partners, and guests to connect to their private networks. The laptops that these visitors bring might not meet system health requirements and can present health risks. By using NAP, administrators can determine that the visiting laptops are not compliant and allow only access to the Internet. Administrators would not typically require or provide any updates or configuration changes to the visiting laptops.

- **Verification of the health state of unmanaged home computers**   Unmanaged home computers that are not a member of the company's Active Directory domain can connect to a managed company network through a VPN connection. Unmanaged home computers provide an additional challenge to administrators because they do not have physical access to these computers. Lack of physical access makes enforcing compliance with health requirements, such as the use of antivirus software, even more difficult. However, with NAP, network administrators can verify the health state of a home computer every time it makes a VPN connection to the company network and limit the access to a restricted network until system health requirements are met.

Extensibility of NAP

NAP is an extensible platform that provides an infrastructure and an API set for adding components that verify and amend a computer's health state and that enforce access restrictions. For a more detailed explanation of NAP architecture and its extensibility, see "Network Access Protection Platform Architecture" at *http://go.microsoft.com/fwlink/?LinkID=90197.*

Limitations of NAP

NAP is not designed to protect a network from malicious users. It is designed to help administrators automatically maintain the health of the computers on the network, which in turn helps maintain the network's overall integrity. For example, if a computer has all the software and configuration settings that the health policies require, the computer is compliant and will be granted the appropriate access to the network. NAP does not prevent an authorized user with a compliant computer from uploading a malicious program to the network or engaging in other inappropriate behavior.

Business Benefits of NAP

The following are the business benefits of NAP:

- **Lower total cost of ownership through centralized configuration and management of system requirements for connection or communication**   NAP provides a central point of configuration to specify the following:

  - ❏ The system health requirements for computers that are connecting to or communicating on your network, which can include malware prevention, software settings, or system configuration settings.

  - ❏ The enforcement behavior for computers that do not meet the requirements. Enforcement behavior can be passive, allowing unlimited access but recording each connection or communication attempt; or active, limiting the access of the noncompliant computer.

  The system requirements and enforcement behavior are centrally configured in the form of health requirement policies on the server that evaluates the client's system settings.

- **Lower total cost of ownership through automated system health or configuration remediation**   NAP-capable computers will automatically install updates for their malware prevention software and make required configuration settings prior to being granted unlimited access to the network. Although most malware prevention software periodically checks for updates to install, NAP requires the updates for network connectivity. Once a NAP-capable computer is compliant, NAP components will automatically perform updates to ensure ongoing compliance.

- **Reduced chance of infection by malware**   Because the NAP platform can enforce system health requirements, NAP-capable computers can be updated and protected against known malware attacks through operating system and antivirus updates on computers prior to allowing them unlimited access. Appropriately configured NAP-enabled networks will have a reduced exposure to malware.

- **Utilization of existing system health and configuration requirements infrastructure**   NAP does not replace your existing system health and configuration infrastructure. Rather, it adds value to the existing components of system health and configuration and extends their role by tying them all together with the common goal of setting and enforcing system health requirements on connecting or communicating computers. Many system configuration, malware prevention, and network security infrastructure vendors support NAP. For a complete list, see Network Access Protection Partners at *http://www.microsoft.com/windowsserver2003/partners/nappartners.mspx.*

Components of NAP

The following sections describe some of the components of the NAP infrastructure to provide a basic understanding of NAP processes. For a more detailed explanation of NAP components and architecture, see the "Network Access Protection Platform Architecture" white paper at *http://go.microsoft.com/fwlink/?LinkID=90197*.

Figure 14-1 shows the components of a NAP-enabled network infrastructure.

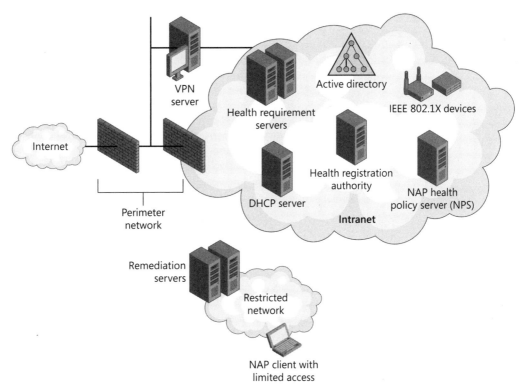

Figure 14-1 Components of a NAP-enabled network infrastructure

The components of a NAP-enabled network infrastructure consist of the following:

- **NAP clients** Computers that support the NAP platform and include computers running Windows Server 2008, Windows Vista, or Windows XP SP3.

- **NAP enforcement points** Computers or network access devices that use NAP or can be used with NAP to require the evaluation of a NAP client's health state and provide restricted network access or communication. NAP enforcement points use a Network Policy Server (NPS) that is acting as a NAP health policy server to evaluate the health state of NAP clients, whether network access or communication is allowed, and the set of remediation actions that a noncompliant NAP client must perform. Examples of NAP enforcement points are the following:

- ❑ **Health Registration Authority (HRA)**   A computer running Windows Server 2008 and Internet Information Services (IIS) that obtains health certificates from a certification authority (CA) for compliant NAP clients.

- ❑ **Network access devices**   Ethernet switches or wireless access points (APs) that support IEEE 802.1X authentication

- ❑ **VPN server**   A computer running Windows Server 2008 and Routing and Remote Access that allows remote access VPN connections to an intranet

- ❑ **DHCP server**   A computer running Windows Server 2008 and the Dynamic Host Configuration Protocol (DHCP) Server service that provides automatic Internet Protocol version 4 (IPv4) address configuration to intranet clients

- ■ **NAP health policy servers**   Computers running Windows Server 2008 and the NPS service that store health requirement policies and provide health state validation for NAP. NPS is the replacement for the Internet Authentication Service (IAS), the Remote Authentication Dial-In User Service (RADIUS) server and proxy provided with Windows Server 2003. NPS can also act as an authentication, authorization, and accounting (AAA) server for network access. When acting as a AAA server or NAP health policy server, NPS is typically run on a separate server for centralized configuration of network access and health requirement policies, as Figure 14-1 shows. The NPS service is also run on Windows Server 2008–based NAP enforcement points, such as an HRA or DHCP server. However, in these configurations, the NPS service is acting as a RADIUS proxy to exchange RADIUS messages with a NAP health policy server.

- ■ **Health requirement servers**   Computers that provide current system health state for NAP health policy servers. For example, a health requirement server for an antivirus program tracks the latest version of the antivirus signature file.

- ■ **Active Directory Domain Services**   The Windows directory service that stores account credentials and properties and Group Policy settings. Although not required for health state validation, Active Directory is required for Internet Protocol Security (IPsec)–protected communications, 802.1X-authenticated connections, and remote access VPN connections.

- ■ **Restricted network**   A separate logical or physical network that contains:

  - ❑ **Remediation servers**   Network infrastructure servers and health update servers that NAP clients can access to remediate their noncompliant state. Examples of network infrastructure servers include Domain Name System (DNS) servers and Active Directory domain controllers. Examples of health update servers include antivirus signature distribution servers and software update servers.

  - ❑ **NAP clients with limited access**   Computers that are placed on the restricted network when they do not comply with health requirement policies.

❑ **Non-NAP-capable computers**   Optionally, computers that do not support NAP can be placed on the restricted network (not shown in Figure 14-1).

System Health Agents and System Health Validators

Components of the NAP infrastructure known as system health agents (SHAs) on NAP clients and system health validators (SHVs) on NAP health policy servers provide health state tracking and validation for attributes of system health. Windows Vista and Windows XP SP3 include a Windows Security Health Validator SHV that monitors the settings of the Windows Security Center. Windows Server 2008 includes the corresponding Windows Security Health Validator SHV. NAP is designed to be flexible and extensible. It can interoperate with any vendor who provides SHAs and SHVs that use the NAP API.

An SHA creates a statement of health (SoH) that contains the current status information about the attribute of health being monitored by the SHA. For example, an SHA for an antivirus program might contain the state of the program (installed and running) and the version of the current antivirus signature file. Whenever an SHA updates its status, it creates a new SoH. To indicate its overall health state, a NAP client uses a System Statement of Health (SSoH), which includes version information for the NAP client and the set of SoHs for the installed SHAs.

When the NAP client validates its system health, it passes its SSoH to the NAP health policy server for evaluation through a NAP enforcement point. The NAP health policy server uses the SSoH, its installed SHVs, and its health requirement policies to determine whether the NAP client is compliant with system health requirements, and if it is not, the remediation actions that must be taken to achieve compliance. Each SHV produces a statement of health response (SoHR), which can contain remediation instructions. For example, the SoHR for an antivirus program might contain the current version number of the antivirus signature file and the name or IP address of the antivirus signature file server on the intranet.

Based on the SoHRs from the SHVs and the configured health requirement policies, the NAP health policy server creates a System Statement of Health Response (SSoHR), which indicates whether the NAP client is compliant or noncompliant and includes the set of SoHRs from the SHVs. The NAP health policy server passes the SSoHR back to the NAP client through a NAP enforcement point. The NAP client passes the SoHRs to its SHAs. The noncompliant SHAs automatically remediate their health state and create updated SoHs, and the health validation process begins again.

Enforcement Clients and Servers

A NAP Enforcement Client (EC) is a component on a NAP client that requests some level of access to a network, passes the computer's health status to a NAP enforcement point that is providing the network access, and indicates health evaluation information to other components of the NAP client architecture. The NAP ECs for the NAP platform supplied in Windows Vista, Windows XP SP3, and Windows Server 2008 are the following:

- An IPsec EC for IPsec-protected communications
- An EAPHost EC for 802.1X-authenticated connections
- A VPN EC for remote access VPN connections
- A DHCP EC for DHCP-based IPv4 address configuration
- A TS Gateway EC for connections to a TS Gateway server

A NAP Enforcement Server (ES) is a component on a NAP enforcement point running Windows Server 2008 that allows some level of network access or communication, can pass a NAP client's health status to NPS for evaluation, and, based on the response from NPS, can provide the enforcement of limited network access. The NAP ESs included with Windows Server 2008 are the following:

- An IPsec ES for IPsec-protected communications
- A DHCP ES for DHCP-based IPv4 address configuration
- A TS Gateway ES for TS Gateway server connections

For 802.1X-authenticated and remote access VPN connections, there is no separate ES component running on the 802.1X switch or wireless AP or VPN server.

Together, ECs and ESs require health state validation and enforce limited network access for noncompliant computers for specific types of network access or communication.

NPS

NPS is a RADIUS server and proxy in Windows Server 2008. As a RADIUS server, NPS provides AAA services for various types of network access. For authentication and authorization, NPS uses Active Directory to verify user or computer credentials and obtain user or computer account properties when a computer attempts an 802.1X-authenticated connection or a VPN connection.

NPS also acts as a NAP health policy server. Administrators set system health requirements in the form of health requirement policies on the NAP health policy server. NAP health policy servers evaluate health state information provided by NAP clients to determine health compliance, and for noncompliance, the set of remediation actions that must be taken by the NAP client to become compliant.

The role of NPS as an AAA server is independent from its role as a NAP health policy server. These roles can be used separately or combined as needed. For example:

- NPS can be an AAA server on an intranet that has not yet deployed NAP.

- NPS can be a combination of AAA server and health policy server for 802.1X-authenticated connections on an intranet that has deployed NAP for 802.1X-authenticated connections.

- NPS can be a health policy server for DHCP configuration on an intranet that has deployed NAP for DHCP configuration.

For more information about NPS and RADIUS, see Chapter 9.

Enforcement Methods

Windows Vista, Windows XP SP3, and Windows Server 2008 include NAP support for the following types of network access or communication:

- IPsec-protected traffic

- IEEE 802.1X–authenticated network connections

- Remote access VPN connections

- DHCP address configurations

Windows Server 2008 and Windows Vista also include NAP support for connections to a TS Gateway server.

Administrators can use these types of network access or communication, known as *NAP enforcement methods*, separately or together to limit the access or communication of noncompliant computers. NPS acts as a health policy server for all these NAP enforcement methods.

The following sections describe the IPsec, 802.1X, VPN, and DHCP enforcement methods.

IPsec Enforcement

With IPsec enforcement, a computer must be compliant to initiate communications with other compliant computers on an intranet in a server isolation or domain isolation IPsec deployment, which require that incoming communications be protected with IPsec. Because IPsec enforcement utilizes IPsec, you can specify requirements for protected communications with compliant computers on a per-IP address or per–TCP/UDP port number basis. IPsec enforcement confines communication to compliant computers after they have successfully connected and obtained a valid IP address configuration. IPsec enforcement one of the strongest forms of limited network access or communication in NAP.

The components of IPsec enforcement consist of an IPsec ES on an HRA running Windows Server 2008 and an IPsec EC in Windows Vista, Windows XP SP3, or Windows Server 2008. The HRA obtains X.509-based health certificates for NAP clients when they prove that they are compliant. These health certificates are then used in conjunction with IPsec policy settings to authenticate NAP clients when they initiate IPsec-protected communications with other compliant NAP clients on an intranet.

For more information about server isolation and domain isolation with IPsec, see Chapter 4, "Windows Firewall with Advanced Security."

802.1X Enforcement

With 802.1X enforcement, a computer must be compliant to obtain unlimited network access through an 802.1X-authenticated network connection, such as to an authenticating Ethernet switch or an IEEE 802.11 wireless AP. For noncompliant computers, network access is limited through a restricted access profile placed on the connection by the Ethernet switch or wireless AP. The restricted access profile can specify an access control list (ACL), which corresponds to a set of IP packet filters configured on the Ethernet switch or wireless AP, or a virtual LAN (VLAN) identifier (ID) that corresponds to the restricted network VLAN. With 802.1X enforcement, health policy requirements are enforced every time a computer attempts an 802.1X-authenticated network connection. 802.1X enforcement also actively monitors the health status of the connected NAP client and applies the restricted access profile to the connection if the client becomes noncompliant.

The components of 802.1X enforcement consist of NPS in Windows Server 2008 and an EAPHost EC in Windows Vista, Windows XP SP3, and Windows Server 2008. 802.1X enforcement provides strong limited network access for all computers accessing the network through an 802.1X-authenticated connection.

VPN Enforcement

With VPN enforcement, a computer must be compliant to obtain unlimited network access through a remote access VPN connection. For noncompliant computers, network access is limited through a set of IP packet filters that are applied to the VPN connection by the VPN server. With VPN enforcement, health policy requirements are enforced every time a computer attempts to obtain a remote access VPN connection to the network. VPN enforcement also actively monitors the health status of the NAP client and applies the IP packet filters for the restricted network to the VPN connection if the client becomes noncompliant.

The components of VPN enforcement consist of NPS in Windows Server 2008 and a VPN EC that is part of the remote access client in Windows Vista, Windows XP SP3, and Windows Server 2008. VPN enforcement provides strong limited network access for all computers accessing the network through a remote access VPN connection.

 Note VPN enforcement with NAP is different than Network Access Quarantine Control, a feature in Windows Server 2003.

DHCP Enforcement

With DHCP enforcement, a computer must be compliant to obtain an IPv4 address configuration that has unlimited network access from a DHCP server. For noncompliant computers, network access is limited by an IPv4 address configuration that allows limited access only to the restricted network. With DHCP enforcement, health policy requirements are enforced every time a DHCP client attempts to lease or renew an IPv4 address configuration. DHCP enforcement also actively monitors the health status of the NAP client and renews the IPv4 address configuration for access only to the restricted network if the client becomes non-compliant.

The components of DHCP enforcement consist of a DHCP ES that is part of the DHCP Server service in Windows Server 2008 and a DHCP EC that is part of the DHCP Client service in Windows Vista, Windows XP SP3, and Windows Server 2008. Because DHCP enforcement relies on a limited IPv4 address configuration that can be overridden by a user with administrator-level access, it is a weak form of limited network access in NAP.

How NAP Works

NAP is designed so that administrators can configure it to meet the individual needs of their networks. Therefore, the actual configuration of NAP will vary according to the administrator's preferences and requirements. However, the underlying operation of NAP remains the same. This section describes how NAP works on the example intranet shown in Figure 14-1. This example intranet is configured for the following:

- Health state validation, health policy compliance, and limited network access for non-compliant NAP clients

- IPsec enforcement, 802.1X enforcement, VPN enforcement, and DHCP enforcement

When obtaining a health certificate, making an 802.1X-authenticated or VPN connection to the intranet, or leasing or renewing an IPv4 address configuration from the DHCP server, each NAP client is classified in one of the following ways:

- NAP clients that meet the health policy requirements are classified as compliant and are allowed unlimited access to the intranet.

- NAP clients that do not meet the health policy requirements are classified as noncompliant and have their access limited to the restricted network until they meet the requirements. A noncompliant NAP client does not necessarily have a virus or some other active threat to the intranet, but it does not have the software updates or configuration settings as required by health requirement policies. A noncompliant NAP client is at higher risk of being compromised and passing on that risk to the intranet. The SHAs on NAP clients can automatically update computers with limited access with the software or configuration settings required for unlimited access. Automatic remediation ensures that noncompliant NAP clients obtain the necessary updates and are granted unlimited access as quickly as possible.

The example intranet in Figure 14-1 contains a restricted network. A restricted network can be created logically or physically. For example, IP filters, static routes, an ACL, or a VLAN identifier can be placed on a NAP client's connection to specify the remediation servers with which they can communicate.

Because most intranets contain a heterogeneous mixture of computers and devices, an administrator might choose to exempt some computers or devices from health policy requirements, for example, computers that require unlimited intranet access and are running Windows Server 2003, Windows 2000 or older versions of Windows, and operating systems other than Windows that do not support NAP. To prevent limited access for these computers, an administrator can optionally configure health requirement policies to grant unlimited access to the intranet for specific non-NAP-capable computers. Ideally, you should update or upgrade your non-NAP-capable computers to support NAP so that all of your computers can have their system health evaluated.

An administrator can also configure an exception policy on the NAP health policy server; exempted computers are not checked for compliance and have unlimited access to the intranet.

The following sections describe the basic processes for IPsec enforcement, 802.1X enforcement, VPN enforcement, and DHCP enforcement for a NAP client.

How IPsec Enforcement Works

The following process describes how IPsec enforcement works for a NAP client that is starting on the example intranet shown in Figure 14-1:

1. The IPsec EC component sends its SSoH indicating its current health state to the HRA.

2. The HRA sends the NAP client's SSoH to the NAP health policy server.

3. The NAP health policy server evaluates the SSoH of the NAP client, determines whether the NAP client is compliant, and sends the resulting SSoHR to the HRA. If the NAP client is not compliant, the SSoHR includes health remediation instructions.

4. If the health state is compliant, the HRA obtains a health certificate for the NAP client. Based on its IPsec policy settings as configured by the administrator, the NAP client can now initiate IPsec-protected communication with other compliant computers using its health certificate for IPsec authentication, and it can respond to communications initiated from other compliant computers that authenticate using their own health certificate.

5. If the health state is not compliant, the HRA sends the SSoHR to the NAP client and does not issue a health certificate. The NAP client cannot initiate communication with other computers that require a health certificate for IPsec authentication. However, the NAP client can initiate communications with remediation servers to correct its health state.

6. The NAP client sends update requests to the appropriate remediation servers.

7. The remediation servers provide the NAP client with the required updates for compliance with health requirements. The NAP client updates its SSoH.

8. The NAP client sends its updated SSoH to the HRA.

9. Assuming that all the required updates were made, the NAP health policy server determines that the NAP client is compliant and sends the SSoHR indicating health compliance to the HRA.

10. The HRA obtains a health certificate for the NAP client. The NAP client can now initiate IPsec-protected communication with other compliant computers.

For information about deploying IPsec enforcement, see Chapter 15, "Preparing for Network Access Protection," and Chapter 16, "IPsec Enforcement."

How 802.1X Enforcement Works

The following process describes how 802.1X enforcement works for a NAP client that is initiating an 802.1X-authenticated connection on the example intranet shown in Figure 14-1:

1. The NAP client and the Ethernet switch or wireless AP begin 802.1X authentication.

2. The NAP client sends its user or computer authentication credentials to the NAP health policy server.

3. If the authentication credentials are valid, the NAP health policy server requests the health state from the NAP client. If the authentication credentials are not valid, the connection attempt is terminated.

4. The NAP client sends its SSoH to the NAP health policy server.

5. The NAP health policy server evaluates the SSoH of the NAP client, determines whether the NAP client is compliant, and sends the results to the NAP client and the Ethernet switch or wireless AP. If the NAP client is not compliant, the results include a limited access profile for the Ethernet switch or wireless AP and the SSoHR containing health remediation instructions for the NAP client.

6. If the health state is compliant, the Ethernet switch or wireless AP completes the 802.1X authentication, and the NAP client has unlimited access to the intranet.

7. If the health state is not compliant, the Ethernet switch or wireless AP completes the 802.1X authentication but limits the access of the NAP client to the restricted network through an ACL or a VLAN ID. The NAP client can send traffic only to the remediation servers on the restricted network.

8. The NAP client sends update requests to the remediation servers.

9. The remediation servers provide the NAP client with the required updates for compliance with health requirement policies. The NAP client updates its SSoH.

10. The NAP client restarts 802.1X authentication and sends its updated SSoH to the NAP health policy server.

11. Assuming that all the required updates were made, the NAP health policy server determines that the NAP client is compliant and instructs the Ethernet switch or wireless AP to allow unlimited access.

12. The Ethernet switch or wireless AP completes the 802.1X authentication, and the NAP client has unlimited access to the intranet.

For information about deploying 802.1X enforcement, see Chapter 15 and Chapter 17, "802.1X Enforcement."

How VPN Enforcement Works

The following process describes how VPN enforcement works for a NAP client that is initiating a VPN connection on the example intranet shown in Figure 14-1:

1. The NAP client initiates a connection to the VPN server.

2. The NAP client sends its user authentication credentials to the VPN server.

3. If the authentication credentials are valid, the NAP health policy server requests the health state from the NAP client. If the authentication credentials are not valid, the VPN connection attempt is terminated.

4. The NAP client sends its SSoH to the NAP health policy server.

5. The NAP health policy server evaluates the SSoH of the NAP client, determines whether the NAP client is compliant, and sends the results to the NAP client and the VPN server. If the NAP client is not compliant, the results include a set of packet filters for the VPN server and the SSoHR containing health remediation instructions for the NAP client.

6. If the health state is compliant, the VPN server completes the VPN connection, and the NAP client has unlimited access to the intranet.

7. If the health state is not compliant, the VPN server completes the VPN connection but, based on the packet filters, limits the access of the NAP client to the restricted network. The NAP client can send traffic only to the remediation servers on the restricted network.

8. The NAP client sends update requests to the remediation servers.

9. The remediation servers provide the NAP client with the required updates for compliance with health requirement policies. The NAP client updates its SSoH.

10. The NAP client restarts authentication with the VPN server and sends its updated SSoH to the NAP health policy server.

11. Assuming that all the required updates were made, the NAP health policy server determines that the NAP client is compliant and instructs the VPN server to allow unlimited access.

12. The VPN server completes the VPN connection, and the NAP client has unlimited access to the intranet.

For information about deploying VPN enforcement, see Chapter 15 and Chapter 18, "VPN Enforcement."

How DHCP Enforcement Works

The following process describes how DHCP enforcement works for a NAP client that is attempting an initial DHCP configuration on the example intranet shown in Figure 14-1:

1. The NAP client sends a DHCP request message containing its SSoH to the DHCP server.

2. The DHCP server sends the SSoH of the NAP client to the NAP health policy server.

3. The NAP health policy server evaluates the SSoH of the NAP client, determines whether the NAP client is compliant, and sends the results to the DHCP server. If the NAP client is not compliant, the results include a limited access configuration for the DHCP server and an SSoHR containing health remediation instructions for the NAP client.

4. If the health state is compliant, the DHCP server assigns an IPv4 address configuration for unlimited access to the NAP client and completes the DHCP message exchange.

5. If the health state is not compliant, the DHCP server assigns an IPv4 address configuration for limited access to the restricted network to the NAP client and completes the DHCP message exchange, sending the SSoHR to the NAP client. The NAP client can send traffic only to the remediation servers on the restricted network.

6. The NAP client sends update requests to the remediation servers.

7. The remediation servers provide the NAP client with the required updates for compliance with health requirement policies. The NAP client updates its SSoH.

8. The NAP client sends a new DHCP request message containing its updated SSoH to the DHCP server.

9. The DHCP server sends the updated SSoH of the NAP client to the NAP health policy server.

10. Assuming that all the required updates were made, the NAP health policy server determines that the NAP client is compliant and instructs the DHCP server to assign an IPv4 address configuration for unlimited access to the intranet.

11. The DHCP server assigns an address configuration for unlimited access to the NAP client and completes the DHCP message exchange.

For information about deploying DHCP enforcement, see Chapter 15 and Chapter 19, "DHCP Enforcement."

> ## How It Works: NAP Component Interaction
>
> System health information, in the form of SSoHs and SSoHRs, between a NAP health policy server and a NAP enforcement point is sent as attributes of a RADIUS message. A NAP health policy server is a RADIUS server, and NAP enforcement points are RADIUS clients.
>
> For IPsec enforcement, system health information between a NAP client and an HRA is sent over Hypertext Transfer Protocol (HTTP) or an encrypted HTTP over Secure Sockets Layer (SSL) session. The NAP client uses HTTP or the HTTP over SSL session to indicate its current system health state and request a health certificate. The HRA uses HTTP or the HTTP over SSL session to send the SSoHR and the health certificate to the NAP client.
>
> For 802.1X enforcement, system health information between a NAP client and a NAP health policy server is sent as Protected Extensible Authentication Protocol (PEAP)–Type-Length-Value (TLV) messages. On the link between the NAP client and the authenticating switch or wireless AP, the PEAP-TLV messages are sent over the EAP over LAN (EAPOL) protocol. Between the authenticating switch or wireless AP and the NAP health policy server, the PEAP-TLV messages are encapsulated and sent as RADIUS attributes of RADIUS messages.
>
> For VPN enforcement, system health information between a NAP client and a NAP health policy server is also sent as PEAP-TLV messages. The PEAP-TLV messages are sent over the Point-to-Point Protocol (PPP)–based logical link between the NAP client and the VPN server created by the VPN connection. Between the VPN server and the NAP health policy server, the PEAP-TLV messages are encapsulated and sent as RADIUS attributes of RADIUS messages.
>
> For DHCP enforcement, system health information between a NAP client and a DHCP server is sent as DHCP options in DHCP messages.

Chapter Summary

NAP is a new platform for Windows Vista, Windows Server 2008, and Windows XP SP3 that includes client and server components to limit the network access or communication of computers until they are compliant with system health requirements. Administrators can configure IPsec enforcement, 802.1X enforcement, VPN enforcement, DHCP enforcement, or all of them, depending on their needs.

IPsec enforcement works by not issuing health certificates to noncompliant NAP clients so that they cannot initiate protected communications with compliant NAP clients. 802.1X enforcement is done by specifying an ACL or VLAN ID that is applied to the 802.1X connection by the Ethernet switch or wireless AP to limit the access to the restricted network. VPN enforcement is done through IP packet filters that are applied to the VPN connection by the VPN server to limit the access to the restricted network. DHCP enforcement is done through an IPv4 address configuration that limits access to the restricted network.

Additional Information

For additional information about NAP, see the following:

- Chapter 15, "Preparing for Network Access Protection"
- Chapter 16, "IPsec Enforcement"
- Chapter 17, "802.1X Enforcement"
- Chapter 18, "VPN Enforcement"
- Chapter 19, "DHCP Enforcement"
- Windows Server 2008 Technical Library at *http://technet.microsoft.com/windowsserver/2008*
- Windows Server 2008 Help and Support
- "Network Access Protection" (*http://www.microsoft.com/nap*)

For additional information about RADIUS and NPS, see the following:

- Chapter 9, "Authentication Infrastructure"
- Windows Server 2008 Technical Library at *http://technet.microsoft.com/windowsserver/2008*
- Windows Server 2008 Help and Support
- "Microsoft Network Policy Server" (*http://www.microsoft.com/nps*)

For additional information about IPsec, see the following:

- Chapter 4, "Windows Firewall with Advanced Security"
- Windows Server 2008 Technical Library at *http://technet.microsoft.com/windowsserver/2008*
- Windows Server 2008 Help and Support
- IPsec (*http://www.microsoft.com/ipsec*)

For additional information about IEEE 802.1X for wireless and wired networks, see the following:

- Chapter 10, "IEEE 802.11 Wireless Networks"
- Chapter 11, "IEEE 802.1X–Authenticated Wired Networks"

- Windows Server 2008 Technical Library at *http://technet.microsoft.com/windowsserver/ 2008*

- Windows Server 2008 Help and Support

- "Wireless Networking" (*http://www.microsoft.com/wifi*)

- "Wired Networking with 802.1X Authentication" (*http://technet.microsoft.com/en-us/ network/bb545365.aspx*)

For additional information about remote access VPNs, see the following:

- Chapter 12, "Remote Access VPN Connections"

- Windows Server 2008 Technical Library at *http://technet.microsoft.com/windowsserver/ 2008*

- Windows Server 2008 Help and Support

- "Virtual Private Networks" (*http://www.microsoft.com/vpn*)

For additional information about DHCP, see the following:

- Chapter 3, "Dynamic Host Configuration Protocol"

- Windows Server 2008 Technical Library at *http://technet.microsoft.com/windowsserver/ 2008*

- Windows Server 2008 Help and Support

- "Dynamic Host Configuration Protocol" (*http://www.microsoft.com/dhcp*)

Chapter 15

Preparing for Network Access Protection

This chapter describes how to prepare your network for Network Access Protection (NAP) from an evaluation of your current network infrastructure to the set of design decisions that you need to make to deploy the components of NAP that are independent of the NAP enforcement method. This chapter assumes the following:

- That you understand the roles of Active Directory, public key infrastructure (PKI), Group Policy, and Remote Authentication Dial-In User Service (RADIUS) elements of a Microsoft Windows–based authentication infrastructure for network access. For more information, see Chapter 9, "Authentication Infrastructure."

- That you understand the components of NAP and NAP enforcement methods. For more information, see Chapter 14, "Network Access Protection Overview."

Evaluation of Your Current Network Infrastructure

Before beginning your NAP deployment, it is helpful to inventory and evaluate your current network infrastructure to ensure that it has the required hosts and access servers and that it meets the requirements for NAP support.

The evaluation of your current network infrastructure falls into the following categories:

- Intranet computers
- Layer 2 attachment to the intranet
- Networking support infrastructure

The following sections explore these categories in detail.

Intranet Computers

Your intranet computers are either candidates for NAP clients or non-NAP-capable clients for possible exception treatment. Your intranet computers can also be classified as managed (members of your Active Directory domain service) or unmanaged.

Managed Computers

Your managed computers can be classified in the following ways:

- **NAP capable** Includes computers running the Windows Vista, Windows XP SP3, or Windows Server 2008 operating systems and other operating systems with a NAP client.

- **Non-NAP-capable** Includes computers running an operating system that does not have a NAP client.

The 802.1X and virtual private network (VPN) NAP enforcement methods do not require that connecting computers be managed for health evaluation, but computers should be managed for authentication and authorization of 802.1X-authenticated and VPN connections to the intranet. For the Internet Protocol security (IPsec) NAP enforcement method, computers can be unmanaged, but the recommendation is that they be managed.

Unmanaged Computers

Your unmanaged computers can be classified in the following ways:

- **NAP capable** Includes computers running Windows Vista, Windows XP SP3, or Windows Server 2008 and other operating systems with a NAP client.

- **Non-NAP-capable** Includes computers running an operating system that does not have a NAP client.

Layer 2 Attachment to the Intranet

Another way to classify computers is by their Layer 2 method of attachment to the intranet.

Wired For computers using wired connections to the intranet, most commonly for desktop user and server computers, you can classify the computers with the following:

- **Authenticated with IEEE 802.1X** Use IEEE 802.1X authentication to authenticate computer use of a switch port. If you want to use the 802.1X enforcement method, ensure that your 802.1X-enabled computers are using a Protected Extensible Authentication Protocol (PEAP)–based authentication method such as PEAP-Microsoft Challenge Handshake Authentication Protocol version 2 (MS-CHAP v2) or PEAP-Transport Layer Security (TLS). A PEAP-based authentication method is required because system health information is transferred between the wired NAP client and the NAP health policy server using PEAP messages. If your 802.1X-enabled computers are using Extensible Authentication Protocol (EAP)–Message Digest 5 (MD5) Challenge Handshake Authentication Protocol (CHAP), configure them to use PEAP-MS-CHAP v2. If your 802.1X-enabled computers are using EAP-TLS, configure them to use PEAP-TLS.

- **Not authenticated with 802.1X** If you want to use the 802.1X enforcement method, you must deploy 802.1X authentication with the PEAP-MS-CHAP v2 or PEAP-TLS authentication methods on your intranet. For more information about how to deploy

802.1X-authenticated wired networks, see Chapter 11, "IEEE 802.1X–Authenticated Wired Networks."

Wireless   For computers using IEEE 802.11 wireless connections to the intranet, most commonly mobile computers, you can classify the computers with the following:

- **Authenticated with IEEE 802.1X**   Use Wi-Fi Protected Access 2 (WPA2)–Enterprise or Wi-Fi Protected Access (WPA)–Enterprise and the IEEE 802.1X standard to authenticate their use of a wireless connection to a wireless access point. If you want to use the 802.1X enforcement method, ensure that your wireless client computers are using a PEAP-based authentication method such as PEAP-MS-CHAP v2 or PEAP-TLS. A PEAP-based authentication method is required because system health information is transferred between the wireless NAP client and the NAP health policy server using PEAP messages. If your wireless clients are using EAP-TLS, configure them to use PEAP-TLS.

- **Not authenticated with 802.1X**   If you are not using 802.1X authentication with WPA2-Enterprise or WPA-Enterprise, upgrade your wireless network immediately to protect your intranet, regardless of whether you want to use the 802.1X enforcement method. If you want to use the 802.1X enforcement method for your wireless connections, use WPA2-Enterprise or WPA-Enterprise with the PEAP-MS-CHAP v2 or PEAP-TLS authentication methods. For more information about how to deploy protected wireless networks, see Chapter 10, "IEEE 802.11 Wireless Networks."

Remote Access

For computers using remote connections to the intranet, most commonly for traveling mobile computers or connections from home, you can classify the computers based on whether the remote access connection is a dial-up or VPN connection. Dial-up remote access connections, increasingly rare for today's intranets because of the convenience of high-speed Internet connectivity, are not subject to NAP health evaluation and enforcement of limited access for noncompliant computers. The VPN enforcement method does not include dial-up remote access connections. If you want to ensure that all Layer 2 connections to your intranet are subject to NAP health evaluation, you should plan on phasing out your dial-up remote access connections. If you cannot eliminate dial-up remote access connections, try to limit dial-up remote access to minimize the risk to your intranet from noncompliant computers.

If you want to use the VPN enforcement method, ensure that your VPN client computers are using a PEAP-based authentication method such as PEAP-MS-CHAP v2 or PEAP-TLS. A PEAP-based authentication method is required because system health information is transferred between the VPN-based NAP client and the NAP health policy server using PEAP messages. If your VPN connections are using MS-CHAP v2, configure them to use PEAP-MS-CHAP v2. If your VPN connections are using EAP-TLS, configure them to use PEAP-TLS.

For more information about deploying remote access VPN connections, see Chapter 12, "Remote Access VPN Connections."

Networking Support Infrastructure

Networking support infrastructure is the services that enable networking across an intranet and include the following:

- **Dynamic Host Configuration Protocol (DHCP)**   If you want to use the DHCP enforcement method with Windows-based DHCP servers, you must upgrade your DHCP servers to Windows Server 2008. For more information, see Chapter 3, "Dynamic Host Configuration Protocol."

- **Domain Name System (DNS)**   Depending on how you implement limited access for noncompliant clients, you might need additional DNS servers. For more information, see Chapter 7, "Domain Name System."

- **Windows Internet Name Service (WINS)**   Depending on how you implement limited access for noncompliant clients, you might need additional WINS servers. For more information, see Chapter 8, "Windows Internet Name Service."

- **Active Directory**   Active Directory domain controllers do not need to be upgraded to Windows Server 2008. However, depending on how you implement limited access, you might need additional Active Directory domain controllers. If your domain controllers are running Windows Server 2008, you should use *read-only domain controllers* (RODCs) for noncompliant clients. An RODC is a new type of domain controller in Windows Server 2008 that can be deployed in locations where physical security cannot be guaranteed. An RODC hosts read-only partitions of the Active Directory database.

- **Group Policy**   Group Policy Objects (GPOs) can be used to centrally configure and propagate NAP client settings to managed computers. You do not need to use a Windows Server 2008–based domain controller. If all of your domain controllers are running Microsoft Windows Server 2003, you must configure NAP client policy settings in a GPO from a computer running Windows Vista or Windows Server 2008.

- **IPsec**   If you want to use IPsec enforcement, you must update your IPsec policy settings in the form of connection security rules to use a health certificate during IPsec authentication in your Active Directory GPOs. As with the NAP client settings, you do not need to use a Windows Server 2008–based domain controller. If all of your domain controllers are running Windows Server 2003, you must configure IPsec policy settings in a GPO from a computer running Windows Vista or Windows Server 2008. For more information about IPsec policy settings, see Chapter 4, "Windows Firewall with Advanced Security."

- **PKI**   If you want to use IPsec enforcement, you must deploy a PKI or you might need to modify your existing PKI to include Windows-based issuing CAs for health certificates. For more information, see Chapter 16, "IPsec Enforcement."

- **VPN**   If you want to use VPN enforcement with Windows-based VPN servers, you must upgrade your VPN servers to Windows Server 2008. For more information, see Chapter 12, "Remote Access VPN Connections."

- **RADIUS**   If you do not have a RADIUS infrastructure, you must deploy one using Windows Server 2008–based RADIUS servers to use any of the NAP enforcement methods. If you have an existing RADIUS infrastructure, you must upgrade your RADIUS servers to Windows Server 2008 to use Network Policy Server (NPS) for NAP health policy evaluation. For more information, see Chapter 9.

NAP Health Policy Servers

The central server that performs health evaluation for NAP is a computer running NPS that is known as a *NAP health policy server*. In this capacity, the computer running NPS is acting as a RADIUS server accepting RADIUS Access-Request messages from NAP enforcement points (RADIUS clients) such as health registration authorities (HRAs), 802.11 wireless access points, 802.1X-capable switches, NAP-enabled VPN servers, and NAP-enabled DHCP servers.

Planning and Design Considerations

When deploying NAP health policy servers, you must consider the following planning and design issues:

- Existing RADIUS infrastructure
- RADIUS server capacity
- NPS logging and reporting mode
- Branch offices
- System health validators

Existing RADIUS Infrastructure

If you have existing RADIUS servers that are running Windows Server 2003 or Windows 2000 Server and Internet Authentication Service (IAS), you must upgrade to Windows Server 2008 on your existing RADIUS servers and configure them as NAP health policy servers.

If you have existing RADIUS servers that are running an operating system other than Windows Server 2003 or Windows 2000 Server, those servers cannot be updated to support NPS and NAP health evaluation. You must deploy separate computers running Windows Server 2008 and NPS as the NAP health policy servers.

If you do not have an existing RADIUS infrastructure, you must install Windows Server 2008 and NPS on either new or existing computers. For example, if your intranet does not use 802.1X authentication for wired connections, 802.11 wireless connections, or VPN connections, you do not need RADIUS servers. However, when you deploy NAP, you need a RADIUS infrastructure to perform health evaluation, regardless of the NAP enforcement method.

RADIUS Server Capacity

For an existing RADIUS infrastructure, in most cases you can use the same RADIUS servers for NAP health evaluation that you are currently using for Layer 2 authentication, authorization, and accounting. In other words, in most cases, you do not need to add additional RADIUS servers to your RADIUS infrastructure to add NAP health evaluation.

If you do not have an existing RADIUS infrastructure, follow the guidance in Chapter 9, and deploy at least two NAP health policy servers for fault tolerance, and configure your NAP enforcement points with primary and secondary RADIUS servers to spread the load between the two NAP health policy servers.

If you need to scale up your RADIUS capacity and spread the load among multiple RADIUS servers, you can deploy a RADIUS proxy layer between the NAP enforcement points and the NAP health policy servers. For more information, see Chapter 9.

NPS Logging and Reporting Mode

The NPS service logs incoming RADIUS requests to a local file or to both a local file and a computer running Microsoft SQL Server, depending on how you configure NPS for logging. NPS logging is important for NAP deployment because you can initially deploy NAP on your intranet in *reporting mode*, in which health compliance is checked but limited network access is not enforced and the user is not informed that their computer is not compliant with system health requirements. In reporting mode, you can analyze the logging information to determine the following:

- Which computers on your intranet are NAP capable
- Of the NAP-capable computers, which of them are compliant

You can use this information to configure NAP-capable computers to be compliant. Reporting mode allows you to fine-tune your NAP deployment before you enable *enforcement mode*, in which noncompliant and non-NAP-capable clients can have limited access to the intranet and users on NAP clients are informed that their computer is not compliant with system health requirements.

As described in Chapter 9, you must ensure that the NPS server can perform logging. If it cannot, it will reject all incoming requests for network access and health evaluation. Therefore, you must ensure that there is enough disk space for local file logging and for SQL Server logging, that there are no configuration or connectivity issues to prevent SQL Server logging, and that there is enough storage space on the computer running SQL Server.

Branch Offices

The decision to deploy NPS servers that perform NAP health evaluation in branch office networks depends on whether the branch office has an existing Active Directory domain controller:

- If the branch office has existing Active Directory domain controllers, you can install NPS on at least two of the domain controllers in the branch office and use them as the NAP health policy servers for the NAP enforcement points of the branch office.

- If the branch office does not have an existing Active Directory domain controller, do not install NPS on servers in the branch office. Instead, have your NAP enforcement points use the RADIUS servers that are present in the main office.

- If the branch office does not have an existing Active Directory domain controller, you can also configure a NAP-based RADIUS proxy in the branch office to use the RADIUS servers that are present in the main office.

System Health Validators

Health policy settings in NPS allow you to define health compliance and noncompliance in terms of the system health validators (SHVs) that are installed on the NAP health policy server. An SHV on the NAP health policy server verifies whether the system health status information sent by its corresponding system health agent (SHA) on a NAP client is compliant for one or more attributes of system health. An SHV can also perform its own evaluation of the NAP client's system health. The result of the evaluation of the NAP client's health by the SHVs is then sent to the NPS service to match a network policy and its configured health policy. For more information about the settings of NPS for NAP health evaluation, see "Health Requirement Policy Configuration" later in this chapter.

Windows Server 2008 includes the Windows Security Health Validator, the SHV that corresponds to the Windows Security Health Agent that is provided with Windows Vista and Windows XP SP3. Using the Windows Security Health Agent and Windows Security Health Validator, you can define system health requirements for the system services of the Windows Security Center in Windows Vista and Windows XP SP3.

Beyond the built-in Windows Security Health Validator SHV, you will need to determine the additional SHVs that you want to use to define system health requirements for your NAP clients. Additional SHVs might be available from the vendors that supply your third-party host firewall, antivirus software, antispyware software, intrusion detection systems, and other security software or infrastructure that you have deployed on your intranet.

Contact your vendors to obtain an SHA that you will install on your NAP clients and the corresponding SHV that you will install on your NAP health policy servers. After you have installed the SHV on the NAP health policy server, you can configure health policies to include the SHV in network policies for compliant and noncompliant NAP clients.

Deployment Steps

To deploy NAP health policy servers, do the following:

1. If needed, follow the steps in Chapter 9 for deploying NPS-based RADIUS servers.

2. Designate which of the RADIUS servers will be NAP health policy servers.

3. If needed, add RADIUS clients for your NAP enforcement points on the RADIUS servers. For example, if RADIUS clients for your wireless access points (APs), authenticating switches, and VPN servers are already configured, and you are not planning to use IPsec or DHCP enforcement, the NAP health policy server in most cases does not need to be configured with any additional RADIUS clients. However, if you are planning to use the IPsec or DHCP enforcement method, you must add RADIUS clients that correspond to your HRAs and DHCP servers.

4. Install and configure the SHVs that you are going to use for health evaluation on the NPS health policy servers, as needed. For example, if you are using just the built-in Windows Security Health Validator SHV, no additional installation is required.

5. Configure NAP health requirement policies as needed using the Configure NAP Wizard. For more information, see "Health Requirement Policy Configuration" later in this chapter.

For additional information about configuring NAP health requirement policies for specific NAP enforcement methods, see the following chapters:

- Chapter 16, "IPsec Enforcement"
- Chapter 17, "802.1X Enforcement"
- Chapter 18, "VPN Enforcement"
- Chapter 19, "DHCP Enforcement"

Ongoing Maintenance

The areas of maintenance for a NAP health policy server are as follows:

- Management of RADIUS clients for NAP enforcement points
- Management of health requirement policies for SHVs

For information on additional areas of maintenance for RADIUS servers, see Chapter 9.

Managing RADIUS Clients for NAP Enforcement Points

When you deploy a new NAP enforcement point, such as a new wireless access point (AP) or VPN server, you must do the following:

1. Add the NAP enforcement point as a RADIUS client to your NPS health policy servers.

2. Configure the NAP enforcement point to use your NAP health policy servers as RADIUS servers.

When you remove a NAP enforcement point, delete the NAP enforcement point as a RADIUS client on your NAP health policy servers.

Managing Health Requirement Policies for SHVs

When you have a new SHV to use in your health requirement policies, you must do the following:

1. Install the corresponding SHA on your NAP clients (if necessary).

2. Install the SHV on your NAP health policy servers.

3. Configure the health requirements for the SHV and your health policies to include the new SHV in their evaluation of system health for compliance or non-compliance.

When you want to remove an SHV, do the following:

1. Configure your health policies to no longer include the new SHV in their evaluation of system health for compliance or non-compliance.

2. Remove the SHV from the NPS health policy server.

3. Remove the corresponding SHA from the NAP clients (if necessary).

Health Requirement Policy Configuration

Health requirement policies on the NAP health policy server determine whether a NAP-capable client is compliant or noncompliant, how to treat noncompliant NAP clients and whether they should automatically remediate their health state, and how to treat non-NAP-capable clients for different NAP enforcement methods.

Components of a Health Requirement Policy

A health requirement policy is a combination of the following:

- Connection request policy
- Health policy
- NAP settings
- Network policy

Connection Request Policies

Connection request policies are an ordered set of rules that allow the NPS service to determine whether a specific connection attempt request or an accounting message received from a RADIUS client should be processed locally or forwarded to another RADIUS server. You can configure connection request policies in the Policies\Connection Request Policies node of the Network Policy Server snap-in. When forwarding messages, the connection request policy specifies a remote RADIUS server group, which you can configure in the RADIUS Clients and Servers\Remote RADIUS Server Groups node of the Network Policy Server snap-in.

When you are configuring the NPS server to perform NAP health evaluation, NPS is acting as a RADIUS server. Therefore, remote RADIUS server groups are not needed. However, connection request policies for local processing of RADIUS request messages might need to be configured or customized for NAP health evaluation.

Health Policies

Health policies allow you to specify health requirements in terms of installed SHVs and whether NAP clients must pass or fail any or all of the selected SHVs.

Figure 15-1 shows an example of a health policy.

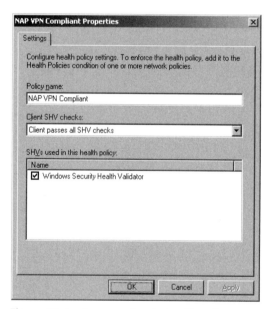

Figure 15-1　An example of a health policy

In the Policy Name box, type the unique name of the policy. In the Client SHV Checks drop-down list, select one of the following:

■ **Client Passes All SHV Checks**　The client's health status in the connection request must pass the health requirements for all of the SHVs selected in the SHVs Used In This Health Policy list. You might select this option to specify that a compliant NAP client is one that must pass the health requirements for all the selected SHVs.

- **Client Fails All SHV Checks**   The client's health status in the connection request must fail all the health requirements for all of the SHVs selected in the SHVs Used In This Health Policy list. You might select this option to specify that a noncompliant NAP client is one that fails the health requirements for all of the selected SHVs.

- **Client Passes One Or More SHV Checks**   The client's health status in the connection request must pass the health requirements of at least one of the SHVs selected in the SHVs Used In This Health Policy list. You might select this option to specify that a compliant NAP client is one that must pass the health requirements of at least one SHV.

- **Client Fails One Or More SHV Checks**   The client's health status in the connection request must fail the health requirements of at least one of the SHVs selected in the SHVs Used In This Health Policy list. You might select this option to specify that a noncompliant NAP client is one that fails any of the SHVs.

In the SHVs Used In This Health Policy list, select the installed SHVs that apply to the policy. By default, the Windows Security Health Validator is listed.

To create a new health policy, in the Network Policy Server console tree, right-click Health Policies, and then click New.

Network Access Protection Settings

Network Access Protection settings, available in the Network Policy Server console tree, in the Network Access Protection node, consist of the following:

- **System Health Validators**   Specifies the configuration of installed SHVs for health requirements and error conditions.

- **Remediation Server Groups**   Specifies the sets of servers that are accessible to non-compliant clients with limited network access for the DHCP and VPN enforcement methods. A remediation server group is a list of servers that noncompliant NAP clients or non-NAP-capable clients can access. The DHCP and VPN servers ensure that non-compliant NAP clients or non-NAP-capable clients can only access the servers in the list. You might have separate groups for noncompliant NAP clients or non-NAP-capable clients or separate groups for different NAP enforcement methods.

System Health Validators   The System Health Validators node displays the set of SHVs that are installed on the NPS server and allows you to configure their settings for health requirements and error conditions. By default, the Windows Security Health Validator SHV is installed. Figure 15-2 shows the properties dialog box of the Windows Security Health Validator SHV.

In this dialog box, you can configure how NPS interprets various error conditions. To configure the health requirements for the Windows Security Health Validator SHV, click Configure. Figure 15-3 shows the default Windows Security Health Validator dialog box.

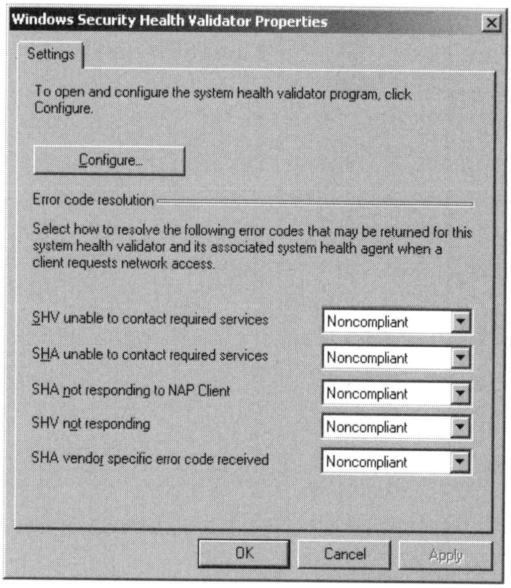

Figure 15-2   The Windows Security Health Validator Properties dialog box

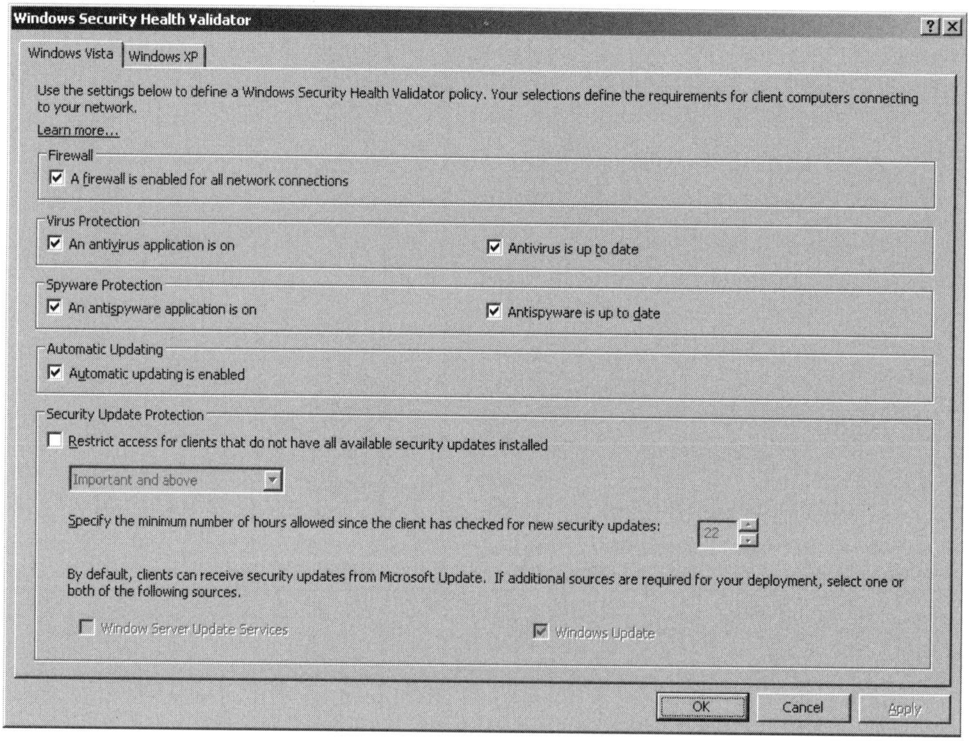

Figure 15-3   The Windows Security Health Validator dialog box

In this dialog box, you can select the health requirements for NAP clients for built-in Windows services that are monitored by the Windows Security Center in Windows Vista (on the Windows Vista tab) and Windows XP SP3 (on the Windows XP tab).

Remediation Server Groups A remediation server group is a list of servers that noncompliant NAP clients or non-NAP-capable clients can access for the VPN and DHCP enforcement methods. You might have separate groups for noncompliant NAP clients or non-NAP-capable clients or separate groups for different NAP enforcement methods.

To create a new remediation server group, in the Network Policy Server console tree, expand Network Access Protection, right-click Remediation Server Groups, and then click New. In the New Remediation Server Group dialog box, you can specify remediation servers by Domain Name System (DNS) name, IPv4 address, or IPv6 address. Figure 15-4 shows an example.

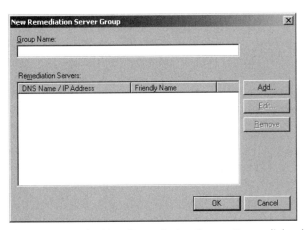

Figure 15-4 The New Remediation Server Group dialog box

Network Policies

Network policies are an ordered set of rules that specify the circumstances under which connection attempts are either authorized or rejected. For each rule, there is an access permission that either grants or denies access, a set of conditions, a set of constraints, and network policy settings. If a connection is authorized, the network policy constraints and settings can specify a set of connection restrictions. For NAP, network policies specify the conditions to check for health requirements and, for noncompliant NAP clients or non-NAP-capable clients, the enforcement behavior.

Access Permission Setting for NAP Regardless of whether NAP health validation is being done for connection attempts that are also authenticated and authorized, you select Grant Access for the access permission so that connection requests are processed for health validation. The connection attempt is authorized, but the network access of noncompliant NAP clients or non-NAP-capable clients can be limited. If you select Deny Access, connection requests are rejected, and no health validation is performed. You can create network policies to explicitly deny access; however, these network policies do not need NAP settings because it is not necessary to validate the system health of a computer that is not allowed access.

Network Policy Conditions for NAP For NAP support, the following conditions have been added to NPS network policies:

- **Health Policy** Specifies a previously configured health policy. If the evaluation of the health settings of a connection attempt matches the health policy, the connection attempt matches this condition of the network policy.

- **NAP-Capable** Specifies whether the client is NAP-capable or not.

- **Policy Expiration** Specifies when the network policy expires and is no longer evaluated. You can use this to transition from a reporting mode to an enforcement mode of NAP operation.

The following are examples of using the Health Policy and NAP-Capable conditions for NAP-based network policies:

- For a network policy that applies only to compliant NAP-capable clients that pass all the health requirements of the installed SHVs, set the Health Policy condition to the Compliant (example name) health policy, which specifies the Client Passes All SHV Checks option.

- For a network policy that applies only to noncompliant NAP-capable clients that fail any of the health requirements of the installed SHVs, set the Health Policy condition to the Noncompliant (example name) health policy, which specifies the Client Fails One Or More SHV Checks option.

- For a network policy that applies only to non-NAP-capable clients, set the NAP-Capable condition to Only Computers That Are Not NAP-Capable.

Network Policy Settings for NAP Network policies in Windows Server 2008 have a set of network policy settings for NAP Enforcement. Figure 15-5 shows an example.

For NAP Enforcement settings, you can specify the following:

- **Allow Full Network Access** Specifies that the connection attempt has unlimited network access. Select this option for network policies defined for compliant NAP clients.

- **Allow Full Network Access For A Limited Time** Specifies that the connection attempt has unlimited network access, but users on noncompliant NAP client computers receive a notification message that they must become compliant by the configured date and time. This is also known as *deferred enforcement mode*.

- **Allow Limited Access** Specifies that the connection attempt has limited network access. Users on noncompliant NAP client computers receive a "This computer is not compliant with the requirements of this network" notification message. Select this option for network policies defined for noncompliant NAP clients or for non-NAP-capable clients. This is also known as *enforcement mode*.

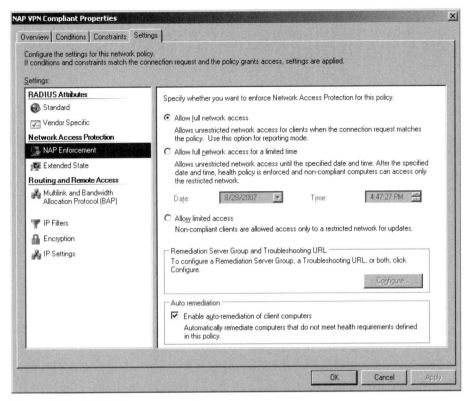

Figure 15-5 NAP Enforcement settings

■ **Enable Auto-Remediation Of Client Computers** Specifies whether the NAP clients must automatically remediate their noncompliant health state.

For limited access, click Configure to specify the remediation server group and troubleshooting URL. Figure 15-6 shows an example of the Remediation Servers And Troubleshooting URL dialog box.

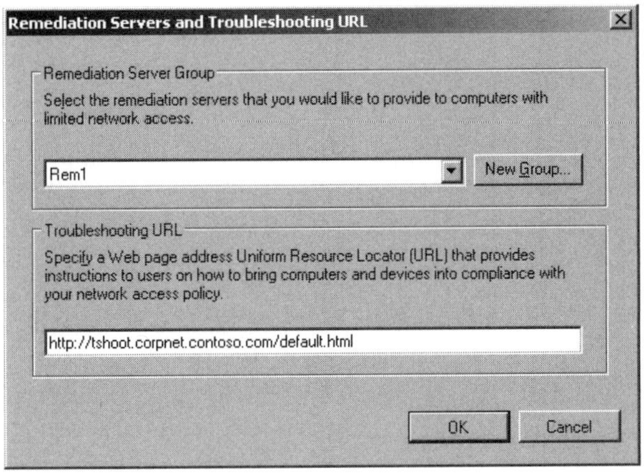

Figure 15-6 Remediation Servers And Troubleshooting URL dialog box

In the Remediation Server Group list, select a previously configured remediation server group, or click New Group to create a new remediation server group.

In the Troubleshooting URL box, type the URL to a Web page of a remediation server for noncompliant NAP clients. This URL is activated when a user clicks More Information in the Network Access Protection dialog box that appears on noncompliant NAP clients. On the Web page, the user can determine how to update the computer so that it is compliant or perform troubleshooting of network access. This URL is also visible in the display of the **netsh nap client show state** command.

The Configure NAP Wizard

You can greatly simplify the initial configuration of NAP health requirement policies by using the Configure NAP Wizard. To run the Configure NAP Wizard, do the following:

1. In the Network Policy Server snap-in, in the console tree, click the NPS (local) or NPS (*RemoteComputerName*) node.

2. In the details pane, click Configure NAP.

The Configure NAP Wizard guides you through the creation of NAP health requirement policies, and it gives you the following choices:

1. On the Select Network Connection Method For Use With NAP page, you can select the network connection method (the NAP enforcement method). The wizard automatically creates a name for the NAP health requirement policy, which you can modify.

2. On the next page (whose title depends on the previously selected network connection method), you can add, edit, or remove RADIUS clients corresponding to your NAP enforcement points. Note that you are not selecting the RADIUS clients to which the health requirement policy applies. The Configure NAP Wizard is just allowing you to add RADIUS clients rather than manually adding them in the RADIUS Clients node of the console tree.

3. Depending on the network method you chose, you might be presented with additional page options, such as DHCP scope or Terminal Service gateway options. Configure these options appropriately.

4. On the Configure Groups page, you can configure computer or user groups to further specify that the network policies created by the wizard apply only to computer accounts that are members of the specified computer groups or only to user accounts that are members of the specified user groups.

5. On subsequent pages, you can configure NAP enforcement method–specific settings. For example, for the 802.1X or VPN enforcement methods, you use the Configure An Authentication Method page to specify the NAP health policy server certificate and the EAP types to use for user or computer-level authentication. For the 802.1X enforcement method, you use the Configure Virtual LANs (VLANs) page to configure the RADIUS

attributes that your wireless APs or authenticating switches use to identify the unlimited access VLAN and the restricted network VLAN.

6.   On the Define NAP Health Policy page, you can configure the SHVs that you want to enforce, auto-remediation behavior, and the behavior for non-NAP-capable computers (restrict their access or allow them unlimited access).

The results of the Configure NAP Wizard are as follows:

■   A connection request policy with the name as specified on the Select Network Connection Method For Use With NAP page.

■   Health policies based on the name specified on the Select Network Connection Method For Use With NAP page and your selections in the wizard. For example, the wizard creates both compliant and noncompliant health policies based on your selections on the Define NAP Health Policy page.

■   Network policies based on the name specified on the Select Network Connection Method For Use With NAP page and your selections in the wizard. For example, the wizard creates up to three network policies: a network policy for compliant NAP clients, a network policy for noncompliant NAP clients, and a network policy for non-NAP-capable clients. These policies can be modified for custom settings or removed as needed.

The new connection request policy and network policies are added to the end of their respective ordered lists, and you can modify the evaluation order as needed.

How NAP Health Evaluation Works

The NPS service on the NAP health policy server uses the following process to perform health evaluation:

1.   When the NPS service on the NAP health policy server receives the RADIUS Access-Request message from a NAP enforcement point, it first determines whether the message originated from an address that corresponds to a configured RADIUS client. If not, the NPS service discards the message. This behavior prevents the NAP health policy server from processing RADIUS messages from RADIUS clients (such as access devices and NAP enforcement points) for which the NPS service has not been configured.

2.   The NPS service then compares the Access-Request message to its configured set of connection request policies. For NAP, the Access-Request message should match a connection request policy that specifies that the NPS service perform the authentication and authorization locally.

3.   The NPS service evaluates the health information in the Access-Request message, which consists of a system statement of health (SSoH) containing one or more statements of health (SoHs). The NPS service passes each SoH to the appropriate SHV for evaluation. The result of the evaluation is a set of statement of health responses (SoHRs) from the SHVs.

4. The NPS service evaluates the Access-Request message and the SoHRs against the network policies. The SoHRs are compared to the Health Policy condition of NAP-based network policies. Recall that the Health Policy condition specifies whether the SHVs must either pass or fail. The NPS service applies the best matching network policy to the Access-Request message. The best matching network policy is either the first matching network policy with a specific source (for Access-Request messages that specify a source tag indicating the type of RADIUS client) or the first matching network policy with an unspecified source (for Access-Request messages that do not specify a source tag).

5. Based on the best matching policy and the Network Access Protection settings of the network policy, the NPS service creates a system statement of health response (SSoHR), which includes the SoHRs from the SHVs and indicates one of the following:

   ❑ The NAP client has unlimited access.

   ❑ The NAP client has limited access. In this case, the SSoHR also indicates whether the client should automatically attempt to remediate its noncompliant health state.

6. The NPS service sends a RADIUS Access-Accept message with the SSoHR to the NAP enforcement point that sent the Access-Request message. If the client has limited access, the Access-Accept message can also contain RADIUS attributes that specify how the NAP client's access is limited.

7. The NAP enforcement point sends the SSoHR to the NAP client.

How It Works: Examples of Health Evaluation Processing for NAP

The following sections describe how the NPS service processes incoming Access-Request messages for access attempts from three different types of clients (a compliant NAP client, a noncompliant NAP client, and a non-NAP-capable client) based on the following configuration:

- **Connection request policies** NPS uses the default Use Windows Authentication For All Users connection request policy, which causes the NPS service to process all RADIUS messages locally rather than forwarding them to another RADIUS server.

- **Health policies** A health policy named MSSHV_Compliant specifies the use of the Windows Security Health Validator SHV and the Client Passes All SHV Checks option.

  A health policy named MSSHV_Noncompliant specifies the use of the Windows Security Health Validator SHV and the Client Fails One Or More SHV Checks option.

- **Network Access Protection settings** The Windows Security Health Validator is configured to require that automatic updating be enabled only on NAP clients.

A remediation server group named REM1 contains a list of the IPv4 addresses for the remediation servers.

■ **Network policies**   A network policy named Compliant_NAP_clients is configured for the following:

❑ Conditions: Health Policy is set to the MSSHV_Compliant policy.

❑ Settings: For NAP Enforcement, the Allow Full Network Access option is selected.

A network policy named Noncompliant_NAP_clients is configured for the following:

❑ Conditions: Health Policy is set to the MSSHV_Noncompliant policy.

❑ Settings: For NAP Enforcement, the Allow Limited Access option is selected, the REM1 remediation server group is selected for the remediation server group, and auto-remediation of client computers is enabled.

A network policy named Downlevel_clients is configured for the following:

❑ Conditions: NAP-Capable is set to Only Computers That Are Not NAP-Capable.

❑ Settings: For NAP Enforcement, the Allow Limited Access option is selected, and for the remediation server group, the REM1 remediation server group is selected.

Example NPS Processing for a Compliant NAP Client

When a compliant NAP client (in our example, a client that has automatic updating enabled) attempts to obtain an IPv4 address configuration from a NAP-enabled DHCP server, the following process occurs:

1. The NAP client sends the DHCP server its SSoH in a DHCP request message, which contains the SoH from the Windows Security Health Agent indicating that automatic updating is enabled.

2. The DHCP server sends the NPS server an Access-Request message containing the SSoH.

3. The NPS server evaluates the Access-Request message against the connection request policies and matches the Use Windows Authentication For All Users connection request policy.

4. The NPS server evaluates system health by passing the SoH to the Windows Security Health Validator, which returns an SoHR indicating that the SoH meets system health requirements.

5. The NPS server evaluates the Access-Request message and the SoHR against the network policies.

6. The Access-Request message and the SoHR match the Compliant_NAP_clients network policy because the Health Policy condition, set to the MSSHV_Compliant

policy, requires that the request pass all the selected SHVs (the Windows Security Health Validator).

7. Based on the Network Access Protection settings of the Compliant_NAP_clients network policy (set to Allow Full Network Access), NPS creates an SSoHR indicating unlimited access and containing the SoHR from the Windows Security Health Validator.

8. NPS sends an Access-Accept message to the DHCP server containing the SSoHR.

9. The DHCP server assigns an unlimited access IP address configuration to the NAP client. During the DHCP message exchange, the DHCP server also passes the SSoHR to the NAP client.

Example NPS Processing for a Noncompliant NAP Client

When a noncompliant NAP client (in our example, one that has automatic updating disabled) attempts to obtain an IPv4 address configuration from a NAP-enabled DHCP server, the following process occurs:

1. The NAP client sends the DHCP server its SSoH in a DHCP request message, which contains the SoH from the default Windows Security Health Agent that indicates that automatic updating is disabled.

2. The DHCP server sends the NPS server an Access-Request message containing the SSoH.

3. The NPS server evaluates the Access-Request message against the connection request policies and matches the Use Windows Authentication For All Users connection request policy.

4. The NPS server evaluates system health by passing the SoH to the Windows Security Health Validator, which returns an SoHR indicating that the system health requirements evaluation failed.

5. The NPS server evaluates the Access-Request message and the SoHR against the network policies.

6. The Access-Request message and the SoHR match the Noncompliant_NAP_clients network policy because the Health Policy condition, set to the MSSHV_Noncompliant policy, requires that the request fail any of the selected SHVs (the Windows Security Health Validator).

7. Based on the Network Access Protection settings of the Noncompliant_NAP_clients network policy (set to Allow Limited Access with the REM1 remediation servers group), NPS creates an SSoHR indicating limited access and containing the SoHR from the Windows Security Health Validator.

8. NPS sends an Access-Accept message to the DHCP server containing the SSoHR and the list of addresses in the REM1 remediation server group.

9. Because the SSoHR indicates limited access, the DHCP server assigns a limited IP address configuration to the NAP client, restricting the network access of the NAP client to the list of addresses in the REM1 remediation server group. During the DHCP message exchange, the DHCP server also passes the SSoHR to the NAP client.

Example of NPS Processing for a Non-NAP-Capable Client

When a non-NAP-capable client attempts to obtain an IPv4 address configuration from a NAP-enabled DHCP server, the following process occurs:

1. The non-NAP-capable client requests an IPv4 address from the DHCP server, but the DHCP request message does not contain an SSoH.

2. The DHCP server sends the NPS server an Access-Request message.

3. The NPS server evaluates the Access-Request message against the connection request policies and matches the Use Windows Authentication For All Users connection request policy.

4. The NPS server evaluates the Access-Request message against the network policies.

5. The Access-Request message matches the Downlevel_clients network policy because the Access-Request message is for a non-NAP-capable client.

6. Based on the Network Access Protection settings of the Downlevel_clients network policy (set to Allow Limited Access with the REM1 remediation servers group), NPS creates an SSoHR indicating limited access.

7. NPS sends an Access-Accept message to the DHCP server containing the SSoHR and the list of IP addresses in the REM1 remediation server group.

8. Because the SSoHR indicates limited access, the DHCP server assigns a limited IP address configuration to the non-NAP-capable client.

Planning and Design Considerations for Health Requirement Policies

You must determine the set of health requirement policies that you need for the following:

■   **Different NAP enforcement methods**   You can have different sets of health requirement policies for the different NAP enforcement methods, as configured by the Configure NAP Wizard, or a single health requirement policy for all of the NAP enforcement methods that you are using on your intranet (manually configured).

■   **Reporting mode and enforcement mode**   In reporting mode, the NAP health policy server logs the NAP evaluation but always allows unlimited access, even for non-compliant NAP clients and non-NAP-capable clients. Reporting mode is done in the initial stages of NAP deployment to determine how many NAP clients on your intranet are compliant or noncompliant. In enforcement mode, noncompliant NAP clients or non-NAP-capable clients can have limited network access.

- **Compliant NAP clients**   A health requirement policy for a compliant NAP client typically allows unlimited access to the intranet.

- **Noncompliant NAP clients**   A health requirement policy for a noncompliant NAP client can allow limited network access in enforcement mode.

- **Non-NAP-capable clients**   A health requirement policy for a non-NAP-capable client can allow unlimited access or be exempted from NAP health evaluation. A health requirement policy for a non-NAP-capable client can also specify limited network access in enforcement mode.

- **Remediation server group**   For enforcement mode, the remediation server group you want for noncompliant NAP clients for the VPN and DHCP enforcement methods.

- **Auto-remediation behavior**   For enforcement mode, whether you want NAP clients to automatically remediate a noncompliant health state. With auto-remediation, a NAP client can attempt to correct its health state without intervention from the user.

- **Settings for the Windows Security Health Validator SHV**   For a NAP client running Windows Vista, you can specify the following:

  - Whether a host-based firewall is enabled for all network connections. Windows Vista includes the Windows Firewall, which by default is enabled on all network connections.

  - Whether an antivirus program is on and whether it is up to date. Windows Vista does not include an antivirus program.

  - Whether an antispyware program is on and whether it is up to date. Windows Vista includes the Windows Defender antispyware program, which is enabled by default.

  - Whether Automatic Updates is enabled. Windows Vista can be configured to enable Automatic Updates.

  - Whether to limit the access of computers that do not have all of the available security updates installed.

For a NAP client running Windows XP SP3, you can specify the following:

  - Whether a host-based firewall is enabled for all network connections. Windows XP SP3 includes the Windows Firewall, which by default is enabled on all network connections.

  - Whether an antivirus program is on and whether it is up to date. Windows XP SP3 does not include an antivirus program.

  - Whether Automatic Updates is enabled. Windows XP SP3 can be configured to enable automatic updates.

  - Whether to limit the access of computers that do not have all the available security updates installed.

Remediation Servers

Remediation servers are the subset of your intranet that noncompliant NAP clients can access when you configure your health requirement policies to enforce limited access. The remediation servers include network infrastructure servers and health update servers. The noncompliant NAP client uses these servers or the resources on these servers to perform remediation, either automatically or manually. It is also possible to configure your health requirement policies to enforce limited access for non-NAP-capable clients.

Remediation servers are not required if you are using reporting mode. In reporting mode you are not limiting the access of noncompliant NAP clients. However, to realize the benefit of NAP to restrict the access of computers that potentially present a risk to the intranet due to noncompliance with health requirements, you must eventually transition to enforcement mode, which requires you to set up remediation servers.

The exact list of remediation servers that a noncompliant NAP client can access for VPN and DHCP enforcement corresponds to the remediation server group specified in the NAP Enforcement setting for the network policy that matched the NAP client's health evaluation. A remediation server group is a list of IPv4 and IPv6 addresses. This list should include network infrastructure servers and health update servers that are needed to remediate noncompliant NAP clients for VPN and DHCP enforcement.

Infrastructure servers include the following:

- DHCP servers to allocate an IPv4 address and other configuration parameters to the noncompliant NAP client so that it can access remediation servers. If you are using the DHCP enforcement method, you do not need to add the NAP-enabled DHCP servers as remediation servers.

- DNS and WINS servers to provide name resolution to noncompliant NAP clients so that they can resolve names and access other remediation servers.

- Active Directory domain controllers so that noncompliant NAP clients can perform domain logons and access domain-based resources such as file shares.

- Internet proxy servers so that noncompliant NAP clients can access the Internet.

- HRAs so that noncompliant NAP clients can obtain a health certificate for the IPsec enforcement method.

Health update servers that might be needed to remediate NAP client system health can include the following:

- **Troubleshooting URL server**   The Web server that hosts the Web page specified in the Troubleshooting URL field of the Remediation Servers And Troubleshooting URL dialog box.

- **Antivirus update servers**   These servers might be located on the Internet. If this is the case and you have Internet proxy servers as remediation servers, you do not need to include the Internet-based antivirus update servers. If you have antivirus update servers deployed on your intranet, you should include them as remediation servers because they will typically be checked first for updates before attempting to access the Internet-based antivirus servers.

- **Antispyware update servers**   Just as with antivirus servers, if you have deployed anti-spyware update servers on your intranet, include them as remediation servers. If they exist only on the Internet, ensure that Internet proxy servers are included in your remediation server groups.

- **Software update servers**   Just as with antivirus servers, if you have deployed software update servers on your intranet, include them as remediation servers. If they exist only on the Internet, ensure that Internet proxy servers are included as remediation servers.

The exact set of health update servers that are needed to remediate NAP clients depends on the SHVs that you are using for health evaluation.

Remediation Servers and NAP Enforcement Methods

The following sections describe how to specify remediation servers for the 802.1X, VPN, and DHCP enforcement methods. The IPsec enforcement method does not use a list of IP addresses to define a set of remediation servers.

802.1X Enforcement

802.1X enforcement uses an access control list (ACL) or a virtual local area network (VLAN) to restrict the access of a noncompliant NAP client. An ACL is a set of IPv4 or IPv6 packet filters configured on the 802.1X access point that is typically identified with a name. The 802.1X access point applies the named ACL to the connection and silently discards all packets that are not allowed by the ACL. A VLAN is a grouping of switch ports to create a separate network. Each VLAN is identified with a VLAN identifier (ID). With VLANs, the 802.1X access point applies the VLAN ID for the restricted network to the connection and traffic from the noncompliant NAP clients is forwarded only to that network. In both cases, traffic from noncompliant NAP clients does not leave the restricted network.

VPN Enforcement

For VPN enforcement, the addresses specified in the remediation server group become a set of IP packet filters that are applied to the VPN connection by the NAP-capable VPN server. The non-compliant NAP client can reach only the servers in the remediation server group regardless of the subnet to which the noncompliant NAP client is logically attached. Packets sent by the non-compliant NAP client to the addresses specified in the remediation server group are forwarded by the VPN server. Packets sent to addresses that are not specified in the remediation server group can be sent by the noncompliant NAP client but are silently discarded by the VPN server.

DHCP Enforcement

For DHCP enforcement, the noncompliant NAP client is assigned an IPv4 address by a DHCP server servicing the subnet to which the NAP client is attached. The addresses specified in the remediation server group and the IPv4 address of the DHCP server become a set of host routes that are added to the noncompliant NAP client's IPv4 routing table. The noncompliant NAP client can reach only the servers in the remediation server group and the DHCP server regardless of the subnet to which the noncompliant NAP client is attached. Packets sent to the DHCP server and the addresses specified in the remediation server group can be sent by the noncompliant NAP client. Packets to other destinations cannot be sent by the noncompliant NAP client.

Planning and Design Considerations for Remediation Servers

In the simplest configuration, you can use all your infrastructure servers and all of your health update servers for all of your enforcement methods. The advantage of this method is simplicity of initial configuration and ongoing maintenance. The disadvantage is that noncompliant NAP clients, which have potentially unsafe configurations, can reach all of your infrastructure servers. However, this security concern can be mitigated by using security technologies such as Windows Firewall on your infrastructure servers to prevent attacks from noncompliant NAP clients. Windows Firewall is enabled by default for servers running Windows Server 2008.

If you want to confine the set of infrastructure servers to the minimum subset needed for noncompliant NAP clients, consider that the current set of network infrastructure servers on your intranet are designed for unlimited access and reflect the load distribution and balancing scheme that is implemented across your intranet. Any computer on the intranet can resolve names and access resources such as domain controllers by using normal DNS and Active Directory processes. Because the infrastructure servers are dependent on each other, to configure a subset of the existing infrastructure servers to operate in a more confined way might require the deployment of separate infrastructure servers that are used only for noncompliant NAP clients.

For example, for the DHCP enforcement method, you can confine the set of DNS servers that are assigned to noncompliant NAP clients through DHCP to a specified list. The noncompliant NAP clients use the DNS servers to locate an Active Directory domain controller. If you want to confine the set of domain controllers that are accessible by a noncompliant NAP client to a specific subset, you must configure the DNS servers that are used by the noncompliant NAP clients to resolve the names associated with Active Directory domain controllers only to the specific domain controllers. This means that these DNS servers cannot be used by compliant NAP clients because they do not reflect the load distribution and balancing scheme that is implemented across the intranet. These DNS servers must be used only by the noncompliant NAP clients and must be managed separately from the DNS servers used by compliant NAP clients. In this example configuration, the domain controllers used by the noncompliant NAP clients might not be situated for optimal performance. For example, the domain controllers might be available only across slow WAN links from the noncompliant NAP client.

Therefore, the tradeoff is between having a higher degree of protection for your infrastructure servers from noncompliant NAP clients (when using a subset of infrastructure servers as remediation servers) and ease of administration and performance across an intranet (when using all of your infrastructure servers as your remediation servers).

The details of how to specify your remediation servers, whether you want to use all of your infrastructure servers or a subset of infrastructure servers, depend on the NAP enforcement method. For more information, see the following chapters:

- Chapter 16, "IPsec Enforcement"
- Chapter 17, "802.1X Enforcement"
- Chapter 18, "VPN Enforcement"
- Chapter 19, "DHCP Enforcement"

Chapter Summary

Preparing your network for NAP consists of evaluating your current network infrastructure, designing NAP health policy servers, determining your health requirement policy configuration, and planning for remediation servers. When evaluating your current network infrastructure, you need to examine the types of computers on your intranet, their method of attachment to the network, whether they are managed or unmanaged, and the networking support infrastructure. When planning your health requirement policy configuration, consider the relationship between connection request policies, health policies, network policies, and the behavior of the NPS service when evaluating the health state of a NAP client. When planning for remediation servers, consider whether you want to use all of your network infrastructure servers or a subset of them.

Additional Information

For additional information about NAP, see the following:

- Chapter 14, "Network Access Protection Overview"
- Chapter 16, "IPsec Enforcement"
- Chapter 17, "802.1X Enforcement"
- Chapter 18, "VPN Enforcement"

- Chapter 19, "DHCP Enforcement"

- Windows Server 2008 Technical Library at *http://technet.microsoft.com/windowsserver/ 2008*

- Windows Server 2008 Help and Support

- "Network Access Protection" (*http://www.microsoft.com/nap*)

For additional information about RADIUS and NPS, see the following:

- Chapter 9, "Authentication Infrastructure"

- Windows Server 2008 Technical Library at *http://technet.microsoft.com/windowsserver/ 2008*

- Windows Server 2008 Help and Support

- "Network Policy Server" (*http://www.microsoft.com/nps*)

For additional information about IPsec, see the following:

- Chapter 4, "Windows Firewall with Advanced Security"

- Windows Server 2008 Technical Library at *http://technet.microsoft.com/windowsserver/ 2008*

- Windows Server 2008 Help and Support

- "IPsec" (*http://www.microsoft.com/IPsec*)

For additional information about IEEE 802.1X for wireless and wired networks, see the following:

- Chapter 10, "IEEE 802.11 Wireless Networks"

- Chapter 11, "IEEE 802.1X–Authenticated Wired Networks"

- Windows Server 2008 Technical Library at *http://technet.microsoft.com/windowsserver/ 2008*

- Windows Server 2008 Help and Support

- "Wireless Networking" (*http://www.microsoft.com/wifi*)

- "Wired Networking with 802.1X Authentication" (*http://www.microsoft.com/technet/ network/wired/default.mspx*)

For additional information about remote access VPN connections, see the following:

- Chapter 12, "Remote Access VPN Connections"

- Windows Server 2008 Technical Library at *http://technet.microsoft.com/windowsserver/ 2008*

- Windows Server 2008 Help and Support
- "Virtual Private Networks" (*http://www.microsoft.com/vpn*)

For additional information about DHCP, see the following:

- Chapter 3, "Dynamic Host Configuration Protocol"
- Windows Server 2008 Technical Library at *http://technet.microsoft.com/windowsserver/2008*
- Windows Server 2008 Help and Support
- "Dynamic Host Configuration Protocol" (*http://www.microsoft.com/dhcp*)

Chapter 16

IPsec Enforcement

This chapter provides information about how to design, deploy, maintain, and troubleshoot the Network Access Protection (NAP) Internet Protocol security (IPsec) enforcement method. This chapter assumes the following:

■ That you understand the role of Active Directory, public key infrastructure (PKI), Group Policy, and Remote Authentication Dial-In User Service (RADIUS) elements of a Windows-based authentication infrastructure for network access. For more information, see Chapter 9, "Authentication Infrastructure."

■ That you understand the role and deployment methods for IPsec. For more information, see Chapter 4, "Windows Firewall with Advanced Security."

■ That you understand the components of NAP and how to prepare your network for NAP. For more information, see Chapter 14, "Network Access Protection Overview," and Chapter 15, "Preparing for Network Access Protection."

Understanding IPsec Enforcement

IPsec enforcement in NAP consists of adding a Health Registration Authority (HRA) and an IPsec Relying Party enforcement client on NAP clients to an IPsec deployment. The HRA is a computer running the Windows Server 2008 operating system and Internet Information Services (IIS). The HRA obtains X.509-based health certificates from a Windows-based certification authority (CA) on behalf of NAP clients when the NAP health policy server has determined that the clients are compliant. NAP clients use health certificates for IPsec authentication when they initiate IPsec-protected communications with other compliant NAP clients on a network. If a NAP client does not have a health certificate, the IPsec peer authentication fails and the NAP client cannot communicate with a compliant IPsec peer. Health certificates are issued by a NAP CA, which is a Windows-based CA for IPsec enforcement.

IPsec enforcement confines the communication on your network and protects network traffic from end-to-end rather than just across a specific physical or logical link. By utilizing IPsec and its configuration flexibility, IPsec enforcement allows to you to set requirements for secure communications with compliant clients on a per-IP address or per–Transmission Control Protocol (TCP) or per–User Datagram Protocol (UDP) port number basis. For example, you could specify IPsec policy settings to secure all Remote Procedure Call (RPC) traffic, subject to IPsec enforcement. IPsec enforcement is one of the strongest and most flexible forms of limited network access in NAP.

The benefits of IPsec enforcement are the following:

- **Tamper-resistant enforcement**   Unlike NAP enforcement methods that rely on the NAP client to restrict network connectivity, IPsec enforcement cannot be bypassed by reconfiguring a NAP client. A NAP client cannot receive a health certificate or initiate communication with a compliant computer that doesn't have a health certificate by manipulating settings on their local computer. Additionally, IPsec enforcement cannot be bypassed through the use of hubs or virtual computer technologies.

- **No infrastructure upgrade needed**   IPsec enforcement works at the Internet layer of the TCP/IP protocol suite and therefore is typically independent of network infrastructure components such as hubs, switches, and routers.

- **Flexible limitations on network access**   With IPsec enforcement, compliant computers can initiate communications with noncompliant computers, but noncompliant computers cannot initiate communications with compliant computers. The administrator specifies the type of traffic that must be authenticated with a health certificate and protected with IPsec through IPsec policy settings. IPsec policy allows for the creation of IP filters that can classify traffic by source IP address, destination IP address, IP protocol number, source and destination TCP port, and source and destination UDP port. By using IPsec policy and IP filter classification, it is possible to limit network access on a per-server or per-application basis.

- **Optional end-to-end encryption**   By specifying IPsec policy settings, you can encrypt IP traffic between IPsec peers for highly sensitive traffic. Unlike IEEE 802.11 wireless LANs, which encrypt frames only from the wireless client to the wireless access point, IPsec encryption is between IPsec peer computers.

IPsec Enforcement Logical Networks

IPsec enforcement typically divides a physical network into three logical networks. A computer is a member of only one logical network at any time. The logical networks are defined in terms of which computers have health certificates and which computers require IPsec authentication with health certificates for incoming communication attempts. The logical networks allow for access limitation and remediation and provide compliant computers with a level of protection from noncompliant computers.

IPsec enforcement defines the following logical networks:

- **Secure network**   The set of computers that have health certificates, require that incoming communication attempts authenticate with health certificates, and share common IPsec policy settings for providing IPsec protection. For example, most server and client computers that are members of an Active Directory infrastructure would be in a secure network. For NAP, NAP health policy servers and health requirement servers are in a secure network. Because a secure network is defined by a common set of IPsec policy settings, there might be multiple secure networks on your network. For example, there might be one secure network that uses Encapsulating Security Payload (ESP) with no encryption for normal traffic between domain members and another secure network that uses ESP with encryption for traffic between domain member clients and specific servers that store confidential data. This chapter assumes a single secure network.

■ **Boundary network** The set of computers that have health certificates but do not require that incoming communication attempts authenticate with health certificates and use IPsec protection. Computers in the boundary network must be accessible to computers on the entire network. These types of computers are the servers needed to assess and remediate NAP client health or otherwise provide network services for computers in the restricted network, such as the HRA and remediation servers. Because computers in the boundary network do not require authentication and protected communication, their health must be closely managed to prevent them from being used to attack computers in the secure network.

■ **Restricted network** The set of computers that do not have health certificates. These are NAP client computers that have not completed health checks or are noncompliant but still require that all incoming communication attempts authenticate with health certificates, are guests, or are non-NAP-capable computers such as computers running versions of Microsoft Windows or other operating systems that do not support NAP.

> **Note** Computers that do not support NAP can be in the secure or boundary networks by obtaining a NAP exemption certificate. NAP exemption certificates can be used in the same way as health certificates for IPsec authentication. Unlike a health certificate, whose validity time is typically on the order of hours, the NAP exemption certificate is typically a long-lived certificate.

Figure 16-1 shows the IPsec enforcement logical networks.

Communication Initiation Processes with IPsec Enforcement

Based on the definition of the three logical networks, the following are the types of initiated communications and their resulting behavior for IPsec enforcement:

■ **Within the secure network** Compliant computers within the secure network have health certificates. When a compliant computer in the secure network initiates communication with another compliant computer in the secure network, it attempts IPsec authentication using its health certificate. Both IPsec peers validate each other's health certificates. IPsec authentication is successful, and subsequent data traffic is protected with IPsec. The result is authenticated peers and protected traffic.

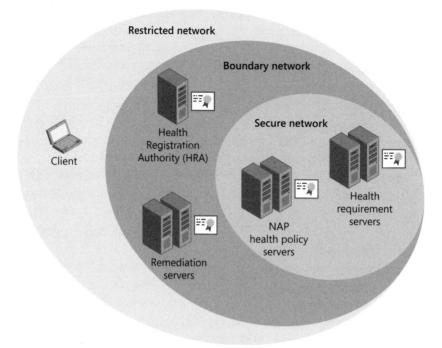

Figure 16-1 IPsec enforcement logical networks

- **Secure network to boundary network** When a compliant computer in the secure network initiates communication with a computer in the boundary network, such as a remediation server, it attempts IPsec authentication using its health certificate. Because computers in the boundary network also have health certificates, both IPsec peers validate each other's health certificates. IPsec authentication is successful, and subsequent data traffic is protected with IPsec. The result is that when a computer in the secure network initiates communication with a computer in the boundary network, peers are authenticated and traffic is protected.

- **Secure network to restricted network** When a compliant computer in the secure network initiates communication with a computer in the restricted network, it attempts IPsec authentication using its health certificate. For a noncompliant NAP client computer that is in the restricted network and requires that all incoming communication attempts authenticate with health certificates, IPsec authentication and communication fail because the NAP client computer cannot submit a health certificate during IPsec negotiation. The result is that when a computer in the secure network initiates communication with a noncompliant NAP client in the restricted network, communication fails. This is the behavior for Windows Vista with no service packs installed. With Windows Vista Service Pack 1, the compliant client in the secure network will be able to communicate with the noncompliant NAP client in the restricted network if both clients have an autoenrolled computer certificate. For a typical non-NAP-capable computer in the restricted network, attempts by a compliant computer in the secure network to negotiate

IPsec protection fails. The computer in the secure network then initiates communication without IPsec protection. The result is that when a computer in the secure network initiates communication with a typical non-NAP-capable computer in the restricted network, peers are unauthenticated and traffic is unprotected.

■ **Within the boundary network** When a computer in the boundary network initiates communication with another computer in the boundary network, such as a remediation server, it attempts IPsec authentication using its health certificate. Because computers in the boundary network have health certificates, both IPsec peers validate each other's health certificates. IPsec authentication is successful, and subsequent data traffic is protected with IPsec. The result is authenticated peers and protected traffic.

■ **Boundary network to secure network** When a computer in the boundary network initiates communication with a computer in the secure network, it attempts IPsec authentication using its health certificate. Because computers in the boundary network have health certificates, both IPsec peers validate each other's health certificates. IPsec authentication is successful, and subsequent IPsec-protected data traffic can begin. The result is that when a computer in the boundary network initiates communication with another computer in the secure network, peers are authenticated and traffic is protected.

■ **Boundary network to restricted network** When a computer in the boundary network initiates communication with a computer in the restricted network, it attempts IPsec authentication using its health certificate. The results are the same as with the communication initiated from computers on the secure network to computers on the restricted network.

■ **Within the restricted network** Computers in the restricted network are typically either not NAP clients or are noncompliant NAP clients that require that all incoming communication attempts authenticate with health certificates. Communications between computers that are not NAP clients are typically not protected with IPsec unless the computers have their own IPsec policy. A NAP client that does not have a health certificate can initiate communications with computers that are not NAP clients. The result is unauthenticated peers and unprotected traffic. However, IPsec authentication and communications between two noncompliant NAP clients will fail because neither of them has health certificates.

■ **Restricted network to boundary network** When a computer in the restricted network initiates unprotected communication with a computer in the boundary network, the boundary network computer allows the unprotected communication and responds with unprotected traffic because the boundary network computer does not require IPsec protection for incoming communication requests. The result is that when a computer in the restricted network initiates communication with a computer in the boundary network, peers are unauthenticated and traffic is unprotected.

■ **Restricted network to secure network** When a computer in the restricted network initiates unprotected communication with a computer in the secure network, the secure network computer drops the unprotected communication packets because it requires IPsec protection for all incoming packets. Because there is no response to the communication requests of the restricted network computer, eventually the communication attempt fails.

Figure 16-2 shows the initiated communication behavior for computers in the secure, boundary, and restricted networks.

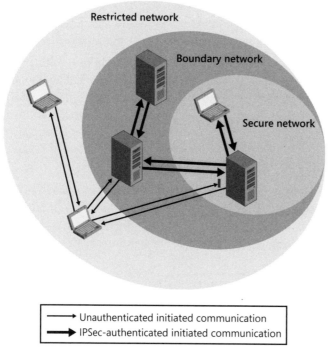

Figure 16-2 Initiated communication between computers in the IPsec enforcement logical networks

The following is a summary of IPsec enforcement:

■ Peers use IPsec protection and peer authentication with health certificates whenever they are located in the secure or boundary networks.

■ IPsec authentication and protection is typically not used when a computer initiates communication with a non-NAP-capable computer in the restricted network and when a computer in the restricted network initiates communication with a computer in the boundary network.

■ Computers in the restricted network cannot initiate communication with computers in the secure network.

Connection Security Rules for IPsec Enforcement

For the IPsec policy settings for IPsec enforcement for computers running Windows Vista or Windows Server 2008, you will configure connection security rules for domain isolation by using the Windows Firewall with Advanced Security snap-in. This new configuration tool provides simplified configuration of IPsec policy settings through the use of the New Connection Security Rule Wizard. For many IPsec enforcement deployments, you will need to configure the following connection security rules:

- A rule for the isolation rule type that requests (but does not require) authentication for both inbound communication and outbound communication. This rule is for the boundary network.

- A rule for the isolation rule type that requires authentication for inbound communication and requests (but does not require) authentication for outbound communication. This rule is for the secure network.

To deploy these connection security rules across your network, you will typically use Active Directory and separate Group Policy Objects (GPOs) for the boundary and secure networks.

For NAP clients running Windows XP SP3, you will need to configure the equivalent policies using the IP Security Polices snap-in. To configure a Windows XP SP3–based NAP client to use its health certificate for IPsec authentication, you must set the HKLM\SYSTEM\Current-ControlSet\Services\PolicyAgent\Oakley\IKEFlags registry value to **0x1c**.

How It Works: Details of IPsec Enforcement

To obtain a health certificate and become a member of the secure network, a NAP client using IPsec enforcement starts up on the network and uses the following process:

1. When the computer starts, the host-based firewall is enabled but does not allow any exceptions. In this state, no other computer can initiate communications with it. At this point, the computer is in the restricted network.

2. The NAP client obtains network access and an IP address configuration.

3. The IPsec Relying Party enforcement client on the NAP client sends its credentials and its System Statement of Health (SSoH) to the HRA.

4. The HRA passes the SSoH to the NAP health policy server in a RADIUS Access-Request message.

5. The NPS service on the NAP health policy server receives the RADIUS Access-Request message, extracts the SSoH, and passes it to the NAP Administration Server component on the NPS server.

6. The NAP Administration Server component passes the Statements of Health (SoHs) in the SSoH to the appropriate system health validators (SHVs).

7. The SHVs analyze the contents of their SoHs and return Statements of Health Response (SoHRs) to the NAP Administration Server.

8. The NAP Administration Server passes the SoHRs to the NPS service.

9. The NPS service compares the SoHRs to the configured set of health requirement policies and creates the System Statement of Health Response (SSoHR).

10. The NPS service sends a RADIUS Access-Accept message with the SSoHR to the HRA.

11. The HRA sends the SSoHR back to the IPsec Relying Party enforcement client. If the NAP client is compliant, the HRA also issues a health certificate to the NAP client.

12. The IPsec Relying Party enforcement client passes the SSoHR to the NAP Agent component on the NAP client.

13. The NAP Agent passes the SoHRs in the SSoHR to the appropriate system health agents (SHAs).

The NAP client removes any existing health certificates if needed and adds the newly issued health certificate to its computer certificate store. With the health certificate and the IPsec policy settings, the NAP client is now a member of the secure network.

The IPsec Relying Party enforcement client performs steps 3–13 whenever an SHA updates its SoH or when the health certificate is about to expire.

If the NAP client is noncompliant, the NAP client performs the following remediation process to become a member of the secure network:

1. Each SHA analyzes its SoHR, and based on the contents, performs the remediation as needed to correct the NAP client's system health state.

2. Each SHA that required remediation passes an updated SoH to the NAP Agent.

3. The NAP Agent collects the updated SoHs from all of the SHAs that required remediation, creates a new SSoH, and passes it to the IPsec Relying Party enforcement client.

4. The IPsec Relying Party enforcement client sends the new SSoH to the HRA.

5. The HRA receives the SSoH and sends it to the NAP health policy server in a RADIUS Access-Request message.

6. The NPS service on the NAP health policy server performs health evaluation and sends a RADIUS Access-Accept message containing the SSoHR to the HRA.

7. The HRA receives the RADIUS Access-Accept message, extracts the SSoHR, and sends it to the NAP client. Because the NAP client is now compliant, the HRA issues the NAP client a health certificate.

Planning and Design Considerations

When planning for the deployment of IPsec enforcement, you must consider the following:

- Active Directory
- PKI
- HRAs
- IPsec policies
- NAP clients

Active Directory

You must consider the following planning and design issues for Active Directory:

- IPsec NAP exemption group
- Security groups or organizational units (OUs) for IPsec policy application
- Security groups or OUs for NAP exceptions

IPsec NAP Exemption Group

You must create an IPsec exemption security group whose members are the remediation servers and HRAs in the boundary network. Remediation servers and HRAs will use certificate autoenrollment to obtain NAP exemption certificates, which are long-lived health certificates that remediation servers and HRAs can use to initiate IPsec-protected communications with computers on the secure network.

Security Groups or OUs for IPsec Policy Application

To create different IPsec policies in the form of connection security rules for computers on the secure network or the boundary network, you must decide how to apply the different sets of Group Policy settings in the form of GPOs. As previously described in this chapter, you need at a minimum a GPO for the IPsec policy for the secure network and a GPO for the IPsec policy for the boundary network. To selectively apply GPOs to the computers of the boundary and secure networks, you can do the following:

- Create security groups for the computers in the boundary network and the secure network, and apply the appropriate GPOs to the security groups by using Group Policy scope filtering.
- Create OUs for the computers in the boundary network and computers in the secure network, and apply the appropriate GPOs to the OUs.

In both cases, you must manage the security group or OU membership as you add remediation servers and computers to your network.

Security Groups or OUs for NAP Exceptions

To exempt computers from IPsec enforcement, you must decide how to group the computers so that they either are not evaluated for health or do not receive an IPsec policy that uses health certificates for IPsec peer authentication. You can use the following methods to exempt computers from IPsec enforcement:

- To prevent NAP evaluation at the NAP health policy server, create a security group whose members contain the computer accounts of exempted computers. On the NAP health policy server, create a network policy that grants access and uses the Windows Groups condition set to the security group for the exempted computers but does not use the Health Policy condition.

- Create an OU whose members contain the computer accounts of exempted computers, and ensure that the GPOs applied to this OU do not contain NAP client settings or connection security rules that specify the use of a health certificate during IPsec peer authentication. With certificate autoenrollment, computers in this OU will obtain NAP exemption certificates to allow communication with clients that require health certificates.

PKI

You must consider the following planning and design issues for your Windows-based PKI for IPsec deployment:

- New PKI or existing PKI
- NAP CA requirements
- Number of NAP CAs
- NAP CAs and certificate revocation lists
- Physical security of NAP CAs
- NAP CA certificate database management
- NAP CA key security
- NAP CA location
- Logical network placement
- Anonymous health certificates

New PKI or Existing PKI

Health certificates are issued by a NAP CA, which must be a Windows-based CA. If you do not already have a Windows-based PKI in place prior to IPsec enforcement deployment, you must deploy a Windows-based PKI in your organization. For more information about deploying a new Windows-based PKI in your organization, see Windows Server 2008 Help and Support, the resources on *http://www.microsoft.com/pki*, or *Windows Server 2008 PKI and Certificate Security* by Brian Komar (Microsoft Press, 2008). For an existing Windows-based PKI, you must create NAP CAs at the issuing CA level in your certificate hierarchy.

Your certificate hierarchy should have a root CA and a level of issuing CAs below the root CA. NAP CAs are at the issuing CA level. Figure 16-3 shows a two-level certificate hierarchy with NAP CAs at the issuing CA level.

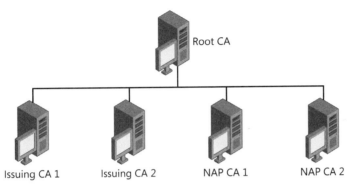

Root CA

Issuing CA 1   Issuing CA 2   NAP CA 1   NAP CA 2

Figure 16-3   Two-level certificate hierarchy with NAP CAs at the issuing CA level

The types of health certificates that are used for IPsec enforcement are as follows:

- Authenticated health certificates for compliant NAP clients (short-lived)

- Anonymous health certificates for compliant NAP clients that are not members of the domain (short-lived)

- NAP exemption certificates for servers in the boundary network (long-lived health certificates)

If servers in the boundary network do not have a valid health certificate, they cannot initiate communication with computers on the secure network. Some boundary network servers, such as the HRA, require communication with computers that can be located on the secure network, such as NAP health policy servers. Therefore, when an HRA does not have a valid health certificate, it cannot communicate with a NAP health policy server on the secure network and cannot verify the health compliance of other NAP clients. Not being able to renew their health certificates, all your NAP clients eventually become members of the restricted network.

To prevent failures of IPsec-protected communication between remediation servers and computers on the secure network, remediation servers are issued an IPsec exemption certificate. The IPsec exemption certificate uses the same certificate template and Enhanced Key Usage (EKU) for system health as health certificates and can be used for IPsec-protected communication between remediation servers and computers in the secure network. However, a typical NAP health certificate is short-lived, on a scale of hours, so that NAP clients must revalidate their system health often. The IPsec exemption certificate, however, is long-lived, on a scale of years.

To automate the issuing and renewal of IPsec exemption certificates to remediation servers, you can configure your PKI for autoenrollment of IPsec exemption certificates to members of the IPsec exemption security group. For more information, see "Deploying IPsec Enforcement" later in this chapter.

NAP CA Requirements

The NAP CA must be able to issue certificates for the EKU with the 1.3.6.1.4.1.311.47.1.1 object identifier (OID). You can use an issuing CA based on the Windows Server 2003 or Windows Server 2008 operating system; however, only NAP CAs running Windows Server 2008 are recommended and supported. For Windows Server 2003–based enterprise CAs, you must configure a custom certificate template for health certificates with this OID. Windows Server 2008–based issuing CAs already have a system health certificate template with this OID.

Although not required, it is highly recommended that the NAP CA be an issuing CA that is dedicated to issuing health certificates. In other words, instead of configuring or designating an existing issuing CA that currently issues computer or user certificates to also issue health certificates, create a new issuing CA that issues just health certificates. The reasons are as follows:

- **Certificate volume and performance**   Health certificates have lifetimes on the scale of hours, rather than years. For a medium or large IPsec enforcement deployment, the sheer number of health certificates might impact an issuing CA's ability to issue other types of certificates.

- **Certificate volume and storage**   Every certificate issued by a CA is also stored in a certificate database for auditing purposes. Because of the number of health certificates that are issued, CA database management becomes an issue. To keep the size of the issuing CA database to manageable levels, it is recommended that you periodically delete the entries in the CA database. Auditing for health certificates after their expiration is typically not needed. If the issuing CA is also issuing long-lived certificates, certificate database management becomes more difficult because the database contains some types of long-lived certificates that you need to keep for auditing purposes.

- **More configuration flexibility**   By using a dedicated NAP CA, you can better control the certificates that it issues, how it issues the certificates, and the properties of those certificates.

Number of NAP CAs

You should have at least two NAP CAs for fault tolerance. If you have a single NAP CA and it becomes unavailable, the HRAs cannot obtain health certificates, and compliant NAP clients cannot receive new health certificates. As a result, compliant NAP clients remain on the restricted network and cannot initiate communications with computers in the secure network.

Additional NAP CAs and HRAs might be needed to ensure adequate performance in a large IPsec enforcement deployment or to distribute NAP CAs in different parts of an organization network, such as branch offices.

NAP CAs and Certificate Revocation Lists

IPsec by default does not perform certificate revocation checking when performing authentication with any type of certificate. Additionally, the lifetime of a typical health certificate is less than the refresh interval of a certificate revocation list (CRL). Therefore, you do not need to plan for CRLs for health certificates in your PKI deployment.

Physical Security of NAP CAs

In some organizations, the physical security of issuing CAs is very high, with the CAs being separated and protected by *hardware security modules* (HSMs), which are computer adapters or external devices that store and physically protect the access to long-term secrets such as the private key of the issuing CA. However, health certificates are short-lived and of limited purpose. In some ways, health certificate are similar to Kerberos tickets. Therefore, the physical security of NAP CAs can often be equivalent to that of Active Directory domain controllers.

NAP CA Certificate Database Management

As previously described, the NAP CA database can become large because of the number of health certificates that are issued. There are two methods for managing the NAP CA certificate database:

- **Automatically**   You can configure the HRA to periodically remove the health certificates from the NAP CA database. This requires that you grant the HRA computer the permissions to manage the CA database. For some PKIs, permission to manage the CA database is very tightly controlled. The recommendation to grant the HRA permission to manage the CA database is based on the NAP CA's role on the network. Recall that the NAP CA should be dedicated to just issuing health certificates; therefore, the HRA would be removing only expired health certificates that do not require long-term storage for security auditing purposes. Additionally, because the HRA requests health certificates on behalf of NAP clients, it should be able to manage the certificates on the NAP CA. This configuration does not introduce any new security vulnerabilities.

  You can control the frequency in seconds at which the HRA removes the health certificates from a NAP CA with the HKLM\Software\Microsoft\HCS\CertDBCleanup-Interval registry value (REG_DWORD type). The default value of the CertDBCleanupInterval registry value is 300 (5 minutes).

■ **Manually** You can use the Certutil tool on the NAP CA with the appropriate permissions to periodically delete records in the NAP CA database, or you can periodically delete the entire NAP CA database. For more information about these methods, see "Ongoing Maintenance" later in this chapter.

If you are not using automatic NAP CA database maintenance, set the CertDBCleanupInterval registry value to **0** on the HRA computer to prevent the HRA from creating error events related to NAP CA database maintenance in the Windows event logs.

The recommendation is that you perform NAP CA database maintenance automatically.

NAP CA Key Security

To protect the integrity of an issuing CA's private key, you can use an HSM. If the NAP CA has the same physical security of your other issuing CAs, you can use HSMs on your NAP CA to provide consistent security protection for all your issuing CAs.

However, as previously described, the dedicated NAP CA has a different role on the network than a CA that is issuing long-lived computer or user certificates. The NAP CA has similar physical security requirements as Active Directory domain controllers. In this case an HSM might not be needed. To provide a level of protection for the private key of a dedicated NAP CA that does not use an HSM, you can configure the lifetime of the NAP CA's certificate, as issued by the root CA or an intermediate CA, to be relatively short. For example, rather than a lifetime on the scale of years, make the lifetime of the NAP CA's certificate six months.

NAP CA Location

You can install the NAP CA on a dedicated computer. However, to save costs and simplify configuration and maintenance, you can install the NAP CA on a server that is also performing other NAP or remediation server functions. For example, you can co-locate the NAP CA on the server in the boundary network that is also being used as the Active Directory domain controller, the HRA, and the NAP health policy server.

Logical Network Placement

The NAP CA can be on the boundary network or the secure network, depending on whether the NAP CA is co-located with another NAP-based remediation server. If the NAP CA is on a dedicated server that does not also run a service for a NAP-based remediation server, place the NAP CA on the secure network.

If the NAP CA is co-located on a server that also runs a service for a NAP-based remediation server, the NAP CA is on the boundary network. For example, if the NAP CA is co-located on a server that is also acting as the HRA and the Active Directory domain controller, the NAP CA is on the boundary network.

Anonymous Health Certificates

When you install an HRA, you are given an option to configure the HRA for just authenticated health certificates or to allow both authenticated and anonymous health certificates. Authenticated health certificates contain both the system health and client authentication EKUs and are issued when the user of the NAP client has authenticated to the domain. Anonymous health certificates contain only the system health EKUs and are issued to compliant NAP clients that are not members of an Active Directory domain. If your network has NAP clients that are not domain members, you can use anonymous health certificates.

If you must use anonymous health certificates, the recommendation is that you create a separate PKI that issues just anonymous health certificates.

Best Practices for the NAP CA

The following are best practices for the NAP CA:

- The NAP CA should be a subordinate CA at the issuing CA level of your certificate hierarchy. You should not use a root CA as the NAP CA.

- For the best performance in a high certificate-volume environment, the NAP CA that is being used for authenticated health certificates should be a standalone CA rather than an enterprise CA. In this environment, a separate NAP CA can be an enterprise CA and issue NAP exemption certificates through autoenrollment.

- The NAP CA should be dedicated to issuing just health certificates.

- Use constraints on health certificates to use only those EKUs that are needed for health and computer authentication and IPsec (the system health authentication and client authentication EKUs).

- The NAP CA should be configured to not issue user certificates.

For more information about configuring certificate and name constraints, see Windows Server 2008 Help and Support or the resources on *http://www.microsoft.com/pki*.

HRAs

You must consider the following planning and design issues for your HRAs:

- Number of HRAs
- Number of health zones
- HRA discovery by NAP clients
- HTTP or HTTP over SSL between NAP clients and HRAs
- Fault tolerance between NAP clients and HRAs
- Load distribution between NAP clients and HRAs
- Fault tolerance between HRAs and NAP CAs

- Load distribution between HRAs and NAP CAs

- Lifetime of health certificates

- HRA location

- HRAs and NAP health policy servers

Number of HRAs

You should have at least two HRAs for fault tolerance. If you have a single HRA and it becomes unavailable, NAP clients cannot receive new health certificates. As a result, compliant NAP clients remain on the restricted network and cannot initiate communications with computers on the secure network.

Additional HRAs might be needed to ensure adequate performance in a large IPsec enforcement deployment or to distribute HRAs in different parts of an organization network, such as branch offices.

Number of Health Zones

A *health zone* is a portion of a network that requires a health certificate from a specific PKI before it will assert system health compliance. In many cases, an IPsec enforcement deployment requires only a single health zone for the entire organization network and therefore a single PKI from which to issue health certificates. However, you might need multiple health zones for the following reasons:

- You have multiple logical intranets that share the same physical network infrastructure. For example, Company A and Company B have deployed their own PKIs and IPsec enforcement. Company A then merges with Company B. A network administrator for the merged company needs to obtain health certificates from both PKIs to perform network administration tasks for both networks.

- You have special health zones for sensitive servers. For example, your finance and human resources departments can contain servers with highly sensitive information. To better protect their assets, IPsec policies applied to these servers require a health certificate from a different PKI.

This chapter describes a single health zone for an intranet.

HRA Discovery by NAP Clients

NAP clients must be able to discover the location of the HRAs on the intranet before beginning the health evaluation process. This automated discovery process can occur with the following methods:

- **Trusted server groups configuration in Group Policy**   You can configure trusted server groups from the Computer Configuration\Windows Settings\Security Settings\Network

Access Protection\NAP Client Configuration node in local or Active Directory–based Group Policy. Each trusted server group corresponds to a different health zone and therefore a different health certificate. If there are multiple trusted server groups, the NAP client will attempt health validation and to obtain a health certificate from the first available server in each group.

The trusted server group is an ordered list of URLs corresponding to the locations of the HRAs. The NAP client attempts to connect to the URL of the first entry in the list. If the NAP client cannot obtain a health certificate from the HRA based on the URL of the first entry in the list, it goes to the second entry, and so on until it reaches the end of the list. The NAP client performs this process for each configured trusted server group.

> **Note**   You can also use the NAP Client Configuration snap-in or the **netsh nap client add|set|delete trustedservergroup** and **netsh nap client add|set|delete server** commands to configure trusted server groups on a NAP client computer. However, if trusted server groups are configured in both the local computer settings and Group Policy, the Group Policy settings will override the local computer configuration.

- **The DNS SRV record for HRAs**   As an alternate way to automatically discover the HRAs on an intranet, a NAP client using the IPsec Relying Party enforcement client also performs a DNS query for SRV records for the FQDN _hra._tcp.*site_name._sites .domain_name*. For example, if a computer's primary domain is contoso.com and is using the default Active Directory site, it will query for the SRV records for _hra._tcp .default-first-site-name._sites.contoso.com. Similar to SRV records used by an Active Directory client to locate domain controllers or global catalogs for a domain, the SRV record for HRAs contains the FQDN of the HRA with which to connect to the HRA, along with a priority setting to control load distribution and balancing. The DNS SRV records for HRAs must be manually configured in the appropriate zones of your DNS namespace. The NAP client ignores the weight and port number settings of the SRV record.

  A NAP client running Windows Server 2008, Windows Vista SP1, or Windows XP SP3 using the IPsec Relying Party enforcement client will query for the HRA SRV records only if it has not been configured with any trusted server groups and has the HKLM\ SYSTEM\CurrentControlSet\Services\napagent\LocalConfig\Enroll\HcsGroups\ EnableDiscovery registry value (DWORD type) set to 1.

  For NAP clients that receive NAP configuration through Group Policy, set the HKLM\SOFTWARE\Policies\Microsoft\NetworkAccessProtection\ClientConfig\ Enroll\HcsGroups\EnableDiscovery registry value (DWORD type) to 1. DNS discovery of HRAs is useful for NAP clients that are not joined to the domain and cannot receive the Group Policy–based trusted server group configuration. Clients that use DNS discovery of HRAs always use HTTPS to communicate with HRAs and the NAP CAs must be enterprise CAs.

> **Note**   If you configure any NAP client setting through Group Policy, the HKLM\SYS-TEM\CurrentControlSet\Services\napagent\LocalConfig\Enroll\HcsGroups\EnableDiscovery registry value will be ignored.

Direct from the Source: Forcing NAP Clients to Retry Unavailable HRAs

When a NAP client is unable to acquire a health certificate from HRA because of a problem with the HRA or some component on which HRA depends, the client will mark the HRA as unavailable. By default, the NAP client will not attempt to obtain a health certificate from this HRA for four hours. When troubleshooting the problem, you can force the NAP client to retry any HRAs that have been marked as unavailable by restarting the Network Access Protection Agent service. You can use the Services snap-in or the **net stop napagent** and **net start napagent** commands at an elevated command prompt. After restarting the Network Access Protection Agent service, check to see whether the client was successful in obtaining a new health certificate.

Greg Lindsay, Technical Writer

Windows Server User Assistance

HTTP or HTTP over SSL Between NAP Clients and HRAs

The communication between NAP clients and the HRAs can be based on either HTTP or HTTP over SSL (HTTPS). With HTTP, certificate request and NAP client identity information is sent as clear text. With HTTPS, certificate request and identity information is sent over an encrypted SSL channel.

HTTPS is more secure, but it requires additional configuration for SSL-based connections. A computer certificate must be installed on the HRA, IIS on the HRA must be configured to use SSL for the HRA Web sites, and the NAP client must have the root CA certificate of the HRA's computer certificate installed in its local certificate store. HTTPS is required when using DNS discovery of HRAs.

HTTP is less secure because the traffic between the NAP client and the HRA is not encrypted. However, HTTP requires fewer configuration steps, and it is easier to troubleshoot NAP client and HRA problems when analyzing the captured network traffic between a NAP client and an HRA.

The recommendation is to use HTTPS for the traffic between NAP clients and the HRAs.

Fault Tolerance Between NAP Clients and HRAs

To provide fault tolerance between NAP clients and HRAs, you must configure the NAP clients with the locations of at least two HRAs. As previously described, you can configure multiple URLs corresponding to your HRAs as entries in a trusted server group in a specified order.

For example, to configure your NAP clients to use a primary HRA (HRA1) and then fail over to a secondary HRA (HRA2), configure your trusted server group with URLs in the following order:

1.   URL to HRA1

2.   URL to HRA2

You can also use Microsoft Cluster Service (MSCS) in Windows Server 2008 to provide fault tolerance for HRAs. For more information, see Windows Server 2008 Help and Support.

Load Distribution Between NAP Clients and HRAs

To distribute the load of health certificate requests across your HRAs, you can configure different groups of NAP clients to use a different ordered list of URLs in the trusted server group. For example, you can do the following:

■   Configure the NAP clients in OU1 to use HRA1 as their primary HRA and HRA2 as their secondary HRA.

■   Configure the NAP clients in OU2 to use HRA2 as their primary HRA and HRA1 as their secondary HRA.

If OU1 and OU2 have roughly the same number of NAP clients, the load of health certificate requests is roughly equally divided between HRA1 and HRA2.

If you are using HTTPS between the NAP client and the HRA, you have the additional option to use an SSL load balancer between your NAP clients and HRAs. The SSL load balancer will distribute the load of HTTPS traffic across the HRAs. This will simplify trusted server group configuration because the group needs to contain only a single entry containing the URL of the SSL load balancer.

You can also use Windows Server 2008 Network Load Balancing (NLB) to provide load balancing for HRAs. For more information, see Windows Server 2008 Help and Support.

Fault Tolerance Between HRAs and NAP CAs

To provide fault tolerance between HRAs and NAP CAs, you must configure the HRAs with at least two NAP CAs. You can configure an HRA with an ordered list of NAP CAs. If the HRA is unable to contact the first NAP CA in the list, it fails over to the second NAP CA, and so on until it goes through the complete list. The HRA will try failed NAP CAs again after five minutes.

For example, to configure an HRA to use a primary NAP CA (CA1) and then fail over to a secondary NAP CA (CA2), use the Health Registration Authority snap-in to configure the HRA with the following ordered list of CAs:

1. CA1

2. CA2

You can also use MSCS in Windows Server 2008 to provide fault tolerance for NAP CAs. For more information, see Windows Server 2008 Help and Support.

Load Distribution Between HRAs and NAP CAs

To distribute the load of health certificate requests across your NAP CAs, you can configure different HRAs to use a different ordered list of NAP CAs. For example, you can do the following:

- Configure HRA1 to use CA1 as its primary NAP CA and CA2 as its secondary NAP CA.
- Configure HRA2 to use CA2 as its primary NAP CA and CA1 as its secondary NAP CA.

Unlike with the communication between NAP clients and HRAs, you cannot use a network load balancer, including Windows Server 2008 NLB, between the HRAs and CAs.

Lifetime of Health Certificates

Changes to the health state on the NAP client will cause the NAP client to perform a new health evaluation and therefore obtain a new health certificate. However, if the health state does not change on the NAP client, it does not perform a new health evaluation.

If the network administrator changes the health requirement policy for IPsec enforcement on the NAP health policy server, it is possible for NAP clients that have health certificates to be noncompliant with the changed health requirement policy. When health requirement policy on the NAP health policy server changes, there is no mechanism to contact NAP clients to perform a new NAP health evaluation.

Therefore, to force the NAP client to periodically verify that its health state is compliant with the current NAP health requirements, the health certificate has a short lifetime. The lifetime of the health certificate is the maximum amount of time that a NAP client with a health certificate can be noncompliant because of changes in health requirement policy.

The default lifetime of health certificates is four hours. If you reduce the default lifetime of health certificates, you reduce the maximum amount of time that a NAP client can be noncompliant because of changes in health requirement policy, but you also increase the frequency with which NAP clients must renew their health certificates. This will increase the load on your HRAs and CAs. The recommendation is that the default lifetime be on the scale of hours and reflect your calculation of load and risk tolerance of the interval between health assessments.

HRA Location

Because HRAs must be able to receive unprotected incoming communications from noncompliant NAP clients, they must be placed on the boundary network. An HRA is a computer running Windows Server 2008 and Internet Information Services (IIS). You can install HRA on a dedicated HRA computer. Alternatively, to save costs and simplify configuration, you can install HRA on an existing server in the boundary network that is providing other types of boundary network services. The recommended co-located configurations for an HRA are as follows:

- Active Directory domain controller computer (boundary network), HRA and NPS acting as the NAP health policy server installed on a single computer (boundary network), and a computer hosting the NAP CA (secure network)

- Active Directory domain controller, HRA, NPS acting as the NAP health policy server, and the NAP CA installed on a single computer (boundary network)

- Active Directory domain controller computer (boundary network), HRA computer (boundary network), NAP health policy server (secure network), and a NAP CA computer (secure network)

- Active Directory domain controller and NPS acting as a NAP health policy server (boundary network), HRA computer (boundary network), and a NAP CA computer (secure network)

HRAs and NAP Health Policy Servers

When the HRA and the NAP health policy server are on separate servers, you must configure the NPS service on the HRA to forward RADIUS requests to the NAP health policy servers. You must use the Network Policy Server snap-in on the HRA and configure a remote RADIUS server group and a connection request policy. The connection request policy causes the NPS service on the HRA to forward requests to a member of the configured remote RADIUS server group.

For fault tolerance between an HRA and the NAP health policy servers, you should have at least two NAP health policy servers and therefore at least two members of the RADIUS server group. For load distribution or balancing between an HRA and the NAP health policy servers, you can configure the priority and weight settings of the members of the remote RADIUS server group. You can set the priority and weight values to be the same to balance the load across multiple NAP health policy servers or specify priority and weight values to prefer one NAP health policy server over another.

For example, to configure two HRAs named HRA1 and HRA2, which have roughly the same amount of requests from NAP clients, for fault tolerance and load balancing between two NAP health policy servers named NPS1 and NPS2, you could configure the following so that:

- For the remote RADIUS server group on HRA1:
  - ❏ NPS1 is the primary remote RADIUS server.
  - ❏ NPS2 is the secondary remote RADIUS server.
- For the remote RADIUS server group on HRA2:
  - ❏ NPS2 is the primary remote RADIUS server.
  - ❏ NPS1 is the secondary remote RADIUS server.

Figure 16-4 shows an example of fault tolerance and load distribution for IPsec enforcement for many NAP clients, two HRAs, two NAP CAs, and two NAP health policy servers.

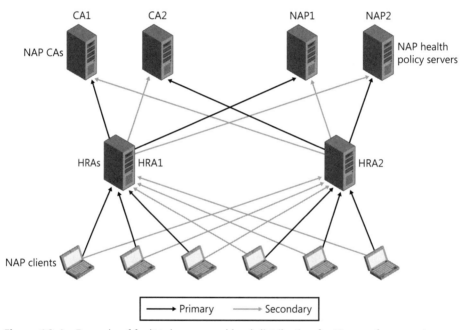

Figure 16-4 Example of fault tolerance and load distribution for IPsec enforcement

IPsec Policies

As described in the "Connection Security Rules for IPsec Enforcement" section earlier in this chapter, IPsec policy settings for IPsec enforcement consist of the following connection security rules:

- An isolation rule for the boundary network that requests (but does not require) authentication for both inbound and outbound communication

- An isolation rule for the secure network that requires authentication for inbound communication and requests (but does not require) authentication for outbound communication

You can also configure additional connection security rules.

NAP Clients

You must consider the following planning and design issues for your NAP clients:

- NAP client operating system
- NAP client domain membership
- Configuration settings
- Configuration methods

NAP Client Operating System

The supported versions of Windows for NAP client functionality that are provided by Microsoft are the following:

- The Windows Vista operating system
- The Windows Server 2008 operating system
- The Windows XP SP3 operating system

Third-party vendors can supply NAP client functionality for other versions of Windows or for non–Windows-based operating systems.

NAP Client Domain Membership

NAP clients should be members of the Active Directory domain to participate in Group Policy–based configuration of NAP client and other settings and the domain isolation environment corresponding to IPsec enforcement. NAP clients that are not domain members can be issued an anonymous health certificate and must be manually configured with NAP client settings and IPsec policy.

Configuration Settings

Consider the following configuration settings for your NAP clients:

- If you are using the Windows Security Health Agent SHA, use Group Policy to enable the Windows Security Center for domain members.
- Enable the IPsec enforcement client.

- Configure NAP client HRA settings.

- Enable automatic startup for the Network Access Protection Agent service.

Configuration Methods

To configure NAP client settings individually, do the following:

- In the NAP Client Configuration snap-in, in the Enforcement Clients node, enable the IPsec enforcement client.

- In the NAP Client Configuration snap-in, in the Health Registration Settings\Trusted Server Groups node, configure NAP client HRA settings.

- In the Services snap-in, enable automatic startup for the Network Access Protection Agent service.

These settings can be configured for NAP clients that are not members of your Active Directory domain.

Manual configuration does not scale to a medium or large intranet. For these environments, use Active Directory and Group Policy settings to do the following:

- Enable the Windows Security Center

- Enable the IPsec enforcement client

- Configure the NAP client HRA settings

- Configure the Network Access Protection Agent service for automatic start-up

On Windows Server 2008, you might need to install the Group Policy Management feature to use the Group Policy management tools such as the Group Policy Management Editor snap-in.

Deploying IPsec Enforcement

The deployment of IPsec enforcement consists of the following tasks:

- Configuring Active Directory

- Configuring PKI

- Configuring HRAs

- Configuring NAP health policy servers

- Configuring remediation servers on the boundary network

- Configuring NAP clients

- Configuring and applying IPsec policies

Configuring Active Directory

To configure Active Directory for IPsec enforcement, do the following:

- Add an IPsec exemption group for computers in the boundary network.

- Create groups or OUs for boundary and secure network computers.

To Add an IPsec Exemption Group

1. In the console tree of the Active Directory Users And Computers snap-in, right-click your domain name, point to New, and then click Group.

2. In the Group Name box, type the name (such as **IPsec NAP Exemption**), and then click OK.

To create a group for the boundary or secure network, do the following:

1. In the console tree of the Active Directory Users And Computers snap-in, right-click your domain name, point to New, and then click Group.

2. In the Group Name box, type the name for the group, and then click OK.

To Create an OU for the Boundary or Secure Network

1. In the console tree of the Active Directory Users And Computers snap-in, right-click your domain name, point to New, and then click Organizational Unit.

2. In the Name box, type the name for the organizational unit, and then click OK.

Using the Active Directory Users And Computers snap-in, add the computer accounts for the boundary or secure network to their appropriate security groups or OUs.

Configuring PKI

To configure your Windows-based PKI for IPsec enforcement, do the following:

- Add a root CA (if needed).

- Create NAP CAs at the issuing CA level.

- Verify NAP CA properties (enterprise CA).

- Create the certificate template for health certificates (enterprise CA).

- Configure the NAP CA to allow non-default lifetimes (enterprise CA).

- Configure the health certificate template for autoenrollment (enterprise CA).

- Publish the certificate template for health certificates (enterprise CA).

- Configure certificate autoenrollment.

Adding a Root CA

If you do not have an existing Windows-based PKI, you must create a root CA and, depending on your organization's needs and security policies, a level of intermediate CAs on computers on the secure network. For information and deployment best practices to deploy a Windows-based PKI, see Windows Server 2008 Help and Support or the resources on *http://www.microsoft.com/pki*.

Creating NAP CAs at the Issuing CA Level

To add a NAP CA on a computer running Windows Server 2008, using Server Manager, install the Active Directory Certificate Services role. For the NAP CA, do not also install the Certification Authority Web Enrollment, Online Responder, or Network Device Enrollment Service roles. During the installation of the Active Directory Certificate Services role, make the NAP CA computer a subordinate, standalone CA at the issuing CA level of your certificate hierarchy unless NAP clients will use DNS discovery of HRAs. In this case, make the NAP CA computer a subordinate enterprise CA. For more information, see Windows Server 2008 Help and Support or the resources on *http://www.microsoft.com/pki*.

To add a NAP CA to a computer running Windows Server 2003, in Control Panel, in Add or Remove Programs, use the Windows Components Wizard to install the Certificate Services component. During the installation of the Certificate Services component, make the NAP CA computer a subordinate CA at the issuing CA level of your certificate hierarchy.

Verifying NAP CA Properties

You must verify that the NAP CA does not require administrator approval for requested certificates by doing the following:

1. In the console tree of the Certification Authority snap-in, right-click the NAP CA name, and then click Properties.

2. Click the Policy Module tab, and then click Properties.

3. Click the Policy Module tab, and then click Properties. On the Request Handling tab, select Follow The Settings In The Certificate Template, If Applicable. Otherwise, Automatically Issue The Certificate.

4. Click OK twice.

Creating the Certificate Template for Health Certificates

For a Windows Server 2003–based NAP CA, you must manually create a System Health Authentication certificate template so that members of the IPsec exemption group can autoenroll a long-lived health certificate. For a Windows Server 2008–based NAP CA, a System Health Authentication certificate template is included.

To Create a Health Certificate Template on a Windows Server 2003–based NAP CA

1. Click Start, click Run, type **certtmpl.msc**, and then press ENTER.

2. In the details pane, right-click Workstation Authentication, and then click Duplicate Template. This template is used because it is already configured with the client authentication EKU.

3. On the General tab, under Template Display Name, type **System Health Authentication**.

4. Select the Publish Certificate In Active Directory check box.

5. Click the Extensions tab, and then click double-click Application Policies.

6. Click Add, and then click New.

7. In the New Application Policy dialog box, under Name, type **System Health Authentication**, and under Object Identifier, type **1.3.6.1.4.1.311.47.1.1**. The Client Authentication application policy will already be present.

8. Click OK three times, and then click the Security tab. Because the WorkStation Authentication template was duplicated, this template should have two application policies: Client Authentication and System Health Authentication.

9. Click Add, type the name of your IPsec NAP exemption group (such as **IPsec NAP Exemption**), and then click OK.

10. On the Security tab, in the Groups Or User Names list, select the name of your IPsec NAP exemption group, and then select the Allow check box next to Autoenroll. Click OK.

For a Windows Server 2008–based NAP CA, you must ensure that the System Health Authentication certificate template has the appropriate permissions for autoenrollment in the IPsec NAP exemption group.

To Configure the Permissions on the System Health Authentication Certificate Template

1. Click Start, click Run, type **certtmpl.msc**, and then press ENTER.

2. In the details pane, right-click System Health Authentication.

3. On the Security tab, click Add, type the name of your IPsec NAP exemption group, and then click OK.

4. Click the name of your IPsec NAP exemption group, select the Allow check boxes next to Enroll and Autoenroll, and then click OK.

To configure the issuing CA to issue the new health certificate template, do the following:

1. From the root CA computer, run the Certification Authority snap-in.

2. In the console tree, expand the root CA name, right-click Certificate Templates, point to New, and then click Certificate Template To Issue.

3. Click System Health Authentication, and then click OK.

Configuring the NAP CA to Allow Non-Default Lifetimes

An enterprise NAP CA must be configured to allow non-default lifetimes. Otherwise, compliant NAP clients will be issued health certificates with the lifetime specified in the health certificate template (on a scale of years), rather than the short-lived lifetime specified in the configuration of the HRA.

To Configure an Enterprise NAP CA to Allow Non-Default Lifetimes

1. At a command prompt on the enterprise NAP CA computer, run the **certutil.exe -setreg policy\EditFlags +EDITF_ATTRIBUTEENDDATE** command.

2. Run the **net stop certsvc** and **net start certsvc** commands to restart the Active Directory Certificate Services service.

Configuring the Health Certificate Template for Autoenrollment

To have the boundary computers (the members of the IPsec NAP exemption group) automatically obtain long-lived health certificates, you must enable certificate autoenrollment in Active Directory by doing the following (Windows Server 2008–based or Windows Server 2003–based CA):

1. Do one of the following:

   ❑ On a computer running Windows Server 2008 with the Group Policy Management feature installed, open the Group Policy Management snap-in. In the console tree, expand Forest, expand Domains, and then click your domain. On the Linked Group Policy Objects pane, right-click the appropriate Group Policy Object (the default object is Default Domain Policy), and then click Edit.

   ❑ On a computer running Windows Server 2003, in the console tree of the Active Directory Users And Computers snap-in, right-click your domain, and then click Properties. Select the Group Policy tab, click the appropriate GPO, and then click Edit.

2. In the console tree of the Group Policy Management Editor snap-in, expand Computer Configuration\Windows Settings\Security Settings\Public Key Policies.

3. In the details pane, double-click Autoenrollment Settings.

4. Verify that Enroll Certificates Automatically is selected, select the Renew Expired Certificate, Update Pending Certificates, And Remove Revoked Certificates check box and the Update Certificates That Use Certificate Templates check box, and then click OK.

Configuring HRAs

To configure an HRA, perform the following tasks:

- Add the HRA to the IPsec NAP Exemption Group.
- Install a computer certificate.

- Configure the Network Policy and Access Services Role.
- Configure the NAP CAs with HRA permissions.
- Configure the properties of the HRA.
- Configure the NPS service on the HRA as a RADIUS proxy.
- Configure IIS for SSL.

Adding the HRA to the IPsec NAP Exemption Group

The HRA computer account must be made a member of the IPsec NAP exemption group so that it will have a long-lived health certificate immediately, allowing it to communicate with computers on the secure network.

To Add an HRA Computer Account to the IPsec NAP Exemption Group

1. In the console tree of the Active Directory Users And Computers snap-in, click the name of your domain.

2. In the details pane, double-click the name of your IPsec NAP exemption group.

3. Click the Members tab, click Add, click Object Types, select the Computers check box, and then click OK.

4. Under Enter The Object Names To Select, type the HRA computer name, and then click OK twice.

Installing a Computer Certificate

If you are using HTTPS to communicate between NAP clients and HRAs, you must install a computer certificate from your PKI on your HRAs. You can install a computer certificate on an HRA in the following ways:

- By using the Certificates snap-in to request a computer certificate
- By using the Certificates snap-in to import a computer certificate
- By requesting a certificate over the Web
- By executing a CAPICOM script that requests a computer certificate
- By configuring autoenrollment for computer certificates

For more information, see "Deploying PKI" in Chapter 9.

Configuring the Network Policy and Access Services Role

The HRA is installed as a role service of the Network Policy and Access Services role using Server Manager.

To Configure the Network Policy and Access Services Role on an HRA Computer

1. Run Server Manager on the HRA computer.

2. Under Roles Summary, click Add Roles.

3. On the Select Server Roles page, select the Network Policy And Access Services check box, and then click Next twice.

4. On the Select Role Services page, select the Health Registration Authority check box, click Add Required Role Services in the Add Roles Wizard window that appears, and then click Next.

5. If you have not previously installed the Web Server role, you are prompted with the Choose The Certificate Server To Use With The Health Registration Authority page. Choose the appropriate option, and then click Next. Figure 16-5 shows an example.

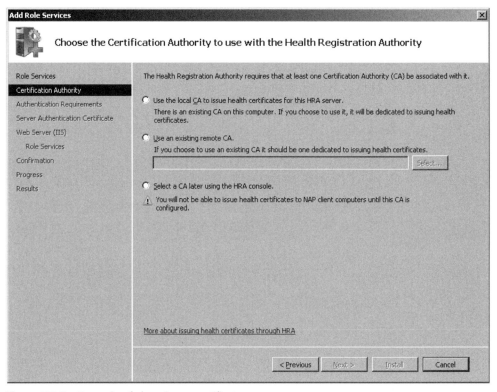

Figure 16-5 Example of choosing a certificate server

6. On the Choose Authentication Requirements For The Health Registration Authority page, choose either Yes, Require Requestors To Be Authenticated As Members Of A Domain (for authenticated health certificates) or No, Allow Anonymous Requests For Health Certificates (for anonymous certificate support), and then click Next. By enabling anonymous certificates, non–domain-joined computers can receive health certificates.

7. On the Choose A Server Authentication Certificate for SSL Encryption page, do one of
    the following:

    ❑   Click Choose An Existing Certificate For SSL Encryption, and then select the
        previously installed computer certificate.

    ❑   Click Create A Self-Signed Certificate For SSL Encryption if you are using a very
        small-scale deployment of NAP or for a test lab. This option requires that you also
        install the self-signed certificate on all your NAP clients.

    ❑   Click Don't Use SSL Or Choose A Certificate For SSL Encryption Later if you do
        not want to use SSL or if the computer certificate that you plan to use for SSL
        encryption has not yet been installed.

    HTTPS between NAP clients and HRAs is recommended but not required. Figure 16-6
    shows an example.

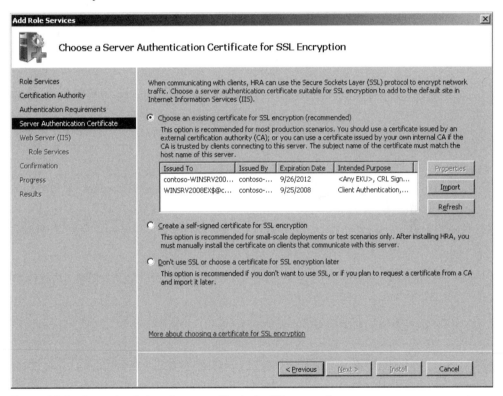

Figure 16-6   Example of choosing a certificate for SSL encryption

8. Click Next.

9. If you have not previously installed the Web Server (IIS) role, you are prompted with the
    Web Server (IIS) and Select Role Services pages. HRAs require only the default Web
    Server (IIS) role services. Click Next on both pages.

10. On the Confirm Installation Selections page, verify your configuration selections, and
    then click Install.

Configuring the NAP CAs with HRA Permissions

The NAP CAs must be configured with permissions to allow the HRA computers to request certificates. The HRA computers can also be granted permission to manage the CA so that it can automatically remove expired certificates from the NAP CA certificate database.

To Configure the NAP CA Permissions

1. In the console tree of the Certification Authority snap-in, right-click the NAP CA name, and then click Properties.

2. Click the Security tab, and then click Add.

3. Click Object Types, select the Computers check box, and then click OK.

4. Under Enter The Object Names To Select, type the names of the HRA computers, and then click OK.

5. Click the name of an HRA computer, or if the NAP CA and HRA are on the same computer, select Network Service. Then select the Request Certificates and Issue And Manage Certificates check boxes. If you are using automatic CA database management, select the Manage CA check box.

6. Click OK.

7. Repeat steps 5 and 6 for all the HRA computers in the list on the Security tab.

> **Note** Selecting the Manage CA permissions is optional. If you do not want to grant the HRA computers the ability to manage the NAP CA database, you should use a manual method to periodically remove the entries of the NAP CA database. For more information, see "Ongoing Maintenance" later in this chapter.

Configuring the Properties of the HRA

Each HRA computer must now be configured with the ordered list of NAP CAs from which it will request health certificates for NAP clients.

To Configure an HRA Computer

1. In the console tree of the Health Registration Authority snap-in, click Certification Authority. Depending on your choice on the Choose The Certificate Server To Use With The Health Registration Authority page when installing the Network Access and Policy Services role, a NAP CA might already be listed in the details pane.

2. To add a NAP CA, right-click Certification Authority, and then click Add Certification Authority.

3. Type the name of the NAP CA, or click Browse to select the NAP CA.

4. Click OK. Repeat steps 2 and 3 as needed to add the complete list.

5. In the details pane, verify that the ordered list of NAP CAs reflects the correct list for this HRA. Reorder the NAP CAs as needed.

6. In the console tree, right-click Certification Authority, and then click Properties.

7. On the Settings tab, specify the appropriate settings such as the lifetime of the health certificates that are requested by the HRA and whether the HRA is using standalone or enterprise CAs.

Repeat this procedure for each HRA computer.

Direct from the Source: Configuring the HRA for an Enterprise CA

The HRA is set by default to use standalone CA mode, which is not compatible with an enterprise issuing CA. When you use an enterprise CA to issue NAP health certificates, or if you use both enterprise and standalone CAs with a single HRA, you must configure CA properties in HRA to use the enterprise operational mode by selecting Use Enterprise Certification Authority in the HRA snap-in properties dialog box or by running the **netsh nap hra set opmode=1** command.

When you enable HRA to use an enterprise CA, you are required to select certificate templates for authenticated and anonymous client requests. The anonymous compliant certificate template must be selected even if you did not choose to enable anonymous certificate requests when installing the HRA. Selecting an anonymous template does not enable anonymous health certificate requests, and it is not required that you select a different template for authenticated and anonymous requests. Unless your deployment includes a requirement that non–domain-joined clients be issued health certificates, you should select the same certificate template for anonymous and authenticated requests.

The authenticated template that you select determines which certificate will be issued to compliant clients with a trusted server group configuration set to use the DomainHRA Web site URL. The anonymous template selected determines the certificate issued in response to requests made to the NonDomainHRA URL.

Greg Lindsay, Technical Writer

Windows Server User Assistance

Configuring the NPS Service on the HRA as a RADIUS Proxy

If the NAP health policy server is located on a different server than the HRA computer, you must configure the NPS service on the HRA computer as a RADIUS proxy. This allows the HRA computer to act as a RADIUS client and send RADIUS-based requests to a NAP health policy server.

To Configure the NPS Service on an HRA Computer as a RADIUS Proxy

1. In the console tree of the Network Policy Server snap-in, expand the RADIUS Clients And Servers node.

2. Right-click Remote RADIUS Server Groups, and then click New.

3. In the New Remote RADIUS Server Group dialog box, in the Group Name box, type the name of the group (for example, **NAP Health Policy Servers**), and then click Add.

4. On the Address tab, type the DNS FQDN, IPv4 address, or IPv6 address of a NAP health policy server.

5. On the Authentication/Accounting tab, in the Shared Secret and Confirm Shared Secret boxes, type the RADIUS shared secret. Do not change the authentication or accounting ports.

6. On the Load Balancing tab, specify the weight and priority for RADIUS traffic to this RADIUS server and failover and failback settings as needed, and then click OK.

7. In the New Remote RADIUS Server Group dialog box, click Add, and then repeat steps 4–6 for each NAP health policy server that this HRA will use to perform health validation for NAP clients.

8. In the console tree of the Network Policy Server snap-in, expand the Policies node.

9. Right-click Connection Request Policies, and then click New.

10. On the Specify Connection Request Policy Name And Connection Type page, type the name of the connection request policy (such as **RADIUS Proxy to NAP Health Policy Servers**), in the Type Of Network Access Server drop-down list, select Health Registration Authority, and then click Next.

11. On the Specify Conditions page, click Add.

12. In the Select Condition dialog box, double-click Day And Time Restrictions.

13. In the Time Of Day Constraints dialog box, click Permitted, click OK and then click Next.

14. On the Specify Connection Request Forwarding page, select Forward Requests To The Following Remote RADIUS Server Group For Authentication, and select the remote RADIUS server group created in step 3. Click Accounting, select Forward Accounting Requests To This Remote RADIUS Server Group, select the remote RADIUS server group created in step 3 from the drop-down list, and then click Next.

15. On the Configure Settings page, click Next.

16. On the Completing Connection Request Policy Wizard page, click Finish.

Configuring IIS for SSL

If you are using HTTPS between NAP clients and HRAs, you must configure IIS on the HRA computer to require SSL encryption for the HRA Web sites.

To Configure IIS on an HRA

1. In the console tree of the Internet Information Services (IIS) Manager snap-in, expand the HRA computer name, then Sites, and then Default Web Site.

2. Click DomainHRA, and then in the details pane, double-click SSL Settings.

3. In the details pane, select Require SSL and optionally, Require 128-bit SSL. The requirement for 128-bit SSL encryption depends on your SSL security requirements. If you do not enable 128-bit SSL, SSL encryption between NAP clients and the HRA will use a 40-bit encryption key.

4. In the Actions pane, click Apply to save the changes.

5. If you have enabled anonymous certificates and want to enable SSL encryption between non–domain-joined NAP clients and the HRA, in the console tree, click NonDomain-HRA, and then in the details pane, double-click SSL Settings.

6. In the details pane, select Require SSL and optionally, Require 128-bit SSL.

7. In the Actions pane, click Apply to save the changes.

Configuring NAP Health Policy Servers

To configure a NAP health policy server, perform the following tasks:

■ Add the Network Policy and Access Services Role.

■ Install SHVs.

■ Configure RADIUS server settings.

■ Configure health requirement policies for IPsec enforcement.

Adding the Network Policy and Access Services Role

To add the Network Policy and Access Services role on a NAP health policy server, you must do the following:

1. On the NAP health policy server computer, run Server Manager.

2. Under Roles Summary, click Add Roles.

3. On the Select Server Roles page, select the Network Policy and Access Services check boxes, and then click Next twice.

4. On the Select Role Services page, click Network Policy Server, and then click Next.

5. On the Confirm Installation Selections page, click Install.

Repeat this procedure for each NAP health policy server.

Installing SHVs

The SHVs that you are using must be installed on each NAP health policy server to be included in the health policy evaluation. The Network Policy and Access Services role includes the Windows Security Health Validator SHV to specify the settings of the Windows Security Center on Windows Vista–based and Windows XP–based NAP clients.

The exact method of installation of additional SHVs will depend on the SHV vendor and can include downloading the SHV from a vendor Web page or running a setup program from a vendor-supplied CD-ROM. Check with your SHV vendor for information about the method of installation.

Configuring RADIUS Server Settings

Each NAP health policy server is a RADIUS server, which might need to be configured with the following RADIUS server settings:

- **UDP ports for RADIUS traffic**   This step is typically needed only if the NAP health policy server is also being used as a RADIUS server for other purposes and other RADIUS clients are using different UDP ports than those defined in the RADIUS RFCs. The default UDP ports used by NAP health policy servers are the same ports as used by the HRAs.

- **RADIUS logging**   You can configure the NPS service to log incoming requests and accounting information in local files or a Microsoft SQL Server database. For more information, see Chapter 9.

You must configure each NAP health policy server with HRAs as RADIUS clients.

To Add a RADIUS Client Corresponding to an HRA

1. In the console tree of the Network Policy Server snap-in, expand RADIUS Clients and Servers, right-click RADIUS Clients, and then click New RADIUS Client.

2. In the New RADIUS Client dialog box, in the Name and Address section, in the Friendly Name box, type a name for the HRA computer. In the Client Address (IP Or DNS) box, type the IPv4 address, IPv6 address, or DNS domain name of the HRA computer. If you type a DNS domain name, click Verify to resolve the name to the correct IP address for the HRA computer.

3. In the Shared Secret section, in the Shared Secret and Confirm Shared Secret boxes, type the shared secret for this combination of NPS server and HRA computer, or click Generate to have the NPS service generate a strong RADIUS shared secret.

4. Select the RADIUS Client Is NAP-Capable check box, and then click OK.

Repeat this procedure for every HRA that will be sending health evaluation requests to the NAP health policy server.

Configuring Health Requirement Policies for IPsec Enforcement

You can create your health requirement policies for IPsec enforcement manually or with the Configure NAP Wizard. Because of the amount of automated configuration being done by the Configure NAP Wizard, this method is recommended and is described in this chapter.

To Create a Set of Policies for IPsec Enforcement

1. In the Network Policy Server snap-in, in the console tree, click NPS.

2. In the details pane, under Standard Configuration, in the drop-down list, select Network Access Protection (NAP), and then click Configure NAP.

3. On the Select Network Connection Method For Use With NAP page, under Network Connection Method, select IPsec With Health Registration Authority (HRA); in the Policy Name box, type a name (or use the name created by the wizard); and then click Next.

4. On the Specify NAP Enforcement Servers Running HRA page, click Next. Because we already added the RADIUS clients corresponding to the HRAs of this NAP health policy server, we do not need to add RADIUS clients.

5. On the Configure User Groups and Machine Groups page, configure computer groups as needed, and then click Next.

6. On the Define NAP Health Policy page, on the Name list, select the SHVs that you want to have evaluated for IPsec enforcement, select the Enable Auto-Remediation Of Client Computers check box if needed, and then click Next.

7. On the Completing NAP Enforcement Policy And RADIUS Client Configuration page, click Finish.

The NAP Wizard creates the following:

- A health policy for compliant NAP clients based on the SHVs selected in the NAP Wizard

- A health policy for noncompliant NAP clients based on the SHVs selected in the NAP Wizard

- A connection request policy for IPsec enforcement requests

- A network policy for compliant NAP clients that allows full access

- A network policy for noncompliant NAP clients that allows limited access

Because the default network policy for NAP clients allows only limited access (enforcement mode), we must modify the network policy for noncompliant NAP clients to allow full access for reporting mode.

To Configure Reporting Mode

1. In the console tree of the Network Policy Server snap-in, expand Policies, and then click Network Policies.

2. In the contents pane, double-click the network policy for noncompliant NAP clients that was created by the NAP Wizard. For example, if you specified "IPsec Enforcement" as the name on the Select Network Connection Method For Use With NAP page of the NAP Wizard, the network policy for noncompliant NAP clients would have the name "IPsec Enforcement Noncompliant."

3. Click the Settings tab, and then select NAP Enforcement.

4. In the network policy properties dialog box, in the details pane, select Allow Full Network Access, and then click OK.

The next step is to ensure that the SHVs that you are using have the correct settings that reflect your health requirements.

To Configure the SHVs for the Required Health Settings

1. In the console tree of the Network Policy Server snap-in, expand Network Access Protection, and then select System Health Validators.

2. In the details pane, under Name, double-click your SHVs, and then configure each SHV with your requirements for system health.

   For example, double-click Windows Security Health Validator, and then click Configure. In the Windows Security Health Validator dialog box, configure system health requirements for Windows Vista–based and Windows XP–based NAP clients.

The next step is to ensure that your health policies are configured for the correct SHVs and conditions to reflect your health requirements.

To Configure the Health Policy Conditions for the Required Health Settings

1. In the console tree of the Network Policy Server snap-in, expand Policies, and then Health Policies.

2. In the details pane, double-click the health policies for compliant and noncompliant NAP clients, and make changes as needed to the health evaluation conditions and the selected SHVs.

Configuring Remediation Servers on the Boundary Network

The first task in configuring remediation servers on the boundary network is to identify the set of servers that noncompliant NAP clients must be able to access. As described in Chapter 14, remediation servers can consist of the following types of computers:

- DHCP servers
- DNS and WINS servers

- Active Directory domain controllers
- Internet proxy servers
- Troubleshooting URL Web servers
- Health update servers

The next step is to place the computer accounts for the remediation servers in the following:

- The IPsec exemption group (so that they can obtain a long-lived health certificate)
- The boundary network OU or security group (so that they can receive boundary network IPsec policy settings)

Depending on the SHAs that your NAP clients are using, you might need to configure your health update servers to provide updates or services to noncompliant NAP clients. See the vendors for your SHAs for information about what needs to be installed and configured.

Configuring NAP Clients

To configure your NAP clients, perform the following tasks:

- Install SHAs.
- Configure NAP clients through Group Policy.
- Configure DNS discovery of HRAs (if needed).
- Add NAP clients to the secure network.

Installing SHAs

Windows Vista–based and Windows XP SP3–based NAP clients include the Windows Security Health Agent SHA. If you are using additional SHAs from third-party vendors, you must install them on your NAP clients. The exact method of installation of additional SHAs will depend on the SHA vendor and can include downloading the SHA from a vendor Web page or running a setup program from a vendor-supplied CD-ROM. Check with your SHA vendor for information about the method of installation.

On an enterprise network, you can use the following methods:

- Network management software such as Microsoft Systems Management Server (SMS) or System Center Configuration Manager 2007 to install software across an organization.
- Login scripts that execute the setup program for the SHA.

Configuring NAP Clients Through Group Policy

Although you can configure NAP clients individually, the best way to centralize the configuration of NAP clients in an Active Directory domain environment is through Group Policy settings, which consists of the following tasks:

- Configuring NAP client settings
- Enabling Windows Security Center
- Configuring the Network Access Protection Agent service for automatic startup

Configuring NAP Client Settings   To configure NAP client settings in Group Policy (equivalent to using the NAP Client Configuration snap-in on an individual Windows Vista–based computer), do the following:

1. Open the Group Policy Management snap-in. In the console tree, expand Forest, expand Domains, and then click your domain. On the Linked Group Policy Objects pane, right-click the appropriate Group Policy Object (the default object is Default Domain Policy), and then click Edit.

2. In the console tree of the Group Policy Management Editor snap-in, expand Computer Configuration\Windows Settings\Security Settings\Network Access Protection\NAP Client Configuration.

3. In the console tree, click Enforcement Clients.

4. In the details pane, double-click the IPsec Relying Party enforcement client.

5. On the General tab, select the Enable This Enforcement Client check box, and then click OK.

6. If you want to specify an image that appears in the NAP client user interface (UI), in the console tree, click User Interface Settings, and then in the details pane, double-click User Interface Settings.

7. On the General tab, type the title and description for the text that appears in the NAP client UI, and then type the path to an image file that appears in the UI, or click Browse and specify its location.

8. If you are using trusted server groups as the method by which NAP clients locate HRAs, in the console tree, expand Health Registration Settings.

9. To add a trusted server group, right-click Trusted Server Groups, and then click New.

10. On the Group Name page, type the name for the group, and then click Next.

11. On the Add Servers page, add the URLs for the HRAs that will be used by the NAP clients to which this Group Policy Object applies.

    For authenticated health certificates using HTTP over SSL, the URL must be in the following form:

    https://**HRA_FQDN**/domainhra/hcsrvext.dll

in which **HRA_FQDN** is the FQDN of the HRA computer (or example, HRA1.corpnet
.contoso.com).

For authenticated health certificates using HTTP, the URL must be in the following
form:

http://**HRA_FQDN**/domainhra/hcsrvext.dll

For anonymous health certificates using HTTP over SSL, the URL must be in the
following form:

https://**HRA_FQDN**/nondomainhra/hcsrvext.dll

For anonymous health certificates using HTTP, the URL must be in the following form:

http://**HRA_FQDN**/nondomainhra/hcsrvext.dll

If you want all the URLs to be SSL-based (contain *https://*), select the Require Server
Verification (https:) For All Servers In The Group check box. If any of the URLs are not
SSL-based (that is, they contain *http://*), clear the Require Server Verification (https:)
For All Servers In The Group check box. Figure 16-7 shows an example of when all the
URLs are SSL-based.

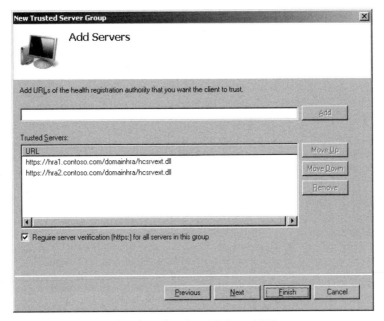

Figure 16-7 Example of configuring SSL-based URLs

12. Verify that all the URLs in the list have the correct syntax.

13. Verify that the URLs in the list are in the correct order.

14. Click Finish to complete the process of adding HRA trusted server groups.

Enabling the Windows Security Center   To use Group Policy to enable the Windows Security Center on NAP clients, do the following:

1. In the console tree of the Group Policy Management Editor snap-in, expand Computer Configuration\Administrative Templates\Windows Components, and then click Security Center.

2. In the details pane, double-click Turn On Security Center (Domain PCs Only).

3. On the Setting tab, click Enabled, and then click OK.

Configuring the Network Access Protection Agent Service for Automatic Startup   To use Group Policy to enable automatic startup of the Network Access Protection Agent service on NAP client settings, do the following:

1. In the Group Policy Management Editor snap-in, in the console tree, expand Computer Configuration\Windows Settings\Security Settings\System Services.

2. In the details pane, double-click Network Access Protection Agent.

3. On the Security Policy Setting tab, select the Define This Policy Setting check box, click Automatic, and then click OK.

Configuring DNS Discovery of HRAs

To configure NAP clients to discover HRAs using DNS SRV records when they are also using Group Policy for NAP client settings, do the following:

1. Remove all existing trusted server group configuration from your NAP client Group Policy settings. If these settings are present, the NAP client will not attempt to discover HRAs using DNS SRV records.

2. On your NAP client computers, create and set the HKLM\SOFTWARE\Policies\ Microsoft\NetworkAccessProtection\ClientConfig\Enroll\HcsGroups\EnableDiscovery registry value (DWORD type) to 1.

Adding NAP Clients to the Secure Network

If you are not using the Computers OU as the OU for your secure network, use the Active Directory Users And Computers snap-in to place the computer accounts of your NAP clients in the secure network OU or security group.

IPsec Enforcement Deployment Checkpoint for Reporting Mode

At this point in the IPsec enforcement deployment, NAP clients on your network have their health state evaluated. Because the IPsec enforcement deployment is in reporting mode, both compliant and noncompliant NAP clients receive health certificates, and the users of noncompliant NAP clients receive no message in the notification area of their desktop warning that their computers do not meet system health requirements. Because you have not yet deployed IPsec policy settings that request or require IPsec protection and authentication with a health certificate, lack of a health certificate will not impair the ability of computers to initiate communications with compliant NAP clients.

While the IPsec enforcement deployment is in reporting mode, you can do the following:

■ Using the Windows Event Viewer snap-in and the Windows Logs\Security event log, perform an analysis of the NPS events on the NAP health policy server to determine which NAP clients are not compliant. Take the appropriate actions to remedy their health state, such as installing missing SHAs or providing health update resources on remediation servers.

■ Check the computer certificate stores of NAP clients to ensure that they are receiving a short-lived health certificate. If not, see the "Troubleshooting" section later in this chapter to determine and correct the problem.

■ Verify that all your remediation servers are being issued long-lived health certificates through autoenrollment.

Configuring and Applying IPsec Policies

After you have verified that the NAP clients are receiving short-lived health certificates and that the remediation servers have received a long-lived health certificate, you can begin config-uring and applying IPsec policies to the computers in the boundary and secure networks. This should be done by performing the following steps:

1. Configure and apply IPsec policy settings for the boundary network.

2. Test clear text and protected communication with the computers in the boundary network.

3. Configure and apply IPsec policy settings for a subset of computers in the secure network.

4. Test clear text and protected communication with the subset of computers in the secure network.

5. Configure the network policy for noncompliant NAP clients for deferred enforcement mode.

6. Configure and apply IPsec policy settings for all the computers in the secure network.

7. Configure the network policy for noncompliant NAP clients for enforcement mode.

The following sections describe these steps in detail.

Configuring and Applying IPsec Policy Settings for the Boundary Network

In this step, you create a GPO containing the IPsec policy settings that requests but does not require IPsec protection for both inbound and outbound communication attempts for computers on the boundary network.

To Configure Boundary Network IPsec Policy Settings

1. On a computer running Windows Server 2008 with the Group Policy Management feature installed, create an MMC containing the Group Policy Management Editor snap-in. In the Select Group Policy Object dialog box, click the Create New Group Policy Object icon, type the name of the new Group Policy Object for the boundary network, and then click OK.

2. In the console tree, under *BoundaryGPOName* [*domain controller name*] Policy, expand Computer Configuration\Windows Settings\Security Settings\Windows Firewall With Advanced Security\Windows Firewall With Advanced Security–LDAP.

3. In the console tree, right-click Windows Firewall With Advanced Security–LDAP, and then click Properties. On the Domain Profile tab, select On (Recommended) in the Firewall State drop-down list, select Block (Default) in the Inbound Connections drop-down list, and select Allow (Default) in the Outbound Connections drop-down list. On the Private Profile tab, select On (Recommended) in the Firewall State drop-down list, select Block (Default) in the Inbound Connections drop-down list, and select Allow (Default) in the Outbound Connections drop-down list. On the Public Profile tab, select On (Recommended) in the Firewall State drop-down list, select Block (Default) in the Inbound Connections drop-down list, select Allow (Default) in the Outbound Connections drop-down list, and then click OK.

4. In the console tree, under Windows Firewall With Advanced Security–LDAP, right-click Connection Security Rules, and then click New Rule.

5. In the New Connection Security Rule Wizard, on the Rule Type page, verify that Isolation is selected, and then click Next.

6. On the Requirements page, select Request Authentication For Inbound And Outbound Connections, and then click Next.

7. On the Authentication Method page, select Computer Certificate, select the Only Accept Health Certificates check box, and then click Browse.

8. Click the name of your root CA, click OK, and then click Next.

9. On the Profile page, verify that the Domain, Private, and Public check boxes are selected, and then click Next.

10. On the Name page, in the Name box, type the name of this rule (for example, **Boundary Network Rule**), and then click Finish.

After the boundary network GPO has been created, apply it to the boundary network OU or security group. For more information, see the *Windows Group Policy Resource Kit: Windows Server 2008 and Windows Vista* by Derek Melber, Group Policy MVP, with the Windows Group Policy Team (Microsoft Press, 2008).

Testing Communication with the Computers in the Boundary Network

After you have applied the boundary GPO to the boundary network security group or OU, do the following:

- Ensure that the remediation servers in the boundary network have received the boundary network GPO settings and have a connection security rule that requests but does not require IPsec protection for both inbound and outbound traffic. For example, you can use the Monitoring node in the console tree of the Windows Firewall with Advanced Security snap-in on a remediation server running Windows Server 2008.

- If the remediation servers have received the boundary network GPO setting, ensure that the remediation servers can initiate communication with NAP clients and non–domain-joined computers and that NAP clients and non–domain-joined computers can initiate communication with the remediation servers.

Communication between NAP clients, non–domain-joined computers, and remediation servers at this stage should be clear text. The IPsec policy on the remediation servers will attempt to negotiate IPsec protection, but it allows fallback to clear for both inbound and outbound communication attempts.

Configuring and Applying IPsec Policy Settings for a Subset of Computers in the Secure Network

Before applying the secure network GPO to all the domain member computers on your network, you should test the secure network GPO and the resulting communication behavior on a subset of your domain member computers by using one of the following:

- A secure test network OU containing test computers. In this case, you can apply the secure network GPO directly to the secure test network OU without affecting other computers on your network.

- A secure test network security group containing test computers. In this case, you must filter the scope of the GPO for just the secure test network security group and apply the secure network GPO to the secure network OU. Because of the scope filtering, the secure network GPO will be applied only to the members of the secure test network security group.

Use the Active Directory Users And Computers snap-in to create either a secure test network OU or a secure test network security group.

Next, create the GPO containing the IPsec policy settings that require IPsec protection for inbound communication attempts and request IPsec protection for outbound communication attempts for computers on the secure network.

To Configure Secure Network IPsec Policy Settings

1. On a computer running Windows Server 2008 with the Group Policy Management feature installed, create a Microsoft Management Console (MMC) containing the Group Policy Management Editor snap-in. Click Browse, and then in the Browse For A Group Policy Object dialog box, click the Create New Group Policy Object icon, type the name of the new Group Policy Object for the secure network, click OK, and then click Finish. Click OK.

2. In the console tree, under *SecureGPOName [domain controller name]* Policy, expand Computer Configuration\Windows Settings\Security Settings\Windows Firewall With Advanced Security\Windows Firewall With Advanced Security–LDAP.

3. In the console tree, right-click Windows Firewall With Advanced Security–LDAP, and then click Properties. On the Domain Profile tab, select On (Recommended) in the Firewall State drop-down list, select Block (Default) in the Inbound Connections drop-down list, and select Allow (Default) in the Outbound Connections drop-down list. On the Private Profile tab, select On (Recommended) in the Firewall State drop-down list, select Block (Default) in the Inbound Connections drop-down list, and select Allow (Default) in the Outbound Connections drop-down list. On the Public Profile tab, select On (Recommended) in the Firewall State drop-down list, select Block (Default) in the Inbound Connections drop-down list, select Allow (Default) in the Outbound Connections drop-down list, and then click OK.

4. In the console tree, under Windows Firewall With Advanced Security–LDAP, right-click Connection Security Rules, and then click New Rule.

5. In the New Connection Security Rule Wizard, on the Rule Type page, verify that Isolation is selected, and then click Next.

6. On the Requirements page, select Require Authentication For Inbound Connections and Request Authentication For Outbound Connections, and then click Next.

7. On the Authentication Method page, select Computer Certificate, select the Only Accept Health Certificates check box, and then click Browse.

8. Click the name of your root CA, click OK, and then click Next.

9. On the Profile page, verify that the Domain, Private, and Public check boxes are selected, and then click Next.

10. On the Name page, in the Name box, type the name of this rule (for example, **Secure Network Rule**), and then click Finish.

For NAP clients that are running Windows XP SP3, you must use the Group Policy Editor snap-in and the IP Security Policies on Active Directory extension at Computer Configuration\Windows Settings\Security Settings to configure and enable an equivalent IPsec policy. Additionally, you must set the HKLM\SYSTEM\CurrentControlSet\Services\PolicyAgent\ Oakley\IKEFlags registry value to **0x1c**. You can do this with a variety of methods including login scripts, through desktop management software such as SMS or Microsoft System Center Configuration Manager 2007, or through Group Policy by using a customized administration (ADM) file.

After the secure network GPO has been created, either apply it to the secure test network OU or filter the scope of GPO for the secure test network security group and apply it to the secure network OU. For more information, see the *Windows Group Policy Resource Kit: Windows Server 2008 and Windows Vista.*

Testing Clear Text and Protected Communication with the Subset of Computers in the Secure Network

After the secure network GPO has been configured and applied to either the secure test network OU or security group, you must test the following types of communications:

- Ensure that the computers in the secure test network received the secure network GPO settings and have a connection security rule that requires IPsec protection for inbound traffic and requests IPsec protection for outbound traffic. For example, you can use the Monitoring node in the console tree of the Windows Firewall with Advanced Security snap-in on a secure test network computer running Windows Vista or Windows Server 2008.

- If the computers in the secure test network have received the secure network GPO setting, verify the following communication behavior:

    - Communication initiated by a computer that is not in the secure test network to a computer in the secure test network is blocked.

    - Communication initiated by a computer in the secure test network to another computer in the secure test network is protected.

    - Communication initiated by a computer in the secure test network to a computer that is not in the secure test network is allowed but not protected.

Communication initiated by computers in the secure test network to all other computers that are not in the secure test network—such as NAP clients, non–domain-joined computers, and remediation servers—at this stage should be clear text. The IPsec policy on the computers in the secure test network will attempt to negotiate IPsec protection, but it allows fallback to clear for outbound communication attempts.

Configuring the Network Policy for Noncompliant NAP Clients for Deferred Enforcement

After testing boundary and secure test network communications, determine the date for deferred enforcement mode (the date for which you will configure the noncompliant NAP client network policy for enforcement mode). On this date, noncompliant NAP clients will not receive a health certificate and will not be able to initiate communications with compliant NAP clients. In deferred enforcement mode for IPsec enforcement, noncompliant NAP clients will still receive a health certificate, but the user will now see a message in the notification area indicating that the computer does not comply with system health requirements.

To Configure Deferred Enforcement Mode

1. In the console tree of the Network Policy Server snap-in, expand Policies, and then click Network Policies.

2. In the contents pane, double-click the network policy for noncompliant NAP clients that was created by the NAP Wizard.

3. Click the Settings tab, and then select NAP Enforcement.

4. In the network policy properties dialog box, in the details pane, select Allow Full Network Access For A Limited Time, specify the date and time that enforcement mode will be configured on the NAP health policy servers, and then click OK.

Perform this procedure on each of your NAP health policy servers.

Configuring IPsec Policy Settings for All of the Computers in the Secure Network

After thorough testing and validation of outbound and inbound communication on the computers in the secure test network as described in the "Testing Clear Text and Protected Communication with the Subset of Computers in the Secure Network" section earlier in this chapter, you can now apply the secure network GPO to all the computers in your secure network. To apply the secure network GPO to the security network OU or group that contains all the domain-joined NAP clients and to ensure that the computers in the security test network OU or group are properly migrated, do one of the following:

- If you are using a secure test network OU and a secure network OU that contains all the domain-joined NAP clients, apply the secure network GPO to the secure network OU, and move the computers in the secure test network OU to the secure network OU.

- If you are using a secure test network OU and a secure network security group that contains all the domain-joined NAP clients, apply the secure network GPO to the secure network OU, and ensure that the computers in the secure test network OU are members of the secure network OU.

- If you are using a secure test network security group and a secure network OU that contains all the domain-joined NAP clients, apply the secure network GPO to the secure network OU, and ensure that the computers in the secure test network security group are members of the secure network OU.

■ If you are using a secure test network security group and a secure network security group that contains all the domain-joined NAP clients, change the scope filtering on the secure network GPO so that it applies to the secure network security group, and ensure that the computers in the secure test network security group are members of the secure network security group.

Configuring the Network Policy for Noncompliant NAP Clients for Enforcement Mode

On the date for enforcement mode, configure enforcement mode on your NAP health policy servers.

To Configure Enforcement Mode

1. In the console tree of the Network Policy Server snap-in, expand Policies, and then click Network Policies.

2. In the contents pane, double-click the network policy for noncompliant NAP clients.

3. Click the Settings tab, and then select NAP Enforcement.

4. In the network policy properties dialog box, in the details pane, select Allow Limited Access, and then click OK.

At this point, the deployment of IPsec enforcement is complete; noncompliant NAP clients will not receive health certificates, and now computers in the secure network require IPsec protection and health certificate–based authentication for inbound connection attempts.

Ongoing Maintenance

The areas of maintenance for an IPsec enforcement deployment are the following:

■ Adding a NAP client

■ Adding a new SHA and SHV

■ Managing NAP CAs

■ Managing HRAs

Adding a NAP Client

To add a NAP client, do the following:

1. Join the NAP client computer to the domain.

2. Install the SHAs on the NAP client computer.

3. Add the computer account of the NAP client to the secure network OU or security group.

For a Windows XP SP3–based NAP client, you must also set the HKLM\SYSTEM\ CurrentControlSet\Services\PolicyAgent\Oakley\IKEFlags registry value to **0x1c**.

For a new non–domain-joined NAP client, follow the steps in "Configuring NAP Client Settings" earlier in this chapter.

Adding a New SHA and SHV

To add a new SHA and SHV to your IPsec enforcement deployment, you must do the following:

1. If needed, install the software or components on your remediation servers for automatic remediation required by the new SHA.

2. Install the required software and SHA on your NAP clients. For more information, see "Configuring NAP Client Settings" earlier in this chapter.

3. Install the SHV on your NAP health policy servers.

4. If needed, on the NAP health policy servers, in the Network Access Protection\System Health Validators node of the NPS snap-in, configure the settings of the SHV for your system health requirements.

5. On the NAP health policy servers, modify the health policies for compliant and non-compliant NAP clients to include the new SHV in its evaluation.

Managing NAP CAs

You must manage NAP CAs when adding or removing a NAP CA from your IPsec enforcement deployment or renewing the NAP CA certificate.

Adding a NAP CA

To add a NAP CA to your IPsec enforcement deployment, do the following:

1. Determine the role of the NAP CA in your IPsec enforcement deployment to provide load distribution and failover to your HRAs.

2. Add the NAP CA to the issuing CA level of your PKI. For more information, see Windows Server 2008 Help and Support or the resources on *http://www.microsoft.com/pki*.

3. Use the Health Registration Authority snap-in on your HRAs, and configure them to use the new NAP CA as appropriate for its role in the IPsec enforcement deployment.

Removing a NAP CA

To remove a NAP CA from your IPsec enforcement deployment, do the following:

1. Determine how the removal of the NAP CA will affect the load distribution and failover scheme for your HRAs.

2. Use the Health Registration Authority snap-in on your HRAs, and configure them to no longer use the NAP CA and to use the remaining NAP CAs for the new load distribution and failover scheme for health certificates.

3. Remove the NAP CA from the issuing CA level of your PKI. For more information, see Windows Server 2008 Help and Support or the resources on *http://www.microsoft .com/pki*.

Manually Removing Database Entries on a NAP CA

If you have decided not to grant HRA computers the permission to manage the CA database of NAP CAs to periodically remove the entries in the NAP CA database, you have two options for manually removing the entries:

- **Use the Certutil tool to delete CA database entries**   You can use the Certutil tool to remove CA database entries and purge the CA database log files at a Windows command prompt, or for NAP CA maintenance, create a scheduled task to periodically run the **certutil** command as a script. The advantage to this method is that the Certification Authority service does not need to be stopped to perform the CA database maintenance. To prevent CA database fragmentation, run the **certutil** script every five or ten minutes.

- **Delete the NAP CA database file**   In this method, you stop the Certification Authority service, delete the NAP CA database file, and then restart the Certification Authority service. You can also use a script and execute the script periodically by using a scheduled task. The disadvantage to this method is that NAP CA cannot issue health certificates while the Certification Authority service is stopped. This might cause your HRAs to switch to a different NAP CA, which can affect your health certificate load distribution.

You can use either of these methods or a combination of methods. For example, you can create a **certutil** script that performs ongoing database maintenance every 10 minutes and a different script to delete the NAP CA database every month.

Renewing the NAP CA Certificate

The certificate assigned to the NAP CA will eventually need to be renewed. You can renew the certificate through autoenrollment or by manual renewal. For the details of these procedures, certificate renewal best practices, and the issues associated with timing issues of an issuing CA certificate and the certificates that it issues, see Windows Server 2008 Help and Support or the resources on *http://www.microsoft.com/pki*.

Managing HRAs

You might need to manage HRAs when adding or removing an HRA from your IPsec enforcement deployment.

Adding an HRA

To add a new HRA to your IPsec enforcement deployment, do the following:

1. Determine the role of the new HRA in your IPsec enforcement deployment to provide load distribution and failover for your NAP clients, NAP CAs, and NAP health policy servers.

2. Join the HRA computer to the domain.

3. Add the HRA computer account to the IPsec exemption group.

4. Install a computer certificate (for HTTPS).

5. Configure the Network Policy and Access Services Role for an HRA.

6. Configure the properties of the new HRA to use the appropriate NAP CAs based on your determined load distribution and failover scheme between HRAs and NAP CAs.

7. Configure the NPS service on the new HRA as a RADIUS proxy to send RADIUS messages to your NAP health policy servers based on your determined load distribution and failover scheme between HRAs and NAP health policy servers.

8. Configure IIS on the new HRA to use SSL for the HRA Web sites (as needed).

9. Configure the appropriate NAP CAs with HRA permissions to request and issue or optionally, to manage the NAP CA database.

10. Configure your NAP health policy servers with a NAP-capable RADIUS client corresponding to the new HRA.

For the details of new HRA configuration, see the "Configuring HRAs" section earlier in this chapter. For the details of configuring the NAP CA, see "Configuring PKI" earlier in this chapter. For the details of configuring NAP health policy servers with a RADIUS client corresponding to the new HRA, see "Configuring NAP Health Policy Servers" earlier in this chapter.

To configure your NAP clients to use the new HRA, add the URLs to the HRA to the appropriate trusted server groups based on your determined load distribution and failover scheme between NAP clients and HRAs. For the details of using Group Policy to configure trusted server groups, see "Configuring NAP Client Settings" earlier in this chapter.

If you are using HRA discovery with DNS, add SRV records to the appropriate DNS zones based on your determined load distribution and failover scheme between NAP clients and HRAs.

Removing an HRA

To remove an HRA from your IPsec enforcement deployment, do the following:

1. Determine how the removal of the HRA will affect the load distribution and failover scheme for your NAP clients, NAP CAs, and NAP health policy servers.

2. From your trusted server groups, delete the URLs to the HRA that is being removed, and modify the remaining URLs in the trusted server groups based on your new load distribution and failover scheme between NAP clients and HRAs.

3. If you are using HRA discovery with DNS, remove the SRV records for the HRA being removed, and modify other SRV records for HRAs based on your new load distribution and failover scheme between NAP clients and HRAs.

4. On all the NAP CAs that the HRA being removed is configured to use, remove all permissions for the computer account of the HRA.

5. On your NAP health policy servers, remove the RADIUS client corresponding to the HRA.

6. Remove the HRA computer.

Troubleshooting

Because of the different components and processes involved, troubleshooting an IPsec enforcement deployment can be a difficult task. This section describes the tools that are provided with Windows Server 2008 and Windows Vista to troubleshoot IPsec enforcement and how to troubleshoot IPsec enforcement starting from the NAP client.

Troubleshooting Tools

Microsoft provides the following tools to troubleshoot IPsec enforcement:

- TCP/IP troubleshooting tools
- The Netsh tool
- The Certification Authority snap-in
- The Certificates snap-in
- NAP client event logging
- HRA event logging
- NPS event logging
- NPS authentication and accounting logging
- IPsec audit logs
- Netsh NAP tracing
- NAP tracing
- Network Monitor 3.1

TCP/IP Troubleshooting Tools

The Ipconfig tool displays the state of a NAP client. At a command prompt on a NAP client, run the **ipconfig /all** command. In the Windows IP Configuration section (the first section in the results display), the state of the NAP client is listed as the System Quarantine State. The System Quarantine State is designated as either Not Restricted or Restricted.

Additional standard TCP/IP troubleshooting tools are Ping and Nslookup to test reachability and name resolution.

The Netsh Tool

Beyond the state of the NAP client as shown in the results of the **ipconfig /all** command, you can gather additional NAP client configuration information by running the following commands:

- **netsh nap client show configuration** Displays the local NAP client configuration including cryptographic service providers (CSPs), hash algorithms, the list of NAP enforcement clients and their state (enabled or disabled), and the state of NAP client tracing

- **netsh nap client show grouppolicy** Displays the same NAP client settings as the **netsh nap client show configuration** command for the settings obtained through Group Policy

- **netsh nap client show state** Displays detailed NAP client state, enforcement client state, and SHA state

- **netsh nap client show trustedservergroup** Displays the list of configured trusted server groups

> **Note** The display for the **netsh nap client show configuration** and **netsh nap client show grouppolicy** commands does not show which set of settings, local or Group Policy–based, is currently active on the NAP client. If any NAP client settings are obtained through Group Policy, the entire set of NAP client settings are specified by Group Policy and all local NAP client settings are ignored.

The Certification Authority Snap-in

Use the Certification Authority snap-in on your NAP CAs to view the list of certificates in the Issued Certificates, Pending Requests, and Failed Requests folders. For example, you can verify that the HRA is removing expired certificates by sorting issued certificates by their expiration date. If the HRA has permission to perform this function, no certificates should be expired for longer than the certificate database cleanup interval (5 minutes by default). Failed requests provide information about certificate requests that reached the CA but did not succeed due to a CA configuration problem. If there are pending requests, health certificates might not be configured to be issued automatically.

Certificates Snap-In

By using the Certificates snap-in for the computer account, you can determine whether a NAP client has a health certificate by looking in the Personal\Certificates node. A health certificate typically has System Health Authentication listed in the Intended Purpose column.

You can also use the Certificates snap-in to determine whether the NAP client has the root CA certificate for the computer certificate of the HRA (when using HTTP over SSL) by looking for the root CA name in the Trusted Root Certification Authorities\Certificates node.

NAP Client Event Logging

Use the Event Viewer snap-in to check the Network Access Protection Client service events in the Windows event log. On computers running Windows Vista or Windows Server 2008, use the Event Viewer snap-in to view events in Applications and Services Logs\Microsoft\Windows\Network Access Protection\Operational. On computers running Windows XP SP3, use the Event Viewer snap-in to view events in the System event log.

HRA Event Logging

Use the Event Viewer snap-in to check the events in the Windows System log that are created by the HRA component.

NPS Event Logging

Use the Event Viewer snap-in to check the Windows Logs\Security event log for NPS events. NPS event log entries contain a lot of information about the NAP health evaluation, including the name of the matching connection request policy (the Proxy Policy Name field in the description of the event) and the matching network policy (the Network Policy Name field in the description of the event). Viewing NPS events in the Windows Logs\Security event log is one of the most useful troubleshooting methods to obtain information about NAP health evaluations.

Netsh NAP Tracing

The Network Access Protection Agent service has an extensive tracing capability that you can use to troubleshoot complex network problems. You can enable netsh NAP tracing by running the **netsh nap client set tracing enable level=basic | advanced | verbose** command. The log files are stored in the *%SystemRoot%*\Tracing folder.

IPsec Audit Logging

Use the Event Viewer snap-in to check for IPsec events in the Windows System log.

Network Monitor 3.1

Use Network Monitor 3.1 or later, a packet capture and analysis tool available as a free download from Microsoft, to capture and view the traffic sent between NAP clients, HRAs, NAP CAs, and NAP health policy servers

You can use Network Monitor for the following:

- To capture the HTTP or HTTPS traffic between the NAP client and the HRA to troubleshoot reachability, TCP connection failures, port blocking on the HRA, HTTP session establishment failures, permissions issues, and SSL negotiation failures.

- To capture the RADIUS traffic between the HRA and the NAP health policy server to troubleshoot reachability, the use of RADIUS port numbers, port blocking on the NAP health policy server, and to determine the contents of RADIUS messages.

- To capture the Health Certificate Enrollment Protocol (HCEP) traffic between the HRA and the CA to troubleshoot reachability, the use of HCEP port numbers, TCP connection failures, port blocking on the CA, and HCEP session negotiation issues.

The proper interpretation of this traffic requires an in-depth understanding of TCP, HTTP, HTTPS, RADIUS, HCEP, and other protocols. You cannot interpret the encrypted portions of HTTPS or IPsec-encrypted traffic by using Network Monitor. Network Monitor captures can be saved as files and sent to Microsoft customer support staff for analysis.

On the Disc   You can link to the download site for Network Monitor from the companion CD-ROM.

Troubleshooting IPsec Enforcement

This section describes how to troubleshoot an IPsec enforcement deployment by starting at the NAP client. This is the approach used by many technical support departments in organizations, and it reflects a multitiered analysis and escalation path to determine the source of a problem and its solution. For example, the IT department of an organization might have the following tiers:

- **Tier 1**   Help desk staff, who can provide an initial assessment of problems and solutions based on an analysis of the client (the NAP client for IPsec enforcement).

- **Tier 2**   Windows network and infrastructure services staff, who manage the remediation servers, HRAs, NAP CAs, and NAP health policy servers.

When troubleshooting IPsec enforcement, it is important to first determine the scope of the problem. If all your NAP clients are experiencing IPsec enforcement problems, issues might exist in your NAP health policy servers. If all your NAP clients that are configured to use a specific HRA or set of HRAs are experiencing IPsec enforcement problems, issues might exist in the HRA configuration, the NAP CA configuration, or the HRA's configured NAP health policy servers. If only specific NAP clients are experiencing IPsec enforcement problems, issues might exist for those individual clients.

Troubleshooting the NAP Client

To troubleshoot the NAP client, do the following:

- Use the Certificates snap-in to verify whether the NAP client has a health certificate installed. If a health certificate is installed, verify the ability to initiate communications with computers in the secure, boundary, and restricted networks. See "Troubleshooting IPsec Policy" later in this chapter.

  If the NAP client does not have a health certificate, try the following steps.

- Verify network reachability from the NAP client to the IP addresses of the HRAs and the other computers on the boundary network. You can use the Ping tool, but because of default Windows Firewall rules, incoming ICMP or ICMPv6 traffic on the HRAs might be blocked.

- Verify name resolution from the NAP client for the names of the HRAs and the other computers on the boundary network. You can use the Ping and Nslookup tools. Verify that the DNS names that the NAP client uses successfully resolve to the correct IPv4 or IPv6 addresses.

- Verify that the Network Access Protection Agent service is started on the NAP client and that it is configured to start automatically. Run the **netsh nap client show state** command to determine the service state and the Services snap-in to configure the Network Access Protection Agent service.

- Verify whether the IPsec Relying Party enforcement client is enabled on the NAP client by running the **netsh nap client show configuration** command. If needed, use the Group Policy Management Editor snap-in (for Active Directory–based GPOs), the NAP Client Configuration snap-in (for the local GPO), or the **netsh nap client set enforcement 79619 enabled** command to enable the IPsec enforcement client.

- If you are using HRA discovery and DNS SRV records, verify that the EnableDiscovery registry value is present in the appropriate location and set to 1 with the Regedit.exe tool. Use the Nslookup tool to query for the _hra._tcp.*site_name._sites.domain_name* name. Verify that the SRV records being returned in the DNS query have the correct IP addresses or FQDNs for the HRAs. You can also review event IDs 39 and 40 in the System event log, which provide details on the success or failure of HRA discovery. If allowed by firewall rules, test reachability to the resolved IP addresses by using the Ping tool. You can also test reachability with a Web browser.

- If you are using trusted server groups, verify that the NAP client is correctly configured with the URLs of the HRAs by running the **netsh nap client show trustedservergroup** command. Use the Group Policy Management Editor snap-in (for Active Directory–based GPOs), the NAP Client Configuration snap-in (for the local GPO), or the **netsh nap client set server** command to correct the trusted server group URLs.

- Verify that the NAP client can successfully reach the Web sites corresponding to the URLs of the HRAs. For trusted server groups, copy the URLs from the display of the **netsh nap client show trustedservergroup** command into the Address bar of Windows Internet Explorer, and try to view the Web site. For URLs that contain */domainhra/ hscrvext.dll*, you should be prompted with a dialog box to type a user name and password.

- Verify that the NAP client has all the appropriate SHAs installed by running the **netsh nap client show state** command. If you are using the Windows Security Health Agent SHA, verify that the Windows Security Center is enabled.

- Use the Windows Firewall with Advanced Security snap-in to verify that the NAP client has received the secure network GPO and its associated connection security rule that requires IPsec authentication for inbound traffic and requests IPsec authentication for outbound traffic.

Beyond these verification steps, use the Event Viewer snap-in on the NAP client to view the NAP client events in Applications and Services Logs\Microsoft\Windows\Network Access Protection\Operational for a Windows Vista–based NAP client and in the System log for Windows XP SP3–based NAP client. Use the NAP client events to perform additional troubleshooting.

For a given attempt to contact an HRA, the NAP client event records a correlation ID. You can use this correlation ID to filter the events on the HRA and examine how the HRA processed the request.

Troubleshooting the HRAs

To troubleshoot the HRAs, do the following:

- Verify network reachability from the HRAs to the IP addresses of the NAP CAs, the NAP health policy servers, and the other computers on the boundary network. You can use the Ping tool, but because of default Windows Firewall rules, incoming ICMP or ICMPv6 traffic on the HRAs might be blocked.

- Verify name resolution from the HRAs for the names of the NAP CAs. You can use the Ping and Nslookup tools. Verify that the DNS names that the HRAs use to resolve to the correct IPv4 or IPv6 address.

- Use Server Manager to verify that the Network Policy and Access Services role is installed with the Network Policy Server and Health Registration Authority role services.

- Use the Services snap-in to verify that the Network Policy Server service and the World Wide Web Publishing Service are started and configured for automatic startup.

- Use the Internet Information Services Manager snap-in to verify that the URLs for authenticated and anonymous health certificates that are configured in the trusted server groups correspond to Web sites on the appropriate HRA. In the console tree, verify that the DomainHRA (authenticated) and NonDomainHRA (anonymous) sites exist when you open the Default Web Site node.

- If you are using HTTP between NAP clients and the HRAs, use the Internet Information Services Manager snap-in to verify that SSL encryption is not enabled on the Domain-HRA (authenticated) and NonDomainHRA (anonymous) sites. Use the Windows Firewall with Advanced Security snap-in to verify that TCP port 80 is open on the HRAs.

- If you are using HTTPS between NAP clients and the HRAs, use the Internet Information Services Manager snap-in to verify that SSL encryption is enabled and correctly configured on the DomainHRA and NonDomainHRA sites. Use the Windows Firewall with Advanced Security snap-in to verify that TCP port 443 is open on the HRAs.

- Run the **netsh nap hra show configuration** command to verify that the HRAs are correctly configured with the NAP CAs.

- Verify that the HRA operational mode is correctly configured. The default HRA mode is to use standalone CA, but the default selection when installing a Windows-based CA is as an enterprise CA. If you add a new enterprise CA to the list of NAP CAs, you must change the default HRA setting to enterprise CA mode.

- If the HRAs are separate from the NAP health policy servers, use the Network Policy Server snap-in to verify that the HRAs are correctly configured. Verify that the connection request policy is configured to forward RADIUS requests to a remote RADIUS server group and that the NAP health policy servers are correctly configured as members of the specified remote RADIUS server group.

Beyond these verification steps, use the Event Viewer snap-in on the HRA to view the HRA events in the Windows Application logs and Security logs for events associated with NAP client requests.

Troubleshooting the NAP CAs

To troubleshoot the NAP CAs, do the following:

- Verify network reachability from the NAP CAs to the IP addresses of the HRAs. You can use the Ping tool, but because of default Windows Firewall rules, incoming ICMP or ICMPv6 traffic on the HRAs might be blocked.

- Verify name resolution from the NAP CAs for the names of the HRAs. You can use the Ping and Nslookup tools. Verify that the DNS names that the NAP CAs are using resolve to the correct IPv4 or IPv6 address.

- Use Server Manager to verify that the Active Directory Certificate Services role is installed.

- Use the Services snap-in to verify that the Active Directory Certificate Services service is started and configured for automatic startup.

- For a Windows Server 2003–based or Windows Server 2008–based enterprise root CA, use the Certificate Templates snap-in to verify that there is a System Health Authentication certificate template configured and available as a new certificate template to issue.

- Use the Certification Authority snap-in to verify that the HRA computers that are requesting health certificates from the NAP CAs have Request and Issue and Manage permissions.

- If you are using automated certificate database management by the HRAs, use the Certification Authority snap-in to verify that the HRA computers that are managing the NAP CA database have Manage CA permissions.

- Verify that the NAP CA is issuing any health certificate requests by checking the contents of the Issued Certificates node of the Certification Authority snap-in.

- Verify whether the NAP CA is denying health certificate requests by checking the contents of the Failed Requests node of the Certification Authority snap-in.

- If you are using an enterprise issuing CA, verify that the HRA is able to enroll itself with a health certificate. This verifies that the HRA has permission to enroll (which is required for an enterprise issuing CA), that the template has been created, and that the template is available to be issued.

Beyond these verification steps, use the Event Viewer snap-in on the NAP CA to view the events in the Windows Security logs for events associated with certificate requests.

Troubleshooting the NAP Health Policy Servers

To troubleshoot the NAP health policy servers, do the following:

- Verify network reachability from the NAP health policy servers to the IP addresses of the HRAs. You can use the Ping tool, but because of default Windows Firewall rules, incoming ICMP or ICMPv6 traffic might be blocked.

- Verify name resolution from the NAP health policy servers for the names of the HRAs. You can use the Ping and Nslookup tools. Verify that the DNS names that the NAP health policy servers use resolve to the correct IPv4 or IPv6 address.

- Use Server Manager to verify that the Network Policy and Access Services role is installed with the Network Policy Server role service.

- Use the Services snap-in to verify that the Network Policy Server service is started and configured for automatic startup.

- Verify that the NAP health policy server is configured with RADIUS clients for all the HRAs that are configured to use the NAP health policy server as a remote RADIUS server. Verify the IP addresses of each RADIUS client.

- In the Properties dialog boxes of each RADIUS client that corresponds to an HRA, on the Settings tab, verify that the RADIUS Client Is NAP-Capable check box is selected.

- Use the Windows Firewall with Advanced Security snap-in to verify that UDP ports 1812 and 1813 are open on the NAP health policy servers.

- Use the Network Policy Server snap-in to verify that the health requirement policies are correctly configured for IPsec enforcement. Verify that there is a correctly configured set of connection request policies, network policies, health policies, and SHVs that reflect your security requirements and the correct behavior for compliant and noncompliant NAP clients. Verify the order of the connection request policies and the network policies.

Beyond these verification steps, use the Event Viewer snap-in on the NAP health policy server to view the NPS events in the Windows Logs\Security event log for events sent by the HRAs for system health validation of NAP clients. To view the NPS events, configure a filter with the Event Sources set to Microsoft Windows Security Auditing and the Task Category set to Network Policy Server.

Troubleshooting Remediation Servers

To troubleshoot remediation servers, do the following:

- Verify that the remediation servers are reachable by members of the restricted network, the boundary network, and the secure network.

- Use the Active Directory Users And Computers snap-in to verify that the remediation servers are members of the IPsec exemption group.

- Use the Certificates snap-in to verify that the remediation servers have a long-lived health certificate installed.

- Use the Windows Firewall with Advanced Security snap-in to verify that the remediation servers have the boundary network IPsec policy settings applied.

Troubleshooting Active Directory

To troubleshoot Active Directory on computers in the boundary and secure networks, do the following:

- Verify that health certificate autoenrollment is enabled for computers in the boundary network.

- Verify the membership of the boundary network security group or OU.

- Verify the membership of the secure network security group or OU.

Troubleshooting IPsec Policy

To troubleshoot IPsec policy on computers in the boundary and secure networks, do the following:

- Verify that the boundary network IPsec policy settings have been applied to the boundary network security group or OU.

- Verify that the secure network IPsec policy settings have been applied to the secure network security group or OU.

Beyond these verification steps, see Chapter 4 for additional IPsec troubleshooting steps.

Chapter Summary

Deploying IPsec enforcement involves configuration of Active Directory, NAP CAs, HRAs, NAP health policy servers, remediation servers, and NAP clients. After an initial configuration in reporting mode, test enforcement mode on a subset of computers. Last, configure enforcement mode for all the computers on the secure network. After deploying enforcement mode, ongoing maintenance of IPsec enforcement consists of adding NAP clients, adding SHAs and SHVs, and managing NAP CAs and HRAs. To troubleshoot IPsec enforcement, verify network connectivity and configuration for NAP clients, HRAs, NAP CAs, NAP health policy servers, and remediation servers.

Additional Information

For additional information about NAP, see the following:

- Chapter 14, "Network Access Protection Overview"
- Chapter 15, "Preparing for Network Access Protection"
- Chapter 17, "802.1X Enforcement"
- Chapter 18, "VPN Enforcement"
- Chapter 19, "DHCP Enforcement"
- Windows Server 2008 Technical Library at *http://technet.microsoft.com/windowsserver/2008*
- Windows Server 2008 Help and Support
- "Network Access Protection" (*http://www.microsoft.com/nap*)

For additional information about Active Directory, see the following:

- *Windows Server 2008 Active Directory Resource Kit* by Stan Reimer, Mike Mulcare, Conan Kezema, and Byron Wright, with the Microsoft Active Directory Team, available both as a stand-alone title and in the *Windows Server 2008 Resource Kit* (both from Microsoft Press, 2008)

- Windows Server 2008 Technical Library at *http://technet.microsoft.com/windowsserver/2008*

- Windows Server 2008 Help and Support

- "Microsoft Windows Server Active Directory" (*http://www.microsoft.com/ad*)

For additional information about PKI, see the following:

- Windows Server 2008 Technical Library at *http://technet.microsoft.com/windowsserver/2008*

- Windows Server 2008 Help and Support

- "Public Key Infrastructure" (*http://www.microsoft.com/pki*)

- *Windows Server 2008 PKI and Certificate Security* by Brian Komar (Microsoft Press, 2008)

For additional information about Group Policy, see the following:

- *Windows Group Policy Resource Kit: Windows Server 2008 and Windows Vista* by Derek Melber, Group Policy MVP, with the Windows Group Policy Team (Microsoft Press, 2008)

- Windows Server 2008 Technical Library at *http://technet.microsoft.com/windowsserver/2008*

- Windows Server 2008 Help and Support

- "Microsoft Windows Server Group Policy" (*http://www.microsoft.com/gp*)

For additional information about RADIUS and NPS, see the following:

- Chapter 9, "Authentication Infrastructure"

- Windows Server 2008 Technical Library at *http://technet.microsoft.com/windowsserver/2008*

- Windows Server 2008 Help and Support

- "Network Policy Server" (*http://www.microsoft.com/nps*)

For additional information about IPsec, see the following:

- Chapter 4, "Windows Firewall with Advanced Security"

- Windows Server 2008 Technical Library at *http://technet.microsoft.com/windowsserver/2008*

- Windows Server 2008 Help and Support

- "IPsec" (*http://www.microsoft.com/IPsec*)

Chapter 17

802.1X Enforcement

This chapter provides information about how to design, deploy, maintain, and troubleshoot 802.1X enforcement with Network Access Protection (NAP).

This chapter assumes the following:

- That you understand the role of the Active Directory, Group Policy, and Remote Authentication Dial-In User Service (RADIUS) elements of a Microsoft Windows–based authentication infrastructure for network access. For more information, see Chapter 9, "Authentication Infrastructure."

- That you have a working IEEE 802.1X–authenticated wireless or wired network. For more information, see Chapter 10, "IEEE 802.11 Wireless Networks," and Chapter 11, "IEEE 802.1X–Authenticated Wired Networks."

- That you understand the components of NAP and how to prepare your network for NAP. For more information, see Chapter 14, "Network Access Protection Overview," and Chapter 15, "Preparing for Network Access Protection."

Overview of 802.1X Enforcement

802.1X enforcement in NAP consists of a NAP health policy server and an 802.1X enforcement client on NAP clients. The NAP health policy server evaluates the health of the NAP client and instructs the *802.1X access point*, either a wireless access point (AP) using 802.1X authentication or an 802.1X-capable switch, to restrict the access of noncompliant NAP clients.

On computers running Windows Vista or Windows Server 2008, the 802.1X enforcement client is named Extensible Authentication Protocol (EAP) Quarantine enforcement client. On computers running the Windows XP operating system with Service Pack 3, there are two different EAP enforcement clients for 802.1X enforcement: the EAP Quarantine enforcement client for wired connections and the Wireless Eapol Quarantine enforcement client for wireless connections.

802.1X enforcement occurs in conjunction with the 802.1X authentication process. After the authentication and health evaluation, a NAP client is in one of the following states:

- Unauthenticated
- Authenticated with unlimited access (a compliant NAP client)
- Authenticated with restricted access (a noncompliant NAP client)

How It Works: Details of 802.1X Enforcement

802.1X enforcement uses an access control list (ACL) or a virtual local area network (VLAN) to restrict the access of the noncompliant NAP client. An ACL is a set of Internet Protocol version 4 (IPv4) or Internet Protocol version 6 (IPv6) packet filters configured on the 802.1X access point. The 802.1X access point applies the ACL to the connection and silently discards all packets that are not allowed by the ACL. A VLAN is multiple switch ports grouped to create a separate network. Each VLAN is identified with a VLAN identifier (ID). With VLANs, the 802.1X access point applies the VLAN ID for the restricted network to the connection, and traffic from noncompliant NAP clients does not leave the restricted network.

The following process occurs when a NAP-capable 802.1X client running Windows Vista connects to an 802.1X access point:

1. The 802.1X client and the 802.1X access point begin the 802.1X authentication process using the EAP over LAN (EAPOL) protocol.

2. The 802.1X access point sends an EAP-Request/Identity message to the EAP client component on the 802.1X client.

3. The EAP client on the 802.1X client responds with an EAP-Response/Identity message that contains the user or computer name of the 802.1X client.

4. The 802.1X access point sends the EAP-Response/Identity message as a RADIUS Access-Request message to the NAP health policy server. For all subsequent EAP-based messages, the logical communication occurs between the NAP health policy server and the EAP client on the 802.1X client, using the 802.1X access point as a pass-through device. Messages between the 802.1X network access device and the NAP health policy server are a series of RADIUS messages.

5. The NAP health policy server sends an EAP-Request/Start Protected EAP (PEAP) message to the EAP client on the 802.1X client.

6. The EAP client on the 802.1X client and the NAP health policy server exchange a series of Transport Layer Security (TLS) messages to negotiate a protected TLS session.

7. The NAP health policy server requires that the 802.1X client authenticate itself using its user or computer credentials and a PEAP authentication method such as PEAP-Microsoft Challenge Handshake Authentication Protocol version 2 (MS-CHAP v2).

8. The 802.1X client authenticates itself to the NAP health policy server using the negotiated PEAP authentication method.

9. The NAP health policy server sends a request for the System Statement of Health (SSoH) to the EAP client on the 802.1X client using a PEAP-Type-Length-Value (TLV) message.

10. The EAP client passes the request for the SSoH to the EAP Quarantine enforcement client, which then queries the NAP Agent component for the SSoH.

11. The EAP Quarantine enforcement client passes the SSoH to the EAP client, which passes it to the NAP health policy server using a PEAP-TLV message.

12. The NPS service on the NAP health policy server extracts the SSoH from the PEAP-TLV message sent in step 8 and passes it to the NAP Administration Server component on the NPS server.

13. The NAP Administration Server component passes the Statements of Health (SoHs) in the SSoH to the appropriate system health validators (SHVs).

14. The SHVs analyze the contents of their SoHs and return Statements of Health Response (SoHRs) to the NAP Administration Server.

15. The NAP Administration Server passes the SoHRs to the NPS service.

16. The NPS service compares the SoHRs to the configured set of health requirement policies and creates the System Statement of Health Response (SSoHR).

17. The NPS service sends a PEAP-TLV message containing the SSoHR to the EAP client on the 802.1X client.

18. The EAP client passes the SSoHR to the EAP Quarantine enforcement client, which passes it to the NAP Agent component.

19. The NAP Agent component passes the SoHRs to the appropriate system health agents (SHAs).

20. If the 802.1X connection is authenticated and authorized, the NPS service sends a RADIUS Access-Accept message to the 802.1X network access device.

    ❑ If the 802.1X connection is restricted, the RADIUS Access-Accept message also contains RADIUS attributes to restrict the traffic of the 802.1X client by specifying an ACL or a VLAN ID.

    ❑ If the 802.1X connection is unlimited, the RADIUS Access-Accept message contains the appropriate RADIUS attributes to allow access to the intranet.

If the NAP client is noncompliant, it can reach only the resources that are specified in the ACL or are located on the restricted network VLAN. The following process performs the automatic remediation required for unlimited network access:

1. Each SHA analyzes its SoHR, and based on the contents, performs the remediation as needed to correct the NAP client's system health state.

2. Each SHA that required remediation passes an updated SoH to the NAP Agent.

3. The NAP Agent collects the updated SoHs from the SHAs that required remediation, creates a new SSoH, and passes it to the EAP Quarantine enforcement client.

> 4. The EAP Quarantine enforcement client restarts 802.1X authentication and sends its SSoH for health validation.
>
> 5. Health validation succeeds, and the 802.1X client has access to the intranet.

With 802.1X enforcement, there are two ways that you can restrict the traffic of noncompliant NAP clients:

- Using an ACL

- Using a VLAN

Using an ACL

When you use an ACL for 802.1X enforcement, the NAP health policy server instructs the 802.1X access point to apply a specified ACL to the noncompliant NAP client computer's connection or port. This ACL has been previously configured on the 802.1X access point and is typically identified with a name. The ACL contains a list of packet filters that correspond to the allowed traffic to and from remediation servers located on the intranet. Figure 17-1 shows the network configuration when using ACLs.

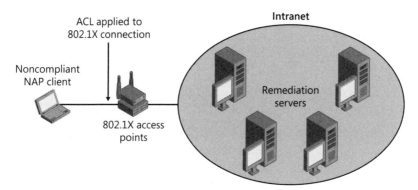

Figure 17-1   Network configuration when using ACLs

When the NAP client successfully authenticates, it typically begins automatic configuration through the Dynamic Host Configuration Protocol (DHCP) for IPv4 or address autoconfiguration for IPv6. For DHCP, the DHCP server typically configures the NAP client with an IPv4 address configuration for the subnet to which the NAP client is attached and a set of domain name system (DNS) servers. The NAP client will use the DNS servers to locate domain controllers and other network resources.

Because different portions of an intranet can use different DHCP servers and network infrastructure servers, the set of packet filters in the ACL for restricted access will typically vary based on the location of a given 802.1X access point on an intranet. For example, in site 1, the

DHCP server is 10.0.0.1 and the DNS server is 10.0.0.2. In site 2, the DHCP server is 192.168.0.1 and the DNS server is 192.168.0.2.

Because a typical 802.1X deployment uses a single network policy for noncompliant NAP clients, you should use a single name for the ACL. On each 802.1X access point, create the ACL and configure the set of packet filters that correspond to the set of remediation servers for the 802.1X access point's location on the intranet.

An advantage to using ACLs for restricted access is that you can isolate the noncompliant NAP clients from each other. The only traffic allowed by the ACL is that between a noncompliant NAP client and the remediation servers. With ACLs, noncompliant NAP clients infected with malware cannot attack other noncompliant NAP clients.

Using a VLAN

When you use VLANs for 802.1X enforcement, the NAP health policy server instructs the 802.1X access point to apply the VLAN ID corresponding to the restricted network to the NAP client's connection. This places the NAP client on the restricted network. Figure 17-2 shows the network configuration when using a restricted network VLAN.

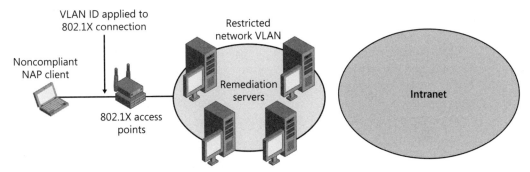

Figure 17-2   Network configuration when using a restricted network VLAN

The restricted network VLAN is a logical subnet that contains the set of remediation servers for noncompliant NAP clients. You must determine which of your intranet network infrastructure servers to place on the restricted VLAN and how to place them on the VLAN. The VLAN should be a self-sufficient IPv4 or IPv6 subnet that contains all the servers needed for basic network connectivity and health update servers, such as the troubleshooting URL Web server.

A disadvantage to using a VLAN for restricted access is the inability to confine the network traffic to only that sent between noncompliant NAP clients and remediation servers. Because there are no packet filters being applied to the noncompliant NAP client's connection on the restricted network, the NAP client can initiate communication with any network node on the restricted network VLAN, including other noncompliant NAP clients. This makes it possible for malware on a noncompliant NAP client to attack other noncompliant NAP clients.

Another disadvantage to using a VLAN for restricted access is that because the restricted VLAN is a different IP subnet, a NAP client's IP address configuration changes when it transitions between being a compliant NAP client and a noncompliant NAP client. The change in IP address configuration might cause temporary disruptions in network connectivity. For example, a change in IP address configuration when transitioning from a noncompliant NAP client to a compliant NAP client during system startup and user logon might cause Group Policy updates or other boot processes to fail.

Planning and Design Considerations

When deploying 802.1X enforcement, you must consider the following in your planning:

- Security group for NAP exemptions
- 802.1X authentication methods
- Type of 802.1X enforcement
- 802.1X access points
- NAP clients

Security Group for NAP Exemptions

To exempt computers from 802.1X enforcement by preventing NAP evaluation at the NAP health policy server, create a security group whose members contain the computer accounts of exempted computers. On the NAP health policy server, create a network policy that grants wireless or wired access and uses the Windows Groups condition set to the security group for the exempted computers but does not use the Health Policy condition.

Because the connection request policy for wired or wireless access with NAP requires the use of PEAP and NAP health evaluation, health evaluation for exempted computers will still be performed and recorded.

802.1X Authentication Methods

Because 802.1X enforcement uses PEAP-TLV messages to transfer system health status and remediation information between the 802.1X access client and the NAP health policy server, you must use a PEAP-based authentication protocol in your protected wireless or wired network solution. Windows Vista, Windows Server 2008, and Windows XP SP3 include support for the following PEAP-based authentication methods:

- PEAP-MS-CHAP v2
- PEAP-TLS

You can also use other PEAP-based authentication methods that are supplied by third-party vendors.

If you are currently using EAP-TLS and either registry-based user or computer certificates or smart cards, you must change your authentication method to use PEAP-TLS prior to deploying 802.1X enforcement.

For more information, see Chapter 10 (for wireless networks) and Chapter 11 (for wired networks).

Type of 802.1X Enforcement

As described in the section "Overview of 802.1X Enforcement," earlier in this chapter, you can implement 802.1X enforcement via ACLs or VLANs. You must decide which type of 802.1X enforcement you will deploy based on your current use of ACLs and VLANs, the capabilities of your 802.1X access points, and administrative preferences. The method of 802.1X enforcement that you choose will determine how you configure 802.1X access points and your health requirement policies for 802.1X enforcement.

802.1X Access Points

You must consider the following planning and design issues for your 802.1X access points:

- ACLs or VLANs for restricted access
- Reauthentication interval

ACLs or VLANs for Restricted Access

The decision to use ACLs or VLANs for restricted access depends on the following:

- Whether your 802.1X access points support ACLs, VLANs, or both.

- If you are already using ACLs to restrict traffic on your intranet, you should use an ACL for 802.1X enforcement. Similarly, if you are already using VLANs to group network access, you should use a VLAN for 802.1X enforcement.

- If you are using a separate VLAN for unauthenticated 802.1X clients, do not use this VLAN for restricted access for noncompliant NAP clients. Create a new VLAN for restricted access for noncompliant NAP clients. Noncompliant NAP clients are authenticated 802.1X clients that might need to access remediation servers to correct their system health. Do not place your remediation servers on the VLAN for unauthenticated 802.1X clients.

- For VLAN-based 802.1X enforcement, create a restricted network VLAN that contains the remediation servers for your intranet.

Reauthentication Interval

Changes to the health state on the NAP client will cause the NAP client to perform a new health evaluation. If the health state does not change, the NAP client does not perform a new health evaluation. If the network administrator changes the health requirement policy for 802.1X enforcement on the NAP health policy server, it is possible for NAP clients that have unlimited access to be noncompliant with the changed health requirement policy. When health requirement policy on the NAP health policy server changes, there is no mechanism to contact NAP clients to perform a new health evaluation. Therefore, to force the NAP client in an 802.1X enforcement deployment to periodically verify that its health state is compliant with the current NAP health requirements, the NAP client must be required to perform a periodic 802.1X reauthentication with its 802.1X access server. The interval for the periodic reauthentication is the maximum amount of time that a NAP client with unlimited access can be noncompliant because of changes in health requirement policy.

The recommended 802.1X reauthentication interval for 802.1X enforcement is 4 hours. If you reduce this reauthentication interval, you reduce the maximum amount of time that a NAP client can be noncompliant because of changes in health requirement policy, but you also increase the frequency with which NAP clients must reauthenticate and perform a new health evaluation. This will increase the load on your NAP health policy servers. The recommendation is that the reauthentication interval is on a scale of hours and that it reflects your calculation of load and risk tolerance of the time interval between health assessments.

Depending on your 802.1X access points, you can configure the 802.1X reauthentication interval with the following:

- The Session-Timeout standard RADIUS attribute
- A vendor-specific attribute (VSA) supported by the 802.1X access point
- The configuration tool for the 802.1X access points

See the documentation for your 802.1X access points to determine how they support the configuration of the 802.1X reauthentication interval.

NAP Clients

You must consider the following planning and design issues for your NAP clients:

- NAP client operating system
- NAP client domain membership
- Configuration settings
- Configuration methods

NAP Client Operating System

The versions of Windows that include NAP client functionality are the following:

- Windows Vista

- Windows Server 2008

- Windows XP SP3

Third-party vendors can supply NAP client functionality for other versions of Windows or for non-Windows–based operating systems.

NAP Client Domain Membership

NAP clients should be members of the Active Directory domain to participate in Group Policy–based configuration of NAP client settings. NAP clients that are not domain members must be manually configured with NAP client settings.

Configuration Settings

Consider the following configuration settings for your NAP clients:

- Enable system health checking for the PEAP authentication protocol.

- If you are using the Windows Security Health Agent SHA for NAP clients running Windows XP SP3 or Windows Vista, enable Windows Security Center for domain members through Group Policy.

- Enable the EAP Quarantine Enforcement Client.

- Enable automatic startup for the Network Access Protection Agent service.

Configuration Methods

You can configure NAP client settings individually with the following:

- Enable system health checking for PEAP in the Authentication tab for the properties of a wired connection or from the Security tab for the properties of a wireless network, in the Protected EAP Properties dialog box, by selecting Enable Quarantine Checks.

- For NAP clients running Windows Vista or Windows Server 2008, enable the EAP Quarantine enforcement client from the Enforcement Clients node of the NAP Client Configuration snap-in.

- For NAP clients running Windows XP SP3, enable the EAP Quarantine enforcement client from a command prompt by running the **netsh nap client set enforcement 79623 enable** command or Wireless Eapol Quarantine enforcement client from a command prompt by running the **netsh nap client set enforcement 79620 enable** command.

- Enable automatic startup for the Network Access Protection Agent service from the Services snap-in.

These settings can be configured for NAP clients that are not members of your Active Directory domain.

Manual configuration does not scale to a medium or large intranet. For these environments, use Active Directory and Group Policy settings to do the following:

- Enable system health checking for PEAP.
- Enable the Windows Security Center.
- Enable the EAP Quarantine or Wireless Eapol Quarantine enforcement clients.
- Configure the NAP Agent service for automatic start-up.

For Windows Server 2008, you might have to install the Group Policy Management feature in Server Manager to use the Group Policy management tools.

Deploying 802.1X Enforcement

The deployment of 802.1X enforcement consists of the following tasks:

- Configuring Active Directory
- Configuring a PEAP-based authentication method
- Configuring 802.1X access points
- Configuring remediation servers on the restricted network
- Configuring NAP health policy servers
- Configuring NAP clients

Configuring Active Directory

For Active Directory, you can optionally configure a security group for exempted computers.

To Create a NAP Exemption Security Group

1. In the console tree of the Active Directory Users and Computers snap-in, right-click your domain name, point to New, and then click Group.

2. In the Group Name box, type the name (such as **NAP Exemptions**), and then click OK.

Using the Active Directory Users And Computers snap-in, add the computer accounts for the exempted computers to the newly created security group.

Configuring a PEAP-Based Authentication Method

If you are not already using a PEAP-based authentication method for 802.1X-authenticated wireless or wired access, you must reconfigure your access clients and the network policy on your NPS servers. For information about configuring the PEAP-MS-CHAP v2 or PEAP-TLS authentication methods, see Chapter 10 and Chapter 11. For third-party PEAP authentication methods, see the third-party documentation for information about configuring Windows-based 802.1X access clients and the NPS servers.

Verify that wired or wireless connections using the PEAP authentication method work properly before continuing your 802.1X enforcement deployment.

Direct from the Source: The Cryptobinding TLV Option

When configuring PEAP authentication methods, one of the available options is to require that cryptographic binding (cryptobinding) TLV responses be received from the authentication peer. This option addresses a vulnerability of PEAP and other authentication protocols to attacks when multiple authentication processes occur independently of each other, with the potential to introduce differing authentication endpoints. This type of attack is commonly known as man-in-the-middle (MITM). This attack is mitigated through the use of cryptobinding TLV responses by validating peers with an additional compound authentication phase and placing restrictions on the reuse of credentials.

On the NPS server, you can access the cryptobinding option through properties of your wired or wireless network policy. On the Settings tab, click Authentication Methods. In EAP Types, click Microsoft: Protected EAP (PEAP), and then click Edit. One of the available options in the Edit Protected EAP Properties dialog box is to Disconnect Clients Without Cryptobinding. On the NAP client, you can access a similar option by reviewing PEAP settings or properties on the Authentication tab of your wired connection or through your wireless profile. In the Protected EAP Properties dialog box, an available option for Disconnect If Server Does Not Present Cryptobinding TLV.

The NPS server will always send a cryptobinding TLV, and there is no option to disable this. If you enable disconnection of clients without cryptobinding as described above, it will additionally enforce receipt of a cryptobinding response from the client computer. If this is not received, the server will reject the connection attempt. On the client side, enabling the cryptobinding option will require that the server send a cryptobinding TLV, and authentication will fail if this is not received by the client. If the cryptobinding option is not enabled on the client and it receives a cryptobinding TLV from the server, it will reply with a cryptobinding TLV response.

Greg Lindsay, Technical Writer

Windows Server User Assistance

Configuring 802.1X Access Points

To use an ACL for 802.1X enforcement, do the following:

- Configure your 802.1X access points with an ACL that restricts the access of noncompliant NAP clients. The ACL must contain a list of packet filters that correspond to the allowed traffic to and from remediation servers located on the intranet.

- Determine how to identify the ACL for restricted network access through a RADIUS attribute for your 802.1X access points. Some 802.1X access points use the standard RADIUS attribute Filter-ID. See your 802.1X access point documentation for information.

To use a VLAN for 802.1X enforcement, do the following:

- If you are already using a VLAN for access to your intranet, that VLAN becomes the VLAN for compliant NAP clients. In this case, you need only create a new VLAN for noncompliant NAP clients that contains the remediation servers on your intranet. See the documentation for your 802.1X access points for information about how to configure VLANs.

- Determine how to indicate the restricted network VLAN through RADIUS attributes for your 802.1X access points. Some 802.1X access points use the following RADIUS or vendor-specific attributes:

    ❑ Tunnel-Medium-Type

    ❑ Tunnel-Pvt-Group-ID

    ❑ Tunnel-Type

    ❑ Tunnel-Tag

See your 802.1X access point documentation for information about how to indicate a VLAN ID for an 802.1X-based connection.

Direct from the Source: The Tunnel-Tag VSA

One of the recommended VSAs used with 802.1X enforcement is Tunnel-Tag. This VSA is used to configure a field within other RADIUS attributes. The value you set for Tunnel-Tag is populated in all RADIUS attributes used in the policy, serving to group these attributes together and identify them as belonging to a particular tunnel. A Tunnel-Tag value is not always required, but using this VSA can help in some instances in relaying attributes to your 802.1X access point. Consult your vendor documentation to determine whether a unique Tag value is required for your switch or access point. For more information about Tunnel-Tag and other RADIUS attributes used with 802.1X NAP, see RFC 2868.

Greg Lindsay, Technical Writer

Windows Server User Assistance

If your 802.1X access points do not support the configuration of the 802.1X reauthentication interval through the Session-Timeout standard RADIUS attribute or through a VSA, see the documentation for your 802.1X access points for information about how to configure the 802.1X periodic reauthentication interval.

Configuring Remediation Servers on the Restricted Network

The first task in configuring remediation servers on the restricted network is to identify the set of servers that noncompliant NAP clients must be able to access. As described in Chapter 15, remediation servers can consist of the following types of computers:

- DHCP servers
- DNS and Windows Internet Name Service (WINS) servers
- Active Directory domain controllers
- Internet proxy servers
- Troubleshooting URL Web servers
- Health update servers

Depending on the SHAs that your NAP clients are using, you might need to configure your health update servers to provide updates or services to noncompliant NAP clients. See the documentation supplied by the vendors for your SHAs for information about what needs to be installed and configured.

Configuring NAP Health Policy Servers

The NAP health policy servers for 802.1X enforcement are the same NPS-based RADIUS servers that are already being used for 802.1X authentication. To configure a NAP health policy server, you must modify the configuration of your existing NPS servers by doing the following:

- Installing SHVs
- Configuring RADIUS server settings
- Configuring health requirement policies for 802.1X enforcement

Installing SHVs

The SHVs that you are using must be installed on each NAP health policy server to be included in the health policy evaluation. The NPS service includes the Windows Security Health Validator SHV to specify the settings of the Windows Security Center on NAP clients running Windows Vista or Windows XP SP3.

The exact method of installation of additional SHVs will depend on the SHV vendor and can include downloading the SHV from a vendor Web page or running a setup program from a vendor-supplied CD-ROM. Check with your SHV vendor for information about the method of installation.

Configuring RADIUS Server Settings

Because the NAP health policy servers are already configured for 802.1X authentication, no changes to typical RADIUS server settings such as RADIUS clients or UDP ports are needed. However, because the 802.1X enforcement deployment will initially use reporting mode, in which noncompliant NAP clients have unlimited access, you might want to change how your NAP health policy servers are logging incoming requests for analysis prior to enabling enforcement mode. You can configure the NPS service to log incoming requests and accounting information in local files or to a Microsoft SQL Server database. For more information, see Chapter 9.

Configuring Health Requirement Policies for 802.1X Enforcement

Because you already have existing network policies for 802.1X-authenticated wireless or wired access, to configure health requirement policies for 802.1X enforcement, you can do one of the following:

- Keep your existing wireless or wired network policies, modify them for compliant NAP clients, and manually create a new connection request policy, health policies for compliant and noncompliant NAP clients, and additional network policies for noncompliant and non-NAP-capable clients.

- Use the Configure NAP Wizard to create a new set of connection request policies, network policies, and health policies for 802.1X-authenticated wireless or wired access, and then manually migrate the custom settings of your existing wireless and wired network policies to the corresponding network policies created by the Configure NAP Wizard. Then, modify your existing wireless and wired network policies.

Because of the amount of automated configuration being done by the Configure NAP Wizard, the second method is recommended and is described in this chapter.

To Create a Set of Policies for 802.1X Enforcement of Wireless or Wired Connections

1. In the Network Policy Server snap-in, in the console tree, click NPS.

2. In the details pane, under Standard Configuration, in the drop-down list, select Network Access Protection (NAP), and then click Configure NAP.

3. On the Select Network Connection Method For Use With NAP page, under Network Connection Method, select IEEE 802.1X (Wireless) or IEEE 802.1X (Wired), and then in the Policy Name box, type a name (or use the name created by the wizard). Figure 17-3 shows an example.

4. Click Next. On the Specify 802.1X Authenticating Switches Or Access Points page, click Next. Because the NAP health policy server is already a RADIUS server to your 802.1X access points, you do not need to add RADIUS clients.

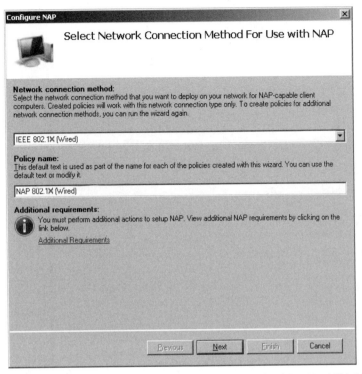

Figure 17-3   The Select Network Connection Method For Use With NAP page

5. On the Configure User Groups and Machine Groups page, configure groups as needed, and then click Next.

6. On the Configure An Authentication Method page, select a computer certificate used by NPS for PEAP authentication, and then select Secure Password (PEAP-MS-CHAP v2), Smart Card Or Other Certificate (EAP-TLS) (for PEAP-TLS), or both as needed. Figure 17-4 shows an example.

7. Click Next. On the Configure Virtual LANs (VLANs) page, in the Organization Network VLAN area, click Configure.

8. In the Virtual LAN (VLAN) Configuration dialog box, on the RADIUS Standard Attributes and Vendor Specific Attributes tabs, configure the attributes needed by your 802.1X access points to specify either the ACL or the VLAN ID for intranet access for compliant NAP clients. See the documentation for your 802.1X access points for information about which attributes to configure to specify the ACL or set the VLAN ID. Figure 17-5 shows an example.

9. Click OK. On the Configure Virtual LANs (VLANs) page, in Restricted Network VLAN, click Configure.

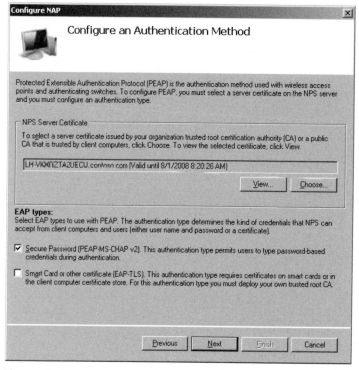

Figure 17-4   The Configure An Authentication Method page

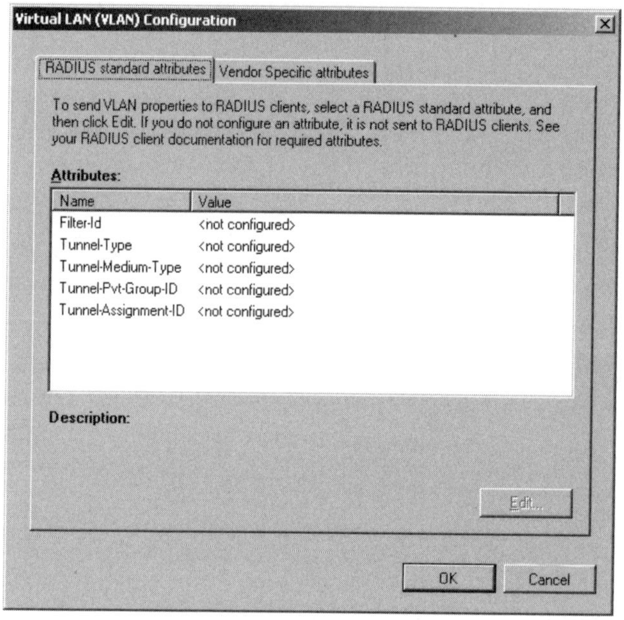

Figure 17-5   The Virtual LAN (VLAN) Configuration dialog box

10. On the RADIUS Standard Attributes and Vendor Specific Attributes tabs, configure the attributes needed by your 802.1X access points to specify either the ACL or the VLAN ID for intranet access. Because you want the initial NAP enforcement mode to be reporting mode (rather than enforcement mode), you must configure the ACL or VLAN ID for intranet access, not restricted access. Additional steps will test the restricted access for noncompliant NAP clients and then configure enforcement mode, in which noncompliant NAP clients will have their network access restricted. Click OK.

11. Click Next. On the Define NAP Health Policy page, select the SHVs that you want to have evaluated for 802.1X enforcement, select the Enable Auto-Remediation Of Client Computers check box as needed, and then select Allow Full Network Access To NAP Ineligible Client Computers, even if you want non-NAP-capable clients to have restricted access. Because you want the initial NAP enforcement mode to be reporting mode (rather than enforcement mode), you must select Allow Full Network Access To NAP Ineligible Client Computers. During the configuration for enforcement mode, you can change the network policy for non-NAP-capable clients to limit their access. Figure 17-6 shows an example.

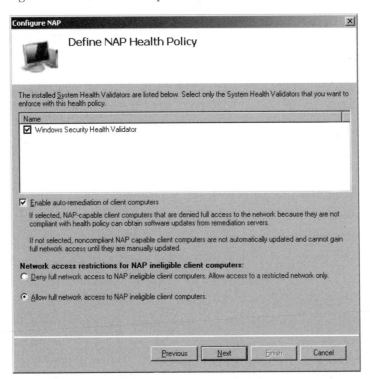

Figure 17-6 The Define NAP Health Policy page

12. Click Next. On the Completing NAP Enforcement Policy And RADIUS Client Configuration page, click Finish.

The Configure NAP Wizard creates the following:

- A health policy for compliant NAP clients based on the SHVs selected in the Configure NAP Wizard

- A health policy for noncompliant NAP clients based on the SHVs selected in the Configure NAP Wizard

- A connection request policy for wireless or wired access requests

- A network policy for compliant NAP clients that allows unlimited access

- A network policy for noncompliant NAP clients that allows restricted access

- A network policy for non-NAP-capable clients

The connection request policy, health policies, and network policies that are created by the Configure NAP Wizard are placed at the bottom of their respective ordered lists. Until you delete or change the order of the existing wireless or wired network policies, the network policies created by the Configure NAP Wizard will not be used for authentication or health evaluation for wireless or wired connections.

You need to ensure that the network policies created by the Configure NAP Wizard have all the correct, customized settings for wireless or wired access that are currently configured for the existing network policies. For example, if your existing network policy for wireless connections contains additional or customized conditions, constraints, or settings, they must be also be configured on the network policies for wireless access created by the Configure NAP Wizard.

The next step is to migrate the custom settings of your existing wireless or wired network policy to the network policies created by the Configure NAP Wizard.

To Configure the Customized Network Policy Settings

1. In the console tree of the Network Policy Server snap-in, expand Policies, and then click Network Policies.

2. In the details pane, double-click your existing wireless or wired network policy.

3. On the Overview tab, in the Network Connection Method area, note whether the Vendor Specific type has been set.

4. On the Conditions tab, note whether there are any additional conditions other than NAS Port Type.

5. On the Constraints tab, note any settings in the list of constraints that have been configured and their configured values.

6. On the Settings tab, note any additional RADIUS standard or vendor-specific attributes that have been configured other than Framed-Protocol and Service-Type. Note any IP filters that have been configured. Click OK.

7. In the details pane, double-click the wireless or wired network policy that was created by the Configure NAP Wizard for compliant NAP clients.

8. On the Overview, Conditions, Constraints, and Settings tabs, configure the custom settings of the existing wireless or wired network policy as determined from performing steps 3 through 6, and then click OK.

9. In the details pane, double-click the wireless or wired network policy that was created by the Configure NAP Wizard for noncompliant NAP clients.

10. On the Overview, Conditions, Constraints, and Settings tabs, configure the custom settings of the existing wireless or wired network policy as determined from performing steps 3 through 6, and then click OK.

11. In the details pane, double-click the wireless or wired network policy that was created by the Configure NAP Wizard for non-NAP-capable computers.

12. On the Overview, Conditions, Constraints, and Settings tabs, configure the custom settings of the existing wireless or wired network policy as determined from performing steps 3 through 6, and then click OK.

In the Configure NAP Wizard, we configured the settings for noncompliant NAP clients to use the unlimited access ACL or VLAN ID. However, because the network policy for noncompliant NAP clients by default allows only limited access (enforcement mode), you must modify this policy to prevent the user from being unnecessarily notified that that user's access is being restricted.

To Configure Reporting Mode

1. In the console tree of the Network Policy Server snap-in, expand Policies, and then click Network Policies.

2. In the details pane, double-click the network policy for noncompliant NAP clients that was created by the Configure NAP Wizard.

3. Click the Settings tab, and then click the NAP Enforcement setting.

4. In the details pane of the network policy properties dialog box, click Allow Full Network Access, and then click OK.

The next step is to ensure that the SHVs that you are using have the correct settings that reflect your health requirements.

To Configure the SHVs for the Required Health Settings

1. In the console tree of the Network Policy Server snap-in, expand Network Access Protection and then System Health Validators.

2. In the details pane, under Name, double-click your SHVs and configure each SHV with your requirements for system health.

   For example, double-click Windows Security Health Validator, and then click Configure. In the Windows Security Health Validator dialog box, configure system health requirements for NAP clients running Windows Vista or Windows XP SP3.

The next step is to ensure that your health policies are configured for the correct SHVs and conditions to reflect your health requirements.

To Configure the Health Policy Conditions for the Required Health Settings

1. In the console tree of the Network Policy Server snap-in, expand Policies, and then Health Policies.

2. In the details pane, double-click the health policies for compliant and noncompliant NAP clients, and make changes as needed to the health evaluation conditions and the selected SHVs.

At this point in the deployment, you have created and configured NAP health requirement policies, but your NAP health policy servers are still using the existing wireless or wired connection request and network policies for wireless or wired access. You must modify the configuration of your connection request policies to ensure that the new connection request policy for 802.1X enforcement is being used for wired or wireless connections.

To Modify Your Connection Request Policies for 802.1X Enforcement

1. In the console tree of the Network Policy Server snap-in, expand Policies and then Connection Request Policies.

2. In the details pane, right-click the name of your existing wireless or wired connection request policy, and then click Disable. When you are confident that the connection request policy that was created by the Configure NAP Wizard is working properly, you can delete this disabled policy.

The connection request policy for wireless or wired connections that was created by the Configure NAP Wizard requires the use of a PEAP-based authentication method and system health checking (the Enable Quarantine Checks check box is selected). The connection attempts of 802.1X clients that do not use a PEAP-based authentication method will be rejected by the NAP health policy server. 802.1X clients that use a PEAP-based authentication method but do not respond to the request for health state will be determined to be non-NAP-capable clients by the NAP health policy server. For example, if a NAP client has system health checking for PEAP disabled (the Enable Quarantine Checks check box is cleared), the NAP client will be determined to be non-NAP-capable.

What you should do with the existing wireless or wired network policies depends on whether you have created a security group that contains computers that are exempted from NAP health evaluation:

- If you created a security group for exempted computers, modify the properties of the existing network policies for wireless or wired access to include group membership in the security group in its conditions.

- If you did not create a security group for exempted computers, move the existing network policies for wireless or wired access so that they are evaluated after the network policies for wireless or wired access that were created by the Configure NAP Wizard.

To modify the conditions of the existing wireless or wired network policies to include the security group for exempted computers, do the following:

1. In the console tree of the Network Policy Server snap-in, expand Policies, and then click Network Policies.

2. In the details pane, double-click the existing network policy for wireless or wired access.

3. On the Conditions tab, click Add. In the Select Condition dialog box, double-click Windows Groups. In the Windows Groups dialog box, click Add Groups, specify the name of the security group for exempted computers, and then click OK three times.

To move the existing wireless or wired network policies so that they are evaluated after the network policies for wireless or wired access that were created by the Configure NAP Wizard, do the following:

1. In the console tree of the Network Policy Server snap-in, expand Policies and then Network Policies.

2. In the details pane, right-click the name of your existing wireless or wired network policy, and then click Move Down.

3. Repeat step 2 as many times as is necessary for the existing wireless or wired network policy to be below the wireless or wired network policies created by the Configure NAP Wizard.

Configuring NAP Clients

To configure your NAP clients, perform the following steps:

- Install SHAs.
- Configure NAP clients through Group Policy.

Installing SHAs

NAP clients running Windows Vista or Windows XP SP3 include the Windows Security Health Agent SHA. If you are using additional SHAs from third-party vendors, you must install them on your NAP clients. The exact method of installation of additional SHAs will depend on the SHA vendor and can include downloading the SHA from a vendor Web page or running a setup program from a vendor-supplied CD-ROM. Check with your SHA vendor for information about the method of installation.

On an enterprise network, you can use the following methods:

- Network management software such as Microsoft Systems Management Server (SMS) or System Center Configuration Manager 2007 to install software across an organization
- Login scripts that execute the setup program for the SHA

Configuring NAP Clients Through Group Policy

Although you can configure NAP clients individually, the best way to centralize the configuration of NAP clients in an Active Directory domain environment is through Group Policy settings, which consists of the following:

- Enabling system health checking for PEAP
- Configuring NAP client settings
- Enabling Windows Security Center
- Configuring the Network Access Protection Agent service for automatic startup

Enabling System Health Checking for PEAP   Although you have already configured your NAP clients to use a PEAP authentication protocol, NAP clients will not respond to a request for their system health state unless the PEAP authentication protocol has system health checking enabled. You can centrally enable system health checking for PEAP through the Group Policy extensions for wired and wireless networks.

To Enable System Health Checking for PEAP in Group Policy

1. Open the Group Policy Management snap-in. In the console tree, expand Forest, expand Domains, and then click your domain. On the Linked Group Policy Objects pane, right-click the appropriate Group Policy Object (the default object is Default Domain Policy), and then click Edit.

2. For wired connections for computers running Windows Server 2008 or Windows Vista, in the console tree of the Group Policy Management Editor snap-in, expand the policy and then Computer Configuration\Windows Settings\Security Settings\Wired Network (IEEE 802.3) Policies.

3. In the details pane, double-click the wired network policy.

4. Click the Security tab, and then click Properties.

5. In the Protected EAP Properties dialog box, select the Enable Quarantine Checks check box, and then click OK twice.

6. For wireless connections, in the console tree, expand Computer Configuration\Windows Settings\Security Settings\Wireless Network (IEEE 802.11) Policies.

7. In the details pane, double-click New Vista Wireless Network Policy.

8. Double-click the appropriate wireless profile, click the Security tab, and then click Properties.

9. In the Protected EAP Properties dialog box, select the Enable Quarantine Checks check box, and then click OK three times.

10. In the details pane, double-click the Windows XP wireless network policy.

11. Click the Preferred Networks tab, double-click the appropriate wireless network, click the IEEE 802.1X tab, and then click Settings.

12. In the Protected EAP Properties dialog box, select the Enable Quarantine Checks check box, and then click OK three times.

Because there are no Group Policy settings to configure the 802.1X authentication properties for wired connection on computers running Windows XP, you must manually enable system health checking for PEAP on NAP clients running Windows XP SP3.

To Manually Enable System Health Checking for PEAP

1. From the Network Connections folder, right-click the wired connection, and then click Properties.

2. Click the Authentication tab, and then click Properties.

3. In the Protected EAP Properties dialog box, select the Enable Quarantine Checks check box, and then click OK twice.

Configuring NAP Client Settings   To configure NAP client settings in Group Policy (equivalent to using the NAP Client Configuration snap-in on an individual computer running Windows Vista), do the following:

1. Open the Group Policy Management snap-in. In the console tree, expand Forest, expand Domains, and then click your domain. On the Linked Group Policy Objects pane, right-click the appropriate Group Policy Object (the default object is Default Domain Policy), and then click Edit.

2. In the console tree of the Group Policy Management Editor snap-in, expand the policy and then Computer Configuration\Windows Settings\Security Settings\Network Access Protection\NAP Client Configuration.

3. In the console tree, click Enforcement Clients.

4. In the details pane, double-click the EAP Quarantine Enforcement Client.

5. On the General tab, click Enable This Enforcement Client, and then click OK.

6. If you want to specify an image that appears in the NAP client user interface (UI), in the console tree, click User Interface Settings, and then in the details pane, double-click User Interface Settings.

7. On the General tab, type the title and description for the text that appears in the NAP client UI, and then type the path to an image file that appears in the UI, or click Browse and specify its location. Click OK.

8. For NAP clients running Windows XP SP3, in the console tree, expand Computer Configuration\Administrative Templates\Windows Components\Network Access Protection.

9. In the details pane, double-click Allow The Network Access Protection Client To Support The 802.1X Enforcement Client Component.

10. On the Setting tab, select Enabled, and then click OK.

Enabling Windows Security Center   To use Group Policy to enable the Windows Security Center on NAP clients that are members of your Active Directory domain, do the following:

1. In the console tree of the Group Policy Management Editor snap-in for the appropriate Group Policy Object, expand Computer Configuration\Administrative Templates\Windows Components, and then click Security Center.

2. In the details pane, double-click Turn On Security Center (Domain PCs Only).

3. On the Setting tab, select Enabled, and then click OK.

Configuring the Network Access Protection Agent Service for Automatic Startup   To use Group Policy to enable automatic startup of the Network Access Protection Agent service on NAP client settings, do the following:

1. In the console tree of the Group Policy Management Editor snap-in for the appropriate Group Policy Object, expand Computer Configuration\Windows Settings\Security Settings\System Services.

2. In the details pane, double-click Network Access Protection Agent.

3. On the Security Policy Setting tab, select the Define This Policy Setting check box, select Automatic, and then click OK.

802.1X Enforcement Deployment Checkpoint for Reporting Mode

At this point in the 802.1X enforcement deployment, NAP clients on your network will have their health state evaluated. Because the 802.1X enforcement deployment is in reporting mode, both compliant and noncompliant NAP clients have unlimited network access to the intranet, and the users of noncompliant NAP clients receive no message in the notification area of their desktop saying that their computers do not meet system health requirements.

While the 802.1X enforcement deployment is in reporting mode, perform an analysis of the NPS events in Windows Logs\Security event log on the NAP health policy servers to determine which NAP clients are not compliant. Take the appropriate actions to remedy their health state, such as installing missing SHAs or providing health update resources on remediation servers.

Testing Restricted Access

Prior to enabling enforcement mode, you must test whether connections of noncompliant NAP clients will be properly assigned the ACL for restricted access or the VLAN ID of the restricted network. To perform this test, do the following:

1. Create a new network policy for noncompliant NAP clients that restricts access for members of a security group containing test computers.

2. Ensure that a noncompliant test computer has its access restricted, is configured with the restricted access ACL or the VLAN ID of the restricted network, and can access only remediation servers on your intranet.

To Create a New Network Policy for the Test Group

1. Designate some NAP client computers on your intranet as test computers for restricted access.

2. Using the Active Directory Users and Computers snap-in, create a security group for testing restricted access, and add the computers determined in step 1 to the group.

3. In the console tree of the Network Policy Server snap-in, expand Policies, and then click Network Policies.

4. Right-click the wireless or wired network policy for noncompliant NAP clients that was created by the Configure NAP Wizard, and then click Duplicate Policy.

5. Double-click the copy of the wireless or wired network policy for noncompliant NAP clients created in step 4.

6. On the Overview tab, in the Policy Name box, type a name for the new network policy. In the Policy State area, select the Policy Enabled check box.

7. On the Conditions tab, click Add. In the Select Condition dialog box, double-click Windows Groups. In the Windows Groups dialog box, click Add Groups, specify the name of the group created in step 2, and then click OK twice.

8. Click the Settings tab. In the RADIUS Attributes area, click Standard. Modify the RADIUS standard attributes to specify either the ACL for restricted access or the VLAN ID of the restricted network. In the RADIUS Attributes area, click Vendor Specific. Modify the vendor-specific attributes as needed to specify either the ACL for restricted access or the VLAN ID of the restricted network.

9. On the Settings tab, under Network Access Protection, click NAP Enforcement. In the details pane, select Allow Limited Access, and then clear the Enable Auto-Remediation Of Client Computers check box.

10. Click Configure. In the Remediation Servers And Troubleshooting URL dialog box, in the Troubleshooting URL box, type the URL to the troubleshooting page on your troubleshooting URL remediation server, and then click OK twice.

11. In the details pane, right-click the name of the duplicated network policy for noncompliant NAP clients, and then click Move Up.

12. Repeat step 11 as many times as is necessary so that the duplicated network policy for noncompliant NAP clients is above the network policy for noncompliant NAP clients that was created by the Configure NAP Wizard.

Next, ensure that the connection for a noncompliant test computer is properly configured with the ACL for restricted access or the VLAN ID of the restricted network.

To Test Restricted Access for a Noncompliant Test Computer

1. Configure a test computer in the security group for testing restricted access to be non-compliant. Depending on your system health requirements, this might be as simple as manually disabling Automatic Updates or Windows Firewall.

2. In the Network Connections folder, force an 802.1X authentication by disabling and then enabling the wireless or wired network adapter.

3. When 802.1X authentication completes, you should see a Network Access Protection message in the notification area of the desktop. You can verify restricted status by running the **ipconfig /all** command.

4. From the test computer, verify that you can reach all the remediation servers and access the troubleshooting URL.

5. From the test computer, verify that you cannot reach servers other than remediation servers on the intranet.

Based on your testing, make any modifications that you need to the duplicated network policy for noncompliant NAP clients, such as the remediation server group, the troubleshooting URL, RADIUS attributes for the restricted access ACL or VLAN restricted network, or the restricted access ACL or VLAN restricted network configuration of your 802.1X access points. If you have made required software for system health and SHA installation software available on remediation servers, ensure that the software and SHAs can be installed from the noncompliant NAP clients.

Configuring the Network Policy for Noncompliant NAP Clients for Deferred Enforcement

After testing restricted network communications for noncompliant NAP clients, determine the date for deferred enforcement mode (the date for which you will configure the noncompliant NAP client network policy for enforcement mode). On this date, noncompliant NAP clients will be placed on the restricted network. In deferred enforcement mode for 802.1X enforcement, noncompliant NAP clients will still be placed on the intranet, but the users will now see a message in their notification area indicating that their computer does not comply with system health requirements.

To Configure Deferred Enforcement Mode

1. In the console tree of the Network Policy Server snap-in, expand Policies, and then click Network Policies.

2. In the details pane, double-click the wireless or wired network policy for noncompliant NAP clients that was created by the Configure NAP Wizard.

3. Click the Settings tab, and then click the NAP Enforcement setting.

4. In the details pane of the network policy properties dialog box, select Allow Full Network Access For A Limited Time, specify the date and time that enforcement mode will be configured on the NAP health policy servers, and then click OK.

Perform this procedure on each of your NAP health policy servers.

Configuring Network Policy for Enforcement Mode

Because you have already configured and tested a network policy that restricts access for non-compliant NAP clients (the duplicated network policy for noncompliant NAP clients), to enable enforcement mode, you will modify this duplicated network policy and disable the original network policy for noncompliant NAP clients that was created by the Configure NAP Wizard.

On the date for enforcement mode, configure enforcement mode on your NAP health policy servers.

To Configure Enforcement Mode

1. In the console tree of the Network Policy Server snap-in, expand Policies, and then click Network Policies.

2. In the details pane, double-click the duplicated network policy for noncompliant NAP clients when you were testing restricted network access.

3. On the Conditions tab, in the Conditions list, click Windows Groups, and then click Remove.

4. On the Settings tab, under Network Access Protection, click NAP Enforcement. In the details pane, under Auto Remediation, select the Enable Auto-Remediation Of Client Computers check box, and then click OK.

5. In the details pane, right-click the original network policy for noncompliant NAP clients that was created by the Configure NAP Wizard, and then click Delete.

At this point, the network policy that you used to test restricted access for noncompliant NAP clients now applies to all of your NAP clients, and the original network policy for noncompliant NAP clients that was created by the Configure NAP Wizard has been deleted.

To limit the access for non-NAP-capable clients, on the date for enforcement mode, you must configure a network policy for non-NAP-capable clients that restricts their access. Because the duplicated network policy for noncompliant NAP clients has already been configured and tested for restricted access, you can duplicate and then modify this policy for non-NAP-capable clients.

To Limit the Access of Non-NAP-Capable Clients

1. In the console tree of the Network Policy Server snap-in, expand Policies, and then click Network Policies.

2. Right-click the duplicated network policy for noncompliant NAP clients, and then click Duplicate Policy. We are duplicating the duplicated network policy for noncompliant NAP clients because it already contains your custom conditions and settings for wireless or wired connections.

3. Double-click the new network policy.

4. On the Overview tab, in the Policy Name box, type a name for the new network policy. In the Policy State area, select the Policy Enabled check box.

5. On the Conditions tab, click Add. In the Select Condition dialog box, double-click NAP-Capable Computers. In the NAP-Capable Computers dialog box, select Only Computers That Are Not NAP-Capable, and then click OK.

6. On the Conditions tab, click the Health Policy condition, click Remove, and then click OK.

7. In the details pane of the Network Policy Server snap-in, move the new network policy so that it is just above the original network policy for non-NAP-capable clients that was created by the Configure NAP Wizard.

8. Right-click the original network policy for non-NAP-capable clients that was created by the Configure NAP Wizard, and then click Delete.

The deployment of 802.1X enforcement is complete. Noncompliant NAP clients and (optionally) non-NAP-capable clients will have their access restricted through either an ACL applied to the 802.1X connection or by placing the connection on the restricted network VLAN.

Ongoing Maintenance

The areas of maintenance for an 802.1X enforcement deployment are as follows:

- Adding a NAP client
- Adding a new SHA and SHV
- Managing 802.1X access points

Adding a NAP Client

To add a NAP client, do the following:

1. Join the NAP client computer to the domain.

2. Install the SHAs on the NAP client computer.

For a new non–domain-joined NAP client, follow the steps in the "Configuring NAP Client Settings" section earlier in this chapter.

Adding a New SHA and SHV

To add a new SHA and SHV to your 802.1X enforcement deployment, you must do the following:

1. If needed, install the software or components on your remediation servers for automatic remediation required by the new SHA.

2. Install the required software and SHA on your NAP clients. For more information, see "Configuring NAP Client Settings" earlier in this chapter.

3. Install the SHV on your NAP health policy servers.

4. If needed, on the NAP health policy servers, in the Network Access Protection\System Health Validators node of the NPS snap-in, configure the settings of the SHV for your system health requirements.

5. On the NAP health policy servers, modify the health policies for compliant and noncompliant NAP clients to include the new SHV in its evaluation.

Managing 802.1X Access Points

For information about managing 802.1X access points, see the "Managing Wireless APs" section in Chapter 10 and the "Managing 802.1X-Capable Switches" section in Chapter 11.

Troubleshooting

Because of the different components and processes involved, troubleshooting an 802.1X enforcement deployment can be a difficult task. This section describes the troubleshooting tools that are provided with Windows Server 2008 and Windows Vista and how to troubleshoot 802.1X enforcement starting from the NAP client.

Troubleshooting Tools

Microsoft provides the following tools to troubleshoot 802.1X enforcement:

- TCP/IP troubleshooting tools
- Netsh tool
- NAP client event logging
- NPS event logging
- NPS authentication and accounting logging
- Netsh NAP tracing
- Network Monitor 3.1

TCP/IP Troubleshooting Tools

The Ipconfig tool displays the state of a NAP client. At a command prompt on a NAP client, run the **ipconfig /all** command. In the Windows IP Configuration section of the display, the state of the NAP client is listed as the System Quarantine State. The System Quarantine State is displayed as either Not Restricted or Restricted.

Additional standard TCP/IP troubleshooting tools are Ping and Nslookup to test reachability and name resolution.

Netsh Tool

Beyond the state of the NAP client as shown in the **ipconfig /all** command, you can gather additional NAP client configuration information by running the following commands:

- **netsh nap client show configuration**   Displays the local NAP client configuration including the list of NAP enforcement clients and their state (enabled or disabled), and the state of NAP client tracing

- **netsh nap client show grouppolicy**   Displays the same NAP client settings as the **netsh nap client show configuration** command for the settings obtained through Group Policy

- **netsh nap client show state**   Displays detailed NAP client state, enforcement client state, and SHA state

> **Note**   The display for the netsh nap client show configuration and netsh nap client show grouppolicy commands does not show which set of settings, local or Group Policy–based, are currently active on the NAP client. If any NAP client settings are obtained through Group Policy, the entire set of NAP client settings is specified by Group Policy and all local NAP client settings are ignored.

NAP Client Event Logging

Use the Event Viewer snap-in to check the events in the Windows event log created by the Network Access Protection Client service. On computers running Windows Vista or Windows Server 2008, use the Event Viewer snap-in to view events in Applications and Services Logs\Microsoft\Windows\Network Access Protection\Operational. On computers running Windows XP SP3, use the Event Viewer snap-in to view events in the System event log.

NPS Event Logging

Use the Event Viewer snap-in to check the Windows Logs\Security event log for NPS events. NPS event log entries contain a lot of information about the NAP health evaluation, including the name of the matching connection request policy (the Proxy Policy Name field in the description of the event) and the matching network policy (the Network Policy Name field in the description of the event). Viewing NPS events in the Windows Logs\Security event log is one of the most useful troubleshooting methods to obtain information about NAP health evaluations.

NPS Logging

By default, NPS will log authentication and accounting data to the *%SystemRoot%*\System32\LogFiles folder in a database-compatible (comma-delimited) text file. You can also configure NPS to perform SQL Server logging and then analyze the NPS authentication and accounting data in a SQL Server database.

Netsh NAP Tracing

The Network Access Protection Agent service has an extensive tracing capability that you can use to troubleshoot complex network problems. You can enable netsh NAP tracing by running the **netsh nap client set tracing state=enable level=basic|advanced|verbose** command. The log files are stored in the *%SystemRoot%*\Tracing folder. Netsh NAP tracing files can be sent to Microsoft customer support staff for analysis.

Network Monitor 3.1

Use Network Monitor 3.1 or later, a packet capture and analysis tool available as a free download from Microsoft, to capture and view the traffic sent between NAP clients, 802.1X access points, and NAP health policy servers. For example, you can use Network Monitor 3.1 to capture the RADIUS traffic between an 802.1X access point and the NAP health policy server to determine the contents of RADIUS messages, such as the RADIUS attributes for specifying the ACL or VLAN ID.

The proper interpretation of this traffic requires an in-depth understanding of RADIUS and other protocols. Network Monitor captures can be saved as files and sent to Microsoft customer support staff for analysis.

> **On the Disc**   You can link to the download site for Network Monitor from the companion CD-ROM.

Troubleshooting 802.1X Enforcement

This section describes how to troubleshoot an 802.1X enforcement deployment by starting at the NAP client. This is the approach used by many technical support departments in organizations and reflects a multitier analysis and escalation path to determine the source of a problem and its solution. For example, the IT department of an organization might have the following tiers:

- **Tier 1**   Help desk staff, who can provide an initial assessment of problems and solutions based on an analysis of the client (the NAP client for 802.1X enforcement)

- **Tier 2**   Windows network and infrastructure services staff, who manage the 802.1X access points, remediation servers, and NAP health policy servers

When troubleshooting 802.1X enforcement, it is important to first determine the scope of the problem. If your wireless or wired clients cannot perform 802.1X authentication, you must troubleshoot that problem independently of NAP and 802.1X enforcement. If all of your wireless or wired clients are experiencing 802.1X enforcement problems, issues might exist in your NAP health policy servers. If all of your wireless or wired clients that are connected to a specific 802.1X access point are experiencing 802.1X enforcement problems, issues might exist in the configuration of the 802.1X access point or its configured NAP health policy servers. If only specific wireless or wired clients are experiencing 802.1X enforcement problems, issues might exist for those individual clients.

Troubleshooting the NAP Client

To troubleshoot the NAP client, do the following:

- Verify whether the NAP client has successfully completed 802.1X authentication using a PEAP-based authentication method. If not, please see the "Troubleshooting" section of Chapter 10 (for wireless networks) or Chapter 11 (for wired networks).

- Verify whether the NAP client is compliant or noncompliant by running the **ipconfig /all** command.

If the NAP client is using a PEAP-based authentication method but is being treated as a non-NAP-capable client, verify that system health checking for PEAP has been enabled on the NAP client (select the Enable Quarantine Checks check box in the Protected EAP Properties dialog box), either through Group Policy or through the properties of the wired connection or wireless network.

If the NAP client is noncompliant and is not autoremediating its health state, verify the following:

- **Network reachability from the NAP client to the IP addresses of the remediation servers on the restricted network** You can use the Ping tool, but because of default Windows Firewall rules, incoming ICMP or ICMPv6 traffic on the remediation servers might be blocked.

- **Name resolution from the NAP client** Use the Ping and Nslookup tools for the names of the remediation servers on the restricted network. Verify that the DNS names that the NAP client uses successfully resolve to the correct IPv4 or IPv6 addresses.

- **That the Network Access Protection Agent service is started on the NAP client and that it is configured to automatically start** Run the **netsh nap client show state** command to determine the service state, and use the Services snap-in to configure the Network Access Protection Agent service.

- **That the EAP Quarantine Enforcement Client is enabled** Run the **netsh nap client show configuration** command. If needed, use the Group Policy Management Editor snap-in (for Active Directory–based GPOs), the NAP Client Configuration snap-in (for the local GPO), or the **netsh nap client set enforcement 79623 enable** command to enable the EAP Quarantine enforcement client.

- **That the NAP client has all the appropriate SHAs installed** Run the **netsh nap client show state** command. If you are using the Windows Security Health Agent SHA, verify that the Windows Security Center is enabled.

Beyond these verification steps, use the Event Viewer snap-in on the NAP client to view the NAP client events in Applications and Services Logs\Microsoft\Windows\Network Access Protection\Operational for a NAP client running Windows Vista and in System for a NAP client Windows XP SP3. Use the NAP client events to perform additional troubleshooting. Note the correlation ID specified in the description of the NAP client events. That correlation ID can be used to find the corresponding event on the NPS server.

Troubleshooting the 802.1X Access Points

To troubleshoot the 802.1X access points, do the following:

- For VLAN-based 802.1X enforcement, verify that the 802.1X access points have been configured correctly with the VLAN IDs of the intranet and the restricted network.

- For ACL-based 802.1X enforcement, verify that the 802.1X access points have been correctly configured with an ACL corresponding to the remediation servers for the location of the 802.1X access point on the intranet.

- Utilize debug mode on 802.1X access points to provide additional detail for 802.1X authentication attempts.

Troubleshooting the NAP Health Policy Servers

To troubleshoot the NAP health policy servers, do the following:

- **Verify that all the RADIUS clients corresponding to 802.1X access points have the RADIUS Client Is NAP-Capable check box cleared on the Settings tab of the properties dialog box of the RADIUS client.**   You can use the Network Policy Server snap-in or the **netsh nps show client** command.

- **Verify that the health requirement policies are correctly configured for 802.1X enforcement.**   You can use the Network Policy Server snap-in or **netsh nps show** commands. Verify that there is a correctly configured set of connection request policies, network policies, health policies, and SHVs that reflect your health requirements and the correct behavior for compliant, noncompliant, and non-NAP-capable clients. Verify the order of the connection request policies and the network policies.

- **Verify that the noncompliant NAP client network policy has been configured to automatically remediate health status.**   You can use the Network Policy Server snap-in or the **netsh nps show np** command.

- **Verify that the network policy for compliant NAP clients is correctly configured.** You can use the Network Policy Server snap-in or the **netsh nps show np** command. For ACL-based 802.1X enforcement, verify the RADIUS standard and vendor-specific attributes to configure the 802.1X access points with the ACL corresponding to intranet access. For VLAN-based 802.1X enforcement, verify the RADIUS standard and vendor-specific attributes to configure the 802.1X access points with the VLAN ID of the intranet.

- **Verify that the network policy for noncompliant NAP clients is correctly configured.** You can use the Network Policy Server snap-in or the **netsh nps show np** command. For ACL-based 802.1X enforcement, verify the RADIUS standard and vendor-specific attributes to configure the 802.1X access points with the ACL corresponding to restricted access. For VLAN-based 802.1X enforcement, verify the RADIUS standard and vendor-specific attributes to configure the 802.1X access points with the VLAN ID of the restricted network.

- **Verify that the network policy for non-NAP-capable clients is correctly configured.** You can use the Network Policy Server snap-in or the **netsh nps show np** command. Verify that the network policy for non-NAP-capable clients is configured with either the ACL or VLAN ID settings for unlimited or restricted access.

Beyond these actions, use the Event Viewer snap-in on the NAP health policy server to view the NPS events in Windows Logs\Security event log for events corresponding to RADIUS messages sent by the 802.1X access points for authentication and system health validation of NAP clients. Use the correlation ID of the NAP client event to locate the corresponding NPS event in the Security log. To view the NPS events, configure a filter with the Event Sources set to Microsoft Windows Security Auditing and the Task Category set to Network Policy Server.

Troubleshooting Remediation Servers

To troubleshoot remediation servers, verify that the remediation servers are reachable by noncompliant NAP clients. For health update servers, verify that they have been correctly configured to provide the resources necessary to remediate the health of a SHA on a NAP client. See the documentation provided by the vendor of the SHA.

Chapter Summary

Deploying 802.1X enforcement involves configuration of Active Directory, 802.1X access points, NAP health policy servers, remediation servers, and NAP clients. After an initial configuration in reporting mode, test enforcement mode on a subset of NAP clients. Last, configure enforcement mode for all 802.1X clients. After deploying enforcement mode, ongoing maintenance of 802.1X enforcement consists of adding NAP clients, adding SHAs and SHVs, and managing 802.1X access points. To troubleshoot 802.1X enforcement, verify network connectivity and configuration for NAP clients, 802.1X access points, NAP health policy servers, and remediation servers.

Additional Information

For additional information about NAP, see the following:

- Chapter 14, "Network Access Protection Overview"
- Chapter 15, "Preparing for Network Access Protection"
- Chapter 16, "IPsec Enforcement"
- Chapter 18, "VPN Enforcement"
- Chapter 19, "DHCP Enforcement"
- Windows Server 2008 Technical Library at *http://technet.microsoft.com/windowsserver/2008*
- Windows Server 2008 Help and Support
- "Network Access Protection" (*http://www.microsoft.com/nap*)

For additional information about Active Directory, see the following:

- *Windows Server 2008 Active Directory Resource Kit* by Stan Reimer, Mike Mulcare, Conan Kezema, and Byron Wright, with the Microsoft Active Directory Team, available both as a stand-alone title and as part of the *Windows Server 2008 Resource Kit* (both from Microsoft Press, 2008)
- Windows Server 2008 Technical Library at *http://technet.microsoft.com/windowsserver/2008*
- Windows Server 2008 Help and Support
- "Windows Server Active Directory" (*http://www.microsoft.com/ad*)

For additional information about Group Policy, see the following:

- *Windows Group Policy Resource Kit: Windows Server 2008 and Windows Vista* by Derek Melber, Group Policy MVP, with the Microsoft Windows Group Policy Team (Microsoft Press, 2008)
- Windows Server 2008 Technical Library at *http://technet.microsoft.com/windowsserver/2008*
- Windows Server 2008 Help and Support
- "Windows Server Group Policy" (*http://www.microsoft.com/gp*)

For additional information about RADIUS and NPS, see the following:

- Chapter 9, "Authentication Infrastructure"
- Windows Server 2008 Technical Library at *http://technet.microsoft.com/windowsserver/2008*
- Windows Server 2008 Help and Support
- "Network Policy Server" (*http://www.microsoft.com/nps*)

For additional information about IEEE 802.1X for wireless and wired networks, see the following:

- Chapter 10, "IEEE 802.11 Wireless Networks"

- Chapter 11, "IEEE 802.1X–Authenticated Wired Networks"

- Windows Server 2008 Technical Library at *http://technet.microsoft.com/windowsserver/2008*

- Windows Server 2008 Help and Support

- "Wireless Networking" (*http://www.microsoft.com/wifi*)

- "Wired Networking with 802.1X Authentication" (*http://www.microsoft.com/technet/network/wired/default.mspx*)

Chapter 18
VPN Enforcement

This chapter provides information about how to design, deploy, maintain, and troubleshoot virtual private network (VPN) enforcement for remote access VPN connections with Network Access Protection (NAP). This chapter assumes the following:

- That you understand the role of Active Directory, Group Policy, and Remote Authentication Dial-In User Service (RADIUS) elements of a Microsoft Windows–based authentication infrastructure for network access. For more information, see Chapter 9, "Authentication Infrastructure."

- That you have a working remote access VPN solution. For more information, see Chapter 12, "Remote Access VPN Connections."

- That you understand the components of NAP and how to prepare your network for NAP. For more information, see Chapter 14, "Network Access Protection Overview," and Chapter 15, "Preparing for Network Access Protection."

Understanding VPN Enforcement

VPN enforcement in NAP consists of a NAP health policy server and a Remote Access Quarantine enforcement client on NAP clients. The NAP health policy server evaluates the health of the NAP client and instructs the remote access VPN server to restrict the access of noncompliant NAP clients.

VPN enforcement occurs in conjunction with the Point-to-Point Protocol (PPP) authentication process for the remote access connection. After the authentication and health evaluation, a NAP client is in one of the following states:

- Unauthenticated
- Authenticated with unlimited access (a compliant NAP client)
- Authenticated with restricted access (a noncompliant NAP client)

How It Works: Details of VPN Enforcement

VPN enforcement uses a set of packet filters to restrict the access of the noncompliant NAP client to the remediation servers on the intranet. A set of Internet Protocol version 4 (IPv4) or Internet Protocol version 6 (IPv6) packet filters is configured on the NAP health policy server. The VPN server applies the packet filters to the remote access connection and silently discards all packets that are not allowed by the filters.

The following process occurs when a NAP-capable VPN client running the Windows Vista operating system connects to a VPN server running the Windows Server 2008 operating system:

1. The VPN client initiates a connection to the VPN server.

2. The VPN server sends an Extensible Authentication Protocol (EAP)–Request/ Identity message to the EAP client component on the VPN client.

3. The EAP client on the VPN client responds with an EAP-Response/Identity message that contains the user name of the VPN client.

4. The VPN server sends the EAP-Response/Identity message as a RADIUS Access-Request message to the NAP health policy server. For all subsequent EAP-based messages, the logical communication occurs between the NAP health policy server and the EAP client on the VPN client, using the VPN server as a pass-through device. Messages between the VPN server and the NAP health policy server are a series of RADIUS messages.

5. The NAP health policy server sends an EAP-Request/Start Protected EAP (PEAP) message to the EAP client on the VPN client.

6. The EAP client on the VPN client and the NAP health policy server exchange a series of Transport Layer Security (TLS) messages to negotiate a protected TLS session.

7. The NAP health policy server requires that the VPN client authenticate itself using its client credentials and a PEAP authentication method such as PEAP-Microsoft Challenge Handshake Authentication Protocol version 2 (MS-CHAP v2).

8. The VPN client authenticates itself to the NAP health policy server using the negotiated PEAP authentication method.

9. The NAP health policy server sends a request for the System Statement of Health (SSoH) to the VPN client by using a PEAP–Type-Length-Value (TLV) message.

10. The EAP client passes the request for the SSoH to the Remote Access Quarantine enforcement client, which then queries the NAP Agent component for the SSoH.

11. The Remote Access Quarantine enforcement client passes the SSoH to the EAP client, which passes it to the NAP health policy server by using a PEAP-TLV message.

12. The NPS service on the NAP health policy server extracts the SSoH from the PEAP-TLV message sent in step 9 and passes it to the NAP Administration Server component.

13. The NAP Administration Server component passes the Statements of Health (SoHs) in the SSoH to the appropriate System Health Validators (SHVs).

14. The SHVs analyze the contents of their SoHs and return Statements of Health Response (SoHRs) to the NAP Administration Server.

15. The NAP Administration Server passes the SoHRs to NPS.

16. The NPS service compares the SoHRs to the configured set of health policies and creates the System Statement of Health Response (SSoHR).

17. The NPS service sends a PEAP-TLV message containing the SSoHR to the EAP client on the VPN client.

18. The EAP client on the VPN client passes the SSoHR to the Remote Access Quarantine enforcement client, which passes it to the NAP Agent component.

19. The NPS service sends a RADIUS Access-Accept message to the VPN server. Then, one of the following occurs:

   ❑ If the VPN connection is unlimited, the RADIUS Access-Accept message does not contain IP packet filters to restrict network access. After the VPN connection completes, the NAP client will have unlimited network access.

   ❑ If the VPN connection has restricted access, the RADIUS Access-Accept message also contains a set of IP packet filters that restrict the traffic of the VPN client to the remediation servers.

If the VPN client is noncompliant, the following process performs the remediation required for unlimited network access:

1. The NAP Agent passes the SoHRs in the SSoHR to the appropriate System Health Agents (SHAs).

2. Each SHA analyzes its SoHR, and based on the contents, performs the remediation as needed to correct the NAP client's system health state.

3. Each SHA that required remediation passes an updated SoH to the NAP Agent.

4. The NAP Agent collects the updated SoHs, creates a new SSoH, and passes it to the Remote Access Quarantine enforcement client, which passes it to the EAP client.

5. The EAP client passes the new SSoH to the NAP health policy server by using a PEAP-TLV message.

6. The NPS service on the NAP health policy server extracts the SSoH from the PEAP-TLV message and passes it to the NAP Administration Server component.

7. The NAP Administration Server component passes the SoHs in the SSoH to the appropriate SHVs.

8. The SHVs analyze the contents of their SoHs and return an SoHR to the NAP Administration Server component.

9. The NAP Administration Server passes the SoHRs to the NPS service.

10. The NPS service compares the SoHRs to the configured set of health policies and creates the SSoHR.

> 11. The NPS service constructs and sends a PEAP-TLV message containing the SSoHR to the EAP client on the VPN client.
>
> 12. The NPS service constructs and sends a RADIUS Access-Accept message to the VPN server that does not include IP packet filters for limited network access.
>
> 13. Upon receipt of the RADIUS Access-Accept message, the VPN server removes the IP packet filters from the VPN connection, allowing the VPN client unlimited network access.

Planning and Design Considerations

When deploying VPN enforcement, you must consider the following in your planning:

- Use of Network Access Quarantine Control
- Security group for NAP exemptions
- Types of packet filtering
- VPN authentication methods
- VPN servers
- NAP clients

Use of Network Access Quarantine Control

Network Access Quarantine Control, a feature of the Windows Server 2003 operating system with Service Pack 1 (SP1), delays normal remote access to a private network until an administrator-provided script has examined and validated the configuration of the remote access computer. When a remote access computer initiates a connection to a remote access server, the user is authenticated, and the remote access computer is assigned an IPv4 address. However, the connection is placed in quarantine mode, in which network access is limited. The administrator-provided script is run on the remote access computer. When the script notifies the remote access server that it has successfully run, and the remote access computer complies with current network policies, quarantine mode is removed, and the remote access computer is granted normal remote access. Network Access Quarantine Control is not the same as VPN enforcement in NAP.

The quarantine restrictions placed on individual remote access connections consist of the following:

- A set of quarantine packet filters that restrict the traffic that can be sent to and from a quarantined remote access client
- A quarantine session timer that restricts the amount of time the client can remain connected in quarantine mode before being disconnected

Network Access Quarantine Control uses a Connection Manager package and a notifier program (Rqc.exe) on the VPN client and the Remote Access Quarantine Agent service (Rqs.exe) on the VPN server. The notifier sends the Remote Access Quarantine Agent service a message indicating that the VPN client has successfully passed the requirements of the script.

If your organization is already using Network Access Quarantine Control, you should consider the following when deploying VPN enforcement with NAP:

■ Coexistence of Network Access Quarantine Control and VPN enforcement

■ Migration of VPN clients from Network Access Quarantine Control to VPN enforcement

Windows Server 2008 supports Network Access Quarantine Control whether you have upgraded a VPN server running Windows Server 2003 with the Remote Access Quarantine Agent service already installed or have installed the Routing and Remote Access role service of the Network Policy and Access Services role.

Network Policy Server in Windows Server 2008 also supports Network Access Quarantine Control whether you have upgraded an Internet Authentication Service (IAS) RADIUS server running Windows Server 2003 or have installed the service when you installed the Network Policy Server role service of the Network Policy and Access Services role. During an upgrade, the remote access policies for Network Access Quarantine Control in IAS will be upgraded to network policies in NPS.

You can now configure VPN enforcement on the Windows Server 2008–based VPN server. The NPS RADIUS server can simultaneously perform Network Access Quarantine Control for non-NAP-capable VPN clients and VPN enforcement for VPN clients that are NAP-capable.

After both types of enforcement are in place and working correctly, you can begin to migrate your remote access clients from Network Access Quarantine Control to VPN enforcement. This is done by upgrading your remote access clients to a version of Windows that supports NAP and then configuring the NAP client for VPN enforcement. Before the upgrade and NAP client configuration, the remote access VPN client will be subject to Network Access Quarantine Control. After the upgrade and NAP client configuration, the remote access VPN client will be subject to VPN enforcement.

> **More Info**   For the details of Network Access Quarantine Control coexistence and migration with VPN enforcement, see the Windows Server 2008 Technical Library at *http://technet.microsoft.com/windowsserver/2008*.

Security Group for NAP Exemptions

To exempt specific users from VPN enforcement by preventing system health evaluation at the NAP health policy server, create a security group whose members contain the user accounts of exempted users. On the NAP health policy server, create a network policy that grants remote access VPN access and uses the Windows Groups condition set to the security group for the exempted users, but does not use the Health Policy condition.

Types of Packet Filtering

To restrict the access of noncompliant NAP clients for VPN enforcement, you can do either or both of the following:

- Configure a remediation server group.
- Configure IPv4 and IPv6 packet filters.

Configuring a Remediation Server Group

When you configure a remediation server group for the NAP Enforcement setting for the network policy for noncompliant NAP clients, you specify the list of IPv4 or IPv6 addresses with which the noncompliant NAP client can communicate. Each address in the list becomes a pair of packet filters: an inbound filter from the VPN client to the address and an outbound filter from the address to the VPN client. Because the filter specification is fairly simple, it is easy to specify and takes less space in the RADIUS message that is sent from the NAP health policy server to the VPN server.

Configuring IPv4 and IPv6 Packet Filters

When you configure IPv4 and IPv6 packet filters for the IP Filters setting for the network policy for noncompliant NAP clients, you can specify the following:

- For inbound IPv4 traffic from the NAP client, the destination address or address range, the IPv4 protocol, Transmission Control Protocol (TCP) source and destination ports, User Datagram Protocol (UDP) source and destination ports, and Internet Control Message Protocol (ICMP) types and codes

- For outbound IPv4 traffic from the NAP client, the source address or address range, the IPv4 protocol, TCP source and destination ports, UDP source and destination ports, and ICMP types and codes

- For inbound IPv6 traffic from the NAP client, the destination address or address range, the IPv6 protocol, TCP source and destination ports, UDP source and destination ports, and ICMP for IPv6 (ICMPv6) types and codes

- For outbound IPv6 traffic from the NAP client, the source address or address range, the IPv6 protocol, TCP source and destination ports, UDP source and destination ports, and ICMPv6 types and codes

Configuring IPv4 and IPv6 packet filters allows more flexibility in specifying the exact types of traffic that are allowed for the noncompliant NAP client. You can use IPv4 and IPv6 packet filters to better protect your remediation servers from potentially malicious noncompliant NAP clients. For example, for the troubleshooting URL remediation server, you can specify an inbound IPv4 filter to the destination IPv4 address of the server and for TCP destination port 80. You can also specify an outbound IPv4 filter from the source IPv4 address of the server and for TCP source port 80. With these filters, no other traffic to the troubleshooting URL Web server is allowed.

However, the filter specification for IPv4 and IPv6 packet filters is fairly complex because so many fields in the traffic are specified. IPv4 and IPv6 packet filters take more space in the RADIUS message that is sent from the NAP health policy server to the VPN server. Therefore, you can use fewer IPv4 or IPv6 packet filters than addresses in a remediation server group.

VPN Authentication Methods

Because VPN enforcement uses PEAP-TLV messages to transfer system health status and remediation information between the remote access VPN client and the NAP health policy server, you must use a PEAP-based authentication protocol in your remote access solution. Windows Vista, Windows Server 2008, and the Windows XP operating system with Service Pack 3 (SP3) include support for the following PEAP-based authentication methods:

- PEAP-MS-CHAP v2
- PEAP-TLS

You can also use other PEAP-based authentication methods that are supplied by third-party vendors.

If you are currently using EAP-TLS and either registry-based user certificates or smart cards, you must change your authentication method to use PEAP-TLS prior to deploying VPN enforcement. For more information, see Chapter 12.

VPN Servers

VPN servers for VPN enforcement must use Windows Server 2008. Windows Server 2003 does not support PEAP-based authentication methods for remote access VPN clients.

Changes to the health state on the NAP client will cause the NAP client to perform a new health evaluation. If the health state does not change, the NAP client does not perform a new health evaluation. If the network administrator changes the health requirement policy for VPN enforcement on the NAP health policy server, it is possible for NAP clients that have unlimited access to be noncompliant with the changed health requirement policy. When health requirement policy changes on the NAP health policy server, there is no mechanism to contact NAP clients to perform a new health evaluation.

For VPN enforcement, there is no recommended method to force the VPN clients to reevaluate their health state with the NAP health policy server. Many VPN connections are short-lived;

they exist for limited periods of time so that users can check e-mail or access an intranet resource. To force the VPN client to reauthenticate and reevaluate their health state could cause connectivity problems because the VPN client can receive a different set of addresses for the VPN connection. For long-lived VPN connections, such as those for users who telecommute, the NAP components on the NAP client, such as SHAs, can periodically validate their health state. When the SHA validation occurs, the health status of the VPN client is also validated.

NAP Clients

You must consider the following planning and design issues for your NAP clients:

- NAP client operating system
- Non-NAP-capable clients
- NAP client domain membership
- Installing NAP client components
- Configuration settings
- Configuration methods

NAP Client Operating System

The versions of Windows that include NAP client functionality are the following:

- Windows Vista
- Windows Server 2008
- Windows XP SP3

Third-party vendors can supply NAP client functionality for other versions of Windows or for non–Windows-based operating systems.

Non-NAP-Capable Clients

You must determine whether non-NAP-capable clients will be allowed unlimited access or restricted access to the intranet. NAP-capable VPN client computers that do not have both the Network Access Protection Agent service started and the Remote Access Quarantine enforcement client enabled will be treated as non-NAP-capable clients.

NAP Client Domain Membership

NAP clients should be members of your Active Directory domain to participate in Group Policy–based configuration of NAP client settings. NAP clients that are not domain members must be manually configured with NAP client settings.

Installing NAP Client Components

With other NAP enforcement methods, installing NAP client components such as the set of SHAs is easier because the computers are all typically part of a managed environment. As domain members, the computers can receive Group Policy settings and have software components automatically installed through desktop management software, such as Microsoft Systems Management Server or Microsoft System Center Configuration Manager 2007, or other methods such as logon scripts.

With VPN enforcement, the VPN client computers can be managed or unmanaged. In some cases, the managed computer is a laptop computer that is rarely connected to the organization's network through a wired or wireless connection. For unmanaged computers, users can initiate remote access VPN connections from home computers or personal laptops that are not members of the organization's domain.

For unmanaged computers and for computers that rarely connect directly to their organization's network, you must provide ways for those computers to install the SHAs needed for health compliance. The following are some of the ways in which you can provide NAP client components to VPN client computers:

- **CMAK package**   You can create a Connection Manager Administration Kit (CMAK) package that contains the SHAs as embedded files and runs a post-connect action to install the SHAs on the NAP clients. This method is not recommended because the CMAK package must contain the SHA installation files for possibly multiple SHAs. This can make the size of the CMAK package very large and impractical to deploy, especially across low-bandwidth connections.

- **Installation points on the Internet**   You can make the SHA installation files available on an Internet Web page. Users must be informed of this location and can install the SHAs before making a remote access VPN connection.

- **Installation points on the remediation servers**   You can make the SHA installation files available on a remediation server. Users can install the SHAs before or after making a remote access VPN connection. If you make the SHA installation files available on the troubleshooting URL Web server, users on noncompliant NAP clients will automatically be informed of its location.

Configuration Settings

Consider the following configuration settings for your NAP clients:

- You must install the software for system health and their corresponding SHAs that are being used to evaluate system health.

- If you are using the Windows Security Health Agent SHA for NAP clients running Windows Vista or Windows XP SP3, enable Windows Security Center manually or, for domain members, through Group Policy. Unmanaged computers running Windows Vista or Windows XP SP3 have Windows Security Center enabled by default.

- Enable the Remote Access Quarantine enforcement client.
- Enable automatic startup for the Network Access Protection Agent service.

Manual Configuration

You must configure NAP client settings individually by doing the following:

- Installing required software and their corresponding SHAs
- For NAP clients running Windows Vista, Windows Server 2008, or Windows XP SP3, enabling the Remote Access Quarantine enforcement client
- For NAP clients running Windows Vista or Windows XP SP3, enabling the Windows Security Center
- Enabling automatic startup for the Network Access Protection Agent service

Automated Configuration for Managed Computers

For managed computers, you can install required software and their corresponding SHAs through desktop management software or other methods, such as logon scripts. Additionally, you can use Active Directory and Group Policy settings to do the following:

- Enable the Windows Security Center.
- Enable the Remote Access Quarantine enforcement client.
- Configure the NAP Agent service for automatic start-up.

For Windows Server 2008, you might have to install the Group Policy Management feature in Server Manager to use the Group Policy management tools.

Deploying VPN Enforcement

The deployment of VPN enforcement consists of the following steps:

- Configuring Active Directory
- Configuring VPN servers
- Configuring a PEAP-based authentication method
- Configuring remediation servers
- Configuring NAP health policy servers
- Configuring NAP clients

Configuring Active Directory

For Active Directory, you can optionally configure a security group for exempted user accounts.

To Create a NAP Exemption Security Group

1. In the console tree of the Active Directory Users And Computers snap-in, right-click your domain name, point to New, and then click Group.

2. In the Group Name box, type the name (such as **NAP Exemptions**), and then click OK.

Using the Active Directory Users And Computers snap-in, add the user accounts for the exempted computers to the newly created security group.

Configuring VPN Servers

If you are not already using an EAP-based authentication method for your remote access VPN connections, you must configure the Windows Server 2008–based VPN server to allow EAP-based authentication.

To Configure Routing and Remote Access Service for EAP-Based Authentication

1. In the console tree of the Routing and Remote Access snap-in, right-click the name of the Routing and Remote Access server, and then click Properties.

2. In the properties dialog box, click the Security tab.

3. On the Security tab, click Authentication Methods.

4. In the Authentication Methods dialog box, select Extensible Authentication Protocol (EAP), and then click OK twice.

Configuring a PEAP-Based Authentication Method

If you are not already using a PEAP-based authentication method for your remote access VPN connections, you must reconfigure your VPN clients and the network policy on your NPS servers. For information about configuring the PEAP-MS-CHAP v2 or PEAP-TLS authentication methods for remote access VPN connections, see Chapter 12. For third-party PEAP authentication methods, see the third-party documentation for information about configuring Windows-based VPN clients and the NPS servers.

Verify that remote access VPN connections using the PEAP authentication method work properly before continuing your VPN enforcement solution.

Configuring Remediation Servers

The first task in configuring remediation servers is to identify the set of servers that non-compliant NAP clients must be able to access. As described in Chapter 15, remediation servers can consist of the following types of computers:

- DNS and WINS servers
- Active Directory domain controllers
- Internet proxy servers

- Troubleshooting URL Web servers
- Health update servers

Depending on the SHAs that your NAP clients are using, you might need to configure your health update servers to provide updates or services to noncompliant NAP clients. See the documentation supplied by the vendors for your SHAs for information about what needs to be installed and configured.

If you are using remediation server groups to restrict access and are using IPv6 over your remote access VPN connections, you must add the IPv6 address that is assigned to the VPN server's Internal adapter to the remediation server group.

To Obtain the IPv6 Address of the Internal Adapter

1. In the console tree of the Routing and Remote Access snap-in, open the IPv6 node, and then click General.

2. In the details pane, click the Internal interface. The IPv6 address assigned to the Internal interface is listed in the IP Address column.

If you are using IPv4 and IPv6 packet filters to restrict access and are using IPv6 over your remote access VPN connections, you must add both inbound and outbound filters for ICMPv6 traffic (protocol 58) to and from the IPv6 address that is assigned to the VPN server's Internal adapter.

Configuring NAP Health Policy Servers

The NAP health policy servers for VPN enforcement are the same NPS RADIUS servers that are already being used for remote access VPN authentication. To configure a NAP health policy server, you must modify the configuration of your existing NPS servers by doing the following:

- Installing SHVs
- Configuring RADIUS server settings
- Configuring health requirement policies for VPN enforcement

Installing SHVs

The SHVs that you are using must be installed on each NAP health policy server to be included in the health policy evaluation. The NPS service includes the Windows Security Health Validator SHV to specify the settings of the Windows Security Center on NAP clients running Windows Vista or Windows XP SP3.

The exact method for installing additional SHVs will depend on the SHV vendor and can include downloading the SHV from a vendor's Web page or running a setup program from a vendor-supplied CD-ROM. Check with your SHV vendor for information about the method of installation.

Configuring RADIUS Server Settings

The NAP health policy servers are already configured for remote access VPN connections. For VPN enforcement, you must select the RADIUS Client Is NAP-Capable check box in the properties dialog box of the RADIUS clients that correspond to your VPN servers. You can change the properties of RADIUS clients from the RADIUS Clients node of the Network Policy Server snap-in. Because the VPN enforcement deployment will initially use reporting mode, in which noncompliant NAP clients have unlimited access, you might want to change how your NAP health policy servers are logging incoming requests for analysis prior to enabling enforcement mode. For more information, see Chapter 9.

Configuring Health Requirement Policies for VPN Enforcement

Because you already have existing network policies for remote access VPN connections, to configure health requirement policies for VPN enforcement, you can do one of the following:

- Keep your existing remote access VPN network policy, modify it for compliant NAP clients, and manually create connection request policies, health policies for compliant and noncompliant NAP clients, and additional network policies for noncompliant and non-NAP-capable clients.

- Use the Configure NAP Wizard to create a new set of connection request policies, network policies, and health policies for VPN-based remote access. Then, manually migrate the custom settings of your existing remote access VPN network policy to the corresponding network policies created by the Configure NAP Wizard. Then, modify your existing remote access VPN network policy.

Because of the amount of automated configuration being done by the Configure NAP Wizard, the second method is recommended and is described in this chapter.

To Create a Set of Policies for VPN Enforcement

1. In the Network Policy Server snap-in, in the console tree, click NPS.

2. In the details pane, under Standard Configuration, in the drop-down list, select Network Access Protection (NAP), and then click Configure NAP.

3. On the Select Network Connection Method For Use With NAP page, under Network Connection Method, select Virtual Private Network (VPN) from the drop-down list, and then in the Policy Name box, type a name (or use the name created by the wizard). Figure 18-1 shows an example.

4. Click Next. On the Specify NAP Enforcement Servers Running VPN Server page, click Next. Because the NAP health policy server is already a RADIUS server to your VPN servers, you do not need to add RADIUS clients.

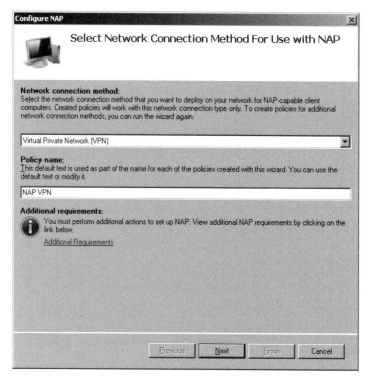

Figure 18-1   The Select Network Connection Method For Use With NAP page

5. On the Configure User Groups and Machine Groups page, add user groups as needed, and then click Next.

6. On the Configure An Authentication Method page, select a computer certificate used by NPS for PEAP authentication, and then select Secure Password (PEAP-MS-CHAP v2), Smart Card Or Other Certificate (EAP-TLS) (for PEAP-TLS), or both as needed. Figure 18-2 shows an example.

7. Click Next. On the Specify A NAP Remediation Server Group And URL page, click Next. Procedures later in this chapter will configure a remediation server group and trouble-shooting URL.

8. On the Define NAP Health Policy page, select the SHVs that you want to have evaluated for VPN enforcement, select the Enable Auto-Remediation Of Client Computers check box as needed, and then select Allow Full Network Access To NAP-Ineligible Client Computers, even if you want non-NAP-capable clients to eventually have restricted access. Because you want the initial NAP deployment to be reporting mode (rather than enforcement mode), you must select Allow Full Network Access To NAP-Ineligible Client Computers. During the configuration for enforcement mode, you can change the network policy for non-NAP-capable clients to limit their access. Figure 18-3 shows an example.

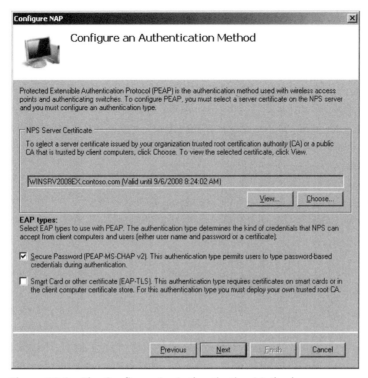

Figure 18-2   The Configure An Authentication Method page

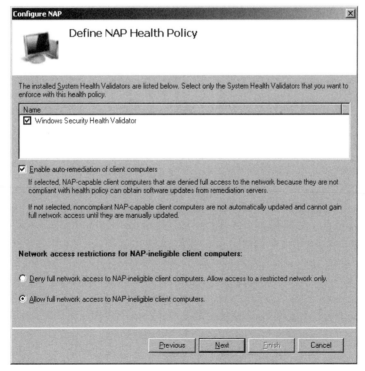

Figure 18-3   The Define NAP Health Policy page

9. Click Next. On the Completing NAP Enforcement Policy And RADIUS Client Configuration page, click Finish.

The Configure NAP Wizard creates the following:

■ A health policy for compliant NAP clients based on the SHVs selected in the Configure NAP Wizard

■ A health policy for noncompliant NAP clients based on the SHVs selected in the Configure NAP Wizard

■ A connection request policy for NAP-based remote access VPN connections

■ A network policy for compliant NAP clients that allows unlimited access

■ A network policy for noncompliant NAP clients that allows restricted access

■ A network policy for non-NAP-capable clients that allows unlimited access

The connection request policy, health policies, and network policies that are created by the Configure NAP Wizard are placed at the bottom of their respective ordered lists. Until you delete or change the order of the existing remote access VPN network policy, the network policies created by the Configure NAP Wizard will not be used for authentication or health evaluation for VPN-based remote access connections.

The next step is to ensure that the network policies created by the Configure NAP Wizard have all of the correct, customized settings for VPN-based remote access that are currently configured for the existing VPN network policy. For example, if your existing network policy for remote access VPN connections contains additional or customized conditions, constraints, or settings, they must be also be configured on the network policies for VPN-based remote access created by the Configure NAP Wizard.

To Configure the Customized Network Policy Settings

1. In the console tree of the Network Policy Server snap-in, expand Policies, and then click Network Policies.

2. In the details pane, double-click your existing remote access VPN network policy.

3. On the Overview tab, in the Network Connection Method area, note whether the Vendor Specific type has been set.

4. On the Conditions tab, note whether there are any additional conditions other than NAS Port Type.

5. On the Constraints tab, note any settings in the list of constraints that have been configured and their configured values.

6. On the Settings tab, note any additional RADIUS standard or vendor-specific attributes that have been configured other than Framed-Protocol and Service-Type. Note any IP filters that have been configured. Click Cancel.

7. In the details pane, double-click the remote access VPN network policy that was created by the Configure NAP Wizard for compliant NAP clients.

8. On the Overview, Conditions, Constraints, and Settings tabs, configure the custom settings of the existing remote access VPN network policy as determined from performing steps 3 through 6, and then click OK.

9. In the details pane, double-click the remote access VPN network policy that was created by the Configure NAP Wizard for noncompliant NAP clients.

10. On the Overview, Conditions, Constraints, and Settings tabs, configure the custom settings of the existing remote access VPN network policy as determined from performing steps 3 through 6, and then click OK.

11. In the details pane, double-click the remote access VPN network policy that was created by the Configure NAP Wizard for non-NAP-capable computers.

12. On the Overview, Conditions, Constraints, and Settings tabs, configure the custom settings of the existing remote access VPN network policy as determined from performing steps 3 through 6, and then click OK.

Because the network policy for noncompliant NAP clients by default allows only limited access (enforcement mode), you must modify this policy to allow unlimited access for reporting mode.

To Configure Reporting Mode

1. In the console tree of the Network Policy Server snap-in, expand Policies, and then click Network Policies.

2. In the details pane, double-click the network policy for noncompliant NAP clients that was created by the Configure NAP Wizard.

3. Click the Settings tab, and then click the NAP Enforcement setting.

4. In the details pane of the network policy properties dialog box, click Allow Full Network Access, and then click OK.

The next step is to ensure that the SHVs that you are using have the correct settings that reflect your health requirements.

To Configure the SHVs for the Required Health Settings

1. In the console tree of the Network Policy Server snap-in, expand Network Access Protection and then System Health Validators.

2. In the details pane, under Name, double-click your SHVs and configure each SHV with your requirements for system health.

    For example, double-click Windows Security Health Validator, and then click Configure. In the Windows Security Health Validator dialog box, configure system health requirements for Windows Vista–based and Windows XP–based NAP clients.

The next step is to configure the health policies created by the Configure NAP Wizard to reflect the conditions for compliant and noncompliant NAP clients for your system health requirements.

To Configure Health Policies for System Health Requirements

1. In the console tree of the Network Policy Server snap-in, expand Policies and then Health Policies.

2. In the details pane, double-click the health policies for compliant and noncompliant NAP clients, and make changes as needed to the health evaluation condition (the Client SHV Checks drop-down box) and the selected SHVs.

At this point in the deployment, you have created and configured NAP health requirement policies, but your NAP health policy servers are still using the existing connection request policy and network policy for VPN-based remote access. You must modify the configuration of your connection request policies to ensure that the new connection request policy for VPN enforcement is being used for VPN connections.

To Modify Your Connection Request Policies for VPN Enforcement

1. In the console tree of the Network Policy Server snap-in, expand Policies and then Connection Request Policies.

2. Right-click the name of your existing remote access VPN connection request policy, and then click Disable. When you are confident that the connection request policy that was created by the Configure NAP Wizard is working properly, you can delete this disabled policy.

The connection request policy for VPN connections that was created by the Configure NAP Wizard requires the use of a PEAP-based authentication method and NAP health evaluation. The connection attempts of VPN clients that do not use a PEAP-based authentication method will be rejected by the NAP health policy server. VPN clients that use a PEAP-based authentication method but do not respond to the request for health state will be determined to be non-NAP-capable clients by the NAP health policy server.

What you should do with the existing remote access VPN network policy depends on whether you have created a security group that contains users that are exempted from NAP health evaluation:

- If you created a security group for exempted users, modify the properties of the existing network policy for VPN-based remote access to include group membership in the security group in its conditions.

- If you did not create a security group for exempted users, move the existing network policy for VPN-based access so that it is evaluated after the network policies that were created by the Configure NAP Wizard.

To modify the conditions of the existing remote access VPN network policy to include the security group for exempted users, do the following:

1. In the console tree of the Network Policy Server snap-in, expand Policies, and then click Network Policies.

2. In the details pane, double-click the existing network policy for VPN-based remote access.

3. On the Conditions tab, click Add. In the Select Condition dialog box, double-click Windows Groups. In the Windows Groups dialog box, click Add Groups, specify the name of the security group for exempted users, and then click OK three times.

To move the existing remote access VPN network policy so that it is evaluated after the network policies that were created by the Configure NAP Wizard, do the following:

1. In the console tree of the Network Policy Server snap-in, expand Policies and then Network Policies.

2. In the details pane, right-click the name of your existing remote access VPN network policy, and then click Move Down.

3. Repeat step 2 as many times as necessary so that the existing remote access VPN network policy is below the network policies that were created by the Configure NAP Wizard.

Configuring NAP Clients

To configure your NAP clients, perform the following tasks:

- Install SHAs.
- Configure managed NAP clients through Group Policy.

Installing SHAs

NAP clients running Windows Vista or Windows XP SP3 include the Windows Security Health Agent SHA. If you are using additional SHAs from third-party vendors, you must install them on your NAP clients. The exact method of installation of additional SHAs will depend on the SHA vendor and can include downloading the SHA from a vendor's Web page or running a setup program from a vendor-supplied CD-ROM. Check with your SHA vendor for information about the method of installation.

On a managed network, you can use the following methods:

- Network management software such as Systems Management Server (SMS) or System Center Configuration Manager 2007 to install software across an organization
- Login scripts that execute the setup program for the SHA

For computers that are not managed, you can install SHAs through a CMAK package with a post-connect action (not recommended), an Internet Web site, or on a remediation server such as the troubleshooting URL Web server.

Configuring NAP Clients Through Group Policy

For managed NAP clients, you can use Group Policy for NAP client settings, which consists of the following:

- Configuring NAP client settings
- Enabling Windows Security Center
- Configuring the Network Access Protection Agent service for automatic startup

Configuring NAP Client Settings   To configure NAP client settings in Group Policy (equivalent to using the NAP Client Configuration snap-in on an individual Windows Vista–based computer), do the following:

1. Open the Group Policy Management snap-in. In the console tree, expand Forest, expand Domains, and then click your domain. On the Linked Group Policy Objects pane, right-click the appropriate Group Policy Object (the default object is Default Domain Policy), and then click Edit.

2. In the console tree of the Group Policy Management Editor snap-in, expand the policy, and then expand Computer Configuration\Windows Settings\Security Settings\Network Access Protection\NAP Client Configuration.

3. In the console tree, click Enforcement Clients.

4. In the details pane, double-click the Remote Access Quarantine Enforcement Client.

5. On the General tab, select the Enable This Enforcement Client check box, and then click OK.

6. If you want to specify an image that appears in the NAP client user interface (UI), in the console tree, click User Interface Settings, and then in the details pane, double-click User Interface Settings.

7. On the General tab, type the title and description for the text that appears in the NAP client UI, and then type the path to an image file that appears in the UI, or click Browse and specify its location. Click OK.

Enabling Windows Security Center   To use Group Policy to enable the Windows Security Center on NAP clients that are members of your Active Directory domain, do the following:

1. In the console tree of the Group Policy Management Editor snap-in for the appropriate Group Policy Object, open Computer Configuration\Administrative Templates\Windows Components, and then click Security Center.

2. In the details pane, double-click Turn On Security Center (Domain PCs Only).

3. On the Setting tab, select Enabled, and then click OK.

Configuring the Network Access Protection Agent Service for Automatic Startup   To use Group Policy to enable automatic startup of the Network Access Protection Agent service on NAP client settings, do the following:

1. In the console tree of the Group Policy Management Editor snap-in for the appropriate Group Policy Object, open Computer Configuration\Windows Settings\Security Settings\System Services.

2. In the details pane, double-click Network Access Protection Agent.

3. On the Security Policy Setting tab, select the Define This Policy Setting check box, select Automatic, and then click OK.

VPN Enforcement Deployment Checkpoint for Reporting Mode

At this point in the VPN enforcement deployment, NAP clients attempting remote access VPN connections will have their health state evaluated. Because the VPN enforcement deployment is in reporting mode, both compliant and noncompliant NAP clients have unlimited network access to the intranet, and the users of noncompliant NAP clients receive no message in the notification area of their desktop saying that their computers do not meet system health requirements.

While the VPN enforcement deployment is in reporting mode, perform an analysis of the NPS events in Windows Logs\Security event log on the NAP health policy servers to determine which NAP clients are not compliant. Take the appropriate actions to remedy their health state, such as installing missing SHAs or providing health update resources on remediation servers.

Testing Restricted Access

Prior to enabling enforcement mode, you must test restricted access for noncompliant NAP clients. To perform this test, you must do the following:

1. Create a new network policy for noncompliant NAP clients that restricts access for members of a security group containing test user accounts.

2. Ensure that a noncompliant test computer making a remote access VPN connection has its access restricted and can access only remediation servers on your intranet.

To Create a Network Policy for Testing Restricted Access

1. Designate some NAP client computers as test computers for restricted access.

2. Using the Active Directory Users And Computers snap-in, create some test user accounts, create a security group for testing restricted access, and then add the test user accounts to the group.

3. In the console tree of the Network Policy Server snap-in, expand Policies, and then click Network Policies.

4. Right-click the remote access VPN network policy for noncompliant NAP clients that was created by the Configure NAP Wizard, and then click Duplicate Policy.

5. Double-click the copy of the network policy for noncompliant NAP clients created in step 4.

6. On the Overview tab, in the Policy Name box, type a name for the new network policy. In the Policy State area, select the Policy Enabled check box.

7. On the Conditions tab, click Add. In the Select Condition dialog box, double-click Windows Groups. In the Windows Groups dialog box, click Add Groups, specify the name of the group created in step 2, and then click OK twice.

8. Click the Settings tab. Under Network Access Protection, click NAP Enforcement. In the details pane, select Allow Limited Access, and then clear the Enable Auto-Remediation Of Client Computers check box.

9. Click Configure. In the Remediation Servers And Troubleshooting URL dialog box, in the Troubleshooting URL box, type the URL to the troubleshooting page on your troubleshooting URL remediation server.

10. In the Remediation Servers And Troubleshooting URL dialog box, click New Group, and then configure the remediation server group for VPN enforcement with the IPv4 or IPv6 addresses of the remediation servers. Click OK twice.

11. If you are also using packet filters, on the Settings tab, under Routing and Remote Access, click IP Filters, and then configure IPv4 and IPv6 input and output packet filters as needed. Click OK.

12. In the details pane, right-click the name of the duplicated network policy for noncompliant NAP clients, and then click Move Up.

13. Repeat step 12 as many times as necessary so that the duplicated network policy for testing noncompliant NAP clients is just above the network policy for noncompliant NAP clients that was created by the Configure NAP Wizard.

To Test Restricted Access for a Noncompliant Test Computer

1. Configure a test computer to be noncompliant. Depending on your system health requirements, this might be as simple as manually disabling Automatic Updates.

2. From the test computer, make a remote access VPN connection to a VPN server.

3. When the VPN connection completes, you should see a Network Access Protection message in the notification area of the desktop. You can verify restricted status by running the **ipconfig** command.

4. From the test computer, verify that you can reach all of the remediation servers and access the troubleshooting Web page.

5. From the test computer, verify that you cannot reach other servers on the intranet.

Based on your testing, make any modifications that you need to the duplicated network policy for noncompliant NAP clients, such as the remediation server group, the troubleshooting URL, or the IPv4 or IPv6 packet filters. If you have made required software for system health and SHA installation software available on remediation servers, ensure that the software and SHAs can be installed from the noncompliant NAP clients.

Configuring Deferred Enforcement

After testing restricted access for noncompliant NAP clients, determine the date for deferred enforcement mode (the date for which you will configure the noncompliant NAP client network policy for enforcement mode). On this date, noncompliant NAP clients will have their access restricted. In deferred enforcement mode for VPN enforcement, noncompliant NAP clients will still have unlimited access to the intranet, but the users will now see a message in their notification area indicating that their computer does not comply with system health requirements.

To Configure Deferred Enforcement Mode

1. In the console tree of the Network Policy Server snap-in, expand Policies, and then click Network Policies.

2. In the details pane, double-click the remote access VPN network policy for noncompliant NAP clients that was created by the Configure NAP wizard.

3. Click the Settings tab, and then click the NAP Enforcement setting.

4. In the details pane, select Allow Full Network Access For A Limited Time, specify the date and time that enforcement mode will be configured on the NAP health policy servers, and then click OK.

Configuring Network Policy for Enforcement Mode

Because you have already configured and tested a network policy that restricts access for noncompliant NAP clients (the duplicated network policy for noncompliant NAP clients for the test user account group), to enable enforcement mode, you will modify this duplicated network policy and disable the original network policy for noncompliant NAP clients that was created by the Configure NAP Wizard. On the date for enforcement mode, configure enforcement mode on your NAP health policy servers.

To Configure Enforcement Mode

1. In the console tree of the Network Policy Server snap-in, expand Policies, and then click Network Policies.

2. In the details pane, double-click the duplicated network policy for noncompliant NAP clients that you used when testing restricted access.

3. On the Conditions tab, in the Condition list, click Windows Groups, and then click Remove.

4. On the Settings tab, under Network Access Protection, click NAP Enforcement. In the details pane, under Auto Remediation, select the Enable Auto-Remediation Of Client Computers check box, and then click OK.

5. In the details pane, right-click the original network policy for noncompliant NAP clients that was created by the Configure NAP Wizard, and then click Delete.

At this point, the network policy that you used to test restricted access for noncompliant NAP clients now applies to all of your NAP clients, and the original network policy for noncompliant NAP clients that was created by the Configure NAP Wizard has been deleted.

To limit the access for non-NAP-capable clients, on the date for enforcement mode, you must configure a network policy for non-NAP-capable clients that restricts their access. Because the duplicated network policy for noncompliant NAP clients already has been configured and tested for restricted access, you can duplicate and then modify this policy for non-NAP-capable clients.

To Limit the Access of Non-NAP-Capable Clients

1. In the console tree of the Network Policy Server snap-in, expand Policies, and then click Network Policies.

2. Right-click the duplicated network policy for noncompliant NAP clients, and then click Duplicate Policy.

3. Double-click the new network policy.

4. On the Overview tab, in the Policy Name box, type a name for the new network policy. In the Policy State area, select the Policy Enabled check box.

5. On the Conditions tab, click Add. In the Select Condition dialog box, double-click NAP-Capable Computers. In the NAP-Capable Computers dialog box, select Only Computers That Are Not NAP-Capable, and then click OK.

6. On the Conditions tab, click the Health Policy condition, click Remove, and then click OK.

7. In the details pane of the Network Policy Server snap-in, move the new network policy for non-NAP-capable clients so that it is just under the original network policy for non-NAP-capable clients that was created by the Configure NAP wizard.

8. Right-click the original network policy for non-NAP-capable clients that was created by the Configure NAP wizard, and then click Delete.

The deployment of VPN enforcement is complete. Noncompliant NAP clients and (optionally) non-NAP-capable clients will have their access restricted to the remediation servers on the intranet.

Ongoing Maintenance

The areas of maintenance for a VPN enforcement deployment are as follows:

- Adding a NAP client
- Adding a new SHA and SHV

Adding a NAP Client

A new NAP client is either a managed computer or an unmanaged computer. To add a NAP client that is a managed computer, do the following:

1. Join the NAP client computer to the domain.

2. Install the SHAs on the NAP client computer.

For a new unmanaged NAP client, follow the steps in "Configuring NAP Client Settings" earlier in this chapter.

Adding a New SHA and SHV

To add a new SHA and SHV to your VPN enforcement deployment, you must do the following:

1. If needed, install the software or components on your remediation servers for automatic remediation required by the new SHA.

2. Install the required software and SHA on your NAP clients. For more information, see "Configuring NAP Client Settings" earlier in this chapter.

3. Install the SHV on your NAP health policy servers.

4. If needed, on the NAP health policy servers, configure the settings of the SHV for the conditions of system health in the Network Access Protection\System Health Validators node of the Network Policy Server snap-in.

5. On the NAP health policy servers, modify the health policies for compliant and non-compliant NAP clients to include the new SHV in its evaluation.

Troubleshooting

Because of the different components and processes involved, troubleshooting a VPN enforcement deployment can be a difficult task. This section describes the troubleshooting tools that are provided with Windows Server 2008 and Windows Vista and how to troubleshoot VPN enforcement starting from the NAP client.

Troubleshooting Tools

Microsoft provides the following tools to troubleshoot VPN enforcement:

- TCP/IP troubleshooting tools
- Netsh tool
- NAP client event logging
- NPS event logging
- NPS authentication and accounting logging
- Netsh NAP tracing
- Tracing
- VPN server event logging
- Network Monitor 3.1

TCP/IP Troubleshooting Tools

The Ipconfig tool displays the state of a NAP client. At a command prompt on a NAP client, run the **ipconfig /all** command. In the Windows IP Configuration section of the display, the state of the NAP client is listed as the System Quarantine State. The System Quarantine State is displayed as either Not Restricted or Restricted.

Additional TCP/IP troubleshooting tools are Ping and Nslookup to test reachability and name resolution.

Netsh Tool

Beyond the state of the NAP client as shown in the **ipconfig /all** command, you can gather additional NAP client configuration information by running the following commands:

- **netsh nap client show configuration** Displays the local NAP client configuration including the list of NAP enforcement clients and their state (enabled or disabled), and the state of NAP client tracing
- **netsh nap client show grouppolicy** Displays the same NAP client settings as the **netsh nap client show configuration** command for the settings obtained through Group Policy
- **netsh nap client show state** Displays detailed NAP client state, enforcement client state, and SHA state

Note The display for the netsh nap client show configuration and netsh nap client show grouppolicy commands does not show which set of settings, local or Group Policy–based, is currently active on the NAP client. If any NAP client settings are obtained through Group Policy, the entire set of NAP client settings is specified by Group Policy and all local NAP client settings are ignored.

NAP Client Event Logging

Use the Event Viewer snap-in to check the events in the Windows event log created by the Network Access Protection Agent service. On computers running Windows Server 2008 or Windows Vista, use the Event Viewer snap-in to view events in Applications and Services Logs\Microsoft\Windows\Network Access Protection\Operational. On computers running Windows XP SP3, use the Event Viewer snap-in to view events in the System event log.

NPS Event Logging

Use the Event Viewer snap-in to check the Windows Logs\Security event log for NPS events. NPS event log entries contain a lot of information about the NAP health evaluation, including the name of the matching connection request policy (the Proxy Policy Name field in the description of the event) and the matching network policy (the Network Policy Name field in the description of the event). Viewing NPS events in the Windows Logs\Security event log is one of the most useful troubleshooting methods to obtain information about NAP health evaluations.

NPS Logging

By default, NPS will log authentication and accounting data to the *%SystemRoot%*\System32\ LogFiles folder in a database-compatible (comma-delimited) text file. You can also configure NPS to perform SQL Server logging and then analyze the NPS authentication and accounting data in an SQL Server database.

Netsh NAP Tracing

The Network Access Protection Agent service has an extensive tracing capability that you can use to troubleshoot complex network problems. You can enable netsh NAP tracing by running the **netsh nap client set tracing state=enable level=basic|advanced|verbose** command. The log files are stored in the *%SystemRoot%*\Tracing folder. Netsh NAP tracing files can be sent to Microsoft customer support staff for analysis.

Tracing

You can use the tracing facility on the VPN client, the VPN server, and the NAP health policy server to obtain detailed component interaction information for VPN enforcement. You can enable components of Windows Server 2008 or Windows Vista to log tracing information to files by using the Netsh tool or by setting registry values. For more information, see "Troubleshooting Tools" in Chapter 12.

VPN Server Event Logging

Use the Event Viewer snap-in to check the events in Windows Logs\System that are created by the Routing and Remote Access service for VPN connections. For more information, see "Troubleshooting Tools" in Chapter 12.

Network Monitor 3.1

Use Network Monitor 3.1, a network sniffer that is available from Microsoft, to capture and view the traffic sent between VPN clients, VPN servers, and NAP health policy servers. For example, you can use Network Monitor 3.1 to capture the RADIUS traffic between a VPN server and the NAP health policy server to determine the contents of RADIUS messages, such as the RADIUS attributes for specifying the IPv4 and IPv6 packet filters.

The proper interpretation of this traffic requires an in-depth understanding of RADIUS and other protocols. Network Monitor captures can be saved as files and sent to Microsoft customer support staff for analysis.

> **On the Disc**   You can link to the download site for Network Monitor from the companion CD-ROM.

Troubleshooting VPN Enforcement

This section describes how to troubleshoot a VPN enforcement deployment by starting at the NAP client. This is the approach used by many technical support departments in organizations and reflects a multi-tier analysis and escalation path to determine the source of a problem and its solution. For example, the IT department of an organization might have the following tiers:

- **Tier 1**   Help desk staff, who can provide an initial assessment of problems and solutions based on an analysis of the client (the NAP client for VPN enforcement)
- **Tier 2**   Windows network and infrastructure services staff, who manage the VPN servers, remediation servers, and NAP health policy servers.

When troubleshooting VPN enforcement, it is important to first determine the scope of the problem. If your VPN clients cannot perform authentication for the VPN connection, you must troubleshoot the authentication problem independently of NAP and VPN enforcement. If all of your VPN clients are experiencing VPN enforcement problems, issues might exist in your NAP health policy servers. If all of your VPN clients that are connected to a specific VPN server are experiencing VPN enforcement problems, issues might exist in the configuration of the VPN server or its configured NAP health policy servers. If only specific VPN clients are experiencing VPN enforcement problems, issues might exist for those individual clients.

Troubleshooting the NAP Client

To troubleshoot the NAP client, do the following:

- Verify whether the NAP client has successfully completed user authentication for the VPN connection. If not, please see the "Troubleshooting" section of Chapter 12.

- Verify whether the NAP client is compliant or noncompliant by running the **ipconfig /all** command.

If the NAP client is noncompliant and is not autoremediating its health state, verify the following:

- **Network reachability from the NAP client to the IP addresses of the remediation servers**   You can use the Ping tool, but because of default Windows Firewall rules, incoming ICMP or ICMPv6 traffic on the remediation servers might be blocked.

- **Name resolution from the NAP client**   Use the Ping and Nslookup tools for the names of the remediation servers. Verify that the DNS names that the NAP client uses successfully resolve to the correct IPv4 or IPv6 addresses.

- **That the Network Access Protection Agent service is started on the NAP client and that it is configured to start automatically**   Run the **netsh nap client show state** command to determine the service state, and use the Services snap-in to configure the Network Access Protection Agent service.

- **That the Remote Access Quarantine Enforcement client is enabled**   Run the **netsh nap client show configuration** command. If needed, use the Group Policy Management Editor snap-in (for Active Directory–based Group Policy Objects), the NAP Client Configuration snap-in, or the **netsh nap client set enforcement 79618 enable** command to enable the Remote Access Quarantine enforcement client.

- **That the NAP client has all of the appropriate SHAs installed**   Run the **netsh nap client show state** command. If you are using the Windows Security Health Agent SHA, verify that the Windows Security Center is enabled.

Direct from the Source: Checking SHA Status

You can install an SHA, but if it doesn't bind and register with the Network Access Protection Agent service, it won't initialize properly and report health status. Use the **netsh nap client show state** command to verify that the SHA is properly initialized. If needed, reinstall the SHA or contact the SHA vendor for more information.

Greg Lindsay, Technical Writer

Windows Server User Assistance

Beyond these verification steps, use the Event Viewer snap-in on the NAP client to view the NAP client events in Applications and Services Logs\Microsoft\Windows\Network Access Protection\Operational for a Windows Vista–based NAP client and in System for a Windows XP SP3–based NAP client. Use the NAP client events to perform additional troubleshooting. Note the correlation ID specified in the description of the NAP client events. The correlation ID can be used to find the corresponding event on the NPS server. Additional VPN NAP events are in Windows Logs\Application with the event source of RasClient.

Troubleshooting the VPN Servers

To troubleshoot the VPN servers, do the following:

■ Verify that the EAP authentication type has been enabled as an authentication method from the Routing and Remote Access snap-in, in the server's properties dialog box, on the Security tab.

Troubleshooting the NAP Health Policy Servers

To troubleshoot the NAP health policy servers, verify the following:

■ **That all of the RADIUS clients corresponding to VPN servers have the RADIUS Client Is NAP-Capable check box selected (on the Settings tab of the properties dialog box of the RADIUS client)** You can use the Network Policy Server snap-in or the **netsh nps show client** command.

■ **That the health requirement policies are correctly configured for VPN enforcement** You can use the Network Policy Server snap-in or **netsh nps show** commands. Verify that there is a correctly configured set of connection request policies, network policies, health policies, and SHVs that reflect your health requirements and the correct behavior for compliant, noncompliant, and non-NAP-capable clients for VPN enforcement. Verify the order of the connection request policies and the network policies.

■ **That the noncompliant NAP client network policy has been configured to automatically remediate health status** You can use the Network Policy Server snap-in or the **netsh nps show np** command.

■ **That the network policy for compliant NAP clients is correctly configured** You can use the Network Policy Server snap-in or the **netsh nps show np** command.

■ **That the network policy for noncompliant NAP clients is correctly configured** You can use the Network Policy Server snap-in or the **netsh nps show np** command. Verify the addresses in the remediation server group or the inbound and outbound IPv4 and IPv6 packet filters. If you are using IPv6 over your VPN connections, verify that the IPv6 address of the Internal adapter of the VPN server has been added to the remediation server group.

■ **That the network policy for non-NAP-capable clients is correctly configured** You can use the Network Policy Server snap-in or the **netsh nps show np** command.

Beyond these verification steps, use the Event Viewer snap-in on the NAP health policy server to view the NPS events in Windows Logs\Security for events corresponding to RADIUS messages sent by the VPN servers for authentication and system health validation of NAP clients. Use the correlation ID of the NAP client event to locate the corresponding NPS event in the Security log. To view the NPS events, configure a filter with the Event Sources set to Microsoft Windows Security Auditing and the Task Category set to Network Policy Server.

Troubleshooting Remediation Servers

Verify that the remediation servers are reachable by noncompliant NAP clients. If you are making required software for system health or SHAs available on remediation servers, verify that the software or SHAs can be installed from a noncompliant NAP client.

For health update servers, verify that they have been correctly configured to provide the necessary resources to remediate the health of a NAP client. See the documentation provided by the vendors of the SHAs that use health update servers.

Chapter Summary

Deploying VPN enforcement involves configuration of Active Directory, VPN servers, NAP health policy servers, remediation servers, and NAP clients. After an initial configuration in reporting mode, test enforcement mode on a subset of VPN clients. Last, configure enforcement mode for all VPN clients. After deploying enforcement mode, ongoing maintenance of VPN enforcement consists of adding NAP clients and adding SHAs and SHVs. To troubleshoot VPN enforcement, verify network connectivity and configuration for NAP clients, VPN servers, NAP health policy servers, and remediation servers.

Additional Information

For additional information about NAP, see the following:

- Chapter 14, "Network Access Protection Overview"
- Chapter 15, "Preparing for Network Access Protection"
- Chapter 16, "IPsec Enforcement"
- Chapter 17, "802.1X Enforcement"
- Chapter 19, "DHCP Enforcement"
- Windows Server 2008 Technical Library at *http://technet.microsoft.com/windowsserver/ 2008*
- Windows Server 2008 Help and Support
- "Network Access Protection" (*http://www.microsoft.com/nap*)

For additional information about Active Directory, see the following:

- *Windows Server 2008 Active Directory Resource Kit* in the *Windows Server 2008 Resource Kit* (both from Microsoft Press, 2008)
- Windows Server 2008 Technical Library at *http://technet.microsoft.com/windowsserver/2008*
- Windows Server 2008 Help and Support
- "Windows Server 2003 Active Directory" (*http://www.microsoft.com/ad*)

For additional information about Group Policy, see the following:

- *Windows Group Policy Resource Kit: Windows Server 2008 and Windows Vista* (Microsoft Press, 2008)
- Windows Server 2008 Technical Library at *http://technet.microsoft.com/windowsserver/2008*
- Windows Server 2008 Help and Support
- "Windows Server Group Policy" (*http://www.microsoft.com/gp*)

For additional information about RADIUS and NPS, see the following:

- Chapter 9, "Authentication Infrastructure"
- Windows Server 2008 Technical Library at *http://technet.microsoft.com/windowsserver/2008*
- Windows Server 2008 Help and Support
- "Network Policy Server" (*http://www.microsoft.com/nps*)

For additional information about remote access VPN connections, see the following:

- Chapter 12, "Remote Access VPN Connections"
- Windows Server 2008 Technical Library at *http://technet.microsoft.com/windowsserver/2008*
- Windows Server 2008 Help and Support
- "Virtual Private Networks" (*http://www.microsoft.com/vpn*)

Chapter 19
DHCP Enforcement

This chapter provides information about how to design, deploy, maintain, and troubleshoot Dynamic Host Configuration Protocol (DHCP) enforcement with Network Access Protection (NAP). This chapter assumes the following:

- That you understand the role of Active Directory, Group Policy, and Remote Authentication Dial-In User Service (RADIUS) elements of a Microsoft Windows–based authentication infrastructure for network access. For more information, see Chapter 9, "Authentication Infrastructure."

- That you have a working DHCP infrastructure for automated Internet Protocol version 4 (IPv4) address configuration. For more information, see Chapter 3, "Dynamic Host Configuration Protocol."

- That you understand the components of NAP and how to prepare your network for NAP. For more information, see Chapter 14, "Network Access Protection Overview," and Chapter 15, "Preparing for Network Access Protection."

Understanding DHCP Enforcement

With DHCP enforcement, a NAP client must be compliant with system health requirements to obtain an unlimited access Internet Protocol version 4 (IPv4) address configuration from a NAP-capable DHCP server. For noncompliant NAP clients, network access is limited by an IPv4 address configuration that allows access only to the restricted network. DHCP enforcement enforces health policy requirements every time a DHCP client attempts to lease or renew an IPv4 address configuration and when the health state of the NAP client changes.

DHCP enforcement in NAP consists of a DHCP enforcement server that is part of the DHCP Server service in the Windows Server 2008 operating system and a DHCP enforcement client that is part of the DHCP Client service in the Windows Vista, Windows XP with Service Pack 3 (SP3), and Windows Server 2008 operating systems. The NAP health policy server evaluates the health of the DHCP client and instructs the DHCP server to restrict the access of noncompliant NAP clients.

How It Works: Details of DHCP Enforcement

DHCP enforcement uses a limited access IPv4 address configuration and a set of host routes to restrict the access of a noncompliant NAP client. The noncompliant NAP client obtains an IPv4 address, a subnet mask of 255.255.255.255, and no default gateway. With this configuration, the noncompliant NAP client cannot send packets to other computers on its subnet or other subnets. The set of host routes correspond to the remediation server group that is configured on the NAP health policy server. With the host routes in its IPv4 routing table, the noncompliant NAP client can send packets to the remediation servers on the intranet.

The following process describes how DHCP enforcement works for a NAP client that is attempting an initial DHCP address configuration:

1. The NAP client sends a DHCP request message containing its System Statement of Health (SSoH) to the DHCP server.

2. The DHCP server sends the SSoH of the NAP client to the NAP health policy server in a RADIUS Access-Request message.

3. The NPS service on the NAP health policy server extracts the SSoH from the Access-Request message and passes it to the NAP Administration Server component.

4. The NAP Administration Server component passes the Statements of Health (SoHs) in the SSoH to the appropriate system health validators (SHVs).

5. The SHVs analyze the contents of their SoHs and return Statements of Health Response (SoHRs) to the NAP Administration Server.

6. The NAP Administration Server passes the SoHRs to NPS.

7. The NPS service compares the SoHRs to the configured set of health requirement policies and creates the System Statement of Health Response (SSoHR).

8. The NPS service sends an Access-Accept message containing the SSoHR to the DHCP server.

   ❏ If the NAP client is noncompliant, the RADIUS Access-Accept message contains a set of IPv4 packet filters corresponding to the IPv4 addresses of the remediation server group to restrict the traffic of the DHCP client. After the DHCP configuration completes, the NAP client will have restricted network access.

   ❏ If the NAP client is compliant, the RADIUS Access-Accept message does not contain the additional packet filters for the remediation server group. After the DHCP configuration completes, the NAP client will have unlimited network access.

9. During the DHCP message exchange, the DHCP server sends the SSoHR to the NAP client.

10. The DHCP client service on the DHCP client passes the SSoHR to the DHCP Quarantine enforcement client, which passes it to the NAP Agent component.

If the DHCP client is noncompliant, the following process performs the remediation required for unlimited network access:

1. The NAP Agent component passes the SoHRs in the SSoHR to the appropriate system health agents (SHAs).

2. Each SHA analyzes its SoHR, and based on the contents, performs the remediation as needed to correct the NAP client's system health state.

3. Each SHA that required remediation passes an updated SoH to the NAP Agent.

4. The NAP Agent collects the updated SoHs, creates a new SSoH, and passes it to the DHCP Quarantine enforcement client, which passes it to the DHCP Client service.

5. The DHCP Client service initiates a new DHCP message exchange to renew its IPv4 address configuration and sends its updated SSoH.

6. The DHCP server sends the updated SSoH to the NAP health policy server in an Access-Request message.

7. The NPS service on the NAP health policy server extracts the SSoH from the Access-Request message and passes it to the NAP Administration Server component.

8. The NAP Administration Server component passes the SoHs in the SSoH to the appropriate SHVs.

9. The SHVs analyze the contents of their SoHs and return an SoHR to the NAP Administration Server component.

10. The NAP Administration Server passes the SoHRs to the NPS service.

11. The NPS service compares the SoHRs to the configured set of health requirement policies and creates the SSoHR.

12. The NPS service constructs and sends an Access-Accept message containing the SSoHR but without the packet filters to the DHCP server.

13. Upon receipt of the RADIUS Access-Accept message, the DHCP server completes the DHCP message exchange with the DHCP client and assigns an IPv4 address configuration for unlimited network access.

Because DHCP enforcement relies on a limited IPv4 address configuration that can be overridden by a user with administrator-level access who can configure a static IPv4 address configuration or add routes to the routing table, it is the weakest form of restricted network access in NAP.

Planning and Design Considerations

When deploying DHCP enforcement, you must consider the following in your planning:

- Security group for NAP exemptions
- DHCP servers
- NAP health policy servers
- Health requirement policies for specific DHCP scopes
- DHCP options for NAP clients
- DHCP enforcement behavior when the NAP health policy server is not reachable
- NAP clients

Security Group for NAP Exemptions

To exempt DHCP client computers from DHCP enforcement by preventing NAP evaluation at the NAP health policy server, create a security group whose members contain the computer accounts of exempted computers. On the NAP health policy server, create a network policy that grants access and uses the Windows Groups condition set to the security group for the exempted computers but does not use the Health Policy condition.

> ### Direct from the Source: DHCP Enforcement Exemption Based on MAC Addresses
>
> Windows Security Groups are the easiest and most efficient method of managing exceptions to your NAP policies. However, they require that machines be joined to your Active Directory to be able to take advantage of them. Many customers have business needs to allow visitors with non-domain-joined machines, such as consultants, vendors, or students, onto the network. With enforcement methods like 802.1X, customers can provide temporary certificates for these scenarios, but this is not an option in DHCP-based enforcement deployments.
>
> In a network using DHCP-based enforcement, the simplest way to exempt a user on a short-term basis is by a media access control (MAC) address. Because MAC addresses are universal, this exemption routine will work with any type of device running any operating system and requires very little end-user interaction. The visitor simply needs to provide their MAC address to the policy administrator, who can then add it directly to an exemption policy. End users can quickly determine their MAC address in the

networking control panel, and many laptop manufacturers even print it on a sticker on the bottom of new systems. Alternatively, IT administrators could determine it on behalf of the user simply by viewing the NPS logs.

Once the MAC address has been identified, a new rule can be created that utilizes the Calling Station ID RADIUS Client Property. This rule could be expressed as "Exempt by MAC Address: Grant access when Calling Station ID matches '001C31123A7A.'" Once your rules are ordered properly, the visitor's connection attempt will match this rule first and will be exempted from policy based purely on its MAC address.

John Morello, Senior Program Manager

Windows Server Customer Connection

DHCP Servers

DHCP servers for DHCP enforcement must use Windows Server 2008. The DHCP Server service in the Windows Server 2003 operating system does not support DHCP enforcement. DHCP servers running Windows Server 2003 must be upgraded to Windows Server 2008.

Changes to the health state on the NAP client will cause the NAP client to perform a new health evaluation through a DHCP renewal of the currently leased configuration. If the health state does not change, the NAP client does not perform a new health evaluation. If the network administrator changes the health requirement policy for DHCP enforcement on the NAP health policy server, it is possible for NAP clients that have unlimited access to be noncompliant with the changed health requirement policy. When health requirement policy changes on the NAP health policy server, there is no mechanism to contact NAP clients to perform a new health evaluation.

For DHCP enforcement, NAP clients reevaluate their health status when they renew their IPv4 address configuration, which happens halfway through their lease time. The recommended lease time for DHCP enforcement is eight hours, requiring a NAP client to renew its IPv4 address and reevaluate its health every four hours. If you reduce the lease time, you reduce the maximum amount of time that a NAP client can be noncompliant because of changes in health requirement policy, but you also increase the frequency with which NAP clients must renew their lease and perform a new health evaluation. This will increase the load on your DHCP and NAP health policy servers.

NAP Health Policy Servers

If you do not already have a RADIUS infrastructure for 802.1X-authenticated or VPN connections, you must deploy NPS-based RADIUS servers for DHCP enforcement. See Chapter 9 for information about deploying a RADIUS infrastructure.

It is also possible to run the NPS service in the role of a NAP health policy server on the DHCP server, eliminating the need for a separate computer for the NAP health policy server. However, this configuration is appropriate only for small networks with a single DHCP server. For intranets with multiple DHCP servers, you should have a separate set of NAP health policy servers.

Health Requirement Policies for Specific DHCP Scopes

On the DHCP server, it is possible to configure a NAP-enabled DHCP scope with a specific name known as a *profile name*. When you create a set of health requirement policies by using the Configure NAP Wizard in the Network Policy Server snap-in, you can identify the profile names to which the policies apply. This allows you the flexibility to create different sets of health requirements on a per-scope basis. For example, you can create a set of health requirement policies that are less restrictive for a subnet of your intranet to which guest computers connect.

DHCP Options for NAP Clients

The DHCP options for restricted access are specified by the restricted state of the noncompliant NAP client (the Subnet Mask DHCP option) and by the set of remediation servers (the Classless Static Routes DHCP option). If you want to specify additional DHCP options to assign to noncompliant NAP clients, you can use the new Default Network Access Protection Class user class. A noncompliant NAP client is automatically assigned the Default Network Access Protection Class user class and will receive options only from that user class, even if the DHCP client is using another user class.

DHCP Enforcement Behavior When the NAP Health Policy Server Is Not Reachable

Based on your network's security requirements, you must decide how to configure DHCP enforcement behavior when the NAP health policy server is not reachable. The Windows Server 2008 DHCP Server service can be configured to assign an unlimited access IPv4 address configuration or a restricted access IPv4 address configuration or to silently discard DHCP messages that are received from DHCP clients. In this case, DHCP clients will either use Automatic Private IP Addressing (APIPA) or their alternate configuration.

NAP Clients

You must consider the following planning and design issues for your NAP clients:

- NAP client operating system
- Non-NAP-capable clients
- NAP client domain membership

- Installing NAP client components
- Configuration settings
- Configuration methods

NAP Client Operating System

The versions of Windows that include NAP client functionality are the following:

- Windows Vista
- Windows Server 2008
- Windows XP SP3

Third-party vendors can supply NAP client functionality for other versions of Windows or for operating systems other than Windows.

Non-NAP-Capable DHCP Clients

You must determine whether non-NAP-capable DHCP clients will be allowed unlimited access or restricted access to the intranet.

NAP Client Domain Membership

NAP clients should be members of your Active Directory domain to participate in Group Policy–based configuration of NAP client settings and to be exempted from NAP health evaluation through security group membership. NAP clients that are not domain members must be manually configured with NAP client settings and cannot be exempted from NAP health evaluation through security group membership.

Installing NAP Client Components

As with other NAP enforcement methods, installing NAP client components such as the set of SHAs is easier when the computers are part of a managed environment. As domain members, the computers can receive Group Policy settings and have software components automatically installed through desktop management software, such as Microsoft Systems Management Server or System Center Configuration Manager 2007, or other methods such as logon scripts.

Configuration Settings

Consider the following configuration settings for your NAP clients:

- If you are using the Windows Security Health Agent SHA for NAP clients running Windows Vista or Windows XP SP3, enable Windows Security Center for domain members through Group Policy. Unmanaged computers running Windows Vista or Windows XP SP3 enable Windows Security Center by default.

- As needed, you must install additional software for system health and their corresponding SHAs that are being used to evaluate system health.

- Enable the DHCP Quarantine enforcement client.

- Enable automatic startup for the Network Access Protection Agent service.

Manual Configuration

To configure NAP client settings individually, do the following:

- Install required software and their corresponding SHAs.

- For NAP clients running Windows Vista, Windows Server 2008, or Windows XP SP3, enable the DHCP Quarantine enforcement client.

- Enable automatic startup for the Network Access Protection Agent service.

Automated Configuration for Managed Computers

For managed computers, you can install required software and their corresponding SHAs through desktop management software or other methods, such as logon scripts. Additionally, you can use Active Directory and Group Policy settings to do the following:

- Enable the Windows Security Center

- Enable the DHCP Quarantine enforcement client

- Configure the NAP Agent service for automatic startup

For Windows Server 2008, you might need to install the Group Policy Management feature in Server Manager to use the Group Policy management tools.

Deploying DHCP Enforcement

The deployment of DHCP enforcement consists of the following tasks:

- Configuring remediation servers
- Configuring NAP health policy servers
- Configuring DHCP servers
- Configuring NAP clients

Configuring Remediation Servers

The first task in configuring remediation servers is to identify the set of servers that non-compliant NAP clients must be able to access. As described in Chapter 15, remediation servers can consist of the following types of computers:

- Domain Name System (DNS) and Windows Internet Name Service (WINS) servers

- Active Directory domain controllers

- Internet proxy servers

- Troubleshooting Uniform Resource Locator (URL) Web servers

- Health update servers

Depending on the SHAs that your NAP clients are using, you might need to configure your health update servers to provide updates or services to noncompliant NAP clients. See the documentation supplied by the vendors for your SHAs for information about what needs to be installed and configured.

Configuring NAP Health Policy Servers

To configure a NAP health policy server, you must modify the configuration of your existing NPS-based RADIUS servers by doing the following:

- Installing SHVs

- Configuring RADIUS server settings

- Configuring health requirement policies for DHCP enforcement

Installing SHVs

The SHVs that you are using must be installed on each NAP health policy server to be included in health policy evaluation. The NPS service includes the Windows Security Health Validator SHV to specify the settings of the Windows Security Center on NAP clients running Windows Vista or Windows XP SP3.

The exact method for installing additional SHVs will depend on the SHV vendor and can include downloading the SHV from a vendor Web page or running a setup program from a vendor-supplied CD-ROM. Check with your SHV vendor for information about the method of installation.

Configuring RADIUS Server Settings

Because DHCP servers do not need to use RADIUS to assign IPv4 address configurations prior to deploying DHCP enforcement, the NAP health policy servers are typically not already configured with the DHCP servers as RADIUS clients. You must add them to the NAP health policy servers by using the NPS snap-in. When configuring the RADIUS client in the New RADIUS Client dialog box, select the RADIUS Client Is NAP-Capable check box.

Additionally, because the DHCP enforcement deployment will initially use reporting mode, in which noncompliant NAP clients have unlimited access, you might want to change how your NAP health policy servers are logging incoming requests for analysis prior to enabling enforcement mode. You can configure the NPS service to log incoming requests and accounting information in local files or a Microsoft SQL Server database. For more information, see Chapter 9.

Configuring Health Requirement Policies for DHCP Enforcement

You can create your Health Requirement Policies for DHCP Enforcement manually or with the Configure NAP Wizard. Because of the amount of automated configuration done by the Configure NAP Wizard, this method is recommended and is described in this chapter.

To Create a Set of Policies for DHCP Enforcement

1. In the Network Policy Server snap-in, in the console tree, click NPS.

2. In the details pane, under Standard Configuration, in the drop-down list, select Network Access Protection (NAP), and then click Configure NAP.

3. On the Select Network Connection Method For Use With NAP page, under Network Connection Method, select Dynamic Host Configuration Protocol (DHCP), and then in the Policy Name box, type a name (or use the name created by the wizard). Figure 19-1 shows an example.

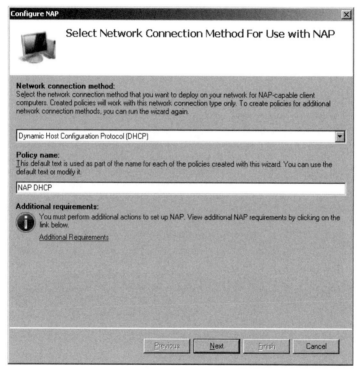

Figure 19-1   The Select Network Connection Method For Use With NAP page

4. Click Next. On the Specify NAP Enforcement Servers Running DHCP Server page, click Add as needed to add RADIUS clients corresponding to your NAP-capable DHCP servers. Click Next.

5. On the Specify DHCP Scopes page, click Add as needed to add the profile names of your DHCP scopes that you want to identify for this set of health requirement policies. For an initial deployment, do not specify any profile names. Click Next.

6. On the Configure User Groups and Machine Groups page, select computer or user groups as needed, and then click Next. For example, if you are using a security group to specify the computers to be evaluated for DHCP enforcement, configure the name of that group on this page. Click Next.

7. On the Specify A NAP Remediation Server Group And URL page, click Next. Procedures later in this chapter will configure a remediation server group and troubleshooting URL.

8. On the Define NAP Health Policy page, select the SHVs that you want to have evaluated for DHCP enforcement, select the Enable Auto-Remediation Of Client Computers check box as needed, and then select Allow Full Network Access To NAP-Ineligible Client Computers, even if you want non-NAP-capable clients to have restricted access. Because you want the initial NAP enforcement mode to be reporting mode (rather than enforcement mode), you must select Allow Full Network Access To NAP-Ineligible Client Computers. During the configuration for enforcement mode, you can change the network policy for non-NAP-capable clients to limit their access. Figure 19-2 shows an example.

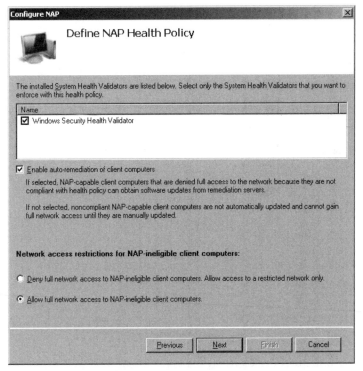

Figure 19-2   The Define NAP Health Policy page

9. Click Next. On the Completing NAP Enforcement Policy And RADIUS Client Configuration page, click Finish.

The Configure NAP Wizard creates the following:

- A health policy for compliant NAP clients based on the SHVs selected in the Configure NAP Wizard

- A health policy for noncompliant NAP clients based on the SHVs selected in the Configure NAP Wizard

- A connection request policy for DHCP-based NAP health evaluation requests

- A network policy for compliant NAP clients that allows unlimited access

- A network policy for noncompliant NAP clients that allows restricted access

- A network policy for non-NAP-capable clients that allows unlimited access

The connection request policy and network policies that are created by the Configure NAP Wizard are placed at the bottom of their respective ordered lists.

Because the network policy for noncompliant NAP clients by default allows only limited access (enforcement mode), you must modify this policy to allow unlimited access for reporting mode.

To Configure Reporting Mode

1. In the console tree of the Network Policy Server snap-in, expand Policies, and then click Network Policies.

2. In the details pane, double-click the network policy for noncompliant DHCP-based NAP clients that was created by the Configure NAP Wizard.

3. Click the Settings tab, and then click the NAP Enforcement setting.

4. In the details pane of the network policy Properties dialog box, click Allow Full Network Access, and then click OK.

The next step is to ensure that the SHVs that you are using have the settings that correctly reflect your health requirements.

To Configure the SHVs for the Required Health Settings

1. In the console tree of the Network Policy Server snap-in, expand Network Access Protection, and then click System Health Validators.

2. In the details pane, under Name, double-click your SHVs, and then configure each SHV with your requirements for system health.

   For example, double-click Windows Security Health Validator, and then click Configure. In the Windows Security Health Validator dialog box, configure system health requirements for Windows Vista–based and Windows XP–based NAP clients.

The next step is to configure the health policies created by the Configure NAP Wizard to reflect the conditions for compliant and noncompliant NAP clients for your system health requirements.

To Configure Health Policies for System Health Requirements

1. In the console tree of the Network Policy Server snap-in, expand Policies, and then click Health Policies.

2. In the details pane, double-click the health policies for compliant and noncompliant NAP clients, and make changes as needed to the health evaluation conditions and the selected SHVs.

To configure a network policy that does not perform health evaluation for the computers that are members of the security group for exempted computers, do the following:

1. In the console tree of the Network Policy Server snap-in, expand Policies, and then click Network Policies.

2. Right-click the DHCP network policy for compliant NAP clients that was created by the Configure NAP Wizard, and then click Duplicate Policy.

3. Double-click the copy of the network policy for compliant NAP clients created in step 2.

4. On the Overview tab, in the Policy Name box, type a name for the new network policy (such as **Exempted Computers**). In the Policy State area, select the Policy Enabled check box.

5. On the Conditions tab, click Add. In the Select Condition dialog box, double-click Windows Groups. In the Windows Groups dialog box, click Add Groups, specify the name of the security group for exempted computers, and then click OK twice.

6. On the Conditions tab, click the Health Policy condition, click Remove, and then click OK.

7. In the details pane, right-click the name of the duplicated network policy created in step 2, and then click Move Up.

8. Repeat step 5 as many times as necessary so that the duplicated network policy is above the network policy for compliant NAP clients that was created by the Configure NAP Wizard.

Configuring NAP Clients

To configure your NAP clients, perform the following steps:

- Install SHAs.
- Configure managed NAP clients through Group Policy.

Installing SHAs

NAP clients running Windows Vista or Windows XP SP3 include the Windows Security Health Agent SHA. If you are using additional SHAs from third-party vendors, you must install them on your NAP clients. The exact method of installation of additional SHAs will depend on the SHA vendor and can include downloading the SHA from a vendor Web page or running a setup program from a vendor-supplied CD-ROM. Check with your SHA vendor for information about the method of installation.

On a managed network, you can use the following methods:

■ Network management software such as Microsoft Systems Management Server (SMS) or System Center Configuration Manager 2007 to install software across an organization

■ Logon scripts that execute the setup program for the SHA

For computers that are not managed, you can install SHAs through a script file or through an intranet Web site.

Configuring Managed NAP Clients Through Group Policy

For managed NAP clients, you can use Group Policy for NAP client settings, which consists of the following:

■ Configuring NAP client settings

■ Enabling Windows Security Center

■ Configuring the Network Access Protection Agent service for automatic startup

Configuring NAP Client Settings   To configure NAP client settings in Group Policy (equivalent to using the NAP Client Configuration snap-in on an individual computer running Windows Vista), do the following:

1. Open the Group Policy Management snap-in. In the console tree, expand Forest, expand Domains, and then click the domain to which your VPN clients belong. On the Linked Group Policy Objects pane, right-click the appropriate Group Policy Object (the default object is Default Domain Policy), and then click Edit.

2. In the console tree of the Group Policy Management Editor snap-in, expand the policy and then Computer Configuration\Windows Settings\Security Settings\Network Access Protection\NAP Client Configuration.

3. In the console tree, click Enforcement Clients.

4. In the details pane, double-click the DHCP Quarantine Enforcement Client.

5. On the General tab, select the Enable This Enforcement Client check box, and then click OK.

6. If you want to specify an image that appears in the NAP client user interface (UI), in the console tree, click User Interface Settings, and then in the details pane, double-click User Interface Settings.

7. On the General tab, type the title and description for the text that appears in the NAP client UI, and then type the path to an image file that appears in the UI or click Browse and specify its location. Click OK.

Enabling Windows Security Center   To use Group Policy to enable the Windows Security Center on NAP clients that are members of your Active Directory domain, do the following:

1. In the console tree of the Group Policy Management Editor snap-in for the appropriate Group Policy Object, open Computer Configuration\Administrative Templates\ Windows Components\Security Center.

2. In the details pane, double-click Turn On Security Center (Domain PCs Only).

3. On the Setting tab, select Enabled, and then click OK.

Configuring the Network Access Protection Agent Service for Automatic Startup   To use Group Policy to enable automatic startup of the Network Access Protection Agent service on NAP clients, do the following:

1. In the console tree of the Group Policy Management Editor snap-in for the appropriate Group Policy Object, open Computer Configuration\Windows Settings\Security Settings\System Services.

2. In the details pane, double-click Network Access Protection Agent.

3. On the Security Policy Setting tab, select the Define This Policy Setting check box, select Automatic, and then click OK.

Configuring DHCP Servers

To configure your DHCP servers for DHCP enforcement, you must do the following:

-   Install and configure the NPS service.

-   Enable and configure Network Access Protection behavior.

-   Configure additional options for noncompliant NAP clients.

-   Configure profile names for specific scopes.

Installing and Configuring the NPS Service

Your NAP-capable DHCP servers exchange the health state information with NAP health policy servers in the form of RADIUS messages. To be able to perform this function, you must install the NPS service on your DHCP servers and configure it as a RADIUS proxy.

To Install the NPS Service on a DHCP Server Computer

1. Run Server Manager on the DHCP server computer.

2. Under Roles Summary, click Add Roles.

3. On the Select Server Roles page, select the Network Policy And Access Services check box, and then click Next twice.

4. On the Select Role Services page, click Network Policy Server, and then click Next.

5. On the Confirm Installation Selections page, verify your configuration selections, and then click Install.

Next, you must configure the NPS service to act as a RADIUS proxy and forward RADIUS requests to your NAP health policy servers.

To Configure the NPS Service as a RADIUS Proxy

1. In the console tree of the Network Policy Server snap-in, expand the RADIUS Clients And Servers node.

2. Right-click Remote RADIUS Server Groups, and then click New.

3. In the New Remote RADIUS Server Group dialog box, in the Group Name box, type the name of the group (for example, **NAP Health Policy Servers**), and then click Add.

4. On the Address tab, type the DNS name, IPv4 address, or IPv6 address of a NAP health policy server.

5. On the Authentication/Accounting tab, in the Shared Secret and Confirm Shared Secret boxes, type the RADIUS shared secret. Do not change the authentication or accounting ports.

6. On the Load Balancing tab, specify the priority and weight for RADIUS traffic to this RADIUS server and failover and failback settings as needed, and then click OK.

7. In the New Remote RADIUS Server Group dialog box, click Add, and then repeat steps 4–6 for each NAP health policy server that this DHCP server will use to perform health validation for NAP clients.

8. In the console tree of the Network Policy Server snap-in, expand the Policies node.

9. Right-click Connection Request Policies, and then click New.

10. On the Specify Connection Request Policy Name And Connection Type page, type the name of the connection request policy (such as **RADIUS Proxy to NAP Health Policy Servers**). In the Type Of Network Access Server drop-down list, select DHCP Server, and then click Next.

11. On the Specify Conditions page, click Add.

12. In the Select Condition dialog box, double-click Day And Time Restrictions.

13. In the Day And Time Restrictions dialog box, click Permitted, click OK, and then click Next.

14. On the Specify Connection Request Forwarding page, under Authentication settings, select Forward Requests To The Following Remote RADIUS Server Group For Authentication, and then select the remote RADIUS server group created in step 3. Click Accounting, select Forward Requests To The Following Remote RADIUS Server Group For Accounting, select the remote RADIUS server group created in step 3 from the drop-down list, and then click Next.

15. On the Configure Settings page, click Next.

16. On the Completing Connection Request Policy Wizard page, click Finish.

17. In the details pane, right-click the new connection request policy, and then click Move Up so that it is above the Use Windows Authentication For All Users default connection request policy.

Enabling and Configuring Network Access Protection Behavior

To enable and configure NAP behavior on a DHCP server, do the following:

1. In the console tree of the DHCP snap-in, expand the server name, right-click IPv4, and then click Properties.

2. Click the Network Access Protection tab. Figure 19-3 shows an example.

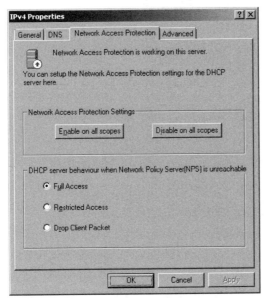

Figure 19-3 The Network Access Protection tab of the IPv4 Properties dialog box

3. Click Enable On All Scopes. To configure the behavior of DHCP enforcement when the NAP health policy server is unavailable, click Full Access, Restricted Access, or Drop Client Packet as appropriate, and then click OK.

Configure Additional Options for Noncompliant NAP Clients

To configure additional DHCP options for noncompliant NAP clients, do the following:

1. In the console tree of the DHCP snap-in, expand the server name and then IPv4.

2. For server options, right-click Server Options, and then click Configure Options. For scope options, expand the scope, right-click Scope Options, and then click Configure Options.

3. In the Server Options or Scope Options dialog box, click the Advanced tab.

4. On the Advanced tab, in the Vendor Class drop-down list, select the appropriate vendor class.

5. In the User Class drop-down list, select Default Network Access Protection Class. Figure 19-4 shows an example.

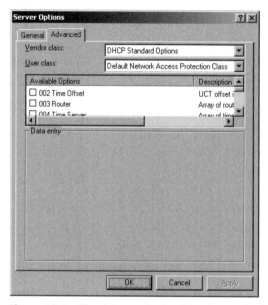

Figure 19-4   The Advanced tab of the Server Options dialog box

6. Configure DHCP options for noncompliant NAP clients as needed, and then click OK.

Configure Profile Names for Specific Scopes

To configure profile names for specific DHCP scopes, do the following:

1. In the console tree of the DHCP snap-in, expand the server name and then IPv4.

2. Right-click the scope, and then click Properties.

3. Click the Network Access Protection tab. Figure 19-5 shows an example.

4. Select Use Custom Profile.

5. In the Profile Name box, type the profile name, and then click OK.

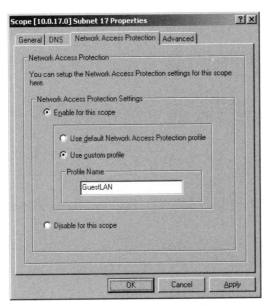

Figure 19-5   The Network Access Protection tab of a DHCP scope properties dialog box

DHCP Enforcement Deployment Checkpoint for Reporting Mode

At this point in the DHCP enforcement deployment, NAP clients attempting to obtain a DHCP address configuration will have their health state evaluated. Because the DHCP enforcement deployment is in reporting mode, both compliant and noncompliant NAP clients have unlimited network access to the intranet, and the users of noncompliant NAP clients receive no message in the notification area of their desktop stating that their computers do not meet system health requirements.

While the DHCP enforcement deployment is in reporting mode, perform an analysis of the NPS events in the Windows Logs\Security event log on the NAP health policy servers to determine which NAP clients are not compliant. Take the appropriate actions to remedy their health state, such as installing missing SHAs or providing health update resources on remediation servers.

Testing Restricted Access

Prior to enabling enforcement mode, you must test restricted access for noncompliant NAP clients. To perform this test, you can do the following:

1. Create a subnet with test DHCP client computers with a corresponding scope configured with the profile name Test on a NAP-capable DHCP server. To configure the scope with the Test profile name, see "Configure Profile Names for Specific Scopes" earlier in this chapter.

2. Create a new network policy for noncompliant NAP clients that restricts access for the Test profile.

3. Ensure that a noncompliant NAP client on the test subnet has its access restricted and can access only remediation servers on your intranet.

To Create a New Network Policy for the Test Profile

1. In the console tree of the Network Policy Server snap-in, expand Policies, and then click Network Policies.

2. Right-click the DHCP network policy for noncompliant NAP clients that was created by the Configure NAP Wizard, and then click Duplicate Policy.

3. Double-click the copy of the network policy for noncompliant NAP clients created in step 2.

4. On the Overview tab, in the Policy name box, type a name for the new network policy. In the Policy State section, select the Policy Enabled check box.

5. On the Conditions tab, click Add. In the Select Condition dialog box, double-click MS-Service Class. In the MS-Service Class dialog box, type **Test**, and then click OK.

6. Click the Settings tab. Under Network Access Protection, click NAP Enforcement. In the details pane, select Allow Limited Access, and then clear the Enable Auto-Remediation Of Client Computers check box.

7. Click Configure. In the Remediation Servers And Troubleshooting URL dialog box, in the Troubleshooting URL box, type the URL to the troubleshooting page on your troubleshooting URL remediation server.

8. In the Remediation Servers And Troubleshooting URL dialog box, click New Group, and then configure the remediation server group for the IPv4 addresses of your remediation servers. Click OK twice.

9. In the details pane, right-click the name of the duplicated network policy for noncompliant NAP clients, and then click Move Up.

10. Repeat step 10 as many times as necessary so that the duplicated network policy for testing noncompliant NAP clients is just above the network policy for noncompliant NAP clients that was created by the Configure NAP Wizard.

Next, ensure that the IPv4 address configuration for a noncompliant NAP client on the test subnet is properly configured for restricted access.

To Test Restricted Access for a Noncompliant Test Computer

1. Configure a NAP client computer on the test subnet to be noncompliant. Depending on your system health requirements, this might be as simple as manually disabling Automatic Updates or Windows Firewall.

2. From the NAP client computer, renew the IPv4 address configuration by running the **ipconfig /renew** command.

3. When the DHCP configuration completes, you should see a Network Access Protection message in the notification area of the desktop. You can verify restricted status by running the **ipconfig** command. You can verify the restricted IPv4 address configuration by running the **ipconfig /all** and **route print** commands. The IPv4 addresses in the remediation server group should be listed as host routes in the IPv4 route table portion of the display of the **route print** command.

4. From the NAP client computer, verify that you can reach all the remediation servers and access the troubleshooting URL.

5. From the NAP client computer, verify that you cannot reach other servers on the intranet.

Based on your testing, make any modifications that you need to the duplicated network policy for noncompliant NAP clients, such as the remediation server group or the troubleshooting URL. If you have made required software for system health and SHA installation software available on remediation servers, ensure that the software and SHAs can be installed from the noncompliant NAP clients.

Configuring Deferred Enforcement

After testing restricted access for noncompliant NAP clients, determine the date for deferred enforcement mode (the date for which you will configure the noncompliant NAP client network policy for enforcement mode). On this date, noncompliant NAP clients will have their access restricted. In deferred enforcement mode for DHCP enforcement, noncompliant NAP clients will still have unlimited access to the intranet, but the users will now see a message in their notification area indicating that their computer does not comply with system health requirements.

To Configure Deferred Enforcement Mode

1. In the console tree of the Network Policy Server snap-in, expand Policies, and then click Network Policies.

2. In the details pane, double-click the DHCP enforcement network policy for noncompliant NAP clients that was created by the Configure NAP Wizard.

3. Click the Settings tab, and then click the NAP Enforcement setting.

4. In the details pane of the network policy properties dialog box, select Allow Full Network Access For A Limited Time, specify the date and time that enforcement mode will be configured on the NAP health policy servers, and then click OK.

Configuring Network Policy for Enforcement Mode

Because you have already configured and tested a DHCP enforcement network policy that restricts access for noncompliant NAP clients (the duplicated network policy for noncompliant NAP clients for the test subnet), to enable enforcement mode, you will modify this duplicated network policy and disable the original DHCP enforcement network policy for noncompliant NAP clients that was created by the Configure NAP Wizard. On the date for enforcement mode, configure enforcement mode on your NAP health policy servers.

To Configure Enforcement Mode

1. In the console tree of the Network Policy Server snap-in, expand Policies, and then click Network Policies.

2. In the details pane, double-click the duplicated DHCP enforcement network policy for noncompliant NAP clients that you were using to test restricted access.

3. On the Conditions tab, in the Condition list, click MS-Service Class, and then click Remove.

4. On the Settings tab, under Network Access Protection, click NAP Enforcement. In the details pane, under Auto Remediation, select the Enable Auto-Remediation Of Client Computers check box, and then click OK.

5. In the details pane, right-click the original network policy for noncompliant NAP clients that was created by the Configure NAP Wizard, and then click Delete.

At this point, the network policy that you used to test restricted access for noncompliant NAP clients now applies to all your NAP clients, and the original network policy for noncompliant NAP clients that was created by the Configure NAP Wizard has been deleted.

To limit the access for non-NAP-capable clients, on the date for enforcement mode, you must configure a network policy for non-NAP-capable clients that restricts their access. Because the duplicated network policy for noncompliant NAP clients has already been configured and tested for restricted access, you can duplicate and then modify this policy for non-NAP-capable clients.

To Limit the Access of Non-NAP-Capable Clients

1. In the console tree of the Network Policy Server snap-in, expand Policies, and then click Network Policies.

2. Right-click the duplicated network policy for noncompliant NAP clients, and then click Duplicate Policy.

3. Double-click the new network policy.

4. On the Overview tab, in the Policy Name box, type a name for the new network policy. In the Policy State area, select the Policy Enabled check box.

5. On the Conditions tab, click Add. In the Select Condition dialog box, double-click NAP-Capable Computers. In the NAP-Capable Computers dialog box, select Only Computers That Are Not NAP-Capable, and then click OK.

6. On the Conditions tab, click the Health Policy condition, click Remove, and then click OK.

7. In the details pane of the Network Policy Server snap-in, right-click the original network policy for non-NAP-capable clients that was created by the Configure NAP Wizard, and then click Delete.

The deployment of DHCP enforcement is complete. Noncompliant NAP clients and (optionally) non-NAP-capable clients will have their access restricted through an IPv4 address configuration that allows access only to the remediation servers on the intranet.

Ongoing Maintenance

The areas of maintenance for a DHCP enforcement deployment are as follows:

- Adding a NAP client
- Adding a new SHA and SHV

Adding a NAP Client

A new NAP client is either a managed computer or an unmanaged computer. To add a NAP client that is a managed computer, do the following:

1. Join the NAP client computer to the domain.

2. Install the SHAs on the NAP client computer.

For a new unmanaged NAP client, follow the steps in "Configuring NAP Client Settings" earlier in this chapter.

Adding a New SHA and SHV

To add a new SHA and SHV to your DHCP enforcement deployment, you must do the following:

1. If needed, install the software or components on your remediation servers for automatic remediation required by the new SHA.

2. Install the required software and SHA on your NAP clients. For more information, see "Configuring NAP Client Settings" earlier in this chapter.

3. Install the SHV on your NAP health policy servers.

4. If needed, on the NAP health policy servers, in the Network Access Protection\System Health Validators node of the NPS snap-in, configure the settings of the SHV for your system health requirements.

5. On the NAP health policy servers, modify the health policies for compliant and non-compliant NAP clients to include the new SHV in its evaluation.

Troubleshooting

Because of the different components and processes involved, troubleshooting a DHCP enforcement deployment can be a difficult task. This section describes the troubleshooting tools that are provided with Windows Server 2008 and Windows Vista and how to troubleshoot DHCP enforcement starting from the NAP client.

Troubleshooting Tools

Microsoft provides the following tools to troubleshoot DHCP enforcement:

- TCP/IP troubleshooting tools
- Netsh tool
- NAP client event logging
- NPS event logging
- NPS authentication and accounting logging
- Netsh NAP tracing
- Network Monitor 3.1

TCP/IP Troubleshooting Tools

The Ipconfig tool displays the state of a NAP client. At a command prompt on a NAP client, run the **ipconfig /all** command. In the Windows IP Configuration section of the display, the state of the NAP client is listed as the System Quarantine State and displayed as either Not Restricted or Restricted.

Additional TCP/IP troubleshooting tools are Ping and Nslookup, used to test reachability and name resolution.

Netsh Tool

Beyond the state of the NAP client as shown in the **ipconfig /all** command, you can gather additional NAP client configuration information by running the following commands:

- **netsh nap client show configuration** Displays the local NAP client configuration including the list of NAP enforcement clients and their state (Enabled or Disabled) and the state of NAP client tracing
- **netsh nap client show grouppolicy** Displays the same NAP client settings as the **netsh nap client show configuration** command for the settings obtained through Group Policy
- **netsh nap client show state** Displays detailed NAP client state, enforcement client state, and SHA state

Note   The display for the netsh nap client show configuration and netsh nap client show grouppolicy commands does not show which set of settings, local or Group Policy–based, is currently active on the NAP client. If any NAP client settings are obtained through Group Policy, the entire set of NAP client settings is specified by Group Policy and all local NAP client settings are ignored.

If any NAP client settings are obtained through Group Policy, the entire set of NAP client settings are specified by Group Policy, and all local NAP client settings are ignored.

NAP Client Event Logging

Use the Event Viewer snap-in to check the events in the Windows event log created by the Network Access Protection Agent service. On computers running Windows Vista or Windows Server 2008, use the Event Viewer snap-in to view events in Applications and Services Logs\Microsoft\Windows\Network Access Protection\Operational. On computers running Windows XP SP3, use the Event Viewer snap-in to view events in the System event log.

NPS Event Logging

Use the Event Viewer snap-in to check the Windows Logs\Security event log for NPS events. NPS event log entries contain a lot of information about the NAP health evaluation, including the name of the matching connection request policy (the Proxy Policy Name field in the description of the event) and the matching network policy (the Network Policy Name field in the description of the event). Viewing NPS events in the Windows Logs\Security event log is one of the most useful troubleshooting methods to obtain information about NAP health evaluations.

NPS Logging

By default, NPS will log authentication and accounting data to the *%SystemRoot%*\System32\ LogFiles folder in a database-compatible (comma-delimited) text file. You can also configure NPS to perform SQL Server logging and then analyze the NPS authentication and accounting data in a SQL Server database.

Netsh NAP Tracing

The Network Access Protection Agent service has an extensive tracing capability that you can use to troubleshoot complex network problems. You can enable Netsh NAP tracing by running the **netsh nap client set tracing state=enable level=basic|advanced|verbose** command. The log files are stored in the *%SystemRoot%*\Tracing folder. Netsh NAP tracing files can be sent to Microsoft customer support staff for analysis.

Network Monitor 3.1

Use Network Monitor 3.1, a network sniffer that is available from Microsoft, to capture and view the traffic sent between DHCP clients, DHCP servers, and NAP health policy servers. For example, you can use Network Monitor 3.1 to capture the RADIUS traffic between a DHCP server and the NAP health policy server to determine the contents of RADIUS messages, such as the RADIUS attributes for specifying the IPv4 packet filters corresponding to the list of remediation servers.

The proper interpretation of this traffic requires an in-depth understanding of RADIUS and other protocols. Network Monitor captures can be saved as files and sent to Microsoft customer support staff for analysis.

On the Disc   You can link to the download site for Network Monitor from the companion CD-ROM.

Troubleshooting DHCP Enforcement

This section describes how to troubleshoot a DHCP enforcement deployment by starting at the NAP client. This is the approach used by many technical support departments in organizations and reflects a multi-tiered analysis and escalation path to determine the source of a problem and its solution. For example, the IT department of an organization might have the following tiers:

- **Tier 1**   Help desk staff, who can provide an initial assessment of problems and solutions based on an analysis of the client (the NAP client for DHCP enforcement)
- **Tier 2**   Windows network and infrastructure services staff, who manage the DHCP servers, remediation servers, and NAP health policy servers

When troubleshooting DHCP enforcement, it is important to first determine the extent of the problem. If your DHCP clients cannot perform any DHCP address configuration, you must troubleshoot that problem independently of NAP and DHCP enforcement. If all your DHCP clients are experiencing DHCP enforcement problems, issues might exist in your NAP health policy servers. If all your DHCP clients that are using a specific DHCP server are experiencing DHCP enforcement problems, issues might exist in the configuration of the DHCP server or its configured NAP health policy servers. If only specific DHCP clients are experiencing DHCP enforcement problems, issues might exist for those individual clients.

Troubleshooting the NAP Client

To troubleshoot the NAP client, do the following:

- Verify whether the NAP client has successfully obtained a DHCP address configuration. If not, please see the "Troubleshooting" section of Chapter 3.

- Verify whether the NAP client is compliant or noncompliant by running the **ipconfig /all** command.

If the NAP client is noncompliant and is not autoremediating its health state, verify the following:

- **Network reachability from the NAP client to the IPv4 addresses of the remediation servers**   You can use the Ping tool, but because of default Windows Firewall rules, incoming Internet Control Message Protocol (ICMP) traffic on the remediation servers might be blocked.

- **Name resolution from the NAP client**   Use the Ping and Nslookup tools for the names of the remediation servers. Verify that the DNS names that the NAP client uses successfully resolve to the correct IPv4 addresses. .

- **That the Network Access Protection Agent service is started on the NAP client and that it is configured to automatically start**   Run the **netsh nap client show state** command to determine the service state, and use the Services snap-in to configure the Network Access Protection Agent service.

- **That the DHCP Quarantine Enforcement Client is enabled**   Run the **netsh nap client show configuration** command. If needed, use the Group Policy Management Editor snap-in (for Active Directory–based Group Policy Objects), the NAP Client Configuration snap-in, or the **netsh nap client set enforcement 79617 enable** command to enable the DHCP Quarantine enforcement client.

- **That the NAP client has all the appropriate SHAs installed**   Run the **netsh nap client show state** command. If you are using the Windows Security Health Agent SHA, verify that the Windows Security Center is enabled.

Beyond these verification steps, use the Event Viewer snap-in on the NAP client to view the NAP client events in Applications and Services Logs\Microsoft\Windows\Network Access Protection\Operational for a Windows Vista–based NAP client and in System for a Windows XP SP3–based NAP client. Use the NAP client events to perform additional troubleshooting. Note the correlation ID specified in the description of the NAP client events. The correlation ID can be used to find the corresponding health evaluation event on the NPS server.

Troubleshooting the DHCP Servers

To troubleshoot DHCP servers for DHCP enforcement, verify the following:

- **That the DHCP server has Network Access Protection enabled**   Use the DHCP snap-in to ensure that NAP is enabled for all scopes from the Network Access Protection tab in the properties dialog box of the IPv4 node.

- **That the DHCP server has NPS installed and configured to forward RADIUS requests to the NAP health policy servers**   Use the NPS snap-in to verify the configuration and processing order of the connection request policy that forwards RADIUS requests to the NAP health policy servers.

- **Network reachability from the DHCP server to the IPv4 addresses of the NAP health policy servers**   You can use the Ping tool, but because of default Windows Firewall rules, incoming ICMP traffic on the NAP health policy servers might be blocked.

- **That the scopes of the DHCP server are NAP enabled and have an appropriate profile name**   Use the DHCP snap-in to ensure that, from the Network Access Protection tab for the properties of your individual scopes, NAP is enabled and that the appropriate profile name is properly configured.

Troubleshooting the NAP Health Policy Servers

To troubleshoot the NAP health policy servers, verify the following:

- **That all the RADIUS clients corresponding to DHCP servers have the RADIUS Client Is NAP-Capable check box selected on the Settings tab of the properties dialog box of the RADIUS client**   You can use the Network Policy Server snap-in or the **netsh nps show client** command.

- **That the health requirement policies are correctly configured for DHCP enforcement**   You can use the Network Policy Server snap-in or **netsh nps show** commands. Verify that there is a correctly configured set of connection request policies, network policies, health policies, and SHVs that reflect your health requirements and the correct behavior for compliant, noncompliant, and non-NAP-capable clients for DHCP enforcement. Verify the processing order of the connection request policies and the network policies.

- **That the network policy for noncompliant NAP clients has been configured to automatically remediate health status**   You can use the Network Policy Server snap-in or the **netsh nps show np** command.

- **That the network policy for compliant NAP clients is correctly configured**   You can use the Network Policy Server snap-in or the **netsh nps show np** command.

- **That the network policy for noncompliant NAP clients is correctly configured**   You can use the Network Policy Server snap-in or the **netsh nps show np** command. Verify the addresses in the remediation server group and the URL for the troubleshooting Web server.

- **That the network policy for non-NAP-capable clients is correctly configured**   You can use the Network Policy Server snap-in or the **netsh nps show np** command.

Beyond these verification steps, use the Event Viewer snap-in on the NAP health policy server to view the NPS events in Windows Logs\Security for events corresponding to RADIUS messages sent by the DHCP servers for system health evaluation of NAP clients. Use the correlation ID of the NAP client event to locate the corresponding NPS event in the Security log. To view the NPS events, configure a filter with the Event Sources set to Microsoft Windows Security Auditing and the Task Category set to Network Policy Server.

Troubleshooting Remediation Servers

Verify that the remediation servers are reachable by noncompliant NAP clients. If you are making required software for system health or SHAs available on remediation servers, verify that the software or SHAs can be installed from a noncompliant NAP client.

For health update servers, verify that they have been correctly configured to provide the necessary resources to remediate the health of an SHA on a NAP client. For more information, see the documentation provided by the vendor of the SHA.

Chapter Summary

Deploying DHCP enforcement involves configuration of Active Directory, DHCP servers, NAP health policy servers, remediation servers, and NAP clients. After an initial configuration in reporting mode, test enforcement mode on subset of NAP clients. Last, configure enforcement mode for all DHCP clients. After deploying enforcement mode, ongoing maintenance of DHCP enforcement consists of adding NAP clients and adding SHAs and SHVs. To troubleshoot DHCP enforcement, verify network connectivity and configuration for NAP clients, DHCP servers, NAP health policy servers, and remediation servers.

Additional Information

For additional information about NAP, see the following:

- Chapter 14, "Network Access Protection Overview"
- Chapter 15, "Preparing for Network Access Protection"
- Chapter 16, "IPsec Enforcement"
- Chapter 17, "802.1X Enforcement"
- Chapter 18, "VPN Enforcement"
- Windows Server 2008 Technical Library at *http://technet.microsoft.com/windowsserver/2008*
- Windows Server 2008 Help and Support
- "Network Access Protection" (*http://www.microsoft.com/nap*)

For additional information about Active Directory, see the following:

- *Windows Server 2008 Active Directory Resource Kit* by Stan Reimer, Mike Mulcare, Conan Kezema, and Byron Wright, with the Microsoft Active Directory Team, available both as a stand-alone title and in the *Windows Server 2008 Resource Kit* (both from Microsoft Press, 2008)

- Windows Server 2008 Technical Library at *http://technet.microsoft.com/windowsserver/ 2008*

- Windows Server 2008 Help and Support

- "Windows Server 2003 Active Directory" (*http://www.microsoft.com/ad*)

For additional information about Group Policy, see the following:

- *Windows Group Policy Resource Kit: Windows Server 2008 and Windows Vista* by Derek Melber, Group Policy MVP, with the Windows Group Policy Team (Microsoft Press, 2008)

- Windows Server 2008 Technical Library at *http://technet.microsoft.com/windowsserver/ 2008*

- Windows Server 2008 Help and Support

- "Windows Server Group Policy" (*http://www.microsoft.com/gp*)

For additional information about RADIUS and NPS, see the following:

- Chapter 9, "Authentication Infrastructure"

- Windows Server 2008 Technical Library at *http://technet.microsoft.com/windowsserver/ 2008*

- Windows Server 2008 Help and Support

- "Network Policy Server" (*http://www.microsoft.com/nps*)

For additional information about DHCP, see the following:

- Chapter 3, "Dynamic Host Configuration Protocol"

- Windows Server 2008 Technical Library at *http://technet.microsoft.com/windowsserver/ 2008*

- Windows Server 2008 Help and Support

- "Dynamic Host Configuration Protocol" (*http://www.microsoft.com/dhcp*)

Glossary

80/20 rule A guideline that suggests using two Dynamic Host Configuration Protocol (DHCP) servers for any network subnet, a technique called DHCP split-scope, in which the primary DHCP server owns 80 percent of the IP addresses and the secondary owns 20 percent. See *DHCP split-scope*.

802.1X An Institute of Electrical and Electronics Engineers (IEEE) standard that provides authenticated network access to Ethernet and 802.11 wireless networks.

802.1X access point An access server that uses Institute of Electrical and Electronics Engineers (IEEE) 802.1X authentication, typically either a wireless access point (AP) using 802.1X authentication or an 802.1X-capable switch.

802.1X enforcement A Network Access Protection (NAP) enforcement method in which a computer must meet system health requirements to obtain unlimited network access through an 802.1X-authenticated network connection, such as to an authenticating Ethernet switch or an Institute of Electrical and Electronics Engineers (IEEE) 802.11 wireless access point (AP).

AAAA resource record A resource record used to map a Domain Name System (DNS) domain name to a host Internet Protocol version 6 (IPv6) address on the network.

access client A computer that requires access to a network or another part of the network. Examples of access clients are dial-up or virtual private network (VPN) remote access clients, wireless clients, or local area network (LAN) clients connected to an authenticating switch.

access control list (ACL) A set of Internet Protocol version 4 (IPv4) or Internet Protocol version 6 (IPv6) packet filters configured on an 802.1X access point, typically identified with a name.

access server A computer that provides access to a network. Examples include remote access servers and wireless access points (APs).

address (A) resource record A resource record (RR) used to map a Domain Name System (DNS) domain name to a host Internet Protocol version 4 (IPv4) address on the network.

Address Resolution Protocol (ARP) A protocol that uses broadcast traffic on the local network to resolve a logically assigned IPv4 address to its physical hardware or media access control (MAC) layer address.

all-user profile A wireless profile that can be used to connect to a specific wireless network by any user with an account on the computer.

answering router A virtual private network (VPN) router that is listening for incoming site-to-site VPN connections.

anycast   A special IPv6 address type that can be assigned to multiple interfaces. The most commonly used example of an anycast address is the Subnet-Router anycast address, which is the subnet prefix with an interface identifier (ID) of zero.

authentication   The process for verifying that an entity or object is who or what it claims to be. Examples include confirming the source and integrity of information, such as verifying a digital signature or verifying the identity of a user or computer.

Authentication Header (AH)   An Internet Protocol security (IPsec) header that provides authentication and integrity, and prevents replay attacks for the entire packet (the Internet Protocol or IP header and the data payload carried in the packet).

auto-static update   The automatic configuration of Internet Protocol version 4 (IPv4) static routes for demand-dial interfaces when you use the Routing Information Protocol (RIP) for IPv4 with Routing and Remote Access.

Automatic Private IP Addressing (APIPA)   A Transmission Control Protocol/Internet Protocol (TCP/IP) feature in the Windows XP operating system and later versions of Windows that automatically configures a unique IP address from the range 169.254.0.1 through 169.254.255.254 with a subnet mask of 255.255.0.0 when TCP/IP is configured for dynamic addressing, a Dynamic Host Configuration Protocol (DHCP) server is not available, and an alternate address is not configured.

Berkeley Internet Name Domain (BIND)   An implementation of Domain Name System (DNS) written and ported to most available versions of the UNIX operating system.

Boolean   A system of base-2 math using a number system consisting of only ones and zeros.

BOOTP relay agent   See *DHCP relay agent*.

boundary network   In Internet Protocol security (IPsec) enforcement for Network Access Protection (NAP), the set of computers that have health certificates but do not require that incoming communication attempts authenticate with health certificates and use IPsec protection.

calling router   A virtual private network (VPN) router that initiates a site-to-site VPN connection.

canonical (CNAME) resource record   A resource record used to map an alternate alias name to a primary canonical Domain Name System (DNS) domain name used in the zone.

certificate revocation list (CRL)   A digitally signed list of unexpired certificates that have been revoked.

certification authority (CA)   An entity responsible for establishing and vouching for the authenticity of public keys belonging to subjects (usually users or computers) or other certification authorities. Activities of a certification authority can include binding public keys to distinguished names through signed certificates, managing certificate serial numbers, and certificate revocation.

Class A IP address   An Internet Protocol (IP) address that ranges from 1.0.0.1 through 126.255.255.254. The first octet indicates the network, and the last three octets indicate the host on the network. Class-based IP addressing has been superseded by Classless Interdomain Routing (CIDR).

Class B IP address   An Internet Protocol (IP) address that ranges from 128.0.0.1 through 191.255.255.254. The first two octets indicate the network, and the last two octets indicate the host on the network. Class-based IP addressing has been superseded by Classless Interdomain Routing (CIDR).

Class C IP address   An Internet Protocol (IP) address that ranges from 192.0.0.1 to 223.255.255.254. The first three octets indicate the network, and the last octet indicates the host on the network. Class-based IP addressing has been superseded by Classless Interdomain Routing (CIDR).

Classless Interdomain Routing (CIDR)   An Internet Protocol (IP) address and routing management method that allocates IP addresses in a way that reduces the number of routes stored on any individual router while also increasing the number of available IP addresses. CIDR replaces class-based IP address allocation.

computer certificate   A certificate that is stored in the local computer certificate store and has the appropriate properties to perform Point-to-Point Protocol (PPP)–based authentication, Secure Sockets Layer (SSL)–based authentication, or Internet Protocol security (IPsec)–based authentication. Also known as a machine certificate.

connection request policy   An ordered set of rules that allow the Network Policy Server (NPS) service to determine whether a specific connection attempt request or accounting message received from a Remote Authentication Dial-In User Service (RADIUS) client should be processed locally or forwarded to another RADIUS server.

coverage volume   The volume around a wireless access point (AP) for which you can send and receive wireless data for any of the supported bit rates.

convergence time   In Windows Internet Name Service (WINS), the time it takes for all WINS servers to be synchronized after an update occurs.

customized Connection Manager (CM) client dialer profile   A self-extracting executable file that is created by a network administrator using the Connection Manager Administration Kit (CMAK). Also known as a package.

Data Encryption Standard (DES)   An encryption algorithm that uses a 56-bit key and maps a 64-bit input block to a 64-bit output block. The key appears to be a 64-bit key, but one bit in each of the eight bytes is used for odd parity, resulting in 56 bits of usable key.

default gateway   The router on the local network that has knowledge of the network prefixes of other networks, so it can forward the packets to other gateways until they are delivered to the one connected to the specified destination.

deferred enforcement mode   A Network Access Protection (NAP) enforcement mode in which noncompliant NAP clients have unlimited network access, but users on noncompliant NAP client computers receive a message that they must become compliant by a configured date and time.

delta CRL   Contains only the certificates revoked since the last base certificate revocation list (CRL) was published, which allows clients to retrieve the smaller delta CRL and quickly build a complete list of revoked certificates.

denial-of-service attack   A situation in which an attacker exploits a weakness or a design limitation of a network service to overload or halt the service so that the service is not available for legitimate users.

DHCP acknowledgment message (DHCPAck)   A message sent by the Dynamic Host Configuration Protocol (DHCP) server to a client to acknowledge and complete a client's request for leased configuration. This message will contain a committed Internet Protocol version 4 (IPv4) address for the client to use for a stated period of time along with other optional client parameters. The DHCP acknowledgment message name is DHCPAck.

DHCP client   Any network-enabled device that supports the ability to communicate with a Dynamic Host Configuration Protocol (DHCP) server for the purpose of obtaining dynamic leased Internet Protocol version 4 (IPv4) configuration and related optional parameters information.

DHCP decline message (DHCPDecline)   A message sent by a Dynamic Host configuration Protocol (DHCP) client to the DHCP server to decline the offer of an Internet Protocol version 4 (IPv4) address on the network. This message is used when the client detects a potential conflict because the IP address is found to be already in use on the network. The DHCP decline message name is DHCPDecline.

DHCP enforcement   A Network Access Protection (NAP) enforcement method in which a computer must meet system health requirements to obtain an Internet Protocol version 4 (IPv4) address configuration for unlimited network access from a Dynamic Host Configuration Protocol (DHCP) server.

DHCP information message (DHCPInform)   A reserved Dynamic Host Configuration Protocol (DHCP) message type used by computers on the network to request and obtain information from a DHCP server for use in their local configuration. When this message type is used, the sender is already externally configured for its Internet Protocol version 4 (IPv4) address on the network, which may or may not have been obtained using DHCP. The DHCP information message name is DHCPInform.

DHCP negative acknowledgment message (DHCPNak)   A message sent by a Dynamic Host Configuration Protocol (DHCP) server to a client to indicate that the Internet Protocol version 4 (IPv4) address that the client requested is not correct for the local IPv4 network served by the DHCP server. This message is most often used when the client computer was moved to a new location, but it could also indicate that the client's lease with the server has expired. The DHCP negative acknowledgment message name is DHCPNak.

DHCP offer message (DHCPOffer)   A message used by Dynamic Host Configuration Protocol (DHCP) servers to offer the lease of an Internet Protocol version 4 (IPv4) address to a DHCP client when it starts on the network. When this message is used, a client can receive more than one offer if multiple DHCP servers are contacted during the DHCP discovery phase, but the client will typically select the first address it is offered. The DHCP offer message name is DHCPOffer.

DHCP option   Address configuration parameters that a Dynamic Host Configuration Protocol (DHCP) service assigns to clients. Most DHCP options are predefined based on optional parameters defined in Request for Comments (RFC) 1542, although extended options can be added by vendors or users.

DHCP relay agent   A host (typically a router but can be a computer) that listens for Dynamic Host Configuration Protocol (DHCP) request broadcast messages and forwards the request as a unicast message to a DHCP server on a different subnet. A DHCP relay agent supports DHCP/BOOTP message relay as defined in Requests for Comments (RFCs) 1541 and 2131.

DHCP release message (DHCPRelease)   A message sent by clients to the Dynamic Host Configuration Protocol (DHCP) server to indicate release of its leased Internet Protocol version 4 (IPv4) address. The client uses this message to cancel its currently active lease. You can perform address release manually using the **ipconfig /release** command at a command prompt. The DHCP release message name is DHCPRelease.

DHCP request message (DHCPRequest)   A message sent by clients to the Dynamic Host Configuration Protocol (DHCP) server to request or renew the lease of its Internet Protocol version 4 (IPv4) address. The client uses this message to select and request a lease from a specific DHCP server, to confirm a previously leased IPv4 address after the client system is restarted, or to extend the current IPv4 address lease for the client. The DHCP request message name is DHCPRequest.

DHCP split-scope   A technique for configuring redundant Dynamic Host Configuration Protocol (DHCP) servers by configuring two DHCP servers with different portions of a single subnet's address space. See *80/20 rule*.

digital signature   See *RADIUS Message Authenticator attribute*.

Domain Name System (DNS)   A hierarchical, distributed database that contains mappings of DNS domain names to various types of data, such as Internet Protocol (IP) addresses. DNS enables the location of computers and services by user-friendly names, and it also enables the discovery of other information stored in the database.

Dynamic Host Configuration Protocol (DHCP)   A Transmission Control Protocol/Internet Protocol (TCP/IP) service protocol that offers dynamic leased configuration of host Internet Protocol version 4 (IPv4) addresses and distributes other configuration parameters to eligible network clients. DHCP provides safe, reliable, and simple TCP/IP network configuration, prevents address conflicts, and helps conserve the use of client IP addresses on the network. DHCP uses a client/server model in which the DHCP server maintains centralized management of IPv4 addresses that are used on the network. DHCP-supporting clients can then request and obtain a lease of an IPv4 address from a DHCP server as part of their network boot process.

Encapsulating Security Payload (ESP)   An Internet Protocol security (IPsec) protocol that provides confidentiality in addition to authentication, integrity, and anti-replay. ESP can be used alone or in combination with Authentication Header (AH). ESP does not normally sign the entire packet unless it is being tunneled. Ordinarily, just the data payload is protected, not the Internet Protocol (IP) header.

end-to-end encryption   Encryption that occurs between the source host and its final destination.

enforcement client (EC)   A component on a Network Access Protection (NAP) client that requests some level of access to a network, passes the computer's health status to a NAP enforcement point that is providing the network access, and indicates health evaluation information to other components of the NAP client architecture.

enforcement mode   A Network Access Protection (NAP) enforcement mode in which noncompliant NAP clients have limited network access. Users on noncompliant NAP client computers will receive a message stating that their computers are not compliant.

enforcement server (ES)   A component on a Network Access Protection (NAP) enforcement point running the Windows Server 2008 operating system that allows some level of network access or communication, can pass a NAP client's health status to a NAP health policy server for evaluation, and, based on the response from server, can provide the enforcement of limited network access.

exclusion range   A range of Internet Protocol version 4 (IPv4) addresses that the Dynamic Host Configuration Protocol (DHCP) server will not assign to clients.

exemptions   In Internet Protocol security (IPsec), a rule that allows specific hosts to bypass IPsec connection security requirements.

group   A collection of user and computer accounts and other groups that can be managed as a single unit.

group scope   A property of a group that determines the extent to which the group is applied within a domain or forest.

group type   A property of a group that determines whether a group can be used to assign permissions to a shared resource (for security groups) or whether a group can be used for e-mail distribution lists only (for distribution groups).

hardware security module (HSM)   A computer adapter or external device that stores and physically protects the access to long-term secrets, such as the private key of an issuing certification authority (CA).

Health Registration Authority (HRA)   A computer running Windows Server 2008 and Internet Information Services (IIS) that obtains health certificates from a Network Access Protection (NAP) certification authority (CA) for compliant NAP clients.

health policies   A named set of settings on a Network Access Protection (NAP) health policy server that allow you to specify health requirements in terms of installed system health validators (SHVs) and whether NAP clients must pass or fail any or all of the selected SHVs.

health requirement policies   The combination of a connection request policy, one or more health policies, one or more network policies, and Network Access Protection (NAP) settings that determine NAP health evaluation and limited access behavior.

health update servers   Servers that contain resources to remediate a noncompliant Network Access Protection (NAP) client's health state.

health zone   A portion of a network that requires a health certificate from a specific public key infrastructure (PKI) before it will assert system health compliance.

hidden network   See *non-broadcast network*.

hosts file   A local text file in the same format as the 4.3 Berkeley Software Distribution (BSD) UNIX /etc/hosts file. This file maps host names to Internet Protocol (IP) addresses, and it is stored in the *%SystemRoot%*\System32\Drivers\Etc folder.

in-addr.arpa domain   A special top-level Domain Name System (DNS) domain reserved for reverse mapping of Internet Protocol version 4 (IPv4) addresses to DNS host names.

inbound filters   Filters on an interface of a Routing and Remote Access server that specify allowed inbound traffic.

incremental zone transfer   In Domain Name System (DNS), a zone transfer request involving only incremental resource record changes between each version of the zone.

Internal interface   A logical interface of a Routing and Remote Access server that represents the connection to all other authenticated remote access clients.

Internet Control Message Protocol (ICMP)   An extension to Internet Protocol version 4 (IPv4), ICMP allows for the generation of error messages, test packets, and informational messages related to IP.

Internet Key Exchange (IKE)   A protocol that establishes the security association and shared keys necessary for two parties to communicate by using Internet Protocol security (IPsec).

Internet Protocol security (IPsec)   A set of industry-standard, cryptography-based protection services and protocols that provides authentication and encryption for IP communications.

Internet Protocol version 4 (IPv4)   A routable protocol in the Transmission Control Protocol/Internet Protocol (TCP/IP) suite that is responsible for IP addressing, routing, and the fragmentation and reassembly of IP packets. IPv4 is the Layer 3 protocol used for the vast majority of network communications, including communications on the Internet.

Internet Protocol version 6 (IPv6)   A routable protocol in the Transmission Control Protocol/Internet Protocol (TCP/IP) suite that is responsible for addressing and routing of IPv6 packets. IPv6 is the new Layer 3 protocol that will eventually replace IP version 4 (IPv4).

Intra-Site Automatic Tunnel Addressing Protocol (ISATAP) address   An Internet Protocol version 6 (IPv6) address in which the 64-bit interface identifier (ID) is either ::0:5EFE:*w.x.y.z*, where *w.x.y.z* is a private Internet Protocol version 4 (IPv4) address, or ::200:5EFE:*w.x.y.z*, where *w.x.y.z* is a public IPv4 address.

ip6.arpa domain   A special top-level Domain Name System (DNS) domain reserved for reverse mapping of Internet Protocol version 6 (IPv6) addresses to DNS host names.

IP address   For Internet Protocol version 4 (IPv4), a 32-bit address used to identify an interface on a node on an IPv4 internetwork. Each interface on the IP internetwork must be assigned a unique IPv4 address, which is made up of the network prefix and a unique host identifier (ID). This address is typically represented with the decimal value of each octet separated by a period (for example, 192.168.7.27). You can configure the IP address statically or dynamically by using Dynamic Host Configuration Protocol (DHCP). For Internet Protocol version 6 (IPv6), a 128-bit address that is assigned at the IPv6 layer to an interface or set of interfaces and that can be used as the source or destination of IPv6 packets.

IPv4 Link-Local (IPv4LL)   See *Automatic Private IP Addressing (APIPA)*.

IPsec enforcement   A Network Access Protection (NAP) enforcement method in which a computer must meet system health requirements to initiate communications with other compliant computers on an intranet in a server isolation or domain isolation Internet Protocol security (IPsec) deployment.

IPsec negotiation   The process that two Internet Protocol security (IPsec) peers use to identify a set of authentication and encryption standards that both peers support.

IPsec policy   Configuration policy that determines which traffic Internet Protocol security (IPsec) examines, how that traffic is secured and encrypted, and how IPsec peers are authenticated.

IPsec SA   See *security association (SA)*.

jitter   A change in latency.

latency   The time it takes for a packet to reach its destination, typically measured in milliseconds (ms).

link encryption   Encryption that occurs on the link between the virtual private network (VPN) client and the VPN server across the Internet.

lmhosts file   A local text file that maps Network Basic Input/Output System (NetBIOS) names (commonly used for computer names) to Internet Protocol version 4 (IPv4) addresses for hosts that are not located on the local subnet. In Windows, this file is stored in the *%SystemRoot%*\System32\Drivers\Etc folder.

local area network (LAN)   A network of computers, printers, and other devices located within a relatively limited area (for example, a building). A LAN enables any connected device to interact with any other on the network.

machine certificate   See *computer certificate*.

Main Mode   Phase 1 of the Internet Protocol security (IPsec) negotiation process. Main Mode negotiation selects a protection suite that both the client and server support, authenticates the computers, and then establishes the master key for the IPsec session.

man-in-the-middle attack   A security attack in which an attacker intercepts and possibly modifies data that is transmitted between two users. The attacker pretends to be the other person to each user. In a successful man-in-the-middle attack, the users are unaware that there is an attacker between them, intercepting and modifying their data.

media access control (MAC) address   The address that is used for communication between network adapters on the same subnet. Each network adapter has an associated MAC address.

name server (NS) resource record   A resource record used in a zone to designate the Domain Name System (DNS) domain names for authoritative DNS servers for the zone.

NAP CA   A Windows-based issuing certificate authority (CA) of health certificates for the Internet Protocol security (IPsec) enforcement method in Network Access Protection (NAP).

NAP enforcement method   A type of network access or communication that is subject to Network Access Protection (NAP) health evaluation.

NAP enforcement point   Computers or network access devices that use Network Access Protection (NAP) or can be used with NAP to require the evaluation of a NAP client's health state and provide restricted network access or communication.

NAP health policy server   Computers running Windows Server 2008 and the Network Policy Server (NPS) service that store health requirement policies and provide health evaluation for Network Access Protection (NAP) clients.

Network Access Protection (NAP)   A new platform for the Windows Server 2008, Windows Vista, and Windows XP SP3 operating systems with architectural components and an application programming interface (API) set that can help IT administrators enforce compliance with health requirement policies for network access or communication.

Network Basic Input/Output System (NetBIOS)   An application programming interface (API) designed by IBM to allow computers to easily communicate over a network. Microsoft adopted NetBIOS and a Layer 2 protocol named NetBIOS Extended User Interface (NetBEUI) as a way for computers running early versions of Windows to network.

Network Policy Server (NPS)   The Microsoft implementation of a Remote Authentication Dial-In User Service (RADIUS) server and proxy in Windows Server 2008. NPS replaces Internet Authentication Service (IAS) in Windows Server 2003.

NetBIOS Extended User Interface (NetBEUI)   A Layer 2 protocol that Microsoft adopted as a way for early versions of Windows to communicate on a local area network.

network address translation (NAT)   A process that translates the internal Internet Protocol version 4 (IPv4) address of each computer on a local area network into an external IPv4 address when that computer connects to the Internet. This process improves the security of the network because internal addresses are not made public.

network policies   An ordered set of rules on a Network Policy Server (NPS) that specify the circumstances under which connection attempts are either authorized or rejected. For each rule, there is an access permission that either grants or denies access, a set of conditions, a set of constraints, and network policy settings. If a connection is authorized, the network policy constraints and settings can specify a set of connection restrictions.

non-broadcast network   An Institute of Electrical and Electronics Engineers (IEEE) 802.11 wireless network with Service Set Identifier (SSID) suppression enabled. Also known as a hidden network.

on-subnet address range   An address range of an intranet subnet to which the virtual private network (VPN) server is attached.

off-subnet address range   An address range that represents a different subnet that is logically attached to the virtual private network (VPN) server.

Open Systems Interconnection (OSI) reference model   A networking model introduced by the International Organization for Standardization (ISO) to promote multi-vendor interoperability. OSI is a seven-layered conceptual model consisting of the application, presentation, session, transport, network, data-link, and physical layers.

outbound filters   Filters on an interface of a Routing and Remote Access server that specify allowed outbound traffic.

package   See *customized Connection Manager (CM) client dialer profile.*

parser   A component included with Network Monitor that can separate the fields of a protocol header and display their structure and values.

perimeter network   A network between an intranet and the Internet that typically contains firewalls and Internet-accessible servers. Also known as a screened subnet or a demilitarized zone (DMZ).

profile   A named list of wireless networks and their configuration settings.

profile name   A name configured on a Network Access Protection (NAP)–enabled Dynamic Host Configuration Protocol (DHCP) scope so that you can specify different health requirement policies for different scopes.

public key infrastructure (PKI)   A system of digital certificates and certification authorities (CAs) that verifies and authenticates the validity of each entity—such as a user, computer, or Windows service—that is participating in secure communications through the use of public key cryptography.

Quality of Service (QoS)   A set of quality assurance standards and mechanisms for data transmission.

Quick Mode   Phase 2 of the Internet Protocol security (IPsec) negotiation process. Quick Mode negotiation occurs after Main Mode negotiation to establish a session key to be used for authentication or encryption until the next Quick Mode negotiation is scheduled to occur.

RADIUS client   An access server that uses the Remote Authentication Dial-In User Service (RADIUS) protocol to send connection requests and accounting messages to a RADIUS server.

RADIUS Message Authenticator attribute   An attribute of a Remote Authentication Dial-In User Service (RADIUS) message that provides cryptographic proof that the message was sent from a computer that has been configured with the same RADIUS shared secret. Also known as the digital signature or signature attribute.

RADIUS proxy   A computer that routes Remote Authentication Dial-In User Service (RADIUS) connection requests and accounting messages between RADIUS clients and RADIUS servers. The RADIUS proxy uses information within the RADIUS message to route the RADIUS message to the appropriate RADIUS client or server.

RADIUS server   A computer that receives and processes connection requests or accounting messages sent by Remote Authentication Dial-In User Service (RADIUS) clients or RADIUS proxies.

read-only domain controllers (RODCs)   A new type of domain controller in Windows Server 2008 that can be deployed in locations where physical security cannot be guaranteed. An RODC hosts read-only partitions of the Active Directory database.

realm name   The part of the account name that identifies the location of the user account, such as the name of an Active Directory domain. For example, for the name *user1@contoso.com, contoso.com* is the realm name.

Redundant Array of Independent Disks (RAID)   A method used to standardize and categorize fault-tolerant disk systems. RAID levels provide various mixes of performance, reliability, and cost.

remediation   The process of updating the health state of a Network Access Protection (NAP) client by changing configuration settings or accessing servers that contain the needed updates, software, scripts, or other resources.

Request for Comments (RFC)   An official document of the Internet Engineering Task Force (IETF) that specifies the details for protocols included in the Transmission Control Protocol/Internet Protocol (TCP/IP) protocol suite. RFCs can be found at *http:// tools.ietf.org/html*.

remediation servers   Network infrastructure servers and health update servers that Network Access Protection (NAP) clients can access to remediate their noncompliant state.

replay attack   An attack in which an attacker with physical access to network media records network communications and then replays them to the server at a later date, typically to submit user credentials without needing to break encryption.

reporting mode   A Network Access Protection (NAP) enforcement mode in which noncompliant NAP clients have unlimited network access and users on noncompliant NAP client computers do not receive a message that their computers are noncompliant.

restricted network   A separate logical or physical network that contains remediation servers and noncompliant Network Access Protection (NAP) clients. In Internet Protocol security (IPsec) enforcement, the set of computers that do not have health certificates.

root authority   The certification authority (CA) at the top of a public key infrastructure (PKI) hierarchy. Also called a root CA.

root hints   Domain Name System (DNS) data stored on a DNS server that identifies the authoritative DNS servers for the root zone of the DNS namespace.

round robin   A simple mechanism used by Domain Name System (DNS) servers to share and distribute loads for network resources. Round robin is used to rotate the order of resource records returned in a response to a query when multiple resource records of the same type exist for a queried DNS domain name.

Router certificate   Also called an Offline request certificate. For a certification authority (CA) for the Windows Server 2008 or Windows Server 2003 operating systems, a special type of user certificate for demand-dial connections.

router-to-router connection   See *site-to-site connection.*

scavenging   A process used by Dynamic Host Configuration Protocol (DHCP) servers to remove the client's resource records automatically when the DHCP lease expires.

scope   The range of Internet Protocol (IP) addresses that are allowed to communicate with the service specified by the Windows Firewall rule.

screened subnet   See *perimeter network.*

secure network   In Internet Protocol security (IPsec) enforcement for Network Access Protection (NAP), the set of computers that have health certificates, require that incoming communication attempts authenticate with health certificates, and share a common set of IPsec policy settings for providing IPsec protection.

security association (SA)   A combination of identifiers that together define Internet Protocol security (IPsec), which protects communication between sender and receiver. An SA must be negotiated before protected data can be sent.

security principal   An Active Directory object that is automatically assigned a security identifier (SID), which can be used to access domain resources.

service (SRV) resource record   A Domain Name System (DNS) resource record used to identify computers that host specific services, specified in Request for Comments (RFC) 2782. SRV resource records are used to locate domain controllers for Active Directory.

Service Set Identifier (SSID)   A name that identifies a specific wireless network. Also known as the wireless network name.

session key   In Internet Protocol security (IPsec), a value that is used in combination with an algorithm to encrypt or decrypt data that is transferred between computers. A session key is created for every pair of computers to provide enhanced security on computers that have multiple simultaneous active sessions.

Signature attribute   See *RADIUS Message Authenticator attribute.*

site-to-site connection   A point-to-point connection between two routers created for the purpose of forwarding traffic between two portions of an intranet over the Internet. Also known as a router-to-router connection.

split tunneling   Concurrent access to both intranet and Internet resources by a remote access virtual private network (VPN) client when a VPN connection is active.

start-of-authority (SOA) resource record   A record that indicates the starting point or original point of authority for information stored in a zone. The SOA resource record (RR) is the first RR created when adding a new zone. It also contains several parameters used by other computers that use Domain Name System (DNS) to determine how long they will use information for the zone and how often updates are required.

Statement of Health (SoH)   Data produced by a system health agent (SHA) that contains the current status information about the attribute of health being monitored by the SHA.

Statement of Health Response (SoHR)   Data produced by a system health validator (SHV) that contains the results of the health validation of a Statement of Health (SoH) or other types of health validation.

static pool of addresses   A manually configured set of address ranges on a Routing and Remote Access server.

subordinate certificate authority (CA)   Child CAs of the root CAs.

system health agent (SHA)   A component of a Network Access Protection (NAP) client that tracks health state for an attribute of system health.

system health validator (SHV)   A component of a Network Access Protection (NAP) health policy server that validates health state for an attribute of system health.

System Statement of Health (SSoH)   Data from a Network Access Protection (NAP) client that includes version information for the NAP client and the set of Statements of Health (SoHs) for the installed system health agents (SHAs).

System Statement of Health Response (SSoHR)   Data from a Network Access Protection (NAP) health policy server that indicates whether the NAP client is compliant or noncompliant and includes the set of Statements of Health Response (SoHRs) from the system health validators (SHVs).

Transmission Control Protocol/Internet Protocol (TCP/IP)   A set of networking protocols widely used on the Internet that provides communications across interconnected networks of computers with diverse hardware architectures and various operating systems. TCP/IP includes standards for how computers communicate and conventions for connecting networks and routing traffic.

transport mode In Internet Protocol security (IPsec), a mode of communication used between two hosts. In transport mode, IPsec tunnels traffic starting at the transport layer, also known as Layer 4. Therefore, IPsec in transport mode can protect the Transmission Control Protocol (TCP) or User Datagram Protocol (UDP) protocol header and the original data, but the Internet Protocol (IP) header itself cannot be protected.

tunnel mode In Internet Protocol security (IPsec), a mode of communication used between two networks. In transport mode, IPsec tunnels traffic starting at the network layer, also known as Layer 3. Therefore, IPsec in transport mode can protect the original Internet Protocol (IP) header itself.

unnumbered connection A point-to-point connection that does not require Internet Protocol (IP) address assignment.

User Datagram Protocol (UDP) A transport layer protocol that offers a connectionless datagram service that guarantees neither delivery nor correct sequencing of delivered packets but provides a payload checksum and upper layer protocol identification that uses source and destination ports.

VPN enforcement A Network Access Protection (NAP) enforcement method in which a computer must meet system health requirements to obtain unlimited network access through a remote access virtual private network (VPN) connection.

Windows Internet Name Service (WINS) A service that provides centralized name resolution for Network Basic Input/Output System (NetBIOS) names. Although Domain Name System (DNS) has replaced WINS as the primary name resolution method for Windows networks, many organizations continue to use WINS for backward compatibility.

wireless network name See *Service Set Identifier (SSID)*.

Zero Configuration Networking See *Automatic Private IP Addressing (APIPA)*.

zeroconf See *Automatic Private IP Addressing (APIPA)*.

zone transfer The synchronization of authoritative Domain Name System (DNS) data between DNS servers. A DNS server configured with a secondary zone periodically queries the master DNS servers to synchronize its zone data.

Index

Joseph Davies

Joseph Davies is a technical writer for the Microsoft Corporation. He has been a writer and instructor of TCP/IP, networking, and security topics since 1992. Since 2001, he has been writing white papers, TechNet articles, Web sites, and Microsoft Press books for the Microsoft Windows networking technology teams. He is the author of TechNet's monthly column "The Cable Guy" (*http://www.microsoft.com/technet/community/columns/cableguy/default.mspx*).

Joseph is co-author of *Deploying Virtual Private Networks with Microsoft Windows Server 2003* (2004), *Microsoft Windows Server 2003 TCP/IP Protocols and Services Technical Reference* (2003), and *Microsoft Windows 2000 TCP/IP Protocols and Services Technical Reference* (2000), all from Microsoft Press. He is author of *Understanding IPv6, Second Edition* (Microsoft Press, 2008), *Windows Server 2008 TCP/IP Protocols and Services* (Microsoft Press, 2008), *TCP/IP Fundamentals for Microsoft Windows* (TechNet, 2006), *Deploying Secure 802.11 Wireless Networks with Microsoft Windows* (Microsoft Press, 2004), and *Understanding IPv6* (Microsoft Press, 2003), which won the Puget Sound Society for Technical Communication (STC) Best of Show and International STC Distinguished Awards.

Tony Northrup

Tony Northrup, CISPP, MCSE, and Microsoft MVP, is a networking consultant and author living near Boston, Massachusetts. Tony has authored or co-authored more than a dozen books on Windows and networking for Microsoft and other publishers, and has written hundreds of articles for TechNet and other technology publications. When he's not consulting or writing, Tony enjoys golf, hiking, and nature photography (which you can see at *http://www.northrup.org*).

Tony is co-author of, among other books, *Windows Vista Resource Kit* (Microsoft Press, 2007), *Home Hacking Projects for Geeks* (O'Reilly, 2004), *MCSA/MCSE Self-Paced Training Kit (Exam 70-299): Implementing and Administering Security in a Microsoft Windows Server 2003 Network* (Microsoft Press, 2004), and *Network Essentials Unleashed* (SAMS/Macmillan, 1998). He is the author of *Windows Server 2003 Troubleshooting Guide* (Microsoft Press, 2005), *NT Network Plumbing* (Hungry Minds, 1998), and *Introducing Windows 2000 Server* (Microsoft Press, 1999).

System Requirements

To use this book's companion CD-ROM, you need a computer equipped with the following minimum configuration:

- The Windows Server 2008, Windows Vista, Windows Server 2003, or Windows XP operating system
- 1 gigahertz (GHz) 32-bit (x86) or 64-bit (x64) processor
- 1 gigabyte (GB) of system memory
- A hard disk partition with at least 1 GB of available space
- Support for DirectX 9 graphics and 32 megabytes (MB) of graphics memory
- Appropriate video monitor
- Keyboard
- Mouse or other pointing device
- CD-ROM drive

To view the online version of this book, you will need Adobe Reader. See *http://www.adobe.com* for information about disk space requirements for Adobe Reader.

To install Microsoft Network Monitor 3.1 from *http://go.microsoft.com/fwlink/?LinkID=92844* or a link on the companion CD-ROM, you need the following additional minimum configuration: A hard disk partition with approximately 25 MB of free disk space.

What do you think of this book?

We want to hear from you!

Do you have a few minutes to participate in a brief online survey?

Microsoft is interested in hearing your feedback so we can continually improve our books and learning resources for you.

To participate in our survey, please visit:

www.microsoft.com/learning/booksurvey/

...and enter this book's ISBN-10 or ISBN-13 number (located above barcode on back cover*). As a thank-you to survey participants in the United States and Canada, each month we'll randomly select five respondents to win one of five $100 gift certificates from a leading online merchant. At the conclusion of the survey, you can enter the drawing by providing your e-mail address, which will be used for prize notification only.

Thanks in advance for your input. Your opinion counts!

* Where to find the ISBN on back cover

ISBN-13: 000-0-0000-0000-0
ISBN-10: 0-0000-0000-0

0 00000 00000   0 0000

Example only. Each book has unique ISBN.

Microsoft®
Press

www.microsoft.com/learning/booksurvey/